Fodor's 2011

WALT DISNEY WORLD

Fodor's Travel Publications   New York, Toronto, London, Sydney, Auckland
www.fodors.com

Be a Fodor's Correspondent

Your opinion matters. It matters to us. It matters to your fellow Fodor's travelers, too. And we'd like to hear it. In fact, we *need* to hear it.

When you share your experiences and opinions, you become an active member of the Fodor's community. That means we'll not only use your feedback to make our books better, but we'll publish your names and comments whenever possible. Throughout our guides, look for "Word of Mouth," excerpts of your unvarnished feedback.

Here's how you can help improve Fodor's for all of us.

Tell us when we're right. We rely on local writers to give you an insider's perspective. But our writers and staff editors—who are the best in the business—depend on you. Your positive feedback is a vote to renew our recommendations for the next edition.

Tell us when we're wrong. We're proud that we update most of our guides every year. But we're not perfect. Things change. Hotels cut services. Museums change hours. Charming cafés lose charm. If our writer didn't quite capture the essence of a place, tell us how you'd do it differently. If any of our descriptions are inaccurate or inadequate, we'll incorporate your changes in the next edition and will correct factual errors at fodors.com *immediately*.

Tell us what to include. You probably have had fantastic travel experiences that aren't yet in Fodor's. Why not share them with a community of like-minded travelers? Maybe you chanced upon a beach or bistro or B&B that you don't want to keep to yourself. Tell us why we should include it. And share your discoveries and experiences with everyone directly at fodors.com. Your input may lead us to add a new listing or highlight a place we cover with a "Highly Recommended" star or with our highest rating, "Fodor's Choice."

Give us your opinion instantly at our feedback center at www.fodors.com/feedback. You may also e-mail editors@fodors.com with the subject line "Walt Disney World Editor." Or send your nominations, comments, and complaints by mail to Walt Disney World Editor, Fodor's, 1745 Broadway, New York, NY 10019.

You and travelers like you are the heart of the Fodor's community. Make our community richer by sharing your experiences. Be a Fodor's correspondent.

Happy Traveling!

Tim Jarrell, Publisher

FODOR'S WALT DISNEY WORLD 2011

Editors: Laura M. Kidder (lead project editor); Carolyn Galgano (hotel and restaurants editor)

Writers: Elise Allen, Nathan Benjamin, Sam Benjamin, Samantha Chapnick, Rona Gindin, Jennifer Greenhill-Taylor, Jennie Hess, Gary McKechnie, Joseph Reed Hayes

Production Editor: Carrie Parker

Maps & Illustrations: David Lindroth; Mark Stroud, Moon Street Cartography, *cartographers;* Bob Blake, Rebecca Baer, *map editors;* William Wu, *information graphics*

Design: Fabrizio La Rocca, *creative director;* Guido Caroti, Siobhan O'Hare, *art directors;* Tina Malaney, Nora Rosansky, Chie Ushio, Jessica Walsh, Ann McBride, *designers;* Melanie Marin, *senior picture editor*

Cover Photo: (Cinderella Castle, Magic Kingdom) © Disney

Production Manager: Amanda Bullock

ISBN 978-1-4000-0461-4

ISSN 1531-443X

SPECIAL SALES

This book is available at special discounts for bulk purchases for sales promotions or premiums. Special editions, including personalized covers, excerpts of existing books, and corporate imprints, can be created in large quantities for special needs. For more information, write to Special Markets/Premium Sales, 1745 Broadway, MD 6-2, New York, New York 10019, or e-mail specialmarkets@randomhouse.com.

AN IMPORTANT TIP & AN INVITATION

Although all prices, opening times, and other details in this book are based on information supplied to us at press time, changes occur all the time in the travel world, and Fodor's cannot accept responsibility for facts that become outdated or for inadvertent errors or omissions. So **always confirm information when it matters,** especially if you're making a detour to visit a specific place. Your experiences—positive and negative—matter to us. If we have missed or misstated something, **please write to us.** We follow up on all suggestions. Contact the Walt Disney World editor at editors@fodors.com or c/o Fodor's at 1745 Broadway, New York, NY 10019.

PRINTED IN CHINA

10 9 8 7 6 5 4 3 2 1

CONTENTS

Fodor's Features

ABOUT THIS BOOK

Our Ratings

In theme-park chapters, ☆, ☆☆, ☆☆☆, or the orange **Fodor's Choice** symbol rates the appeal of the attraction to the audience noted. "Young children/kids" refers to kids ages 6 and under, many of whom won't meet the height requirements of most thrill rides anyway. Since youngsters come with different confidence levels, exercise your own judgment with the scarier rides.

In non-theme-park chapters, black stars in the margin highlight things we deem **Highly Recommended,** places that our writers, editors, and readers praise again and again for excellence. The very best attractions, properties, and experiences get our highest rating, the orange **Fodor's Choice** symbol, throughout this book.

By default, there's another category: any place we include in this book is by definition worth your time, unless we say otherwise. And we will.

Disagree with any of our choices? Care to nominate a place or suggest that we rate one more highly? Visit our feedback center at www.fodors.com/feedback.

Budget Well

Hotel and restaurant price categories from ¢ to $$$$ are defined in the Where to Eat and Where to Stay chapters. For attractions, we always give standard adult admission fees; reductions are usually available for children, students, and senior citizens. Want to pay with plastic? **AE, D, DC, MC, V** following restaurant and hotel listings indicate whether American Express, Discover, Diners Club, MasterCard, and Visa are accepted.

Restaurants

Unless we state otherwise, restaurants are open for lunch and dinner daily. We mention dress only when there's a specific requirement and reservations only when they're essential or not accepted—it's always best to book ahead.

Hotels

Hotels have private bath, phone, TV, and air-conditioning and operate on the European Plan (aka EP, meaning without meals), unless we specify that they use the Continental Plan (CP, with a continental breakfast), Breakfast Plan (BP, with a full breakfast), or Modified American Plan (MAP, with breakfast and dinner), or are all-inclusive (AI, including all meals and most activities). We always list facilities but not any extra fees they might incur. Find out what's included when you book.

Listings
★	Fodor's Choice
★	Highly recommended
✉	Physical address
✛	Directions or Map coordinates
⌂	Mailing address
☎	Telephone
🖷	Fax
⊕	On the Web
✐	E-mail
🎫	Admission fee
☉	Open/closed times
Ⓜ	Metro stations
▭	Credit cards

Hotels & Restaurants
🛏	Hotel
↰	Number of rooms
⚭	Facilities
¶⚬¶	Meal plans
✕	Restaurant
⚘	Reservations
🏛	Dress code
⌇	Smoking
⚲♀	BYOB

Outdoors
🏌	Golf
⛺	Camping

Other
☺	Family-friendly
⇨	See also
✉	Branch address
☞	Take note

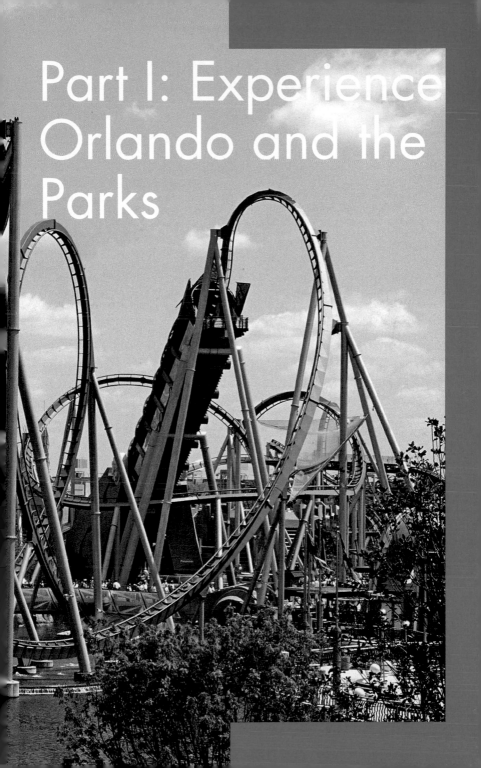

Part I: Experience Orlando and the Parks

WHAT'S NEW IN ORLANDO AND THE PARKS

Once a thriving citrus-growing region, Orlando saw its tourism star rise soon after Disney opened the Magic Kingdom in 1971. In the decades since, Mickey's empire has ballooned, SeaWorld has made a splash with Shamu, and Universal Studios has brought big-screen thrills to life. Today Orlando's meeting and convention business thrives with resort hotel numbers second only to those of Las Vegas.

Visitors see Orlando as a shiny vacation kingdom bolstered by cartoon characters. Residents see it as a city on the rise, albeit one that's too reliant on a single industry—namely, tourism. Local officials have responded to these sentiments by courting and welcoming new industry to the area, and, as a result, Orlando is becoming an increasingly sophisticated city.

Today's Orlando . . .

. . . is evolving rapidly. Downtown Orlando is honing a hip edge, a growing high-tech corridor is attracting young professionals, and a new medical research center is springing up near Orlando International Airport. Sports fans and concertgoers are lining up for tickets to downtown's Amway Center, home of Orlando's NBA team, the Orlando Magic. And plans are underway for construction of an elaborate downtown performing arts center that would dwarf the aging Bob Carr Performing Arts Center.

. . . is enjoying a theme-park growth spurt. At Disney, the horizon is bright with plans for a major Fantasyland expansion in the Magic Kingdom plus an overall 10-year growth plan that includes up to 11,000-plus new hotel rooms and a possible fifth theme park. In fact, Disney is collaborating with Best Friends Pet Care to open an on-site luxury pet resort with grooming, boarding, and a doggy day camp. Development is also under way near Disney's northeast border for construction of a 900-acre resort area with a Four Seasons property, family vacation homes, and a golf course to replace Disney's dormant Eagle Pines course. Finally, two new Disney cruise ships will set sail from Port Canaveral, Florida, in 2011 and 2012.

SeaWorld opened the thrill coaster, Manta, and updates its live shows regularly. Universal Studios debuted its long-anticipated Wizarding World of Harry Potter.

Theme parks also are staying cutting-edge with interactive exhibits and attractions. Verizon and Disney have even teamed up to offer phone services that update you on real-time attraction availability, Disney

WHATS HOT IN ORLANDO AND THE PARKS NOW

Stargazing is an ever-popular pastime at the Orlando Science Center's Crosby Observatory. But the starstruck can also engage in "stargaping"—as in **celebrity sighting.** While park hopping, you could run into just about any pop-culture icon. Whose theme-park-lovin' mugs might you snap? Tina Fey, Tom Cruise and Katie Holmes, Britney Spears, Miley Cyrus, Mariah Carey, Michael Douglas and Catherine Zeta-Jones, Gwen Stefani—the list goes on. Celeb chefs like Cat Cora and Emeril Lagasse kick things up a notch when they're in town. Famous locals include In Sync's Joey Fatone and actress-singer Mandy Moore, sports figures Tiger Woods and Warren Sapp, comedian Wayne Brady, and actor Wesley Snipes.

More and more, **metro area pets** are being given the celebrity treatment. Dog-owning foodies in Orlando

At one point during the Harry Potter and the Forbidden Journey adventure at Universal's Islands of Adventure, you're propelled into the midst of a Quidditch match.

character locations, and other in-park "breaking news."

. . . is a nosher's paradise. Area restaurants are innovating and impressing with a variety of ethnic, farm-to-table, and vegan menus. Trendy truffle fries are hot at The Ravenous Pig in Winter Park; classics like foie gras are always in style at Le Coq au Vin. Orlando has three master sommeliers—at this writing, that's just one fewer than New York City and Chicago.

Celebrity chefs, including Cat Cora, Todd English, Emeril Lagasse, and Norman Van Aken, have taken over numerous Orlando dining rooms. Disney chef Scott Hunnel makes dinner a royal occasion at Victoria & Albert's, Central Florida's only AAA Five-Diamond restaurant. Even theme-park chefs are setting new standards, offering options that range from sushi at the counter-service Sunshine Seasons in Epcot to blueberry- and pistachio-crusted grilled pork at Mythos Restaurant in Islands of Adventure. As the owners of Le Coq au Vin aptly advise: "Bon Appetit y'all!"

and Winter Park take their best friends for a nosh at spots like Harmoni Market and K Restaurant and Wine Bar. Dogs-about-town often frequent Winter Park Farmer's Market and Fleet Peeple's Park, and there are several popular pooch boutiques like the Doggie Door on North Park Avenue in Winter Park.

Orlando **architecture** is turning heads these days as the downtown skyline undergoes enhancement, lakefront manses compete for attention, and buildings about town earn design raves. The city's eclectic shape features the country's second-largest convention center (Chicago's is the largest), with its open-air bridge and moving sidewalks; the rustic bayou-themed House of Blues; the observatory-capped Orlando Science Center; and the love-it-or-hate-it downtown LYNX bus station, with its wavy, whimsical lines.

WHAT'S WHERE

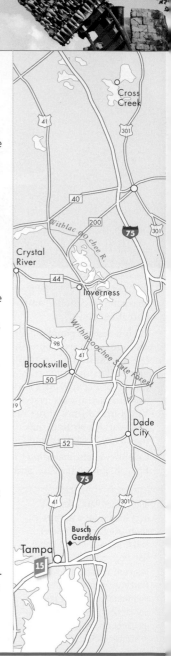

The following numbers refer to chapters.

4-**8** Walt Disney World Resort. Disney welcomes you to four theme parks: Magic Kingdom, Animal Kingdom, Epcot, and Hollywood Studios. All are packed with rides, attractions, shows, and interactive experiences. The 40-square-mi resort also delivers Blizzard Beach and Typhoon Lagoon water parks and the lively Downtown Disney area full of restaurants, shops, and entertainment diversions like the House of Blues and Cirque du Soleil. What else is there? Only a 220-acre sports complex, 34 hotels, lodges, and campsites, full-service spas, golf courses, character meals, dinner shows, and a wedding pavilion.

9-**11** Universal Orlando Resort. The area's big-thrill destination, Universal Orlando, brings movies to life at Universal Studios and delivers gravity-defying rides and special-effects surprises at Islands of Adventure. Nearby Wet 'n Wild is full of watery rides and adventures. Three on-site Universal resorts, including a Hard Rock Hotel, offer themed accommodations, and 12 partner hotels pick up the slack. CityWalk is the nightlife hub for themed restaurants, bars, movies, and clubs, and Hard Rock Live is the big-ticket

concert venue for every act from Megadeath to Lady Gaga.

12-**13** SeaWorld Orlando. Marine life takes the stage at SeaWorld Orlando, where killer whales and other marine mammals perform and thrill seekers find their adrenaline rush on coaster and simulator attractions. Sister park Discovery Cove is a daylong, swim-with-the-dolphins beach escape. SeaWorld also invites you to a day of water play at Aquatica water park.

14 Orlando and Environs. Those who venture beyond the parks to downtown Orlando, International Drive, Kissimmee, Winter Park, and Cape Canaveral on the east coast will discover new sights and experiences worth exploring. For Old Florida kitsch, you can't beat Gatorland and its "jaw-inspiring" creature features. Experience the g-forces of a space-shuttle liftoff, Kennedy Space Center Visitor Complex.

15 Tampa Bay Area. Tampa's Busch Gardens adventure park and nearby Ybor City make a visit to Central Florida's west coast appealing. But there's much more: culture vultures flock across the bay to St. Petersburg for concerts, major-league ball, and museums like the Salvador Dalí Museum, while eco-adventurers veer north to the Nature Coast.

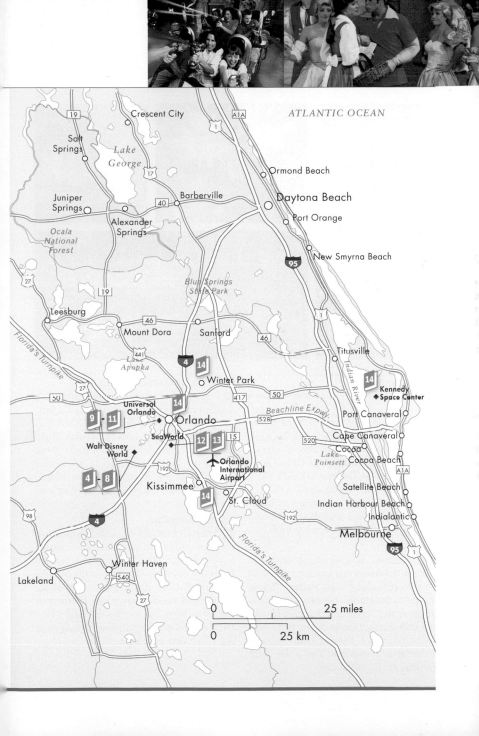

TOP ATTRACTIONS

Magic Kingdom

(A) Disney's most-visited theme park welcomes you with a barbershop quartet serenade and the fragrance of fresh-baked cookies. Cinderella Castle beckons and magical lands have classic attractions—from Adventureland's Pirates of the Caribbean to Tomorrowland's sleek Space Mountain. Wide-eyed children meet Mickey Mouse, ride their first roller coaster, and fly high with Peter Pan and Dumbo. Few adults can resist going.

Epcot

(B) Top reasons to visit begin with the hands-on Innoventions exhibits and end with the not-to-be-missed Soarin' "hanggliding" adventure. History is entertaining at the American Adventure and Spaceship Earth. Count down to launch on Mission: Space. Dine at Tutto Italia or another great restaurant. End a day with fireworks at IllumiNations.

Disney's Hollywood Studios

(C) Film- and TV-inspired adventures lure audiences to The American Idol Experience, Indiana Jones Epic Stunt Spectacular, and Toy Story Midway Mania! Thrill seekers get their kicks at Twilight Zone Tower of Terror and Rock 'n' Roller coaster Starring Aerosmith. The Magic of Disney Animation highlights Walt and his cartoons.

Animal Kingdom

(D) Animals from several continents share the spotlight in habitats that mimic native environments. You'll see some critters from the open-air safari vehicles of Kilimanjaro Safaris; you'll spot others along landscaped trails. Shows like Festival of the Lion King draw crowds. Rides like DINOSAUR and Expedition Everest push the adrenaline envelope.

Universal Studios
(E) Universal is known for action, adventure, and a touch of irreverence. From Terminator 2 3D to Revenge of the Mummy, attractions score points with fans of contemporary film. City street reproductions set the movie back lot scene. Younger kids love Woody Woodpecker's Kid Zone.

Islands of Adventure
(F) The Wizarding World of Harry Potter draws crowds to this park, which is already known for such draws as The Amazing Adventures of Spider-Man and the Incredible Hulk Coaster. There's also whimsical Seuss Landing.

SeaWorld and Discovery Cove
(G) Lagoons are populated by all manner of sea creatures, and shows are well done. Kraken and Manta are first-rate coasters, and Shamu's Happy Harbor makes young kids gleeful. Discovery Cove lets you swim with dolphins.

I-Drive
International Drive, 7 mi northeast of Disney, is a busy commercial strip with attractions like Ripley's Believe it or Not! Odditoruim, WonderWorks, Wet 'n Wild water park, and Fun Spot.

Kennedy Space Center
About an hour's drive east of Orlando the center has exhibits about space exploration; interactive rides like the Shuttle Launch Experience; an astronaut memorial and a hall of fame; and an IMAX theater.

Busch Gardens Tampa
(H) It's a 335-acre adventure park with free-roaming animals. It's an amusement park with six roller coasters. It's an entertainment venue with Broadway-style theater extravaganzas and 4-D movies. It's all in Tampa, just 84 mi southwest of Orlando.

IF YOU LIKE

Thrill Rides

Many people love high-speed launches and stomach-churning multiple inversions. Simulator rides that produce similar results are just as popular. Strap on your seat belt and prepare for liftoff!

■ **Roller Coasters.** Coaster fans can't get enough of the Incredible Hulk at Islands of Adventure, Manta at SeaWorld, and Rock 'n' Roller Coaster at Disney's Hollywood Studios. There's also Expedition Everest at Animal Kingdom, Space Mountain at Magic Kingdom, Hollywood Rip Ride Rockit at Universal Studios, and SheiKra at Busch Gardens.

■ **Simulators.** Soarin' at Epcot gives you the sensation of hang gliding over California. Wild Arctic at SeaWorld takes you on a virtual helicopter ride above polar ice caps. The Simpsons Ride at Universal Studios is a cartoonish romp, and the Amazing Adventures of Spider Man uses 3-D technology and special effects to the max for high-voltage thrills. At DisneyQuest and WonderWorks you can "build," then ride, your own simulated roller coaster. Pretend you're an astronaut at Kennedy Space Center's Shuttle Launch Experience.

■ **Wet Rides.** Hot Florida days and wet thrill rides go together like burgers and fries. Cool off at Journey to Atlantis at SeaWorld; Popeye and Bluto's Bilge-Rat Barges and Dudley Do-Right's Ripsaw Falls at Islands of Adventure; Splash Mountain at the Magic Kingdom; and Kali River Rapids at Animal Kingdom.

■ **Waterslides.** Wedgie alert: get your bikini in a bunch on Humunga Kowabunga speed slide at Typhoon Lagoon, Summit Plummet at Blizzard Beach, Bomb Bay at Wet 'n Wild, and Dolphin Plunge at Aquatica.

Special Effects and Interactive Fun

Bubbles burst on your nose. A 3-D snake threatens from the big screen. Cartoons come to life. Aliens attack. Anything's possible when theme-park attractions throw special effects, animation magic, and hands-on action into the mix.

■ **Theater Shows.** If you get a kick out of special-effects surprises in 3-D films, these top shows should be on your itinerary: Shrek 4-D at Universal Studios; It's Tough to Be a Bug! at Animal Kingdom; Mickey's PhilharMagic at Magic Kingdom; Honey, I Shrunk the Audience at Epcot; and MuppetVision 3-D at Hollywood Studios.

■ **Interactive Rides.** Competitive streak? These scored rides, complete with hands-on laser guns or spring-action shooters, are just the ticket: Men in Black: Alien Attack at Universal Studios; Toy Story Midway Mania! at Hollywood Studios; Buzz Lightyear's Space Ranger Spin at Magic Kingdom.

■ **Audio-Animatronics.** Disney's Audio-Animatronics characters pop up in every park, and some of the figures can be quite convincing. Among the best: the wicked witch of The Great Movie Ride "Oz" sequence at Hollywood Studios; the President Obama figure at the Hall of Presidents and Captain Jack Sparrow of Pirates of the Caribbean, both at Magic Kingdom; and the monstrous yeti of Expedition Everest at Animal Kingdom.

■ **Cartoon Magic.** Animation brings characters to life on dozens of rides and attractions, from nutty Homer at Universal's The Simpson's Ride to wacky Mushu of the Disney film *Mulan* at The Magic of Disney Animation in Hollywood Studios.

Animal Antics

Alligators don't just hang out in Orlando's many large lakes—they also headline 'gator-wrestling shows and whole-chicken feeding frenzies at Gatorland. If reptiles aren't your thing, consider the options.

■ **Natural Habitats.** Frolic with dolphins and snorkel amid stingrays at Discovery Cove's Dolphin Lagoon and Tropical Reef. SeaWorld's Penguin Encounter and other attractions feature many animals and fish in re-created environments. At Animal Kingdom you'll see Bengal tigers along the Maharajah Jungle Trek; lowland gorillas at Pangani Forest Exploration Trail; and Galapagos tortoises at Discovery Island Trails. Myombe Reserve at Busch Gardens is a rain-forest environment with gorillas and chimps.

■ **Safaris.** Kilimanjaro Safaris at Animal Kingdom is a bumpy adventure in open-air vehicles through African habitats. No 20-minute safari is the same (except for the poaching storyline), as the elephants, hippos, lions, zebras, and other animals are constantly on the move. At Busch Gardens the off-road Rhino Rally safari passes crocs, rhinos, and hippos.

■ **Performances.** SeaWorld is the top park in which to see animals trained to entertain. Shamu makes a huge splash in the show Believe. Sea lions, otters, and walruses astound you at the Clyde and Seamore Take Pirate Island dramedy. At the Pets Ahoy show, dogs, cats, parrots, and even a pig play for laughs.

■ **Critter Connections.** At Rafiki's Planet Watch in Animal Kingdom there are exotic animal encounters and a petting yard with animals from around the world. At SeaWorld you can feed and pet dolphins at Key West and stroke rays at Stingray Lagoon.

Parades, Fireworks, and Shows

Lights, fireworks, action! You'll get your fill at Orlando's theme parks. The Magic Kingdom alone uses 683 pieces of pyro nightly for its dazzling 12-minute Wishes fireworks and music show. If you love a parade, find your section of curb and park it early.

■ **Daytime Pageants.** You can set your watch by the Magic Kingdom's daily 3 PM Disney character parade, Celebrate a Dream Come True. Mickey's Jammin' Jungle Parade is a safari of fun at Animal Kingdom, and Block Party Bash is a daily interactive dance event at Hollywood Studios.

■ **Nighttime Spectacles.** The Magic Kingdom's Wishes explodes almost nightly over Cinderella Castle, and the SpectroMagic parade with millions of twinkling lights charms crowds several times weekly along Main Street, U.S.A. Epcot's nightly IllumiNations combines music, flames, fireworks, and fountains in a 13-minute display of near-cosmic proportion. Get a seat early for Fantasmic! at Hollywood Studios, a (usually twice a week) 25-minute fireworks, laser, lights, and dancing-fountains show starring Sorcerer Mickey Mouse.

■ **Explosive Action.** The Eighth Voyage of Sinbad at Islands of Adventure juices up its storyline with 25 minutes of physical stunt work, plus water explosions, flames, and fireworks. Indiana Jones Epic Stunt Spectacular! has dynamic action sequences straight from the film. Car, boat, and motorcycle stunts take the stage at the Lights, Motors, Action! Extreme Stunt Show (both at Hollywood Studios).

Luxury Resorts

Orlando attracts millions of visitors each year, and it stands to reason that some are big spenders. Here are our favorite upscale lodging resorts that offer an array of amenities from first-rate service, fine food, and pampering spas to championship golf courses, attractive architecture, and a general ambience of luxury.

■ **Animal Kingdom Lodge.** One of the few places at Disney where the exotic animals strolling past your window are real. The soaring thatch-roofed lobby is breathtaking, and staff tells stories about their African homelands.

■ **Grand Floridian Resort & Spa.** A hotel in the Victorian style, complete with broad verandas, that allows guests to feel as though they've traveled back in time to an era when they were truly pampered.

■ **Portofino Bay Hotel.** The hotel is as close a clone to the Mediterranean town as you'll find; it's easy to imagine yourself in Italy, sunbathing in a formal Italian garden, drinking Campari and enjoying La Dolce Vita, contemplating a fine Italian dinner or a visit to the restful spa.

■ **Waldorf Astoria Orlando.** While it's not an exact copy of the famed Manhattan original, it's a thoroughly updated ode to Waldorf luxury, with a Guerlain spa, fine restaurants, and a championship golf course.

Family- and Budget-Friendly Stays

Families flock to this theme-park-oriented area, which means that there are endless budget options that can accommodate the entire clan.

■ **All-Star Sports, Music & Movies Resorts.** Each section of this sprawling resort is geared to a particular interest, providing fun for kids, and a break for parents' wallets. The Music resort pays homage to genres from Broadway show tunes to country, jazz, and rock n' roll; the pools are shaped like a guitar and a piano. In the Movies resort, huge characters from classic Disney films frame each building. The Sports resort celebrates baseball, football, basketball, and more, and has a pool shaped like a baseball diamond.

■ **Fort Wilderness Resort Campground or Cabins.** Whether you are a camper or not, this relatively unknown and inexpensive part of Disney World offers a unique glimpse of Florida wilderness, along with entertainment, such as the ridiculously funny Hoop Dee Doo Revue, which makes the kid in all of us erupt with laughter. If you don't have a tent, staff will provide one and put it up!

■ **Lake Buena Vista Resort.** Close enough to Disney to watch the fireworks from your balcony, this hotel has something for every member of the family: free Wi-Fi, free shuttles to Disney and outlet malls, a fun pool, and, best of all, it's within walking distance to Downtown Disney's entertainment complex.

■ **Nickelodeon Family Suites by Holiday Inn.** Sponge Bob and Co. are as familiar to kids as Mickey and Minnie, and this reasonably priced hotel complex is located near Disney, but allows for an escape to something completely different.

Foodie Experiences

The Orlando dining scene does not only consist of hamburgers and hot dogs. You can also find five-star dining and creative cuisine mixed in among the sea of food courts and fast-food chains.

■ **Boma.** African-inspired dishes like spiced roasted chicken and curried-coconut seafood stew are a hit with parents and kids at this casual and excellent buffet in the Animal Kingdom Lodge.

■ **Luma on Park.** Under the deft guidance of chef Brandon McGlamery, over-the-top delicious takes on creative American fare are served in a stylish see-and-be-seen space right on Winter Park's tony Park Avenue.

■ **Primo, by Melissa Kelly.** Melissa Kelly's farm-to-table ethos is in full effect at the Orlando outpost of the chef's famed Italian-organic Maine restaurant. Here produce is grown in the hotel garden, so diners can expect all of the dishes to be prepared with the freshest ingredients.

■ **The Ravenous Pig.** From a charcuterie platter on which every salami is made entirely from scratch to a small inventive menu that changes every day based on what's fresh in the market (plus the best burger in town), this comfortable newcomer is worth the drive.

Theme Restaurants

Part of the fun of Orlando is the over-the-top theme parks, and the restaurants to match. Here are our favorite restaurants where ambience and decor are just as prized as what is on the plate.

■ **Cuba Libre.** This expansive eatery replicates the streets of Cuba, and if you close your eyes, sip a mojito, and snack on some *papas rellenas*, you'll almost feel like you're in Havana.

■ **50s Prime Time Café.** Head back in time at this replica of a kitschy, classic American diner. Clips of sitcoms like I Love Lucy and The Donna Reed Show play in the background as diners chow down on comfort-food favorites like meat loaf and fried chicken.

■ **Sci-Fi Dine-In Theater Restaurant.** Dine-in at this (fake) drive-in, where standard American fare, like salads, sandwiches, and burgers are served to you as you sit in a faux convertible and watch movie clips from classic sci-fi flicks from the 50s and 60s.

■ **Three Broomsticks.** Harry Potter fans should look no further than this tavern at the new Wizarding World of Harry Potter attraction. Dine here and you'll feel like you're in the heart of Hogsmeade, rather than the heart of Orlando.

ORLANDO EVENTS

If you've been to Orlando and its parks and enjoyed the top attractions at least once, it may be time to think about a special trip around one of the many festivals and events slated throughout the year.

The year-end holiday season is particularly festive. Decorations go up and events begin around Thanksgiving and continue through early January. It pays to book a trip during the first few weeks of December, when there's a lull between Thanksgiving and Christmas crowds.

Decor devotees should plan time for a trip through Disney to visit meticulously adorned resort hotel lobbies and to marvel at intricate gingerbread-house displays. Kids can reveal their deepest wishes to Santa at Downtown Disney Marketplace.

Winter

Don't miss Epcot's nightly, included-with-admission **Candlelight Processional,** with celebrity narrators retelling the Christmas story accompanied by a choir and orchestra. Line up early for the America Gardens Theatre event or snag reserved seating by purchasing the Candlelight lunch or dinner package (about $35–$60 for adults, $15 or more for children ages 3–9).

At Islands of Adventure the season takes a curmudgeonly turn during **Grinchmas,** a stage show based on the popular Dr. Seuss book. You'll hear an original Mannheim Steamroller musical score and six songs by a cast including the Grinch and the Whos from Whoville.

Mickey's Very Merry Christmas Party spreads holiday cheer at the Magic Kingdom during scheduled November and December evenings. It "snows" on Main Street, U.S.A. Hot cocoa and cookies, seasonal stage shows, and a holiday parade and fireworks add to the fun that's priced lower than one day's park admission.

At Disney's Hollywood Studios you can see the long-running holiday-time **Osborne Family Spectacle of Dancing Lights.** Disney's Animal Kingdom unwraps **Mickey's Jingle Jungle Parade** for the holiday festivities.

The Wild Arctic attraction at SeaWorld becomes **The Polar Express Experience** from mid-November through early January, when you can enjoy a multisensory ride past classic scenes from the popular film based on the Caldecott-medal-winning book *The Polar Express.* Shows starring sea lions, otters, Shamu, and even the Sesame Street gang are performed throughout the holidays.

At least 40,000 athletes from around the globe lace up their running shoes each January during the **Walt Disney World Marathon** weekend. Donald, Mickey, and Goofy challenge racers to a half marathon, a full marathon, or both. There are also a 5K family fun run, kids' races, and a Health and Fitness Expo at ESPN Wide World of Sports complex.

Spring

During **Mardi Gras at Universal Studios,** beads, stilt walkers, and floats keep the spirit of New Orleans alive on Saturday nights from February through April. Live bands straight from the Big Easy perform, and you can slurp up authentic New Orleans–style food and drinks.

For more than 50 years, the juried **Winter Park Sidewalk Art Festival** (⊕ *www.wpsaf. org*) has taken over Park Avenue and Central Park in posh Winter Park during the third weekend of March. More than 300,000 visitors typically show up to enjoy exhibits by 225 or more artists, nosh on curly fries and gyros, and listen to live music.

Summer

During June's **Gay Days Orlando** (⊕ *www. gaydays.com*), parties and tours are organized throughout the metro area and the parks for the gay, lesbian, bisexual, and transgendered community and their families and friends.

Kissimmee's Lakefront Park launches its own **City of Kissimmee July 4th Celebration** at 5 PM with live music, karaoke, bingo, food, and a water-ski show before the pyrotechnics. **A Flashback 4th of July** in the city of Celebration near Walt Disney World features a festival-themed costume contest tied to a past decade (50s, 70s—a different era each year), plus live music, games, and fireworks. Downtown Orlando draws thousands to its free **Lake Eola Park Fireworks** event that begins late afternoon with games, food, and live entertainment.

Fall

Florida's longest-running professional golf event (40 years and counting), the **Children's Miracle Network Classic** (⊕ *www. childrensmiraclenetworkclassic.com*), takes place each fall when golf greats descend on the Disney links for a shot at the purse and a chance to help improve the lives of children. Past Classic champs include Tiger Woods, Jack Nicklaus, Payne Stewart, and Vijay Singh.

For six weeks (late September through mid-November) the **Epcot International Food & Wine Festival** transforms the park into a food-and-wine wonderland with tasting seminars, culinary demonstrations, and a constant stream of celebrity chefs. Dine around the world at international marketplaces selling tasty bites, or splurge on wine schools.

Kids in costumes own the streets of the Magic Kingdom during their quest for treats (no tricks!) at **Mickey's Not-So-Scary Halloween Party,** a gently spooky celebration on scheduled evenings throughout September and October. Party tickets are priced below regular park admission, and it's easier to meet the characters and avoid ride queues.

Blood-curdling screams are the night music of **Halloween Horror Nights,** the wildly popular fright-fest at Universal Studios. Chill-inducing haunted houses and scare zones populated by characters from your worst nightmares guarantee delicious terrors for less than the price of regular park admission.

For more than three decades, November's **Festival of the Masters,** a juried art festival at Downtown Disney, has welcomed top artists showcasing works from clay, wood, and metal, to oils, watercolors, and jewelry.

The **Macy's Holiday Parade** at Universal Studios replicates the New York original with balloon, floats, and marching bands from across the country. Holiday shows in the park star Barney, the Blues Brothers, and other Universal celebs.

ORLANDO WEDDINGS AND HONEYMOONS

Orlando and its theme parks have become increasingly popular shower, wedding, and honeymoon destinations. The area appeals to starry-eyed Gen Y couples and, more and more, older couples, some marrying for the second time and many bringing family and friends in for the wedding-vacation-reunion of a lifetime. They come from across the United States and throughout the world, and their ideas of the perfect wedding vary greatly.

One bride made an entrance in Cinderella's glass coach; her groom rode in on a white horse. A thrill-seeking couple took the freefall plunge on the Twilight Zone Tower of Terror at Disney's Hollywood Studios. Two couples, on separate occasions, tied the knot in the middle of their Walt Disney World Marathon run, exchanging vows in front of Cinderella Castle at the Magic Kingdom. Moonlight on the Ritz-Carlton lawn set the scene for another couple's romantic vow exchange, and a rooftop Orlando wedding wowed yet another couple's guests with a 360-degree view of the downtown skyline and scenic Lake Eola Park.

Pre-Wedding Events

Showers and bachelor and bachelorette parties are easy to arrange in a city where there's so much to do. At Disney, the Mad Hatter can show up for a bridesmaid's tea event at the Grand Floridian. Parties can begin with dinner and a wine tasting at Hannibal's wine cellar in Winter Park before moving on to a local nightclub. Grooms who stay at Portofino Bay like to party at Universal CityWalk, because no driving is required—a ferry will shuttle them back to the hotel.

For rehearsal dinners (or wedding receptions) Disney pulls out the stops to stage events ranging from an after-hours

reception at the Lion King Theater in Animal Kingdom to an internationally themed event at one of the World Showcase countries in Epcot.

Weddings

You can opt for a traditional ceremony at Disney's Wedding Pavilion on the Seven Seas Lagoon by the Grand Floridian Resort & Spa. Designed with the charming features of a Victorian summerhouse, the pavilion is an airy room with a view of Cinderella Castle just across the lagoon. Alternatively, you can plan an informal beachside vow-exchange at a lakeside Disney resort; a garden or gazebo ceremony; an over-the-top, Cinderella-style wedding; or a Broadway-themed blowout.

Downtown Orlando and historic Winter Park are popular wedding destinations, as well, says Lisa Konecny, owner of E Events (⊕ *www.e-eventsdesign.net*). The Grand Bohemian Hotel stages amazing rooftop ceremonies. Konecny and her team have planned rooftop weddings and receptions at other downtown buildings, including one with a panoramic view of the skyline and Lake Eola.

Other top wedding spots are downtown's Orange County Regional History Center; the City Arts Factory in the arts district, where exhibits constantly change; the Mennello Museum of American Art in the city's Loch Haven area; and Casa Feliz, a historic Spanish home-museum in Winter Park.

According to Konecny, couples who hire E Events tend to be a bit older and are sophisticated. They also like to hold the wedding ceremony and reception in one location, making Orlando the perfect choice. The area is rife with professional entertainers who are available for receptions. Theme-park musicians and other

performers often contract out at reasonable prices, and there's a lot of diversity, from zydeco and salsa bands to groups that specialize in swing music.

Heather Snively, owner of Weddings Unique (www.weddingsunique.com), says Orlando attracts a lot of couples planning second marriages, couples with children, and those seeking a wedding–family reunion–minivacation packaged as one. Resort hotels like the Ritz, Waldorf Astoria, and Portofino Bay at Universal feature romantic backdrops for the ceremony, plus smaller ballrooms ideal for receptions.

The hotels can also support activities ranging from spa parties to golf outings for those in the wedding party. Snively and her team plan up to 40 weddings a year from soup to nuts, working closely with in-house resort coordinators to smooth out every detail and with travel agents to make arrangements for guest travel.

Honeymoons

Central Florida resorts cater to honeymooners with special packages. Honeymoon suites with whirlpools and other amenities create the backdrop for romance that's enhanced with extras like champagne and chocolate-covered strawberries. Resort pools with cabanas, beaches, waterfalls, swaying palms, and poolside margarita delivery make the subtropical setting seem as exotic as a tropical island.

Disney's Fairy Tale Honeymoons division helps you customize a vacation package and even offers a Honeymoon Registry if your guests wish to contribute to your post-wedding getaway rather than give a traditional gift. There are package deals to be had at Walt Disney World resorts and at Disney's Vero Beach Resort. Some couples make their wedding dreams or vow renewals come true at sea, where the honeymoon follows immediately.

Planning Tips

If you're dreaming about a central Florida wedding, keep these tips from the experts in mind:

■ Hire a reputable planner long before the big date. Though you'll pay a fee for your planner, he or she will be an advocate with barter power when dealing with vendors.

■ For a destination wedding, build in plenty of time to book travel arrangements and accommodations for all who plan to attend.

■ If your budget is tight, plan your Orlando wedding between Monday and Thursday during non-peak season for the lowest hotel rates.

■ Split the wedding-planning tasks with your partner. If the groom is focused more on the reception's music, food, and beverages, the bride can focus on, say, wedding flowers and photography.

■ Let your wedding planner arrange romantic escapes from your guests, especially if you plan to wed *and* honeymoon in Orlando. If everyone's staying at the Gaylord Palms Resort or the Hard Rock Hotel, have your wedding planner book you a spa package at the Waldorf Astoria or Ritz-Carlton.

■ Start your research by visiting several Orlando-area wedding-planner Web sites; the Orlando/Orange County Convention & Visitor's Bureau site at orlandoinfo. com/weddings; and Disney's Fairy Tale Weddings & Honeymoons at disney-weddings.disney.go.com.

DISNEY CRUISES

More than a dozen years after Disney Cruise Line (DCL) first set sail with the *Disney Magic* and the *Disney Wonder*, it launches its third ship, Disney Dream, in 2011 and its fourth, Disney Fantasy, in 2012, increasing its cruise-ship guest capacity to more than 13,000. Disney's making waves with innovations aboard the Dream, from its shipboard high-speed AquaDuck waterslide coaster, the first of its kind in the industry, to "virtual" portholes in inside staterooms that provide real-time views from outside the ship.

The cruise line continues to offer its popular excursions from Port Canaveral, Florida, to the Bahamas and Key West, Florida, as well as to eastern and western Caribbean destinations with stops that include Grand Cayman, Cozumel, and St. Thomas. All Caribbean and Bahamian cruises include at least one stop at Disney's gem of a private island, Castaway Cay. DCL also offers a lineup of alternative sailings to the Mexican Riviera, the Mediterranean, and Alaska.

A big Disney plus: you can combine an ocean getaway with a stay at Walt Disney World for a seamless land-and-sea vacation. You check in just once: your room key at your Disney resort hotel becomes both your boarding pass at Disney's terminal at Port Canaveral and the key to your stateroom.

Cruise Packages

Packages include room, meals (there are extra charges at the exclusive restaurants though), and most shipboard activities, but not shore excursions or, generally, transportation to and from the ship. Prices vary greatly depending on the package options you choose, the stateroom, the destination, the time of year you sail, and which week you book. A three-night

Disney Dream cruise starts at about $389 per person based on double occupancy and not including taxes and fees.

Booking early might help you secure a better rate, but you might also get a bargain by booking at the last minute on a ship that hasn't filled. ◼TIP➜ Dig for a discount on your Disney cruise with a travel agent who specializes in cruises. Find one at ⊕ *www.travelsense.org.*

To book any Disney cruise, check into vessels and staterooms, find out about shore excursions and more, contact the **Disney Cruise Line** (☎ *800/370–0097* ⊕ *www. disneycruise.com*).

Staterooms

Disney Magic and Disney Wonder each have 875 staterooms, 73% of which have ocean-view rooms and 44% of which have private verandas. Disney Dream is a larger ship with 1,250 staterooms—88% are outside rooms, and 90% of those offer private verandas.

Cabins are ranked by category and range from standard inside staterooms (category 11 on the Dream; categories 11 and 12 on the Magic or Wonder; 169–184 square feet, sleeps three to four) to deluxe family staterooms with verandas (category 4 on all ships, 256–304 square feet, sleeps five). Luxurious concierge suites are top-of-the-line, with every amenity from whirlpool bathtubs to walk-in closets.

Budget-minded cruisers often are tempted to stick with the least expensive option, the inside stateroom, but if you choose this option you'll give up a valued amenity on Disney ships—the split bathroom. It features a vanity, sink, and full tub and shower in one area and a vanity, sink, and toilet in another—a real time-saver when it's time for you and your cabin mates to

freshen up before excursions or evening dinners and shows.

Quite a few of the staterooms have a clever pull-down bunk-bed setup that saves space until bedtime and draws cheers from children. All rooms are elegantly appointed with natural wood furniture.

Disney does a commendable job of keeping rooms and much of the rest of the ship smoke-free while setting aside some deck, bar, and private veranda areas for smokers.

For Guests with Disabilities

Accessible staterooms for people with disabilities have ramps, handrails, fold-down shower seats, and handheld showerheads; special communications kits are available with phone alerts, amplifiers, and text typewriters. Assistive-listening systems are available in the ships' main theaters, and sign-language interpretation is offered for live performances on specified cruise dates.

Shore Excursions

At various ports of call Disney offers between one and two-dozen organized excursions, from snorkeling and diving to sightseeing and shopping. For example, at Grand Cayman you can visit a butterfly farm or sign up for a trip to Stingray City, not really a city, but a long sandbar where you can swim with hundreds of rays. During a stop at Cozumel you can explore the Mayan ruins of Tulum and strike a bargain for handcrafted Mexican hats, toys, and knickknacks. All activities are rated from "leisurely" to "strenuously active."

Adult Activities

Poolside games, wine tastings, dessert-making, and even navigational demonstrations by the ship's bridge officers are among the adults-only diversions. Each

ship's spa is a don't-miss for those who need some pampering—book early!

For a romantic dinner, the intimate, adults-only **Palo** (Magic, Wonder and Dream) offers sweeping ocean views. Expect a fantastic wine list and dishes like grilled salmon with creamy risotto and grilled filet mignon with a port-wine reduction and Gorgonzola cheese sauce. Reserve early for this hot ticket. The champagne brunch on four-night-or-longer cruises is another great Palo dining event.

The art nouveau decor in the *Dream's* exclusive 80-seat restaurant, **Remy,** is a nod to the movie *Ratatouille*, and, of course, the cuisine is French-inspired. The eight or nine tasting dishes served each night might include fresh asparagus with black truffle and *vin jaune*, lobster nage, or Japanese Wagyu beef with garlic-potatoe puree and petite carrots. Wine pairings are amazing; so are the pastries. Book as far ahead of your trip as possible.

DID YOU KNOW?

Mickey Mouse was the inspiration for the Disney ships' colors—black hull, white superstructure, yellow trim and lifeboats, and giant red funnels. The ships recall classic ocean liners of the 1930s, and when the captain hits the horn, it plays the first seven notes of "When You Wish Upon a Star."

Children's Activities

On all three ships, there's nearly an entire deck reserved for kids. When you drop them off, pick up a pager to stay in touch with the activities counselors. Babysitting is available on the Magic and Wonder for children under 3 at **Flounder's Reef Nursery** for $6 per hour (two-hour minimum) and $5 an hour for each additional sibling. Disney also offers a groundbreaking online service, Babies Travel Lite, which lets parents order all their baby's travel products, including diapers and formula, and have them shipped to their stateroom before the cruise begins. Similar services are offered at the Dream's **It's a Small World Nursery.**

The well-run **Oceaneer Club** on the Magic and Wonder provides nonstop activities for kids ages 3 to 7. Little ones have a ball in the playroom designed to look like Captain Hook's pirate ship. They can scramble around on a rope bridge, watch a Disney movie, and do crafts at the **Toy Story Boot Camp.** Counselors tailor activities to kids ages 3 to 4 and 5 to 7 separately. On the Dream, the Club space welcomes children ages 3 to 10.

Kids 8 to 12 can head for the high-tech **Oceaneer Lab** on the Magic and Wonder. There are science experiments, sports challenges, and karaoke jams. A program inspired by the *High School Musical* craze features a Mad Cap Caper talent show. With their parent's permission, children can check themselves in and out of the Lab as they please. On the Disney Dream the expanded Lab space is open to children 3 to 10. The Dream also ventures into tween territory with a new club, **Edge,** that offers high-tech entertainment for 11- to 13-year-olds in their own loft-style space.

Teens up to age 17 chill out at a getaway called the **Stack** on the *Disney Magic,* **Aloft** on the *Wonder, and* **Vibe** *on the Dream.* They can tune in to music, watch plasma-screen TVs, play board and video games, or just hang out and meet new friends. Organized activities for teens include trivia games and evening dance parties. Internet message-, photo-, and video-posting also are available.

Restaurants

Coordinators arrange for you to alternate restaurants each night so you can sample a variety of offerings. Disney also offers early and late dinner seatings. Early ones are best for families with small children. Also, look into the Dine and Play option, where servers speed up the kids' service, then the ship's activity counselors whisk youngsters off so older family members can relax. If you miss your seating altogether, you can always find a casual dining option.

At **Animator's Palate**, scenes featuring Disney characters change from black-and-white to Technicolor as the meal progresses on the Magic and Wonder; on the Dream diners are surrounded by an artist's studio where famous film scenes line the walls and fiber-optic "brush pillars" paint oversized ceiling "palettes" vibrant colors. Dining is slightly more formal at **Lumiere's,** on the *Magic,* where beef tenderloin, lamb shank, and other entrées are served French-style in a classic ocean-liner-style dining room.

At **Triton's,** on the *Wonder,* seafood, roast duck, pasta, and other selections are served in an elegant, art deco, under-the-sea-theme dining room. The Dream's **Royal Palace,** inspired by Disney's princess films, serves crowned rack of lamb, beef Wellington, and other royal dishes. At

the Caribbean-theme **Parrot Cay** restaurant (Magic and Wonder), the mood is both casual and festive. On the Dream, **Enchanted Garden** is the whimsical, more casual rotation restaurant. Character breakfasts and high tea with Wendy of *Peter Pan* fame are options aboard the *Magic* (but not the *Wonder*).

After-Dark Entertainment

During the **Pirates IN the Caribbean** themed evening, swashbuckling servers dish up Caribbean and Bahamian taste treats, an "arrr" or two, a cup of grog, and (on seven-night cruises) a pirate bandanna for every guest at dinner. After dinner, you head off to a deck party where Captain Hook, Mr. Smee, and others appear for some high-spirited action, dancing, and fireworks.

Lavish shows and variety acts entertain families every night of every cruise. The big hit on Disney Wonder is Toy Story–The Musical, a larger-than-life stage version of the film classic. The Golden Mickeys on the Wonder and Magic is a high-tech salute to the animation of Walt Disney in the form of a Hollywood-style award ceremony. Twice Charmed: An Original Twist on the Cinderella Story, is a Broadway-style production on Disney Magic that begins where the original Cinderella story ended.

Disney Dreams . . . An Enchanted Classic is a sweet bedtime story starring Peter Pan, Aladdin, Ariel, and other Disney characters combining animation, pyrotechnic and laser features, snow effects, and mechanisms that let characters "fly" more convincingly. The Dream premieres the first full-scale musical revue dedicated to Disney's famous animated villains in Villains Tonight! Each ship also has a **cinema** screening classic Disney films, and

every guest will have the opportunity to experience a show or film featuring the digital 3-D enhancements.

There are also many things geared to adults. At the **Cove Café** on all ships you can enjoy a gourmet coffee, watch TV, check e-mail, and socialize. **Beat Street,** a nightclub on the *Magic,* has the Rockin' Bar D dance club and Sessions, a piano bar. **Route 66,** the *Wonder*'s nightclub, has the WaveBands dance club and the Cadillac Lounge piano bar. If you're looking for something more low-key, check out **Diversions,** a sports pub on both ships.

On the new ship Dream, Disney expands its nightlife offerings at **The District**, with lounges, a pub, sky bar, and nightclub. Movie fans can see first-run films at the ships' plush Buena Vista Theatre, where full-length features really pop with digital 3-D technology.

Castaway Cay

Disney has its own private Bahamian island, Castaway Cay, with white-sand beaches, towering palms, and swaying hammocks—it's a key stop on many Disney cruises. You can relax on the beach, or join a snorkeling or parasailing excursion. Castaway Ray's Stingray Adventure lets adults and kids age 5 and up touch, feed, and even snorkel with stingrays in an island lagoon.

If you're not traveling with children or if you've dropped them off at Scuttle's Cove to take part in the kids' programs, hop a tram to Serenity Bay. This is a beach just for adults, where you can melt under the influence of a cabana sheltered Swedish massage or sip a rum punch from Castaway Air Bar. A lunch buffet is served on both the family and adult ends of the island. Sand-accessible wheelchairs are available for guests who need them.

ORLANDO GOLF COURSES

The International Association of Golf Tour Operators voted Orlando the "North American Golf Destination of the Year 2010" for good reason. There are 177 golf courses and 23 golf academies in the area. Sunny weather almost year-round doesn't hurt, and, though most of Florida is extremely flat, many of the courses feature hills that make them more challenging.

Resort hotels often let nonguests use their golf facilities. Some country clubs are affiliated with particular hotels, and their guests can play at preferred rates. Twilight discounts often apply after 2 PM in busy seasons and after 3 PM the rest of the year; the discount is usually half off the normal rate. Because golf is so incredibly popular, courses regularly raise rates.

In general, even public courses have dress codes, so call ahead for specifics and be sure to reserve tee times. Greens fees usually vary by season, and virtually all include mandatory cart rental, except for the few 9-hole walking courses.

GOLFPAC Travel (⊠ *483 Montgomery Pl., Altamonte Springs* ☎ *407/260–2288 or 800/327–0878* ⊕ *www.golfpactravel.com*) packages golf vacations and arranges tee times at more than 78 Orlando courses. Rates vary based on hotel and course, and 60 to 90 days' advance notice is recommended to set up a vacation.

Walt Disney World

Where else would you find a sand trap shaped like the head of a well-known mouse? Disney has four championship courses—all on the PGA Tour route—plus a 9-hole walking course. All have a driving range, pro shop, locker room, and a snack bar–restaurant. Any guest at a WDW hotel who checks in specifically

to play golf enjoys free cab fare to the course.

Greens Fees. There are lots of variables, with prices ranging from $29 for a youngster 17 or under to play 9 holes at Oak Trail walking course to an adult non-hotel guest paying $174 for 18 holes at Osprey Ridge in peak season. Rates change frequently, though, so confirm when booking. Disney guests get a price break, and you should ask about twilight discount rates. If you only plan to play once, leave the gear at home—you can rent shoes, range balls, and clubs at any location.

Tee Times and Reservations. Tee times are available daily from dawn until dusk. You can book them up to 90 days in advance if you're staying at a WDW-owned hotel, 60 days ahead if you're staying elsewhere, and you must cancel them at least 48 hours out.

One-on-one instruction from PGA-accredited professionals is available at the Palm and Magnolia courses. Prices for private lessons vary: 45-minute lessons cost $75 for adults and $50 for youngsters 17 and under. For tee times and private lessons, call **Walt Disney World Golf & Recreation Reservations** (☎ *407/939–7529*).

The Lake Buena Vista course winds among Downtown Disney–area town houses and villas. Greens are narrow, and hitting straight is important because errant balls risk ending up in someone's bedroom. Be prepared for the famous island green on the 7th. ⊠ *Lake Buena Vista Dr.* ⚑ *18 holes, 6,819 yards, par 72, USGA rating 72.7.*

The Magnolia, played by the pros in the Disney–Oldsmobile Golf Classic, is long but forgiving, with extra-wide fairways. More than 1,500 magnolia trees line the course. ⊠ *Shades of Green, 1950 W.*

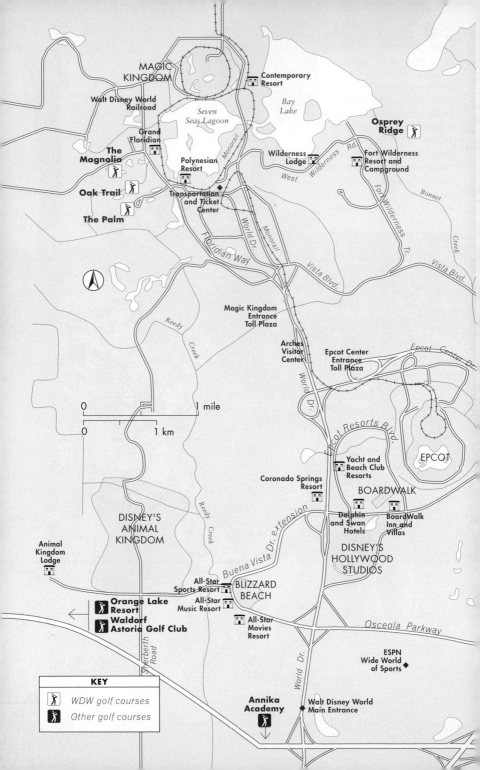

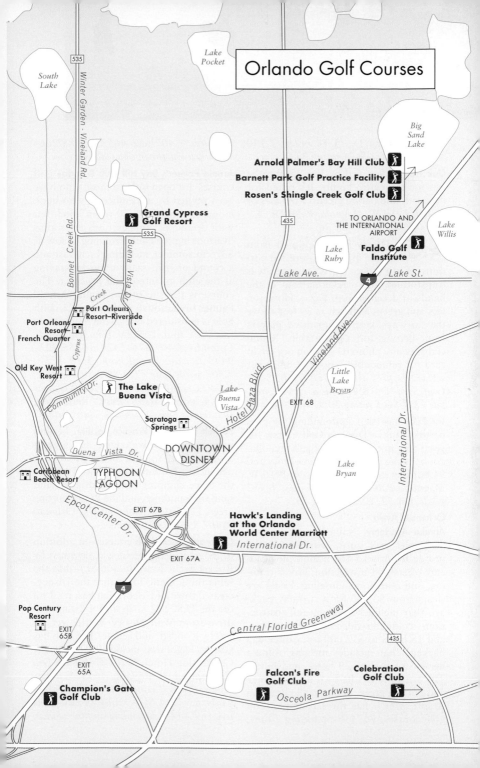

Magnolia-Palm Dr. 🏌 *18 holes, 7,190 yards, par 72, USGA rating 73.9.*

Oak Trail is designed by Ron Garl to be fun for the entire family. It's noted for its small, undulating greens. ⊠ *Shades of Green, 1950 W. Magnolia-Palm Dr.* 🏌 *9 holes, 2,913 yards, par 36.*

★ **Fodor's Choice** **Osprey Ridge**, sculpted from some of the still-forested portions of the huge WDW acreage, was transformed into a relaxing tour in the hands of designer Tom Fazio. However, tees and greens as much as 20 feet above the fairways keep competitive players from getting too comfortable. Rental clubs require photo ID and a major credit card for refundable deposit of $500 per set. ⊠ *Osprey Ridge Golf Club, 3451 Golf View Dr.* 🏌 *18 holes, 7,101 yards, par 72, USGA rating 73.9.*

The Palm has been confounding the pros participating in Disney's Golf Classic for years. It's not as long as the Magnolia, nor as wide, but it has 9 water holes and 94 bunkers. ⊠ *Shades of Green, 1950 W. Magnolia-Palm Dr.* 🏌 *18 holes, 6,957 yards, par 72, USGA rating 73.*

Orlando Area

Annika Academy. Named for its owner and chief golf guru, world-renowned pro golfer Annika Sorenstam, the academy offers golf instruction, fitness training, and nutrition counseling. Prices are steep: from $2,500 for a two-day package that includes lodging, golf instruction, computer/video swing analysis, and 18 holes to $12,000 for a three-day package that includes meeting Annika herself for a clinic, 9 holes, and lunch. The academy has its own driving range and putting green, and is at the Reunion Resort, which has three championship golf courses. ⊠ *7450 Sparkling Court,*

Reunion ☎ *407/662–4653 or 888/266–4522* ⊕ *www.theannikaacademy.com.*

Arnold Palmer's Bay Hill Club & Lodge golf courses are open only to those who have been invited by a member or who book lodging at the club's 70-room hotel. But with double-occupancy rates for rooms overlooking the course running as low as $375 in summer, including breakfast and a round of golf, many consider staying at the club an interesting prospect. The course is the site of the annual Arnold Palmer Invitational, and its par-72, 18th hole is considered one of the toughest on the PGA tour. ⊠ *9000 Bay Hill Blvd., Orlando* ☎ *407/876–2429 or 888/422–9445* ⊕ *www.bayhill.com* 🏌 *18 holes, 7,207 yards, par 72, USGA rating 75.1; 9 holes, 3,409 yards, par 36* ☒ *Greens fees included in room rates* ☞ *Restaurant, spa, tennis, private lessons, club rental.*

Barnett Park Golf Practice Facility, besides having an attractive course, has a great asset: it's free. You just show up to use the net-enclosed driving range (with 10 pads), the three chipping holes with grass and sand surroundings, and the 9-hole putting green. ⊠ *4801 W. Colonial Dr., Orlando* ☎ *407/836–6248* ☒ *Free.*

Celebration Golf Club course—in addition to its great pedigree (it was designed by Robert Trent Jones Jr. and Sr.)—has the same thing going for it that the Disney-created town of Celebration has: it's 1 mi off the U.S. 192 strip and a 10-minute drive from Walt Disney World, yet it's lovely, wooded, and serene. The club has golf packages that include lodging at the Celebration Hotel. ⊠ *701 Golf Park Dr., Celebration* ☎ *407/566–4653* ⊕ *www. celebrationgolf.com* 🏌 *18 holes, 6,783 yards, par 72, USGA rating 73* ☒ *Greens fees $69–$145, depending on time of year,*

time of day, and whether you're a Florida or Celebration resident; daily discount rates begin at 2 PM ☞ Restaurant, pro shop, private lessons, club rental.

★ **Champions Gate Golf Club**, with the onsite David Leadbetter Golf Academy, has two distinct courses designed by Greg Norman. The 7,406-yard International has the feel of the best British Isles courses, whereas the 7,048-yard National course is designed in the style of the better domestic courses, with a number of par-3 holes with unusual bunkers. The club is less than 10 mi from Walt Disney World at Exit 72 on I-4. ✉ *1400 Masters Blvd., Champions Gate* ☎ *407/787–4653 Champions Gate, 407/787–3330 or 888/633–5323 Leadbetter Academy* ⊕ *www.championsgategolf.com* ⚐ *International: 18 holes, 7,406 yards, par 72, USGA rating 73.7. National: 18 holes, 7,048 yards, par 72, USGA rating 72.0* ⛳ *Greens fees $65–$187, depending on time of year and time of day. Golf lessons at Leadbetter Academy are $225 per hr and $1,750 per day for private lessons; group lessons are $325 for 3 hrs; a 3-day minischool is $975; a 3-day complete school is $3,000* ☞ *Pro shop, golf school, private lessons, club rental.*

Falcon's Fire Golf Club, designed by Rees Jones, has strategically placed fairway bunkers that demand accuracy off the tee. This club is just off the Irlo Bronson Highway and is convenient to the hotels in the so-called Maingate area. ✉ *3200 Seralago Blvd., Kissimmee* ☎ *407/239–5445* ⊕ *www.falconsfire.com* ⚐ *18 holes, 6,901 yards, par 72, USGA rating 73.8* ⛳ *Greens fees $79–$145, $49 after 2 PM* ☞ *Tee times 8–60 days in advance. Restaurants, private and group lessons, club*

rental, lockers, driving range, putting green.

Faldo Golf Institute by Marriott is the team effort of world-famous golf pro Nick Faldo and Marriott Corp. An extensive-curriculum golf school and 9-hole golf course occupy the grounds of the corporation's biggest time-share complex, Marriott's Grande Vista. Here you can do anything from taking a one-hour, $125–$160 lesson with a Faldo-trained pro to immersing yourself in a three-day extravaganza ($955–$1,345) in which you learn more about golf technique than most nonfanatics would care to know. The Faldo Swing Studio offers high-tech teaching methods. The course, designed by Ron Garl, is geared to make you use every club in your bag—and perhaps a few you may elect to buy in the pro shop. ✉ *Marriott Grande Vista, 12001 Avenida Verde, Orlando* ☎ *407/903–6295 or 888/463–2536* ⊕ *www.gofaldo.com* ⚐ *9 holes, 2,400 yards, par 32.*

Grand Cypress Golf Resort, fashioned after a Scottish glen, is comprised of three 9s: the North, South, and East courses, and the 18-hole New Course. In addition, the Grand Cypress Academy of Golf, a 21-acre facility, has lessons and clinics. The North and South courses have fairways constructed on different levels, giving them added definition. The New Course, designed by Jack Nicklaus, was inspired by the Old Course at St. Andrews, and has deep bunkers, double greens, a snaking burn, and even an old stone bridge. ✉ *1 N. Jacaranda, Orlando* ☎ *407/239–1909 or 800/835–7377* ⊕ *www.grandcypress. com* ⚐ *North: 9 holes, 3,521 yards, par 36. South: 9 holes, 3,472 yards, par 36. East: 9 holes, 3,434 yards, par 36. New: 18 holes, 6,773 yards, par 72. New Course*

USGA rating 71.9. ⊠ Greens fees $120–$250 ☞ Tee times New Course 8–5; all others 7:30–5. Restaurant, club rental, shoe rental, locker room, driving range, putting green, free valet parking.

Hawk's Landing Golf Club at the Orlando World Center Marriott, originally designed by Joe Lee, was extensively upgraded with a Robert E. Cupp III design in 2000. The 220-acre course includes 16 water holes, lots of sand, and exotic landscaping. ⊠ Orlando World Center Marriott, 8701 World Center Dr., Orlando ☎ 407/238–8660 or 800/567–2623 ⊕ www.golfhawkslanding.com ⅃ 18 holes, 6,810 yards, par 72, USGA rating 72.6 ⊠ Greens fees $89–$169 ☞ Tee times 7 days in advance for public, 90 days in advance for World Center guests. Restaurants, private and group lessons, club and shoe rental.

Orange Lake Resort, about five minutes from Walt Disney World's main entrance, has two 18-hole courses (the Legends and the Reserve) and two 9-hole courses (Crane's Bend, Legends Walk). The Legends is a signature Arnold Palmer–designed championship course; the Reserve was designed by Mike Dasher and has unique land and water challenges. Crane's Bend is family-friendly. Legend's Walk is an executive walker's course open until 9 PM nightly, where children 15 and younger play free. The signature hole for the entire group of courses is the Island Oak, No. 13, a 432-yard, par-4 hole in the Pines section (the back 9) of the Legends Course. ⊠ 8505 W. Irlo Bronson Memorial Hwy., Kissimmee ☎ 407/239–1050 or 888/640–6522 ⊕ www.orangelakegolf.com ⅃ The Legends: 18 holes, 7,072 yards, par 72, USGA rating 72.2. The Reserve: 18 holes, 6,670 yards, par 71, USGA rating 72.6. Crane's Bend: 9 holes, 1,901 yards, par

30. Legend's Walk: 9 holes, 1,581 yards, par 30 ⊠ Greens fees $50–$125 for resort guests; $80 –$155 nonguests ☞ Tee times 30 days in advance preferred. Restaurant, private and group lessons, club rental, lighted driving range, putting green.

Rosen's Shingle Creek Golf Club, designed by David Harman, lies alongside a lovely creek, the headwaters of the Everglades. The course is challenging yet playable, with dense stands of oak and pine trees and interconnected waterways. The golf carts even have GPS yardage systems. Universal Studios and the Orange County Convention Center are within a few minutes' drive. ⊠ 9939 Universal Blvd., Orlando ☎ 407/996–9933 or 866/996–9933 ⊕ www.shinglecreekgolf.com ⅃ 18 holes, 7,205 yards, par 72, USGA rating 69.8 ⊠ Greens fees $69 –$129 ☞ Tee times 7–dusk. Restaurant, club rental, shoe rental, driving range, putting green.

The Waldorf Astoria Golf Club is a championship Rees Jones–designed course with a five-tee system for all playing levels. It winds through a scenic wetland preserve, with bunkers reminiscent of century-old hazards. Majestic stands of pine and cypress line the fairways; Jones maintained natural elements while enhancing the land's existing contours. ⊠ 14224 Bonnet Creek Resort La., Orlando ☎ 407/597–3782 or 888/924–6531 ⊕ www.waldorfastoriagolfclub.com ⅃ 18 holes, 7,113 yards, par 72, USGA rating 74.6 ⊠ $125 (seasonal) ☉ Tee times 7–6. Restaurant, club rental, shoe rental, locker room, driving range, putting green, free valet parking.

DOING ORLANDO AND THE PARKS RIGHT

by Jennie Hess

Taumata Racer, Aquatica

You don't have to wish upon a star to make all your Orlando vacation dreams come true. Your trip will be memorable, whether you're traveling with small children, tweens, or teens or the whole gang of friends or family; whether you're on your honeymoon or flying solo.

Gather (or cyber-gather) all your travel companions together to create a wish list. Then, as you create your itinerary, consider everyone's needs and plan accordingly.

Got small children? Know their theme-park limits to prevent meltdowns, and factor in time away from crowded parks for a laid-back visit to smaller attractions. And, to avoid disappointments, don't wait to get to the parks to determine ride height restrictions.

Teens and tweens may want to head for some rides on their own. Determine theme-park meeting locations, and be sure everyone carries a cell phone in case they encounter longer ride lines and delays.

If the guys are planning to hit the links and the gals want a spa day, don't wait until you're in town to reserve a tee time or a facial-mani-pedi package.

What follows are suggestions (and a few quick tips) on how you can do Orlando and the parks right—regardless of who's in your group. For more planning tips and insights, check out Chapter 1.

Shamu's Happy Harbor play area, SeaWorld

Pirates of the Caribbean, Magic Kingdom

FAMILIES WITH SMALL KIDS

Things will go more smoothly if you stick to routines. It's easier than you think. During naptime, for instance, you can relax on a bench while your toddler snoozes in her stroller and the rest of the family heads for a park attraction. Finding sights for wee ones is easy in the parks and outside.

Magic Kingdom. This is the top Disney destination for families with tots; Fantasyland is filled with age-appropriate attractions. Pooh's Playful Spot lets squirmy kids burn up some energy.

SeaWorld. Dolphins, whales, and other marine mammals mesmerize young children. Most shows are captivating, and Shamu's Happy Harbor is a wet, wonderful play area.

Typhoon Lagoon. It sets an idyllic waterpark scene for families with small children. Ketchakiddie Creek is a favorite splash zone.

Orlando Science Center. Exhibits—many of them interactive—at this center near downtown Orlando let kids experience science and the world around them.

Downtown Disney Marketplace. A kiddie train, splash fountains, a LEGO Imagination Center, Bibbidi Bobbidi Boutique (think princess makeovers) are among the attractions for kids.

FAMILIES WITH TWEENS

You and your tweens will have more fun together if you involve them in pre-trip planning. Let each child scope out best bets on Orlando- and theme-park Web sites, then gather to compare notes and create a rough itinerary. Here are a few suggestions to jumpstart the research.

Magic Kingdom. Who ever really outgrows this classic? Tweens love rides ending in "mountain"—Space, Splash, and Big Thunder. The Haunted Mansion and Pirates of the Caribbean are both cool.

Islands of Adventure. This theme-park will be a hit with tweens who love thrill rides and/or superheroes like Spider-Man. For muggle fans of J.K. Rowling's books, the Wizarding World of Harry Potter is a must-see.

Disney's Animal Kingdom. The exotic animals and safari are highlights, but so are scream-inducing Expedition Everest, DINO-SAUR, and Kali River Rapids.

Aquatica. Orlando's newest water park has water-slide thrills and a tube slide through a Commerson's dolphin habitat.

Fun Spot. Tweens love the go-kart racetrack best, but the carnival-style rides and arcades are a big draw, too.

WonderWorks. Tweens can "build" their own coaster, and then ride it; lie on a bed of nails; and pilot a simulated fighter jet.

Incredible Hulk Coaster, Islands of Adventure

Sleuths Mystery Dinner Show, Orlando

FAMILIES WITH TEENS

Let teens make their own "gotta do" list and head out on their own. (Chances are at least some of the sights below will make it to every list.) Stay in touch by texting updates and meeting for meals.

Disney's Hollywood Studios. Teens rave about The Twilight Zone Tower of Terror and Rock 'n' Roller Coaster Starring Aerosmith. Competing in Toy Story Midway Mania! and voting for contestants in The American Idol Experience are other cool options.

Islands of Adventure. Older kids are drawn to the action here—from the Amazing Adventures of Spider-Man to the Incredible Hulk Coaster.

Universal Studios. Teens love Hollywood Rip Ride Rockit, Revenge of the Mummy, and the irreverent The Simpsons Ride.

Blizzard Beach and Wet 'n Wild. Blizzard stands out for its wintry theme, mix of thrills, and laid-back "beach" scene. Wet 'n Wild has loud music and big-thrill slides.

Universal CityWalk. It gets high marks for trendy shopping, movie theaters, and concerts. The theatrics of Blue Man Group is a big teen draw around the corner.

Spa with Mom. Mother-daughter facials and pedicures make for a fun morning or afternoon at Orlando spas like the Buena Vista Palace or Disney's Grand Floridian.

LARGE, MIXED GROUPS

Look into Disney's vacation-planning program, Grand Gatherings. Just remember that group members will be happier campers with some "me" time factored in. Here are some suggestions for shared and individual experiences.

Behind-the-Scenes Park Tours. Tours at SeaWorld, Magic Kingdom, Epcot, and Animal Kingdom are great shared experiences. Note that the more people you have on the expensive but oh-so-cool VIP tour at Universal, the better value it is.

Dinner shows. Some area favorites are Medieval Times in Kissimmee, Sleuths Mystery Dinner Show on I-Drive, Disney's Hoop-Dee-Doo Revue, and SeaWorld's Makahiki Luau.

Discovery Cove. Book a "beach" day here to share the experience of swimming with the dolphins. Meals and snacks are included.

Epcot. Everyone can fan out here to take in the attractions of Future World or World Showcase and then gather for dinner at a reserved table to share experiences.

Spa Visits and Golf Expeditions. These are perfect "breakaway" activities. And there are options for both at Disney and in the greater Orlando area.

Spring Training. In March, it's easy to arrange a group outing to a ballgame in one of several central Florida locations.

Cirque du Soleil – *La Nouba*

Disney's Animal Kingdom.

COUPLES

Let us count the ways to be romantic in Orlando . . . there are too many to list here. Even if the kids are along for the trip, you can carve out time together by using a hotel's sitter service or by packing the children off to a resort kids' club.

Victoria & Albert's. Splurge on a dinner fit for royalty at the Grand Floridian's elegant eatery, central Florida's only AAA Five-Diamond restaurant. Reserve months ahead.

Spa Treatments for Two. Top spas for couples pampering include those in the Ritz Carlton, Waldorf Astoria, Grand Floridian, Portofino Bay, Gaylord Palms, and Walt Disney World Dolphin.

Cirque du Soleil. Hold hands and share the wonder of the surreal show, *La Nouba*, at Downtown Disney West Side.

Wekiwa Springs State Park. Escape here for a picnic and/or to rent a canoe and share quiet time on the river.

Islands of Adventure and CityWalk. Plan a wild and crazy evening of roller-coaster thrills and then belly up to the bar for a cheeseburger in paradise at Jimmy Buffet's Margaritaville.

Lake Eola. Paddle a swan-shaped boat together at this lake in downtown Orlando. Then share flatbread and sip champagne at Eola Wine Company across the street.

SINGLES (OR GROUPS OF FRIENDS)

It's nice to have a traveling companion, but there's an advantage to visiting on your own—you can cover a lot more territory. Single but traveling with friends? You still may want to split up to sample from your own play list.

Animal Kingdom. Animal-loving singles can linger longer at this park to watch behaviors of many exotic creatures along Discovery Trail, the Oasis, Maharajah Jungle Trek, and Pangani Forest Exploration Trail.

Winter Park. On a day trip to this this town you can shop Park Avenue, take a scenic boat tour, and see the Tiffany collection at the Morse Museum of American Art.

Disney's Boardwalk. Let nostalgia take hold on a lakeside stroll. Or hop into a surrey or onto a bicycle built for two. Watch dueling pianos at Jellyrolls or a game at ESPN Club.

Run through the parks. Plan your visit in January and compete in the Walt Disney World Half- or Full Marathons—run both, and you'll go home with a Goofy medal as well as a Donald (half) and a Mickey (full)!

Tour new Worlds. Spend seven hours on Disney's Backstage Magic Tour of Magic Kingdom, Epcot, and Hollywood Studios. Or take one of SeaWorld's Spotlight tours into the penguin or dolphin backstage habitats.

Planning an Orlando Vacation

WORD OF MOUTH

"Get the Park Hopper Pass. You'll want to visit all the parks. Check out dining with Disney characters. My daughter loved the princess breakfast. Now that she's 13, she prefers Universal Studios. If you have time, spend a day there, too. One of the most memorable experiences was [swimming with the dolphins] at Discovery Cove."

—KendraM

ORLANDO TRANSPORTATION PLANNER

Getting Here

All the major and most discount airlines fly into **Orlando International Airport** (*MCO* ☎ *407/825-2001* ⊕ *www. orlandoairports.net*).

The **Beachline Expressway** (aka Beeline Expressway or Route 528), a toll road, gets you from the airport to area attractions. Depending on the location of your hotel, follow it west, and either exit at SeaWorld for the International Drive (I-Drive) area or stay on it to Interstate 4, and head west for Disney and U.S. 192–Kissimmee or east for Universal and downtown Orlando.

The **Central Florida Greenway (SR 417)** is a faster way from the airport to Disney than the Beachline, but tolls are heftier

Magical Express

If you're staying at a Disney hotel, this free service will deliver your luggage from your home airport to your hotel (and back again) *and* shuttle you to and from your resort. ■TIP→ You must book before departure (☎ 866/599-0951; ⊕ www. disneysmagicalexpress.com); have your flight information handy.

Getting Around

If you're spending your entire vacation on Disney property, you can use its fleet of buses, trams, boats, and monorail trains exclusively. If you're staying outside the Disney resort—or want to visit a non-Disney attraction—you'll need to use cabs, shuttles (your hotel may have a free one), and/or rental cars. Some hotels also offer shuttles to and from Universal and SeaWorld, which don't have transit systems.

CABS, SHUTTLES, AND PUBLIC TRANSPORTATION

Many non-Disney hotels offer free airport shuttles. If yours doesn't, cab fare from the airport to the Disney area runs $55–$75. Try **Star Taxi** (☎ *407/857-9999*) or **Yellow Cab Co.** (☎ *407/422-2222*). **Town & Country Transportation** (☎ *407/828-3035*) charges $75 one-way for a town car. The **Mears Transportation Group** (☎ *407/423-5566* ⊕ *www.mearstransportation.com*) offers shuttle and charter services throughout the Orlando area. The **I-Ride Trolley** (☎ *407/248-9590* ⊕ *www.iridetrolley. com*) serves most attractions in the I-Drive area (including SeaWorld). It won't get you to Disney or Universal. The **LYNX** (☎ *407/841-5969* ⊕ *www.golynx.com*) bus system provides service throughout Orlando.

CAR RENTAL

Rates vary seasonally and can begin as low as $30 a day/$149 a week for an economy car (excluding 6.5% rental car tax). If you're staying on Disney property but want to rent car for a day, you might get a better daily rate if you reserve for two or more days, then return the car early. (Just be sure there aren't any penalties for this.)

ROAD CONDITIONS AND SERVICE

Rush hours are weekdays 6–10 AM and 4–7 PM. Dial *511 for traffic advisories (www.fl511.com). Dial *347 (*FHP) for the Florida Highway Patrol. Most Florida highways are also patrolled by Road Rangers, a free roadside service. The **AAA Car Care Center** (☎ *407/824-0976*) near the Magic Kingdom provides emergency services, including free towing even for non-AAA members on Disney property weekdays 7–7, Saturday 7–4.

Transit Times and Costs

AIRPORT TO:	BY SHUTTLE	BY TAXI/CAR
Magic Kingdom	30–45 min.; $33 round trip (RT); $20 one way (OW)	35 min.; approx. $62 (taxi fare)
Downtown Disney	30–45 min.; $33 RT; $20 OW	25–30 min.; approx. $45
Animal Kingdom/ Hollywood Studios	30–45 min.; $33 RT; $20 OW	35 min.; approx. $55
Universal	30–40 min.; $33 RT; $20 OW	20 min.; approx. $40
Kissimmee	30–45 min.; $33 RT; $20 OW	30 min.; approx. $50
I-Drive (Doubletree Castle)	30–40 min.; $29 RT; $18 OW	20 min.; approx. $35
Downtown Orlando	30 min.; $28 RT; $17 OW	30 min.; approx. $35

MAGIC KINGDOM TO:	BY SHUTTLE	BY TAXI/CAR
Downtown Disney	N/A (use Disney transportation)	10–15 min.; approx. $25
Animal Kingdom/ Hollywood Studios	N/A (use Disney transportation)	15 min.; approx. $20
Universal	N/A	25 min.; approx. $35
Kissimmee	30 min.; $18 RT	25–30 min.; approx. $30
I-Drive (Doubletree Castle)	35 min.; $18 RT	30 min.; approx. $35
Downtown Orlando	N/A	40 min.; approx. $40

UNIVERSAL TO:	BY SHUTTLE	BY TAXI/CAR
Magic Kingdom	N/A	20 min.; approx. $20
Downtown Disney	N/A	20 min.; approx. $25
Animal Kingdom/ Hollywood Studios	N/A	30 min.; approx. $40
Kissimmee	30 min.; $18 RT	25 min.; approx. $45
I-Drive (Doubletree Castle)	25 min.; $18 RT	5–10 min.; approx. $10
Downtown Orlando	N/A	10 min.; approx. $25

Orlando Routes

1

Beachline Expressway: Toll road from the airport to International Drive (I-Drive) and Disney (roughly $2). Also good for Universal, SeaWorld, and Space Coast.

Interstate 4: Main east–west highway between Tampa and Daytona; it follows a north–south track through Orlando. ■TIP→ Think north when I-4 signs say east (toward Daytona, say), and south when they say west (toward Tampa). Key exits are:

–Exit 64B: Magic Kingdom/U.S. 192; *heavy* peak-season traffic near this exit.

–Exit 65: Animal Kingdom, ESPN Wide World of Sports

–Exit 67: Epcot/Downtown Disney, Typhoon Lagoon, Universal; less-congested exit.

–Exit 68: Downtown Disney, Typhoon Lagoon.

–Exits 71 and 72: SeaWorld

–Exits 72, 74A, and 75A: I-Drive

–Exits 74B and 75A: Universal Orlando Resort

Semoran Blvd: main road to Winter Park. Heavily traveled but moves well; plenty of amenities.

Spacecoast Parkway or Irlo Bronson Memorial Highway (U.S. 192): Runs east–west to Kissimmee or Universal and downtown Orlando. Continues east to Space Coast. Crosses I-4 at Exits 64A and 64B.

ORLANDO THEME PARKS PLANNER

Area Contacts

Florida Tourist Board:
☎ 850/488–5607 ⊕ www.
visitflorida.com

**Kennedy Space Center/
Space Coast:** ☎ 321/
449–4444 ⊕ www.
kennedyspacecenter.com

**Kissimmee/St. Cloud
Visitors Bureau:** ☎ 407/944–
2400 ⊕ www.floridakiss.com

Orlando Visitors Bureau:
☎ 407/363–5872 or
800/972–3304 ⊕ www.
visitorlando.com

**Space Coast Office of
Tourism:** ☎ 321/433–4470
⊕ www.space-coast.com

**Tampa Bay and Com-
pany:** ☎ 800/368–2672
or 813/223–1111 ⊕ www.
visittampabay.com

**Winter Park Welcome Cen-
ter:** ☎ 407/599–3399 ⊕ www.
cityofwinterpark.org

Disney Packages

Cruises: Disney Cruise Line ships have activities and ameni-
ties to thrill family members of all ages. From Florida's Port
Canaveral you can sail to the Bahamas, Caribbean, or
Panama Canal.

Fairy Tale Weddings & Honeymoons. Some 1,500 couples
tie the knot at Disney World every year. At the Fairy Tale
Wedding Pavilion and many other locations, the bride
can ride in a Cinderella coach, have rings borne to the
altar in a glass slipper, and spend time with Mickey and
Minnie at the reception. Check out the interactive Web site,
disneyweddings.disney.go.com.

Magic Your Way Vacations. These packages bundle hotel,
parks admission, and an array of add-on options—dining
plans, airfare, Park Hopper passes, spa treatments—that
make it easy to customize your trip. They can also offer
good value for money. Just do your homework so you'll
know that, if you *aren't* interested in seeing Cirque du
Soleil, it's best not to splurge on the Platinum Plan, which
includes tickets to this show. You'll also be sure to determine how many park meals and snacks you'll truly need
before investing in a dining plan.

Grand Gatherings. If you're planning a group trip, you
must look into this service. It allows groups of eight or more
to tailor entertainment and meals to their needs. Contact
central reservations for information.

Universal Packages

Vacation Package. Universal offers its own plans and
ever-changing roster of deals to help you maximize value.
(When starting your research, check out the "Hot Deals"
section of the Web site.) Basic packages include hotel and
park admission, but can be expanded to include airfare;
dining; rental cars; show tickets; spa treatments; admission
to SeaWorld, Wet'n Wild, Aquatica, Busch Gardens, and
Discovery Cove; and a VIP treatment that lets you skip
many theme-park lines. Note, though, that this last perk is
free to guests at Universal hotels.

Parks Tickets

Per-day, per-person, at-the-gate admissions range from roughly $40–$50 at Aquatica or Wet 'n Wild to about $70–$80 at Universal, Disney, and SeaWorld. Discovery Cove runs between $189 without a dolphin swim to $299 with it, though prices vary seasonally. Combo ticket plans can save money, but be sure to weigh what they offer against your needs.

DISNEY

Magic Your Way: With this plan, the more days you stay, the greater your per-day savings. For instance, a one-day ticket costs $79 for anyone age 10 and up, whereas a five-day ticket costs $228 (or just under $46 per day). There are also add-ons:

Park Hopper: This lets you move from park to park within a single day and adds $52 to the price of a ticket, no matter how many days your ticket covers. The flexibility is fantastic—you can spend the day at Animal Kingdom, for example, then hit Magic Kingdom for fireworks.

Water Parks Fun and More: With this $52-per-ticket add-on, you get admission to Typhoon Lagoon, Blizzard Beach, and other Disney attractions.

No Expiration: This add-on (prices vary) lets you use your ticket for more than one trip to Disney (e.g., use five days of a seven-day Magic Your Way ticket on one visit and two days on another).

UNIVERSAL, SEAWORLD, BUSCH GARDENS TAMPA

Universal Parks: A one-day Park to Park ticket is $109 (ages 10 and up); a seven-day version is nearly $170 (a better per-day value at just over $24 a day). Add the Express PLUS (prices vary) option to skirt ride lines; City-Walk Party Pass (roughly $12) for one-night venue access; CityWalk Party Pass and Movie (almost $21) for a free movie; and Length of Stay Wet'n Wild pass (about $48).

SeaWorld and Busch Gardens Parks: There are various ticket plans for SeaWorld Orlando parks and Busch Gardens Tampa Bay, which are all run by one company.

Orlando FlexTicket: This gives you up to 14 consecutive days' unlimited entry to (but not parking at) Universal and SeaWorld parks and select CityWalk venues. It costs nearly $260 (ages 10 and up). The Flex Ticket Plus (nearly $300) includes admission to Busch Gardens and free shuttle service between it and various Orlando locations.

Parks Planning Contacts

DISNEY

Central Reservations: ☎ 407/932–7639 (407/W-DISNEY)

Dining: ☎ 407/939–3463 (407/WDW-DINE)

Fairytale Weddings & Honeymoons: ☎ 321/939–4610; ⊕ disneyweddings.disney.go.com

Golf: ☎ 407/939–4653 (407/WDW-GOLF)

Hotel: ☎ 407/939–7429

Vacation Packages: ☎ 407/939–7675

Tickets: ☎ 407/939–1289

Web Site: ⊕ disneyworld.disney.go.com

SEAWORLD

Discovery Cove: ☎ 877/557–7404 ⊕ www.discoverycove.com

SeaWorld: ☎ 888/800–5447 ⊕ www.seaworld.com/orlando

UNIVERSAL

Main Number: ☎ 407/363–8000

Dining: ☎ 407/224–3613; 407/224–4012 for character meals

Hotel: ☎ 888/273–1311

Vacation Packages: ☎ 877/801–9720

Web Site: ⊕ www.universalorlando.com

Disney *Magic Your Way* Price Chart

TICKET OPTIONS								
TICKET	1-DAY	2-DAY	3-DAY	4-DAY	5-DAY	6-DAY	7-DAY	10-DAY
BASE TICKET								
Ages 10-up	$79	$156	$219	$225	$228	$231	$234	$243
Ages 3-9	$68	$133	$187	$192	$195	$198	$201	$210
Base Ticket admits guest to one of the four major theme parks per day's use. Park choices are: Magic Kingdom, Epcot, Disney's Hollywood Studios, Disney's Animal Kingdom. 8- and 9-day tickets are also available.								
ADD: Park Hopper	$52	$52	$52	$52	$52	$52	$52	$52
Park Hopper option entitles guest to visit more than one theme park per day's use. Park choices are any combination of Magic Kingdom, Epcot, Disney's Hollywood Studios, Disney's Animal Kingdom.								
ADD: Water Parks Fun & More	$52 2 visits	$52 2 visits	$52 3 visits	$52 4 visits	$52 5 visits	$52 6 visits	$52 7 visits	$52 10 visits
Water Parks Fun & More option entitles guest to a specified number of visits to a choice of entertainment and recreation venues. Choices are Blizzard Beach, Typhoon Lagoon, DisneyQuest, Disney's Oak Trail golf course, and Wide World of Sports.								
ADD: No Expiration	n/a	$18	$24	$52	$73	$84	$115	$210
No expiration means that unused admissions on a ticket may be used any time in the future. Without this option, tickets expire 14 days after first use.								

MINOR PARKS AND ATTRACTIONS		
TICKET	AGES 10-UP	AGES 3-9
Typhoon Lagoon or Blizzard Beach 1-Day 1-Park	$45	$39
DisneyQuest 1-Day	$41	$35
Disney's ESPN Wide World of Sports	$13.50	$10
Cirque du Soleil's *La Nouba*	$69–$120	$56–$97
*All prices are subject to Florida sales tax		

Get wet on the 12-story Summit Plummet at Disney's Blizzard Beach.

Universal Orlando Ticket Price Chart

TICKET OPTIONS					
TICKET	**1-DAY**	**2-DAY**	**3-DAY**	**4-DAY**	**7-DAY**
BASE TICKET					
Ages 10-up	$79	$110	$125	$135	$160
Ages 3-9	$69	$97	$110	$118	$140

Base Ticket admits guest to one park per day, either Universal Studios or Islands of Adventure.

ADD: Park-to-Park option	$30	$15	$15	$10	$10

Park-to-Park Ticket allows guest to go back and forth between Universal Studios and Islands of Adventure.

ADD: Wet 'n Wild Length of Stay Ticket	$48	$48	$48	$48	$48

Wet 'n Wild Length of Stay Ticket gives guest admission to the water park for 14 consecutive days, beginning with the first day of use.

ADD: CityWalk Party Pass	$12	$12	$12	$12	$12
CityWalk Party Pass and Movie	$21	$21	$21	$21	$21

CityWalk Party Pass gives guest one-night access to CityWalk clubs and venues (some of which require you to be at least 21). CityWalk Party Pass and Movie adds to that a free movie at the AMC Universal Cineplex 20.

ADD: 1- and 2-Park Express PLUS Pass	$26 off-season, $56 peak season				

Gives guest access to much shorter lines at Universal Studios and Islands of Adventure rides. (Note that this pass is included in the room rate at Universal Resort hotels.)

All prices are subject to Florida sales tax

Universal Orlando.

By Elise Allen

There's magic in Orlando . . . and we don't just mean the NBA team. The city and its environs teem with magical experiences, both natural and Imagineered. With endless joys and excitements for people of all ages, it's no wonder that more than 50 million people visit every year.

The most obvious source of Orlando's magic is Disney World. And with four theme parks, two water parks, 20 or so themed hotels, shopping districts, and countless dining options, you could spend a lengthy vacation entirely on Disney property and still not see it all.

Universal Studios and Islands of Adventure offer their own thrills, including the new Wizarding World of Harry Potter. There's also Sea-World, Discovery Cove—where you can have the truly magical experience of swimming with the dolphins—and Busch Gardens Tampa. To take a break from the theme parks, you can visit Winter Park's Charles Hosmer Morse Museum for what may well be the world's largest collection of Tiffany glass; go hiking, swimming, or canoeing in Wekiwa Springs State Park; or head to Space Coast.

You could also just take it easy. Even in the midst of a whirlwind theme-park tour, you can laze by the pool, indulge in a spa treatment, play a round of golf, or leisurely shop an afternoon away.

The key to an ideal Orlando vacation is planning. Figure out well in advance who's going, what everyone wants to do on this trip, and what you'll save for the next. If your stay will center around theme parks, decide which parks to visit on which days, buy your ticket and hotel package, and make meal reservations—all long before leaving home.

When you're actually in Orlando, though, try to be flexible. Your plans form the backbone of your trip and you want it to be strong, but things will come up—moods will change, plans will alter. That's OK. For the most part, it's not difficult to change segments of your itinerary once you're on the ground. Planning is key to enjoying Orlando and all it offers, but so is taking a deep breath, allowing for the occasional detour, and going with the flow of your vacation.

CREATING YOUR DREAM ORLANDO VACATION

1

Say the words "dream vacation" to 10 people, and they'll picture 10 completely different experiences. The best way for you to make your dream come true is to keep in mind who's traveling while you're doing the planning.

Throughout this chapter (and the rest of the guide) we offer advice specifically geared to the following types of travelers: families with small kids; families with tweens; families with teens; couples; singles or groups of friends; and large, mixed groups (like family reunions).

Start your planning by looking at the big picture and then moving on to the details. To help, we offer possible answers to five questions—the ones most asked by people planning Orlando trips. They are:

- What should we see and do?
- When should we go (and how long should we stay)?
- Where should we stay?
- Where should we eat?
- How much will we spend?

Your own answers to these questions will form the backbone of your dream trip. It bears repeating, however, that although a successful trip requires careful planning, it also requires flexibility. Fussy kids, friends or relatives unable to agree, an unforeseen stormy day are just some of the things that can ruin your plans. Sticking with a blueprint when it no longer makes sense is madness. This is, after all, a vacation. Plans are important, but so is happiness.

Stay relaxed, stay flexible, and have a great trip!

WHAT SHOULD WE SEE AND DO?

FAMILIES WITH SMALL KIDS

For a happy, low-stress trip, cater to your kids' desires. That doesn't mean buying or doing everything they want, but it does mean being mindful of their needs, schedules, and patience levels. Choose your parks wisely. Sure, Islands of Adventure's Seuss Landing is terrific for small kids, but most of the other rides at that park are geared to older kids. Water parks are fun, but height restrictions can frustrate wannabe riders who don't make the cutoff.

■ TIP→ Even rides geared to small kids can have frightening sounds or darkness. Research attractions on YouTube, so you know what's what.

Get thee to the Magic Kingdom! There's absolutely no better spot, possibly in the entire universe, for small kids than this wonderland. Everything about it lives up to its "magical" name: the horse-drawn carriages clopping down Main Street, U.S.A.; the spires of Cinderella Castle; the classic characters, readily accessible and eager to share an autograph and a huge hug.

TIPS FOR SENIOR CITIZENS

People 65 and older are vibrant and active, more likely to characterize themselves by family or interest (solo travelers, couples on a second—or third—honeymoon, or grandparents) than by age.

One good time to think of age is when it comes to discounts! Being over 65 can mean perks like reduced fares or specials on airfare, hotels, and restaurants. Two examples include the I-Ride Trolley that cruises International Drive, and offers a 25-cent fare for passengers age 65 and over; and the LYNX public transportation system, which offers various AdvantAge fares for passengers age 65 and over.

You can find a wealth of senior discounts through the American Association of Retired Persons (AARP), which, despite the name, you don't have to be retired to join. Membership is open to anyone age 50 or older, costs only $16 a year, and entitles you to a wide variety of services and discounts. These are updated regularly on the AARP Web site, *www.aarp.org.*

■ TIP→ Introduce small kids to giant versions of even beloved characters tentatively; some kids are intimidated at first.

Whichever parks you hit, bring or rent a stroller. Your child may have plenty of energy and be a great walker on a normal day, but pounding the pavement under the hot sun for several hours really take its toll. Avoid meltdowns before they hit by keeping a ready supply of snacks and handheld games or activities. When kids are full and have things to do, they're less likely to get fussy while waiting in long lines.

■ TIP→ When the adults in your party want to hit grown-up rides, take advantage of Baby Swap. Universal and Disney both offer this service on rides that are inappropriate for small children. Though each company handles it slightly differently, the gist is the same: one adult waits in line while the other watches the kids, and then the other adult gets to skip to the front of the line for his or her turn.

FAMILIES WITH TWEENS

Pick a theme park, any theme park. Even if they've outgrown Disney characters, your tweens will still love the thrills of Space Mountain at the Magic Kingdom, Rock 'n' Roller Coaster and Tower of Terror at Hollywood Studios, and Misson: SPACE at Epcot. Animal Kingdom combines exciting attractions like Kali River Rapids and Expedition Everest with the coolness factor of live lions, elephants, giraffes, and other animals on the Kilimanjaro Safari.

More adventurous tweens will chomp at the bit to prove their mettle on Islands of Adventure's monster roller coasters. And fans of the J.K. Rowling stories will adore the Wizarding World of Harry Potter. Sea-World is also a great choice for this age, and it combines theme-park attractions with educational opportunities (shhhh). In warm weather, water parks Blizzard Beach, Typhoon Lagoon, Wet 'n Wild, and Aquatica are huge draws.

Your theme-park vacation will be most successful if you combine thoughtful planning with flexibility and spontenaity. There's a lot to be said for having the wonder of a child!

Its great fun to share your favorite big-deal rides with your kids, and, at this age they can take advantage of just about everything—if they're ready, that is. Some tweens leap at the chance to ride up front in the Incredible Hulk Roller Coaster, others will still be frightened by Space Mountain. No need to rush into anything. The bigger rides will be there for you to enjoy together when your kids are older.

FAMILIES WITH TEENS

Universal Studios and Islands of Adventure are fantastic teen choices, with thrill rides like Incredible Hulk Coaster, Revenge of the Mummy, and Hollywood Rip Ride Rockit. Teens will also love the late-night bustle of CityWalk, with its funky, neon-lit stores, throngs of people, live music, and nightclubs that open their doors to younger patrons on teen nights. At Disney's Hollywood Studios kids 14 and older can audition for the American Idol Experience, where the best singer of the day wins a chance to audition for the real *American Idol* TV show.

An Orlando vacation is a great time to give older teens some space. The bus and monorail system at Walt Disney World offers the opportunity for them to get around without relying on you for a ride. Just be sure you all keep your cell phones on, so you can keep in touch.

■TIP→ Use cell phone-based GPS (Loopt is one such service) to pinpoint the location of your teens.

As much as you might be dying for family bonding time, at this age your teen will be happier if he or she can bring a friend. Before offering an invitation, talk to the parents of the potential guest. Agree up front about expenses, who's paying, and how much supervision will be offered. Written permission—signed by the guest's parents and notarized—will be needed to fly. Such documentation, plus insurance info, will also be needed to get health care in the event of an emergency.

Of course, with freedom can come extravagance. Little things like arcade games or soft drinks and virgin cocktails ($1 to $5 each) add up in a hurry. Set a budget, and encourage your teens to stick to it.

■ TIP→ Giving teens prepaid debit cards will help both you and them stay on or under budget.

COUPLES

Believe it or not, there are plenty of opportunities for quality together time in the theme parks. Swimming with the dolphins at Discovery Cove is an unforgettable experience, especially when shared with the one you love. What's more romantic than a whirlwind trip around the world? It's possible at Epcot's World Showcase. And you can always grab onto one another for dear life on the Tower of Terror at Disney's Hollywood Studios or on Dueling Dragons at Universal's Islands of Adventure.

Winter Park, just northeast of Orlando, is a great romantic getaway thanks to its Old South charm and its myriad boutiques, museums, and eateries. And on the scenic boat tour of the town's waterways you may just find yourselves holding hands.

After dark, stroll arm-in-arm through the Magic Kingdom, with all of Main Street, U.S.A. and Cinderella Castle lit up and fireworks above. Later, go club-hopping into the wee hours at Universal's CityWalk.

SINGLES OR GROUPS OF FRIENDS

If you're a theme-park aficionado, oh my, are you in the right place. Even if you're not a big fan, the parks here are so good that you have to visit at least one. ■ TIP→ Use super-fast-moving single-rider lines to board crowded rides faster. Rides with such lines include Animal Kingdom's Expedition Everest and Epcot's Test Track; Universal Studios's Revenge of the Mummy and Hollywood Rip, Ride, Rockit; Islands of Adventure's Amazing Adventures of Spider-Man and Incredible Hulk Coaster; and SeaWorld's Journey to Atlantis.

You non-theme-parkers are still in the right place. Orlando has all kinds of other options. Enjoy a blissful spa day at Disney's Grand Floridian, the Ritz-Carlton Orlando Grande Lakes, or the Waldorf Astoria. Play golf at the Disney World Resort, or tackle one of the other fantastic courses in and around Orlando. Shopping here is a treat, too, with many malls and outlets at your disposal.

In the evening you can head to Universal's CityWalk and make some memories with karaoke at the Rising Star or with a music show at Hard Rock Live. On Disney property you can hit the BoardWalk for Jellyrolls' dueling pianos and sing-alongs or for Atlantic Dance's DJs and live bands. You can also hang with locals at Orlando institutions like Social or Wally's.

To make the trip truly memorable, push the envelope. Try racing NASCAR vehicles at the Richard Petty Driving Experience; call Bob's Balloons to see the Disney area by hot-air balloon; or let the Space Coast inspire you, and take to the skies yourself with Space Coast Skydiving.

TIPS FOR PEOPLE WITH DISABILITIES

The theme parks have many amenities and services for people with mobility issues or vision or hearing impairments. Park information centers can answer specific questions and dispense general information about this. Both Walt Disney World and Universal Studios publish free guidebooks that detail amenities and services (allow six weeks for delivery).

Most hotels have been renovated to comply with the Americans with Disabilities Act (ADA). Outside Disney properties, however, the definition of accessibility seems to differ from hotel to hotel. Some places may be fully accessible by ADA standards for people with mobility problems—with things like roll-in showers or wheelchair-accessible buffets—but not for people with hearing or vision impairments, for example.

In most properties only elevators and room-number plaques are Braille-equipped, though some employees are trained on assisting guests with visual impairments. Flashing or vibrating phones and alarms and closed-captioning are more common; an industry-wide effort to teach some employees sign language is under way.

MOBILITY CONCERNS
Many theme-park attractions are accessible to guests with mobility problems. Note that in some you may be required to transfer to a wheelchair if you use an electronic convenience vehicle (ECV). In others, you must transfer from your wheelchair or ECV to the ride vehicle and must have a traveling companion who can assist you, if needed, as park staff are not allowed to do so.

Probably the most comfortable course is to bring your wheelchair from home. If your chair is wider than 24½ inches and longer than 32 inches (44 inches for ECVs), consult theme-park-attraction hosts and hostesses before getting in line. Also note that thefts of wheelchairs while their owners are inside attractions are rare but have been known to occur. Take the precautions you would in any public place.

Wheelchair rentals are available from area medical-supply companies, most of which will deliver to your hotel. You can also rent by the day in major theme parks.

VISION AND HEARING IMPAIRMENTS
Attractions in the parks typically have both a visual element that makes them appealing without sound and an audio element that conveys the charm even without the visuals.

Many attractions are equipped for assisted-listening, handheld-captioning, and other devices, which you can pick up (for a deposit but no fee) at Guest Relations stations at park entrances. Some rides or shows also have closed-caption TV monitors and/or sign-language interpreters, though the latter are available only on certain days (check schedules at Guest Relations).

Service animals are permitted, unless a ride or special effect could spook or traumatize them. Large Braille maps are posted at centralized areas.

LARGE GROUPS

Getting everyone to agree on what to do is tricky. Preschoolers will be content on Dumbo, but older thrill-seekers will want faster-paced rides. Grandparents might rather play golf than traipse around a water park. And those doing the planning may find themselves also doing the mediating—far more frustrating than fun.

Orlando offers some terrific things you can do as a large group. Behind-the-scenes or customized VIP theme-park tours, dinner shows, Cirque du Soleil, the Kennedy Space Center, and spring-training games in the Tampa area are wonderful all-ages experiences. As for theme parks, Disney's Animal Kingdom probably has the most universal appeal.

> ### ORLANDO WEATHER
>
> January and February can be cold, with temps occasionally dropping to freezing at night. Spring is gorgeous: sunny and temperate. April and May can be nippy or warm enough for the water parks. Summer is hot and humid—water parks are the best ways to keep cool. Crowds are thick and lines are long, but hours are extended. Late summer and fall comprise hurricane season, but late in September through November days are bright and beautiful and temperatures cooler.

Be sure to schedule apart time; not every moment has to be a group hug. You can splinter into smaller groups during the day, so some can go shopping in Winter Park, some can hit the links, some can attack a theme park, come can lounge by the pool. When you meet up for dinner, you'll all have stories to share.

■TIP→ Consider using Disney's Grand Gatherings program. Accessible both online and over the phone, the program helps groups of eight or more travel well together. You get access to Grand Gatherings Travel Planners, who will help you make the most of your trip. There are also experiences only accessible to Grand Gatherings, such as a special dinner and safari package at Animal Kingdom or an International Dinner at Epcot plus VIP viewing for Illuminations.

WHEN SHOULD WE GO?

Let's be honest: there is no "empty" time at Orlando's theme parks. Crowds thin in January, after New Year's, and stay reasonable until around President's Day. From that point through Labor Day, though, crowds are either heavy (as in mid-February through early June and again in late August) or very heavy.

Things lighten up after Labor Day, but grow busy again around Columbus Day. After that comes another light patch until right around Thanksgiving, which is huge in the parks. There's a slight lull in early December, right between Thanksgiving and Christmas vacations.

■TIP→ If your schedule demands that you go at a peak time, you can always get a break from the crowds by planning non-theme-park days. Visit the Kennedy Space Center early in the workweek, when you'll avoid both weekend crowds and late-week school field trips. Eschew Saturday

Just saying "magic" and "Disney" in the same sentence brings to mind Cinderella Castle aglow at night, surrounded by dazzling fireworks.

theme-park madness in favor of a trip to charming Winter Park, where you can stroll a farmers' market between 7 AM and 1 PM. Stick around to roam the grassy parks, visit small museums and galleries, or maybe catch a matinee at the Winter Park Playhouse.

If you'd rather not venture far from the parks, you can escape the crowds by simply slipping back to your hotel for a spa treatment, a swim, a walk around the grounds, a paddleboat ride—many of Orlando's hotels offer such a variety of recreation options that they're practically theme parks themselves.

CONSIDERATIONS FOR DIFFERENT TYPES OF TRAVELERS

As always, the makeup of your travel group will determine when it's best to go. In this case, however, it boils down to two types of travelers: those with school-age kids and those without them.

TRAVELING WITH KIDS

It's a dilemma: you want to plan a great vacation and avoid the crowds, but can you really rationalize taking the kids out of school to visit a theme park? It's a tough call, and the best plan is to consult with your child's teachers first. Ideally, they can advise you on the best time of the school year to go and create a study plan to ensure your child's education isn't compromised during the trip.

For elementary-school kids there are ways of making the trip educational. For example, your child could write about the different countries featured at Epcot in lieu of a missed homework assignment; do a report

HOW LONG SHOULD WE STAY?

The baseline is a day for every theme park you visit, plus two travel days. So, to have a rich, full experience in all six of the Disney and Universal theme parks, you'd need eight days. To include SeaWorld or one of the water parks or a non-theme-park attraction, add another day—for a total of nine days. Phew!

If you're selective, though, you can have a great five- to seven-day trip, *including* two travel days. Families with young kids might spend full days at only a few theme parks. Those with tweens or teens might do two parks in a day, but take in only the highlights. Singles, couples, or groups might might take the full-day park-tour approach or mix the half-day park-highlights approach—perhaps with half days of down time (rather than at other parks).

How long you stay might also affect your hotel choice. The longer and more varied the trip, the farther from the theme parks you can stay. The shorter the trip and/or the more time you plan to spend in Disney or Universal parks, the better off you are staying on or very near Disney or Universal property.

SAMPLE ITINERARIES

Below are a few sample three- and five-day itineraries to which you should add two travel days. These are our dream trips. We're happy to share them, but, for best results, you really should create your own!

FAMILIES WITH SMALL KIDS
Duration: 3 Days

Plans: Day 1—Magic Kingdom early, with a nap or pool break back at the hotel, returning for the evening Wishes fireworks show or

Spectromagic parade. Day 2—the whole family by the hotel pool or the kids busy in the hotel's children's program while Mom and Dad head to Downtown Disney or the Board-Walk. Day 3—Hollywood Studios from morning through to the afternoon Block Party Bash; enjoy the Hoop-Dee-Doo Revue dinner show.

Other Recommendations: Use Magical Express airport-transfer service; stay on Disney property; get the basic Disney meal plan; buy two-day Magic Your Way parks tickets (which you don't need to use on consecutive days). Work in a character meal on arrival or departure day.

FAMILIES WITH TWEENS
Duration: 5 Days

Plans: Day 1—Magic Kingdom highlights in the morning; Epcot later in the day with dinner at World Showcase followed by Illuminations!. Day 2—a day at Blizzard Beach or Typhoon Lagoon water parks, or, if it's raining or cold, at DisneyQuest. Day 3—kids head to the hotel's kids' program; Mom and Dad rent a car and head to Winter Park. Day 4—Islands of Adventure, with the Wizarding World of Harry Potter first thing. Day 5—SeaWorld or Kennedy Space Center.

Other Recommendations: Take a cab from the airport, and a rental car back. Stay at a Disney or Lake Buena Vista property; skip the Disney or Universal meal plans. Add the Park Hopper option to the one-day Disney ticket, but skip the Water Parks and More option. Consider Universal's Express PLUS Pass.

HOW LONG SHOULD WE STAY?

FAMILIES WITH TEENS
Duration: 3 Days

Plans: Day 1—a full day at Universal Studios. Day 2—teens spend time by the pool while Mom and Dad play golf or hit a spa; dinner together followed by an evening—together or apart—at CityWalk. Day 3—a full day at Islands of Adventure.

Other Recommendations: Take a shuttle or cab to and from the airport, stay at a Universal property; do the Universal Meal Deal on theme-park days. Consider taking in Blue Man Group on the night out at City-Walk. Buy multiday Universal tickets online in advance to save; invest in Universal's Express PLUS Pass.

SINGLES, COUPLES, OR GROUPS OF FRIENDS
Duration: 3 Days

Plans: Day 1—morning at hotel pool or spa, lunch at the hotel, late afternoon Magic Kingdom highlights and dinner at California Grill with a view of Wishes fireworks. Day 2—take a balloon ride over Orlando, golf a championship course, swim with the dolphins at Discovery Cove, or drive NASCAR-style at the Richard Petty Driving Experience. Day 3—full day at Disney's Animal Kingdom, Epcot, Universal's Studios, or Islands of Adventure with dinner and a night out in Orlando.

Other Recommendations: If it's a special occasion, book a car service to and from the airport. Use shuttles or cabs the rest of the time.

Don't bother with park meal plans, but do splurge on a luxury hotel with lots of amenities (on or off theme-park property): Disney's Grand Floridian; Universal's Portofino Bay; Orlando's Ritz-Carlton, Waldorf Astoria, or Gaylord Palms.

Consider buying two-day Magic Your Way Disney tickets and getting Universal's Express PLUS Pass (free if you stay at a Universal hotel).

LARGE, MIXED GROUPS
Duration: 2 to 5 days—depending on how well you all get along.

Plans: Large, mixed groups have the most flexibility. On any given day there are bound to be some members heading to a theme park, some going out shopping or to play golf, and some relaxing by the pool or in a spa. So those who want to take in a theme park every day can do so (and will always have someone to go with), and those who don't will always have someone with whom to share the alternatives.

Just be sure to plan get-togethers: a meal or two, an evening or two (perhaps for a show like Cirque du Soleil), an afternoon or two—if not a full day—maybe at SeaWorld, a water park, or Kennedy Space Center.

Other Recommendations: Use the Magical Express and Grand Gatherings services, opt for some version of the Disney meal plan, and stay on-site. Otherwise choose an all-suites hotel in a location that's convenient, regardless of who's doing what—perhaps a central I-Drive spot.

If group plans involve more than one day of sightseeing—say one day in Winter Park and another at Kennedy Space Center, or a spring-training baseball game in the Tampa Area—rent a van. Otherwise rely on in-park transportation, hotel shuttles, or cabs.

on the animals of SeaWorld; or prepare a talk about what he or she learned at the Kennedy Space Center.

■ TIP→ **To avoid crowds and meltdowns, families with young children should visit theme parks in the morning and evening. Leave the hot afternoons for naps and down time at the hotel pool.**

Note that although it may be fine to take younger kids out of school for a few days, missing several days of middle or high school could set your child back for the rest of the semester. If you do go during school vacations like the rest of the world, all is not lost. Take advantage of Extra Magic Hours, Fastpass, or Universal's front-of-the-line privileges when you can; retreat to your hotel when you need to; and simply make peace with the crowds so you can enjoy your vacation.

TRAVELING WITHOUT KIDS

It's very simple: avoid crowds by planning around school vacations. If water parks aren't a priority, early January is a great time, specifically about a week after New Year's. Kids will be back in school, and the Walt Disney World Marathon weekend will be over, so those crowds will be gone. If you love water parks, go after Labor Day, when kids are back in school. The Florida weather will still be hot enough to make the waterslides a joy.

WHERE SHOULD WE STAY?

When it comes to Orlando lodging, no matter who you are and where you decide to stay, you should book months in advance (at least six months for hotels at Disney). This is particularly important for travel when rates are lowest, specifically early January to mid-February, late April to mid-June, and mid-August to early December.

Your choices include resorts on Disney property (most owned and operated by Disney), those on Universal property, and those not in or affiliated with either park. Each type of property merits consideration.

HOTELS ON DISNEY AND UNIVERSAL PROPERTY

If you're interested solely in attractions at Disney or Universal, in-park hotels are best. For starters, they offer such convenient transportation options that you probably won't need a rental car—a huge cost savings.

Walt Disney World's massive campus is tied together by a dizzying array of complimentary monorails, buses, and water taxis. All will easily get you anywhere on the property you want to go. Universal provides complimentary shuttles and water taxis between its two theme parks and on-site hotels, though the hotels and parks are also within walking distance of one another.

Universal and Disney's on-site hotels also offer many special perks—some designed to save money, some designed to save time. Note that these perks don't necessarily extend to non-Disney-owned hotels on Disney property, so ask for those specifics before booking.

1

WHERE SHOULD WE STAY?

	VIBE	PROS	CONS
Disney	Thousands of rooms at every price; convenient to Disney parks; free transportation all over WDW complex.	Perks like early park entry, and Magical Express, which lets you circumvent airport bag checks.	Without a rental car, you likely won't leave Disney. On-site buses, while free, can take a big bite of time out of your entertainment day.
Universal	On-site hotels offer luxury and convenience. There are less expensive options just outside the gates.	Central to Disney, Universal, SeaWorld, malls, and I–4; free water taxis to parks from on-site hotels.	On-site hotels are pricey; expect heavy rush-hour traffic during drives to and from other parks.
I-Drive	A hotel, convention-center, and activities bonanza. A trolley runs from one end to the other.	Outlet malls provide bargains galore; diners enjoy world-class restaurants; it's central to parks; many hotels offer free shuttles.	Transportation can be pricey, in cash and in time, as traffic is often heavy. Crime is up, especially after dark, though area hotels and businesses have increased security.
Kissimmee	It's replete with mom 'n' pop motels and restaurants and places to buy saltwater taffy.	It's just outside Disney, very close to the Magic Kingdom. Lots of Old Florida charm.	Some motels here are a little seedy. Petty crime in which tourists are victims is rare—but not unheard-of.
Lake Buena Vista	Many hotel and restaurant chains here. Adjacent to WDW, which is where almost every guest in your hotel is headed.	Really close to WDW; plenty of dining and shopping options; easy access to I–4.	Heavy peak-hour traffic. As in all neighborhoods near Disney, a gallon of gas will cost 10%–15% more than elsewhere.
Central Orlando	Parts of town have the modern high-rises you'd expect. Other areas have oak-tree-lined brick streets winding among small, cypress-ringed lakes.	Lots of locally owned restaurants and some quaint B&Bs. City buses serve the parks. There's good access to I–4.	You'll need to rent a car. And you will be part of the traffic headed to WDW. Expect the 25-mi drive to take at least 45 minutes.
Orlando International Airport	Mostly business and flight-crew hotels and car rental outlets.	Great if you have an early flight or just want to shop in a mall. There's even a Hyatt on site.	Watching planes, buses, taxis, and cars arrive and depart is all the entertainment you'll get in.

BABYSITTING IN ORLANDO

If you're staying in a room, suite, or condo and need to rent baby equipment, such as a stroller, bassinet, high chair, or even pool toys, call **A Baby's Best Friend** (☎ *407/891–2241, 888/461–2229 toll-free in U.S.* ⊕ *www.abbf.com*) for swift delivery and fair rates. You can order online. The company also carries CD and DVD players, refrigerators, and microwaves.

If you want to plan an adults-only evening, consider **The Kid's Nite Out** (☎ *407/828–0920 or 800/696–8105* ⊕ *www.kidsniteout.com*) program, which works with hotels throughout Orlando. It provides in-room babysitting for children ages 6 weeks to 12 years. Fees start at $14 an hour for one child, and increase by $2.50 for each additional child. There's a four-hour minimum, plus a transportation fee of $10 for the sitter to travel to your hotel room.

When you make a reservation, you must provide a credit-card number. There's a 24-hour cancellation policy; if you cancel with less than 24 hours' notice, your credit card is charged the four-hour minimum fee ($56 for one child, higher rates for multiple children booked). The service recommends booking from two weeks to 90 days in advance.

HOTELS OFF THEME-PARK PROPERTY

If you plan to visit several parks or go sightseeing elsewhere in Central Florida, consider off-site hotels. Those closest to Disney are clustered in a few principal areas: along I-Drive; in the U.S. 192 area and Kissimmee; and in the Downtown Disney–Lake Buena Vista Area, just off Interstate 4 Exit 68.

Nearly every hotel in these areas provides frequent (sometimes free) transportation to and from Disney or even Universal. In addition, there are some noteworthy and money-saving, if far-flung, options in the greater Orlando area. One suburban caveat: traffic on Interstate 4 in Orlando experiences typical freeway gridlock during morning (7–9 AM) and evening (4–6 PM) rush hours.

■TIP→ Anyone can visit Disney hotels. To save money and still have on-site resort experiences, stay at a moderately priced hotel off-site and then visit the animals at the Animal Kingdom Lodge, say, or rent a boat at the Grand Floridian.

CONSIDERATIONS FOR DIFFERENT TYPES OF TRAVELERS

Whether you stay on theme-park property or off, prioritize your needs. A great spa is wonderful, but if you're running around with three small kids, will you actually use it? Do you want luxury or rustic simplicity? A splurge or a super-saver?

In addition, weigh what you get for the money. Sure, you might spend more on a room at a Disney or Universal resort than at an off-site property. But if staying at a cheaper off-site hotel means renting a car or spending a lot on cab rides, you might not ultimately be saving that much. Conversely, if you're planning to split your time between, say,

Disney, Universal, and SeaWorld, you probably won't make full use of all the Disney or Universal perks and might be better off shopping for a good-deal, conveniently located, off-site hotel with free theme-park shuttle service.

Finally, if you're traveling with children, be sure to mention their ages when you make reservations. Sometimes hotels have special features, such as rooms with bunk beds, just for families. Such things aren't necessarily offered up front, so be sure to ask.

■ TIP→ Regardless of whether you stay at hotels nearby the theme-parks or at on-site resorts, it can take between 20 minutes and an hour to get to and from park entrances.

FAMILIES WITH SMALL KIDS

If this is a Disney trip, stick with Disney hotels: the transportation system makes it simple to scoot back for a nap or some down time at the pool.

Many Disney properties are designed to appeal to kids, some with great children's facilities and programs. At the value-priced All-Star Movies Resort, small kids love the giant *Toy Story* figures and Disney-movie themes everywhere. The Polynesian Resort's Neverland Club has an enchanting Peter Pan–themed clubhouse and youngsters-only dinner show. Parents rave about the Sand Castle Club at the Yacht and Beach Club resorts. What's more, most of these clubs are open from late afternoon until midnight, so parents can slip out for a romantic meal while the kids play games, do art projects, and enjoy a snack or dinner.

■ TIP→ Delight kids with a wake-up call from Mickey while staying at a Disney resort.

If you do stay off-site, book a hotel geared to small children. The Nickelodeon Family Suites by Holiday Inn, in Lake Buena Vista, offers suites whose separate kid-friendly bedrooms are decorated with images of cartoon characters. It also has live shows featuring Nick characters, a Nickelodeon-themed pool, and tons of kids' activities.

East of International Drive the connected JW Marriott and Ritz-Carlton Orlando Grande Lakes resorts have rooms with adjoining kids' suites, complete with miniature furniture and toys. The Ritz also has a Kids Club with a play area and daily scheduled activities.

Wherever you stay, inquire about child equipment. Most hotels—and certainly all owned by Disney—have amenities such as cribs. (Some hotels require you to reserve cribs in advance. Ask whether there will be an additional charge, and make sure the crib meets current child-safety standards.)

FAMILY WITH TWEENS

With tweens you don't really need a hotel that's super-close to a theme park, so your selection is greater. Even properties that seem adult-oriented have offerings that tweens will love. The "lazy river" pools at the Omni Orlando Resort at ChampionsGate and the JW Marriott, for instance, are generally big hits.

Many hotels also have supervised camp-style programs, with trained counselors and fun, active, outdoorsy things to do. These are great for

DISNEY AND UNIVERSAL RESORT PERKS

1

DISNEY PERKS

Extra Magic Hours. You get special early and late-night admission to certain Disney parks on specified days. Call ahead for details so you can plan your early- and late-visit strategies.

Free Parking. Parking is free for Disney hotel guests at Disney hotel and theme-park lots.

Magical Express. If you're staying at a Disney hotel you don't need to rent a car or think about finding a shuttle or taxi or worry about baggage handling thanks to this free service.

At your hometown airport you'll check your bags in and won't see them again till you get to your Disney hotel. At Orlando International Airport you'll be met by a Disney rep who will lead you to a coach that takes you to your hotel. Your luggage will be delivered separately, and usually arrives in your room an hour or two after you do.

On departure, the process works in reverse (though only on some participating airlines, so check in advance). You get your boarding pass and check your bags at the hotel. At the airport you go directly to your gate, skipping check-in. You won't see your bags until you're in your hometown airport. Participating airlines include American, Continental, Delta, JetBlue, Northwest, Southwest, and United.

Charging Privileges. You can charge most meals and purchases throughout Disney to your hotel room.

Package Delivery. Anything you purchase at Disney—at a park, a hotel, or in Downtown Disney—can be delivered to the gift shop of your Disney hotel for free.

Priority Reservations. Disney hotel guests get priority reservations at Disney restaurants and choice tee times at Disney golf courses up to 30 days in advance.

Guaranteed Entry. Disney theme parks sometimes reach capacity, but on-site guests can enter even when others would be turned away.

UNIVERSAL PERKS

Head-of-the-Line Access. Your hotel key lets you go directly to the head of the line for most Universal Orlando attractions. Unlike Disney's Fastpass program, you don't need to use this at a specific time; it's always good.

Priority Seating. Many of Universal's restaurants offer priority seating to those staying at on-site hotels.

Charging Privileges. You can charge most meals and purchases throughout Universal to your hotel room.

Delivery Services. If you buy something in the theme parks, you can have it sent directly to your room, so you don't have to carry it around.

Free Loaners. Some on-site hotels have a "Did You Forget?" closet that offers everything from kid's strollers to dog leashes to computer accessories. There's no fee for using this service.

arrival and departure days, when you probably don't want to schlep to a park, but you also don't want to hear the dreaded "I'm so bored." Standouts are the Camp Holiday program at the Holiday Inn SunSpree Resort Lake Buena Vista; and the Camp Hyatt program at the Hyatt Regency Grand Cypress, near Downtown Disney. The latter is a top-class resort with sprawling grounds that are almost on top of Walt Disney World property, so it's perfect for families who want to be near the Mouse but need to take a break from Disney each night.

FAMILY WITH TEENS

A great hotel pool is a major boon for teens, who might not want to spend all their time in the theme parks. Stormalong Bay, the pool complex shared by the Yacht and Beach Club, has it all: a lazy river, water-slide, sandy-bottom pool, and an elevated tanning deck. This location is also surrounded by the shops, restaurants, and leisure activities of Disney's BoardWalk—a great place for teens to explore on their own.

Teens are usually partial to Universal's thrills, so the South Pacific–themed Royal Pacific Resort here is also an excellent choice. It has a lagoon-style swimming pool with a sandy beach; "dive-in" movies on select nights; a fitness center with a whirlpool, steam room, and sauna; a nightly torch-lighting ceremony; and an authentic luau. The rock-and-roll–themed Hard Rock Hotel is also a great Universal option.

■ TIP➔ If at all possible, book more than one room. As they say, the family that sleeps together . . . hates each other in the morning. Teens are used to their own space; crabby moods stemming from being crammed together will put a damper on the vacation. When booking, request connecting rooms—with a door connecting your room to that of your teen—as opposed to adjoining rooms, which only means that your rooms are next to each other.

If booking more than one room is too pricey, look into accommodations at all-suites hotels or family suites at regular hotels. These larger quarters are often reasonably priced. Just be sure to check on the hotel's definition of "suite." Sometimes it's merely an L-shape room with a sitting area (i.e., there's no door separating you from your teen). The key question is: do your suites have two separate rooms?

SINGLES OR GROUPS OF FRIENDS

If you're traveling solo, you'll never feel lonely at a theme-park hotel. Consider one in Disney's BoardWalk area—perhaps the BoardWalk Inn and Villas, Disney's Yacht Club, or Disney's Beach Club. From here you're just steps from shopping, dining, and nightlife. Similarly, Universal hotels like the elegant Portofino Bay Hotel are just a blink away from the shopping and the hopping nightlife of CityWalk. Plus, Portofino has a spa.

If theme parks really aren't your thing, you can still get your wow factor by staying at a hotel like the Gaylord Palms Resort. The interior of this place is like a Cecil B. DeMille movie—about Florida. Just walking around in the 4-acre atrium is an adventure, with indoor gardens evoking the Everglades and old St. Augustine. There's also lots to do on-site, including dining, shopping, pampering yourself at the spa, or working out in the large fitness center.

COUPLES

Luxury properties like the Ritz-Carlton Orlando Grande Lakes spell romance. Ultraluxurious rooms, restaurants, and spa programs, plus a championship golf course, make this resort one of the best in the Orlando area. Another romantic option is downtown's less pricey but oh-so sexy little Eō Inn & Urban Spa, which sometimes offers couples packages with spa treatments for two.

If you and your sweetie are Disneyphiles, Disney's five-star Grand Floridian Hotel absolutely drips with Victorian romance, and the Animal Kingdom Lodge offers the romantic delights of sunsets over the savanna and giraffes and zebras munching leaves just below your balcony. The Port Orleans Resort–French Quarter, in Downtown Disney, is a great, more affordable choice for couples.

LARGE GROUPS

All-suites properties are the logical choice. If you're coming mainly for the theme parks, stay on Disney or Universal grounds, as the many perks—especially those involving transportation—will definitely make life easier. Some Disney properties with suites include Fort Wilderness Resort Cabins, Beach Club Villas, BoardWalk Inn and Villas, and the new Bay Lake Tower at the Contemporary Resort. At the Universal properties, ask for suite availability.

If you plan to spend time away from the parks or will be shuttling between Universal and Disney, consider reserving an apartment or condo. This works best for families who thrive on the chaos of communal living. (It also works better if you assign chores. It's just not fair if one or two people consistently do all the work.)

The only potential hang-up to the apartment-condo scenario is who gets the master suite. If it's a birthday, anniversary, or retirement event, the big room naturally goes to the guest(s) of honor. Otherwise, the decision isn't so straightforward. One solution: donate it to some of the kids. The suite will be plenty big for a slumber party, and you'll love the fact that their war-torn bathroom is blissfully out of sight.

If your family members tend to get in each other's hair, you're better off reserving a block of hotel rooms. Add a courtesy suite, and you have all the benefits of togetherness, plus a place to retreat to when you need it. Talk to a hotel agent to figure out how many people each room can accommodate comfortably, and how many rooms you'll need.

WHERE SHOULD WE EAT?

Reservations are strongly recommended throughout Orlando. Indeed, make reservations for Disney restaurants and character meals at both Universal and Disney at least 90 (and up to 180) days out. And be sure to ask about the cancellation policy—at a handful of Disney restaurants, for instance, you may be charged penalties if you don't give 24- to 48-hours' notice.

Downtown Disney Marketplace is a dining and nightlife hub. It's also great for shopping, with, among other things, the world's largest Disney store—appropriately named World of Disney.

MEAL PLANS

Disney Magic Your Way Dining Plan allows you one table-service meal, one counter-service meal, and one snack per day of your trip at more than 100 theme-park and resort restaurants. For more money, you can upgrade the plan to include more; to save, you can downgrade to a counter-service-only plan.

Adding the plan to a vacation package costs about $42 per adult, per day, and less than $12 per child age 3–9, per day. This includes taxes but not gratuities. Used wisely, this plan is a steal; but Disney makes out like a bandit when you don't use all the meals on your plan, so absolutely do so. Plan ahead, and use "extra" meals to your advantage by swapping two table-service meals for a Disney dinner show, say, or an evening at a high-end restaurant like California Grill.

Universal Meal Deal is a daylong, all-you-can-eat offer at walk-up eateries inside Universal Studios and Islands of Adventure. Daily prices are $25 and $13 (both parks), and $21 and $11 (one park) for ages 10 and over and kids under 10, respectively. All-you-can-drink soft drinks are $9 daily for all. A valid unlimited Meal Deal ticket lets you purchase a $6 add-on ticket good for one entrée at participating City-Walk restaurants.

CONSIDERATIONS FOR DIFFERENT TYPES OF TRAVELERS

1

FAMILIES WITH SMALL KIDS

If you're traveling with small children you really should include a character meal. Walt Disney World offers breakfast, lunch, dinner, or snacks at each of its four parks and some of its resorts. Some are buffets; others are family-style or pre-plated. Regardless of the format, Mickey, Donald, Goofy, Chip 'n' Dale, Cinderella, and other favorites show up to sign autographs and pose for snapshots.

At Universal, Islands of Adventure's Confisco Grille has a character breakfast Thursday and Sunday. At Christmastime there's a Grinchmas character breakfast at Islands of Adventure featuring the Grinch and friends. Universal's hotels also have character dinners on select nights.

As soon as you find out which characters your children most want to see, call the Disney or Universal dining reservations line to find out what's available and book it. If you haven't reserved ahead, you could try showing up early to one of the meals—the chances are slim that you'll get in, but who knows? May you'll wish upon a star and get lucky. ⇨ *For more details on character meals, see Chapter 3, Where to Eat.*

■ TIP→ If your children are theme-park newbies, have your character meal near the end of a visit, so they'll be used to seeing the large and sometimes frightening figures.

When it comes to choosing a sit-down restaurant for a family meal that doesn't involve a Disney or Universal character, you really just have to know how much formality your kids can or can't handle. That being said, Disney and Universal know their audience, and most restaurants can—and expect to—accommodate children. One exception is Victoria & Albert's, which doesn't allow small kids.

FAMILIES WITH TWEENS

Many tweens are ready to be a little daring in their dining, and Orlando can oblige them. The restaurants of Epcot's World Showcase offer delicacies from all over the world. Another great spot is the Animal Kingdom Lodge's casual buffet restaurant, Boma, where African-inspired dishes like spiced roasted chicken and curried-coconut seafood stew are a hit with parents and kids alike.

The kitsch factor at restaurants in Disney's Hollywood Studios is perfect for tweens. The '50s Prime Time Café looks like a 1950s kitchen. Many tables have their own TVs that air clips of 1950s shows, and "Mom" serves up old-style American comfort food. The Sci-Fi Dine-In Theater builds its booths into top-down convertible cars that face a big screen where you can watch '50s and '60s sci-fi and monster flicks as you munch burgers, sandwiches, and other basic American fare.

Universal's Islands of Adventure also has a variety of themed casual eateries, many based around superheroes or other classic characters. The new Three Broomsticks restaurant is sure to be a hit, as it's themed to make you feel as if you're dining in the world of Harry Potter.

TIPS FOR EATING WITH SMALL KIDS

Avoid arriving overly hungry. Famished children are notoriously miserable, and Murphy's Law dictates that the hungriest people in the restaurant will be served last. Avert disaster with the Cheerios or graham crackers you have stashed in your bag.

Order for the kids first. There's no shame in staggering your family's meals, regardless of the type of restaurant; the timing will benefit everyone. Before your server even finishes saying, "Hello my name is...," place your order for the little ones. Request grown-up drinks and fare when the server returns.

Let them eat cake. Here's a brazen approach to the staggered meal: feed kids their main dish via room service or counter service at the park, and later let them eat dessert while you enjoy a restaurant dinner. Consider it the tactical approach to parenting.

Be realistic. The time to introduce a new food to your child is not at the end of a long day, when she's missed her nap and she's starving.

And, realistically, an unadventurous palate at home is likely to be equally unadventurous on the road.

Be creative. Don't feel shackled by the children's menu, and don't despair if there isn't one: many restaurants will be happy to adjust grown-up meals. Linguine without the clam sauce and chicken Parmesan without the Parmesan (but maybe with ketchup) are good bets. Most resort restaurants are used to this; off-site restaurants may or may not be. Ask ahead about the kitchen's flexibility, and find out whether kiddie meals have grown-up prices.

Know when to give up. The fancy macaroni-and-cheese made with real cheddar just isn't the same as the freeze-dried cheese-food product your children love at home. The restaurant's pasta is too saucy, or your child is simply cranky. Whatever the cause of the fussiness—especially if it escalates into a meltdown—be considerate of the hapless diners around you. Pay your bill and leave. Enjoy your doggie bags back in your hotel room after the kids have gone to bed.

FAMILIES WITH TEENS

CityWalk is filled with high-energy themed eateries that teens will love. A consistent favorite is the Hard Rock Cafe, which plays a constant stream of music videos and has walls covered with rock memorabilia.

The Latin Quarter thrums with nightly live music on the patio, and brings together the style of all 21 Latin American nations. Its decor is meant to make diners feel like they're dining alfresco near an ancient temple. Pat O'Briens replicates the famous New Orleans watering hole, complete with crawfish, jambalaya, po'boys, and other favorites. Teens will especially enjoy the nonalcoholic Hurricanes.

On Disney property the ESPN Club is a great choice for teen sports fans. Even its bathrooms are equipped with video monitors, so you don't have to miss a second of a great game.

COUPLES

Truly, you'd be hard-pressed to find more romantic restaurants than the ones on Disney property. Jiko, for example, at the Animal Kingdom Lodge, pairs superb southern-African cuisine with an exceptional wine list and incredibly knowledgeable servers. The atmosphere is intimate, and you can step outside afterward for a moonlit walk along the savannah. The California Grill, atop the Contemporary Hotel, receives high praise for its innovative American cuisine and incredible Magic Kingdom views. Reserve months in advance for a window seat during the fireworks, or cuddle on the balcony as you take in the spectacle.

If you really want to go all out, there's absolutely nothing like Victoria & Albert's, in the Grand Floridian. Treat yourself to a seven-course prix-fixe meal at the restaurant many consider to be central Florida's best. The Victorian dining room and costumed servers transport you to another time and place, and every mouthful is a delight.

Universal CityWalk offers exceptional New Orleans cuisine at Emeril's. Outside the theme-parks, Norman's at the Ritz Carlton has great views and sophisticated New World cuisine.

SINGLES OR GROUPS OF FRIENDS

With the freedom to travel, you're in a prime position to try the best Orlando has to offer outside the theme parks. At Bonefish Grill you and a primarily local crowd can enjoy standout seafood, including grilled sea bass, tilefish, and rainbow trout. It's served in a casually elegant dining room on Sand Lake Road (aka Restaurant Row).

At Seasons 52, another Sand Lake establishment, what's on the menu this month won't be on it next month, as the kitchen uses only the freshest seasonal ingredients. Dishes are as healthful as they are delicious: meat and fish tend to be grilled, not fried or baked, and desserts are decadent but served in shot-glass sizes. Seek out Le Coq au Vin in south-central Orlando for such French country fare as bronzed grouper with roasted pecans and the namesake chicken with red-wine sauce.

LARGE GROUPS

Dinner shows are great for large groups. Food is plentiful and often quite good, and the entertainment keeps younger family members engaged for longer than usual. Luaus are perfect large-group dining events, and Orlando has several of them. There's the Spirit of Aloha show at Disney's Polynesian Resort, the Wantilan Luau in the Royal Pacific Resort at Universal, and the Makahiki Luau at SeaWorld.

Disney's Fort Wilderness Resort has a couple of dinner-show options. While enjoying the Hoop-Dee-Doo Musical Review, an Old West–themed vaudeville-style show, you dine on ribs, fried chicken, corn, and other down-home favorites. At Mickey's Backyard BBQ, held March through December, everyone loves the burgers, hot dogs, and watermelon, and the little kids go crazy over the chance to get up and dance with Mickey, Minnie, and friends.

Many off-park venues also offer themed dining. At Arabian Nights in Kissimmee your meal occurs as part of a princess' birthday. Things get dramatic when an uninvited guest threatens the festivities, resulting in an extravaganza on horseback. You enjoy it all while eating prime rib or vegetable lasagna, while your kids feast on chicken tenders or pasta.

You'll probably want to organize a special dinner at some point during the trip. If you're not working within a meal plan, you might worry that such an event will bust your budget. It doesn't have to. Group-sales offices at many restaurants can help arrange gala dinners for any budget. And many eateries—even lower-priced ones—offer private rooms and special menus for groups. Ask a concierge or other hotel staffer for suggestions about such restaurants.

■ TIP➔ Arrange to have your big event at lunch, which tends to be cheaper than dinner.

HOW MUCH WILL WE SPEND?

If you're traveling to Orlando, be prepared to spend and spend—and spend some more. Even if you get great deals on transportation and hotel, your credit-card balance will seem to increase and cash will seem to evaporate out of your wallet in the hot Orlando sun.

COSTS

First there are the usual vacation costs: pet boarding, airfare, trip insurance, ground transportation, lodging, and food. Then there are the vacation costs that you tend to take for granted but which add up: gratuities, souvenirs, and sundries (e.g., more sunscreen, bottled water, new batteries).

In Orlando you have to add another whole layer to the cost of a trip, starting with, of course, theme-park tickets. Although prices for these vary greatly depending on the park, the plan, the ages of those in your group, you can peg admission at roughly $70 per day per person. For a family of four visiting three parks, that's close to $850.

What's more, costs for food and other items inside the parks are generally higher than elsewhere. For instance, a snack of churros and sodas can set a family of four back almost $25. To all this you have to add to extras such as character meals, babysitting, cover charges, show tickets, greens fees, and spa treatments.

At this point you might begin to panic. Don't. Take your trip planning and budgeting step by step, and you'll soon find that there are lots of ways to make an Orlando vacation financially accessible.

BUDGETING

We can't stress enough the importance of creating a formal budget for a trip to Orlando and carrying it with you—so you'll be more likely to stick to it. If you do this for all your vacations, great. You're a step ahead. If you don't do this, have we got a plan for you!

SAMPLE COSTS AT WALT DISNEY WORLD	
20 oz. bottle of water $2	Souvenir T-shirt $16–$35
20 oz. bottle of soda $2–$2.50	Roll of film (36 shots) $9.49
Cup of coffee $2–$2.25	1 G digital memory card $17.95
Cheeseburger $6.10	Autograph book $6.95
French fries $2.50	Plush character toys $12–$100
Ice-cream treat $2.50–$4	

THREE-STEP BUDGETING PLAN

Step 1: Create Your Dream Itinerary. First, go back through this chapter and answer the first four trip-planning questions. Your answers will enable you to create a wish list of theme parks and other sights and activities to enjoy (be sure to dream big). Slot these into a day-by-day itinerary to determine how long your dream trip should be and possibly even when to go. Having an itinerary can also help you figure out where to stay and eat.

Step 2: Create Your Dream Budget. Use your dream itinerary—and the decisions made because of it—to create your dream budget. In addition to calculating costs for parks tickets, other entertainments and activities, hotel, transportation, and food, be sure to include estimated daily totals for things like tips, souvenirs, and sundries. Also include kennel costs, trip insurance, and babysitting fees if applicable.

■ TIP→ Most of us lowball costs. To offset this, add in another 2% to 5% of the total budget. The percentage you use should depend on how well you generally police spending.

When you calculate the total cost of your trip, remember that at this point you're still dreaming big. Take a deep breath and move on to Step 3.

Step 3: Create Your Real Budget (and Itinerary). OK. So your dream-vacation budget has, most likely, an astronomical total. Now it's time to bring everything back down to earth. This might mean spending more time researching discounts, lower rates, or package deals. It might also mean reassessing your priorities.

Perhaps you'll book a cheaper hotel so you can spend more days at Disney. Or maybe you'll splurge on lodging and take in fewer parks. You might move your trip up or back a month to get a lower airfare or plan a shorter trip to lower costs overall. Regardless, by making some adjustments you'll soon have a more realistic trip—in terms of both your budget and, no doubt, your itinerary.

SAVING MONEY

IN GENERAL

Shop around. Seem obvious? Not necessarily so. Did you know, for instance, that Internet prices aren't always the lowest? Travel agents may *still* be able to get you better deals, simply because it's their business to know their way around the reservations thicket. And online

TIPPING IN ORLANDO

Whether they carry bags, deliver food, or clean rooms, hospitality workers rely on tips to help them earn a living. Although you'll ultimately base tips on how involved the service is and how well it's performed, here are some guidelines:

In transit, tip airport skycaps and shuttle drivers $1 to $2 per bag and taxi drivers 15% to 20% of the fare. At hotels go with $1 to $2 per bag for bellhops, $1 or $2 per night per guest for housekeeping, $5 to $20

for special concierge service, and $1 to $2 for parking valets or doormen who hail cabs.

Tip the caddies 15% of the greens fee, and spa therapists and waitstaff in full-service restaurants 15% to 20% of the total bill. Tip bartenders and cocktail waitresses 10% to 15% of the total check.

prices can be dramatically different from site to site—room costs alone can vary by as much as 200%. What's more, not all chains or carriers are represented on all sites. This is especially true of the smaller or discount airlines. You might also find the cheapest fare or best promotional room rate on an airline or hotel-chain Web site. Note also that you can sometimes get a better price if you call a hotel's local toll-free number (if available) rather than a central reservations number.

Use aggregator sites to compare prices. Web sites like Kayak.com, Mobissimo.com, Sidestep.com, and Travelgrove.com cull the best prices for airfares, hotels, and rental cars from many places. Most aggregators compare the major online travel-agent–booking-engine sites such as Expedia, Travelocity, and Orbitz. They also look at some car-rental and airline Web sites. Some aggregators also compare such things as trip insurance or vacation packages.

■ TIP→ Booking directly with Disney rarely yields the lowest price. For everything but parks tickets and dining plans (whose prices are fixed), you'll get better deals with major on-line booking sites.

Investigate credit-card privileges. Even if your credit card doesn't give you frequent-flier miles for purchases, you may still be eligible for discounts on travel products or services. Visit the company's Web site to check on hotel deals or promotions.

Have the best deals find you. On Expedia, Travelocity, and other sites you can sign up to receive e-mails the moment a fare to Orlando meets your price requirements. TravelZoo.com and FareCompare.com send e-mails alerting you to great deals on packages and airfares, respectively. And many airlines e-mail a list of weekly specials (typically on Tuesday or Wednesday for the next or following weekend).

Consider what organizations you belong to. Are you a member of the American Dental Association or the American Bar Association? Are you U.S. military personnel? Even if you do nothing more than carry your membership card and pay yearly dues, you can take advantage of low rates that many organizations and unions negotiate with hotels and car-rental companies.

Look into group discounts. Depending on its size, your brood may qualify for rates normally offered to schools and corporations. Talk to group-sales professionals, and ask about discounts on flights as well as hotels (for multiroom blocks), theme parks, and shows.

ON THE THEME PARKS

Buy park tickets when you book your trip. This not only enables you to avoid any price increases that happen before you arrive, it also lets you take advantage of online discounts that parks like Universal and SeaWorld offer. For Discovery Cove, you must book well in advance as attendance is limited to 1,000 people a day.

Save money with a multiday park pass. Theme-park admission can be pricey, but multiday packages are always available, and these often include additional benefits, such as early entry to the park.

Skip the theme parks on days you arrive and depart. It's not worth spending money for just a couple of hours in the parks. Instead, use those days to lounge around your hotel pool or to visit Downtown Disney, Disney's BoardWalk, or Universal CityWalk.

Don't Sweat the Wee Ones. Babies and tots under 3 get into the parks for free—one less cost to worry about.

ON HOTELS

Watch out for the term "from" when pricing hotels. That baseline figure, although an effective come-on, might apply to an undesirable hotel. The minimally acceptable, midlevel options could be quite a hike up.

Always ask about packages and special rates. High-end hotel chains catering to business travelers are often busy only on weekdays; to fill rooms they often drop rates dramatically on weekends. And most hotels have special package deals or corporate rates.

Ask about incidental costs. Seemingly petty details such as surcharges on local phone calls, local occupancy taxes, early check-in fees, resort amenity fees, energy surcharges, and parking can really add up. Some hotels tack on hidden gratuities, too.

ON MEALS

Stay at an all-suites hotel with in-room kitchens. Making some of your own meals will reduce your costs—as will bringing all your own essentials.

Stock up at a supermarket on the way to the hotel. That's especially advisable if you're staying put for a while. You'll get better prices here than at hotel shops.

Plan to have lunch at that fancy restaurant. Menus at lunch often vary only slightly from those at dinner, but prices at lunch can be much lower.

ON AIRFARE

Keep tabs on prices. To determine when to buy tickets, check out Fare-Compare.com, which has historical and current airfares, and Bing.com/travel, which uses Farecast technology to predict fare changes based on historical data. Unlike many other sites, AirfareWatchDog.com includes rates for budget airlines in its research.

AT-HOME EXPENSES

TYPE OF EXPENSE	TOTALS
House Sitter Total	$
Pet Sitter/Boarding Total	$
Babysitter Total	$
Subtotal:	$

TRANSPORTATION

TYPE OF EXPENSE	TOTALS
Airfare (ticket price x no. of tickets)	$
Estimated Airport Transfers (to/from home airport and Orlando airport)	$
Trip Insurance Total	$
Est. Shuttle/Bus Fare (est. per-person daily round-trip cost x no. of days x no. of people)	$
Est. Cab Fare (est. total daily fare—including 10% to 20% tip—x no. of days)	$
Rental-Car Cost (including insurance)	$
Est. Gasoline Cost (miles you plan to drive divided by car's gas mileage x average per-gallon gas cost to/from/within Orlando)	$
Est. Parking Cost (at home airport and/or in Orlando)	$
Est. Skycap/Airport Shuttle Driver Tips ($1–$2 per bag x no. of legs on your trip)	$
Subtotal:	$

FOOD AND HOTEL

TYPE OF EXPENSE	TOTALS
Hotel Costs (room rate including tax x no. of nights x no. of rooms)	$
Est. Hotel Tips ($1–$2 per night per guest for housekeeping; $5–$20 for each concierge service; $2 per trip in or out for parking valets)	$
Est. Meal Costs (est. daily per-person cost for three meals x no. of days x no. of people)	$
OR	
Adult Meal Plan Cost (meal-plan option x no. of adults)	$
Child Meal Plan Cost (meal-plan option x no. of children)	$
Est. Restaurant Tips (10% to 20% of total meal costs)	$
Est. Snack Costs (est. daily per-person cost x no. of days x no. of people)	$
Subtotal:	$

ENTERTAINMENT

TYPE OF EXPENSE	TOTALS
Adult Disney Ticket (x no. of adults)	$
Child Disney Ticket (x. no. of children)	$
Adult Universal Ticket (x no. of adults)	$
Child Universal Ticket (x. no. of children)	$
Adult SeaWorld Ticket (x no. of adults)	$
Child SeaWorld Ticket (x. no. of children)	$
Est. Adult Total for Other Attractions/Activities (x no. of adults)	$
Est. Child Total for Other Attractions/Activities (x. no. of children)	$
Est. Total Nightlife Cost (e.g., bar tabs, cover charges, movies/show tickets, tips)	$
Est. Total Babysitting Costs	$
Subtotal:	$

SHOPPING

TYPE OF EXPENSE	TOTALS
Adult Souvenir Budget (daily allowance x no. of days x no. of adults)	$
Child Souvenir Budget (daily allowance x no. of days x no. of chlldren)	$
Sundries Allowance (no. of days x daily allowance for extra sunscreen, camera/photo expenses, baby supplies, miscellanous tips, etc.)	$
Subtotal:	$

TRIP TOTAL 1	$
Extra 2% to 5% of Total 1 (for a more realistic total)	$
TRIP TOTAL 2	$

ORLANDO DISCOUNTS AND DEALS

Pick up local coupon books. **Entertainment Travel Editions** (☎ 800/445-4137 ⊕ www. entertainment.com) has one for around $30 with discounts on rental cars, admission fees, and meals.

Look into **Orlando/Orange County Convention and Visitors Bureau** offerings. The free Orlando Magicard (☎ 800/643-9492 ⊕ www. orlandoinfo.com/magicard) provides discounts for many attractions, restaurants, and stores. The CVB also sells park ticket plans (☎ 800/255-5786 or 407/363-5872 ⊕ www. orlandoticketsales.com).

Mousesavers.com aims to give readers the scoop on ways to score discounts on all things Disney: www. mousesavers.com. *For the most part it doesn't offer specific discounts, but it does provide great advice on where you can ferret out your own. In a few cases, such as with its recommended non-Disney hotels, Mousesavers has negotiated added perks like free breakfasts. The site also lists many discounts for a long list of other Orlando parks and attractions, including all the biggies.*

Though Disney doesn't always publicize it, it does offer many of its own discounts and promotions, all of which the independent Web site **DIS** (⊕ www.wdwinfo.com/discounts.

html) compiles and shares. The site also includes discounts and promotions for the Universal parks and properties.

If you're active-duty or retired military, National Guard, Army Reserve, a disabled veteran, foreign military stationed with U.S. armed forces, or a Department of Defense civilian with military ID, you can also stay at the on-site **Shades of Green Resort** (☎ 407/824-1403 ⊕ www. shadesofgreen.org) for a fraction of what it costs to stay at other Disney resorts. You can also buy up to three rooms so nonmilitary members of your party can stay with you.

Members of the military are also eligible to purchase discounted and tax-free park tickets, including the Magic Your Way Stars and Stripes Pass. The resort's ticket office is open 8 AM to 9 PM. (You can buy these tickets at the main entry gate, too, but tax will then be included.) Shades of Green also sells heavily discounted tickets to Orlando's other attractions, including both Universal parks, SeaWorld, Busch Gardens, Kennedy Space Center, Wet 'n Wild, and many more. Military personnel and their spouses can also buy tickets for a select number of nonmilitary guests. You do not need to stay at Shades of Green resort to qualify for any of its attractions discounts.

Pick your days and times wisely. Look for departures on Tuesday, Wednesday, and Saturday, typically the cheapest days to travel. Flights on these days are often less crowded as well. Also check on prices for departures at different times of day.

Investigate flights to secondary airports. Flights to Daytona's airport, 45 minutes from Orlando, may be cheaper and have better availability, especially during high season. Area car-rentals rates might also be lower.

Fly on a holiday. Just as the most expensive fares tend to be on the days or weekends at either side of a holiday, some of the least expensive are on the holiday itself, especially Christmas and Thanksgiving. Just be sure that the airfare cost savings isn't completely eaten up by hotel, car-rental, and other costs made more expensive by the holiday.

Ask about child and senior fares. In this age of troubled airlines, it's rare to find discounts of any kind. But it never hurts to ask.

ON CAR TRAVEL

Calculate the cost of a drive to Orlando. Input your route and the make and model of your car on AAA's fuel-cost calculator (*www.fuelcostcalculator. com*) and voilà! (The figures assume there are no traffic jams.) Gas prices are updated regularly. Use it to budget for a road trip and to compare that to the cost of flying.

Find the cheapest gas. Gas prices are greatly influenced by state gas taxes. A Web site operated by the U.S. Environmental Protection Agency, *www.fueleconomy.gov*, gives national and regional average prices. Also helpful are sites like Gas Buddy (*www.gasbuddy.com*) and Gas Price Watch (*www.gaspricewatch.com*), which use consumer tips to rank prices in a particular area.

Decide whether you'll really need a rental car. If you're staying on Disney or Universal property, you most likely will not. If you'll be traveling, price out those trips by cab, then see if it pays to have a rental car. Don't forget the costs of gas and parking in your estimate.

Check out weekly rates and packages. Even if you only want to rent for five or six days, ask for the weekly rate; it may very well be cheaper than the daily rate for that period of time. Adding a car rental onto your air-hotel vacation package may be cheaper than renting a car separately.

Don't forget the locals. Price local companies as well as the majors. Avoiding the chains and renting through local agencies can save you big bucks, particularly in touristy areas like Florida, where competition is stiff. The potential downsides include limited counter office hours, infrequent shuttle service, limited car selection, and no guaranteed road-side assistance.

Ask about fees and surcharges. Most agencies impose a surcharge on drivers under age 25 (some won't rent to drivers under 25; for others the cutoff age is 21). Airports often add surcharges, which you can sometimes avoid by renting from an agency whose office is just off airport property. Don't assume that bringing the car back early will save you bucks. If you return your car before the minimum number of days (often five) specified in a weeklong contract, the weekly rate could revert to a much higher daily rate.

Check prices on different-size cars. Most of us assume that renting a compact car is less expensive than a standard-size model. But smaller cars are more popular with renters, so prices may be lower for the larger models. Check the fees. You may be pleasantly surprised.

Get smart about fuel. Pass on the option of paying the rental agency for a tank of gas rather than refueling the car yourself before you return it. In some cases the per-gallon rate is much higher than you'd pay at a gas station. Even if the per-gallon rate is lower, you'll be charged for an entire tank of gas whether you use it all or not (it's hard to work it so you can coast in on empty upon return). Plan to fill up the tank yourself, at a station away from the drop-off point, to get better prices.

PACKING

In Orlando, casual, comfortable clothing is best. Men need a jacket and tie in only a handful of restaurants. It can get quite cool in December, January, and February. In general, though, be prepared for a range of temperatures in winter by packing clothing that you can layer.

In summer you'll want a sun hat and a rain poncho in case of sudden thunderstorms (or for watery theme-park rides). On hot summer days the perfect theme-park outfit begins with generous amounts of sunscreen, followed by shorts made of a breathable, quick-drying material, topped by a T-shirt or tank top. At any time of the year pockets are useful for Fastpass tickets and park maps.

WHAT TO PACK

Remember the itinerary you created and used to create a budget? Well, that same itinerary is very useful when it comes time to pack, too. Next to each day's activities, note the outfits—including shoes—and gear you'll need. Use these notes to create a custom packing list.

Study your list, noting how many times you've cited specific items. If shorts are listed seven times for a week, for instance, consider cutting the number down to two or three pairs. Do you really need several pairs of shoes, or can you make do with a pair of sneakers for park-walking and a pair of flip-flops for the pool? The right pair of elegant sandals can work with both day and evening outfits. If you plan to run, your running shoes can double as walk-around shoes. As for toiletries, try to make your daily routine more travel-friendly. Why pack hand, body, and face creams when one all-purpose moisturizer will do?

HOW TO PACK

Place a copy of your packing list in your personal documents kit—as a checklist for when you're repacking to head home, for reference on the next trip, and as a record in case your luggage is lost or stolen.

Pare every ounce of extra weight. The small stuff adds up. Packing pros know, for instance, to remove facial tissues from their bulky boxes and slip them into resealable plastic bags. Ditto for baby wipes—useful for waterless hand washing and, some contend, stain removal. Also weed out valuables you'd hate to lose. (If you do take good jewelry, make a point of never removing it, even when sleeping; once it's off, it's too easy to forget.)

If you're traveling with a spouse or companion, figure out where you don't need to double up. She's got the shampoo? You'll get the toothpaste. A pair of people flying together could also pack some of each

ORLANDO VACATIONS PLANNING TIMELINE

1 YEAR OUT

■ If you're planning a trip with a large group, get a firm commitment from everyone and a sense of what they want to do. Determine the trip dates and length of stay, and create a rough itinerary and a budget. Then start booking the big things: airfare, hotels, and parks tickets.

■ If your group trip centers on Walt Disney World and includes at least eight guests over the age of 3, you qualify for a Grand Gatherings vacation. Now's the time to contact Disney's Grand Gatherings office at 407/934-7639 and start planning.

6 MONTHS OUT

■ Small groups and families, couples, and singles should create itineraries and budgets and research and book your flights, hotel, rental car (if necessary), and parks tickets.

■ Make reservations for spa treatments, shows, and character or other special theme-park meals like a romantic dinner at Victoria & Albert's or the California Grill.

■ Arrange for the swim-with-the-dolphin experience at SeaWorld's Discovery Cove.

■ Large groups should book special Disney dining and entertainment experiences through Disney's Grand Gatherings (407/934-7639).

3 MONTHS OUT

■ Reserve meals at special restaurants outside the theme parks.

■ Reserve theme-park events that weren't available until now, such as Disney's Pirate Adventure and the Wonderland Tea Party.

■ Reserve spots at hotel day camps or kids' clubs, and line up babysitting services.

■ If your child is bringing a friend, get notarized permission from the parents for that child to travel with you.

60 DAYS OUT

■ Make a packing list for each travel companion.

■ Make sure your kids have the clothes they need—they may have outgrown last summer's bathing suits—and start shopping so you have time to find just the right thing (and perhaps to return or exchange the wrong thing for the right one).

■ Make kennel reservations or arrange for a pet sitter.

■ Book a house sitter.

30 DAYS OUT

■ Make pretrip manicure, haircut, or other appointments.

■ Check your luggage for damage (particularly the zippers) or for anything that might have spilled inside on a previous trip.

■ Buy any new luggage you need.

■ Make sure clothes, shoes, and other gear are clean and ready for the trip.

2 TO 3 WEEKS OUT

■ Go over your plans and start gathering all your documents (tickets, hotel-reservation confirmation printouts, etc.). If there are issues, deal with them right away.

■ Arrange to have your mail held at the post office or ask a neighbor to pick it up.

ORLANDO VACATIONS PLANNING TIMELINE

■ Stop newspaper delivery or ask a neighbor to bring it in for you.

■ Arrange for lawn and houseplant care or snow removal during your absence (if necessary).

■ Go over your packing lists again. Finish shopping.

1 WEEK BEFORE THE TRIP
■ Finalize your packing list, and start gathering items.

■ Buy film or digital media, and check the batteries in your camera.

■ Refill prescription medications with an adequate supply.

■ Get traveler's checks if you use them (remember to keep a separate record of the serial numbers). Get a supply of $1 bills for tipping baggage handlers (at the airport, hotel, etc.).

■ Put valuables in a safety deposit box.

■ Pay any bills that will be due while you're gone.

■ Leave your itinerary, the hotel's phone number, and a house key with a relative or friend.

■ Purchase small games or toys to keep young travelers occupied while en route to Orlando.

3 DAYS BEFORE
■ Confirm your flights; departure times are sometimes subject to change.

■ Put a card with your name, address, and telephone number inside each suitcase.

■ Fill out the exterior luggage tags.

■ Do last-minute laundry and housework.

■ Arrange for transportation to the airport (if applicable).

■ Pull out the luggage, and begin packing.

1 DAY BEFORE
■ Take pets to the kennel.

■ Water houseplants and the lawn.

■ Dispose of perishables in the refrigerator.

■ Mail any last-minute bills.

■ Set timers for the indoor lights.

■ Reorganize your wallet. Remove anything you won't need (check-cashing cards, department store or gas credit cards, etc.), and put it all in an envelope.

■ Finish packing.

DEPARTURE DAY!
■ Turn off the water if there's danger of frozen pipes while you're away.

■ Adjust the thermostat, and double-check the door locks.

■ Arrive at the airport two hours before your departure time.

■ Slip your car keys, parking claim checks, and airline tickets in your carry-on luggage.

■ Have your photo IDs ready for airport check-in.

person's essentials in the other's suitcase. That way, if one bag doesn't make it to the destination, both will still be covered.

When it's time to fill your suitcase, pile everything you plan to bring on your bed or dresser. Eye your clothes and cull a few more items. If you pack directly into your suitcase, you'll be tempted to throw in a few extra items (trust us, you will). Once you've made the final edit, pack only what's in front of you. If you've followed our advice, your suitcase should be a lean, mean, traveling machine.

PACKING TIPS FOR KIDS

Give everyone his or her own bag. Individual suitcases (preferably different colors—red for one, blue for another) help you locate items in a hurry. This will make life easy at the airport, as even little kids are not only capable of toting around a mini Pullman—they often enjoy it.

Pack one communal carry-on. A family bag of essentials saves heartache if some of your luggage is temporarily lost. Include an outfit for everyone, as well as prescriptions and other must-haves. A communal bag also simplifies car travel, giving quick access to overnight necessities for midway stops instead of having to unpack the whole car.

Consider creative carry-ons. Soft coolers that don't go beyond airline size limits make great carry-on luggage. Roomy and crushable, they're perfect for nonbreakable items (such as those extra outfits) and help you cut your food bill by becoming picnic baskets for snacks.

CAR-TRAVEL PACKING TIPS

Check the trunk. Trunks are prone to dampness—wetness from one big storm can remain in your trunk for long periods, then creep into luggage. Line the bottom of your trunk with a waterproof tarp or, better yet, with some kind of slightly elevated platform that allows air to circulate between the base of your trunk and the goods stored in it.

Separate your "getting there" and "there" clothes. If your Orlando trip involves a hotel stay or stays along the way, keep the clothing you plan to use once you arrive in one piece of luggage at the back of the trunk or under other bags. Put the clothing you need during the drive in lighter and smaller duffel bags or luggage stowed in an easy to reach place.

Keep essential road-trip items handy. Pack the emergency kit last and in a place where it's easily accessible. Also keep books, electronic entertainment gadgetry, and the cell-phone charger handy.

Organize with plastic drawers. You can buy cheap, stackable plastic drawers at most department stores. Put a few of these in your trunk, filling one with books and maps and another with toiletries, and you'll have an efficient system for even the longest trip from home.

PACKING CHECKLIST

1

ON THE PLANE
What to Wear

■ Your bulkiest clothes and outerwear

■ A sweater or other coverup

■ Loose clothing in soft, natural fibers

■ Low-heeled leather or canvas slip-on shoes

What to Carry

■ Travel documents

■ Money, valuables

■ Electronics, breakables

■ 311-compliant toiletries kit

■ Prescription medications

■ Eyeglasses, sunglasses

■ Change of clothes

■ Reading material, paper, pens

■ Neck pillow

■ Sleep mask, earplugs

■ Soft slippers or warm socks

ADULT STUFF

■ 1 pair of khakis or other dressy-casual trousers

■ 1 pair of jeans

■ 1 pair of long pants that convert to shorts or capris

■ 1 pair of shorts or capris

■ 1 sundress or set of casual-dressy separates

■ 1 coordinating blazer (men) or elegant wrap (women)

■ 2 collared shirts (e.g., oxfords, polos, etc.)

■ 3 T-shirts or turtlenecks

■ 1 pullover sweater or cardigan

■ 1 pareo or sarong

■ Workout outfit (including sports bra if applicable)

■ 1 pair of sneakers good for walking *and* your sport of choice (e.g., running, tennis)

■ 1 pair of dressy boots or shoes

■ 1 pair of sandals or flip-flops

■ Necessary accessories: scarves, belt, handbag, hosiery or socks, sunglasses

■ Sleepwear, underwear

■ Bathing suit, goggles, cap

■ Sun hat

■ Rain poncho or all-purpose windbreaker, jacket with a zip-out lining, or winter coat (wear on the plane)

■ Umbrella

■ Any larger toiletries

■ Collapsible tote bag or day pack and duffel (for big shoppers)

■ If winter, hats, scarves, gloves (even central Florida has cold snaps)

PACKING CHECKLIST

KIDS STUFF
For Really Young Ones

- Two outfits and pajamas per day

- Outerwear, socks, undershirts

- Swimsuit, swim diapers, diaper cover

- Diapers, rash cream, changing pad

- Baby wipes, baby powder

- Toilet-seat adapter or potty seat

- Car seat

- Baby carrier

- Collapsible stroller

- Baby formula

- Can opener, if needed

- Bottles or holders, liners, nipples, rings, caps

- Bottle brush

- Breast pump

- Baby cereal

- Bibs

- Terrycloth hand towels

- Collapsible hook-on high chair

- Blankets

- Sleepwear

- Pacifiers

- Nightlight

- Portable crib

- Safety gizmos

For Older Kids, Tweens, and Teens

- One outfit per day

- Two extra tops

- An extra pair of pants

- One dress outfit

- Sweatshirt, sweater

- Windbreaker, outerwear

- Shoes, extra laces

- Socks, undies

- Two swimsuits, swim goggles

- Snacks

- Familiar foods

- Drinks

- Toys, books, games, iPod or MP3 player, DVDs and players

- A tote for all the toys, books, games, iPod or MP3 players, DVDs and players

Where to Stay

WORD OF MOUTH

"You MUST go to the Grand Floridian Hotel and see how they decorate for the holidays. No pictures can do it justice. It is a grand old hotel, . . . with a real life-sized Gingerbread house, and a Christmas tree that I have never seen so big. If you can afford it, it is worth it to stay at this hotel."

—JillDavis

Updated by Jennifer Greenhill-Taylor

With tens of thousands of lodging choices available in the Orlando area, from tents to deluxe villas, there is no lack of variety in price or amenities. Narrowing down the possibilities can be part of the fun.

About 50 million visitors come to the Orlando area each year, making it the most popular tourism destination on the planet. More upscale hotels are opening, as visitors demand more luxurious surroundings, such as crisp, white duvet covers and luxe linens, tasteful and refined decor, organic toiletries, or ergonomic chairs and work desks and more. But no matter what your budget or desires, lodging comes in such a wide range of prices, themes, color schemes, brands, meal plans, and guestroom amenities, that visitors will have no problem finding something that fits. Area resorts offer characters in costume performing for the kids, water parks, and massive indoor amusements, like the Gaylord Palms, which offers re-creations of the Everglades, old St. Augustine, and Key West under a gargantuan glass roof, giving visitors the illusion of having visited more of Florida than they expected.

The area around the expanded Orange County Convention Center is going more upscale as the center draws savvy conventioneers who bring their families along to visit the theme parks. Despite tough economic times, several big resorts opened their doors, including the first Waldorf Astoria outside New York, the Hilton Orlando Bonnet Creek, and smaller hotels such as the European-inspired Mona Lisa. Many of the new and existing hotels are joining the trend in green lodging that is expanding in the area, bringing recycling, water conservation, and other environmentally conscious amenities to the table.

But the number of hotel rooms means you can still find relative bargains throughout the Orlando area, even on Disney property, by researching your trip well and shopping wisely.

DID YOU KNOW?

The All-Star Sports, Music, and Movies Resorts all are thematically designed. Goofy is the pitcher in the baseball diamond-shaped pool at the Sports Resort; a piano shaped-pool can be found at the Music resort; and a huge Buzz Lightyear figure stands tall at the Movies Resort.

WHERE TO STAY PLANNER

Lodging Strategy

The vast array of hotels and resorts in the Orlando area may seem daunting to first-time visitors. But fret not—our expert writers and editors have done a lot of legwork. The selections here represent the best the area has to offer—from budget picks to the most luxurious resorts. Scan "Best Bets" on the following pages for top recommendations by price and experience. Or find a review quickly in the listings, organized alphabetically within neighborhood or theme park. Happy hunting!

With Kids

Few hotels in this area are not kid-friendly. A quick way to tell whether a hotel welcomes children: a "lazy river" pool, water playground, or character meals. Walt Disney World's on-site resorts obviously will have children's facilities and programs. Many other hotels in the area have supervised children's programs with trained counselors and planned activities. A step in your research is to ask, before booking, whether your hotel offers a children's program, babysitting services, or a kids-eat-free policy in their restaurant. This is a market in which travelers with youngsters can expect a lot.

Reservations

You can book many accommodations—Disney-owned hotels and some non-Disney-owned hotels—through the **WDW Central Reservations Office** (☎ 407/934-7639 ⊕ www.disneyworld.com). People with disabilities can call **WDW Special Request Reservations** (☎ 407/939-7807). When booking by phone, expect to chat with a robot first, then a real person. Packages can be arranged through the **Walt Disney Travel Co.** (☎ 407/934-7639 ⊕ www. disneyworld.com). Avoid checkout headaches by asking about the resort fee. Many hotels and resorts charge this fee, and few tell you until checkout, so make sure to ask about it in advance.

Facilities

All hotels and resorts in Central Florida have air-conditioning, and most have cable or satellite TV, coffeemakers, in-room irons, and ironing boards. Those in the moderate and expensive price ranges often have bathrobes and hair dryers. High-speed wireless access (Wi-Fi) is now common even at budget properties, but some hotels still charge a daily fee for Internet service. If being connected is important, it's best to ask. Most hotels, even the budget ones, have a pool, and many have fitness facilities.

If a particular amenity is important to you, ask for it; many hotels will provide extras upon request. Double-check your bill at checkout, and if a charge seems unreasonable, this is the time to have it remedied. If you're traveling with pets, note the hotel's pet policies. Some hotels require substantial cleaning fees. A big note to smokers: most of the hotels and resorts in Central Florida are entirely smoke-free, meaning even smoking outdoors on hotel property is frowned upon or prohibited.

Prices and Price Chart

In the Orlando area there's an inverse relationship between temperature and room rates. The hot and humid weather in late summer and fall brings low prices and possibly hurricanes. Conversely, the balmy days of late February, March, and April attract lots of visitors; hotel owners charge accordingly. One note about hurricane season—it officially begins in June, but a hurricane in Florida before August is a rarity. Rates are often low from early January to mid-February, from late April to mid-June, and from mid-August to the third week in November.

Always call several places—availability and special deals can drive room rates at a $$$$ hotel down into the $$ range—and don't forget to ask whether you're eligible for a discount. You can always save by preparing a few meals in a room, suite, or villa with a kitchenette or kitchen. Web sites will often offer a better room rate, so compare the prices offered on the Web and through the hotel's local or toll-free number (it one is available). Always ask about special packages or corporate rates.

WHAT IT COSTS

	¢	$	$$	$$$	$$$$
FOR TWO PEOPLE	Under $100	$100–$174	$175–$249	$250–$350	over $350

Price categories reflect the range between the least and most expensive standard double rooms in nonholiday high season, based on the European Plan (with no meals) unless otherwise noted. County and resort taxes (10%–12%) are extra

Using the Maps

Throughout the chapter, you'll see mapping symbols and coordinates (⊹ 3:F2) after property names or reviews. Maps are located within the chapter. The first number after the ⊹ symbol indicates the map number. Following that is the property's coordinate on the map grid.

In This Chapter

Spotlight On

2

WALT DISNEY WORLD

Disney-operated hotels are fantasies unto themselves. Each is designed according to a theme (quaint New England, the relaxed culture of the Polynesian Islands, an African safari village, etc.) and each offers the same perks: free transportation from the airport and to the parks, the option to charge all your purchases to your room, special guest-only park-visiting times, and much more. If you stay on-site, you'll have better access to the parks and you'll be more immersed in the Disney experience.

MAGIC KINGDOM RESORT AREA

Take I–4 Exit 62, 64B, or 65.

The ritzy hotels near the Magic Kingdom all lie on the monorail route and are only minutes away from the park. Fort Wilderness Resort and Campground, with RV and tent sites, is a bit farther southeast of the Magic Kingdom, and access to the parks is by bus.

$$$–$$$$ 🖼 **Contemporary Resort.** You're paying for location and tradition when you stay here. The first hotel to open here, nearly 40 years ago, has been completely renovated several times to maintain a sleek, modern look. The monorail runs through the lobby, so it takes just minutes to get to the Magic Kingdom and Epcot. Upper floors of the main tower (where rooms are more expensive) offer great views of activities in and around the Magic Kingdom, including the nightly fireworks and the boat traffic on Bay Lake and the Seven Seas Lagoon. For the fireworks alone, at least one dinner at the California Grill (atop the building) is worth the pricey dinner tab. **Pros:** easy access to Magic Kingdom; Chef Mickey's is here, the epicenter of the character-meal world; launching point for romantic sunset Bay Lake cruises. **Cons:** a mix of conventioneers and vacationers (there's an on-site convention center) means that it is sometimes too frenzied for the former and too staid for the latter; among the most kid-intensive of the pricier Disney hotels, so if you don't like children around, look elsewhere. ☎ *407/824–1000 ❥1,013 rooms, 25 suites ♿ In-room: safe, refrigerator, Wi-Fi. In-hotel: 3 restaurants, room service, tennis courts, pools, gym, beachfront, children's programs (ages 4–12), laundry facilities, laundry service, Wi-Fi hotspot* ▭ *AE, D, DC, MC, V* ✥ *1:B1.*

$$$ 🖼 **Fort Wilderness Resort Cabins.** This 700-acre campground is a resort in itself, with cabins and campsites. With its dozens of entertainment options, including biking, outdoor movies, and singing around the campfire—and the very popular Hoop-Dee-Doo Musical Review and Backyard BBQ character event—a family can have a truly memorable vacation in real Florida wilderness. The cabins, which resemble log mobile homes, can accommodate four grown-ups and two youngsters. **Pros:** cabins don't constitute roughing it (they have air-conditioning); you can save a fortune by cooking, but you don't have to, thanks to the three-meals-a-day restaurant and nightly barbecue. **Cons:** shuttle to Disney theme parks is free, but slow; coin-op laundry is pricey ($2 to wash, $2 to dry). ☎ *407/824–2900 ❥421 cabins ♿ In-room: kitchen,*

BEST BETS FOR ORLANDO AND THE PARKS LODGING

With thousands of hotels to choose from, ask yourself first what your family truly wants to do in Orlando during your visit. This invariably leads to an on-property vs. off-property debate, and more questions. To assist you, here are our top recommendations by price (any property listed here has at least some rooms in the noted range) and experience. The very best properties—those that provide a particularly remarkable experience in their price range—are designated in the listings with the Fodor's Choice logo.

Fodor's Choice ★

All-Star Resorts, p. 102

Best Western Lake Buena Vista Resort, p. 106

Animal Kingdom Lodge, p. 103

Coronado Springs Resort, p. 102

Fort Wilderness Resort Campground, p. 100

Grand Floridian Resort & Spa, p. 100

Hyatt Regency Grand Cypress Resort, p. 133

Mona Lisa Suite Hotel, p. 123

Nickelodeon Family Suites by Holiday Inn, p. 133

Portofino Bay Hotel, p. 112

Ritz-Carlton Orlando Grande Lakes, p. 119

Royal Pacific Resort, p. 113

Waldorf Astoria Orlando, p. 134

By Price

¢

Best Western Lake Buena Vista Resort, p. 106

Fort Wilderness Resort Campground, p. 100

Parc Corniche Condominium Suite Hotel, p. 118

Sheraton Safari Hotel, p. 134

$

All-Star Resorts, p. 102

Hyatt Place Orlando/ Universal, p. 112

Mona Lisa Suite Hotel, p. 123

Pop Century Resort, p. 103

$$

Coronado Springs Resort, p. 102

Nickelodeon Family Suites by Holiday Inn, p. 133

Royal Pacific Resort, p. 113

Walt Disney World Dolphin or Swan, p. 106

$$$

Animal Kingdom Lodge, p. 103

Contemporary Resort, p. 90

Fort Wilderness Resort Cabins, p. 90

Hyatt Regency Grand Cypress Resort, p. 133

Portofino Bay Hotel, p. 112

Ritz-Carlton Orlando Grande Lakes, p. 119

$$$$

Grand Floridian Resort & Spa, p. 100

Polynesian Resort, p. 100

Waldorf Astoria Orlando, p. 134

By Experience

MOST KID-FRIENDLY

All-Star Resorts, p. 102

Contemporary Resort, p. 90

Nickelodeon Family Suites by Holiday Inn, p. 133

Pop Century Resort, p. 103

BEST POOLS

Hyatt Regency Grand Cypress Resort, p. 133

JW Marriott Orlando Grande Lakes, p. 117

Portofino Bay Hotel, p. 112

Ritz-Carlton Orlando Grande Lakes, p. 119

BEST FOR BUSINESS

Doubletree Hotel at the Entrance to Universal Orlando, p. 109

Hilton Orlando, p. 116

Hyatt Place Orlando/ Universal or Convention Center, p. 112, p. 116

Peabody Hotel, p. 118

Rosen Plaza Hotel, p. 119

Westin Imagine, p. 119

HOTELS AT A GLANCE

Hotel Name	Location/Nearest Park	Price	Best For	Pool (y/n)	Restaurant (y/n)	Bar (y/n)	Spa (y/n)	Children's Programs (y/n)	Shuttle to Parks (y/n)
Contemporary Resort	Magic Kingdom	$$$–$$$$	Couples, Families w/ children 10 and under	y	y	y	y	y	y
Fort Wilderness Resort Cabins	Magic Kingdom	$$$	Families w/ children 10 and under, Families with teens and tweens	y	y	y	n	y	y
★ Fort Wilderness Resort Campground	Magic Kingdom	¢	Families w/ children 10 and under, Families with teens and tweens	y	y	n	n	y	y
★ Grand Floridian Resort & Spa	Magic Kingdom	$$$$	Couples, Families w/ children 10 and under, Seniors	y	y	y	y	y	y
Polynesian Resort	Magic Kingdom	$$$$	Couples, Families w/ children 10 and under	y	y	y	n	y	y
Wilderness Lodge	Magic Kingdom	$$$–$$$$	Mixed groups	y	y	y	n	y	y
Beach Club Villas	Epcot	$$$$	Couples, Seniors	y	y	n	n	n	y
Caribbean Beach Resort	Epcot	$$	Singles, Couples	y	y	n	n	n	y
★ Coronado Springs Resort	Epcot	$$	Singles, Couples	y	y	y	n	n	y
★ Yacht and Beach Club Resorts	Epcot	$$$$	Couples, Families with teens and tweens, Seniors	y	y	y	y	y	y
★ All-Star Sports, Music, Movies Resorts	Animal Kingdom	$	Families w/ children 10 and under	y	y	y	n	y	y
★ Animal Kingdom Lodge	Animal Kingdom	$$$–$$$$	Mixed groups	y	y	y	n	y	y
Pop Century Resort	Animal Kingdom	$	Families w/ children 10 and under, Families with teens and tweens	y	y	y	n	n	y
Old Key West Resort	Downtown Disney	$$$–$$$$	Couples, singles	y	y	y	y	n	y

Hotel	Location	Price	Who It's For						
Port Orleans Resort-French Quarter	Downtown Disney	$$	Couples, singles	y	y	y	n	n	y
Port Orleans Resort-Riverside	Downtown Disney	$$	Couples, singles	y	y	y	n	n	y
Saratoga Springs Resort	Downtown Disney	$$$–$$$$	Couples, Families with teens and tweens	y	y	y	y	n	y
Shades of Green	Magic Kingdom	$–$$	Mixed groups	y	y	y	n	n	y
Walt Disney World Dolphin	Epcot	$$–$$$	Families w/ children 10 and under, teens and tweens	y	y	y	y	y	y
Walt Disney World Swan	Epcot	$$–$$$	Couples, Families with teens and tweens	y	y	y	y	y	y
★ Best Western Lake Buena Vista Resort	Downtown Disney	$–$	Couples, Families with teens and tweens	y	y	y	n	n	y
Buena Vista Palace Hotel & Spa	Downtown Disney	$$–$$$	Families w/ children 10 and under, teens and tweens	y	y	y	y	y	y
Doubletree Guest Suites	Downtown Disney	$–$$	Couples, Families w/ children 10 and under, teens and tweens	y	y	y	n	n	y
Hilton in the WDW Resort	Downtown Disney	$$–$$$	Mixed groups	y	y	y	y	y	y
Holiday Inn in the WDW Resort	Downtown Disney	$	Couples, Families with teens and tweens	y	y	y	n	n	y
Regal Sun Resort	Downtown Disney	$$	Families w/ children 10 and under	y	n	y	n	n	y
Comfort Suites Orlando/Universal	Universal Orlando	$–$	Singles, Families with teens and tweens	y	n	n	n	n	y
Doubletree Hotel at Entrance to Universal	Universal Orlando	$–$	Singles, Families with teens and tweens	y	y	n	n	n	y
Hard Rock Hotel	Universal Orlando	$$$–$$$$	Couples, Singles, Families with teens and tweens	y	y	y	y	n	y
Holiday Inn Hotel & Suites Orlando/Universal	Universal Orlando	$–$	Couples, Singles	y	y	y	n	n	y

HOTELS AT A GLANCE

Hotel Name	Location/ Nearest Park	Price	Best For	Pool (y/n)	Restaurant (y/n)	Bar (y/n)	Spa (y/n)	Children's Programs (y/n)	Shuttle to Parks (y/n)
★ Hyatt Place Orlando/Universal	Universal Orlando	$–$$	Singles	y	y	y	n	n	y
★ Portofino Bay Hotel	Universal Orlando	$$$–$$$$	Couples, Seniors	y	y	y	y	n	y
Royal Pacific Resort	Universal Orlando	$$–$$$	Couples, Singles	y	y	y	n	y	y
Bluegreen Resorts, The Fountains	I-Drive	$$	Mixed groups	y	y	y	n	y	y
The Doubletree Castle	I-Drive	$$	Families w/ children 10 and under	y	y	y	n	n	y
Doubletree Resort Orlando-International Drive	I-Drive	$$	Couples, Singles	y	y	y	n	n	y
Embassy Suites Orlando International Drive South/Convention Center	I-Drive	$–$$	Couples, singles	y	y	y	n	n	y
Enclave Suites at Orlando	I-Drive	¢–$	Families w/ children 10 and under	y	y	n	n	n	y
Floridays Resort	I-Drive	$–$$	Mixed groups	y	y	y	n	n	y
Four Points by Sheraton Orlando Studio City	I-Drive	$	Couples, Singles	y	y	y	n	n	y
Hilton Orlando	I-Drive	$$–$$$	Couples, Seniors	y	y	y	y	n	y
Hyatt Place Orlando/Convention Center	I-Drive	$–$$	Couples, Singles	y	y	y	n	n	n

Hotel	Location	Price	Best for						
Hyatt Place Orlando/Convention Center	I-Drive	$–$$	Couples, Singles	y	y	y	n	n	n
JW Marriott Orlando Grande Lakes	I-Drive	$$–$$$	Mixed groups	y	y	y	y	n	y
Lake Eve Resort	I-Drive	$–$$	Couples, Seniors	y	y	y	n	n	y
Marriott Residence Inn SeaWorld International Center	I-Drive	$$	Couples, Singles	y	y	y	n	n	y
Parc Corniche Condominium Suite Hotel	I-Drive	c	Mixed groups	y	y	y	n	n	y
Peabody Orlando	I-Drive	$$–$$$	Couples, Seniors	y	y	y	y	n	y
Renaissance Orlando Resort at SeaWorld	I-Drive	$–$$	Couples, Singles	y	y	y	y	n	y
★ Ritz-Carlton Orlando Grande Lakes	I-Drive	$$$–$$$$	Couples, Seniors	y	y	y	y	y	y
Rosen Plaza Hotel	I-Drive	$–$$	Mixed groups	y	y	y	y	n	y
Rosen Shingle Creek	I-Drive	$$–$$$$	Mixed groups	y	y	y	y	n	y
Westin Imagine	I-Drive	$$$–$$$$	Couples, Singles	y	y	y	y	y	y
Wyndham Orlando Resort	I-Drive	$	Families with teens and tweens	y	y	y	y	n	y
Baymont Inn & Suites	Kissimmee	c–$	Families w/ children 10 and under, teens and tweens	y	y	n	y	y	y
Best Western Lakeside	Kissimmee	c	Families w/ children 10 and under	y	y	y	n	n	y
Gaylord Palms Resort	Kissimmee	$$$–$$$$	Mixed groups	y	y	y	y	y	y
Omni Orlando Resort at ChampionsGate	Kissimmee	$$–$$$	Seniors	y	y	y	y	y	y

HOTELS AT A GLANCE

Hotel Name	Location/ Nearest Park	Price	Best For	Pool (y/n)	Restaurant (y/n)	Bar (y/n)	Spa (y/n)	Children's Programs (y/n)	Shuttle to Parks (y/n)
Reunion Resort & Club Wyndham Grand Resort	Kissimmee	$$$–$$$$	Mixed groups	y	y	y	y	y	n
Saratoga Resort Villas at Orlando Maingate	Kissimmee	$	Families w/ children 10 and under	y	y	y	y	n	y
Seralago Hotel & Suites Maingate East	Kissimmee	¢	Families w/ children 10 and under	y	y	y	n	n	y
Celebration Hotel	Celebration	$$–$$$	Mixed groups	y	y	y	n	n	y
★ Mona Lisa Suite Hotel	Celebration	$–$$	Couples, Singles	y	y	y	n	n	y
Caribe Royale All-Suites Resort & Convention Center	Lake Buena Vista Area	$–$$	Families w/ children 10 and under	y	y	y	n	n	y
Country Inn & Suites by Carlson	Lake Buena Vista Area	¢–$	Couples, Families w/ children 10 and under	y	n	n	n	n	y
Embassy Suites Hotel Lake Buena Vista	Lake Buena Vista Area	$–$$	Couples, Singles	y	y	n	n	n	y
Hawthorn Suites Resort Lake Buena Vista	Lake Buena Vista Area	¢–$	Couples, Singles	y	n	y	n	n	y
Hilton Orlando Bonnet Creek	Lake Buena Vista Area	$$$–$$$$	Couples, Seniors	y	y	y	y	y	y
Holiday Inn SunSpree Lake Buena Vista	Lake Buena Vista Area	¢–$	Families w/ children 10 and under, teens and tweens	y	y	y	n	y	y

Name	Area	Price	Clientele							
★ Hyatt Regency Grand Cypress Resort	Lake Buena Vista Area	$$$–$$$$	Mixed groups	y	y	y	y	y	y	y
Marriott Village at Little Lake Bryan	Lake Buena Vista Area	$–$$	Mixed groups	y	y	y	n	n	y	y
★ Nickelodeon Family Suites by Holiday Inn	Lake Buena Vista Area	$$–$$$	Families w/ children 10 and under		y	y	n	n	y	y
Orlando World Center Marriott	Lake Buena Vista Area	$$–$$$	Couples, Seniors	y	y	y	n	y	y	y
Sheraton Safari Hotel	Lake Buena Vista Area	¢–$	Families w/ children 10 and under	y	y	y	n	n	n	y
★ Waldorf Astoria Orlando	Lake Buena Vista Area	$$$–$$$$	Couples, Seniors	y	y	y	y	y	y	y
Wyndham Bonnet Creek	Lake Buena Vista Area	$$–$$$	Families w/ children 10 and under	y	y	y	n	n	y	y
The Courtyard at Lake Lucerne	Central Orlando	$–$$	Ccuples	n	n	n	n	n	n	n
Eo Inn & Urban Spa	Central Orlando	$–$$	Couples, Singles	n	n	n	y	n	n	n
Grand Bohemian	Central Orlando	$$–$$$	Couples, Singles	y	y	y	n	n	n	n
Sonesta Orlando Downtown	Central Orlando	$–$$	Mixed groups	y	y	y	n	n	n	n
The Florida Hotel & Conference Center	Orlando International Airport	$–$$	Couples, Seniors	y	y	y	n	n	n	n
Hyatt Regency Orlando International Airport	Orlando International Airport	$$–$$$	Mixed groups	y	y	y	n	n	n	n
Park Plaza Hotel	Winter Park	$$–$$$	Couples, Seniors	n	y	y	n	n	n	n

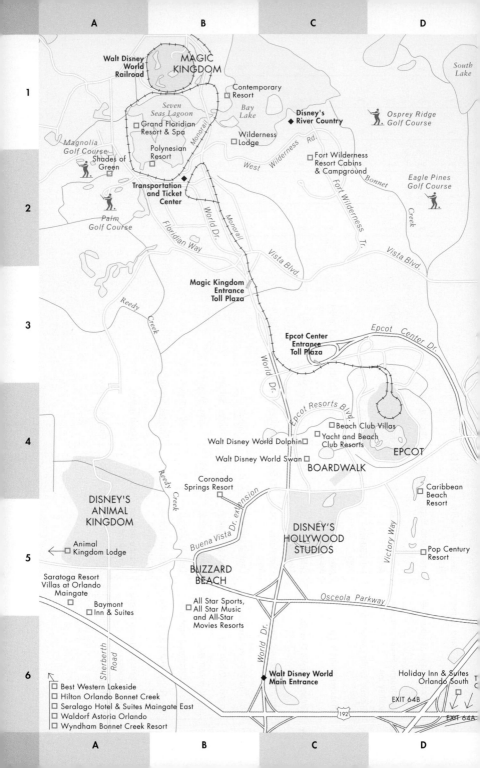

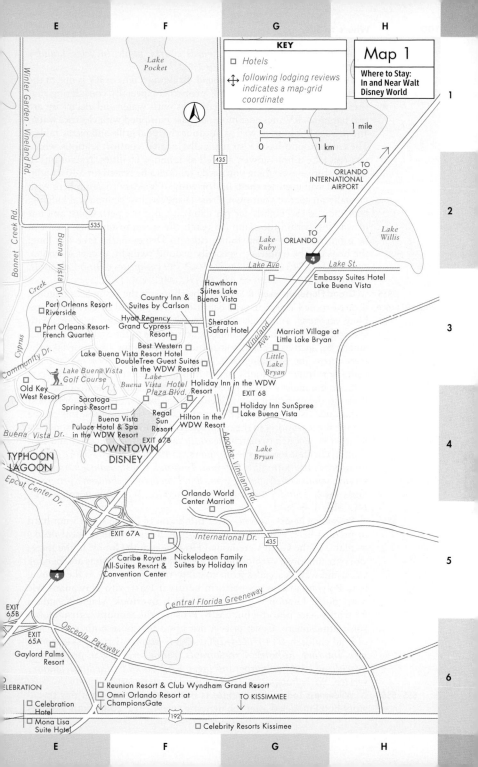

KEY

□ *Hotels*

⬦ *following lodging reviews indicates a map-grid coordinate*

Map 1

Where to Stay: In and Near Walt Disney World

0 ———— 1 mile
0 ———— 1 km

E F G H

1
2
3
4
5
6

Lake Pocket

Winter Garden - Vineland Rd.

435

TO ORLANDO INTERNATIONAL AIRPORT

535

Lake Ruby

TO ORLANDO

Lake Ave.

Lake St.

4

Lake Willis

Bonnet Creek Rd.

Buena Vista Dr.

Creek

Cyprus

Community Dr.

Hawthorn Suites Lake Buena Vista

Embassy Suites Hotel Lake Buena Vista

Port Orleans Resort-Riverside

Country Inn & Suites by Carlson

Hyatt Regency Grand Cypress Resort

Sheraton Safari Hotel

Vineland Ave.

Marriott Village at Little Lake Bryan

Little Lake Bryan

Port Orleans Resort-French Quarter

Best Western Lake Buena Vista Resort Hotel

DoubleTree Guest Suites in the WDW Resort

Lake Buena Vista Golf Course

Lake Buena Vista Hotel

Lake Buena Vista Plaza Blvd.

Holiday Inn in the WDW Resort

EXIT 68

Old Key West Resort

Saratoga Springs Resort

Regal Sun Resort

Holiday Inn SunSpree Lake Buena Vista

Apopka-Vineland Rd.

Buena Vista Palace Hotel & Spa in the WDW Resort

Hilton in the WDW Resort

Lake Bryan

EXIT 67B

Buena Vista Dr.

TYPHOON LAGOON

DOWNTOWN DISNEY

Epcot Center Dr.

EXIT 67A

Orlando World Center Marriott

International Dr.

435

Caribe Royale All-Suites Resort & Convention Center

Nickelodeon Family Suites by Holiday Inn

4

EXIT 65B

Central Florida Greeneway

EXIT 65A

Osceola Parkway

Gaylord Palms Resort

CELEBRATION

Reunion Resort & Club Wyndham Grand Resort

Omni Orlando Resort at ChampionsGate

TO KISSIMMEE

Celebration Hotel

192

Mona Lisa Suite Hotel

Celebrity Resorts Kissimmee

E F G H

Internet. In-resort: restaurant, tennis courts, pools, bicycles, laundry facilities ▤ *AE, D, DC, MC, V* ✛ *1:C2.*

¢ ⛺ **Fort Wilderness Resort Campground.** Bringing a tent or RV is one of the
Fodor'sChoice cheapest ways to stay on WDW property, especially considering that
★ sites accommodate up to 10. Tent sites with water and electricity are real bargains. RV sites cost more, but are equipped with electric, water, and sewage hookups as well as outdoor charcoal grills and picnic tables. The campground has 15 strategically located comfort stations where you can take a hot shower, as well as laundry facilities, restaurants, a general store—everything you need. Tents can be rented for $30 a night, and staff will even set them up for you, so it's easy to camp here with virtually no gear of your own. **Pros:** Disney's most economical lodging; pets allowed ($5 nightly fee per campsite, not per pet). **Cons:** amount of walking within the camp (to reach the store, restaurants, etc.) can be a bit much for some; shuttle rides to Disney parks take too long; the bugs can be irritating especially around twilight, except in winter. ☎ *407/824–2742 or 407/934–7639* ↘ *799 campsites* ⅋ *In-hotel: pools, laundry facilities, tennis* ▤ *AE, D, DC, MC, V* ✛ *1:C2.*

$$$$ ⛆ **Grand Floridian Resort & Spa.** On the shores of the Seven Seas Lagoon,
Fodor'sChoice this red-roofed Victorian is all delicate, white-painted gingerbread, ram-
★ bling verandas, and brick chimneys. It's Disney's flagship resort, with everything from its best-appointed guest rooms to the high-quality hotel amenities, such as a dock from which you can rent a boat or take the ferry across the adjoining lake. Although you won't look out of place walking through the lobby in flip-flops, afternoon high tea and a pianist playing nightly in the lobby are among the more genteel touches. **Pros:** on the monorail route; Victoria & Albert's, one of Disney's best restaurants, is located here; if you're a couple with no kids, this can be among the least noisy of the on-property Disney hotels. **Cons:** some say it's not ritzy enough to match the room rates; conference center and convention clientele lend to the stuffiness. ☎ *407/824–3000* ↘ *867 rooms, 90 suites* ⅋ *In-room: safe, Internet. In-hotel: 6 restaurants, bars, room service, tennis courts, pools, gym, spa, beachfront, children's programs (ages 4–12), laundry facilities, laundry service, Wi-Fi hotspot* ▤ *AE, D, DC, MC, V* ✛ *1:A1.*

$$$$ ⛆ **Polynesian Resort.** You may not think you're in Fiji, but it's not hard to pretend here, especially after downing a few of the tropical drinks available in the Great Ceremonial House—aka the lobby. In the three-story atrium lobby orchids bloom alongside coconut palms and banana trees, and water cascades from volcanic-rock fountains. At the evening luau Polynesian dancers perform before a feast with Hawaiian-style roast pork. Lagoon-view rooms—which overlook Magic Kingdom fireworks—are peaceful but costly. **Pros:** on the monorail; great aloha-spirit atmosphere. **Cons:** pricey; not good for those bothered by lots of loud children. ☎ *407/824–2000* ↘ *847 rooms, 5 suites* ⅋ *In-room: safe, Internet. In-hotel: 4 restaurants, room service, bar, pools, gym, beachfront, children's programs (ages 4–12), laundry facilities, laundry service, Wi-Fi hotspot* ▤ *AE, D, DC, MC, V* ✛ *1:B2.*

$$$–$$$$ ⛆ **Wilderness Lodge.** The architects outdid themselves with this seven-story hotel modeled after the majestic turn-of-the-20th-century lodges

2

of the American Northwest. The five-story lobby, supported by tower-ing tree trunks, has an 82-foot-high, three-sided fireplace made of rocks from the Grand Canyon and lighted by enormous tepee-shaped chande-liers. Two 55-foot-tall hand-carved totem poles complete the illusion. The hotel's showstopper is its Fire Rock Geyser, a faux Old Faithful that erupts with sometimes alarming regularity, near the large pool, which begins as an artificially heated hot spring in the lobby. This hotel is a good option if you're a couple without kids looking for more serenity than is found at Disney's other hotels. **Pros:** high wow-factor architec-ture; boarding point for romantic Bay Lake sunset cruises. **Cons:** ferry toots its horn at every docking; no direct shuttle to Magic Kingdom. ☎ *407/824–3200 📞 727 rooms, 31 suites ⚙ In-room: safe, Internet. In-hotel: 3 restaurants, room service, pool, bicycles, children's programs (ages 4–12), laundry facilities, laundry service, Wi-Fi hotspot ☰ AE, D, DC, MC, V ✛ 1:B1.*

EPCOT RESORT AREA

Take I–4 Exit 67.

From the Epcot resorts you can walk or take a boat to the International Gateway entrance to Epcot, or you can take the shuttle from your hotel or drive to the Future World (front) entrance.

$$$$ 🏨 **Beach Club Villas.** Each villa in this pale-turquoise-and-white water-front area has a separate living room, kitchen, and one or two bed-rooms. Interiors are warm neutral colors with white iron bedsteads. Private balconies on the upper levels or porches at street level ensure that you can enjoy your morning coffee with a view of the lake. The villas are marketed as time-share properties for Disney Vacation Club members, but available rooms are also rented on a per-night basis. You'll have access to all the facilities of the adjacent Yacht and Beach Club resorts, including the Stormalong Bay water park. **Pros:** short walk to the Disney BoardWalk area; in-suite kitchens let you save money on meals. **Cons:** can be noisy; not close to Magic or Animal kingdoms. ☎ *407/934–8000 📞 205 villas ⚙ In-room: safe, Internet. In-hotel: res-taurant, room service, tennis courts, pools, gym, beachfront, laundry service, Wi-Fi hotspot ☰ AE, D, DC, MC, V ✛ 1:C4.*

$$ 🏨 **Caribbean Beach Resort.** Six palm-studded "villages," all awash in dizzying pastels and labeled with names straight from the Caribbean, each with its own pool, share 45-acre Barefoot Bay and its white-sand beach. Bridges connect to a 1-acre path-crossed play and picnic area called Parrot Cay. You can rent boats to explore the lake, or rent bikes to ride along the 1½-mi lakefront promenade. **Pros:** plenty of on-site outdoor activities, like volleyball, giving the place a lush summer-camp feel; convenient to Epcot, Disney's Hollywood Studios, and Downtown Disney. **Cons:** you don't truly feel swept away to a tropical island; the only swimmable waters are in the pools, not the lake; walks from your room to the beach or a restaurant can be up to 15 minutes. ☎ *407/934–3400 📞 2,112 rooms ⚙ In-room: safe, Internet. In-hotel: restaurant, room service, pools, beachfront, bicycles, laundry facilities, laundry service, Wi-Fi hotspot ☰ AE, D, DC, MC, V ✛ 1:D4.*

$$ ☷ **Coronado Springs Resort.** Because of its 95,000-square-foot convention
Fodor's Choice   center and the adjacent 60,000-square-foot ballroom, and moderate
★   price, this is Disney's most popular convention hotel. Since the meeting space is in its own wing, the resort is also popular with families who appreciate its casual Southwestern architecture, its lively, Mexican-style food court, and its elaborate swimming pool, which has a Mayan pyramid with a big slide. **Pros:** great pool with a play area–arcade for kids and a bar for adults; lots of outdoor activities. **Cons:** some accommodations are a half-mile from the restaurants; standard rooms are on the small side; kids may find the subdued atmosphere boring. ☎ 407/939–1000 ➾ 1,917 rooms ♿ In-room: safe, Internet. In-hotel: 2 restaurants, room service, bar, pools, gym, spa, bicycles, laundry service, Wi-Fi hotspot ☰ AE, D, DC, MC, V ✛ 1:B4.

$$$$ ☷ **Yacht and Beach Club Resorts.** These big Seven Seas Lagoon inns seem straight out of a Cape Cod summer, with their nautical decor and waterfront locale. The five-story Yacht Club has hardwood floors, a lobby full of gleaming brass and polished leather, an oyster-gray clapboard facade, and evergreen landscaping; there's even a lighthouse on its pier. At the Beach Club, a croquet lawn and cabana-dotted white-sand beach set the scene. Stormalong Bay, a 3-acre water park with slides and whirlpools, is part of this club. **Pros:** location, location, location—it's easy to walk to Epcot and the BoardWalk, and Disney's Hollywood Studios is a fun, 20-minute ferry ride away. **Cons:** distances within the hotel—like, from your room to the front desk—can seem vast; high noise factor. ☎ 407/934–8000 Beach Club, 407/934–7000 Yacht Club ➾ 1,213 rooms, 112 suites ♿ In-room: safe, Internet, Wi-Fi. In-hotel: 4 restaurants, room service, tennis courts, pools, gym, beachfront, bicycles, children's programs (ages 4–12), laundry service, Wi-Fi hotspot ☰ AE, D, DC, MC, V ✛ 1:C4.

ANIMAL KINGDOM RESORT AREA

Take I–4 Exit 64B.

In the park's southwest corner, Disney's third resort area comprises the fabulous Africa-theme Animal Kingdom Lodge, plus two budget-price hotel complexes: All-Star Village, not far from U.S. 192, and the Pop Century Resort, on Osceola Parkway.

$ ☷ **All-Star Sports, All-Star Music, and All-Star Movies Resorts.** Stay here if you
☾   want the quintessential Disney-with-your-kids experience, or if you're
Fodor's Choice   a couple that feels all that pitter-pattering of little feet is a reasonable
★   tradeoff for a good deal on a room. (Hint: for a little peace, request a room away from pools and other common areas.) In the Sports resort Goofy is the pitcher in the baseball-diamond pool; in the Music resort you'll walk by giant bongos; and in the Movies resort huge characters like *Toy Story*'s Buzz Lightyear frame each building. Each room has two double beds, an armoire, and a desk. These are the smallest rooms in any Disney hotel, which helps keep the room rate down. **Pros:** unbeatable price for a Disney property. **Cons:** no kids' clubs or programs, possibly because this is on the bottom tier of Disney hotels in terms of room rates; distances between rooms and on-site amenities can seem

vast. ☎ *407/939–5000 Sports, 407/939–6000 Music, 407/939–7000 Movies* ⇌*1,700 rooms, 215 family suites at Music; 1,920 rooms at Movies and Sports* ⬧ *In-room: safe, Internet. In-hotel: room service, bars, pools, laundry facilities, laundry service, Internet terminal* ▭ *AE, D, DC, MC, V* ✛ *1:B5.*

$$$–$$$$ ▦ **Animal Kingdom Lodge.** Giraffes, zebras, and other wildlife roam three
Fodor's Choice 11-acre savannas separated by the encircling arms of this grand hotel,
★ designed to resemble a "kraal" or animal enclosure in Africa. Entering the vast atrium lobby is like entering a cathedral, with a roof formed of thatch rather than marble. A massive clay chimney structure dominates the right-hand side of the four-story lobby. Cultural ambassadors give talks about their African homelands, the animals, and the artwork on display; evenings include storytelling sessions around the fire circle on the Arusha Rock terrace. **Pros:** extraordinary wildlife and cultural experiences; excellent on-site restaurants, Jiko, Boma and Sanaa. **Cons:** shuttle to parks other than Animal Kingdom can take more than an hour; guided savanna tours available only to guests on the concierge level, where the least expensive room is $100 a night higher than the least expensive rooms in other parts of the hotel. ☎ *407/934–7639* ⇌*972 rooms, 499 suites or villas* ⬧ *In-room: safe, Internet. In-hotel: 3 restaurants, bar, pools, gym, spa, children's programs (ages 4–12), laundry facilities, laundry service, Wi-Fi hotspot* ▭ *AE, D, DC, MC, V* ✛ *1:A5.*

$ ▦ **Pop Century Resort.** Giant jukeboxes, 65-foot-tall bowling pins, an oversized Big Wheel and Rubik's Cube, and other pop-culture memorabilia are scattered throughout the grounds. Items from mood rings to eight-track tapes are incorporated into the architecture; wall-mounted shadow boxes display toys, fashions, and fads from each decade since the 1950s. A big food court and a cafeteria serve reasonably priced fare. **Pros:** great room rates; hotel provides a trip down memory lane; proximity to ESPN Wide World of Sports and Disney's Hollywood Studios. **Cons:** big crowds at the front desk; big crowds (and noise) in the food court; small rooms; lots of small kids around. ☎ *407/934–7639* ⇌*2,880 rooms* ⬧ *In-room: safe, Internet. In-hotel: room service, bar, pools, gym, laundry service, Wi-Fi hotspot* ▭ *AE, D, DC, MC, V* ✛ *1:D5.*

DOWNTOWN DISNEY RESORT AREA

Take I–4 Exit 64B or 68.

The Downtown Disney–Lake Buena Vista resort area, east of Epcot, has a variety of mid-price and upscale hotels, all of which offer shuttles to all of the parks.

$$$–$$$$ ▦ **Old Key West Resort.** A red-and-white lighthouse helps you find your way through this marina-style resort. Freestanding villas resemble turn-of-the-20th-century Key West houses, with white clapboard siding, delicate ornamental woodwork, and private balconies that overlook the waterways winding through the grounds. The resort is part of the Disney Vacation Club network, but rooms are rented to anyone when they're available. **Pros:** quiet and romantic; abundance of accommodations with whirlpool baths. **Cons:** distances between rooms

Disney's Animal Kingdom Lodge

and restaurants, recreation facilities, bus stops; $9.95 fee for Internet, no Wi-Fi. ☎ *407/827–7700* ↘ *761 units* ⚷ *In-room: safe, Internet. In-hotel: restaurant, tennis courts, pools, gym, spa, bicycles, laundry facilities, laundry service* ☐ *AE, D, DC, MC, V* ⊕ *1:E3.*

$$ 🏨 **Port Orleans Resort–French Quarter.** Ornate Big Easy–style row houses with wrought-iron–trimmed balconies cluster around squares planted with magnolias. Lamp-lighted sidewalks are named for French Quarter thoroughfares. Because this place is relatively quiet, it appeals more to couples than families with kids, although, like any WDW hotel, it is not devoid of youngsters. The food court serves Crescent City specialties such as jambalaya and beignets, and to give it even more New Orleans flavor, Mardi Gras colors and parade-float props are scattered around. **Pros:** authentic, fun New Orleans–style atmosphere; lots of water recreation options, including boat rentals. **Cons:** even though there are fewer kids here, public areas can still be quite noisy; shuttle service is slow; food court is the only on-site dining option. ☎ *407/934–5000* ↘ *1,008 rooms* ⚷ *In-room: safe, Internet, refrigerator. In-hotel: pool, bicycles, laundry facilities, laundry service, Wi-Fi hotspot* ☐ *AE, D, DC, MC, V* ⊕ *1:E3.*

$$ 🏨 **Port Orleans Resort–Riverside.** Buildings look like plantation-style mansions (in the Magnolia Bend section) and rustic bayou dwellings (in the Alligator Bayou section) and you can typically pick which section you want. The registration area looks like a steamboat interior, and the 3½-acre, old-fashioned swimming-hole complex called Ol' Man Island has a pool with slides, rope swings, and a nearby play area. **Pros:** carriage rides; river cruises; lots of recreation options for kids. **Cons:** shuttle can be slow; no shortage of extremely noisy youngsters, if that's a concern. ☎ *407/934–6000* ⌇ *2,048 rooms* ⚇ *In-room: safe, Internet. In-hotel: restaurant, pools, gym, bicycles, laundry facilities, laundry service* ▭ *AE, D, DC, MC, V* ✛ *1:E3.*

$$$–$$$$ ⛶ **Saratoga Springs Resort.** This large Disney Vacation Club has hundreds of units on 16 acres. Three- and four-story buildings, decorated inside and out to look like the 19th-century resorts of upstate New York, overlook a giant pool with artificial hot springs and faux boulders. Standard rooms have microwaves and refrigerators; suites have full kitchens. There are 60 tree-house cabins that let you live a sort of Swiss Family Robinson life. Rich woods, Early American–style furniture, and overstuffed couches lend a homey, country-chic look. **Pros:** in-room massage available; abundance of rooms with whirlpool baths. **Cons:** it's a fair hike from some accommodations to the restaurant and other facilities. ☎ *407/934–7639* ⌇ *924 units* ⚇ *In-room: safe, Internet. In-hotel: restaurant, tennis courts, pools, gym, spa, bicycles, Wi-Fi hotspot* ▭ *AE, D, DC, MC, V* ✛ *1:F4.*

OTHER ON-SITE HOTELS

Although not operated by the Disney organization, the Swan and the Dolphin just outside Epcot, Shades of Green near the Magic Kingdom, and the hotels along Hotel Plaza Boulevard near Downtown Disney call themselves "official" Walt Disney World hotels. While the Swan, Dolphin, and Shades of Green have the special privileges of on-site Disney hotels, such as free transportation to and from the parks and early park entry, the Downtown Disney resorts have their own systems to shuttle hotel guests to the parks.

MAGIC KINGDOM RESORT AREA

$–$$ ⛶ **Shades of Green.** Operated by the U.S. Armed Forces Recreation Center, the resort is open only to active-duty and retired personnel from the armed forces, as well as reserves, National Guard, active civilian employees of the Department of Defense, widows or widowers of service members, disabled veterans, and Medal of Honor recipients. Rates vary with your rank, but are significantly lower than at Disney hotels open to the public. You'll find family suites that sleep up to eight adults each, and two swimming pools surrounded by expansive decks and lush, tropical foliage. A little-known fact is that the resort is a short walk from the Polynesian, so it's easy to use the monorail stop at the Polynesian to expedite your travels around Disney World. **Pros:** large standard rooms; on Disney's shuttle line; Army–Air Force Exchange store discounts deeply for people with military IDs. **Cons:** daily fee for Internet usage. ☎ *407/824–3600 or 888/593–2242* ⊕ *www.shadesofgreen.org* ⌇ *586 rooms, 19 suites* ⚇ *In-room: safe, refrigerator, Internet. In-hotel: 4 restaurants, room service, bars, tennis courts, pools, gym, laundry facilities, laundry service, Wi-Fi hotspot* ▭ *AE, D, MC, V* ✛ *1:A2.*

EPCOT RESORT AREA

Take I–4 Exit 67.

$$–$$$ ▦ **Walt Disney World Dolphin.** World-renowned architect Michael Graves designed the neighboring Dolphin and Swan hotels. Outside, a pair of 56-foot-tall sea creatures bookend this 25-story glass pyramid. The fabric-draped lobby resembles a giant sultan's tent. All rooms have either two queen beds or one king, with pillow-top mattresses, down comforters with crisp white duvet covers, and overstuffed pillows. These amenities make the beds here some of the kingdom's most comfortable. The pool's cave and waterfall complex is so inviting that even the kids won't complain if you escape from the midday heat at the Magic Kingdom or Epcot for a relaxing cool-down. **Pros:** access to all facilities at the Walt Disney World Swan; easy walk or boat ride to BoardWalk; good on-site restaurants. **Cons:** self-parking is $10 a day; a $10 a day "resort fee" covers Wi-Fi and Internet access, use of health club, and local phone calls; room-charge privileges stop at the front door, and don't extend to the Disney parks. ⊠ *1500 Epcot Resorts Blvd., Lake Buena Vista* ☏ *407/934–4000 or 800/227–1500* ⊕ *www.swandolphin. com* ↻ *1,509 rooms, 112 suites* ⌂ *In-room: safe, Internet. In-hotel: 9 restaurants, room service, bars, tennis courts, pools, gym, spa, beachfront, children's programs (ages 4–12), Wi-Fi hotspot* ☰ *AE, D, DC, MC, V* ⊹ *1:C4.*

$$–$$$ ▦ **Walt Disney World Swan.** Facing the Dolphin across Crescent Lake, the Swan is a twin in many ways to its sister hotel, but with two 46-foot swans gracing the rooftop, so you can tell from a distance which hotel is which. The Grotto, a 3-acre water playground complete with waterslides, waterfalls, and all the trimmings, lies between and is shared by the Dolphin and Swan, and Disney's BoardWalk and the Fantasia Gardens miniature-golf complex are nearby. You can walk for miles around here and always be in a super-pleasant Disney environment. **Pros:** charge privileges and access to all facilities at the Dolphin (but not inside Disney World); easy walk to BoardWalk; free boats take you to the BoardWalk and Epcot; good on-site restaurants. **Cons:** like the Dolphin, the Swan levies a $10 per night resort fee, which includes in-room Internet access, health club privileges, and 60 minutes a day of free local phone calls. ⊠ *1200 Epcot Resorts Blvd., Lake Buena Vista* ☏ *407/934–3000 or 800/248–7926* ⊕ *www.swandolphin.com* ↻ *756 rooms, 55 suites* ⌂ *In-room: safe, Internet. In-hotel: 8 restaurants, room service, bars, tennis courts, pools, gym, spa, beachfront, children's programs (ages 4–12), Wi-Fi hotspot* ☰ *AE, D, DC, MC, V* ⊹ *1:C4.*

DOWNTOWN DISNEY RESORT AREA

Take I–4 Exit 68.

¢–$ ▦ **Best Western Lake Buena Vista Resort.** A near-total face-lift during 2010
Fodor's Choice   gave this Best Western resort, just minutes away from Downtown Dis-
★   ney, a real boost. Guest rooms received new carpeting, bedding, luxury linens, and crisp duvets; bathrooms were tiled in Italian ceramics. All rooms have private balconies with updated furnishings and spectacular views of the nightly Disney fireworks. Disney shuttles are available,

2

but you can walk to Downtown Disney in 10 minutes or less. **Pros:** free Wi-Fi and parking, not to mention the price, makes this one of the best bargains on Hotel Row; close to Downtown Disney. **Cons:** inconvenient to Universal and downtown Orlando. ⊠ *2000 Hotel Plaza Blvd., Lake Buena Vista* ☎ *407/828–2424 or 800/937–8376* ⊕ *www. lakebuenavistaresorthotel.com* ⤴ *325 rooms* ⅙ *In-room: Wi-Fi. In-hotel: 3 restaurants, room service, pools, gym, laundry facilities, laundry service, Wi-Fi hotspot* ⊟ *AE, D, DC, MC, V* ✢ *1:F3.*

$$–$$$ ☷ **Buena Vista Palace Hotel & Spa.** This hotel gets kudos as much for its on-site charms as for its location, just yards from Downtown Disney. As a guest, you receive free transportation to all Disney parks, the chance to sign up for Disney character meals at your hotel, and access to Disney golf courses, just as in the Disney on-property hotels. **Pros:** easy walk to Downtown Disney; spa is huge and luxurious. **Cons:** inconvenient to Universal and downtown Orlando; daily fee for Wi-Fi. ⊠ *1900 Buena Vista Dr., Lake Buena Vista* ☎ *407/827–2727* ⊕ *www.buenavistapalace. com* ⤴ *1,014 rooms, 209 suites* ⅙ *In-room: safe, refrigerator, Internet. In-hotel: 4 restaurants, room service, tennis courts, pools, gym, spa, children's programs (ages 4–12), laundry facilities, laundry service, Wi-Fi hotspot* ⊟ *AE, D, DC, MC, V* ✢ *1:F4.*

$–$$ ☷ **Doubletree Guest Suites in the WDW Resort.** The modern, clean lines of this low-rise resort can be glimpsed amid the trees of Hotel Row. Guests have access to Disney golf courses and transportation to parks. There's a special "registration desk" for kids, where they can get coloring books, balloons, and chocolate-chip cookies. **Pros:** within walking distance of Downtown Disney; free shuttle to all Disney attractions. **Cons:** inconvenient to Universal and downtown Orlando; $10 self-parking fee. ⊠ *2305 Hotel Plaza Blvd., Lake Buena Vista* ☎ *407/934– 1000 or 800/222–8733* ⊕ *www.doubletreeguestsuites.com* ⤴ *229 units* ⅙ *In-room: safe, refrigerator, Internet, Wi-Fi. In-hotel: 2 restaurants, room service, bars, tennis courts, pool, gym, laundry facilities, laundry service, Wi-Fi hotspot* ⊟ *AE, D, DC, MC, V* ✢ *1:F3.*

$$–$$$ ☷ **Hilton in the WDW Resort.** Befitting the fantasy world most theme-park visitors seek, the entrance is behind a waterfall, leading into a starkly modern, newly renovated lobby. Although not huge, rooms are decorated in a restrained, neutral palette, with flat-screen TVs and work tables. Many on the upper floors have great views of Downtown Disney, just a short walk away. **Pros:** close to Downtown Disney. **Cons:** pricier than similar lodgings farther from Disney; Internet and Wi-Fi fee; inconvenient to Universal and downtown Orlando. ⊠ *1751 Hotel Plaza Blvd., Lake Buena Vista* ☎ *407/827–4000, 800/782–4414 reservations* ⊕ *www.hilton.com* ⤴ *814 rooms, 27 suites* ⅙ *In-room: safe, Internet, Wi-Fi. In-hotel: 7 restaurants, room service, pools, gym, children's programs (ages 3–12), laundry facilities, laundry service, Wi-Fi hotspot* ⊟ *AE, DC, MC* ✢ *1:F4.*

$ ☷ **Holiday Inn in the WDW Resort.** The very modern lobby, with its glass-roofed atrium, muted colors, contemporary furnishings, and linen sheers over floor-to-ceiling windows, indicates the hotel's low-key elegance. Rooms reflect the same ambience, with crisp white linens, minimalist wood furniture and headboards, and flat-screen TVs. Some of the rooms

Buena Vista Palace Hotel & Spa

have balconies that face the parks, offering a view of the evening fireworks. **Pros:** walking distance to Downtown Disney; free transportation to all Disney parks; free Wi-Fi and wired Internet access. **Cons:** no free shuttle to Universal or SeaWorld; not convenient to Orlando ⊠ *1805 Hotel Plaza Blvd., Downtown Disney, Lake Buena Vista* ☎ *407/828–8888 or 800/423–0908* ⊕ *www.hiorlando.com* ↴ *323 rooms* ⛉ *In-room: safe, Internet, Wi-Fi (free). In-hotel: restaurant, room service, bars, pool, gym, safe, laundry service, Wi-Fi hotspot, parking* ⊟ *AE, D, DC, MC, V* ✛ *1:F4.*

$–$$ 🎏 **Regal Sun Resort.** Any hotel within walking distance to Downtown Disney is a great draw, and one with a swimming pool and water-playground complex that will entice kids away from the Magic Kingdom during the midday heat is even better. Kids programs, and a separate kids' recreation area make it a good choice for families. Guests have the choice of several on-site eateries, along with access to Disney golf courses. **Pros:** within walking distance of Downtown Disney; free shuttle to all Disney attractions. **Cons:** inconvenient to Universal and downtown Orlando; daily resort fee of $15. ⊠ *1850 Hotel Plaza Blvd., Lake Buena Vista* ☎ *407/828–4444 or 800/624–4109* ⊕ *www. regalsunresort.com* ↴ *619 rooms, 7 suites* ⛉ *In-room: safe, refrigerator, Internet, Wi-Fi. In-hotel: 3 restaurants, room service, bar, tennis courts, pools, laundry service, Wi-Fi hotspot* ⊟ *AE, DC, MC, V* ✛ *1:F4.*

UNIVERSAL ORLANDO AREA

Take I–4 Exit 74B or 75A, unless otherwise noted.

Universal Orlando's on-site hotels were built in a little luxury enclave that has everything you need, so you never have to leave Universal property. In minutes you can walk from any hotel to CityWalk, Universal's dining and entertainment district, or take a ferry that cruises the adjacent artificial river.

If the on-property Universal hotels are a bit pricey for your budget, don't worry, a burgeoning hotel district has sprung up across Kirkman Road, offering convenient accommodations and some less expensive room rates. Although these off-property hotels don't have the perks of the on-site places, you'll probably be smiling when you see your hotel bill.

¢–$ ▦ **Comfort Suites Orlando/Universal Studios.** The pale-brick exterior with Victorian-style architectural touches makes the place look like a dorm in a small-town college, but the amenities inside are more extensive than normal college-student fare. Each studio has a full kitchen, complete with microwave, stovetop, refrigerator, dishes, and dishwasher. There's a business center, fitness center, and game room on-site, and the neighborhood has lots of entertainment and dining options. **Pros:** half-mile walk to area shops and restaurants; low room rates, free shuttle to Universal and SeaWorld. **Cons:** free full breakfast, but no on-site restaurant or room service. ⊠ *5617 Major Blvd., Orlando* ☏ *407/363–1967 or 800/951–7829* ⊕ *www.comfortorlando.com* ⤴ *150 suites* & *In-room: kitchen, refrigerator, Wi-Fi. In-hotel: pool, laundry facilities, Wi-Fi hotspot* ▭ *AE, D, DC, MC, V* ✛ *2:D1.*

¢–$ ▦ **Doubletree Hotel at the Entrance to Universal Orlando.** The name sounds awkward, but it's very descriptive, and the conveniently located hotel is a hotbed of business-trippers and pleasure-seekers thanks to a location right at the Universal Orlando entrance. Don't worry about noisy conventioneers—the meeting and convention facilities are isolated from the guest towers. **Pros:** within walking distance of Universal and area shops and restaurants; free shuttle to Universal. **Cons:** on a fast-lane tourist strip; need a rental car to reach Disney, I-Drive, or downtown Orlando; daily fee for Wi-Fi in room. ⊠ *5780 Major Blvd., I–4 Exit 75B* ☏ *407/351–1000* ⊕ *www.doubltreeorlando.com* ⤴ *742 rooms, 15 suites* & *In-room: safe, Wi-Fi. In-hotel: restaurant, room service, pool, gym, laundry facilities, laundry service, Wi-Fi hotspot* ▭ *AE, D, DC, MC* ✛ *2:D1.*

$$$–$$$$ ▦ **Hard Rock Hotel.** Inside the California Mission–style building you'll find rock memorabilia from an Elvis jump suit to the slip Madonna wore in her "Like a Prayer" video. Rooms have black-and-white photos of pop icons, 32-inch flat-panel TVs, and iHome docking stations, and, best of all, your hotel key card lets you bypass lines at Universal. **Pros:** shuttle, water taxi, or short walk to Universal and CityWalk; preferential treatment at Universal rides; charge privileges on your room extend to the two other on-property Universal hotels. **Cons:** rooms and meals are pricey; loud rock music in public areas may annoy some people; fee for gym and in-room Wi-Fi. ⊠ *5800 Universal Blvd., Universal Orlando*

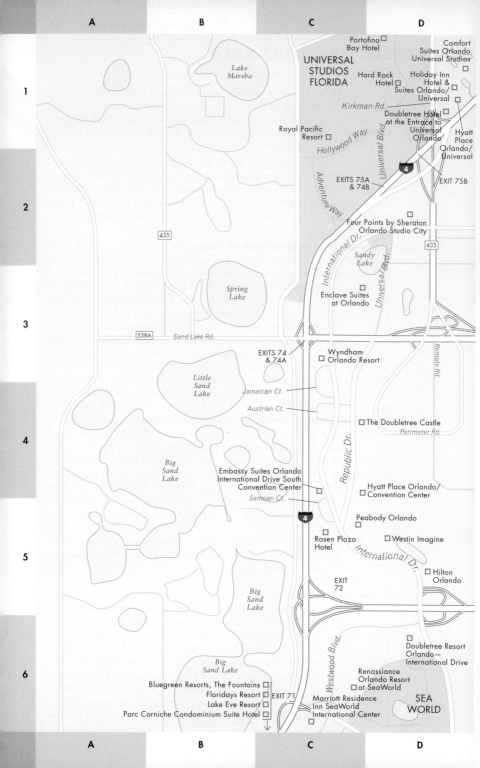

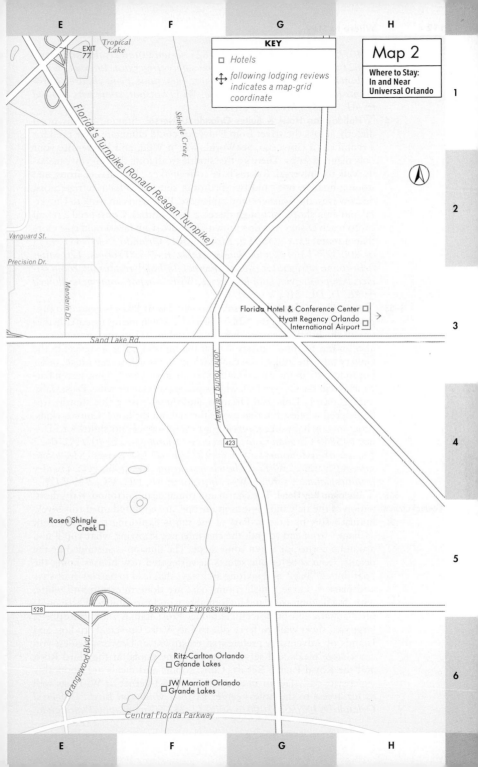

☎ 407/503–7625 or 800/232–7827 ⊕ www.universalorlando.com ⇨ 621 rooms, 29 suites ⸜ In-room: safe, refrigerator, Internet, Wi-Fi. In-hotel: 3 restaurants, room service, bars, pool, gym, children's programs (ages 4–14), laundry service, Wi-Fi hotspot, some pets allowed ▭ AE, D, DC, MC, V ⊹ 2:D1.

¢–$ ▣ **Holiday Inn Hotel & Suites Orlando/Universal.** Staying at this hotel directly across the street from Universal could eliminate your need for a rental car if Universal, SeaWorld, Wet 'n Wild, and I-Drive are your only planned stops. There's a free shuttle to all four, though you can easily walk to Universal. Rooms have coffeemakers, hair dryers, irons, and ironing boards; one- and two-bedroom suites also have refrigerators, microwaves, dishwashers, and tableware. **Pros:** you can walk to Universal and area shops (although there's a free shuttle). **Cons:** need a rental car to reach Disney and downtown Orlando. (Cab fare would cost more than a rental car.) ⊠ 5905 S. Kirkman Rd., Orlando ☎ 407/351–3333 or 800/327–1364 ⊕ www.hiuniversal.com ⇨ 390 rooms, 120 suites ⸜ In-room: refrigerator (some), Internet. In-hotel: restaurant, room service, bar, pool, gym, laundry service, Wi-Fi hotspot, some pets allowed ▭ AE, D, DC, MC, V ⊹ 2:D1.

$–$$ ▣ **Hyatt Place Orlando/Universal.** This new Hyatt Place is geared to support what Hyatt calls the "24/7" lifestyle, which means essentially that any of the hotel amenities that are available at 3 in the afternoon are also on tap for hotel guests at 3 in the morning. For instance, in the Gallery (aka the lobby) you can check in at a touch-screen kiosk, order hot food 24/7 in the casual Gallery Kitchen, or watch a big-screen flat-panel TV in the Gallery Den while sipping espresso or wine. **Pros:** walking distance to Universal Orlando, and there's also a free shuttle; free high-speed wireless Internet access throughout the hotel. **Cons:** no kids' programs or babysitting service; no room service; no shuttles to Disney. ⊠ 5859 Caravan Court, Universal Orlando area ☎ 407/351–0627 ⊕ www.orlandouniversal.place.hyatt.com ⇨ 151 rooms ⸜ In-room: safe, refrigerator, Wi-Fi. In-hotel: restaurant, bar, pool, gym, laundry facilities, laundry service, Wi-Fi hotspot ▭ AE, DC, MC, V ⊹ 2:D1.

$$$
Fodor'sChoice
★
   ▣ **Portofino Bay Hotel.** The charm and romance of Portofino, Italy, destination of the rich and famous in Europe, are conjured up at this lovely luxury resort by Loews. Part of the fun is exploring this waterfront "village" from end to end; the charm is not knowing what you'll find around a corner, or down some steps. The illusion is sustained by the details, from cobblestone streets to variegated row houses lining the boat-dotted "bay," and inviting archways that lead to narrow stairways and piazzas. Large, plush rooms here are done in cream and white, with down comforters and high-quality wood furnishings. Three pools offer aquatic fun or peaceful sunning. **Pros:** Italian villa atmosphere; large spa; short walk or ferry ride to CityWalk, Universal Studios, and Islands of Adventure; preferential treatment at Universal rides; you can charge meals and services (and use the pools) at the Hard Rock and the Royal Pacific Resort. **Cons:** rooms and meals are noticeably expensive; daily fee for in-room high-speed Internet or Wi-Fi, as well as for access to the fitness center. ⊠ 5601 Universal Blvd., Universal Orlando ☎ 407/503–1000 or 800/232–7827 ⊕ www.universalorlando.

com ☞ *699 rooms, 51 suites �& In-room: safe, Internet, Wi-Fi. In-hotel: 3 restaurants, room service, bar, pools, gym, spa, children's programs (ages 4–14), laundry service, Wi-Fi hotspot, some pets allowed ▭ AE, D, DC, MC, V ✛ 2:D1.*

$$–$$$
Fodor's Choice
★

🏨 **Royal Pacific Resort.** The entrance—a broad, covered footbridge high above a tropical stream—sets the tone for the Pacific Rim theme of this hotel, which is on 53 acres planted with lush shrubs, soaring bamboo, and palms. The focal point is a 12,000-square-foot lagoon-style pool, which has a small beach and an interactive water-play area. All guest rooms have bright, tropical bed coverings, bamboo ceiling accents, and electronics that include iPod-station clock radios and 32-inch flat-panel televisions, plus in-room Wi-Fi. Emeril Lagasse's restaurant, Tchoup Chop, draws crowds. The hotel hosts Polynesian-style luaus every Saturday. **Pros:** preferential treatment at Universal rides; serene, Zen garden vibe. **Cons:** rooms can feel cramped; $10-a-day fee for Internet access unwarranted given rates. ✉ *6300 Hollywood Way, Universal Orlando* ☎ *407/503–3000 or 800/232–7827* ⊕ *www.universalorlando. com* ☞ *1,000 rooms, 113 suites �& In-room: safe, Wi-Fi. In-hotel: 3 restaurants, room service, bars, pool, gym, children's programs (ages 4–14), laundry facilities, laundry service, Wi-Fi hotspot, some pets allowed ▭ AE, DC, MC, V ✛ 2:C1.*

ORLANDO METRO AREA

INTERNATIONAL DRIVE

Take I–4 Exit 72, 74A, or 75A, unless otherwise noted.

The sprawl of newish hotels, restaurants, malls, and dozens of small attractions known as International Drive—"I-Drive" to locals—makes a convenient base for visits to Walt Disney World, Universal, and other Orlando attractions. Parallel to Interstate 4, this four-lane boulevard stretches from Universal in the north to Kissimmee in the south.

If you're planning a day visiting I-Drive attractions, consider the I-Ride Trolley, which travels the length of I-Drive from Florida's Turnpike to the outlet center on Vineland Avenue, stopping at Wet 'n Wild and SeaWorld. (This trolley does not go to Universal Orlando, even though it's nearby.) I-Ride is a more worthy transportation tool than you might think. Lots of hotels don't offer shuttle service to Disney, even for a fee; but you can ride I-Ride to hotels that do offer the fee-based Disney shuttle, which, depending on the size of the family or group, can be cheaper than a cab.

$$ 🏨 **Bluegreen Resorts, The Fountains.** Like a summer camp for the whole family, this huge condo community, on the southern end of International Drive, rents out lodging to nonowners of the condos, just like a regular hotel. On the edge of Lake Eve, the resort has a dock with boat rentals, and two meandering, palm-tree-lined pools (the biggest is 6,000 square feet), with waterslides, fountains, an indoor-outdoor area, and hot tubs. A 20,000-square-foot recreational center, with a store and a kids' club, has all sorts of organized activities going on

Portofino Bay Hotel

inside, like bingo, kids' karaoke, face painting, and a regular session of "Margarita Madness" for adults, all of which give little reason to ever be bored. **Pros:** self-contained resort that you'd never have to leave to have a great vacation. **Cons:** roughly equidistant between Disney and Universal, this resort is close to neither; nothing outside the resort is within easy walking distance. ⊠ *12400 International Dr. S, I-Drive areaOrlando* ☎ *407/905–4100* ⊕ *www.bluegreenonline.com* ⇗ *539 rooms* ⚶ *In-room: safe, kitchen, Internet. In-hotel: 2 restaurants, bar, pools, water sports, gym, bicycles, children's programs (ages 4–10), laundry service, Wi-Fi hotspot* ▬ *AE, D, DC, MC, V* ⊹ *2:C6.*

$$ 🍴 **The Doubletree Castle.** You won't really think you're in a castle at this midprice hotel, although the gold-and-silver spires, medieval-style mosaics, arched doorways, hotel "creature" in the entry hall (it's benign, and won't scare the kids), and a bevy of British tourists may make you feel like reading Harry Potter. Take your book to either the rooftop terrace or the inviting courtyard, which has a big, round swimming pool. A 2010 renovation of all rooms upgraded the furniture, bringing flat-screen TVs and upscale bedding. Two good restaurants, Café Tu Tu Tango and Vito's Chophouse, are connected by a walkway to the hotel, and Pointe Orlando, a popular dining, entertainment, and shopping complex is an easy walk. **Pros:** kid-friendly; easy walk to I-Drive eateries and attractions; theme-park shuttle ($10 per person, round-trip), including Disney (a rarity in this neighborhood). **Cons:** on a congested stretch of I-Drive; $10.95 fee for Wi-Fi. ⊠ *8629 International Dr., I-Drive area, Orlando* ☎ *407/345–1511 or 800/952–2785* ⊕ *www.doubletreecastle.com* ⇗ *216 rooms* ⚶ *In-room: safe, Internet,*

2

Wi-Fi. In-hotel: 2 restaurants, room service, bar, pool, gym, laundry service, Wi-Fi hotspot ▭ *AE, D, DC, MC, V* ✛ *2:D4.*

$$ ⊡ **Doubletree Resort Orlando – International Drive.** On 28 acres just south of the convention center, this 17-story hotel welcomes families as well as conventioneers. The resort underwent a name change and completed a $35 million renovation in late 2009, making it the largest Doubletree Resort in the world. The updated decor brings the serenity of Indonesia to the hectic I-Drive area. It's about midway between the airport and Disney, less than a mile from SeaWorld, and a five-minute drive from Universal. **Pros:** on-site miniature golf course; free theme-parks shuttle. **Cons:** few shops and restaurants within walking distance; fee for Internet use. ✉ *10100 International Dr., I-Drive area, Orlando* ☏ *407/352–1100 or 800/327–0363* ⊕ *www.doubletreeorlandoidrive. com* ⌖ *1,094 rooms, 35 suites* ♿ *In-room: safe, Internet, Wi-Fi. In-hotel: 3 restaurants, room service, pools, gym, spa, laundry service, Wi-Fi hotspot* ▭ *AE, D, DC, MC, V* ✛ *2:D6.*

$–$$ ⊡ **Embassy Suites Orlando International Drive South/Convention Center.** An airy, eight-story atrium with palm trees and fountains greets guests when they enter this all-suites hotel, giving the feel of luxury to this moderately priced lodging. The rooms and amenities continue the sensation: upscale beds and bedding, two flat-screen TVs, and a health club with sauna. And the only additional fee is for Wi-Fi—breakfast, evening drinks, and the shuttle to Disney and Universal are all free. **Pros:** easy walk to Convention Center and Pointe Orlando; free shuttle to Disney and Universal; walking distance to Convention Center and lots of shopping and dining. **Cons:** on congested stretch of I-Drive; Internet–Wi-Fi fee of $9.95 a day. ✉ *8978 International Dr., I-Drive area, Orlando* ☏ *407/352–1400 or 800/433–7275* ⊕ *www.embassysuitesorlando.com* ⌖ *244 suites* ♿ *In-room: Internet, Wi-Fi. In-hotel: restaurant, room service, pool, gym, Wi-Fi hotspot* ▭ *AE, D, DC, MC, V* ⦿| *BP* ✛ *2:C4.*

¢–$ ⊡ **Enclave Suites at Orlando.** With three 10-story buildings surrounding a private lake, a restaurant, and recreation area, this all-suites lodging is less a hotel than a condominium complex. Here what you would spend for a normal room in a fancy hotel gets you an apartment with a living room, a full kitchen, two bedrooms, and a small terrace with a lake view. There's free transportation to Universal, SeaWorld, and Wet 'n Wild. **Pros:** good deals on spacious suites; within walking distance of I-Drive eateries and attractions; free breakfast. **Cons:** area traffic can be a hassle; public facilities, like the pools, are not exceedingly large, considering the size of the resort; transportation to Disney is $12 per person round-trip. ✉ *6165 Carrier Dr., I-Drive area, Orlando* ☏ *407/351–1155 or 800/457–0077* ⊕ *www.enclavesuites.com* ⌖ *321 suites* ♿ *In-room: safe, kitchen, refrigerator, Internet, Wi-Fi. In-hotel: restaurant, tennis court, pools, gym, laundry facilities, laundry service, Wi-Fi hotspot* ▭ *AE, D, DC, MC, V* ⦿| *BP* ✛ *2:D3.*

$–$$ ⊡ **Floridays Resort.** The ad slogan of the place is "in the middle of the Magic," but if you interpret that to mean you'll see Disney World out your balcony window, you'll be disappointed. This 35-acre resort is indeed in the middle, about halfway between Disney and Universal Orlando, which means it is not close to either, and it's within walking distance of virtually nothing. But the resort is a destination in itself, and offers shuttles to the parks for those who get tired of Florida living at this self-described "oasis." This all-suite resort has all the amenities you'll need for perfect Florida days, including a couple of swimming pools, a health club, a game room, two eateries, a business center, and more. **Pros:** great, self-contained environment for a family vacation; it's on the I-Ride Trolley route. **Cons:** too far to walk to almost anything meaningful; grocery shopping via shuttle or I-Ride can be problematic. ⊠ *12562 International Dr., I-Drive area, Lake Buena Vista* ☎ *407/238–7700* ⊕ *www.floridaysresort.com* ⤳ *432 suites* ☼ *In-room: safe, kitchen, Internet. In-hotel: restaurants, bar, pools, gym, laundry service, Wi-Fi hotspot* ▭ *AE, D, DC, MC, V* ✛ *2:C6.*

$ 📺 **Four Points by Sheraton Orlando Studio City.** Atop this Sheraton is a giant silver ball with the hotel's name on it, so it's hard to miss. The lobby and guest rooms were totally renovated in 2010, giving the hotel a very contemporary feel and a more family-friendly ambience. In a clear bid for tech-savvy guests, the "living room" portion of the lobby has a big-screen TV and free computer workstations, and there's free Wi-Fi throughout the hotel. **Pros:** convenient to Universal; free shuttle to theme parks and outlet malls; great night views from upper floors. **Cons:** located on an unattractive stretch of I-Drive. ⊠ *5905 International Dr., I-Drive area, Orlando* ☎ *407/351–2100 or 800/327–1366* ⊕ *www.starwoodhotels.com/fourpoints* ⤳ *301 rooms* ☼ *In-room: safe, Internet, Wi-Fi. In-hotel: restaurant, room service, bar, pool, laundry service, Wi-Fi hotspot* ▭ *AE, D, DC, MC, V* ✛ *2:D2.*

$$–$$$ 📺 **Hilton Orlando.** From the spacious entry, where sparkling crystal chandeliers light the space, to the restrained decor throughout the hotel, this hotel exudes elegance. With 175,000 square feet of meeting space inside the hotel and a direct walkway to the Convention Center, the target clientele is clearly corporate groups. But Hilton courts conventioneers with families, so the place is laden with amenities: a big, lazy-river-style pool, basketball court, and a kids' club. **Pros:** free shuttle to Universal Studios, SeaWorld; 13 mi from Orlando International Airport. **Cons:** about 80% of the guests here will be conventioneers; no free shuttle to Disney World; fee of $14.95 daily for Internet. ⊠ *6001 Destination Pkwy., Universal Blvd.Orlando* ☎ *407/313–4300* ⊕ *www.hilton.com* ⤳ *1,400 rooms* ☼ *In-room: Wi-Fi, Internet. In-hotel: 7 restaurants, room service, bars, golf course, tennis court, pools, gym, spa, laundry service, Wi-Fi hotspot, some pets allowed* ▭ *AE, D, DC, MC, V* ✛ *2:D5.*

$–$$ 📺 **Hyatt Place Orlando/Convention Center.** Youngish, high-tech-consuming business travelers and vacationing families will find value here because of the location. While it's three blocks from the Orange County Convention Center, it's also just a block from a highly tourist-friendly part of I-Drive, making it an easy walk to dozens of restaurants, shops, and attractions like Pointe Orlando, a restaurant, movie theater, and shopping complex. Like other Hyatt Places, this one is hooked into the 24/7 lifestyle, with a computer touch screen in the lobby restaurant from which you can order food at all hours (kitchen staff is always on duty). At the 24-hour "E-Center" you'll have use of a desktop computer and free printouts. **Pros:** convenient to Convention Center and Pointe Orlando. **Cons:** no kids' program or babysitting services; no theme-park shuttles. ⊠ *8741 International Dr., I-Drive area* ☎ *407/370–4720 or 888/492–8847* ⊕ *www.orlandoconventioncenter.place.hyatt.com* ⇋ *149 rooms* ⚕ *In-room: safe, refrigerator, Internet, Wi-Fi. In-hotel: restaurant, bar, pool, gym, laundry service, Wi-Fi hotspot* ⊟ *AE, DC, MC, V* ✛ *2:D4.*

$$–$$$ ▦ **JW Marriott Orlando Grande Lakes.** With more than 70,000 square feet of meeting space, this hotel caters to a convention clientele. But because it's part of a lush resort that includes a European-style spa and a Greg Norman–designed golf course, it also appeals to those looking to relax. The good news about this place is that you get Ritz-Carlton amenities at JW Marriott prices. Wander down a long connector hallway to the adjoining Ritz-Carlton, where you can use your room charge card in the restaurants and shops. **Pros:** pool is great for kids and adults; shares amenities with the Ritz, including a world-class, albeit expensive, health and beauty spa; shuttle service to SeaWorld and Universal. **Cons:** things are spread out on the grounds; you need a rental car to reach Disney and other area offerings. ⊠ *4040 Central Florida Pkwy., I-Drive area, Orlando* ☎ *407/206–2300 or 800/576–5750* ⊕ *www.grandelakes.com* ⇋ *1,000 rooms, 64 suites* ⚕ *In-room: Wi-Fi. In-hotel: 5 restaurants, room service, bars, golf course, pool, gym, spa, laundry service, laundry facilities, Wi-Fi hotspot* ⊟ *AE, D, DC, MC, V* ✛ *2:F6.*

$–$$ ▦ **Lake Eve Resort.** Even though the address is on International Drive (in the newer section of the big tourism thoroughfare, south of Central Florida Parkway), this all-suites resort actually offers serenity as its salient attribute. The hotel building is set well off the street, and the primary visual element you will experience outside the windows is Lake Eve, a place of refuge for migratory birds that don't seem to care that an interstate highway and a major tourism strip are each about a half-mile away. You probably would not want to stay here without a rental car, but the resort offers some great perks, like free shuttles to Disney. **Pros:** relatively secluded, especially for I-Drive. **Cons:** too far to walk anywhere. ⊠ *12388 International Dr. S., Orlando* ☎ *866/934–7985 or 407/597–0370* ⊕ *www.lakeeveresort.com* ⇋ *176 suites* ⚕ *In-room: safe, kitchen, Wi-Fi. In-hotel: restaurant, bar, pool, gym, laundry service, Wi-Fi hotspot* ⊟ *AE, D, DC, MC, V* ✛ *2:C6.*

$$ ▦ **Marriott Residence Inn SeaWorld International Center.** The longish name hints at all the markets the hotel is attempting to tap: SeaWorld, I-Drive, and the Convention Center. All are within a 2-mi radius; all are served by hotel shuttles. A free breakfast is served daily, and several nearby restaurants will deliver to your room. The recreation area around the pool is like a summer camp, with a basketball court, playground equipment, picnic tables, and gas grills. **Pros:** well-equipped kitchens; free breakfast. **Cons:** not much within walking distance; hard to find from Interstate 4, even though you can see the hotel from the freeway. ⊠ *11000 Westwood Blvd., I–4 Exit 72, I-Drive area, Orlando* ☎ *407/313–3600 or 800/331–3131* ⊕ *www.residenceinnseaworld.com* ⇋ *350 suites* ⚕ *In-room: kitchen, Internet, Wi-Fi. In-hotel: safe, restau-*

rant, bar, pool, gym, laundry facilities, laundry service, Wi-Fi hotspot, some pets allowed ⊟ *AE, D, DC, MC, V* ⵋ❍ⵋ *BP* ✦ *2:C6.*

¢ ⊞ **Parc Corniche Condominium Suite Hotel.** Set back from International Drive a bit, the hotel offers a good deal for a family that loves golf and theme parks. A golf course next to the property offers hotel residents a discount, and the Nick Faldo Golf Institute is just across International Drive. Each of the one- and two-bedroom suites, which are soothingly decorated in pale yellows and blues, with brightly patterned bedspreads, has a kitchen (with a dishwasher) plus a patio or balcony with golf-course views. A free continental breakfast is served daily. SeaWorld is only a few blocks away. **Pros:** great for golf lovers; well-equipped kitchens; free theme-parks shuttle; free breakfast. **Cons:** not much within walking distance; $4 daily fee for Internet access. ✉ *6300 Parc Corniche Dr., I-Drive area, Orlando* ☎ *407/239–7100 or 800/446–2721* ⊕ *www. parccorniche.com* ⟿ *210 suites* ␣ *In-room: Wi-Fi. In-hotel: restaurant, bar, room service, golf course, pools, gym, laundry facilities, laundry service, Wi-Fi hotspot* ⊟ *AE, D, DC, MC, V* ⵋ❍ⵋ *CP* ✦ *2:C6.*

$$–$$$ ⊞ **Peabody Orlando.** The famed Peabody ducks have a bigger playground to waddle through, as the hotel's $450-million expansion opened in late 2010. The five coddled canards still exit their elevator at 11 AM and march to a rousing Sousa tune along the lobby to the fountain in the atrium, where they entertain guests until just past teatime. Then they proceed back to the elevator, and are whisked away to their pricey penthouse aerie. Many more guests can join in the fun, as the luxury hotel doubled its number of guest rooms, added restaurants, an expanded spa, a new pool, and a huge amount of meeting space. **Pros:** adjacent to Convention Center (business travelers take note); good spa; short walk to shops and restaurants. **Cons:** pricey; $15 optional daily hotel service fee includes Wi-Fi; on a congested section of I-Drive. ✉ *9801 International Dr., I-Drive area, Orlando* ☎ *407/352–4000 or 800/732–2639* ⊕ *www.peabodyorlando.com* ⟿ *1,641 rooms, 193 suites, 5 penthouse suites* ␣ *In-room: safe, Internet, Wi-Fi, refrigerator (some). In-hotel: 13 restaurants, bars, room service, tennis courts, pool, gym, spa, Wi-Fi hotspot* ⊟ *AE, D, DC, MC, V* ✦ *2:C5.*

$–$$ ⊞ **Renaissance Orlando Resort at SeaWorld.** The 10-story atrium brims with ponds and palm trees, much of which you can ogle from above as you float skyward in sleek glass elevators. The rooms are equipped with nice touches like high-speed Internet connections, beds with crisp white duvets, and stylish furniture. While the hotel has a solid convention clientele, it doesn't ignore families. There are children's activities throughout the year, and fire pits have been installed on the pool terrace for the marshmallow-roasting crowd. **Pros:** across from SeaWorld; shuttles to Disney ($13 round-trip) and Universal, SeaWorld, and Aquatica (free). **Cons:** unless you're near an elevator, it's a long walk around each floor to reach rooms; shuttles to Disney aren't free; many conventioneers afoot; $14.95 daily Internet fee. ✉ *6677 Sea Harbor Dr., I-Drive area, Orlando* ☎ *407/351–5555 or 800/468–3571* ⊕ *www.renaissancehotels. com* ⟿ *781 rooms* ␣ *In-room: safe, Internet, Wi-Fi. In-hotel: 5 restaurants, room service, tennis courts, pool, gym, spa, laundry service, Wi-Fi hotspot* ⊟ *AE, D, DC, MC, V* ✦ *2:C6.*

$$$–$$$$ ⊡ **Ritz-Carlton Orlando Grande Lakes.** Orlando's first and only Ritz is
Fodor'sChoice   a particularly extravagant link in the luxury chain. Service is exem-
★   plary, from the fully attended porte-cochere entrance to the 18-hole
golf course and 40-room spa. Rooms and suites have large balconies,
elegant wood furnishings, down comforters, and decadent marble baths
(with separate showers and tubs). All rooms underwent a renovation in
2010, to be complete by early 2011. An enclosed hallway connects the
Ritz to the nearby JW Marriott Hotel, where you'll find more restau-
rants and a kid-friendly water park. **Pros:** truly luxurious; impeccable
service; great spa; golf course; shares amenities with Marriott. **Cons:**
pricey; need a rental car to reach Disney and area shops and restau-
rants; $9.50 daily fee for Wi-Fi. ⊠ *4012 Central Florida Pkwy., Orlando*
☎ *407/206–2400 or 800/576–5760* ⊕ *www.grandelakes.com* ⇆ *584
rooms, 64 suites* ⚅ *In-room: Wi-Fi. In-hotel: 6 restaurants, room ser-
vice, bars, golf course, pool, gym, spa, children's programs (ages 5–12),
laundry service, Wi-Fi hotspot* ▭ *AE, D, DC, MC, V* ✛ *2:F6.*

$–$$ ⊡ **Rosen Plaza Hotel.** Harris Rosen, Orlando's largest independent hotel
owner, loves to offer bargains, and you can definitely find one here. The
hotel finished a total renovation of the guest rooms in 2010, with new
tile in bathrooms, flat-screen TVs, and mini-refrigerators. Although it's
essentially a convention hotel, leisure travelers like the prime location
and long list of amenities. With the BAGS service, you can get your airline boarding pass and check your suitcases in the hotel lobby, so you
can go straight to the gate at Orlando International. **Pros:** within walking
distance of I-Drive eateries and attractions; guests in all seven Rosen-
owned hotels in Orlando get priority reservations at the 18-hole golf
course at Rosen's Shingle Creek, a couple of blocks away from the Rosen
Plaza. **Cons:** Convention Center traffic can be bad; daily Internet fee.
⊠ *9700 International Dr., I-Drive area, Orlando* ☎ *407/996–9700 or
800/627–8258* ⊕ *www.rosenplaza.com* ⇆ *810 rooms* ⚅ *In-room: safe,
Internet. In-hotel: 3 restaurants, room service, bar, pool, laundry facilities, laundry service, Wi-Fi hotspot* ▭ *AE, D, DC, MC, V* ✛ *2:C5.*

$$$–$$$$ ⊡ **Rosen Shingle Creek.** It may be close to the Convention Center, but
make no mistake: this place has plenty for those seeking fun and relax-
ation. There's the 13,000-square-foot spa, for instance, and the cham-
pionship golf course and golf academy. There are also four swimming
pools and recreation options that include fishing and nature trails. The
architecture recalls the Spanish Revival palaces you find in Palm Beach
County. **Pros:** golf course; spa; free shuttle to Universal, SeaWorld,
Aquatica; BAGS check-in service; the only four-star-level resort in town
with a self-service coin laundry. **Cons:** large grounds mean long walks
to on-site amenities; no shuttle to I-Drive or Disney; daily fee for Wi-Fi.
⊠ *9939 Universal Blvd., I-Drive area, Orlando* ☎ *407/996–9939,
866/996–6338 reservations* ⊕ *www.rosenshinglecreek.com* ⇆ *1,500
rooms, 109 suites* ⚅ *In-room: safe, Internet. In-hotel: 6 restaurants,
room service, golf course, tennis courts, pools, gym, spa, laundry facili-
ties, laundry service, Wi-Fi hotspot* ▭ *AE, D, DC, MC, V* ✛ *2:E5.*

$$$–$$$$ ⊡ **Westin Imagine.** Directly across Universal Boulevard from the mam-
moth Orange County Convention Center, this 12-story hotel attracts
scores of conventioneers, but it's also strategically situated near

Ritz-Carlton Orlando Grande Lakes

SeaWorld, Universal Orlando, and I-Drive one block away, and welcomes families. The hotel has some inviting amenities like a big lagoon pool and huge pool-deck area with outdoor hot tubs. **Pros:** free shuttle to SeaWorld and Universal; easy walk to Convention Center, Pointe Orlando, I-Drive; kids' programs. **Cons:** no Disney shuttle; 20–25 minutes away from Disney World. ⊠ *9501 Universal Blvd., I-Drive area* ☎ *888/946–9501* ⊕ *www.westinimagineorlando.com* ↩ *315 rooms* ⚷ *In-room: safe, Internet. In-hotel: 3 restaurants, room service, bar, tennis courts, pool, gym, spa, children's program, Wi-Fi hotspot* ⊟ *AE, D, DC, MC, V* ✛ *2:D5.*

$ ⊡ **Wyndham Orlando Resort.** Two-story villas, palm trees, turquoise pools, and romantic lagoons evoke a Caribbean getaway. And you can't beat the location, just five minutes from Universal and the shops and restaurants of I-Drive, and only a short drive to the west for the upscale restaurants and shops of Sand Lake Road's restaurant row. There's a free shuttle to Universal and SeaWorld, and one to Disney for $16 round-trip. **Pros:** convenient to Universal, SeaWorld, I-Drive, and outlet malls. **Cons:** daily Internet fee; no free shuttle to Disney, which is about 30 minutes away. ⊠ *8001 International Dr., I-Drive area, Orlando* ☎ *407/351–2420 or 800/996–3426* ⊕ *www.wyndham. com* ↩ *1,052 rooms* ⚷ *In-room: safe, refrigerator, Internet. In-hotel: 3 restaurants, room service, pools, gym, spa, laundry service, Wi-Fi hotspot, some pets allowed* ⊟ *AE, D, DC, MC, V* ✛ *2:C3.*

KISSIMMEE

Take I–4 Exit 64A, unless otherwise noted.

If you're looking for anything remotely quaint, charming, or sophisticated, move on. With a few exceptions (the Gaylord Palms Resort, the Mona Lisa, Celebration), the U.S. 192 strip—aka the Irlo Bronson Memorial Highway—is a neon-and-plastic strip crammed with bargain-basement motels, fast-food spots, nickel-and-dime attractions, over-priced gas stations, and minimarts.

In past years, when Disney was in its infancy, this was the best place to find affordable rooms.But now that budget hotels have cropped up all along I-Drive, you can often find better rooms closer to the theme parks. There are exceptions, however—some of the older hotels have maintained decent standards and kept their prices very interesting.

One Kissimmee caveat: beware of the word "maingate" in many hotel names. It's a good 6 mi from Kissimmee's "maingate" hotel area to the Walt Disney World entrance. The "maingate west" area, however, is only about 2 mi from the park. Of course, the greater the distance from Walt Disney World, the lower the room rates.

¢–$ **Baymont Inn & Suites.** This six-story inn certainly gives guests value for their money. The kids' suites have queen beds for the adults and an extra room for the kids with bunk beds, a TV, CD player, video and board games. And there are options to get your kids out in the sunshine without leaving the hotel, like a sand volleyball court and pool complex with an adjacent wading pool. **Pros:** kids' play area in main restaurant; free Disney, Universal, and SeaWorld shuttle; golf and tennis centers nearby; bargain room rates. **Cons:** feels very much on the tourist strip. ✉ *7601 Black Lake Rd., 2 mi west of I-4* ☎ *407/396–1100* ⊕ *www.baymontinns.com* ⊃ *295 rooms, 30 suites* ♿ *In-room: safe, refrigerator, Internet, Wi-Fi. In-hotel: restaurant, room service, pool, gym, laundry facilities, laundry service, Wi-Fi hotspot, some pets allowed* ═ *AE, D, DC, MC, V* ✛ *1:A5.*

¢ **Best Western Lakeside.** Fifteen two-story, balconied buildings make up this 27-acre hotel complex, which is a long way west of Kissimmee and quite close to Disney. A small lake offers pedal boating, and a miniature-golf course on property offers family fun. Children's activities include arts and crafts, movies, or a play area. **Pros:** this is one of the few Orlando hotels with a sub-$60 rate that is not a dump; feels almost like a family summer camp on an idyllic lake; free breakfast for kids 10 and under; Disney shuttle. **Cons:** on a stretch of highway that you wouldn't want to walk along. ✉ *7769 W. Irlo Bronson Memorial Hwy., 2 mi west of I-4* ☎ *407/396–2222 or 800/848–0801* ⊕ *www.bestwesternlakeside.com* ⊃ *651 rooms* ♿ *In-room: safe, refrigerator, Internet, Wi-Fi. In-hotel: 2 restaurants, room service, bar, pools, gym, children's programs (ages 4–12), laundry facilities, laundry service* ═ *AE, D, DC, MC, V* ✛ *1:A6.*

$$$–$$$$ **Gaylord Palms Resort.** Built in the style of a grand turn-of-the-20th-century Florida mansion, this resort is meant to awe. Inside its enormous atrium, covered by a 4-acre glass roof, are re-creations of Florida icons such as the Everglades, Key West, and old St. Augustine. A renovation

scheduled to be completed in late 2010 brings new carpeting, wallpaper, upgraded bed linens, and bigger flat-screen TVs to the rooms, which carry on the Florida themes with colorful, tropical decorations. With two pool areas and the huge Relache spa, the hotel connives to make you never want to leave. **Pros:** you could have a great vacation without ever leaving the grounds; free shuttle to Disney. **Cons:** rooms are pricey; not much within walking distance (although the hotel is so big that you can take quite a hike inside the building); shuttles to Universal and SeaWorld are available, but through an outside firm, at a price. ⊠ *6000 Osceola Pkwy., I–4 Exit 65* 🕾 *407/586–0000* ⊕ *www.gaylordpalms. com* ⤤ *1,406 rooms, 86 suites* ♿ *In-room: safe, Internet. In-hotel: 5 restaurants, bars, pools, gym, spa, children's programs (ages 4–12), laundry service, Wi-Fi hotspot* ☰ *AE, D, DC, MC, V* ✛ *1:E6.*

$$–$$$ ⊡ **Omni Orlando Resort at ChampionsGate.** Omni took over a 1,200-acre golf club with two Greg Norman–designed courses and a David Leadbetter academy to create this huge Mediterranean-style complex south of Disney. With a 70,000-square-foot conference center, the resort definitely attracts the corporate crowd. But there's family appeal, too, thanks to a lazy-river-style pool (one of the most popular in the Orlando area) and excellent children's programs. The hotel is a 10-minute drive from Disney, but you don't have to drive—it offers a free shuttle (well, sort of free; it's part of the $16 a day resort fee). **Pros:** big European-style spa; huge, water-park-style pool; good restaurant; golf school and two golf courses. **Cons:** rooms and food are pricey; $16 a day resort fee for Internet, shuttles, newspapers, gym. ⊠ *1500 Masters Blvd., I–4 Exit 58, ChampionsGate* ✛ *South of Kissimmee* 🕾 *407/390–6664 or 800/843–6664* ⊕ *www.omnihotels.com* ⤤ *720 rooms, 32 suites, 57 villas* ♿ *In-room: Internet, Wi-Fi. In-hotel: 5 restaurants, room service, bars, golf courses, tennis courts, pools, gym, spa, children's programs (ages 1–12), laundry facilities, laundry service, Wi-Fi hotspot* ☰ *AE, D, DC, MC, V* ✛ *1:E6.*

$$$–$$$$ ⊡ **Reunion Resort & Club Wyndham Grand Resort.** It occupies on a former orange grove, far from the bustle of Interstate 4, and yet it's only 12 minutes from Disney. A stay here includes access to three private world-caliber golf courses designed by Tom Watson, Arnold Palmer, and Jack Nicklaus. (And the property adjoins the ANNIKA Academy, operated by LPGA great Annika Sorenstam, if you want to polish your game.) The resort was developed as a residential and vacation-home complex, but its condo-style villas are available on a per-night basis. **Pros:** secluded atmosphere; proximity to Disney and ChampionsGate area; free Internet. **Cons:** no Disney shuttle, so you'll need a rental car. ⊠ *7593 Gathering Dr., Reunion* 🕾 *407/396–3200 or 888/418–9611* ⊕ *www.reunionresort.com* ⤤ *60 units* ♿ *In-room: safe, Internet. In-hotel: restaurant, room service, bar, golf courses, pools, gym, spa, bicycles, children's programs (ages 4–12), laundry facilities, laundry service* ☰ *AE, D, DC, MC, V* ✛ *1:E6.*

$ ⊡ **Saratoga Resort Villas at Orlando Maingate.** The tile-roof-and-stucco villas have between one and three bedrooms, living and dining areas, and well-equipped kitchens. Because there is a full kitchen, you can cook your own meals, but room-service dining is also available. Families

2

can play on the championship miniature-golf course, and wander the mile-long walkways along landscaped waterways. **Pros:** rates are hard to beat; free shuttle to Disney. **Cons:** on unattractive tourist strip; can't really walk around off the grounds; $12 a night resort fee. ⊠ *4787 W. Irlo Bronson Hwy.Kissimmee* ☎ *407/397–0555 or 800/303–0427* ⊕ *www.saratogaresortvillas.com* ⟿ *150 villas* ⚬ *In-room: safe, Internet. In-hotel: restaurant, room service, bar, pool, gym, spa, laundry facilities, Wi-Fi hotspot* ⊟ *AE, D, DC, MC, V* ⊹ *1:A5.*

¢ ⯐ **Seralago Hotel & Suites Maingate East.** It's within walking distance of the Old Town shopping and entertainment complex and 3 mi from Disney. Special kids' suites have an area designed to look like a Wild West fort, with bunk beds, TVs, and video games. All rooms have kitchenettes with refrigerators and microwaves. Kids under 10 eat free (with a paying adult) at the restaurant, which is only open for breakfast. **Pros:** easy walk to shops and restaurants; free shuttle to all Disney parks, free Wi-Fi. **Cons:** on a touristy strip of highway. ⊠ *5678 W. Irlo Bronson Memorial Hwy. Kissimmee* ☎ *407/396–4488, 800/366–5437, or 800/465–4329* ⊕ *www.orlandofamilyfunhotel.com* ⟿ *614 rooms, 110 suites* ⚬ *In-room: kitchen, Wi-Fi. In-hotel: restaurant, room service, bar, tennis courts, pools, laundry facilities, laundry service, Wi-Fi hotspot* ⊟ *AE, D, DC, MC, V* ⊹ *1:A6.*

CELEBRATION

$$–$$$ ⯐ **Celebration Hotel.** Like everything in the Disney-created town of Celebration, this 115-room hotel borrows from the best of the 19th, 20th, and 21st centuries. The lobby resembles those of Victorian grandes dames, with hardwood floors and decorative millwork throughout. Rooms may look as if they date from the early 1900s, but each has a plasma-screen TV and high-speed Internet access. Even though it's less than 1 mi south of the U.S. 192 tourist strip in Kissimmee, the hotel's surroundings are serene. The restaurants, shops, cinema, and more of downtown Celebration are right around the corner. **Pros:** a mere block from good restaurants; rental bikes and golf carts make touring a breeze; free shuttle to Celebration Golf and Fitness Center. **Cons:** shuttle to Disney is $22 per family of four, round-trip; need a rental car (or lots of cab money) to get around off-site. ⊠ *700 Bloom St., Celebration* ☎ *407/566–6000 or 888/499–3800* ⊕ *www.celebrationhotel. com* ⟿ *115 rooms* ⚬ *In-room: Internet, Wi-Fi. In-hotel: 2 restaurants, pool, gym, laundry service, Wi-Fi hotspot, some pets allowed* ⊟ *AE, D, DC, MC, V* ⊹ *1:D6.*

$–$$ ⯐ **Mona Lisa Suite Hotel.** Much like a European boutique hotel in style,
Fodor's Choice the Mona Lisa is very human in scale, and crisply minimalist in decor.
★ An oversized closeup detail from Leonardo da Vinci's Mona Lisa greets visitors at the entrance to the unpretentiously welcoming lobby, and hand-painted details from other art masterworks adorn the public areas. On the edge of the Disney-created community of Celebration, the hotel is a brief shuttle ride away from the restaurants, cafés, and shops in the village. The buildings form an oasis of calm around the circular pool and a palm-tree-planted tropical island in the middle. **Pros:** free shuttle to downtown Celebration and all the theme parks; golf privileges at Celebration Golf; spa privileges at Celebration Day Spa; concierge service.

Cons: busy U.S. 192 is close by; $12-a-day resort fee; if you want to go anywhere besides Celebration and the parks, you'll need a car. ✉ *225 Celebration Pl., Celebration* ☎ *866/404–6662 or 407/964–7000* ⊕ *www.monalisasuitehotel.com* ⤳ *240 suites: 93 one bedroom, 147 two bedroom* ⚒ *In-room: safe, kitchen, Wi-Fi. In-hotel: 2 restaurants, room service, bar, pool, Wi-Fi hotspot, parking (paid)* ⊟ *AE, D, DC, MC, V* ✛ *1:D6.*

LAKE BUENA VISTA AREA

Many people stay in resorts a bit farther northeast of Downtown Disney because, though equally grand, they tend to be less expensive than those right on Hotel Plaza Boulevard. If you're willing to take a five-minute drive or shuttle ride, you might save as much as 35% off your room tab.

$–$$ ⛌ **Caribe Royale All-Suites Resort & Convention Center.** This big pink palace of a hotel, with flowing palm trees and massive artificial waterfalls, underwent a huge renovation in 2009–10, in which bathrooms, bedrooms, carpets, and linens were updated in the suites and the TVs throughout the property were replaced with flat-screens with HD cable. Huge ballrooms attract corporate conferences, but there are key family-friendly ingredients, too: free transportation to Disney (10 minutes away) and a huge children's recreation area, including a big pool with a 65-foot slide and interactive water-play area. **Pros:** family-friendly; great pool area; good on-site restaurants; free shuttle to Disney; reciprocal room-charge privileges at the restaurants in the Buena Vista Suites hotel next door. **Cons:** too far to walk to shops and restaurants; daily fee for Internet is $9.99. ✉ *8101 World Center Dr., Orlando* ☎ *407/238–8000 or 800/823–8300* ⊕ *www.cariberoyale.com* ⤳ *1,338 suites, 120 villas* ⚒ *In-room: kitchen (some), refrigerator, Internet, Wi-Fi. In-hotel: 4 restaurants, room service, bars, tennis court, pool, gym, laundry facilities, laundry service, Wi-Fi hotspot* ⊟ *AE, D, DC, MC, V* ⦿⦿ *BP* ✛ *1:F5.*

¢–$ ⛌ **Country Inn & Suites by Carlson.** The signature lobby fireplace looks a little ridiculous in Orlando, but the in-room amenities and proximity to Downtown Disney (½ mi away) make this hotel a good bet for families. Guests can book what the hotel calls a one-bedroom Country Kids Suite, with two beds, two TVs (one of which is hooked up for video games), a refrigerator, and a microwave. **Pros:** refrigerators in every room; free shuttle to Disney; free continental breakfast. **Cons:** no on-site restaurant; no room service (but there are plenty of restaurants nearby). ✉ *12191 S. Apopka Vineland Rd., Orlando* ☎ *407/239–1115 or 800/456–4000* ⊕ *www.countryinns.com* ⤳ *170 rooms, 50 suites* ⚒ *In-room: safe, refrigerator, Internet. In-hotel: pool, gym, laundry facilities, Wi-Fi hotspot* ⊟ *AE, D, DC, MC, V* ⦿⦿ *CP* ✛ *1:F3.*

$–$$ ⛌ **Embassy Suites Hotel Lake Buena Vista.** The peach facade of this hotel, designed in faux California Mission style, is clearly visible from Interstate 4. It's only a mile from Downtown Disney, 3 mi from SeaWorld, and 7 mi from Universal Orlando, making it an ideal location for park hoppers. The atrium lobby, loaded with vegetation and soothed by the sounds of a rushing fountain, is a great place to enjoy the free cooked-to-order breakfast and evening cocktails. The resort offers seasonal

Continued on page 132

ORLANDO SPAS:
Escape from the Theme Parks
by Jennie Hess

If you hit the ground running after arriving in Orlando, at some point you may need to shift your pace from "fast forward" to "pause." If so, head directly to one of Orlando's resort spas. The area has enough standout pampering palaces to indulge every theme-park-weary parent, aching golfer, parched sunbather, and Disney princess.

Each of Orlando's resort spas is known for something special, whether it's the Balinese four-hand massage at the Mandara or customized Guerlain therapies at the Waldorf. Several spas draw on Florida's citrus-producing region to offer refreshing orange, grapefruit, and lime therapies. And you can go global with massage techniques from Japan, Thailand, Polynesia, and Sweden.

Families who want to stay together can even spa together at treatment centers specializing in youth facials, massages, and manicure/pedicure (aka mani/pedi) packages. The Grand Floridian Spa & Health Club offers its My First Facial experiences; the Ritz-Carlton Orlando treats kids like royalty with the Princess Fizzing Manicure and Pedicure.

Make your spa excursion special by planning enough time to use complimentary whirlpools, saunas, and steam rooms. Most spas offer free access to impressively equipped fitness centers and relaxation rooms stocked with herbal teas, fresh fruits, and other goodies. Book treatments early, and ask about gratuities—often 18% to 20%—which may or may not be included in your treatment or package.

Pictured above: The Spa at Shingle Creek—mother and daughter getting treatment

TOP SPOTS

WALDORF ASTORIA SPA BY GUERLAIN

Don't try to pour your own tea—your gracious valet is there to serve and make you comfortable. Spa slippers aren't one-size-fits many—they're sized to fit you. Instead of fancy therapies, the Guerlain treatments on the spa menu are kept simple so that therapists can focus on customizing them to meet your needs.

The extraordinary Exceptional Orchidée Impériale Treatment facial (2 hours, $420) babies your face with two therapies to detoxify and invigorate, two masks targeted to your needs, and a custom eye contour treatment. Meanwhile, your hands are pampered with warm paraffin and wrapped in mitts to soften them, and your tootsies and calves are massaged and moisturized to the max.

Can't bear to leave? Soak up the good karma stretched out on a chaise lounge by the whirlpool, where natural light streams through a window.

BODY TREATMENTS Massage: Deep tissue, four hand, lymphatic drainage, pregnancy and postnatal, reflexology, Swedish. **Exfoliation:** Floral-extract body polish. **Wraps/Baths:** Replenishing wrap with algae, hydrotherapy and balneotherapy baths. **Other:** Men's Firming Abdomen Treatment; men's facials.

BEAUTY TREATMENTS Epilation, facials, mani/pedi. Hair/scalp conditioning, hair cutting/styling.

PRICES Body treatments: $95–$540. **Facials:** $180–$420. **Mani/pedi:** $55–$220.

✉ 14200 Bonnet Creek Resort La., Orlando, FL 32821 ☎ 407/597–5360 ⊕ www.waldorfastoriaorlando.com. ♿ Parking: Valet only, complimentary with spa validation, but please tip ▭ AE, MC, V.

Balneotherapy

RITZ-CARLTON ORLANDO GRANDE LAKES

Prepare to be "wowed" as you enter this lavish, grand-palazzo-style spa—Orlando's largest with 40 treatment rooms. It won't take long to relax as you float past gauzy drapes, shed your tourist togs, and don an ultra-plush robe.

Did we say "relax?" Go for the two-hour Relax Body Ritual ($330), a signature organic treatment package using products made from fruits like cranberry and pomegranate. A therapist treats you to a full-body smoothing exfoliation, a hydrating body wrap (catnap optional), massage, and a hydrotherapy soak—you control the jets to suit your mood.

Alternatively, you could go "green" with the Eco-Rooftop Hammock Experience in a private outdoor sanctuary. Fully clothed, you'll rock gently in your hammock during a treatment regimen of cranial sacral, reflexology, and shiatsu massage.

BODY TREATMENTS Massage: four hand, Hawaiian lomi lomi, neuromuscular, rain-forest stone (hot stones and Vichy shower), reflexology, shiatsu, Thai. **Exfoliation:** organic scrubs and polishes. **Wraps/Baths:** seaweed and vitamin rich wraps; Vichy shower; hydrotherapy baths. **Other:** men's facials, manicures, pedicures; Princess Fizzing mani/pedi (ages 2–10); teen facials (14–17).

BEAUTY TREATMENTS Eye-lift treatment, facials, mani/pedi, microdermabrasion, nonsurgical face lift, peels. Hair cutting/styling.

PRICES Body treatments: $75–$350. **Facials:** $130–$330. **Mani/pedi:** $35–$175.

✉ 4024 Central Florida Pkwy, Orlando, FL 32837 ☎ 407/393–4200 ⊕ www.ritzcarlton.com/orlando ♿ Parking: Self-parking at J.W. Marriott next door; valet parking discounted to $5 with spa validation stamp ▭ AE, MC, V.

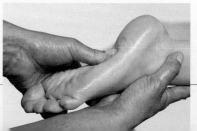

Reflexology

HONORABLE MENTIONS

Disney's Grand Floridian Resort & Spa

DISNEY'S GRAND FLORIDIAN RESORT & SPA

This 10,000-square-foot Victorian-style spa sits on the edge of Disney's Seven Seas Lagoon, and the resort's beach chairs are complimentary to sun worshippers who book a treatment.

If you want to feel like a million dollars, cash in on the spa's exclusive Aurum Manus (Hands of Gold) therapy so you can be massaged with warmed organic oils and smooth, semiprecious stone spheres like jade, crystal, and sodalite (50 minutes, $150; 80 minutes, $205). This holistic treatment is a real stress reliever as it stimulates vital points of the body's energy meridians.

Bring the family—there's a couples treatment room and a menu of "first" facials and massages for kids ages 4–12 (though youths aged 13–17 can also receive spa treatments if accompanied by an adult).

BODY TREATMENTS Massage: Aromatherapy, reflexology, sports, Swedish. **Exfoliation:** Sugar scrub, olive oil-and-salt body polish. **Wraps/Baths:** Clay mask and other body wraps incorporated into therapies and baths including ginger lime, juniper algae, lavender vanilla, rose sallow thorn, ylang ylang. **Other:** My First Facial or My First Massage (ages 4–12); gentleman's facial.

PRICES Body Treatments: $75–$375. **Facials:** $70–$190. **Mani/pedi:** $55–$110.

✉ 4111 North Floridian Way, Lake Buena Vista, FL 32830 ☎ 407/82–2332 to spa, 407/824–3000 to salon, ⊕ www.relaxedyet.com ♿ Parking: Complimentary self parking ▬ AE, MC, V.

THE SPA AT SHINGLE CREEK

Florida's settlers would have marveled at the luxury of the Spa at Shingle Creek, a resort near the Orange County Convention Center. The romance of Old Florida envelops you during the Calusa Cocoon (50 minutes, $120), which begins with a skin-silkening apricot scrub. Next, your therapist massages a blend of essential oils like lavender and ylang ylang into your skin before wrapping you like a papoose in a foil-like blanket.

A scalp massage completes the blissful experience. The signature Creekside Citrus and Cedar Massage (50 minutes, $130; 80 minutes, $175) invigorates with white-cedar, spruce, and lime oils and a body and scalp massage.

A cup of ginger-peach tea paired with oatmeal cranberry cookies in the spa lounge helps prolong the tranquility.

BODY TREATMENTS Massage: aromatherapy, ashiatsu, craniosacral, four hands, pregnancy, reflexology, scalp, hot stone, stretching, couples. **Exfoliation:** Sugar, fruit, and sea-salt scrubs. **Wraps:** Fruit, mud, and vitamin body masks and wraps. **Other:** Hot-towel hydrotherapy; gentleman's facial; youth facials and mani/pedis.

PRICES Body Treatments: $110–$225. **Facials:** $110–$220. **Mani/pedi:** $35–$85.

✉ 9939 Universal Blvd., Orlando, FL 32819 ☎ 407/996–9939 ⊕ www.spaatshinglecreek.com ♿ Parking: Complimentary valet or self-parking with spa validation (please tip valet) ▬ AE, MC, V.

Shingle Creek

Buena Vista Palace Hotel & Spa

MANDARA SPA

A Balinese paradise in landlocked central Florida? You'll find it at Mandara Spa at the Walt Disney World Dolphin Resort.

The signature Four Hand Massage (50 minutes, $240) delivers a blend of shiatsu, Hawaiian lomi lomi, Swedish, Thai, and Balinese massage. The Balinese Body Polish with Massage features a fragrance choice of coffee, lime and ginger, or Balinese boreh made from spices like clove, ginger, and nutmeg (50 minutes, $130; 75 minutes, $190).

Other southeast Asian indulgences are on the menu, including a super-hydrating Coconut Rub and Milk Ritual Wrap (50 minutes, $145; 75 minutes, $205) and the Frangipani Nourishing Hair & Scalp Treatment add-on ($30).

There's also a Mandara Spa in the Loew's Portofino Bay Hotel at Universal.

BODY TREATMENTS **Massage:** Balinese, couples, deep tissue, reflexology, shiatsu, Swedish. **Exfoliation:** salt, herb, and spice-blend scrubs. **Wraps:** clay, seaweed. **Other:** shirodhara; men's massage and facial; mani/pedis, facials, and massages for children 8 and up with adult companion.

PRICES **Body treatments:** $60–$255. **Facials:** $130–$240. **Mani/pedi:** $35–$130.

✉ Walt Disney World Swan & Dolphin Resort, 1500 Epcot Resorts Blvd., Lake Buena Vista, FL 32830 ☎ 407/934-4772 ⊕ www.mandaraspa. com ♿ Parking: Complimentary valet and self parking with spa validation ▭ AE, MC, V.

BUENA VISTA PALACE HOTEL & SPA

When you've exhausted your shopping agenda, you can drop in and settle back for the signature Royal Velvet Sugar Scrub, featuring mango-ginger sugar crystals and moisturizing mango body butter (80 minutes, $175). While you're at it, treat those tired gams to the add-on Theme Park Leg Relief Wrap (25 minutes, $75).

The ultra-relaxing, skin-smoothing European Rose Body Treatment (80 minutes, $160) guarantees you'll glow after your sun-dried rose clay wrap and cream-based body polish.

The atmosphere is intimate, and the prices are as reasonable as you'll find at a resort spa. Girlfriend gatherings with martinis and canapés by the secluded outdoor pool are a hit.

BODY TREATMENTS. **Massage:** craniosacral, deep tissue, hot stone, reflexology, shiatsu, Swedish. **Exfoliation:** cream-based body polish, sugar scrub. **Wraps:** clay, organic mud, seaweed. **Other:** men's facials; massages, facials, and body treatments for children 11–16 if accompanied by an adult.

PRICES **Body treatments:** $110–$180. **Facials:** $120–$200. **Mani/pedi:** $50–$85.

✉ 1900 N. Buena Vista Dr., Lake Buena Vista, FL 32830 ☎ 407/827-3200 ⊕ www.buenavistapalace.com ♿ Parking: Self parking and complimentary valet parking with spa validation ▭ AE, MC, V.

Resort/Spa name	Body Treatments	Facials	Mani/Pedis	Couples Treatments	Youth Treatments by age	Fitness Center	Sauna	Steam Room
Buena Vista Palace	$110–$180	$120–$200	$50–$85	yes	11–16	yes	yes	yes*
Disney's Grand Floridian	$55–$240	$70–$190	$55–$110	yes	4–17	yes	yes	yes
Mandara Spa at WDW Dolphin Resort	$59–$255	$130–$240	$35–$130	yes	8–18	no	no	yes
Ritz-Carlton	$95–$350	$130–$330	$35–$175	yes	2–10 and 14–17	yes	yes	yes
Shingle Creek	$65–$225	$110–$220	$35–$85	yes	10 and up	yes	yes	yes
Waldorf Astoria	$95–$540	$180–$420	$55–$220	yes	no	yes	yes	yes

*Available for women only

Spa at Ritz-Carlton Orlando Grande Lakes

GLOSSARY

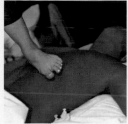

ashiatsu

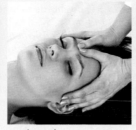

craniosacral

sports massage

abhyanga Herbal-oil massage sometimes performed by two therapists and often followed by a hot-towel treatment.

aromatherapy Massage and other treatments using plant-derived essential oils intended to relax the skin's connective tissues and stimulate the flow of lymph fluid.

ashiatsu Deep-tissue massage in which the therapist uses only his or her feet, usually while holding onto bars suspended from the ceiling over the massage table.

ayurveda A traditional Indian medical practice that uses oils, massage, herbs, and diet and lifestyle modification to restore balance to the body.

Balinese massage One of many traditional massages from the Indonesian island of Bali. Sessions may incorporate the use of essential oils, kneading strokes, stretching, accupressure, and reflexology.

balneotherapy Water-based treatment using geothermal hot springs, mineral water, or seawater to improve circulation, strengthen immunity, and relieve pain and stress.

body polish Use of scrubs, loofahs, and other exfoliants to remove dead skin cells.

craniosacral Massage therapy focusing on the skull and spine.

hot-stone massage Massage using smooth stones heated in water and applied to the skin with pressure or strokes or simply rested on the body.

hydrotherapy Underwater massage, alternating hot and cold showers, and other water-oriented treatments.

lomi lomi Traditional Polynesian massage employing long, gentle strokes. Stretching, healing rituals, and prayers may also be part of the treatment.

microdermabrasion Removing the top layer of skin (usually on the face) by brushing it with an abrasive substance to diminish the appearance of fine lines and even out pigmentation.

lymphatic drainage Massage technique designed to stimulate lymph-system circulation and help the body drain away toxins and excess water.

reflexology Massage on the pressure points of feet, hands, and ears.

salt glow Rubbing the body with coarse salt to remove dead skin. Also called salt scrub or rub.

shiatsu Japanese massage that uses pressure applied with fingers, hands, elbows, and feet.

shirodhara Ayurvedic massage in which warm herbalized oil is trickled onto the center of the forehead, then gently rubbed into the hair and scalp.

sports massage A deep-tissue massage to relieve muscle tension and residual pain from workouts.

sugar scrub Rubbing the body with an exfoliating product made with sugar.

Swedish massage Stroking, kneading, and tapping to relax muscles. It was devised at the University of Stockholm in the 19th century by Per Henrik Ling.

Thai massage Deep-tissue massage and passive stretching to ease stiff, tense, or short muscles.

thalassotherapy Water-based treatments that incorporate seawater, seaweed and algae.

Vichy shower Treatment in which a person lies on a cushioned, waterproof mat and is showered by overhead water jets.

outdoor movies by the pool (all Disney movies, of course). **Pros:** convenient to Downtown Disney; free shuttle to all Disney parks; within walking distance of restaurants and shops. **Cons:** public areas are noisy; daily Internet fee of $9.95; no shuttle to other parks. ✉ *8100 Lake St., Orlando* ☎ *407/239–1144, 800/257–8483, or 800/362–2779* ⊕ *www. embassysuites.com* ↪ *334 suites* ♿ *In-room: safe, refrigerator, Internet. In-hotel: 2 restaurants, room service, tennis court, pool, gym, Wi-Fi hotspot* ⊟ *AE, D, DC, MC, V* ⍾⊙⍾ *BP* ✣ *1:G3.*

¢–$ 🆃 **Hawthorn Suites Resort Lake Buena Vista.** Every suite has a bedroom and a full kitchen, but if you don't want to cook early in the morning, there's a free hot breakfast buffet, even though there is no on-site restaurant other times of the day. Free cocktails on weekday late afternoons is also a pleasant perk. Another freebie is the Disney shuttle. Downtown Disney is 1 mi away, and it's a pleasant walk if you're inclined for a springtime stroll, but can be a grind in the high summer heat. **Pros:** affordable; full kitchens; walk to shops; free Disney shuttle. **Cons:** pool area gets noisy; four-night minimum during peak season in March and April. ✉ *8303 Palm Pkwy., Orlando* ☎ *407/597–5000 or 866/756–3778* ⊕ *www.hawthornlakebuenavista.com* ↪ *120 suites* ♿ *In-room: safe, kitchen, refrigerator, Wi-Fi. In-hotel: room service, bar, pool, laundry facilities, Wi-Fi hotspot* ⊟ *AE, D, DC, MC, V* ⍾⊙⍾ *CP* ✣ *1:G3.*

$$$–$$$$ 🆃 **Hilton Orlando Bonnet Creek.** Next door to the Waldorf Astoria hotel, and connected to it via a convention hall, the hotel is part of the Bonnet Creek resort area, right next to Disney World's own vast forest lands. The hotel is not quite as plush as the Waldorf, but it is an amenity-laden property just the same. It targets corporate meetings, but also offers great appeal for families, with its 2-acre lagoon pool, children's program, and, of course, transportation to Disney World. Guests at the Hilton can use facilities at the Waldorf, including the Waldorf Astoria Spa by Guerlain and the Waldorf restaurants. **Pros:** wonderful setting for a hotel—Disney is just moments away, but the views southwest over the golf course and forest beyond give it a remote air; next door to the Waldorf, with its amenities easily at hand; free Disney shuttle. **Cons:** nothing within walking distance; you will need to rent a car; $10 a day Internet-access fee. ✉ *14100 Bonnet Creek Resort Lane, Bonnet Creek, Orlando* ☎ *407/597–5500* ⊕ *www.hiltonbonnetcreek.com* ↪ *1,000 rooms, 36 suites* ♿ *In-room: safe, Internet, Wi-Fi. In-hotel: 4 restaurants, room service, bars, golf course, pools, gym, spa, children's programs (ages 4–12), laundry service, Wi-Fi hotspot* ⊟ *AE, D, DC, MC, V* ✣ *1:A6.*

¢–$ 🆃 **Holiday Inn SunSpree Lake Buena Vista.** This family-oriented hotel, which underwent a huge renovation in 2010, does a lot to keep the kids happy. There's a children's registration desk, a CyberArcade, and a small theater where movies are offered throughout the day, in addition to a restaurant where kids 12 and under eat free. A nightly resort fee covers shuttles to all parks, lobby movies, Internet, poolside activities, and more. **Pros:** extremely kid-friendly; great deal for families; you can walk to some off-property restaurants, and a very handy, 24-hour convenience store, without crossing the street. **Cons:** too noisy at times for adults; street is a tad busy for pedestrians to try to cross, especially at night. ✉ *13351 Rte. 535, Orlando* ☎ *407/239–4500 or 800/366–6299* ⊕ *www.kidsuites.com* ⤳ *507 rooms* ⟐ *In-room: safe, refrigerator, Wi-Fi. In-hotel: restaurant, bar, pool, gym, seasonal children's programs (ages 4–12), laundry facilities, laundry service, Wi-Fi hotspot* ☰ *AE, D, DC, MC, V* ✛ *1:G4.*

$$$–$$$$
Fodor's Choice
★
🔲 **Hyatt Regency Grand Cypress Resort.** On 1,500 acres just outside Disney's north entrance, this spectacular resort has a private lake with watercraft, three golf courses, and miles of trails for strolling, bicycling, jogging, and horseback riding. The resort completed a $65-million renovation in 2010, upgrading guest rooms and public spaces. Tropical birds, plants, and a museum's treasure of Asian sculpture fill the 18-story atrium, which can be viewed from the glass-fronted elevators. Rooms overlooking Disney have a spectacular view of the evening fireworks at Epcot and the Magic Kingdom, and guests can watch the giant hot-air balloon rise and lower at Downtown Disney. Accommodations are divided between the hotel and the **Villas of Grand Cypress** (✉ *1 N. Jacaranda Dr., Orlando* ☎ *407/239–1234 or 800/835–7377*), with 200 villas. **Pros:** great Sunday brunch at La Coquina; huge pool; lots of recreation options, including nearby equestrian center. **Cons:** pricey; shuttle to Disney is part of the $18 daily resort fee; inconvenient to Universal Orlando, SeaWorld, and downtown Orlando. ✉ *1 Grand Cypress Blvd., Orlando* ☎ *407/239–1234 or 800/233–1234* ⊕ *www.hyattgrandcypress.com* ⤳ *750 rooms* ⟐ *In-room: safe, Internet. In-hotel: 5 restaurants, room service, golf courses, tennis courts, pools, gym, spa, bicycles, children's programs (ages 4–12), laundry service, Wi-Fi hotspot* ☰ *AE, D, DC, MC, V* ✛ *1:F3.*

$–$$
🔲 **Marriott Village at Little Lake Bryan.** The private, gated Marriott Village has three hotels. The **Courtyard** welcomes families and business travelers with 3,000 square feet of meeting space and large standard rooms decorated with yellow and green floral patterns and blond-wood furniture. The indoor-outdoor pool has a swim-up bar. At **SpringHill Suites,** accommodations have kitchenettes, separate sleeping and dining areas, and Sony Playstations, and the hotel serves a free, hot breakfast. The **Fairfield Inn** is the least expensive of the three, but rooms are as bright and pleasant, if not quite as amenity laden. Continental breakfast is included in the rates, and there are several chain restaurants in the complex. Best of all, there's an on-site Disney planning center, where you can buy park tickets. **Pros:** lots of informal dining options; lower room rates than hotels on the other side of Interstate 4; you can walk to a few chain restaurants just off of the hotel property. **Cons:** Disney shuttle costs $7 per person round-trip (hotels across Interstate 4 have free shuttles). ✉ *8623 Vineland Ave., Orlando* ☎ *407/938–9001 or 877/682–8552* ⊕ *www.marriottvillage.com* ⤳ *650 rooms, 450 suites* ⟐ *In-room: safe, refrigerator, Internet. In-hotel: 8 restaurants, room service, bars, pools, gym, children's programs (ages 4–12), laundry facilities, laundry service, Wi-Fi hotspot* ☰ *AE, D, DC, MC, V* 🍴 *CP* ✛ *1:G3.*

$$–$$$
☾
Fodor's Choice
★
🔲 **Nickelodeon Family Suites by Holiday Inn.** The Nickelodeon theme extends everywhere, from the suites, where separate kids' rooms have bunk beds and SpongeBob wall murals, to the two giant water-park pools. Kids will look forward to wake-up calls from Nickelodeon stars,

character breakfasts, live entertainment, mass slimings, and a 3-D movie theater. The accommodations are so thoroughly designed for kids that it is not the best place for those without youngsters. **Pros:** extremely kid-friendly; free Disney, Universal Orlando, and SeaWorld shuttles; massive discounts (up to 50% off standard rates) for active-duty military; you can save about $20 on a room a night with memberships like AAA and AARP; mini-golf course. **Cons:** not within walking distance of Disney or Downtown Disney; may be too frenetic for folks without kids. ⊠ *14500 Continental Gateway, Orlando* ☎ *407/387–5437 or 866/462–6425* ⊕ *www.nickhotels.com* ↻ *777 suites* ⚒ *In-room: safe, kitchen (some), refrigerator, Internet. In-hotel: 7 restaurants, room service, pools, gym, children's programs (ages 4–12), laundry facilities, laundry service, Wi-Fi hotspot* ▭ *AE, D, DC, MC, V* ✛ *1:F5.*

$$–$$$ ⊡ **Orlando World Center Marriott.** With 2,000 rooms, this is one of Orlando's largest hotels, and it's very popular with conventions. (In fact, at 400,000 square feet, it has more convention space within the hotel than any other hotel in Orlando, which means more than any hotel in Florida. The place is a convention factory.) But children are always welcome, and there are scheduled programs planned just for kids. The pool complex is vast, with serene areas for quiet sunbathing, and a waterfall, cave, and slide feature that kids will love. **Pros:** good steak house on-site; golf course; lobby Starbucks. **Cons:** Internet fee of $14.95 and up daily; on-site restaurants have expense-account-size prices; nothing worth seeing within walking distance; in fact, the hotel fronts a highway that doesn't encourage pedestrians. ⊠ *8701 World Center Dr., I–4 Exit 65, Orlando* ☎ *407/239–4200 or 800/228–9290* ⊕ *www.marriottworldcenter.com* ↻ *2,000 rooms, 98 suites, 259 villas* ⚒ *In-room: Internet. In-hotel: 7 restaurants, room service, golf course, pools, gym, spa, children's programs (ages 4–12), laundry facilities, laundry service, Wi-Fi hotspot* ▭ *AE, D, DC, MC, V* ✛ *1:F5.*

¢–$ ⊡ **Sheraton Safari Hotel.** From the pool's jungle motif to the bamboo enclosures around the lobby pay phones, this little piece of Africa in the hotel district adjacent to Downtown Disney is a trip. Although there are some leopard skin–print furniture coverings and wild-animal portraits on the walls, the guest rooms are relatively sedate. Watch your kids play on 79-foot-long python waterslide in the pool area while you sip drinks and snack at the poolside Monkey Bar, or imbibe inside at Zanzibar. **Pros:** kid-attractive pool area; short walk to shops and restaurants; free Disney shuttle; small pets allowed with deposit. **Cons:** pool area can get loud; close to Downtown Disney, but a tad too far to walk there (about 1 mi). ⊠ *12205 Apopka Vineland Rd., Orlando* ☎ *407/239–0444 or 800/423–3297* ⊕ *www.sheratonsafari.com* ↻ *489 rooms, 96 suites* ⚒ *In-room: safe, kitchen (some), refrigerator (some), Internet. In-hotel: 2 restaurants, room service, pool, gym, Wi-Fi hotspot* ▭ *AE, D, DC, MC, V* ✛ *1:F3.*

$$$–$$$$ ⊡ **Waldorf Astoria Orlando.** While it doesn't duplicate the famed Waldorf
Fodor's Choice   Astoria Hotel in New York, the Waldorf Astoria Orlando echoes the
★   original with imagination and flair, from the clock under the dome in the center of the circular lobby to tiny, black-and-white accent tiles on the floors of the guest rooms. Rooms are decorated with understated

elegance, using black-and-white highlights against rich beige-and-gold neutrals. Beds and linens are as plush and comfy as you'll find anywhere in the world. If you want a butler, one is available. If you want a massage, the Guerlain spa exudes relaxation the minute you walk in the door. If golf is your choice, a vast Rees Jones–designed course fills the view from the lobby, bar, or balcony rooms. The hotel connects to and shares a convention hall and meeting space with the Hilton Bonnet Creek. Pros: a lavish and luxurious hotel, spa, and golf resort, next to Disney. Cons: if you can bear to leave the cabana you'll need a car to see anything else in the area. ⊠ *14200 Bonnet Creek Resort La., Orlando* ☎ *407/597-5500* ⊕ *www.waldorfastoriaorlando.com* ⤢ *328 rooms, 169 suites* ⟁ *In-room: safe, Internet. In-hotel: 5 restaurants, room service, bars, golf course, pool, gym, spa, children's programs (ages 4–12), laundry service, Wi-Fi hotspot* ⊟ *AE, D, DC, MC, V* ✢ *1:A6.*

$$-$$$ ⛨ **Wyndham Bonnet Creek Resort.** Despite being within close proximity to Disney property, the resort seems remote, as the entry road passes through pristine Florida forest and bamboo-laden landscaping. Seven multistory condo towers, with architecture that echoes Florida's Spanish heritage, sit around a large, serene lake; some have pools and restaurants, but for those that don't, pleasant paths connect one building to the next. The hotel portion of the resort is expected to open in mid-2011; until then, condos are for rent just as though you were at a hotel. Pros: practically in Mickey's lap; free shuttle to Disney parks; lots of activities. Cons: not convenient to Universal or downtown Orlando; on-site food choices are limited. ⊠ *9560 Via Encinas, Bonnet Creek Lake Buena Vista* ☎ *407/238-3500 or 800/251-8736* ⊕ *www.wyndhamvacationresorts.com* ⤢ *1,596 units* ⟁ *In-room: safe, kitchen, refrigerator, Internet. In-hotel: 3 restaurants, room service (limited), bars, pools, gym, children's programs (ages 4-12), laundry facilities, parking (free)* ⊟ *AE, D, DC, MC, V* ✢ *1:A6.*

CENTRAL ORLANDO

Take Exit 83B off Interstate 4 westbound, Exit 84 off Interstate 4 eastbound.

Central Orlando, north of Walt Disney World and the I-Drive area, is a thriving business district on weekdays and attracts a club and restaurant crowd on weekend nights.

$-$$ ⛨ **The Courtyard at Lake Lucerne.** These four beautifully restored Victorian houses that surround a palm-lined courtyard were architectural treasures more than 50 years before Disney came to Orlando, and have kept their own brand of magic even now, as they collectively make up one of the better historic inns you'll find in the southeast United States. Although it's almost under an expressway bridge, there's no traffic noise. You can sit on one of the porches and imagine yourself back in the time when citrus ruled and the few visitors arrived at the old railroad station on Church Street, six blocks away. Pros: serenity; great Victorian architecture; short walk to Lake Eola and downtown restaurants. Cons: far from theme parks and I-Drive; walking in some parts of downtown can be a bit dicey. ⊠ *211 N. Lucerne Circle E, Downtown*

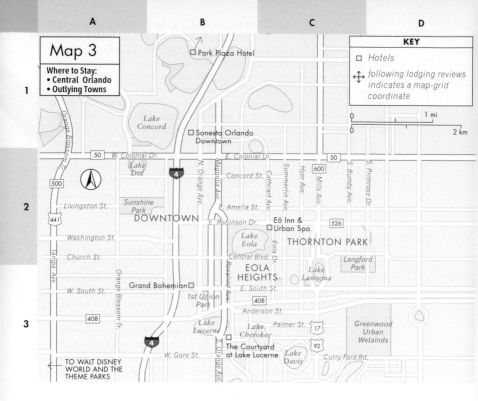

Orlando, Orlando ☎ 407/648–5188 ⊕ www.orlandohistoricinn.com
⤳ 15 rooms, 15 suites ⚒ In-room: Wi-Fi. In-hotel: Wi-Fi hotspot, laundry services ═ MC, V ⅋ CP ⊕ 3:B3.

$–$$ ⛉ **Eō Inn & Urban Spa.** The entrance is at the rear of the building, behind Panera Bread, the bakery–restaurant that occupies the ground floor. Consequently, this three-story boutique hotel in a 1923 building is an undiscovered charmer. The spa does a brisk business on its own, but as a hotel guest you can always get in for a Swedish massage or a beauty treatment. Best of all, Lake Eola, with its 1-mi walking path, is across the street—treat yourself to a king suite, with a balcony overlooking the lake. **Pros:** good spa; very short walk to Lake Eola, Thornton Park and downtown; these areas have plenty of restaurants and are safe to walk to at night. **Cons:** you have to battle Interstate 4 traffic; Disney is 30–45 minutes away. (Don't believe the hotel Web site statement that Disney is 20 minutes away. Without lights and a siren on your car, or a helicopter, that won't happen.) ⊠ 227 N. Eola Dr., off E. Robinson St., Thornton Park, Orlando ☎ 407/481–8485 or 888/481–8488 ⊕ www. eoinn.com ⤳ 17 rooms ⚒ In-room: Wi-Fi. In-hotel: spa, laundry service, Wi-Fi hotspot ═ AE, D, DC, MC, V ⊕ 3:C2.

$$–$$$ ⛉ **Grand Bohemian.** This European-style property is downtown Orlando's only luxury hotel, and is part of the locally owned Kessler chain. Opposite city hall, the Grand Bohemian showcases more than 100 pieces of art from the Kessler collection—including a rare Imperial Grand Bösendorfer piano, which sits in a posh ground-floor lounge. Rooms have dark-wood furnishings with brushed-silver accents. **Pros:** art gallery; quiet, adult-friendly atmosphere; great restaurant; sophisticated entertainment; short walk to Lake Eola and downtown restaurants and clubs. **Cons:** kids may find it boring; meals are relatively expensive. ⊠ *325 S. Orange Ave., Downtown Orlando,* ☎ *407/313–9000 or 866/663–0024* ⊕ *www.grandbohemianhotel.com* ⤣ *249 rooms, 36 suites* ♿ *In-room: Wi-Fi. In-hotel: restaurant, room service, bar, pool, gym, parking (paid)* ⊟ *AE, D, DC, MC, V* ✛ *3:B3.*

$–$$ 🖵 **Sonesta Orlando Downtown.** A business hotel with a 20,000-square-foot conference center, this relatively undiscovered gem's location also holds value for families. Within walking distance are pleasant little Lake Ivanhoe and a neighborhood with a handful of small restaurants and antiques shops, and downtown Orlando's clubs and restaurants are only a few blocks south. This is a good base from which to see the "real" Orlando, miles away from the nearest tourist strip. **Pros:** easy walk to pleasant downtown lakes; close to museum district, arts, and antiques district; you can jump on Interstate 4 and be in Daytona Beach (60 mi away) about as quickly as you can be in Downtown Disney; the bulk of the heavy Interstate 4 traffic is between the hotel and Disney, not between the hotel and points east and north. **Cons:** no children's program or babysitting services; distance and traffic between hotel and Disney. ⊠ *60 S. Ivanhoe Blvd.,Downtown Orlando,* ☎ *407/425–4455* ⊕ *www.sonesta.com/orlando* ⤣ *340 rooms* ♿ *In-room: safe, refrigerator, Wi-Fi. In-hotel: restaurant, room service, bar, pool, gym, laundry facilities, laundry service* ⊟ *AE, DC, MC, V* ✛ *3:B1.*

ORLANDO INTERNATIONAL AIRPORT

The area around the airport, especially the neighborhood just north of the Beachline Expressway, has a surfeit of hotels, mostly used by business travelers and airline staff. They're worth checking out if you have an early departure.

$–$$ 🖵 **The Florida Hotel & Conference Center.** Five miles from the airport gates, the Florida Hotel is midway between Orlando International and I-Drive. You're in for a treat if you like to shop: the hotel is connected to the upscale Florida Mall, with seven major department stores and 250 specialty shops. The hotel feels upscale, too, with polished marble floors, fountains in the lobby, and a good in-house restaurant, Cricket's. **Pros:** access to the mall's shopping and dining options; in-room spa services; short drive to airport. **Cons:** neighborhood is less than scenic; besides the interior of the adjoining mall, there's nothing to walk to around the hotel; Disney is 18 mi away; no free shuttles. ⊠ *1500 Sand Lake Rd., at S. Orange Blossom Trail, Orlando International Airport, Orlando* ☎ *407/859-1500 or 800/588–4656* ⊕ *www.thefloridahotelorlando. com* ⤣ *511 rooms* ♿ *In-room: Internet, refrigerator. In-hotel: restaurant, room service, pool, gym, laundry service* ⊟ *AE, D, DC, MC, V* ✛ *2:H3.*

$$–$$$ 🖵 **Hyatt Regency Orlando International Airport.** If you have to catch an early-morning flight, this hotel inside the main terminal complex is a good option. Counting the time you spend waiting for the elevator,

your room is a five-minute walk from the nearest ticket counter. Rooms have views of either the runways or a 10-story-tall terminal atrium; terminal-side rooms have balconies. Hemisphere, the hotel's upscale restaurant, offers an eclectic menu that changes seasonally and spectacular runway views. **Pros:** quiet and sublime; if you're a people-watcher, it doesn't get much better than the view from your terminal-side balcony; terminal's 24-hour shopping and dining options are available; shuttles to Disney and Universal (for a fee). **Cons:** nothing around but the airport; downtown Orlando and the theme parks are at least 30 minutes away. ⊠ *9300 Airport Blvd., Orlando International Airport, Orlando* ☎ *407/825–1234 or 800/233–1234* ⊕ *www.orlandoairport. hyatt.com* ☎ *445 rooms* ♿ *In-room: Internet. In-hotel: 2 restaurants, room service, pool, gym, laundry service, Wi-Fi hotspot* ⊟ *AE, D, DC, MC, V* ✧ *2:H3.*

WINTER PARK

Take I–4 Exit 87 or 88.

Home of Rollins College, Winter Park is greater Orlando's poshest and best-established area. Brick streets overhung by moss-draped oaks lead to flower-bedecked Park Avenue, the main drag. Chichi shops and restaurants line its east side, and a beautifully landscaped park graces the west side. It feels a million miles from the tourist trail, but it's just a short drive from the major attractions.

$$–$$$ 🏨 **Park Plaza Hotel.** Small and intimate, this 1922 establishment feels almost like a private home. The best accommodations are front garden suites with a living room that opens onto a balcony usually abloom with impatiens and bougainvillea. Balconies are so covered with shrubs and ferns that they are somewhat private, inspiring romantic interludes. A half-dozen sidewalk cafés and many more upscale boutiques and shops surround the hotel. Park Plaza Gardens, the restaurant downstairs, offers quiet atrium dining and excellent food. **Pros:** romantic; great balconies overlooking Park Avenue; shops and restaurants adjacent; in-house restaurant is in a brick-walled courtyard; Amtrak station is about a block away. **Cons:** the railroad tracks are a lot closer than the station, and you can sometimes hear train noise at night; no small children allowed; small rooms; Disney is 60 minutes away. ⊠ *307 Park Ave. S, Winter Park* ☎ *407/647–1072 or 800/228–7220* ⊕ *www. parkplazahotel.com* ☎ *27 rooms* ♿ *In-room: Wi-Fi. In-hotel: restaurant, room service, parking (free), laundry service, Wi-Fi hotspot, no kids under 5* ⊟ *AE, DC, MC, V* ✧ *3:B1.*

Where to Eat

WORD OF MOUTH

"[Jiko] turned out to be the best meal, by far! A little expensive, but so worth it!"

—lenapresti

Updated by
Rona Gindin

You'll find the all-American-standby burger-and-fries combo everywhere in Orlando, yet the ambitious chefs behind Orlando's theme-park and independent restaurants provide loads of better options—much better. Locally sourced foods, creative preparations, and clever international influences are all the rage here, giving even die-hard foodies surprisingly satisfying meals. Theme-park complexes have some of the best restaurants in town, although you may opt for a car rental to seek out the local treasures.

The signs of Orlando *getting it*—of moving beyond its menu mediocrity—is most evident in the last place one would look: Disney's fast-food outlets. Every eatery on Disney property offers a vegetarian option, and kiddie meals come with healthful sides and drinks unless you specifically request otherwise.

Around town, locals flock to The Ravenous Pig, a gastropub where the menu changes every day; Luma on Park, a suave home of thoughtfully created cutting-edge meals; and any number of dining establishments competing to serve the very finest steak. Orlando's culinary blossoming began in 1995, when Disney's signature California Grill debuted featuring farm-to-table cuisine and wonderful wines by the glass. Soon after, celebrity chefs started opening shop.

Orlando's destination restaurants can be found in the theme parks, as well in it the outlying towns. Sand Lake Road is now known as Restaurant Row for its eclectic collection of worthwhile tables. Here you'll find fashionable outlets for sushi and seafood, Italian and chops, Hawaiian-fusion and upscale Mexican. Heading into the residential areas, the neighborhoods of Winter Park (actually its own city), Thornton Park, and College Park are prime locales for chow. Scattered throughout

Central Florida, low-key ethnic restaurants specialize in the fare of Turkey, India, Peru, Thailand, Vietnam—you name it. Prices in these family-owned finds are usually delightfully low.

WALT DISNEY WORLD AREA

MAGIC KINGDOM

Dining options in the Magic Kingdom are mainly counter service, and every land has its share of fast-food places selling burgers, hot dogs, grilled-chicken sandwiches, and salads. Each has a different regular and children's menu. The walkways are peppered with carts dispensing smoked turkey legs, popcorn, ice-cream bars, lemonade, bottled water, and soda. The Magic Kingdom's no-liquor policy fits the theme park most suited for little kids, but it does not extend to the rest of Walt Disney World.

$$$$
AMERICAN

✕ **Cinderella's Royal Table.** Cinderella and other Disney princesses appear at breakfast time at this eatery in the castle's old mead hall; you should book reservations up to 180 days in advance to be sure to see them. The Once Upon a Time Breakfast offers all-you-can-eat options such as scrambled eggs, sausages, bacon, French toast, and beverages. The Fairytale Lunch, a prix-fixe table-service meal, includes entrées like pan-seared salmon with herbed rice and pasta pomodoro. The prix-fixe dinner features selections such as roast lamb chops with herb pesto and roast prime rib of beef with cabernet sauce. When you arrive at the Cinderella Castle, a photographer snaps a shot of your group in the lobby. A package of photographs will be delivered to your table during your meal. ⊠ *Cinderella Castle* ☎ *407/939–3463* ⚞ *Reservations essential* ▭ *AE, D, DC, MC, V* ✛ *1:B1.*

$$$
AMERICAN

✕ **Liberty Tree Tavern.** This "tavern" is dry, but it's a prime spot on the parade route, so you can catch a good meal while you wait. Order colonial-period comfort food for lunch like hearty pot roast cooked with a cabernet wine–and–mushroom sauce, or turkey and dressing with mashed potatoes. The restaurant is decorated in lovely Williamsburg colors with Early American–style antiques and lots of brightly polished brass. ⊠ *Liberty Square* ☎ *407/824–6461* ▭ *AE, D, DC, MC, V* ✛ *1:B1.*

$$–$$$
ITALIAN

✕ **Tony's Town Square Restaurant.** Inspired by the animated classic *Lady and the Tramp,* Tony's offers everything from spaghetti with meatballs to a New York strip steak, to a catch of the day served with pancetta-tossed orzo pasta. There's no wine list, but you can get the lemonade punch in a collector's mug. The most tempting desserts are the lemon-walnut layer cake or the pistachio crème brûlée. If you can't get a table right away, you can watch *Lady and the Tramp* in the waiting area. ⊠ *Main St., U.S.A., Liberty Sq.* ☎ *407/939–3463* ▭ *AE, D, DC, MC, V* ✛ *1:B1.*

WHERE TO EAT PLANNER

Eating Out Strategy

Where should we eat? With thousands of eateries competing for your attention, it may seem like a daunting question. But fret not—our expert writers and editors have done most of the legwork. The selections here represent the best this city has to offer—from hamburger-joints to fine dining. Search "Best Bets" for top recommendations by price, cuisine, and experience. Or find a review quickly in the listings, organized alphabetically within theme park or neighborhood. Dive in, and enjoy!

Smoking

Florida law forbids smoking in all enclosed restaurant areas except stand-alone bars. Smoking is not necessarily permitted even on patios, so call ahead to find out a restaurant's policy.

Using the Maps

Throughout the chapter, you'll see mapping symbols and coordinates (✛ 3:F2) at the end of each review. Maps are located within the chapter. The first number after the ✛ symbol indicates the map number. Following that is the property's coordinate on the map grid.

What to Wear

Because tourism is king around Orlando, casual dress is the rule. Flip-flops and cutoffs are acceptable in just about all fast-food and mid-priced restaurants. While it's best to dress up for the ritzier restaurants, don't be shocked to find diners beside you in Levi's and polo shirts. Men need jackets only in the most exclusive establishments.

Prices and Price Chart

If you're staying at one of Disney's lodging facilities, you may find one of the Disney Dining Plan deals to be of great value. The options are tweaked annually, but each plan entitles you to a certain number of meals and snacks per day in restaurants of specific categories. For 2010, the resort offered six options as part of a Magic Your Way vacation package. To learn more, visit ⊕ *www.disneyworld. com* and type Disney Dining Plans into the search box. Universal Orlando offers an all-you-can-eat-from-lunch-on deal for the walk-up eateries inside the two theme parks (but not the restaurants in CityWalk). Tickets can be purchased at the theme-park ticket office, at participating restaurants, or at ⊕ *www.universalorlando.com/dining. For more information on the meal plans offered at both Disney and Universal, refer to chapter 1, Planning Your Trip.*

Credit cards are widely accepted. If you plan to use a credit card, it's a good idea to double-check its acceptability when making reservations or before sitting down to eat. Some restaurants are marked with a price range ($$–$$$, for example). This indicates one of two things: either the average cost straddles two categories, or, that if you order strategically, you can get out for less than most diners spend.

WHAT IT COSTS

	¢	$	$$	$$$	$$$$
AT DINNER	under $8	$8–$14	$15–$21	$22–$30	over $30

Prices are per person for a median main course, at dinner, excluding tip and tax of 6.5 %.

Reservations

All WDW restaurants and most restaurants elsewhere in greater Orlando take reservations. For restaurant reservations within Walt Disney World, call ☎ *407/939–3463* (*WDW–DINE*) or book online at ⊕ *www.disneyworld.com/ dining.* Reservations are accepted 180 days in advance. You can also get plenty of information on the Web site, including the hours, price range, and specialties of all Disney eateries. Menus are posted online and tend to be up-to-date except for the more upscale eateries, which tend to vary their menus regularly. For Universal Orlando reservations, call ☎ *407/224–9255* (theme parks and CityWalk) or *407/503–3463* (hotels). Learn about the complex's 50-plus restaurants at ⊕ *www.universalorlando.com;* press the Dining tab.

In reviews, reservations are mentioned only when they're essential or not accepted. Unless otherwise noted, the restaurants listed are open daily for lunch and dinner.

Tipping and Taxes

In most restaurants, tip the waiter 15%–20% of the food and beverage charges before tax. Tip at least $1 per drink at the bar, and $2 for valet parking.

With Kids

Theme parks or no theme parks, Orlando is a family-oriented town, and its restaurants not only welcome children—they expect them. All but the most exclusive dining rooms (Victoria & Albert's, Christini's Ristorante Italiano) stock high chairs, children's menus, and some kind of time-killer like a paper menu with games and crayons.

Mealtimes

When you're touring the theme parks, you can save a lot of time by eating in the off-hours. Lines at the counter-service places can get very long between noon and 2 PM, and waiting in line for food can get more frustrating than suffering the queue for a ride. Try eating lunch at 11 AM and dinner at 5 PM, or lunch at 2:30 PM and dinner at 9 PM.

In This Chapter

Spotlight On

3

BEST BETS FOR ORLANDO AND THE PARKS DINING

If it can be fried and put under a heat lamp you can probably find it in Orlando, but the dining scene both within the parks and the city itself has long transcended fast food. Quality restaurants operate within the parks, Downtown Disney, and several Orlando neighborhoods. Here are our top recommendations, organized by price, cuisine, and experience. The restaurants we consider the very best are indicated in the listings with the Fodor's Choice logo.

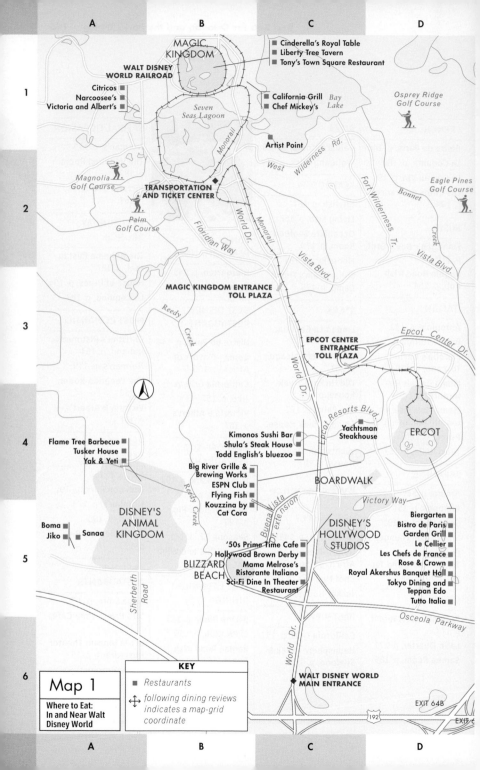

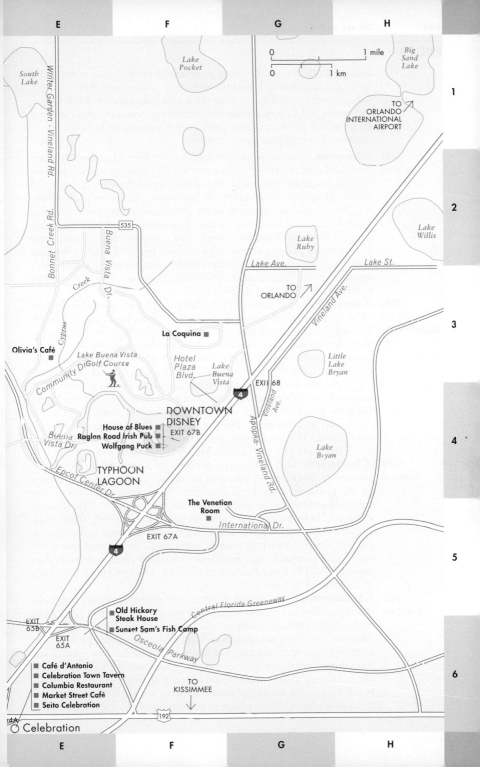

EPCOT

Epcot's World Showcase offers some of the finest dining in Orlando. Every pavilion has at least one and often two or even three eateries. Where there's a choice, it's between a relatively expensive full-service restaurant and a more affordable, ethnic fast-food spot, plus carts and shops selling snacks ranging from French pastries to Japanese ices—whatever's appropriate to the pavilion.

$$$$
GERMAN

✗ **Biergarten.** Oktoberfest runs 365 days a year here. The cheerful, sometimes raucous, crowds are what you would expect in a place with an oompah band. The menu and level of frivolity are the same at lunch and dinner. Mountains of sauerbraten, bratwurst, chicken or pork schnitzel, German sausage, spaetzle, apple strudel, Bavarian cheesecake, and Black Forest cake await you at the all-you-can-eat buffet. And if you aren't feeling too Teutonic, there's also rotisserie chicken and roast pork. Patrons pound pitchers of all kinds of beer and wine on the long communal tables—even when the yodelers, singers, and dancers aren't egging them on. Prices change seasonally. ⊠ *Germany* ☎ *407/939–3463* ☰ *AE, D, DC, MC, V* ✛ *1:D4.*

$$$$
FRENCH
Fodor's Choice
★

✗ **Bistro de Paris.** The great secret in the France pavilion—and, indeed, in all of Epcot—is the Bistro de Paris, upstairs from Les Chefs de France. The sophisticated menu changes regularly and reflects the cutting edge of French cooking; representative dishes include pan-seared scallops, venison medallions with caramelized apple and cranberries, and rack of lamb with thyme, ratatouille, and a thin onion tart. Come late, ask for a window seat, and plan to linger to watch the 9 PM Epcot light show. Moderately priced French wines are available by the bottle and the glass. If you like French cuisine but don't know much about it, the six-course, prix-fixe meal, $54 per person without wine, or $89 with wine parings, is a good way to go. ⊠ *France Pavilion, World Showcase* ☎ *407/939–3463* ☰ *AE, D, DC, MC, V* ☉ *No lunch* ✛ *1:D4.*

$$$$
AMERICAN

✗ **Garden Grill.** Solid family-style dinner fare is served here as the restaurant revolves, giving you an ever-changing view of each biome on the Living with the Land boat ride. The restaurant offers an all-you-can-eat family-style meals with visits from Chip 'n' Dale. Typical choices include roast turkey with cranberry-orange relish, flank steak with mushroom wine jus, plus kiddie favorites like mac and cheese or chicken nuggets. Except for the Princess meals in Norway, this is the only Epcot restaurant that has Disney character meet-and-greets during meals. ⊠ *The Land Pavilion* ☎ *407/939–3463* ☰ *AE, D, DC, MC, V* ☉ *No lunch* ✛ *1:D4.*

$$$$
CANADIAN

✗ **Le Cellier Steakhouse.** This charming eatery with stone arches and dark-wood paneling has a good selection of wine and Canadian beer. Aged beef is king, although many steaks appear only on the dinner menu. The prix-fixe menu has choices ranging from salt-crusted prime rib to salmon prepared two ways. But you can also order à la carte. Even though the menu changes periodically (gone are the buffalo steaks, alas), there are always nonbeef options such as veal T-bone with black-bread-panzanella salad, and potato gnocchi with grilled eggplant and pesto broth. Desserts pay tribute to the land up north with crème brûlée made with maple sugar, and a Canadian Club chocolate cake. ⊠ *Canada Pavilion* ☎ *407/939–3463* ⊟ *AE, D, DC, MC, V* ✦ *1:D4.*

$$$ ✕ **Les Chefs de France.** What some consider the best restaurant at Disney was created by three of France's most famous chefs: Paul Bocuse, Gaston Lenôtre, and Roger Vergé. Classic escargots, a good starter, are prepared in a casserole with garlic butter; you might follow up with roasted breast of duck and leg confit, or grilled beef tenderloin with black pepper sauce. Make sure you finish with crepes *au chocolat.* The nearby Boulangerie Pâtisserie offers tarts, croissants, éclairs, napoleons, and more, to go. ⊠ *France Pavilion* ☎ *407/939–3463* ⊟ *AE, D, DC, MC, V* ✦ *1:D4.*

FRENCH

Fodor's Choice

★

3

$$ ✕ **Rose & Crown.** If you're an Anglophile and you love a beer so thick you could stand a spoon up in your mug, this is the place to soak up both the suds and British street culture. "Wenches" serve up traditional English fare—fish-and-chips, cottage pie (ground beef with onions, carrots, and peas, topped with Duchess potatoes), and the ever-popular bangers and mash (sausage over mashed potatoes). Potato-and-leek soup or Scotch egg make good appetizers. Vegetarians will even find a tasty vegetarian shepherd's pie. For dessert, try the sticky toffee pudding or lemon pie. The terrace has a splendid view of IllumiNations. ⊠ *United Kingdom* ☎ *407/939–3463* ⊟ *AE, D, DC, MC, V* ✦ *1:D4.*

BRITISH

$$$$ ✕ **Royal Akershus Banquet Hall.** This Norwegian restaurant has become the site of character buffets at all three meals, with an array of Disney princesses, including Ariel, Belle, Jasmine, Snow White, Mulan, Mary Poppins, and even an occasional cameo appearance by Cinderella. The ever-changing Norwegian menu at this restaurant is as extensive as you'll find on this side of the Atlantic. Appetizers are offered buffet style, and usually include herring, goat-milk cheese, peppered mackerel, and gravlax (cured salmon served with mustard sauce) or *fiskepudding* (a seafood mousse with herb dressing). For your main course, chosen à la carte, you might try traditional ground pork and beef *kjottkake* (dumplings), or mustard-glazed seared salmon. Aquavit, wine, and specialty drinks are offered. ⊠ *Norway* ☎ *407/939–3463* ⊟ *AE, D, DC, MC, V* ⌕ *Reservations essential* ✦ *1:D4.*

SCANDINAVIAN

$$–$$$ ✕ **Tokyo Dining and Teppan Edo.** What were once three restaurants in a complex called Mitsukoshi (which is also the name of a giant Tokyo department store) have evolved into two restaurants, **Teppan Edo,** a teppanyaki steak house were chefs do performance cooking at 20 grills, and **Tokyo Dining.** Menu standouts at Teppan Edo include the New York strip, the filet mignon, and the Tori chicken breast. Teppan Edo also has a small sushi selection, and a kids' menu that avoids the typical mac and cheese, and instead offers Teppan-style chicken or shrimp with rice and veggies. Tokyo Dining is the part of the twin-restaurant operation that is more stylish and bustling and specializes in sushi, serving a wider variety than its neighbor, with the addition of tempura dishes like shrimp, scallops, or veggies. Both restaurants have something great to watch: Teppan Edo has the performing chefs; Tokyo Dining has a great view of the Japan pavilion. ⊠ *Japan* ☎ *407/939–3463* ⊟ *AE, D, DC, MC, V* ✦ *1:D4.*

JAPANESE

EPCOT INTERNATIONAL FOOD & WINE FESTIVAL

For six autumn weeks, Epcot hosts the Epcot International Food & Wine Festival, attracting folks more interested in a fine phyllo than a photo op with Cinderella.

(Above) A family digs in at the Epcot International Food & Wine Festival. (Bottom right) Diners at Epcot's Teppan Edo. (Top right) Marinated strawberries with basil served at the Argentina kiosk.

The festival is essentially a compendium of food- and beverage-related offerings, some free with the price of Epcot admission, others costing anywhere from $3 to a few hundred. Guests can attend wine seminars, have cookbooks signed by authors, and sample tapas-sized portions of foods from around the world. And that's just the basics. Throughout the six-week shindig, Disney and guest chefs host brunches, lunches, and wine-pairing dinners at Epcot and in hotels, some posh, others festive, and yet more T-shirt and shorts-friendly. The headliners change annually but might include names like Jacques Torres, Bobby Deen, or Allen Susser. The festival's food and beverage lineup changes annually, but for more information and to make reservations (during festival season only, generally midsummer through early November), call ☎ *407/939–3378* or visit ⊕ *www.disneyworld. com/foodandwine.*

MASTER OF THE HOUSE

Visitors with a serious interest in the fruit of the vine should consider enrolling in one of the festival's Wine School classes, taught by a Master Sommelier (North America has only 103). Each three-hour course focuses on a single subject, such as the wines of a particular region of France, a certain type of varietal, or "Taste Wine Like a Master." Classes conclude with with a food and wine reception.

SHOPPING FOR A SNACK

The heart of the Food & Wine Festival—and the most approachable event for hungry tourists on a budget—takes place around Epcot's World Showcase. Ordinarily a miniature world of 11 pavilions themed around one country apiece, the area takes on new life as 25 "international marketplaces" take up residence.

Each of the 25 marketplaces, from Brazil to Bangkok, offers a taste of one country, selling approximately three appetizer-size food items and a few beverages that pair well—nearly all for $3 to $7 apiece. Indisputably popular creations like the garlicky escargots at the France counter and the cheddar-cheese soup ladled out endlessly at Canada are keepers; regulars might revolt if those were absent at any time. Still, a majority of the menu can change in a given year. Attendees who stop by every autumn might taste Indian potato-onion dosa crepes (with a tart mango lassi drink or a Kingfisher Premium Lager Beer) and Chilean rock shrimp ceviche (with Marques Chardonnay) one time, an Irish fisherman's pie (with Bunratty Meade honey wine) and a Moroccan kefta beef patty (with a tangerine mimosa) another.

At a few marketplaces, a certain item is featured instead of a locale. The Welcome Center, for instance, pours a bounty of bubbly. A cheese marketplace called Mouse Catch generally puts together a good variety of dairy products. And the all-American Hops & Barley Market often specializes in fare U.S. citizens can be proud of, such as New England lobster rolls and Samuel Adams beers.

Lines tend to get very long, especially on weekends when locals pour in for their regular fix of foreign fare, so consider timing your tour in off hours when most spots have shorter waits.

FESTIVAL OF THE SENSES

Every Saturday evening throughout the festival, food and wine enthusiasts clad in cocktail attire saunter into the gala, "Party for the Senses." Billed as a "grand tasting," the bash is a huge all-you-can-eat fancy food fest. In a dramatically decorated, high-ceilinged room, 10 to 15 chefs from around the country host one food station apiece, serving a hearty appetizer-size portion of one passionately prepared dish. Some are Disney chefs eager to show their talents, while others are known nationally. Big names such as François Payard, Allen Susser, and Walter Staib have been known to participate. Wines and beers are poured freely throughout the night, and the display of exquisite cheeses always makes for a tempting snack. Live entertainment such as acrobats and vocalists gives attendees something to watch while taking a break between bites. The price is approximately $135 per person plus park admission.

$$$ ✗ **Tutto Italia.** After a generation as the culinary pillar of the Italy section
ITALIAN at Epcot, L'Originale Alfredo di Roma Ristorante disappeared in summer 2007 and was replaced by Tutto Italia, located in the same building, with the same formality—servers wear white shirts and black ties. Even though typical diners are wearing shorts, a T-shirt, and flip-flops, they're still welcome at the starch-tablecloth-covered tables, where they can enjoy a four-course Italian meal. Offerings include a braised pork shank with polenta and apple gremolata, lobster ravioli with truffled tomato sauce, and spaghetti and meatballs with a slant—these are made with veal and pomodoro sauce. Desserts include mocha tiramisu and cannoli stuffed with chocolate, sweet ricotta, and candied orange. Expect a wait at peak lunch and dinner times; outdoor seating is also available. ⊠ *Italy* ☎ *407/939–3463* ⚖ *Reservations essential* ▤ *AE, D, DC, MC, V* ✛ *1:D4.*

DISNEY'S HOLLYWOOD STUDIOS

The Studios tends to offer more casual American cuisine than the other parks. In other words, it's cheeseburger city. However, there are some good, imaginative offerings, too. There are four ways to book dinner packages that include the Fantasmic! after-dark show: by phone, in person at a Disney hotel, at the park's Guest Services, and at Hollywood Junction.

$$ ✗ **50's Prime Time Café.** Who says you can't go home again? If you grew
AMERICAN up in middle America in the 1950s, just step inside. While *I Love Lucy*
Fodor'sChoice and *The Donna Reed Show* clips play on a television screen, you can
★ feast on meat loaf, pot roast, or fried chicken, all served on a Formica tabletop. At $15, the meat loaf is one of the best inexpensive dinners in any local theme park. Enjoy it with a malted-milk shake or root-beer float (or a bottle of wine). The place offers some fancier dishes, such as olive oil–poached salmon, which are good but out of character with the diner theme. If you're not feeling totally wholesome, go for Dad's Electric Lemonade (rum, vodka, blue curaçao, sweet-and-sour mix, and Sprite), which is worth every bit of the $10.25 price tag. Just like Mother, the menu admonishes, "Don't put your elbows on the table!" ⊠ *Hollywood Blvd.* ☎ *407/939–3463* ▤ *AE, D, DC, MC, V* ✛ *1:C5.*

$$$ ✗ **Hollywood Brown Derby.** At this reproduction of the famous 1940s
AMERICAN Hollywood restaurant, the walls are lined with movie-star caricatures, just as in Tinseltown. The specialty is the Cobb salad, which by legend was invented by Brown Derby founder Robert Cobb; the salad consists of finely chopped lettuce enlivened by loads of tomato, bacon, turkey, blue cheese, chopped egg, and avocado, all tossed table-side. Other menu choices include grilled salmon with spinach and warm bacon vinaigrette; and house-cured duck pastrami with vanilla–white balsamic–melon-pear salad. If you request the Fantasmic! dinner package, make a reservation for no later than two hours before the start of the show. ⊠ *Hollywood Blvd.* ☎ *407/939–3463* ▤ *AE, D, DC, MC, V* ✛ *1:C5.*

$$ ✗ **Mama Melrose's Ristorante Italiano.** To replace the energy you've no
ITALIAN doubt depleted by miles of theme-park walking, you can load up on carbs at this casual Italian restaurant that looks like an old warehouse. Good main courses include Italian sausage served atop rigatoni pasta

with tomato-basil sauce, and grilled tuna with tomato risotto and olive-caper butter. Wood-fired flatbreads are available as an entrée choice here (a great bargain at $12 and up) with toppings ranging from pepperoni to grilled chicken with sun-dried tomato pesto. The sangria, available by the carafe, flows generously. Ask for the Fantasmic! dinner package if you want priority seating for the show. ⊠ *Streets of America* ☎ *407/939–3463* ▭ *AE, D, DC, MC, V* ✛ *1:C5.*

$$–$$$
AMERICAN

✕ **Sci-Fi Dine-In Theater Restaurant.** If you don't mind zombies leering at you while you eat, then head to this enclosed faux drive-in, where you can sit in a fake candy-color '50s convertible and watch trailers from classics like *Attack of the Fifty-Foot Woman* and *Teenagers from Outer Space.* The menu includes choices like slow-roasted barbecue ribs, a beef-and-blue-cheese salad, sautéed shrimp with bow-tie pasta, and a huge Reuben sandwich with fries or melon slices. The hot-fudge sundaes are delicious. ⊠ *Echo Lake* ☎ *407/939–3463* ▭ *AE, D, DC, MC, V* ✛ *1:C5.*

DISNEY'S ANIMAL KINGDOM

Disney's Animal Kingdom is far from a foodie destination, but Disney's highly themed zoo does offer variety, including an African-themed buffet, a Chinese restaurant with table service, and surprises like a tea stand, a fruit market, and picnic lunches packaged to go.

¢–$
FAST FOOD

✕ **Flame Tree Barbecue.** This counter-service eatery is one of the relatively undiscovered gems of Disney's culinary offerings. There's nothing fancy here, but you can dig into ribs, barbecued chicken, and pulled pork and barbecued beef sandwiches with several sauce choices. For something with a lower calorie count, try the smoked turkey served in a multigrain bun, or a great barbecued chicken and crisp green salad with vinaigrette dressing. The outdoor tables, set beneath intricately carved wood pavilions, make great spots for a picnic, and they're not usually crowded. ⊠ *Discovery Island* ▭ *AE, D, DC, MC, V* ✛ *1:A4.*

$$$$
AMERICAN

✕ **Tusker House.** This restaurant offers all-buffet dining three meals a day, starting with a character breakfast (Donald's Safari Breakfast), and lunch and dinner without Donald and his crew. Tusker's offers healthier fare like spice-rubbed rotisserie chicken, curry chicken, carved top sirloin roast, rotisserie pork loin, along with the standard kids' fare like mac and cheese and chicken drumsticks served with mashed potatoes. Prices change seasonally. ⊠ *Harambe* ☎ *407/939–3463* ⌖ *Reservations essential* ▭ *AE, D, DC, MC, V* ✛ *1:A4.*

$$
ASIAN

✕ **Yak & Yeti.** The location of this pan-Asian cuisine, sit-down eatery—the only full-service restaurant inside Disney's Animal Kingdom—certainly makes sense. It's just at the entrance to the Asia section, in a two-story, 250-seat building that is pleasantly faux-Asian, with cracked plaster walls, wood carvings, and tile mosaic tabletops. Standout entrées include the roast duckling with orange-wasabi, and the tempura shrimp with coconut-ginger rice and plum sauce. Also tasty, if not authentically Asian, are the baby back ribs with a hoisin barbecue sauce and sweet chili slaw. ⊠ *Disney's Animal Kingdom* ☎ *407/939–3463* ▭ *AE, D, DC, MC, V* ✛ *1:A4.*

DOWNTOWN DISNEY

Downtown Disney is a shopping and dining complex that is broken into three sections: Marketplace, which is known more for its shopping but boasts quite an array of restaurants; Pleasure Island, originally a nightlife complex that now has some over-the-top themed eateries; and West Side, with its enviable lineup of dining spots plus entertainment venues. There is no cover charge to enter any part of Downtown Disney.

$$
AMERICAN

✕ **House of Blues.** You're unlikely to like this place unless you enjoy listening to high-decibel music during your meal. But if you do, this is a great place to chow down from an eclectic menu that offers everything from baby back ribs to shrimp and scallop diablo, to a tasty and healthy Thai salad with chicken skewers and Thai noodles. The smoked pulled-pork sandwich with Jim Beam barbecue sauce is a great menu mainstay item, as is the brick-oven pizza. A worthy dessert is the white-chocolate banana-bread pudding. The Gospel Sunday Brunch offers a Southern cooking buffet and live gospel music. Reservations are available only for Sunday brunch. ⊠ *West Side* ☎ *407/934–2583* ⊕ *www.houseofblues. com* ☰ *AE, D, DC, MC, V* ✛ *1:F4.*

$$$
AMERICAN

✕ **Olivia's Café.** This is like a meal at Grandma's—provided she lives in Key West and likes to gussy up her grub with trendy twists. The menu ranges from fennel-dusted grouper with black beans and rice to grilled pork chops with chipotle barbecue sauce and smoked-cheddar grits. Desserts are indulgent, such as the banana-bread-pudding sundae with bananas Foster topping and vanilla ice cream. The outdoor seating, which overlooks a waterway, is a nice place to dine any time the midsummer's heat is not bearing down. ⊠ *Old Key West Resort* ☎ *407/939–3463* ☰ *AE, D, DC, MC, V* ✛ *1:E3.*

$$$
IRISH

✕ **Raglan Road Irish Pub.** Some would argue that the phrase "authentic Irish pub at Disney's Pleasure Island" is oxymoronic, particularly when that pub seats 600 people. But if Irish grub's your thing, Raglan's is on target: the shepherd's pie is higher quality than the usual version, prepared with beef and lamb and jazzed up with house spices. And you don't have to settle for plain fish-and-chips here (though you can for $17); there's also panfried lemon sole and chips. Three massive and ornate bars, all imported from Ireland and all more than a century old, help anchor the pub. The entertainment alone makes this place worth the visit. A good, four-person Irish house band, Tuskar Rock, performs nightly, as does Danielle Fitzpatrick, herself an Irish import, who performs lively folk dances on stage each evening. ⊠ *Pleasure Island* ☎ *407/938–0300* ⊕ *www.raglanroadirishpub.com* ☰ *AE, D, MC, V* ✛ *1:F4.*

$$$–$$$$
AMERICAN

✕ **Wolfgang Puck.** There are lots of choices here, from wood-oven pizza at the informal Puck Express to fine-dining meals in the upstairs formal Dining Room. There's also a sushi bar and an informal café; the café is quite literally a happy medium, and may be the best bet for families hoping for a bit of elegance without the pressure of a formal dinner. At Express try the barbecue chicken, or spinach and mushroom pizza. At the café, midprice entrées like bacon-wrapped meat loaf, and pumpkin ravioli with brown butter sauce, fried sage, and port wine glaze are winners, and you can always try the pizza pie that made

An evening at Victoria & Albert's.

Puck famous: smoked salmon with dill cream, red onion, chili oil, and chives. The Dining Room always offers inspired entrées like lobster risotto with lemon preserve. Three- and four-course menus are priced at $50 and $60, respectively. ✉ *West Side* ☎ *407/938–9653* ⊕ *www.wolfgangpuckorlando.com* ▭ *AE, DC, MC, V* ✢ *1:F4.*

DISNEY'S BOARDWALK

This pedestrian-friendly retail and entertainment area is lined with a variety of good eateries. It becomes liveliest in the evenings.

$$ ✕ **Big River Grille & Brewing Works**. Strange but good brews, like Pale
AMERICAN Rocket Red Ale, Southern Flyer Light Lager, and Gadzooks Pilsner, abound here at Walt Disney World's only microbrewery. You can dine inside among the giant copper brewing tanks, or sip your suds outside on the lake-view patio. The menu emphasizes meat and fish, with pork ribs slow-cooked in red barbecue sauce, a flame-grilled meat loaf made with ground beef and Italian sausage, and grilled Atlantic salmon fillet with dill butter. The garlic–mashed potatoes are a perfect accompaniment. ✉ *Disney's BoardWalk* ☎ *407/560–0253* ⊕ *www.bigrivergrille.com* ▭ *AE, D, DC, MC, V* ✢ *1:C4.*

$ ✕ **ESPN Club**. Not only can you watch sports on a big-screen TV here
AMERICAN (the restaurant has 108 monitors), but you can also periodically see ESPN programs being taped in the club itself and be part of the audience of sports-radio talk shows. Food ranges from an outstanding half-pound burger, made with Angus chuck, to an excellent Reuben with plenty of corned beef, sauerkraut, and cheese. If you want an appetizer, try the Macho Nachos, crispy corn tortilla chips piled high with spicy

ili, shredded cheddar cheese, sour cream, spicy salsa, and sliced jalapeños. This place is open quite late by Disney standards—until 2 AM on Friday and Saturday. Beware, the place can be pretty loud during any broadcast sports event, especially football games. ⊠ *Disney's Board-Walk* ☎ 407/939–5100 ▭ *AE, D, DC, MC, V* ✥ *1:C4.*

$$$$
SEAFOOD

✕ **Flying Fish.** One of Disney's better restaurants, Flying Fish is whimsically decorated with murals along the upper portion of the walls paying tribute to Atlantic seaboard spots of the early 1900s. This is a place where you put on your "resort casual" duds to "dine," as opposed to putting on your flip-flops and shorts to "chow down." The chefs take the food so seriously that the entire culinary team takes day trips to local farms to learn their foodstuffs' origins. Flying Fish's best dishes include potato-wrapped red snapper, which is so popular it has been on the menu for several years, and oak-grilled Bay of Fundy salmon. ⊠ *Disney's BoardWalk* ☎ 407/939–2359 ▭ *AE, D, DC, MC, V* ◷ *No lunch* ✥ *1:C4.*

$$$
MEDITERRANEAN

✕ **Kouzzina by Cat Cora.** Celebrity-chef Cat Cora and Disney joined forces in 2009 to open an upbeat family-oriented Greek restaurant along the BoardWalk. From an exhibition *kouzzina* (Greek for kitchen), the culinary team puts out hearty portions of Cora's family favorites, including the familiar starter *spanakopita* (spinach pie) and an amazing side dish of brussels sprouts sautéed with lemon and capers. Entrées range from a sweet cinnamon-stewed chicken to a whole fish panroasted with braised greens, olives, fennel, and smoked chili. Be sure to get a refreshing, sweet, coffee frappé to go with your *loukoumades* (donuts with warm honey) or Greek cookies. ⊠ *Disney's BoardWalk* ☎ 407/939–3463 ▭ *AE, D, DC, MC, V* ✥ *1:C4.*

WDW RESORTS

$$$$
AMERICAN

✕ **Artist Point.** If you're not a guest at the Wilderness Lodge, a meal here is worth it just to see the giant totem poles and huge rock fireplace in the lobby. The specialty at this restaurant, which specializes in the foods of the American Northwest, is cedar-plank salmon, served sometimes with sourdough bread dumpling, broccolini, and mulled-red-wine brown butter (worth its $34 price tag). There's a good Northwestern U.S. wine list, and a wine-pairing option for an additional cost. ⊠ *Wilderness Lodge* ☎ 407/939–3463 ◿ *Reservations essential* ▭ *AE, D, DC, MC, V* ✥ *1:C1.*

$$$$
AFRICAN
Fodor's Choice
★

✕ **Boma—Flavors of Africa.** Boma takes Western-style ingredients and prepares them with an African twist—then invites guests to walk through an African marketplace–style dining room to help themselves at the extraordinary buffet. The dozen or so serving stations have entrées such as roasted pork, chicken, beef, and fish served with tamarind and other robust sauces; intriguing salads; and some of the best hummus this side of the Atlantic. Don't pass up the soups, as the hearty chicken corn porridge is excellent. The zebra dome dessert is chocolate mousse covered with white chocolate and striped with dark chocolate. All meals are prix fixe, and prices change seasonally. The South African wine list is outstanding. ⊠ *Disney's Animal Kingdom Lodge* ☎ 407/939–3463 ◿ *Reservations essential* ▭ *AE, D, DC, MC, V* ◷ *No lunch* ✥ *1:A5.*

$$–$$$ ✕ **California Grill.** The view of the surrounding Disney parks from this
AMERICAN 15th-floor restaurant is as stunning as the food, especially at night,
when you can watch the nightly Magic Kingdom fireworks from the
dining room. The menu changes regularly, but choices might include
seared bison with white corn–and-mushroom "risotto," turnips, chest-
nuts, and pinot noir–juniper emulsion; or handmade cavatelli pasta with
wild mushrooms, buttercup squash, winter kale, and truffle-mascar-
pone cream. ⊠ *Contemporary Resort* ☎ *407/939–3463* ⚓ *Reservations
essential* ⊟ *AE, D, DC, MC, V* ✛ *1:B1.*

$$$$ ✕ **Chef Mickey's.** This is the holy shrine for character meals, with Mickey,
AMERICAN Minnie, or Goofy around for breakfast and dinner—it's not a quiet spot
to read the *Orlando Sentinel*. Folks come here for entertainment and
comfort food. The breakfast buffet includes omelets cooked to order,
mountains of pancakes, and even a breakfast pizza. The dinner buffet
doesn't disappoint with prime rib, baked ham, and changing specials
like beef tips with mushrooms or tamarind-glazed salmon. Finish off
your meal at the all-you-can-eat dessert bar of sundaes and chocolate
cake. ⊠ *Contemporary Resort* ☎ *407/939–3463* ⊟ *AE, D, DC, MC,
V* ✛ *1:B1.*

$$$$ ✕ **Citricos.** Although the name implies that you might be eating lots
ECLECTIC of local citrus-flavor specialties, you won't necessarily find them here,
although citrus fruit is woven in subtly, in drinks like the "Citropolitan"
martini, infused with lemon-and-lime liqueur, and in tropical-fruit crème
brûlée for dessert. But you will find an ambitious menu that's funda-
mentally American with influences of Europe's low-fat, high-flavor cuisines, namely Tuscan, Provençal, and Spanish-Mediterranean. Standout
entrées include oak-grilled swordfish with fingerling potatoes, roasted
fennel tossed with applewood-smoked bacon and violet-mustard cream;
and braised veal shank with carrot-potato puree, roasted vegetables,
and toasted citrus gremolata. The wine list, one of Disney's most
extensive, includes vintages from around the world. ⊠ *Grand Floridian* ☎ *407/939–3463* ⚓ *Reservations essential* ⊟ *AE, D, DC, MC, V*
✛ *1:A1.*

$$$$ ✕ **Jiko.** The name of this restaurant means "the cooking place" in Swa-
AFRICAN hili, and it is certainly that. The dining area surrounds two big, wood-
Fodor's Choice burning ovens and a grill area where you can watch cooks in North
★ African–style caps working on your meal. The menu here is more African-inspired than purely African, but does include authentic entrées like
Swahili curry shrimp from an East African recipe and short ribs with
a Kenyan coffee-barbecue sauce. The menu changes periodically, but
typically includes entrées such as maize-crusted wreckfish with tomato-
butter sauce, and chicken with goat-cheese potatoes, preserved lemon,
and harissa. The restaurant offers more than 65 wines by the glass,
including a large selection of African vintages. And if you want to have
a private party (for up to 40 people), the wine room decorated with
African sculptures is the place to have it. ⊠ *Disney's Animal Kingdom
Lodge* ☎ *407/939–3463* ⚓ *Reservations essential* ⊟ *AE, D, DC, MC,
V* ☾ *No lunch* ✛ *1:A5.*

$ ✕ **Kimonos.** Knife-wielding sushi chefs prepare world-class sushi and
JAPANESE sashimi but also other Japanese treats like soups and salads at this sleek

3

hotel sushi bar, where dark teak woods dominate the decor and servers wear kimonos. Popular rolls include the Dragon Roll (giant shrimp, tuna, and avocado), Dancing Eel Roll (crab, avocado, and eel), and the Bagel Roll (smoked salmon, cream cheese, and scallion). Cocktails are a draw here, too, along with entertainment in the form of nightly karaoke. ⊠ *Walt Disney World Swan* ☎ *407/934–3000* ⊟ *AE, D, DC, MC, V* ⊗ *No lunch* ✛ *1:C4.*

$$$$
SEAFOOD
✕ **Narcoossee's.** The dining room, with Victorian-style columns, high ceilings, and hardwood floors, makes a great place not only to enjoy great steaks and seafood, but to gaze out the windows at the nightly fireworks shows over the Seven Seas Lagoon. (The restaurant has its own elegant style, and its managers expect your wardrobe to have that quality too—no shorts or flip-flops.) Among the best menu choices are the grilled salmon with shrimp risotto, or the surf-and-turf centerpiece: Maine lobster and a tender filet mignon. The name of the place, incidentally, was not a word coined by Disney Imagineers—it's the name of a river and a small Central Florida town, both of which predate Disney. ⊠ *Grand Floridian Resort* ☎ *407/939–3463* ⊟ *AE, D, DC, MC, V* ✛ *1:A1.*

$$
AFRICAN
Fodor's Choice
★
✕ **Sanaa.** Most of the flavors are from India, yet Sanaa is really a celebration of the Spice Islands—locales off the coast of Africa that for centuries hosted traders from the world's corners. Exotic yet approachable lunches and dinners make Sanaa a true find on the outer edges of the Disney empire; views of zebras and giraffes right out the picture windows are another draw. Mustard seed–crusted scallops and pulled duck with red curry sauce are good starters. For the main course, be sure to try the shrimp in green curry sauce—only spicy upon request. ⊠ *Disney's Animal Kingdom Villas* ☎ *407/989–3463* ⊟ *AE, D, DC, MC V* ✛ *1:A5*

$$$$
STEAK
✕ **Shula's Steak House.** The hardwood floors, dark-wood paneling, and pictures of former Miami Dolphins coach Don Shula make this restaurant resemble an annex of the NFL Hall of Fame. Among the best selections are the porterhouse and prime rib. Finish the 48-ounce porterhouse and you get a signed picture of coach Don Shula, plus your name will be displayed on a virtual plaque on the restaurant's Web site. If you're not a carnivore, go for the Norwegian salmon, the Florida snapper, or the huge (up to 4 pounds) Maine lobster. ⊠ *Walt Disney World Dolphin* ☎ *407/934–1362* ⊟ *AE, D, DC, MC, V* ⊗ *No lunch* ✛ *1:C4.*

$$$$
AMERICAN
Fodor's Choice
★
✕ **Todd English's bluezoo.** Celebrity-chef Todd English oversees this cutting-edge seafood eatery, a sleek, modern restaurant that resembles an underwater dining hall, with blue walls and carpeting, aluminum fish suspended from the ceiling, and bubblelike lighting fixtures. The menu is creative and pricey, with entrées like the 2-pound Maine "Cantonese lobster," fried and tossed in a sticky soy glaze; and Florida grouper with black-truffle spaetzle, black radish, and black-truffle vinaigrette. If you don't care for fish, alternatives include salted, braised pork loin with apple kraut, German potato, and apple-mustard glaze. The pear mille-feuille—caramelized puff pastry with poached pears and vanilla ice cream, topped with caramel whipped cream and tonka-bean

Continued on page 167

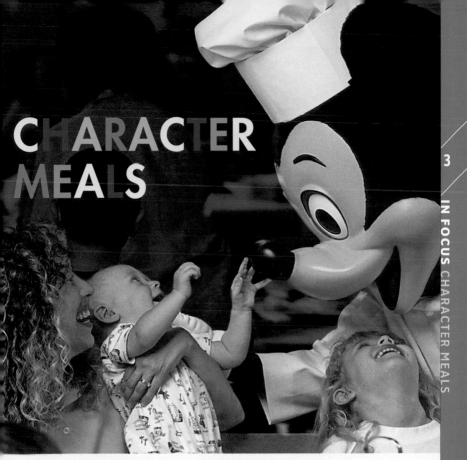

CHARACTER MEALS

Little ones get personal attention from Mickey Mouse at Chef Mickey's.

Character meals are larger-than-life experiences that might be the high point of your child's visit to Walt Disney World or Universal. Mickey, Minnie, Spidey, and more come alive and welcome your kids as if they were old friends. By Joseph Hayes

These meals, ranging from Alice in Wonderland–themed tea parties to Mickey Mouse–hosted barbecues (and everything in between) are unique, one-on-one opportunities where characters pose for pictures and engage with the little ones. Kids adore hugging or getting an autograph from their favorites; even tots who may be shy at first, will usually warm up to their most-loved character.

Here we give our picks for the best character breakfast, lunch, and dinner options at both Walt Disney World and Universal, and provide a comprehensive chart, listing all dining experiences for every budget, location, and character preference. Choose the meal that's best for your family, and watch as your youngsters go giddy over meeting Cinderella or Scooby Doo.

BREAKFAST: TOP PICKS

WDW

PRINCESS STORYBOOK DINING at Akershus Royal Banquet Hall, Epcot. Belle, Jasmine, Snow White, the Little Mermaid's Ariel and many more princesses could appear at this medieval castle-styled Norwegian building. $37.26 adult; $22.35 child.

CHEF MICKEY'S FUN TIME BUFFET, Disney's Contemporary Resort. Kids love seeing the monorail pass overhead while greeting the Big Cheese. Chef Mickey's Buffet combines space-age Disney styling with Mickey Mouse, Donald, and the gang, plus the ever-popular Mickey-shaped waffles. $30.88 adult; $17.03 child.

'OHANA'S BEST FRIENDS BREAKFAST WITH LILO & STITCH, Disney's Polynesian Resort. The intergalactic Stitch and his human friend, Lilo, join your family in a tropical setting for this very popular breakfast. Every 30 minutes, Mickey and Pluto join in while kids parade around the restaurant with maracas and wide grins. $19 adult; $11 child.

UNIVERSAL

CONFISCO GRILLE, Islands of Adventure. Young explorers love breakfast with The Cat in the Hat and Spider-Man at Universal's Islands of Adventure for its motley crew of characters. The Simpsons; Scooby Doo; Cat In The Hat, Spider-Man, and beasts from Whoville can show up at any time. Sun. and Thurs.; $17.95 adult; $11.95 child, plus park admission.

Bibbidi Bobbidi Boutique rolls out the welcome mat for boys with its "Cool Dude" treatment.

DRESS UP

If your little ones want to look like a princess when meeting a princess, head to **The Bibbidi Bobbidi Boutique** (407/939–7895) in the World of Disney Store at Downtown Disney's Marketplace, where little girls can transform into fairytale princesses or pop divas. There's also a branch right in **Cinderella Castle**. Boys can get their buccaneer on at **The Pirates League** (407/939–2739), next to the Pirates of the Caribbean ride, with costumes, eye patches, and gold teeth. Bibbidi Bobbidi Boutique packages range from **$49.95–$189.95**; Pirates League, **$29.95**.

Prices for meals at Disney are prepaid and include tax.

BREAKFAST OPTIONS

CHARACTER MEAL	LOCATION	POSSIBLE CHARACTERS	PRICES; ADULT/CHILD	HOURS
WALT DISNEY WORLD				
Cinderella's Royal Table	Cinderella Castle, Magic Kingdom	Cinderella, the Royal family, Jasmine, Sleeping Beauty, Snow White, Belle	$49.65*/$32.22*	Daily
Princess Storybook Dining	Akershus Royal Banquet Hall, Norway Pavilion, Epcot	Ariel, Belle, Jasmine, Snow White, Aurora, Mulan, Alice, and Mary Poppins	$37.26/$22.35	Daily
Chef Mickey's Fun Time Buffet	Disney's Contemporary Resort	Mickey, Minnie, Goofy, Pluto and Donald	$30.88/$17.03	Daily
Donald's Safari Breakfast	Tusker House Restaurant, Animal Kingdom	Donald, Daisy, Goofy, Mickey	$19/$11	Daily
'Ohana's Best Friends Breakfast with Lilo & Stitch	Disney's Polynesian Resort	Mickey, Pluto, Lilo, Stitch	$19/$11	Daily
Supercalifragilistic Breakfast	1900 Park Fare at Disney's Grand Floridian	Mary Poppins, Alice, Mad Hatter	$25/$14	Daily
Beach Club Breakfast Buffet	Cape May Café at Disney's Yacht and Beach Club Resorts	Goofy, Donald	$19/$11	Daily
Playhouse Disney's Play 'n Dine	Hollywood & Vine, Disney's Hollywood Studios	Jo Jo and Goliath, June and Leo, Playhouse Pals	$27/$15	Daily
A Buffet with Character	Crystal Palace, Magic Kingdom Adventureland	Winnie the Pooh, Tigger, Eeyore, Piglet	$26.62/$14.09	Daily
Good Morning Character Breakfast	Garden Grove at Walt Disney World Swan Resort	Goofy, Pluto	$19/$12	Sat., Sun.
Watercress Café Character Breakfast	Buena Vista Palace Resort	Minnie, Pluto, Goofy	$24/$13	Sun.
Covington Mill Character Breakfast	Hilton in the Walt Disney World Resort	Mickey, Minnie	a la carte	Sun.
UNIVERSAL				
Universal Orlando Character Dining	Confisco Grill, Universal Islands of Adventure	The Simpsons, the Scooby Doo gang, Cat In The Hat, Spider-Man, and beasts from Whoville	$17.95*/$11.95*	Sun., Thurs.

*Plus park admission

3

IN FOCUS CHARACTER MEALS

LUNCH (OR TEA): TOP PICKS

WDW

PLAYHOUSE DISNEY'S PLAY 'N DINE, Disney's Hollywood Studios. The Hollywood & Vine Restaurant brings Disney Channel stars to life. JoJo and Goliath from *JoJo's Circus*, and June and Leo from Disney's *Little Einsteins* march around the room, singing and dancing to the delight of their energetic fans. This is a great choice for toddlers. $27 adult; $15 child.

A BUFFET WITH CHARACTER AT THE CRYSTAL PALACE, Magic Kingdom. A lovely Victorian setting is the perfect place for the old-fashioned and lovable Winnie the Pooh and friends to greet your kids. This is the only meal where you can find characters from the Hundred Acre Wood. Lunch includes upscale goodies for adults, and a separate kids buffet featuring pizza and mac 'n cheese. $28.72 adult; $15.97 child.

MY DISNEY GIRL'S PERFECTLY PRINCESS TEA PARTY, Disney's Grand Floridian Resort. Girls ages 3 to 11 enjoy the princess experience with Mom (or Dad). Dressing up is encouraged, and lunch, featuring tea and sandwiches, is served on china plates (apple juice and peanut butter for the little darlings; cheeses and finger sandwiches for adults). Princess Aurora (Sleeping Beauty herself) may make an appearance. Little ones receive a special Disney Girl Princess doll, jewelry, and a photo scrapbook; a nice parting gift considering the hefty price. $89.54 adult; $174.75 child.

Leo (from the *Little Einsteins*) pictured here at Disney's Hollywood studios

TEA PARTY

Tea and Mad Hatter reigns at the Wonderland Tea Party. A kids-only affair (Moms, take a stroll through the Grand Floridian Hotel or book a massage at its Spa), "tea" consists of apple juice and cupcakes served by a very silly Hatter (the girls love him) and Alice (girls dress like her). Dress-up is encouraged but not required. Games and stories fill the hour for approximately 25 attendees from ages 4 to 12, and autographed photos are the parting gift. $42.60 child.

Alice at Wonderland Tea Party

Prices for meals at Disney are prepaid and include tax.

WDW LUNCH OPTIONS

CHARACTER MEAL	LOCATION	POSSIBLE CHARACTERS	PRICES; ADULT/ CHILD	HOURS
Princess Storybook Dining	Akershus Royal Banquet Hall, Norway Pavilion, Epcot	Ariel, Belle, Jasmine, Snow White, Princess Aurora, Mulan, Alice, Mary Poppins	$39.39/23.42	Daily
Cinderella's Royal Table	Cinderella Castle, Magic Kingdom	Jasmine, Sleeping Beauty, Snow White, and Belle	$53.38/$33.46	Daily
Playhouse Disney's Play 'n Dine	Hollywood & Vine, Disney's Hollywood Studios	JoJo and Goliath (*JoJo's Circus*), and June and Leo from Disney's *Little Einsteins*	$27/$15	Daily
A Buffet with Character	Crystal Palace, Magic Kingdom Adventureland	Winnie the Pooh, Tigger, Eeyore, Piglet	$28.72/$15.97	Daily
TEA PARTIES				
My Disney Girl's Perfectly Princess Tea Party	Grand Floridian Hotel	Princess Aurora, Rose Petal	$84.54/$174.75	Weds., Thurs., Fri.
Wonderland Tea Party	Grand Floridian Hotel	Mad Hatter, Alice	$42.60 child	Daily

Sleeping beauty, Ariel and Cinderella's mouse at Akershus Royal Banquet Hall.

DINNER: TOP PICKS

WDW

MICKEY'S BACKYARD BBQ at the Fort Wilderness Resort. This dinner show has everything from dancing and foot-stomping country music, to finger-food goodies like hotdogs and fried chicken. Cowboy Mickey Mouse is the star of the show. Thurs. and Sat., Mar.–Dec; $50.99 adult; $29.99 child.

CINDERELLA'S HAPPILY EVER AFTER DINNER at Disney's Grand Floridian Resort. A dinner buffet of worldly cuisine is complete with Cinderella, Prince Charming, and their family (including the wicked steps) making the rounds. $36 adult; $18 child.

UNIVERSAL

TRATTORIA DEL PORTO, Loews Portofino Bay Hotel. Delectable Italian cuisine will please parents, while Shrek and Scooby Doo distract the kids. Characters appear on Friday nights between 6:30 and 9:30 PM, coinciding with Bambino Pasta Cucina, when young ones can make their own pasta. Pricing is à la carte.

THE KITCHEN, Hard Rock Hotel at Universal Orlando. Spider-Man and Dr. Seuss characters appear on Saturdays from 6 to 9 PM. The special child-only Kids' Crib area, supplies crayons and cartoon videos, allowing parents to have a break while everyone enjoys their meals. Pricing is à la carte.

Prices for meals at Disney are prepaid and include tax.

Above, Ariel pictured at Cinderella's Royal Table signing autographs. Below, Cinderella at Cinderella Castle.

THE HARDEST TICKET IN TOWN

The magic of fairy tale has never been better realized than at **Cinderella Castle**, where the presence of Princess Charming herself makes this the hottest character meal ticket in Disney-town. With only 130 seats for breakfast, lunch, or dinner, reservations are scarce. Cinderella greets your family in the Castle lobby, pictures (included in the price) are taken, then you are whisked up to your table, where Fairy Godmother and Wicked Step-sisters alike stop chairside to chat and sign autographs.

DINNER OPTIONS

CHARACTER MEAL	LOCATION	POSSIBLE CHARACTERS	PRICES; ADULT/CHILD	HOURS
WALT DISNEY WORLD				
Mickey's Backyard BBQ	Fort Wilderness Resort	Mickey, Minnie, and friends	$50.99/$29.99	Thurs. and Sat., Mar.–Dec.
Cinderella's Happily Ever After Dinner	Grand Floridian Resort	Cinderella, Prince Charming, and Step-sisters	$36/$18	Daily
Cinderella's Royal Table	Cinderella Castle, Magic Kingdom	Cinderella, the Royal family, Jasmine, Sleeping Beauty, Snow White, Belle	$59.61/$35.95	Daily
Chip 'n' Dale's Harvest Feast	Garden Grill, Epcot	Mickey, Chip 'n' Dale, Pluto	$37.27/$18.10	Daily
Princess Storybook Dining	Akershus Royal Banquet Hall, Norway Pavilion, Epcot	Ariel, Belle, Jasmine, Snow White, Princess Aurora, Mulan, Alice, Mary Poppins	$44.72/$24.48	Daily
A Buffet with Character	Crystal Palace, Magic Kingdom Adventureland	Winnie the Pooh, Tigger, Eeyore, Piglet	$39.40/$19.16	Daily
Character Dinner	Garden Grove at Walt Disney World Swan Resort	Goofy, Pluto	$18.99/$11.99	Daily
Chef Mickey's Fun Time Buffet	Disney's Contemporary Resort	Mickey, Donald, Minnie	$38.33/$19.16	Daily
UNIVERSAL				
Universal Orlando Character Dining	Trattoria del Porto at Loews Portofino Bay Hotel	Shrek, Scooby Doo	a la carte	Fri.
Universal Orlando Character Dining	The Kitchen at Hard Rock Hotel	Spiderman, Dr. Seuss characters	a la carte	Sat.
Universal Orlando Character Dining	Loews Royal Pacific Resort	Scooby Doo, Woody Woodpecker, Shrek	a la carte	Tues., Sat.

Above, Mickey's Backyard BBQ; Left, JoJo at Disney's Hollywood Studios

3

IN FOCUS CHARACTER MEALS

FAQ

Belle making friends at Cinderella's Royal Table.

■ **How do I make reservations?** Call Disney's Dining Reservation Center at ☎ 407/939-3463 for meals at Disney properties, or check the Disney Dining website at ⊕ www.disney-world.com/dining. Universal reservations can be made at ☎ 407/224-9255 (theme parks and CityWalk) or ☎ 407/503-3463 (hotels), or online at ⊕ www.universalorlando.com. Resort hotels can be contacted individually; many don't require reservations. Check for last minute cancellations; walking up to the podium and asking for an available table will often bring results.

■ **How far in advance should I book a character meal?** At Disney, reservation dates open 180 days in advance and go very quickly. Disney Resort hotel vacationers can book 180 days from the start of their stay rather than the actual desired date, giving them an edge. The most popular meals require a credit card deposit at the time of reservation, which may be charged if cancelled less than 48 hours in advance. Universal character meals, which are

relatively easy to get, usually require 30 to 90 days advance booking.

■ **How do I know which characters will be at the meal?** You don't. Cast-members change daily, and all anyone can offer is that you may see a certain list of characters, but usually not all of them. Characters tend to be site-specific and you will see most of the princesses at the castle at any one time.

■ **Are all meals prix-fixe, and what are the different types of meals offered? Buffet, family-style, pre-plated?** Most breakfasts are all-you-can-eat buffets; certain offerings are family-style table service and may be easier for parties if you have multiple children. Lunches are both buffet and family style; most dinners are buffet or pre-plated. Prices for meals at the Disney parks include tax.

■ **What should I bring to a character meal?** Don't forget your own camera, autograph book and a large Sharpie (it's hard to handle a tiny pen with big gloves).

ice cream—is worth its $14 price tag. ⊠ *Walt Disney World Dolphin* ☎ *407/934–1111* ⊕ *www.thebluezoo.com* ☰ *AE, D, DC, MC, V* ☺ *No lunch* ✛ *1:C4.*

$$$$
CONTINENTAL
Fodor's Choice
★

✕ **Victoria & Albert's.** At this ultraposh award-winning Disney restaurant, two servers dressed in his-and-hers Victorian costumes anticipate your every need. This is one of the plushest fine-dining experiences in Florida—a regal meal in a tasteful Victorian-style room—a space so sophisticated that children under 10 aren't on the guest list. The six-course, prix-fixe menu changes daily. Appetizer choices might include chorizo-crusted duck, or walnut oil–seared duck with hearts of palm and cheese fondue; entrées may be Florida black grouper with artichokes, fennel, leeks, and *jamón Ibérico* (Spanish ham), or Kurobuta pork tenderloin and belly with beets and sherry-bacon vinaigrette. For most of the year, there are two seatings, at 5:45 and 9 PM. In July and August, however, there's generally just one seating at 6:30 PM. Make your reservations at least 90 and up to 180 days in advance. Disney considers this the biggest of the big-deal restaurants on the property, and most longtime Disney World fans do, too. ⊠ *Grand Floridian* ☎ *407/939–3862* ⚑ *Reservations essential* ⓜ *Jacket required* ☰ *AE, D, DC, MC, V* ☺ *No lunch* ✛ *1:A1.*

$$$$
STEAK

✕ **Yachtsman Steak House.** Aged grain-fed beef, the attraction at this casual steak house in the ultrapolished Yacht and Beach Club, can be seen mellowing in the glassed-in butcher shop near the entryway. The chefs are proud of their beef here, and the quality seems to prove it. Meats are hand-cut on the premises. The 12-ounce New York strip with peppercorn-brandy sauce and potato gratin is quite tasty, but at $42, it's not soft on your wallet. You can also try a cowboy steak, filet mignon, porterhouse—or lamb, chicken, rainbow trout, or the vegetarian potato-and-leek ravioli. An artisanal cheese platter and nice selections of dessert wines and scotches round out the menu. ⊠ *Yacht and Beach Club* ☎ *407/939–3463* ☰ *AE, D, DC, MC, V* ☺ *No lunch* ✛ *1:C1.*

UNIVERSAL ORLANDO AREA

With dozens of restaurants, including the world's largest Hard Rock Cafe, Universal Orlando is a culinary force. Islands of Adventure has from one to six eateries—not all of them strictly burgers-and-fries affairs—in each of its lands. Universal Studios Florida has yet more places for lunch and dinner. And at CityWalk, a dining-retail-entertainment complex that you have to pass as you leave the two theme parks, you'll find even more tempting eateries.

UNIVERSAL STUDIOS

Behind-the-scenes movie action is the theme at Universal Studio Florida, and dining options are purposely cliché versions of restaurants you might see on the silver screen: an old-fashioned Italian joint, a '50s drive-in, an Irish pub, and a seafood house, for example. Be sure to

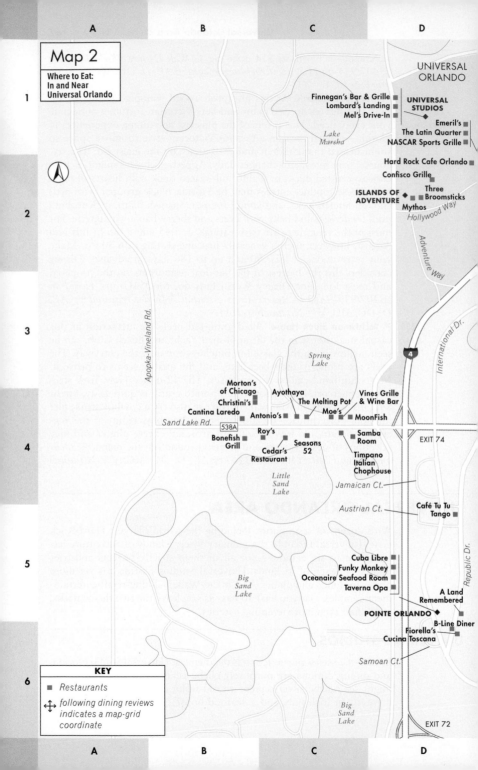

Map 2

**Where to Eat:
In and Near
Universal Orlando**

**UNIVERSAL
ORLANDO**

A **B** **C** **D**

1

Finnegan's Bar & Grille ■
Lombard's Landing ■
Mel's Drive-In ■

**UNIVERSAL
STUDIOS** ◆
Emeril's ■
The Latin Quarter ■
NASCAR Sports Grille ■

Hard Rock Cafe Orlando ■

Confisco Grille ■

*Lake
Marsha*

**ISLANDS OF
ADVENTURE** ◆ ■ ■ Three
■ Broomsticks
Mythos

Hollywood Way

2

Adventure Way

3

*Spring
Lake*

[4] **4**

International Dr.

Morton's
of Chicago ■
Christini's ■ ■

Ayothaya ■
The Melting Pot ■

Vines Grille
& Wine Bar ■

Cantina Laredo ■

Antonio's ■ ■
Moe's ■

■ MoonFish

Sand Lake Rd.

538A

Roy's ■

4

Bonefish
Grill ■

Cedar's
Restaurant ■

Seasons
52 ■

■ Samba
Room

*Little
Sand
Lake*

Timpano
Italian
Chophouse

EXIT 74

Jamaican Ct.

Republic Dr.

Austrian Ct. ■ Café Tu Tu
Tango ■

5

*Big
Sand
Lake*

Cuba Libre ■
Funky Monkey ■
Oceanaire Seafood Room ■
Taverna Opa ■

A Land
Remembered ■

POINTE ORLANDO ◆ ■

B-Line Diner ■

Fiorella's ■
Cucina Toscana

Samoan Ct.

6

Apopka-Vineland Rd.

KEY

■ *Restaurants*

✛ *following dining reviews
indicates a map-grid
coordinate*

*Big
Sand
Lake*

EXIT 72

A **B** **C** **D**

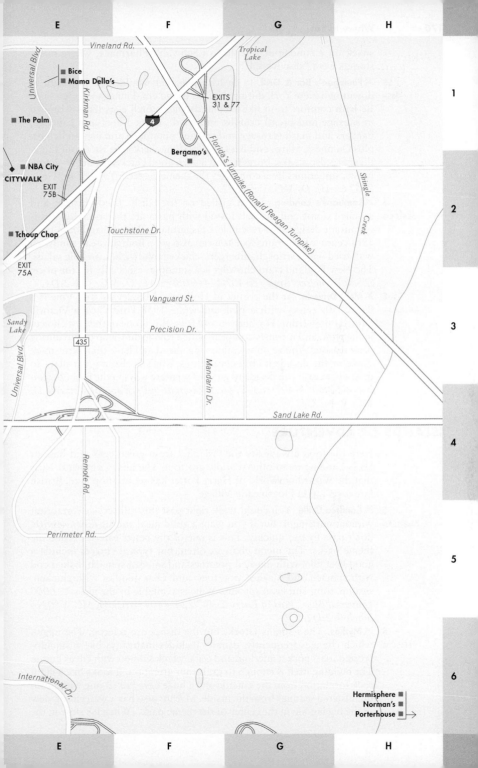

snack on a sundae at a replica of Schwab's Pharmacy, where many starlets were "discovered."

$$
IRISH
✗**Finnegan's Bar & Grill.** In an Irish pub that would look just right in downtown New York during the Ellis Island era, Finnegan's offers classic Irish comfort food like shepherd's pie, Scotch eggs (eggs wrapped in sausage and bread crumbs and fried), corned beef and cabbage, bangers and mash (sausage and mashed potatoes), and fish-and-chips, plus Guinness, Harp, and Bass on tap. If shepherd's pie isn't your thing, there are also steaks, burgers, and a darn good chicken salad. Irish folk music, sometimes live, completes the theme. ✉ *New York* ☎ *407/363–8757* ▭ *AE, D, MC, V* ✛ *2:E2.*

$
SEAFOOD
✗**Lombard's Landing.** Fresh grilled or fried fish, fried shrimp, and steamed clams and mussels tossed with pasta are the specialty at this restaurant designed to resemble a Fisherman's Wharf warehouse from 19th-century San Francisco. You can also get a Boursin steak sandwich with fried onion strips, hamburgers, chicken sandwiches, and big salads. The New England clam chowder is a standout, especially for the price. ✉ *San Francisco/Amity* ☎ *407/224–6400* ▭ *AE, D, MC, V* ✛ *2:D1.*

¢–$
AMERICAN
✗**Mel's Drive-In.** At the corner of Hollywood Boulevard and Vine is a flashy '50s eatery with a pink-and-white 1956 Ford Crown Victoria parked out in front. For burgers and fries, this is one of the best choices in the park, and it comes complete with a roving doo-wop group during peak seasons. You're on vacation—go ahead and have that extra-thick shake or the decadent chili-cheese fries. Mel's is also a great place to meet up, in case you decide to go your separate ways in the park. ✉ *Hollywood Blvd.* ☎ *407/363–8766* ⌦ *Reservations not accepted* ▭ *AE, D, MC, V* ✛ *2:D1.*

ISLANDS OF ADVENTURE

Here the food always fits the "island," from green eggs and ham at Seuss Landing to an otherworldly grotto in The Lost Continent. Now that the Wizarding World of Harry Potter has set up shop here, British fare is on tap in Hogsmeade Village.

$
AMERICAN
✗**Confisco Grille.** You could walk right past this full-service restaurant without noticing it, but if you want a good meal and sit-down service, don't pass by too quickly. This is one of the better eateries inside the theme parks. The menu changes often, but typical entrées include a good beef fillet with mashed potatoes and sautéed spinach, baked cod with spinach and mashed potatoes, and Thai noodles with chicken, shrimp, tofu, and bean sprouts. Wine is available by the glass. ✉ *6000 Universal Blvd., Port of Entry* ☎ *407/224–4404* ▭ *AE, D, MC, V* ☯ *No lunch* ✛ *2:D2.*

$
ECLECTIC
✗**Mythos.** The name is Greek, but the dishes are eclectic. The menu, which changes frequently, usually includes mainstays like pistachio-crusted roast pork tenderloin and cedar-plank salmon with citrus butter. The building itself is enough to grab your attention. It looks like a giant rock formation from the outside and a huge cave (albeit one with plush upholstered seating) from the inside. Mythos also has a waterfront view of the big lagoon in the center of the theme park. (When it's slow in the

park, Mythos is only open for lunch.) ⊠ *6000 Universal Blvd., Lost Continent* ☎ *407/224–4534* ▭ *AE, D, MC, V* ✛ *2:D1.*

$–$$ ✕ **Three Broomsticks.** For the first time ever, Harry Potter fans can taste
BRITISH   pumpkin juice and butterbeer, cauldron cakes and treacle fudge. The otherworldly goodies are sold along with traditional English fare such as fish-and-chips, shepherd's pie, and Cornish pasty at Three Broomsticks, part of Universal Orlando's new Wizarding World of Harry Potter attraction. Rickety staircases and gaslit chandeliers bring a bit of overcast Hogsmeade to sunny Orlando. ⊠ *6000 Universal Blvd., Wizarding World of Harry Potter* ☎ *407/224–4534* ▭ *AE, D, MC, V* ✛ *2:D2.*

CITYWALK

Restaurants, bars, clubs, shops, live entertainment, movie theaters—even a cigar bar and a high-end tattoo parlor—make Universal CityWalk an attraction on its own. The upbeat expanse serves as the entrance to both Universal Orlando theme parks—you can't reach the parks from the parking lot without walking through—and is an after-dark destination for tourists and locals alike.

$$$$ ✕ **Emeril's.** The popular eatery is a culinary shrine to Emeril Lagasse, the
CREOLE   famous Food Network chef who occasionally makes an appearance.
Fodor's Choice   And while the interior of the restaurant with its modernistic interior
★   of 30-foot ceilings, blond woods, a second-story wine loft, and lots of galvanized steel looks nothing like the Old French Quarter, the hardwood floors and linen tablecloths create an environment befitting the stellar nature of the cuisine. Entrées may include andouille-crusted red snapper with toasted pecans and crispy shoestring potatoes; bone-in rib eye with Emeril's Worcestershire sauce; chili-glazed rotisserie duck with wild-mushroom bread pudding; and double-cut pork chops with caramelized sweet potatoes. And Emeril knows your 9-year-old is not a New York food critic, so there are kids' offerings like cornmeal-fried gulf shrimp. Reservations are usually essential, but there's a chance of getting a walk-in seating if you show up for lunch (11:30 AM) or early for dinner (5:30 PM). ⊠ *6000 Universal Blvd.* ☎ *407/224–2424* ⊕ *www.emerils.com* ⌕ *Reservations essential* ▭ *AE, D, MC, V* ✛ *2:D2.*

$$ ✕ **Hard Rock Cafe Orlando.** Built to resemble Rome's Colosseum, this
AMERICAN   1,000-seat restaurant is the largest of the hundred-odd Hard Rocks in the world, but getting a seat at lunch can still require a long wait. The music is always loud and the walls are filled with rock memorabilia. Appetizers range from spring rolls to chicken tenders to smoke-grilled chicken wings. The most popular menu item is still the cheeseburger, but the barbecue combo and the fajitas are strong contenders. If you don't eat meat, try the grilled salmon fillet with white-cheddar mashed potatoes. ⊠ *6050 Universal Blvd.* ☎ *407/351–7625* ⊕ *www.hardrockcafe.com* ⌕ *Reservations not accepted* ▭ *AE, D, DC, MC, V* ✛ *2:D2.*

$$ ✕ **Latin Quarter.** This grotto-like restaurant and club, with domed ceil-
LATIN AMERICAN   ings and stone walls, is one of those jumping-by-night, dormant-by-day spots, but the food is good all the time. Cuisines from 21 Latin nations are on the menu, as is a wide selection of South American beers. Good entrée choices include the Caribbean-crusted mahimahi with blackened

scallops and roasted red pepper sauce; marinated *churrasco* (grilled skirt steak) with chimichurri sauce; paella with chorizo and four seafood ingredients; red snapper with a crispy coconut batter and mango-wine sauce; and guava-spiced spare ribs. This place can be a little loud in the evening, especially when a DJ entertains, but the live Latin music has a grand energy. Listen to live Spanish guitar music on the patio nightly. ⊠ *6000 Universal Blvd.* ☎ *407/224–2800* ⊕ *www.universalorlando. com* ⊟ *AE, D, MC, V* ⊹ *2:D1.*

$ ✕ **NASCAR Sports Grille.** Filled with race-car simulator games and racing
AMERICAN   memorabilia, this eatery might not look like the place to grab a sublime meal, but that's not the case. This theme restaurant has a reputation as a good place for grub. Selections worth trying include the Southern-style pot roast, and the slow-roasted baby back rib platter with sweet potatoes; the Talladega cheeseburger with a side of fries is a cut above the standard theme-park burger. ⊠ *6000 Universal Blvd.* ☎ *407/224–7223* ⊕ *www.nascarsportsgrille.com* ⊟ *AE, D, MC, V* ⊹ *2:E2.*

UNIVERSAL HOTELS

$$$–$$$$ ✕ **Bice Ristorante.** Trendy, pricey Bice is the Orlando unit of an interna-
ITALIAN   tional upscale chain of Italian restaurants. Bice (pronounced "*BEACH*-ay") is an Italian nickname for Beatrice, as in Beatrice Ruggeri, who founded the original Milan location of this family restaurant in 1926. But the word "family" does not carry the connotation "mom and pop" here, where cream-colored starched linens set the stage for sophisticated cuisine. The restaurant retains its frescoed ceilings, marble floors, and picture windows overlooking great views of the artificial (but appealing) bay just outside. The food is expensive (a simple spaghetti Bolognese with homemade pasta is $25), but some of the entrées that seem worth it include the osso buco with saffron risotto and the roasted rack of lamb with sautéed spinach. ⊠ *Loews Portofino Bay Hotel, 5601 Universal Blvd.* ☎ *407/503–1415* ⊕ *www.orlando.bicegroup.com* ⊟ *AE, DC, MC, V* ⊘ *No lunch* ⊹ *2:E1.*

$$$ ✕ **Mama Della's Ristorante.** The premise here is that Mama Della is a
ITALIAN   middle-aged Italian housewife who has opened up her home as a restaurant. "Mama" is always on hand (this is a coveted job for middle-aged actresses who do a good Italian accent), strolling among the tables, wearing an apron and making small talk. The food is no theme-park fantasy—it's excellent. The menu has Italian classics like chicken marsala, veal parmigiana, and spaghetti with meatballs and Bolognese sauce; all of the pastas are made in-house. Outdoor seating on a patio offers viewing of the hotel's nightly Musica Della Notte (Music of the Night) opera show. ⊠ *Loews Portofino Bay Hotel, 5601 Universal Blvd.* ☎ *407/503–3463* ⊕ *www.loewshotels.com* ⊟ *AE, D, DC, MC, V* ⊘ *No lunch* ⊹ *2:E1.*

$$$$ ✕ **The Palm.** With its dark-wood interior and hundreds of framed celeb-
STEAK   rity caricatures, this restaurant resembles its famed New York City namesake. As you might guess, a hearts of palm salad is a specialty here, but for most diners the steaks are the star of the show. Aged beef is the

predominant house specialty, and the 16-ounce strip steak cooked on a hot stone with onions and peppers is another standout. For fish lovers, the peppercorn-encrusted Atlantic salmon is a tasty option. ✉ *Hard Rock Hotel, 5800 Universal Blvd.* ☎ *407/503–7256* ⊕ *www.thepalm. com* ▭ *AE, D, DC, MC, V* ◷ *No lunch* ✢ *2:E1.*

$$$ ✕ **Tchoup Chop.** With its cathedral ceiling, the inside of this restaurant
HAWAIIAN looks almost churchlike in a modern-glitzy kind of way, and the food at Emeril Lagasse's Pacific-influenced restaurant is certainly righteous. Following the theme of the Royal Pacific Resort, the decorators included lots of bamboo, bright glazed tile, an exposition kitchen and a long zero-edge pool with porcelain lily pads running the length of the dining room. The menu combines Lagasse's signature bold flavors with Polynesian fusion cooking. Entrées change seasonally, but representative dishes include mochi-seared sea scallops with butternut squash risotto and creamy Thai curry-lobster sauce, and smoked-sea-salt grilled fillet of beef tenderloin. ✉ *Royal Pacific Resort, 6300 Hollywood Way* ☎ *407/503–2467* ⊕ *www.emerils.com* ⟁ *Reservations essential* ▭ *AE, D, DC, MC, V* ✢ *2:E2.*

ORLANDO METRO AREA

KISSIMMEE

Although Orlando is the focus of most theme-park visitors, Kissimmee is actually closer to Walt Disney World; it offers a huge number of dining choices, although many are of the "burger barn" variety in accordance with the area's budget lodging options. But there are notable exceptions. To visit the area, follow Interstate 4 to Exit 64A. Allow about 15 to 25 minutes to travel from WDW, or about 35 minutes from I-Drive—although the restaurants featured below are minutes from Walt Disney World's southern tip.

$$$$ ✕ **Old Hickory Steakhouse.** The purposely shabby dining rooms are a
STEAK playful movie-set kind of edifice designed for effect; be assured, the service is as polished as at any serious steak house. Dine on the deck under the soaring glass atrium, and you'll overlook the hotel's simulated Everglades wildlife. The experience is designed to entertain, and it does; the food is worth the roughly $75 a person you'll spend for dinner before wine or an artisanal cheese plate. ✉ *Gaylord Palms Resort, 6000 W. Osceola Pkwy., I–4 Exit 65* ☎ *407/586–1600* ⊕ *www.gaylordpalms. com* ▭ *AE, DC, MC, V* ◷ *No lunch* ✢ *1:E6.*

CELEBRITY CHEFS

Emeril Lagasse was the first headliner to hit Orlando's tourist corridor, bringing his New Orleans sass to Universal CityWalk in 1999.

(Above) Barbecue shrimp served at Emeril's Orlando. (Bottom right) Chef Cat Cora. (Top right) Emeril's Pacific-influence restaurant, Tchoup Chop.

Since then Orlando has become a hot spot for celebrity chef hangouts. Emeril opened a second, Polynesian-themed eatery called Tchoup Chop, and Roy Yamaguchi (Roy's Orlando), Norman Van Aken (Norman's), Melissa Kelly (Primo), Todd English (bluezoo), Kevin Dundon (Raglan Road), and most recently Cat Cora (Kouzzina), set up shop here too.

Meanwhile, a few local chefs have fostered their own foodie followings. Clifford Pleau, who broke boundaries as the opening chef of Disney's California Grill, later went on to create the popular, upscale Seasons 52 chain with Darden Restaurants. Winter Park natives James and Julie Petrakis met at the Culinary Institute of America and eventually founded The Ravenous Pig, a respected gastropub. And Greg Richie, who gained acclaim as the first on-site chef at Roy's Orlando, developed his own fan base and is now at Emeril's Tchoup Chop.

FARM TO TABLE

Preferring to cook with organic fruits and vegetables, the chefs at Melissa Kelly's Primo took to tilling themselves. The culinary team built two sprawling gardens at the JW Marriott Orlando Grande Lakes, which houses Kelly's Italian-organic restaurant. Stroll through at any time to see strawberries and rosemary peeking through the soil, maybe zucchini or kale, red oak lettuce, and deep purple eggplants.

3

EMERIL LAGASSE
Emeril's Orlando and Emeril's Tchoup Chop

Lagasse built his reputation as a Creole cook with exceptionally bold flavors in New Orleans and imported his signature style to Emeril's Orlando. When he opened Tchoup Chop, though, he made the menu Polynesian-fusion to match the theme of its host hotel. So while roasted redfish with andouille crust gives a taste of the French Quarter at Emeril's, you're more likely to think of tiki huts at Tchoup Chop, where Kiawe-smoked baby back ribs are a typical menu choice.

ROY YAMAGUCHI
Roy's Orlando

Melding childhood experiences in Asia and Hawaii, master chef Roy Yamaguchi blends flavors from all corners of the Pacific Rim. For guests in his Orlando dining room (it's one of 33 globally), that means creative classics like crunchy, golden lobster pot stickers and macadamia-crusted mahimahi. Yamaguchi gives local chefs the freedom to create a sizeable portion of their menus, which is why you might find Hawaiian-style misoyaki butterfish here and nowhere else.

CAT CORA
Kouzzina by Cat Cora

Cat Cora's family is Greek, yet she was raised in the deep South. As a result her

menu has a host of Greek influences—olive oil, lemon, garlic, and olives are abundant—yet the food is approachable for the steak-and-taters crowd. So what if the pork chop is cooked over oak and served with citrus-fennel marmalade? Once you have the Cat's Ouzo-tini, an all-American-style martini made with authentic Greek Metaxa Ouzo, you'll be up for anything.

NORMAN VAN AKEN
Norman's

He first called it New World Cuisine while others used the world Floribbean. No matter the terminology, Van Aken was among the first to mix and match elements of Floridian foods with those from Latin America and the Caribbean. Today he throws Asia into the mix, too, conjuring up intensely flavorful foods from ceviches (tossed table-side) to spicy ice creams, and a Mongolian-marinated veal chop that's to die for.

TODD ENGLISH
Todd English's bluezoo

English first made headlines in Boston at a storefront restaurant called Olives, which drew crowds for straightforward food that he calls "interpretive rustic Mediterranean cuisine." Today English oversees an empire of restaurants. In Orlando seafood is the theme, and here our finned friends are frequently gussied up with cutting-edge cooking techniques.

$$$$
SEAFOOD

✗ **Sunset Sam's Fish Camp.** Often restaurants with a great decor or an architectural gimmick don't bother to back it up with good food. But that's not the case with Sunset Sam's. The cuisine here, focused on great fish offerings, is on par with the grand look of the place, with its 60-foot sailboat floating in a giant indoor lagoon. Starters are big enough to be a meal, and include crispy coconut-fried shrimp and Blue Hill Bay mussels in curried coconut-lime broth. Entrées are pricey but not exorbitant, and include blackened swordfish, seared ahi tuna, and salmon with avocado-mango salsa. For dessert, go for the traditional key lime pie or perhaps a trio of small desserts served in shot glasses. ✉ *Gaylord Palms Resort, 6000 W. Osceola Pkwy., I–4 Exit 65, Gaylord Palms Resort* ☎ *407/586–1101* ⊕ *www.gaylordpalms.com* ⊟ *AE, D, DC, MC, V* ✛ *1:E6.*

CELEBRATION

If this small town with early-20th-century-style homes and perfectly manicured lawns reminds you a bit of Main Street, U.S.A., in the Magic Kingdom, it should. The utopian residential community was created by Disney, with all the Disney attention to detail. Every view of every street is warm and pleasant, though the best are out the windows of the town's Market Street–area restaurants, most of which face a pastoral (though man-made) lake. Homes here are on the expensive side, and restaurants reflect the upscale nature of the local customers. To get here, take Interstate 4 to Exit 64 and follow the CELEBRATION signs.

$$
ITALIAN

✗ **Café d' Antonio.** The wood-burning oven and grill are worked pretty hard here, and the mountains of hardwood used in the open kitchen flavor the best of the menu—the pizza, the grilled fish and chicken, the steaks and chops, and even the lasagna. Standouts include *pappardella al salmon* (wide, ribbon pasta with salmon, sweet peas, and a brandy-and-cheese sauce) and ravioli stuffed with lobster and ricotta cheese, tossed in tarragon cream with brandy and capers. At lunch you can pick your own ingredients for a personal, wood-oven pizza. As at the rest of Celebration's restaurants, there's an awning-covered terrace overlooking the lake. ✉ *691 Front St.* ☎ *407/566–2233* ⊕ *www.antoniosonline. com* ⊟ *AE, D, MC, V* ✛ *1:H6.*

$$
AMERICAN

✗ **Celebration Town Tavern.** This New England–cuisine eatery, operated by a family with Yankee roots, has a double personality. The interior is a brass, glass, and dark-wood-paneling kind of place, while the outside patio has table seating plus the Paddy O' Bar. The food ranges from landlubber treats like baby back ribs, prime rib, and gargantuan burgers to exquisite seafood including Ipswich clams and 2-pound lobsters, plus, on occasion, a salute to the Sunshine State with its Florida stone crabs in season. While the place has a clearly ultra-affluent demeanor, there are plenty of menu choices right out of a working-class Boston bar—meatball hoagies, Philly cheesesteak sandwiches, and Buffalo-style chicken wings. For dessert there's great—what else?—Boston cream pie. ✉ *721 Front St.* ☎ *407/566–2526* ⊕ *www.thecelebrationtowntavern. com* ⊟ *AE, D, MC, V* ✛ *1:H6.*

$$$ ✕ **Columbia Restaurant.** Celebration's branch of this family-owned high-

LATIN AMERICAN   end chain is generally as good as the original in Tampa, which has been operating for a century now. Start with the black bean cakes with guacamole and sour cream, or the empanadas stuffed with beef, roasted corn, and black beans. For your main course, zero in on the paella—either *à la Valenciana*, with clams, shrimp, scallops, squid, chicken, and pork mixed into tasty yellow rice; or the *paella campesina*, a "farmer's" paella from Spain, with no seafood, but beef, pork, and chicken. The best dessert, *brazo gitano cien anos* (sponge cake with strawberries that is soaked in syrup and Spanish sherry and flambéed table-side), was created for the restaurant chain's 100th anniversary in 2005, and is well worth its price just for the show. ⊠ *649 Front St.* ☎ *407/566–1505* ⊕ *www.columbiarestaurant.com* ⊟ *AE, D, DC, MC, V* ✦ *1:H6.*

$$ ✕ **Market Street Café.** The menu at this upscale diner ranges from the

AMERICAN   house-special baked-potato omelet and other breakfast classics served all day, like waffles and French toast, to comfort classics like beef Stroganoff and homemade chicken potpie. In addition to a hearty version of the quintessential American hamburger (best enjoyed with a creamy milk shake), there's also a salmon-and-veggie burger for the cholesterol wary. An outdoor seating section in front of the restaurant makes for a pleasant dining destination. ⊠ *701 Front St.* ☎ *407/566–1144* ⚑ *Reservations not accepted* ⊟ *AE, D, MC, V* ✦ *1:H6.*

$$$ ✕ **Seito Celebration.** Operated by the Seils, the Japanese family that owns

JAPANESE   four Seito Sushis in Central Florida, this quiet and casual eatery offers the same excellent sushi as its sister locations. You can dine on your favorite rolls while overlooking the lake in the center of Celebration. Selections range from the quintessentially Eastern Seito Roll (tuna, salmon, and crab) to a highly Occidental TGIF Roll (tuna, shrimp, avocado, and whitefish). Non-sushi entrées like salmon teriyaki and a tender filet mignon are also available. The house specialties, which include marinated sea bass, are worthwhile and inexpensive. Although cold tofu may sound like a health-food-freak's revenge, it's actually a great appetizer here, livened up with ginger, scallions, and soy sauce. The restaurant also offers several prix-fixe meals, with a representative sampling of the chef's best work. ⊠ *671 Front St., Suite 100* ☎ *407/566–1889* ⊕ *www.seitosushi.com* ⊟ *AE, D, DC, MC, V* ✦ *1:H6.*

INTERNATIONAL DRIVE

A number of restaurants are scattered among the hotels that line International Drive—the best along the manicured area near the convention center. Many are branches of chains, from fast-food spots to theme coffee shops and up, but the food found here can be quite good. To get to the area, take Interstate 4 Exit 72 or 74A. Count on it taking up to half an hour from the Kissimmee area or from a WDW property.

$$$$ ✕ **A Land Remembered.** The name of this award-winning restaurant is

AMERICAN   somewhat enigmatic (it's named for a novel about Florida by Patrick Smith) but then, so is the location—it's in the golf clubhouse of the Rosen Shingle Creek resort. But if you're a steak lover, it's worth your while to find this place, as chef Dan Nestor has obvious skill. Notable choices include the 1½-pound slab of prime rib, and if the sticker shock of its price doesn't get you, the 24-ounce porterhouse with a Vidalia onion sauce shouldn't disappoint the most ardent beef connoisseur. If you don't like beef, you're still in a good place here, with choices that include spit-roasted free-range chicken with tangerine and thyme butter, and lamb Tequesta, rubbed with roasted garlic and dry mustard. ✉ 9939 *Universal Blvd., Rosen Shingle Creek, International Drive* ☎ 407/996–3663 ⊕ *www.landrememberedrestaurant.com* ▭ AE, DC, MC, V ✛ 2:D5.

$$$ ✕ **B-Line Diner.** As you might expect from its location in the Peabody
AMERICAN Hotel, this slick, 1950s-style diner with gray-vinyl counter seats is not exactly cheap, but the salads, sandwiches, and griddle foods are tops. The classic combo—a thick, juicy burger with fries and a milk shake—is done beautifully. And there are lots of selections you'd never expect to find here, like New York strip steak with chipotle butter, pan-seared mahimahi with root vegetables, and wok-fried udon noodles with shrimp. It's open 24 hours, so if you crave eggs Benedict (with applewood-smoked Canadian bacon) at 3 AM, B-Line is the place to go. The restaurant was scheduled to undergo a renovation and menu change in 2010. ✉ *Peabody Orlando, 9801 International Dr.* ☎ 407/352–4000 ⊕ *www.peabodyorlando.com* ▭ AE, D, DC, MC, V ✛ 2:D6.

$$$ ✕ **Bergamo's Italian Restaurant.** If you like Broadway show tunes with
ITALIAN your spaghetti and opera with your osso buco, then head here for the booming voices as well as the good food, both of which are provided by servers in black vests. Management does not rely on the entertainment alone to fill seats: the food is very worthwhile. Start with the assorted antipasti, which gets you a sampling of roasted peppers, roasted marinated mushrooms, frittata, and bruschetta with white anchovies. Then try the linguine *pescatore* (fisherman's linguine), with lobster, shrimp, crabmeat, and mussels; or the classic osso buco with risotto Milanese. ✉ 5250 *International Dr., I–4 Exit 74A or 75A* ☎ 407/352–3805 ⊕ *www.bergamos.com* ▭ AE, D, DC, MC, V ◔ No lunch ✛ 2:D4.

$$ ✕ **Café Tu Tu Tango.** The food here is served tapas-style—everything is
ECLECTIC appetizer-size but plentiful, and inexpensive. The eclectic menu is fitting for a restaurant on International Drive. If you want a compendium of cuisines at one go, try the black-bean soup with cilantro sour cream, the baby lamb chops with "gingerapple" glaze, the pan-seared shrimp and chicken pot stickers, or the chipotle chicken *ropa vieja*. The wine list includes more than 50 wines from several countries, both by the bottle and the glass. The restaurant is designed to resemble an artist's loft; artists paint at easels while diners sip drinks like Matisse Margaritas. ✉ 8625 *International Dr.* ☎ 407/248–2222 ⊕ *www.cafetututango.com* ⌨ *Reservations not accepted* ▭ AE, D, MC, V ✛ 2:D5.

$$$ ✕ **Cuba Libre.** This restaurant, a branch of a popular chain that began
CUBAN in Philadelphia, is not exactly like the down-home *Cubano* kinds of eateries you'll find in the Calle Ocho district of Miami, but it presents great Caribbean cooking in an Orlando sort of way—with movie-set-style flair. The restaurant concept is from chef Guillermo Pernot, a James Beard Award winner and one of the creators of what is called "New Latin Cuisine." Main dishes of note include the slow-cooked,

guava-glazed barbecued ribs, and the *churrasco a la Cubana* (grilled skirt steak), the daily staple in Cuban restaurants in Miami or Havana. There's also a worthwhile pressed Cuban sandwich and a good version of a traditional Latin dish *ropa vieja*, shredded beef brisket with tomatoes, bell peppers, and onions in a red wine sauce. For the mojitos, including a splendid grilled pineapple version, the sugarcane is juiced on the premises. ✉ *9101 International Dr., Pointe Orlando* ☎ *407/226–1600* ⊕ *www.cubalibrerestaurant.com* ▭ *AE, DC, MC, V* ✛ *2:D5.*

$$$$
ITALIAN
✕ **Fiorella's Cucina Toscana.** This quiet little eatery—tucked behind the Orange County Convention Center on Universal Boulevard in the Westin Imagine Orlando—is just off International Drive, and the Tuscan cooking makes it worth the short trip. The decor is vibrant but not gaudy, with dark woods accented by bright, custom-made glass flowers and other objects on the walls. Worthy dinner selections include bresaolo carpaccio with truffle oil and pickled shallots, Maine lobster ravioli in sherried lobster sauce, and Black Angus tenderloin of beef with Gorgonzola cheese and fingerling potatoes. ✉ *9501 Universal Blvd., Westin Imagine Hotel, International Drive area* ☎ *407/233–2200* ⊕ *www.fiorellasorlando.com* ▭ *AE, DC, MC, V* ✛ *2:D56.*

$$$$
AMERICAN
✕ **Funky Monkey Wine Company.** Funky Monkey brings to the convention-center area its enticing mix of creative American cuisine, sushi, interesting wines, and occasional entertainment—including drag shows. Each table is treated to a plate of edamame tossed with lime juice and minced garlic instead of the typical bread basket. Butternut squash ravioli, bacon-wrapped pork tenderloin with soy-ginger glaze, and grilled shrimp on blue-cheese polenta are typical entrée choices. For a respite from touristy watering holes, grab a grape-purple seat at the low-key bar and get a chardonnay by the glass with a plate of panko-almond crusted fried goat cheese or pan-roasted mussels with key lime. ✉ *9101 International Dr., Suite 1208, Pointe Orlando, International Drive* ☎ *407/418-9463* ⊕ *www.funkymonkeywine.com* ▭ *AE, D, DC, MC, V* ☯ *No lunch Sun.* ✛ *2:D5.*

$$$$
AMERICAN
Fodor's Choice
★
✕ **Norman's.** Celebrity-chef Norman Van Aken brings impressive credentials to the restaurant that bears his name, as you might expect from the headline eatery in the first and only Ritz-Carlton in Orlando. Van Aken's culinary roots go back to the Florida Keys, where he's credited with creating "Floribbean" cuisine, a blend that is part Key West and part Caribbean – although he now weaves in flavors from all continents. The Orlando operation is a formal, sleek restaurant with marble floors, starched tablecloths, waiters in black-tie, and a creative, if expensive, menu. The offerings change frequently, and are offered à la carte and in four-, five-, and seven-course tasting menus. In addition to ceviches tossed table-side, classics from Norman's include yucca-stuffed crispy shrimp with sour-orange sauce, pan-cooked yellowtail with citrus butter, and grilled pork "Havana" with "21st-century" mole and smoky plantain crema. ✉ *Ritz-Carlton Grande Lakes, 4000 Central Florida Pkwy.* ☎ *407/393–4333* ⊕ *www.normans.com* ▭ *AE, D, DC, MC, V* ☯ *No lunch* ✛ *2:H6.*

$$$
SEAFOOD
✕ **Oceanaire Seafood Room.** Don't let the 1930s-era ocean-liner interior fool you: as theme restaurants go, this place is a good one, packing

everything from—depending on the season—Florida wahoo, Alaskan Bairdi tanner, or Ecuadorian swordfish. The straightforward preparation here—grilled or broiled, brushed with sea salt, olive oil, and fresh lemon juice—is also a welcome break from some of this eatery's more flamboyant counterparts. The chefs change the menu every day based on what's fresh. Lobster bisque and clams casino are standouts, as are the grand shellfish platter and the grilled black Florida grouper. Make sure to save room for the caramel deluxe brownie or a flashy favorite, the baked Alaska, which is flamed at the table. ⊠ *9101 International Dr., Suite 1002, Pointe Orlando, International Drive* ☎ *407/363–4801* ⊕ *www. theoceanaire.com* ⊟ *AE, DC, MC, V* ⊗ *Closed Sun. No lunch* ✛ *2:D5.*

$$$$ ✕ **Primo.** James Beard Award winner Melissa Kelly cloned her Italian-
ITALIAN   organic Maine restaurant in an upscale Orlando hotel and brought her
Fodor's Choice   farm-to-table sensibilities with her. Here the daily dinner menu pays
★   tribute to Sicily's lighter foods with produce grown in a hotel garden. Homemade cavatelli is tossed with wild mushrooms and spinach and topped with shaved truffles. Duck breast is glazed with chestnut honey and paired with house-made pancetta, apple compote, roasted turnips, and braised red cabbage. Desserts are just as special, with the likes of Meyer lemon–scented crème brûlée and a bowl of hot zeppole tossed in organic cinnamon and sugar. *JW Marriott Orlando, Grande Lakes* ⊠ *4040 Central Florida Pkwy , South Orlando32837* ☎ *407/393–4444* ⊕ *www.primorestaurant.com* ⊜ *Reservations essential* ⊟ *AE, D, DC, MC, V* ⊗ *No lunch* ✛ *2:H6.*

$$ ✕ **Taverna Opa.** This high-energy Greek restaurant bills itself as offering
GREEK   "fun with a capital F," possibly because the ouzo flows like a mountain stream, the Greek music almost reaches the level of a rock concert, and the roaming belly dancers actively encourage diners to take part in the mass Zorba dancing (which often happens on the tops of dining tables). The only thing missing is the Greek restaurant tradition of throwing dinner plates, made up in part by the throwing of torn-up paper napkins, which sometimes reaches near-blizzard level. The food, by the way, is also excellent. Standouts include traditional staples like *spanakopita* (phyllo pastry with spinach and feta cheese), *saganaki* (the traditional flaming cheese appetizer), *avegolemono* (lemony chicken-rice soup), and perhaps the most famous Greek entrée, *moussaka* (layers of roasted eggplant, potatoes, and ground meat, topped with béchamel sauce). The best dessert is the *baklava* (phyllo filled with walnuts, cinnamon, cloves, and honey). ⊠ *9101 International Dr., Pointe Orlando* ☎ *407/879–2481* ⊕ *www. tavernaoparestaurant.com* ⊟ *AE, D, DC, MC, V* ✛ *2:D5.*

LAKE BUENA VISTA

Lake Buena Vista, just to the east of Downtown Disney, is essentially a collection of midscale hotels, convention hotels, and chain restaurants catering to off-site visitors to Disney World. The restaurants tend to be well run, well kept, and affordable, with a few destination dining rooms dotting the area.

CLOSE UP

Popular Chain Restaurants

When all you want is a quick bite, consider these chain restaurants.

Brooklyn Pizza: Thin crusts and good ingredients make for decent New York–style pies at Brooklyn Pizza, a local chain that has arguably the best Meat Lovers option in town. In the tourist areas, you'll find branches on International Drive (inside Magical Midway) and near the airport. ⊕ www. brooklynpizzafl.com

Bubbalou's Bodacious Bar-B-Que: A trio of local smokeries serve up mounds of Southern barbecue, from baby back ribs to pulled-pork sandwiches. The restaurant on Kirkman Road and Conroy-Windermere Road is minutes from Universal Orlando. ⊕ www.bubbalous.com

Einstein's Bros. Bagels: For a light breakfast or lunch, Einstein's satisfies with a menu of bagels, wraps, salads, and sandwiches ordered at the counter and delivered to the table. ⊕ www.einsteinbros.com

First Watch: Breakfast and lunch classics make First Watch a popular choice for locals, who line up on weekends for Key West "crepeggs" (a crepe filled with eggs that have been scrambled with turkey, avocado, bacon, tomatoes, and Monterey Jack cheese), and Floridian French Toast with bananas, kiwi, and berries. Sandwiches and salads are also on the menu. ⊕ www.firstwatch.com

Five Guys Burgers and Fries: Five Guys has a nearly cultlike following for its freshly ground beef. Fifteen toppings are available for no charge, and the fries are cut from potatoes in the stores. Munch on peanuts while you wait. ⊕ www.fiveguys.com

Jimmy John's: Lunchtime lines are out the door at Orlando's six Jimmy John's, where the "world's greatest gourmet sandwiches" are essentially subs and clubs. ⊕ www.jimmyjohns.com

Johnny Rockets: Burgers, chili dogs, and frothy milk shakes are served in a vibrant, '50s-diner-style environment here. There are branches on International Drive and in Winter Park. ⊕ www.johnnyrockets.com

Panera Bread: Fresh-baked pastries, bagels, and espresso drinks are the mainstays here, although you can grab a hearty and inexpensive meals like smoked-chicken panini on onion focaccia or a bowl of soup served in a hollowed-out sourdough loaf and still have change left from a $10 bill. ⊕ www.panerabread.com

Pei Wei Asian Diner: Bold flavors from all corners of the Asian continent come together at these polished-looking fast-casual restaurants, where a hearty noodle bowl, orange-peel beef, or sweet-and-sour tofu will come in at under $10. ⊕ www.peiwei.com

Pizza Fusion: The owners of the burgeoning chain claim to be as concerned with saving the world as they are with serving flavorful organic fare. What guests reap are tasty organic pies along with salads and sandwiches. ⊕ www.pizzafusion.com

TooJay's Gourmet Deli: A New York deli it ain't, but the TooJay's chain offers a welcome pastrami fix for those with a yen for salty meat on crusty seeded rye. In fact, Central Florida's six restaurants all have extensive menus with everything from chopped liver to shrimp salad, matzo ball soup to roast turkey dinners. ⊕ www.toojays.com

$$$$ ✕ **La Coquina.** This restaurant, just outside Disney property, bills itself
FRENCH   as French with an Asian influence. It's essentially two restaurants, both
open September through June. On Saturday evenings, guests at the
Chef's Kitchen eat an $89 prix-fixe seven-course dinner ($128 with wine
pairings) in the kitchen, which is decorated beautifully. Dishes might be
leaf-wrapped snapper with tomato-parsley fondue or squab with black
couscous Parmesan. Come for Sunday brunch, when La Coquina's generous buffet selection of goodies with free-flowing champagne and live
piano music makes the price ($64 adults, $32 kids) almost seem like
a bargain. For brunch, you're seated in the dining room, but your
waiter takes you into the kitchen. It's set up like a European marketplace, where you pick out what you want to eat and watch the chef
cook it to order—perhaps agave-glazed rack of lamb with eggplant and
herb cheese, or roast tenderloin of buffalo with cippolini onions, goat
cheese, beet napoleon, and arugula leaves. ☒ *Hyatt Regency Grand
Cypress, 1 Grand Cypress Blvd., Lake Buena Vista Area* ☏ *407/239–
3853* ⊕ *www.hyattgrandcypress.com* ⊟ *AE, D, DC, MC, V* ☉ *Open
Sat. night and Sun. brunch.* ✛ *1:F3.*

$$$$ ✕ **The Venetian Room.** Inside the Caribe Royale All-Suite Hotel & Con-
CONTINENTAL   vention Center, one of Lake Buena Vista's many convention hotels, this
place was definitely designed for execs on expense accounts. But the
serene, luxurious, and romantic atmosphere makes it a great place for
dinner with your significant other. The architecture alone is enough to
lure you in. It's designed to look like Renaissance Venice: the entryway has a giant copper dome over the door and the dining room has
dark-wood furniture, crystal chandeliers, and carpets that could grace
a European palace. A good starter is the seared diver scallops with por-
cini asparagus risotto and pancetta crisp, although the ultrarich lobster
bisque is hard to resist. You can follow that with a good filet mignon,
or blood-orange duck l'orange. ☒ *Caribe Royale All-Suite Hotel &
Convention Center, 8101 World Center Dr., Lake Buena Vista Area*
☏ *407/238–8060* ⊕ *www.thevenetianroom.com* ⊟ *AE, D, DC, MC,
V* ☉ *No lunch* ✛ *1:F5.*

SAND LAKE ROAD

This part of Orlando is an anomaly: It's a growing collection of appealing strip centers filled with restaurants—from fast-casual panini and
Asian-food restaurants to fine-dining establishments—that's about equidistant from well-to-do residential neighborhoods, Walt Disney World,
Universal Orlando, SeaWorld, and International Drive. The result is
known as Restaurant Row, and it's the only place in town where locals
dine beside convention-goers and adventuresome theme-park visitors.
From Interstate 4, take the Sand Lake Road exit, 74A.

$$–$$$ ✕ **Antonio's Ristorante Sand Lake.** This Italian fine-dining establishment—
ITALIAN   a convention-oriented facility with a lovely, earthy Tuscan decor and
private party rooms—has great service and a good chef with plenty of
talent. Tasty creations include *lombata al forno,* a veal chop stuffed
with prosciutto, fontina cheese, and spinach, sautéed and finished in the
wood-fire oven; ravioli *de argosta* (ravioli with lobster, brandy, and a

cream sauce); and the lasagna with ground beef, also baked in a wood-fired oven. ⊠ *7559 W. Sand Lake Rd., The Fountains at Bay Hill, I–4 Exit 74A* ☎ *407/363–9191* ⊕ *www.antoniosonline.com* ▭ *AE, D, DC, MC, V* ☯ *Closed Sun. No lunch* ✛ *2:C4.*

$$$–$$$$

THAI

✕ **Ayothaya.** Although it is not as fancy or as highly themed as its Sand Lake neighbors, the menu here is solid. Start with the mandatory (if you are a true Thai fan) chicken satay or the Thai dumplings with shrimp and chicken stuffing, or go for the Ayothaya sampler, with chicken satay, spring rolls, tulip dumplings (dumplings stuffed with chicken and crabmeat with sweet-and-sour sauce), crab cakes, fried wonton, and Thai shrimp rolls. There's no sensible need to eat more after that, but forge ahead and try any of the standout curry or noodle dishes. ⊠ *7555 Sand Lake Rd., The Fountains at Bay Hill* ⊕ *www.ayothayathaicuisineoforlando. com* ☎ *407/345–0040* ▭ *AE, MC, V* ✛ *2:C4.*

$$–$$$

SEAFOOD

✕ **Bonefish Grill.** After polishing its culinary act in the Tampa Bay area, this Florida-based seafood chain has moved into the Orlando market with four casually elegant eateries that offer seafood from around the world. Anglers (waiters) serve standout dishes like wood-grilled salmon in mango sauce, mahimahi in a pan-Asian sauce, and pistachio-crusted rainbow trout. Meat lovers may prefer the center-cut, wood-grilled filet mignon or the boneless pork chop with fontina cheese. For the record, there's no bonefish on the menu. It's an inedible game fish, caught for sport (and usually released). ⊠ *7830 Sand Lake Rd., I–4 Exit 74A* ☎ *407/355–7707* ⊕ *www.bonefishgrill.com* ▭ *AE, D, DC, MC, V* ☯ *No lunch* ✛ *2:B4.*

$–$$

MEXICAN

✕ **Cantina Laredo.** You can tell this is an upscale Mexican eatery first by the Porsches in the parking lot, and then by the aged Mexican tequila that fetches up to $75 a bottle on the menu. Among the great *platos especiales* (special plates) is *camaron poblano asada*—a Mexican steak wrapped around a mild poblano pepper stuffed with shrimp and Jack cheese. But if you want representative Mexican dining, go for the Laredo Platter, comprised of a cheese chile relleno (breaded, mild pepper, stuffed with cheese and fried), handmade tamale, a chicken enchilada, and a taco *al carbon* made with shredded steak. If you walk in from the front, you may never notice the small covered dining area out back that faces a courtyard with a spectacular fountain; a pleasant setting for a lovely meal. ⊠ *8000 Via Dellagio Way, Dellaggio* ☎ *407/345–0186* ⊕ *www.cantinalaredo.com* ▭ *AE, D, DC, MC, V* ✛ *2:B4.*

$$

MIDDLE EASTERN

✕ **Cedar's Restaurant.** This family-owned Lebanese eatery, set in a major upscale strip shopping center that's become part of Restaurant Row serves Middle Eastern standards like shish kebab, baba ghanoush, and hummus, as well as tasty daily specials. One of the best of the regular entrées is the *samak hara* (sautéed red snapper topped with onions, tomatoes, and cilantro). More formal than the average Orlando-area Middle Eastern restaurant, Cedar's has tables with white-linen tablecloths and diners who tend to sport resort-casual attire. A belly dancer performs on Saturday evenings. ⊠ *7732 W. Sand Lake Rd., Plaza Venezia, I–4 Exit 74A* ☎ *407/351–6000* ⊕ *www.orlandocedars.com* ▭ *AE, D, DC, MC, V* ✛ *2:C4.*

3

$$$$ ✕ **Christini's Ristorante Italiano.** Locals, visitors, and theme-park execs
ITALIAN alike love to spend money at Christini's, one of the city's fanciest places
for northern Italian cuisine. Try the chicken marsala or the veal scallop-
pine, topped with roasted peppers, prosciutto, and provolone, and then
flambéed in sherry and brandy. The multicourse dinner often takes a
couple of hours or more, but if you like Italian minstrels at your table,
this place should please you. ✉ *7600 Dr. Phillips Blvd., Dr. Phillips
Marketplace* ☎ *407/345–8770* ⊕ *www.christinis.com* ▭ *AE, D, DC,
MC, V* ⊗ *No lunch* ✦ *2:B4.*

¢–$ ✕ **Moe's Southwest Grill.** Moe's is a great fast-food alternative with most
SOUTHWESTERN meals costing well south of $10. This is an immensely casual fast-food
joint with music blaring over the sound system, but by no means a dive.
It has a youthful vibrancy, and makes a great place for a quick meal. The
Moe in this equation could almost be the guy who cavorted with Larry
and Curly. There are several oddly named dishes, including an "Ugly
Naked Guy" taco, "The Homewrecker" (formerly called "The Other
Lewinsky," but updated when the world forgot Monica), and "Joey
Bag of Donuts." But the food is more sublime than the nomenclature.
The burritos here are gargantuan. In fact, the Joey Jr. special, a smaller
burrito and a soft drink, is enough to feed the average adult. ✉ *7541D
W. Sand Lake Rd., I–4 Exit 74A* ☎ *407/264–9903* ✉ *847 S. Orlando
Ave., Winter Park* ☎ *407/629–4500* ⊕ *www.moes.com* ⌔ *Reservations
not accepted* ▭ *AE, D, MC, V* ✦ *2:C4.*

$$$ ✕ **MoonFish.** MoonFish is a splashy-looking restaurant that caters to
SEAFOOD the convention crowd with private rooms, polished service and high
prices—but the food is quite good. The menu is a blend of Pan-Asian,
Pacific Rim, Cajun, and Floribbean fare. Specialties range from almond-
fried lobster tail to seared bluefin tuna mignon. The restaurant also
specializes in aged beef, which you can view in a big refrigerated cabi-
net as you walk in the door, served up in every variety. If you want to
indulge yourself, try the Oscar Mignon, a sirloin with hollandaise and
a crabmeat topping. ✉ *7525 W. Sand Lake Rd.,The Fountains at Bay
Hill,I–4 Exit 74A* ☎ *407/363–7262* ⊕ *www.fishfusion.com* ▭ *AE, D,
DC, MC, V* ✦ *2:C4.*

$$$$ ✕ **Morton's of Chicago.** Morton's looks like a sophisticated private club,
STEAK and youngsters with mouse caps are not common among the clientele of
this nationwide chain's Orlando restaurant. It's not unusual for checks
to hit $80 a head, but if beef is your passion, this is the place you'll
want to go. Center stage in the kitchen is a huge broiler, kept at 900°F
to sear in the flavor of the porterhouses, sirloins, T-bones, and other
cuts of aged beef. Soufflés are a specialty here and there are four: choco-
late, raspberry, lemon, and Grand Marnier. (Order at the beginning
of your meal.) The wine list has about 500 vintages from around the
world. ✉ *Dr. Phillips Marketplace, 7600 Dr. Phillips Blvd., Suite 132*
☎ *407/248–3485* ⊕ *www.mortons.com* ▭ *AE, DC, MC, V* ✦ *2:B4.*

$$$–$$$$ ✕ **Roy's.** Chef Roy Yamaguchi has more or less perfected his own cui-
HAWAIIAN sine type replete with tropical fruit–based sauces and lots of imagina-
tion. The menu changes seasonally, but typical dishes include treats
like Hawaiian-style butterfish with a sizzling Chinese vinaigrette or
hibachi-style grilled Atlantic salmon with Japanese citrus sauce. If your

Bite-size desserts at Seasons 52.

tastes remain on the mainland, go for classics like garlic-honey-mustard beef short ribs or the "Cowboy" center-cut 16-ounce, bone-in rib eye. The crunchy golden lobster pot stickers are one of the best appetizers in Orlando. The three-course prix-fixe menu, at $35 per person, is a relative bargain, as you get your choice from three appetizers, four entrées, and two desserts. ✉ *7760 W. Sand Lake Rd., Plaza Venezia, I–4 Exit 74A* ☎ *407/352–4844* ⊕ *www.roysrestaurant.com* ▭ *AE, D, DC, MC, V* ☽ *No lunch* ✛ *2:C4.*

$$$ ✕ **Samba Room.** This big, vibrant restaurant is a good version of a Nuevo
LATIN AMERICAN Latino experience, which puts contemporary spins on traditional Latin American flavors. You may agree once you taste the pork *barbacoa* cooked in banana leaves. To sample the extensive menu, go for tapas-style appetizers, including the Peruvian calamari and the empanada sampler. A standout on the main-course menu is rum-teriyaki-glazed salmon, and another is the skirt steak with chimichurri sauce. For dessert, try the banana crème brûlée or the *pudin de zanahoria* (sweet carrot cake). There is live Latin music nightly and free wireless access. ✉ *7468 W. Sand Lake Rd., Plaza Venezia, I–4 Exit 75A* ☎ *407/226–0550* ⊕ *www.sambaroom.net* ▭ *AE, D, MC, V* ✛ *2:C4.*

$$ ✕ **Seasons 52.** Parts of the menu change every week at this innova-
AMERICAN tive restaurant, which serves different foods at different times of year,
Fodor'sChoice depending on what's in season. Meals here tend to be healthful yet
★ hearty and very flavorful. You might have the grilled rack of lamb with Dijon sauce, pork tenderloin with polenta, or salmon cooked on a cedar plank and accompanied by grilled vegetables. An impressive wine list with dozens of selections by the glass complements the long and color-ful menu. Another health-conscious concept adopted at Seasons 52 is

the "mini indulgence" dessert: classics like chocolate cake, butterscotch pudding, and rocky-road ice cream served in portions designed not to bust your daily calorie budget. Although the cuisine is haute, the prices are modest—not bad for a snazzy, urbane, dark-wood-walled bistro and wine bar. It has live music nightly to boot. ⊠ *7700 Sand Lake Rd., I–4 Exit 75A* ☎ *407/354–5212* ⊠ *463 E. Altamonte Dr., I–4 Exit 92, Altamonte Springs* ☎ *407/767–1252* ⊕ *www.seasons52.com* ▭ *AE, D, DC, MC, V* ✛ *2:C4.*

$$$ ╳ **Timpano Italian Chophouse.** You may feel like you're on the set of the
ITALIAN   movie *Oceans 11*—the original version—as you slide into the black-leather booth at a table with a starched tablecloth and a cabaret lamp, while Frank Sinatra croons in the background and the waiters sing along—but the place is not boisterous or silly; it's laid-back, if loud. American beef definitely gets plenty of attention here, but that doesn't cancel out any of the Italian flair. A very worthy appetizer is the tuna carpaccio with kalamata olives, red onions, and lemon aioli served with Timpano's signature flatbread. Along with the 12-ounce New York strip and 16-ounce double-bone pork chops, there's a credible version of veal marsala with herbs and tomatoes and a fine rock shrimp–and–lobster ravioli. ⊠ *7488 W. Sand Lake Rd., Plaza Venezia, I–4 Exit 75A* ☎ *407/248–0429* ⊕ *www.timpanochophouse.net* ▭ *AE, D, DC, MC, V* ✛ *2:C4.*

$$$$ ╳ **Vines Grill & Wine Bar.** Live jazz and blues music fills the night at the
AMERICAN   bar section of this suave restaurant, but the food and drink in the snazzy main dining room are headliners in their own right. The kitchen specializes in thick, double-cut Kurobuta pork chops plus sublime fish dishes like crab-crusted black grouper. The wine list here is extensive, with offerings from Napa Valley, New Zealand, Australia, Chile, Italy, and France. The crowd tends to dress up, but suit jackets and ties are not required. ⊠ *7533 W. Sand Lake Rd., I–4 Exit 74A* ☎ *407/351–1227* ⊕ *www.vinesgrille.com* ▭ *AE, D, DC, MC, V* ☙ *No lunch* ✛ *2:C4.*

CENTRAL ORLANDO

The center of Orlando shows what the town as a whole was like before it became a big theme park. Quiet streets are lined with huge oaks covered with Spanish moss. Museums and galleries are along main thoroughfares, as are dozens of tiny lakes, where herons, egrets, and, yes, alligators, peacefully coexist with human city dwellers. This is quintessential urban Florida. The restaurants in this area, a good half hour from the Disney tourism area via Interstate 4, tend to have more of their own sense of character and style than the eateries going full tilt for your dollars in Kissimmee and Lake Buena Vista or on International Drive.

$$–$$$ ╳ **Amura.** Amura, Japanese for "Asian village," is a local chain of high-
JAPANESE   end Japanese restaurants; two of the three also have teppanyaki dining. The downtown unit is lively and hip, while the two suburban outposts are quieter and nearly luxurious—and priced accordingly. The sushi menu has about 40 choices, from *aoyagi* (round clams) to yellowtail tuna. The Mexican roll—with avocado, shrimp, and jalapeño peppers—makes for an unusual appetizer. For a taste of many non-sushi items, try the Tokyo Plate, piled high with chicken teriyaki, salmon teriyaki,

ginger pork, California roll, and tempura veggies. ⊠ *55 W. Church St. 170, Downtown Orlando* ☎ *407/316–8500* ⊕ *www.amura.com* ▭ *AE, D, DC, MC, V* ☺ *No lunch Sun.* ✛ *3:D6.*

$$$ ✕ **The Boheme Restaurant.** The Grand Bohemian, a downtown, boutique,
ECLECTIC luxury hotel, is the setting for one of the central city's better restaurants. As a prelude to your main, try the calamari served with tomatoes, olives, Asiago, and Moroccan aioli. For a main course, consider sea bass in cilantro truffle oil with mashed potatoes and asparagus, or the crab ravioli with Asiago cheese in a vodka-cream sauce. At breakfast, the French toast is an excellent way to awaken your palate. The Sunday brunch here is a worthwhile experience: you can get carved New York strip steak and stone crab legs as well as omelets. ⊠ *Grand Bohemian Hotel, 325 S. Orange Ave., Downtown Orlando* ☎ *407/313–9000* ⊕ *www.grandbohemianhotel.com* ⚔ *Reservations essential* ▭ *AE, D, DC, MC, V* ✛ *3:B6.*

$$$ ✕ **Cityfish.** In downtown Orlando's trendy Thornton Park district, this
SEAFOOD casual dining spot aims to be urbane and caters to locals, but if your kids are wearing mouse ears when you go here you won't be frowned upon. With the general ambience of a city sports bar—including flat-screen TVs on all the walls—Cityfish dispenses basic, well-prepared, fresh fish, served up simply with a few creative twists, such as the seafood nachos layered with shrimp and scallops, corn, black beans, salsa, and shredded cheese. The big patio filled with tables shaded by large umbrellas is a great place to spend a few unhurried hours in spring or fall. ⊠ *617 E. Central Blvd., Thornton Park* ☎ *407/849–9779* ⊕ *www. cityfishorlando. com* ⚔ *Reservations not accepted* ▭ *AE, D, MC, V* ✛ *3:E6.*

$$$ ✕ **HUE.** On the ground floor of a condo high-rise a short stroll from
ECLECTIC Lake Eola, this place makes an effort to have a hip, contemporary menu to match its striking decor. While it may not be quite as cool as its press clippings, the food is both good and eclectic, with offerings ranging from blackened fish tacos with cheddar cheese, tri-color tortilla chips, and black bean–corn salsa in a flour tortilla to double-cut pork chops in Asian barbecue sauce. The oven-roasted Chilean sea bass with Asiago tapenade and roasted-garlic mashed potatoes is the signature dish. The large outdoor dining area is perfect for people-watching. Brunch is served Sunday 11 AM–4 PM; it's a "disco" brunch once a month. ⊠ *629 E. Central Blvd., Thornton Park* ☎ *407/849–1800* ⊕ *www.huerestaurant.com* ▭ *AE, D, DC, MC, V* ✛ *3:E6.*

¢–$ ✕ **Johnny's Fillin' Station.** In a building that once housed a grocery store
AMERICAN and then a lemonade stand, this burger joint and sports bar is a monument to the fact that good eating can sometimes be had in extremely humble surroundings. Orlando residents rave about the burgers, which are straightforward half-pounders infused with what the management calls a "family recipe." Generous portions of onions, tomatoes, and other less common ingredients—like grilled mushrooms and peppers—make these burgers wonderfully sloppy. Make sure to grab extra napkins. The bacon-and-blue cheeseburger is the most popular item on the menu. This place is also a sports bar with a pool table and dart boards and can get loud and crowded. ⊠ *2631 Ferncreek Ave., South Orlando* ☎ *407/894–6900* ⊕ *www.johnnysfillinstation.com* ▭ *D, MC, V* ✛ *3:D6.*

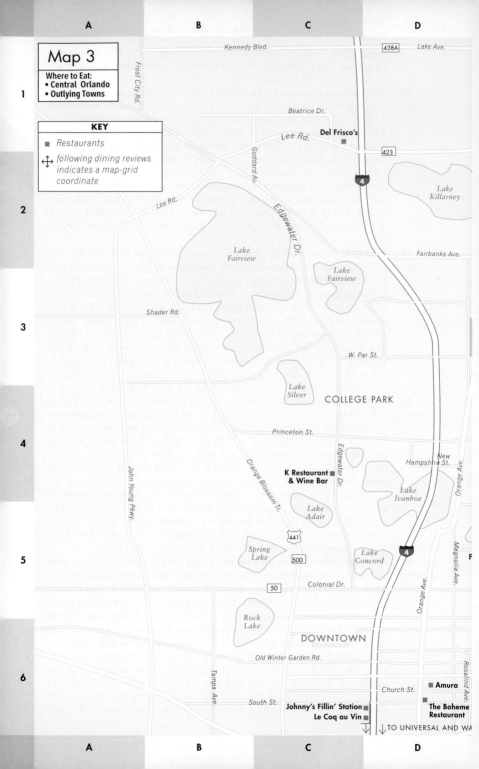

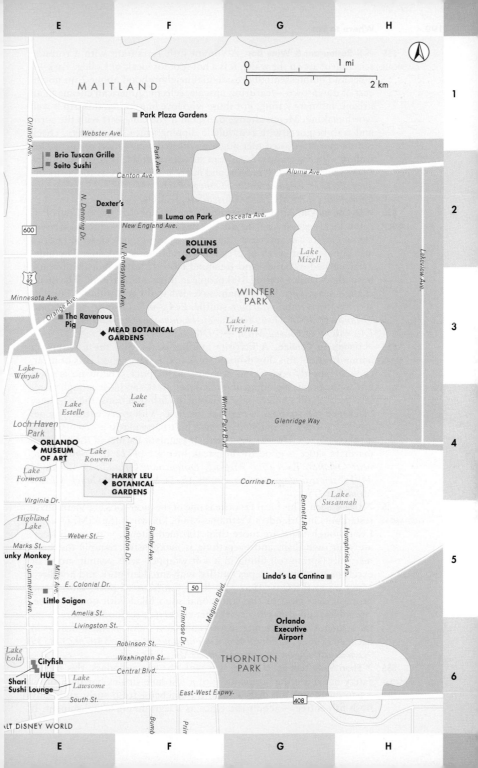

$$$

AMERICAN

✕**K Restaurant & Wine Bar.** A vibrant little restaurant with a rotating selection of art on the walls, K is a hot spot for locals of College Park—a quiet and quintessentially residential neighborhood about 2 mi northeast of downtown—featuring upscale, eclectic, American cuisine in an urbane, intimate setting. For those who love fine dining, this trip is well worth making. Menus change daily, but if you can, start with the corn-and-crab-beignets with remoulade dipping sauce. For entrées, check out the porcini-dusted filet mignon with red wine sauce, or the grilled wahoo with roast corn, fava-bean succotash, and lemon-thyme butter. There is an extensive wine list, and many selections are available by the glass. ✉ *1710 Edgewater Dr., College Park* ☎ *407/872–2332* ⊕ *www.kwinebar.com* ▭ *MC, V* ☽ *Closed Sun.* ✛ *3:C4.*

$$$

FRENCH

✕**Le Coq au Vin.** After decades under the care of chef-owner Louis Perrotte, local legend Le Coq au Vin has new owners—and a different menu. Guests can still treat themselves to rich French classics, but can also choose from a list of creative, Florida-influenced fare. The hideaway, owned by Sandy and Reimund Pitz, is located in a small house in south Orlando, seating 100 people in three dining rooms. The menu changes seasonally, but the namesake dish is always available. For dessert, try the Grand Marnier soufflé. ✉ *4800 S. Orange Ave., South Orlando* ☎ *407/851–6980* ⊕ *www.lecoqauvinrestaurant.com* ▭ *AE, DC, MC, V* ☽ *Closed Mon.* ✛ *3:D6.*

$$$

STEAK

✕**Linda's La Cantina.** A favorite among locals since the Eisenhower administration, this down-home steak house serves good cuts of meat, cooked expertly and served at a reasonable price. The menu is short and to the point, including about a dozen steaks and just enough ancillary items to fill a single page. Among the fish selections, the 12-ounce blackened red snapper is perhaps the best. With every entrée you get a heaping order of spaghetti (which isn't particularly noteworthy) or a baked potato. The chicken, veal, or eggplant Parmesan topped with marinara sauce is good for nonsteak lovers. ✉ *4721 E. Colonial Dr., near Orlando Executive Airport, Downtown Orlando* ☎ *407/894–4491* ⊕ *www.lindaslacantina.com* ▭ *AE, D, MC, V* ☽ *No lunch. Closed Mon.* ✛ *3:G5.*

$

VIETNAMESE

✕**Little Saigon.** This local favorite is one of the nicer-looking Vietnamese restaurants in Orlando's Vietnamese hub, known as the ViMi District. Even though there are more than 100 menu items, you can still create your own dish, and everything is inexpensive. Sample the summer rolls (spring-roll filling in a soft wrapper) with peanut sauce, or excellent Vietnamese crepes (stuffed with shredded pork and noodles). Move on to the *Com Heo Xao Bong Cai* (sautéed pork, onion, and broccoli over rice) or the traditional soup filled with noodles, rice, vegetables, and your choice of either chicken or seafood. Be sure to try the strong, sweet Vietnamese iced coffee—it's almost like a dessert in itself. ✉ *1106 E. Colonial Dr., Downtown Orlando* ☎ *407/423–8539* ⊕ *www.littlesaigonrestaurant.com* ▭ *MC, V* ✛ *3:E5.*

$$$

JAPANESE

✕**Shari Sushi Lounge.** Resplendent with chrome and glass, this trendy eatery has more the atmosphere of a fast-lane singles bar than of an Asian oasis, but the dishes from the kitchen—fresh sushi and daily fresh fish entrées—acquit the place as a legit dining establishment. If you're here for the sushi, the place will not disappoint—there are 25 different varieties, including sea urchin and baby octopus. Start with the *tako* salad, a delicious arrangement of octopus, cucumber, enoki mushrooms, mandarin oranges, and spicy kimchi sauce, or Wagyu steak that you cook yourself on a hot stone. Then move on to one of the entrées like shrimp tempura or sake salmon—an 8-ounce fillet steamed with sake, garlic, soy sauce, lime juice, and grated ginger. ⊠ *621 E. Central, Thornton Park* ☎ *407/420–9420* ⊕ *www.sharisushilounge.com* ⊟ *AE, D, DC, MC, V* ⊘ *No lunch* ✛ *3:E6.*

3

ORLANDO INTERNATIONAL AIRPORT

$$$$ ✕ **Hemisphere Steak & Seafood.** The view competes with the food on the
ECLECTIC ninth floor of the Hyatt Regency Orlando International Airport hotel. Although Hemisphere overlooks major runways, you don't get any jet noise, just a nice air show. Entrées change seasonally, but always include steaks such as Harris Ranch New York strip and Australian Wagyu-style Kobe rib eye, as well as selections like double-cut lamb chops, and cedar-plank-roasted wild salmon with mustard-ginger glaze. Even though it's been open for years, a lot of experienced travelers consider this place something of an undiscovered gem because the kitchen is so skilled. ⊠ *Hyatt Regency Orlando Airport* ☎ *407/825–1234 Ext. 1900* ⊕ *www.orlandoairport.hyatt.com* ⊟ *AE, DC, MC, V* ⊘ *No lunch. Closed Sun.* ✛ *2:H6.*

$$$ ✕ **Porterhouse.** Porterhouse is a mid- to upscale steak house located in
STEAK an airport hotel, but run with the loving attention of an independent enterprise. Opened in 2005, it's in the Orlando Airport Marriott, which has regular shuttle service to and from the terminals. The dining room is casual, with dark-wood walls and butcher paper covering the tabletops. The beef is a treat, but if it's not your ideal meal, alternatives include blackened sturgeon with shrimp butter and shoestring fries, and grilled salmon with porcini orzo. ⊠ *7499 Augusta National Dr., Orlando Airport Marriott* ☎ *407/851–9000* ⊕ *www.porterhouseorlandosteakhouse. com* ⊟ *AE, D, DC, MC, V* ⊘ *No lunch* ✛ *2:H6.*

WINTER PARK

Winter Park is a charming suburb on the northern end of Orlando, 25 minutes from Disney. It's affluent, understated, and sophisticated—and can be pleasurable when you need a break from the theme parks. It has four restaurant hubs: Park Avenue, Orange Avenue, Hannibal Square, and Winter Garden Village. To get into the area, follow Interstate 4 to Exit 87.

$$$ ✕ **Brio Tuscan Grille.** Head to this trendy restaurant for wood-grilled
ITALIAN meats and fish, Italian classics like chicken piccata, and plenty of pasta. Try the strip steak topped with Gorgonzola, or the shrimp-and-scallop linguine with black pepper–cream sauce. A good appetizer choice is the bruschetta, a wood-baked flatbread covered with toppings like sliced steak or roasted red peppers with mozzarella. The dining room's Italian archways are elegant, it's frescoed walls schmaltzy in a grand trattoria sort of way, and the sidewalk tables are a good option on cool days.

✉ *480 N. Orlando Ave., Winter Park* ☎ *407/622–5611* ✉ *4200 Conroy Rd., Mall at Millenia, Orlando* ☎ *407/351–8909* ⊕ *www.brioitalian. com* ☰ *AE, MC, V* ✚ *3:E2.*

$$$ ✗ **Del Frisco's Prime Steak & Lobster.** Locals like this quiet, uncomplicated, **STEAK**   family-run steak house, which delivers carefully prepared food and attentive service in a traditional setting of red leather and dark wood. When your steak arrives—still sizzling on a hot plate—the waiter asks you to cut into it and check that it was cooked as you ordered. The menu is simple: rib eyes, porterhouses, filet mignon. Seafood such as jumbo lump-blue-crab cakes, lobster, shrimp, and salmon fill out the "surf" side of the menu. ✉ *729 Lee Rd., Winter Park* ☎ *407/645–4443* ⊕ *www.delfriscosorlando.com* ☰ *AE, D, DC, MC, V* ☉ *Closed Sun. No lunch* ✚ *3:C2.*

$$ ✗ **Dexter's.** A trio of Central Florida restaurants, Dexter's is a low-key **ECLECTIC**   concept with a wildly creative menu, surprisingly low prices, a good wine list, and a faithful following among locals. Two of the best-selling entrées are the chicken tortilla pie—a stack of puffy, fried tortillas layered with chicken and cheese—and the Bourbon Street Jambalaya, with andouille sausage and salmon. The rotating fish of the day features whatever's freshest in season. In addition to a core menu shared by the three restaurants, each of the three units has its own "café" menu that's made up of specialties designed by that unit's on-site chef. There's always live music on Thursday night. ✉ *558 W. New England Ave.* ☎ *407/629–1150* ⊕ *www.dexwine.com* ⚤ *Reservations not accepted* ☰ *AE, D, DC, MC, V* ✚ *3:E2.*

$$$ ✗ **Luma on Park.** Although Luma on Park is a 21st-century place, serv-**AMERICAN**   ing what it calls "progressive American cuisine," it's also very much **Fodor's**Choice   in line with Winter Park's 19th-century past. The chic contemporary ★   setting includes terrazzo floors accented by plush carpets and seating areas in alcoves that create a cozy feel. A high point is the wine cellar, which holds 80 varieties of fine wine, all available by the half glass, glass, and bottle. The menu changes frequently and always includes pastas and salumi prepared from scratch. On recent visits standouts included two appetizers: roasted turnip-pear soup with Aleppo-pepper oil, and lacinato kale ravioli with toasted-garlic brodo. Notable entrées include Faroe Island ocean trout with quinoa, maitake mushrooms and tangerine broth, and Niman Ranch pork schnitzel with sage–brown-butter grits and honey-glazed cranberries. The restaurant offers a three-course, prix-fixe dinner Sunday through Tuesday for $35 per person, $45 with wine pairings. ✉ *250 S. Park Ave.* ☎ *407/599–4111* ⊕ *www. lumaonpark.com* ⚤ *Reservations essential* ☰ *AE, MC, V* ✚ *3:F2.*

$$$ ✗ **Park Plaza Gardens.** Sitting at the sidewalk café and bar is like sitting **CONTINENTAL**   on the main street of the quintessential American bustling town. But the locals know the real gem is hidden inside—an atrium with live ficus trees, a brick floor, and brick walls that give the place a Vieux Carré feel. Chef John Tan's menu is composed of traditional continental fare with elements of American, French, and Asian flavors, like rack of lamb or tenderloin topped with Boursin cheese. One dish with the Florida touch is baked grouper with lemon jasmine rice and tomato-ginger

Delectable dining at The Ravenous Pig.

coulis. ⊠ *319 Park Ave. S* ☎ *407/645–2475* ⊕ *www.parkplazagardens.com* ▭ *AE, D, MC, V* ✛ *3:F1.*

$$$
AMERICAN
Fodor's Choice
★

✕ **The Ravenous Pig.** A trendy, vibrant gastropub in one of Orlando's most affluent enclaves, the Pig is arguably Orlando's most popular foodie destination. Run by husband-and-wife chefs James and Julie Petrakis, the restaurant dispenses delicacies such as roast suckling pig with rye gnocchi dumplings, and grilled cobia (a white-fleshed Florida fish) with collards and persimmon chutney. The menu changes daily, but often includes less expensive pub fare like lobster tacos and homemade pretzels with a taleggio-porter fondue. A good dessert is the "Pig Tails," essentially a basket full of piping hot, pig tail–shaped doughnuts with a chocolate-espresso dipping sauce. There's an ample-size bar area separate from the dining room. ⊠ *1234 N. Orange Ave.* ☎ *407/628–2333* ⊕ *www.theravenouspig.com* ⌖ *Reservations essential* ▭ *AE, D, MC, V* ✆ *Closed Sun. and Mon.* ✛ *3:D5.*

$$
JAPANESE

✕ **Seito Sushi.** Tucked into a corner of Winter Park Village, this pleasant eatery combines two great elements: sushi and sidewalk dining. Order a Japanese beer (or some hot sake) and sample the raw fish offerings, including the signature Seito roll, composed of tuna, white tuna, salmon, and crabmeat in a cucumber skin with ponzu sauce. Another favorite roll is the lobster Katsu, with deep-fried lobster topped with snow crab and avocado. There's also plenty of inspired cooked cuisine, including tasty sea bass with Asian rice, excellent salmon teriyaki, and even a good New York strip steak. Top off your meal with some red-bean ice cream or fried bananas. ⊠ *510 N. Orlando Ave., Winter Park Village* ☎ *407/644–5050* ⊕ *www.seitosushi.com* ▭ *AE, MC, V* ✛ *3:E2.*

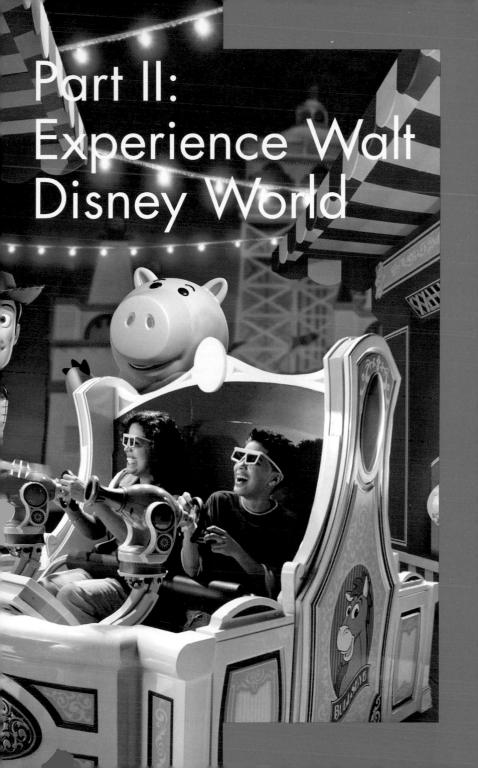

Part II: Experience Walt Disney World

WELCOME TO WALT DISNEY WORLD

TOP REASONS TO GO

★ **Nostalgia:** Face it—Mickey and company are old friends. And you probably have childhood pictures of yourself in front of Cinderella Castle. Even if you don't, nobody does yesteryear better: head to Main Street, U.S.A. or Hollywood Boulevard and see.

★ **Memories in the Making:** Who doesn't want to snap photos of Sis on the Dumbo ride or of Junior after his Splash Mountain experience? The urge to pass that Disney nostalgia on to the next generation is strong.

★ **The Thrills:** For some this means roller-coasting to an Aerosmith sound track or simulating space flight; for others it's about cascading down a water-slide or going on safari.

★ **The Chills:** If the Pirates of the Caribbean cave doesn't give you goose bumps, try the Haunted Mansion or Twilight Zone Tower of Terror.

★ **The Spectacle:** The list is long: fireworks, laser-light displays, arcade games, parades. . . .

1 **Magic Kingdom.** Disney's small but emblematic park is home to the iconic Space Mountain and Pirates of the Caribbean ride.

2 **Epcot.** Future World's focus is science, technology, and hands-on experiences. In the World Showcase you can tour 11 countries without getting jet lagged.

3 **Disney's Hollywood Studios.** Amazing attractions at this re-creation of old-time Hollywood include Rock 'n' Roller Coaster starring Aerosmith and Twilight Zone Tower of Terror.

4 **Disney's Animal Kingdom.** Around and amid a 100-acre wildlife preserve are an Asian-themed water ride, an African safari ride, and shows.

5 **6** **Water Parks.** Blizzard Beach's best (worst?) ride is the 55-mph dead-drop from Summit Plummet. Water babies love Typhoon Lagoon's Ketchakiddie Creek.

7 **Downtown Disney.** It's a shopping, dining, entertainment hub in three parts: the Marketplace, Pleasure Island, and the West Side.

8 **BoardWalk.** At this lakeside district you can dine, shop, ride a bicycle built for two, or cut a rug in an old-style dance hall.

CENTRAL FLORIDA

Orlando

9 Celebration. Disney's utopian residential community near Kissimmee recalls the Magic Kingdom's Main Street, U.S.A., but without swarms of tourists.

GETTING ORIENTED

Walt Disney World straddles Orange and Osceola counties to the west of Interstate 4. Four exits will get you to the parks and resort areas: 64B, 65, 67, and 68. To reach hotels along I-Drive use Exit 72, 74A, or 75A.

WALT DISNEY WORLD PLANNER

Operating Hours

Walt Disney World operates 365 days a year. Opening and closing times vary by park and by season, with the longest hours during prime summer months and year-end holidays. The parking lots open at least an hour before the parks do.

In general, openings hover around 9 AM, though certain attractions might not start up till 10 or 11 AM. Closings range between 5 and 8 PM in the off-season and between 8 and 10, 11, or even midnight in high season. Downtown Disney and BoardWalk shops stay open as late as 11 PM.

EXTRA MAGIC HOURS

The Extra Magic Hours program gives Disney resort guests free early and late-night admission to certain parks on specified days—call ahead for information about each park's "magic hours" days to plan your early- and late-visit strategies.

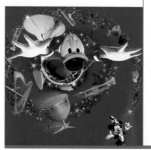

Getting In and Around

At the gate, the per-person per-day price is $79 adults (ages 10 and older) and $68 children (ages 3–9). You can buy tickets at the Ticket and Transportation Center (TTC) in the Magic Kingdom, from booths at other park entrances, in all on-site resorts if you're a guest, at the Disney store in the airport, and at various other sites around Orlando. You can also buy them in advance online—the best way to save time and money.

If you opt for a multiday ticket, you'll be issued a nontransferable pass that uses your fingerprint for ID. Slide your pass through the reader, just like people with single-day tickets, and also slip your finger into the V-shape reader.

PARKING AND IN-PARK TRANSPORT

Parking at Disney is free to resort guests; all others pay $14 for cars and $15 for RVs and campers. Parking is free for everyone at Typhoon Lagoon, Blizzard Beach, Downtown Disney, and the BoardWalk. Trams take you between the theme-park lots (*note your parking location!*) and turnstiles. Disney's buses, boats, and monorails whisk you from resort to park and park to park. If you're staying on Disney property, you can use this system exclusively. Either take a Disney bus or drive to Typhoon Lagoon and Blizzard Beach. Once inside the water parks, your can walk, swim, slide, or chill out. Allow up to an hour for travel between parks and hotels on Disney transportation.

FASTPASS

Fastpass helps you avoid lines, and it's included in regular park admission. Insert your theme-park ticket into the machines near several attractions. Out comes your Fastpass, printed with a one-hour window of time during which you can return to get into the fast line. *Don't forget to take your park ticket back, too.* You can't make a Fastpass for another attraction until you're within the window of time for your first appointment. It's best to make appointments only for the most popular attractions and to make new ones as soon as existing ones mature. Strategy is everything.

Doing Disney Right

If you remember nothing else, keep in mind these essential strategies, tried and tested by generations of Disney fans.

■ **Buy tickets before leaving home.** It saves money and gives you time to look into all the ticket options. It also offers an opportunity for you to consider vacation packages and meal plans. Before you can sing "M-I-C-K-E-Y" you'll be organized and ready for a fun, successful Disney trip.

■ **Make dining reservations before leaving home.** If you don't, you might find yourself eating fast food (again) or leaving Disney for dinner. On-site restaurants, especially those featuring character appearances, book up fast.

■ **Arrive at least 30 minutes before the parks open.** We know, it's your vacation and you want to sleep in. But you probably want to make the most of your time and money, too. Plan to be up by 7:30 am each day to get the most out of your park visits. After transit time, it'll take you 15-20 minutes to park, get to the gates, and pick up your park guide maps and *Times Guide*.

■ **See top attractions in the morning.** And we mean *first thing*. Decide in advance on your can't-miss attractions, find their locations, and hotfoot it to them before 10 AM.

■ **Use Fastpass.** Yes, use the Fastpass. It's worth saying twice. The system is free, easy, and it's your ticket to the top attractions with little or no waiting in line.

■ **Use Baby Swap.** Disney has a theme-park "rider switch" policy that works like this: one parent waits with the baby or toddler while the other parent rides the attraction. When the ride ends, they switch places with minimal wait.

■ **Build in rest time.** Who wants to become overly hot, tired, and grumpy? Start early and then leave the parks around 3 or 4 PM, thus avoiding the hottest and most crowded period. After a couple of hours' rest at your hotel, head back for a nighttime spectacle or to ride a big-deal ride or two (lines often are shorter around closing time).

■ **Create an itinerary, but leave room for spontaneity.** Decide which parks to see on each day, and know your priorities, but don't try to plot your trip hour by hour. If you're staying at a Disney resort, find out which parks have Extra Magic Hours on which days.

■ **Eat at off hours.** To avoid the mealtime rush hours have a quick, light breakfast at 7 or 8 AM, lunch at 11 AM, and dinner at 5 or 6 PM.

Other Disney Services

If you don't mind shelling out $175–$315 an hour (with a six-hour minimum), you can take a customized **VIP Tour** with guides who help you park hop and get good seats at parades and shows. These tours don't help you skip lines, as at Universal, but they make navigating easy. Groups can have up to 10 people, and it pays to book up to three months ahead.

At **character meals**—breakfasts, lunches, or dinners—Mickey, Belle, or other characters sign autographs and pose for photos. Book through Disney's dining reservations line up to 180 days out; these hugging-and-feeding frenzies are wildly popular. They're also a good way to spend the morning on check-out day.

Disney Contacts

Dining Reservations:
☎ 407/939–3463

Golf Reservations:
☎ 407/939–4653

Guest Info: ☎ 407/824–4321

VIP Tours: ☎ 407/560–4033

WDW Travel Company:
☎ 407/939–1289

Web: ⊕ www.disneyworld.com

DISNEY NEWS

Mickey Mouse. Tinker Bell. Cinderella. What would childhood be like without the magic of Disney? When kids (and let's be honest, adults, too) want to go to "the" theme park, they're heading to Disney. Here you're walking amid people from around the world and meeting characters like Snow White and Donald Duck while rides whirl nonstop and the irrepressible "It's a Small World" tune and lyrics run through your head. You can't help but believe dreams really do come true here.

The secret to enjoying Disney is to have a good plan and the flexibility to take detours when magical moments occur. You probably can persuade your children to rush to the big-deal rides early in the morning when timing matters most, but don't expect them to keep up that pace all day. Cushion your itinerary with extra time, so they can pause when the spirit moves them. Let your motto be "quality over quantity." It's better to tour the parks in a relaxed fashion. Why disappoint your little ones by passing up the chance to hobnob with Princess Jasmine in your hurry to get to Pirates of the Caribbean—only to find a 30-minute wait at the ride entrance.

It's also important that your kids are involved in the vacation planning and are aware of the need for a park strategy. Let each family member choose one or two top rides or attractions for each park. Everything else should be icing on the cake. Run through the plan before you enter the park; if children know ahead of time that souvenirs are limited to one per person and that ice-cream snacks come after lunch, they're likely to be more patient than if they're clueless about your plans and dazzled by every merchandise cart they encounter.

What's New

In 2008 Disney closed the six Pleasure Island nightclubs at Downtown Disney to transform the area into a dining, shopping, family entertainment destination. So far, a well-received restaurant, Paradiso 37, has opened, and a Latin chicken-restaurant chain, Pollo Campera, known for its healthful options, is slated to replace the Marketplace's McDonald's.

Tethered on the West Side, the Characters in Flight helium balloon now affords 400-foot-high, 360-degree, fair-weather kingdom views. Disney's Wide World of Sports, south of Hollywood Studios off of Osceola Parkway, has been given an ESPN theme and name change to ESPN Wide World of Sports and will soon unveil a 100-lane bowling center.

Meanwhile, in the Magic Kingdom, Mickey's Toontown Fair is slated to close, making way for a Fantasyland expansion—the biggest thing to happen here since Mickey's Birthdayland opened in 1988 and then morphed into Toontown Fair. The "re-imagined" Fantasyland is expected to open in 2013 with a new Dumbo ride, a three-ring-circus tent, and a *Beauty and the Beast*–themed castle, complete with a library for Story Time with Belle. Over at Hollywood Studios, the force will be with you in a big way with the 3-D immersion version of the Star Tours attraction.

Disney Cruise Line has expanded its fleet, with the new *Disney Dream;* a fourth vessel, the *Disney Fantasy,* is slated to launch in 2012. Disney also has more lodging, dining, and shopping area plans on the drawing board, so stay tuned. . . .

DISNEY'S OTHER WORLDS

Try to budget in a few hours to explore Disney's "other" places. Several of them are no-admission-required charmers; one is a high-tech, high-cover-charge gaming wonderland.

DISNEY'S BOARDWALK

In the good ol' days, Americans escaped their city routines for seaside, breeze-swept boardwalks. **Disney's BoardWalk** is within walking distance of Epcot and across Crescent Lake from Disney's Yacht and Beach Club Resorts and fronting a hotel of the same name. You'll be drawn to some good restaurants (including Kouzzina, developed by Iron Chef Cat Cora), bars, souvenir shops, surreys, saltwater taffy vendors, and performers. After sunset, the mood is festive. If you're here when Epcot is ready to close, you can watch the park fireworks from the bridge that connects BoardWalk to the Yacht and Beach Club Resorts.

DOWNTOWN DISNEY

East of Epcot and close to Interstate 4 (I–4) along a large lake, this shopping, dining, and entertainment complex has three areas: the Marketplace, Pleasure Island, and West Side. You can rent lockers, strollers, or wheelchairs, and there are two Guest Relations (aka Guest Services) centers.

Marketplace

In the **Marketplace,** the easternmost Downtown Disney area, you can meander along winding sidewalks and explore hidden alcoves. Children love to splash in fountains that spring from the pavement and ride the miniature train and old-time carousel ($2). Toy stores entice with creation-stations and too many treasures to comprehend. There are plenty of spots to grab a bite or sip a cappuccino along the lakefront. The Marketplace is open from 9:30 AM to 11 PM.

Pleasure Island

When it was a nightlife destination, the Downtown Disney area known as **Pleasure Island** charged admission after dark for access to its bars, comedy clubs, and dance spots. But the nightclubs have closed and the place is undergoing a makeover to be completed in 2012. That said, Raglan Road Irish Pub and Restaurant still offers live Irish music six nights a week, and the upscale cigar bar, Fuego Cigars by Sosa, serves wine and spirits. A few restaurants and shops beckon as you stroll from the Marketplace to West Side.

West Side

The main attractions in Downtown Disney's hip **West Side** are the House of Blues Music Hall, Cirque du Soleil, and DisneyQuest virtual indoor theme park and arcade. You can also ride the Characters in Flight ($16 ages 10 and up; $10 ages 3–9) helium balloon that's tethered here, shop in boutiques, or dine in such restaurants as the Wolfgang Puck Café and Planet Hollywood. Shops open at 10:30 AM, and closing time is between 11 PM and 2 AM.

CELEBRATION

This Disney-created community, where every blade of grass in every lawn seems perfect, is as picturesque as a movie set—although, to some critics, it would be one used in *The Stepford Wives*. But **Celebration** is a great showcase of American architecture and urban planning. It's also a delightful place to spend a morning or afternoon.

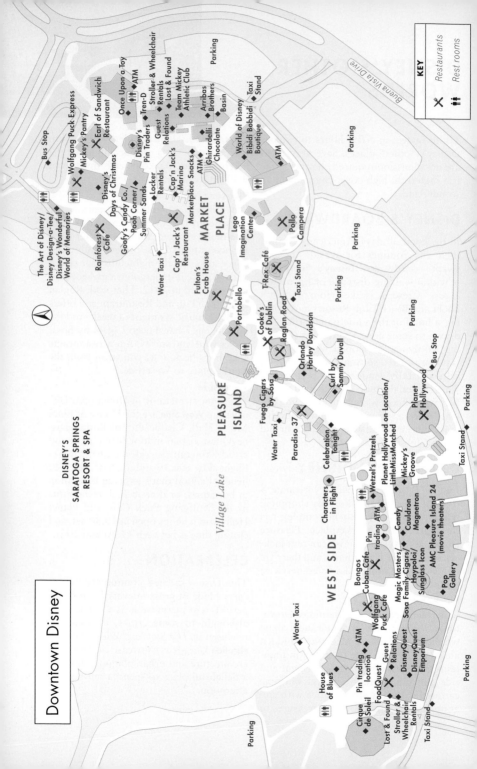

Downtown Disney

KEY

✕ *Restaurants*

👫 *Rest rooms*

Buena Vista Drive

DISNEY'S SARATOGA SPRINGS RESORT & SPA

Village Lake

MARKET PLACE

PLEASURE ISLAND

WEST SIDE

Parking

Bus Stop

The Art of Disney/
Disney Design-a-Tee/
Disney's Wonderful
World of Memories

Wolfgang Puck Express

Mickey's Pantry

Earl of Sandwich
Restaurant

Once Upon a Toy

Tren-D

ATM

Stroller & Wheelchair
Rentals

Lost & Found

Team Mickey
Athletic Club

Arribas
Brothers

Taxi
Stand

Basin

Rainforest
Cafe

Disney's
Days of Christmas

Disney's
Pin Traders

Guest
Relations

World of Disney

Bibidi Bobbidi
Boutique

Ghirardelli
Chocolate

ATM

Goofy's Candy Co./
Pooh Corner/
Summer Sands

Cap'n Jack's
Marina

Water Taxi

Cap'n Jack's
Restaurant

Locker
Rentals

Marketplace Snacks

ATM

Lego
Imagination
Center

Pollo
Campera

Fulton's
Crab House

Portobello

T-Rex Café

Taxi Stand

Parking

Cooke's
of Dublin

Raglan Road

Orlando
Harley Davidson

Curl by
Sammy Duvall

Parking

Fuego Cigars
by Sosa

Water Taxi

Paradiso 37

Celebration
Tonight

Planet Hollywood on location/
LittleMissMatched

Planet
Hollywood

Bus Stop

Parking

Characters
in Flight

Wetzel's Pretzels

Mickey's
Groove

Taxi Stand

Bongos
Cuban Cafe

Pin
trading

ATM

Magic Masters/
Sosa Family Cigars/
Hoypoloi/
Sunglass Icon

Candy
Cauldron
Magnetron

AMC Pleasure Island 24
(movie theaters)

Wolfgang
Puck Cafe

Pop
Gallery

Water Taxi

House
of Blues

Pin trading

ATM

Guest
location

Relations

FoodQuest

Cirque
de Soleil

Lost & Found

Stroller &
Wheelchair
Rentals

DisneyQuest

DisneyQuest
Emporium

Parking

Taxi Stand

DISNEYQUEST

On Disney's West Side, in a five-story virtual-reality mini-theme park, is **Disney-Quest,** where you'll pay a hefty cover to participate in high-tech virtual adventures and play video games. To be fair, you can play all day, and there are cutting-edge games and interactive adventures that make the admission worthwhile. It's also a great place for teens and older tweens (children under 10 must be accompanied by an adult).

In **Explore Zone,** fly through the streets of Agrabah with the help of a virtual-reality helmet on Aladdin's Magic Carpet Ride. Take a Virtual Jungle Cruise down the roiling rapids of a prehistoric world, and paddle (yes, *really* paddle) to adventure amid volcanoes, dinosaurs, and other cretaceous threats. At Pirates of the Caribbean: Battle for Buccaneer Gold, you and the gang must brave the high seas and sink pirate ships to acquire treasure.

In the **Score Zone,** battle super villains while flying, headset firmly intact, through a 3-D comic world in Ride the Comix. Escape evil aliens and rescue colonists during Invasion! An ExtraTERRORestrial Alien Encounter. Or hip-check your friends in a life-size Mighty Ducks Pinball Slam game.

In the **Create Zone** learn the secrets of Disney animation at the Animation Academy. Create your own twisted masterpiece at Sid's Create-A-Toy, based on the popular animated film *Toy Story.* Or, at Living Easels, make a *living* painting on a giant electronic screen. Thrills await at Cyberspace Mountain, where you can design your own roller coaster on a computer screen, then climb aboard a 360-degree pitch-and-roll simulator for the ride of your dreams. At Radio Disney Song-Maker, produce your own hit.

Classic free-play machines like Pac Man reside in the **Replay Zone.** You can also sit with a partner in an asteroid cannon–equipped bumper car and blast others to make their cars do a 360-degree spin in Buzz Lightyear's AstroBlaster.

Attractions all are wheelchair accessible, but most require transfer from wheelchair to the attraction itself. You can, however, wheel right on to Pirates of the Caribbean: Battle for Buccaneer Gold, Aladdin's Magic Carpet Ride, and Mighty Ducks Pinball Slam. Rent wheelchairs ($12 per day for hand operated, $50 for electric plus $100 refundable credit-card deposit) at the DisneyQuest Emporium or in the Marketplace at Guest Relations. Guide dogs are permitted in all areas but aren't allowed to ride several attractions. Strollers are *not* permitted, though, oddly, there are baby-changing stations in both men's and women's restrooms.

Four attractions have height requirements: Cyberspace Mountain (51 inches), Buzz Lightyear's Astro Blaster (51 inches), Mighty Ducks Pinball Slam (48 inches), and Pirates of the Caribbean (35 inches). Little ones 2–7 can enjoy a Kids' Area on the fourth floor, where they can play smaller versions of video and other games like air hockey, basketball, and bowling.

Lost and Found is at the admissions window, film can be purchased at the Emporium, and cash is available at ATMs inside the House of Blues merchandise shop not far from the DisneyQuest entrance. ☎ 407/828–4600 ⌨ *$41 adults, $35 children 3–9, excluding sales tax ☉ Sun.–Thurs. 11:30–10, Fri. and Sat. 11:30–1.*

A MAN, A MOUSE, A LEGACY By Jennie Hess

Walt Disney once said, "I only hope that we never lose sight of one thing—that it was all started by a mouse." His legendary mouse, Mickey, took the world by storm in 1928 in the theatrical debut of the animated short film *Steamboat Willie*. Today, Walt is Mickey, Mickey is Walt, and their legacy is legendary.

Above: Walt Disney; below: Mickey from *Fantasia*, 1940; right: *Pinocchio*, 1940

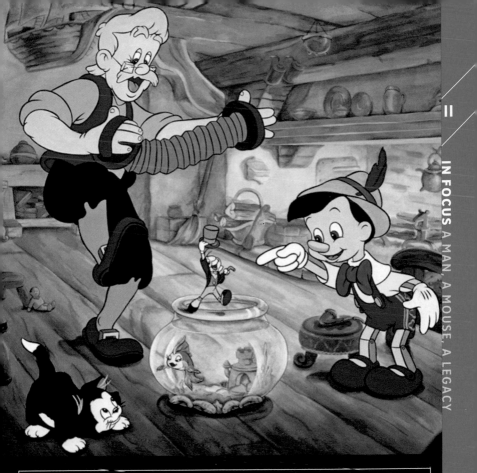

There's a tale still told (and disputed) that Walt imagined Mickey while on a train from New York to California, after a disastrous meeting where he lost the rights to a character called Oswald the Lucky Rabbit. Walt's friend and colleague, gifted Dutch cartoonist Ub Iwerks, first drew Mickey, but it was Walt who gave him a voice and personality.

He planned to name the mouse Mortimer, but his wife, Lilian, insisted the name didn't fit the cheerful little rodent.

The man behind the mouse, Walter Elias Disney, was born December 5, 1901, in Chicago. His early Midwestern years were spent nurturing his love of drawing. After driving an ambulance for the Red Cross in France during World War I, Walt returned to the States and worked for an ad company, where he met Ub.

Though Mickey appeared in the silent short *Plane Crazy* in May of 1928, the amiable mouse didn't really take a bow until the November debut of *Steamboat Willie*. Walt's use of synchronized sound made all the difference. By 1937, Walt and company had released their first animated feature-length film, *Snow White and the Seven Dwarfs*.

The many films that followed formed the creative and financial bedrock for a legacy of one theme park after another. But perhaps the greatest legacy of Walt and his mouse is that they both make memories for generation upon generation.

TIMELINE

	Hollywood studio opens	*Steamboat Willie* released	*Snow White* wins special Oscar
1920		**1930**	**1940**

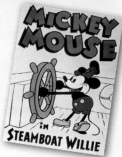

Shirley Temple presents Disney with one big and seven dwarf-size Oscars for *Snow White*, 1939; right: *Snow White*; *Steamboat Willie* poster, 1928

A Mouse Is Born

1920s–30s

Walt and his brother, Roy, establish a Hollywood studio in 1923. Animated shorts *Plane Crazy* and *Steamboat Willie*, starring both Mickey and Minnie, are released in 1928. Thereafter, Walt and his artists create dozens of Mickey shorts like 1930's *The Chain Gang*, when an orange pup named Pluto first appears.

Two years later, a good-natured dog, Goofy, debuts as an audience extra in *Mickey's Revue*. His spasmodic laugh earns him a series of his own animated short films. Hot-tempered Donald Duck and his loyal girlfriend, Daisy, follow.

In 1937, America's first full-length animated feature, *Snow White and the Seven Dwarfs*, becomes the highest-grossing feature of its time. *Gone with the Wind* doesn't blow by that record until 1939, the same year that Disney's groundbreaking feature earns a special Academy Award: one full-size Oscar and seven dwarf Oscars presented by Shirley Temple.

■ **Visit:** Walt Disney: One Man's Dream; The Magic of Disney Animation (⇨ *Ch. 6*),

Goofy

Characters Come to Life

1940s–50s

Fans of all ages flock to see successive hits, from *Pinocchio* and *Fantasia* (both 1940) to *Dumbo* (1941) and *Bambi* (1942). Though *Fantasia* is panned by some, it earns Academy Awards kudos for innovating in the area of visualized music—specifically, animation set to music by composers such as Bach, Tchaikovsky, and Beethoven and recorded under the direction of conductor Leopold Stokowski.

During World War II, the Disney studio springs to patriotic action with a series of military training and propaganda films. After the war, the animation wizards cast a spell over the

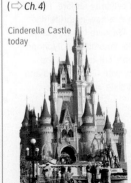

Left: *Dumbo*, 1941 and *Lady and the Tramp*; right:
entrance to Sleeping Beauty's Enchanted Castle,
Disneyland, late 1960s

country with Cinderella (1950),
Alice in Wonderland (1951),
Peter Pan (1953), *Lady and the
Tramp* (1955), *Sleeping Beauty*
(1959), and others.

During this period, Walt's
love for nature leads him to
produce 13 true-life adventure films, eight of which win
Oscars. Walt also brings his
first live-action adventure
film, *Treasure Island*, to the
screen. All the while he and
his brother, Roy, begin dreaming up a new adventure
altogether—Disneyland.

The first Disney theme park
opens on July 17, 1955, in
Anaheim, California. Many of
its attractions and rides have
themes based on Disney film
successes. Drawing on his
lifelong train infatuation, Walt

encircles the park with the
Disneyland Railroad.

■ **Visit:** Cinderella Castle
(⇨ *Ch. 4*).

■ **Ride:** Cinderella's Golden
Carrousel, Peter Pan's Flight,
Snow White's Scary Adven-
ture, and Dumbo the Flying
Elephant (⇨ *Ch. 4*)

■ **See:** Mickey's PhilharMagic
(⇨ *Ch. 4*)

Cinderella Castle
today

1960s–70s

A Magical New Frontier

In the early 1960s, Walt
purchases 27,500 Orlando
acres—an area twice the
size of Manhattan. Sadly,
he dies (December 1966) before
Walt Disney World opens.

On October 1, 1971, the Magic
Kingdom gates swing open,
and a sleek monorail glides
to the Contemporary and the
Polynesian resort hotels. In
November, a 640-acre west-
ern-style camping resort, Fort
Wilderness, opens.

■ **Visit:** Magic Kingdom
(⇨ *Ch. 4*)

■ **Ride:** The Monorail
(⇨ *Ch. 4*)

Above: Disney Paris; Mickey hat; right: EPCOT during food and wine festival

1980s–90s

A Worldlier Walt

Prior to his death, Walt begins work on what he hopes will be an ideal city. He names the project Experimental Prototype Community of Tomorrow. After the Magic Kingdom opens, Disney executives use some of Walt's ideas to create EPCOT Center. What opens in 1982 is the second Florida theme park—celebrating the world's cultures, the past, and the future—rather than an experimental community.

The 1980s are banner years for Disney Parks and Resorts. In 1983, the company's first international park—Tokyo Disneyland—opens. In 1989, Florida's third park, Disney-MGM Studios (later Disney's Hollywood Studios) premiers with celebrity fanfare. Not far from it, a new nightlife district, Pleasure Island, pumps up the volume, and Typhoon Lagoon, crashes onto the scene with 6-foot waves and thrill-slide appeal.

The decade that follows is no less ambitious. In 1992 Euro Disney Resort (now Disneyland Paris) becomes the Mouse's second international destination; the first Disney cruise ships are launched from Port Canaveral, Florida; and the fourth Florida park, Disney's Animal Kingdom, earns raves for its authentic habitats. The icing on the Magic Kingdom's 20th anniversary cake? The animation studio is once again making big-screen hits with *Beauty and the Beast* (1991), *Aladdin* (1992), and *The Lion King* (1994)

■ **Visit:** Spaceship Earth (⇨ *Ch. 5*); The Great Movie Ride (⇨ *Ch. 6*); Kilimanjaro Safaris (⇨ *Ch. 7*); Typhoon Lagoon (⇨ *Ch. 8*)

Aladdin

Finding Nemo's, Dory and Nemo

A Hidden Mickey at Epcot

Hidden Mickeys began as an inside joke among Disney Imagineers, the creative folks behind the theme parks. When finishing an attraction, they'd slip a Mickey into the motif to see who might notice. You can get a list of Hidden Mickeys at any Guest Relations location or at ⊕ www.hiddenmickeys. org. Here are just a few to get you started, though:

Big Thunder Mountain Railroad (Magic Kingdom). As your train nears the station, look to your right for three rusty gears on the ground.

DINOSAUR (Animal Kingdom). Stare at the bark of the painted tree in the far left background of the wall mural at the entrance.

Haunted Mansion (Magic Kingdom). As you move through the ballroom, notice the Mouse-eared place setting on the table.

Spaceship Earth (Epcot). Mickey smiles down from a constellation behind the loading area.

Twilight Zone Tower of Terror *(Hollywood Studios).* In the boiler room, look for a water stain on the wall after the queue splits.

New Millennium

To Infinity and Beyond!

■ The new millennium sends the Mouse into overdrive. Hong Kong Disneyland opens (2005), as do several World attractions, among them one with a *Toy Story* theme, and another with a *Nemo* theme. Disney World also adds to its accommodations, bringing the total to 28,000 rooms, 3,000 Disney Vacation Club villas, and 800 campsites. New eateries like Kouzzina by Cat Cora at Disney's Boardwalk open as does a luxurious on-Disney-property Waldorf Astoria, the second in the nation.

Looking ahead, it seems as if pixie dust will permeate the World for years to come.

The Four Seasons is planning a posh resort, and Disney is breaking ground on its Art of Animation Resort, slated to open in late 2012 adding 2,000 rooms and suites to the World's inventory. Disney is also prepping the Magic Kingdom's Fantasyland for an expansion, and Disney Cruise Line is anticipating the launch of two new cruise ships.

■ **Visit:** Soarin' and The Seas with Nemo & Friends (⇨ *Ch. 5*); Toy Story Midway Mania! (⇨ *Ch. 6*); Expedition Everest (⇨ *Ch. 7*)

Toy Story's Buzz Lightyear

DISNEY SHOPPING

It doesn't matter where you happen to land on Disney property—there's certain to be a shop close by overflowing with trendy Mickey merchandise, classic Disney keepsakes, or unique worldly treasures. Check your budget, and dive right in.

Lots of little girls go gaga over Disney's ubiquitous princess costumes and accessories, but they also clamor for trendy mismatched socks, tanks, and jammies at LittleMissMatched shop in Downtown Disney's West Side. As for boys, well, you can't pry them away from the Magic Kingdom's pirate paraphernalia or LEGO Imagination Center's brick-building stations in Downtown Disney Marketplace.

Adults have many shopping options, too, including authentic German beer steins and French perfumes at Epcot's World Showcase and stunning handcrafted art pieces, including menorahs and mezuzahs, at Hoypoloi in Downtown Disney's West Side. Safari hats are cool buys at Animal Kingdom, and hand-painted animation cels are hot tickets at Hollywood Studios. Even Disney's two water parks tempt sunbathers with branded beach towels and swimwear.

SAVVY SHOPPING

Who can resist a Cinderella snow globe, Mickey Mouse watch, or any one of a million colorful seemingly must-have treasures? It's easy to blow a bundle at Disney. Here are a few tips to help you keep things in check:

■ TIP➜ Agree on a spending limit. Do this for each family member, and stick to it. Children are less likely to buy the first thing they see if they know the budget is set.

■ TIP➜ Window-shop first, spend later. Often, you can find merchandise you saw in a given park at a Downtown Disney shop, and waiting till later cuts down on unnecessary impulse buys. If, however, you're in a park and find a must-buy-on-the-spot item, have the shop deliver it for free to the park's Package Pick-up station or to your Disney hotel room.

■ TIP➜ Ask shop clerks about sale items. Many shops discount seasonally or all year-round. That said, discounted items may not be displayed to catch your eye. Look for sale items first—and if you can't find them, just ask.

■ TIP➜ Don't worry about missed shopping ops. If you return home and regret that you didn't buy that snow globe, don't despair! Call WDW's Merchandise Mail Order service at ☎ 407/363–6200.

TOP AREAS

Though you can't turn a Disney corner without seeing a store or merchandise cart, certain areas within the parks and Downtown Disney offer the best shopping opportunities. And it really pays to know where these opportunities are: not only can you maximize your time, but you can also minimize your spending.

Downtown Disney

Why spend valuable touring time shopping in the theme parks when you can come here (for no entry fee) on your first or last day? The perfect place for one-stop souvenir shopping, Downtown Disney has dozens of stores, including the vast, hard-to-top World of Disney, the super-kid-friendly LEGO Imagination Center, and the über-hip Tren-D clothing and accessory shop.

Epcot World Showcase

Fine goods and trinkets from all over the world, some handcrafted, are sold at the pavilions representing individual countries here. Check out the Japanese and Chinese kimonos, Moroccan fezzes, French wines, Norwegian sweaters, and Mexican wood carvings. A United Kingdom shop even helps you research your family coat of arms, which you can buy as a paper printout or dressed up with paint or embroidery.

Main Street, U.S.A., Magic Kingdom

The Main Street buildings, with forced-perspective architecture and elaborately decorated facades, beckon, but don't waste precious touring time shopping in the morning. Come back later for custom-made watches, hand-blown crystal, cookware, princess dresses, mouse ears, and, of course, fairy tale-themed snow globes.

Discovery Island, Animal Kingdom

Although there are some great shops in Africa and Asia, many of the goods are concentrated in this hub. You'll find plush panda and leopard backpacks for kids, several types of safari hats, and even a "Green Corner" at Disney Outfitters, where earth-minded jewelry, "lucky" bamboo plants, and organic cotton T-shirts are hits.

Hollywood Boulevard, Hollywood Studios

If you're a size 0 or 2 like soap-opera diva Susan Lucci, you may want to take home the pink coat she wore on *All My Children* ($1,000 at Sid Cahuenga's One-of-a-Kind shop just inside the park). Or you can buy more affordable togs at the Boulevard's Keystone Clothiers (adults), L.A. Prop Cinema Storage (kids), and Mickey's of Hollywood (all in the family).

TOP SOUVENIRS

If you're scratching your head trying to figure out what could be the most memorable souvenir, you've got options—from the classic to the unexpected.

Make-Your-Own Mouse Ear Hat. For $12 and up, you can customize your ears—from fuzzy pink to shiny silver—at The Chapeau in the Magic Kingdom.

Indiana Jones Fedora. This brown wool-felt fedora (about $37) is a Halloween favorite. Pick one up at Indiana Jones Adventure Outpost in Hollywood Studios.

Zulu Basket. Uniquely patterned telephone-wire baskets at Mombasa Marketplace in the Animal Kingdom ($23–$52) are woven by South Africa's Zulu people.

Kimono. Kids' and adults' poly-rayon or silk kimonos, at China or Japan shops in Epcot ($33–$170), never go out of style.

Princess Dress. Many a little girl's treasure is her Cinderella, Aurora, Belle, or Ariel dress ($60) from Tinker Bell's Treasures, Magic Kingdom, or World of Disney, Downtown Disney Marketplace.

Double Light Saber. Let double the force be with you! At Tatooine Traders in Hollywood Studios, kids can customize a light saber ($19.99 single; $22.95 double) with crystals, hilts, and blades.

Mickey Computer Mouse. A wireless mouse styled after the Big Cheese's white-gloved hand is $30 at Mickey's of Hollywood in Hollywood Studios.

Plush Character Toy. Dumbo, Goofy, Nemo—you name the character, and there's a plush toy—in one of many sizes and at just about any Disney park or Downtown Disney. Prices run about $10 to $50.

TOP 50 DISNEY SHOPS

MAGIC KINGDOM

Main Street, U.S.A.

The Chapeau. Classic monogrammed mouse ears are always in style. But the really hot ears are those you customize yourself from a selection of beanies, ears, patches, and other doodads. The hats may not stay on all day, though, so consider saving this purchase until later. Or buy a Disney baseball cap to block the sun.

Crystal Arts. It dazzles with Arribas Brothers engraved crystal pieces like a sparkling Cinderella coach or an iconic glass slipper in one of many sizes (though none will fit your foot!). Don't miss visiting the glass studio and its 2,100°F furnaces in the back, where a glassblower explains the process while creating wineglasses and bowls. Fascinating!

The Emporium. At 17,000 square feet, it's the largest souvenir shop in any of the parks. You'll find thousands of Disney character products, from sunglasses to plush toys. Princess items rock for little girls—a set of three princess clip magnets is just $7. Mickey and Minnie oven mitts are $12 each. Inquire about marked-down merchandise.

Uptown Jewelers. It's a treasure chest of jewelry, figurines, and Disney lithographs. In the Watchmaker's corner, artists sketch Disney characters and themes (Tinker Bell, anyone?) for the faces that are built into $200 to $350 watches.

Adventureland

Agrabah Bazaar. It has the expected Aladdin-wear and Jasmine costumes. But you'll also find maracas and other inexpensive percussion instruments, gold- and silver-plated bangles with tiny Mickey ears attached, and snappy leather and straw hats for the jungle or desert.

Pirate's Bazaar. Just outside the Pirates of the Caribbean, you can stock up on pirate hats, swords, flintlocks, and hooks-for-hands. The ultimate scalawag topper is a Captain Jack Sparrow hat complete with braids ($32).

Frontierland

Big Al's. This merchandise cart across the walkway from the Country Bear Jamboree has Davy Crockett coonskin caps, fancy cowboy hats, Pocahontas garb, and other gear that draws oohs and ahs from cowboy and -girl wannabes.

Liberty Square

Ye Old Christmas Shop. Shoppers who arrive after Christmas discover discounts up to 75% on ornaments. Next Christmas will be magical with a $22 princess stocking. Character ornaments, Mickey wedding top hats, and Minnie bridal veils are always in stock

Fantasyland

Tinker Bell's Treasures. Sparkly, shimmering dresses, hats, dolls, jewelry, and Tinker Bell pajamas and slippers are all the rage. You can even take home your very own Cinderella Castle. Boys can get a complete pirate costume here.

EPCOT

Future World

Mouse Gear. The usual Disney suspects—plush toys, Mickey cookware, Disney pins, Epcot-themed sweatshirts and T-shirts—are all at this Future World emporium. A few gems include the $17 World Showcase–theme drumsticks for budding musicians and gauzy scarves for fashionistas.

World Showcase

Enoteca Castello. This Italy pavilion shop sells some of the country's popular wines, olive oils, pastas, and sweets. And if you want to age like Sophia Loren, try the virgin-olive-oil soap, just $14.95 for a pump bottle.

Historic Research Center. The focus at this United Kingdom outpost is tracking down your family name and coat of arms. Take home a printout of the latter for $40. Drop the bigger bucks for a framed, embroidered or hand-painted version.

Il Bel Cristallo. For chic Italian totes, accessories, and collectibles, stop at this Italy pavilion. You'll also find fragrances by Gucci, Ferragamo, and Valentino.

La Signature. In the France pavilion, follow your nose for a sniff and a spritz of high-end French perfumes. Guerlain fragrances, cosmetics, and skin-care products like the Orchidée Impériale eye cream ($185) draw fans from around the globe.

Les Vins de France. Enjoy tasting some wine and shopping for a bottle or two of your favorite. A fun, practical souvenir is the $20 sparkly Mickey wine stopper.

The Market. Morocco's open-air market is like something out of an Indiana Jones movie. It's a maze of shops selling straw bags and colorful carpets. It's also a great place to pick up something really different, like a Moroccan fez for $17 or belly-dancing gear, including a bright scarf ($55), finger cymbals ($8), and a CD ($24) with all the music you need to wow your audience.

Mitsukoshi. Hello Kitty, one of Japan's most popular toys, is on hand here. Another toy favorite is a four-inch collectible Bebichhichi doll with pacifier ($17.50). Dress up with a washable poly kimono ($33) or a more luxurious silk version ($170), or check out the shimmering pearl jewelry. You'll be tempted to take home some sweets after watching a Japanese Candy Art demonstration just outside the store.

The Plaza de los Amigos. Descend a ramp at this Mexico shop to find sombreros ($15 or $20), baskets, pottery, and leather goods. You can have a brightly hued poncho just like America Ferrera wore in the pilot of TV's *Ugly Betty* for $37.

Puffin's Roost. In Norway, Viking wannabes go crazy for the soft toy spears and shields ($11–$14). The $13 plush puffins are sweet for tots, and you can find Norwegian pewter, leather goods, and colorful sweaters.

Queen's Table. This United Kingdom shop is devoted to smelling good, or smelling like David Beckham—his signature scent is available here.

Weinkeller. In Germany, you can buy a wine-flight passport ($20) here for two 2-ounce samples of German wine—Reislings and ice wines are popular—as well as two samples each of Italian and French wines at the Italy and France pavilions (or you can pick up the same passport when visiting those other two countries).

Yong Feng Shangdian. China's sprawling bazaar has a huge selection of tea sets ranging in style from traditional to contemporary ($110—but sometimes on sale) and fragranced candles that are sure to align your chi. Butterfly hair combs and brocade pajamas are beautiful, but the hottest items are little Buddha statues, available for $8 and up.

HOLLYWOOD STUDIOS

Hollywood Boulevard

Keystone Clothiers. This shop pops with stylish clothing and accessories for adults. Handbags and totes sport classic Mickey or 1930s Sleeping Beauty artwork. Black-and-silver "I Love Mickey" bangles ($14) make a statement. Character-themed clothing for men, like the gray, red, and white Grumpy tie ($30), elicit smiles.

L.A. Prop Cinema Storage. The sherbet-green Tinker Bell fleece hoodie has a matching backpack ($43). Little girls gravitate toward the Tinker Bell Fashion Set of tiny dolls and costumes ($13). Boys want to check out the Toy Story spring-action shooter ($12).

Mickey's of Hollywood. The largest store in this park is a mini-version of the Magic Kingdom's Emporium with toys, T-shirts, and doodads. Blue velvety Sorcerer's Apprentice hats have Mouse ears, plus a moon and stars that light up ($36.95.) You'll find kooky Koosh ball pens featuring Pixar and princess characters for $5.95 and a computer mouse styled like Mickey's white-gloved hand.

Sid Cahuenga's One-of-a-Kind. Enter this kitschy little bungalow to find Dick Van Dyke's pastel striped jacket from *Mary Poppins* ($65,000). A signed Russell Crowe *Gladiator* portrait goes for $350. Sid's even sells celebrity clothing—a coat worn by Susan Lucci on *All My Children* will set you back $1,000. Movie posters, in comparison, are a steal.

Echo Lake

Indiana Jones Adventure Outpost. Almost as popular as the pirate hats in the Magic Kingdom are the Indiana Jones felt fedoras ($37) sold at this outpost near the stunt amphitheater. Small kids can get a complete Indy play set with fedora, machete, pistol, and gems for $20.

Tatooine Traders. This spot outside of the Star Tours ride is jammed with kids clamoring to build their own light sabers ($19.99 single; $22.95 double) complete with crystals, hilts, and blades.

Streets of America

The Writer's Stop. A cup of coffee or a spot of tea pairs well with some browsing here. If you happen to hit it right, you might get a book signed by a celebrity author.

Youse Guys Moychindice. This shop on New York Street sells CDs of Los Lawn Boys, the rockin' band that plays sets on the street under the moniker Mulch, Sweat, & Shears—Live in Concert!

Animation Courtyard

Animation Gallery. If you appreciate the art of animation, this is the place. It's loaded with interesting art pieces, some valuable, some not. You can watch artists hand paint animation cels; you can also buy limited-edition hand-painted cels that include "Goofy Moments," and "Off to Neverland" ($125–$290). You'll also find statuettes, posters, and animation books.

Sunset Boulevard

Sunset Club Couture. It's the one shop you don't want to miss on Sunset Boulevard. Super-soft vintage T-shirts star Mickey in a scene from 1928's animated short *Plane Crazy* and others ($33). Vintage Donald Duck in 1934's *The Wise Little Hen* makes for a fun ball cap ($20). And women's clothing runs the gamut from campy Chip 'n Dale "I'm Nuts fer Ya," tees to gold-thong sandals. Customized watches like those sold at the Magic Kingdom's Uptown Jewelers are sold here, too.

ANIMAL KINGDOM

Discovery Island

Creature Comforts. This spot close to the border at Africa specializes in kiddie togs. You can get a Minnie Mouse leopard-ears headband ($13), small panda and leopard backpacks ($22), and plenty of princess merchandise.

Disney Outfitters. The Outfitters, situated near the Tip Board, features its own "green corner," with sustainable jewelry of hemp, straw, bamboo, and recycled materials, plus organic cotton T-shirts ($25–$32). There's a broad selection of upscale men's and women's apparel, as well as jewelry and pottery handcrafted by African artisans.

Island Mercantile. To the left as you enter Discovery Island from the Oasis is Animal Kingdom's largest shop. It stocks clothing, cookware, photo frames, and lots of logo souvenirs. Safari hats, caps, and straw hats range from $17–$30, and you can buy a pair of safari pants that folds up into its own pocket to carry as a pack ($31). These could come in handy when you emerge soaked from Kali River Rapids.

Dinoland

Chester & Hester's Dinosaur Treasures. Dinophiles can't resist the finds here. It has a big display of quite large and scary-looking, yet soft and huggable, T-rex, velociraptor, and other dinosaur figures ($12–$20). Beyond the prehistoric, the shop has a build-your-own Mr. Potato Head station, and an attractive bin of rocks for collectors.

Africa

Mombasa Marketplace and Ziwani Traders. In Harambe Village, this is a great stop for unusual items like the Zulu-made colorful telephone wire baskets, dishes from Zimbabwe, and South African wines such as a Porcupine Ridge cabernet. Young kids like to play with the small figurines ($2.95 and $3.95) of giraffes, elephants, rhinos, and other critters they just saw on their Kilimanjaro Safaris ride.

Asia

Bhaktapur Market. At this gem of a shop you'll find bejeweled sandals and thongs ($19) and gorgeous, colorful print scarves of silk, satin, or India chiffon ($30–$35). There's also a good chance you'll find something on the clearance shelves— anything from a calligraphy kit to a soap and candle set.

DOWNTOWN DISNEY

Marketplace

Disney Design-A-Tee. Tucked next to the long-standing Art of Disney gallery, this shop wows creative types with eight touch-screen computer stations where you can select your Hanes shirt (color, size, style), then choose from among hundreds of Disney images (contemporary and vintage) to complete your design. ($23.95 children's size; $26.95 adult size). These are perfect for a family-reunion keepsake.

LEGO Imagination Center. An impressive backdrop of large and elaborate LEGO sculptures and piles of colorful LEGO bricks wait for children and their parents to build toy castles, cars, or cold-fusion chambers. A covered outdoor play area is a great place to experiment with the bricks at building stations before buying. Ask a clerk to point out the discounted merchandise shelf.

Mickey's Mart. The sign proclaims EVERYTHING $10 AND UNDER—undoubtedly a welcome sight for those who've been reaching for their wallets a lot. If children

are pushing for a trinket, head to the "4 for $10" quick-fix shelves stocked with little toys and souvenir mugs, magnets, photo frames, and kiddie cups.

Once Upon A Toy. Toy rooms are themed to boys with kinetic train displays and Star Wars sets and to girls with castles and a My Little Pony Creation Station. There are lots of classic games redesigned with Disney themes, like the Haunted Mansion Game of Life. You can test-drive many of the toys, and, at the Mr. Potato Head Creation Station, you can fill a box with assorted lips, noses, and even Mickey ears ($20).

Pin Traders. It's nice to know that you can visit the biggest and best location for pin collectors without paying park admission. There are so many pins lining the walls, including many hard-to-find limited-edition pins, that you could go cross-eyed. And there's a pin-trading station staffed by a Disney cast member who'll help you find that Snow White or teacup pin.

Tren-D. The newest Marketplace boutique has "hip" and "eclectic" written all over it. Chic sundresses with subtle Mickey-ear designs are perfect for an evening at Cirque du Soleil or dinner at House of Blues. Designer items are from Billabong, Judith Jack, Kidada Jones, and Roxy.

World of Disney. At *the* Disney superstore—with 50,000 square feet of shopping and nearly half a million Disney items—beware of sensory overload. Themed shopping areas like the princess room ($65 for that Cinderella dress or Ariel costume) help steer your to just the right toys, clothing, housewares, and more. The Bibbidi Bobbidi Boutique, similar to one at the Magic Kingdom, does princess makeovers ($50–$240). Disney media, from software

to CDs, is everywhere, and there's candy for every sweet tooth.

West Side

Hoypoloi. It's easy to lose track of time in this little oasis of fine art, handcrafted jewelry, and Zen paraphernalia. Big sellers include solid bronze frogs by Frogman; signed, digitized paintings by Alan Foxx; Zen art boxes for "living in the moment;" and handsome menorahs and mezuzahs.

LittleMissMatched. Girls and their moms are goofy for the candy-colored T-shirts, jammies, duffels, and miss matched socks (a pack of three pairs of knee-high socks for $12) at this new West Side shop. Seasonal sales run periodically, and there's a good chance you can dress up with quirky flair for a bargain.

Magic Masters. At this small shop you'll usually find someone demonstrating card or coin tricks and other close-up magic. If you buy, they'll teach you how to do that particular feat of prestidigitation before you leave.

Magnetron. As the name implies, this place sells magnets—some 20,000 of them. So what's the big attraction? Well, they light up, change color, glow in the dark, and come in every shape, size, color, and pop-culture character (check out magneto-Elvis). You'll find lots of fun, inexpensive souvenirs.

Sosa Family Cigar Company. Cigars are kicking ash at this family-owned business, and Thursday through Saturday evenings you can watch an expert roll stogies by hand. There's even a humidor filled with the finest cigars for aficionados. Smoking!

DISNEY NIGHTLIFE

After dark, your theme-park experience takes on a new energy, and beyond the parks you can have your pick of dinner shows, music performances, bars, lounges, and one mind-blowing Cirque du Soleil performance.

Stay late at a park to enjoy parades or fireworks, or check out the hopping bar scene at Epcot's Rose & Crown Pub. You can have a foot-stomping, ribs-and-chicken hoedown at the dinner show in the Fort Wilderness Resort. Or you can say "aloha" at the Polynesian Resort's luau. Just a stroll or quick boat ride from Epcot there's a carnival-like atmosphere of sweet shops, games of chance, fine dining, and entertainment for all at Disney's Board-Walk. Or head over to Downtown Disney for a House of Blues concert or cigars and martinis at Fuego Cigars by Sosa at Pleasure Island. The lights here shine brightly long into the night. For information on entertainment, call the Disney operator at ☎ 407/824–2222.

TOP NIGHTLIFE DESTINATIONS

Downtown Disney. Though Pleasure Island's nightclubs have closed, you can still find some great bars and lounges here including Raglan Road Irish Pub and Restaurant and Bongo's Cuban Café.

Boardwalk. A piano bar, a dance club, a brewpub, and an ESPN Club sports bar offer lots of options.

Disney Resorts. With more than a dozen on-property resorts, the hotel bar and lounge scene is lively. You don't have to be a resort guest to visit these nightspots, which range from boisterous to mellow.

Epcot. Four words: Rose & Crown Pub! Great piano sets by the Hat Lady, and,

on busy nights, four-to-six-deep-at-the-bar guarantees good times at this United Kingdom watering hole. A more relaxing bar scene is at Cava de Tequila in the Mexico pavilion. Tequila flight, anyone?

FIREWORKS, LIGHT SHOWS, AND PARADES

Electrical Water Pageant. This 10-minute floating parade of sea creatures is composed of tiny lights, with an electronic score highlighted by Handel's Water Music. If you're by Bay Lake and the Seven Seas Lagoon, look for it from the beaches at the Polynesian (at 9), the Grand Floridian (9:15), Wilderness Lodge (9:35), Fort Wilderness (9:45), the Contemporary (10:10), and, in busy seasons, the Magic Kingdom (10:25). Times vary; check with Guest Relations.

Fantasmic! Hollywood Studios' 25-minute special-effects blockbuster is held after dark, usually twice weekly, in an often-packed 6,500-seat amphitheater. Mickey Mouse in the guise of the Sorcerer's Apprentice emcees a revue packed with villains and heroes, drama, song and dance, light effects, pyrotechnics, and scenes from Disney films projected onto water screens. Arrive at least an hour early; you may get wet if you sit close to the front. Consider the Fantasmic! dinner package, which includes seats in a VIP area.

Illuminations. Epcot's 13-minute show, which takes place over the reflective World Showcase lagoon, usually begins at 9 PM, and features lasers, fireworks, fountains, and a floating sphere that displays video scenes. Good vantage points include the patios of the Rose & Crown Pub (United Kingdom) and Cantina de

San Angel (Mexico) or between boat docks at the World Showcase entrance. For a front-row spot, arrive at least an hour beforehand.

SpectroMagic. Millions of tiny lights decorating the floats, carriages, and even costumes of the Magic Kingdom's parade will mesmerize you. Kids can't tear their eyes away from the 20-minute spectacle. This is a seasonal parade; times vary, so check the park's *Times Guide* before you set out. Take your place on the curb at least 40 minutes ahead of time.

Wishes. The 12-minute Magic Kingdom show exemplifies the magic of Disney. To the accompaniment of classic Disney melodies, fireworks are launched from 11 locations around the park, as Jiminy Cricket reminds you that "anything your heart desires" can come true. The best place to watch is Main Street—try to snag the few seats on the second floor of the Walt Disney World train station or elsewhere near the front of the park so you can make a quick exit. Check your park *Times Guide* for performances, which vary seasonally.

CIRQUE DU SOLEIL

La Nouba, a surreal show by the world-famous Cirque du Soleil company, starts at 100 mph and accelerates through 90 minutes of acrobatics, avant-garde staging, costumes, choreography, and a grand finale that makes you doubt Newton's law of gravity. The story of La Nouba—derived from the French phrase *faire la nouba* (live it up)—is alternately mysterious, dreamlike, comical, and sensual. A cast of 72 international performers takes the stage in this specially constructed, 70,000-square-foot venue. In 2010, world-renowned juggler Anthony Gatto

joined the cast with an exhilarating nine-minute act. Call ahead for good seats (there are three categories of seating) and hire a babysitter if necessary. Though the show doesn't charge for tots under age 3 who can sit on a lap, you wouldn't want to miss one minute of this class act. ☎ *407/939–7600 reservations* ⊕ *www.cirquedusoleil.com* ✉ *$73.49–$127.80 adults, $59.76–$111.83 children 3–9* ☉ *Performances Tues.–Sat. 6 and 9.*

TOP BOARDWALK NIGHTSPOTS

Atlantic Dance Hall. Atlantic Dance is a high-energy Top 40 dance club with a huge screen showing videos requested by the crowd. The parquet dance floor is set off by furnishings of deep blue, maroon, and gold, and the ceiling glows with gold stars and twinkling lights. Signature martinis are in demand, and you can get cognac, a cappuccino, and light bites to burn off on the dance floor. ☎ *407/939–2444* ✉ *No cover* ☉ *Tues.–Sat. 9 PM–2 AM.*

Big River Grille & Brewing Works. Disney World's only brewpub has intimate tables where brew masters tend to their potions. You can order a $5.95 sampler with up to six 4-ounce shots of whatever's on tap that day, usually including Red Rocket, Southern Flyer Light Lager, Gadzooks Pilsner, and Steamboat Pale Ale. Upscale pub grub and sandwiches pair well. There's also a sidewalk café. ☎ *407/560–0253* ✉ *No cover* ☉ *Daily 11:30 AM–midnight.*

ESPN Club. The sports motif here is carried into every nook and cranny—the main dining area looks like a sports arena, with a basketball-court hardwood floor and a giant scoreboard that projects the day's big game. There are more than 100 TVs

throughout (even in the restrooms). The place is packed for big games; call ahead to see if special seating rules are in effect. ☎ *407/939–1177* 💳 *No cover* 🕙 *Daily 11:30 AM–1 AM.*

Jellyrolls. In this rockin', boisterous piano bar comedians act as emcees and play dueling grand pianos nonstop. The steady stream of conventions at Disney makes this the place to catch CEOs doing the conga to Barry Manilow's "Copacabana"—if that's your idea of a good time. ☎ *407/560–8770* 💳 *$10 cover after 7 PM* 🕙 *Daily 7 PM–2 AM.*

TOP DOWNTOWN DISNEY NIGHTSPOTS

Bongos Cuban Café. Latin rhythms provide the beat at this enterprise with a pre-Castro theme owned by pop singer Gloria Estefan. Four bars are especially busy on weekends, when a Latin band kicks it up a notch with *muy caliente* music. Samba, tango, salsa, and merengue rhythms roll throughout the week. ☎ *407/828–0999* 🕙 *Sun.–Thurs. 11 AM–10:30 PM; Fri. and Sat. 11 AM–1:30 AM*

House of Blues. The restaurant serves up live blues performances Friday and Saturday and rib-sticking Mississippi Delta cooking all week long. The attached concert hall has showcased such artists as Aretha Franklin, David Byrne, Steve Miller, Willie Nelson, and Journey. ☎ *407/934–2583* 💳 *Covers vary* 🕙 *Daily, performance and restaurant times vary.*

TOP DISNEY RESORT NIGHTSPOTS

Dinner Shows

Hoop-Dee-Doo Revue. The Pioneer Hall Players perform romantic ballads, corny tunes, and slapstick. You chow down on barbecued ribs, fried chicken, corn on the cob, strawberry shortcake, and all the fixin's. Prime-time shows sell out months in advance in busy seasons. ✉ *Fort Wilderness Resort* ☎ *407/939–3463 for reservations up to 180 days in advance, 407/824–2803 for dietary restrictions* 💳 *$52.99–$65.99 adults, $26.99–$33.99 children 3–9, including tax and gratuity. Prices vary by seat selection* 🕙 *Daily 5, 7:15, and 9:30.*

Spirit of Aloha. It's an outdoor barbecue with colorful South Pacific–style entertainment. Fire jugglers and hula-drum dancers are entertaining for the whole family, and the hula dancers' navel maneuvers are something to see. ✉ *Polynesian Resort* ☎ *407/939–3463 for reservations up to 180 days in advance, 407/824–1593 for dietary restrictions* 💳 *$54.99–$67.99 adults, $27.99–$34.99 children 3–9, including tax and gratuity. Prices vary by seat selection* 🕙 *Tues.–Sat. 5:15 and 8.*

Resort Bars

Mizner's. A stylish, refined alcove named after Florida Renaissance architect Addison Mizner is tucked away at the far end of Grand Floridian's second-floor lobby. It's a tasteful getaway where you can unwind with a glass of champagne, a martini, or a Manhattan. The extensive drink menu includes multiple single-malt scotch whiskies and after-dinner cognacs and ports. ✉ *Grand Floridian* 🕙 *Daily 5 PM–11 PM.*

What's classier (or more classic) than having dinner and seeing a show? Cirque du Soleil's spectacle, *La Nouba*, is one of the classiest shows in town.

Narcoossee's. Inside the restaurant is a bar that serves ordinary beer in expensive yard glasses, but the porch-side views of the Seven Seas Lagoon, the nightly Electrical Water Pageant, and the Magic Kingdom fireworks are worth the premium you pay. ✉ *Grand Floridian* ☺ *Daily 5:30 PM–10 PM.*

Rix Lounge. The decor is contemporary mixed with traditional Mexican, and includes warm coral, orange, and pink tones with art-glass chandeliers. There's a decent-sized dance floor that stays busy thanks to a DJ. Martinis, mojitos, and margaritas pair well with tapas and the hip ambience. ✉ *Coronado Springs Resort* ☺ *Tues.–Sat. 5 PM–2 AM.*

Territory Lounge. The frontier theme here honors the Corps of Discovery (look overhead for a Lewis and Clark Expedition trail map). In between drinks, check out the surveying equipment, daguerreotypes, parka mittens, maps, and what the lounge claims is a pair of Teddy Roosevelt's boots. ✉ *Wilderness Lodge* ☺ *Daily 4:30–midnight.*

Victoria Falls. The exotic safari theme incorporates leather directors' chairs, native masks, and the gurgling of a stream that flows from the lobby and through the lounge to cascade over rockwork into a small pool at the Boma restaurant below. This is a great spot to watch a game and sip South African wines and beers or the signature South African margarita. Arrive early and check out the zebras, giraffes, and other animals on the lodge's savannah. ✉ *Animal Kingdom Lodge* ☺ *Daily 4 PM–midnight.*

The Wave Lounge. A big U-shape bar lends this large place a community watering-hole feel. Warm-tone furniture contrasts with a cool blue color scheme, and a dark ceiling with twinkling lights mimics starlight. The innovative spirits menu features wines from Australia and New Zealand. Organic ales from Orlando Brewing are popular, and there's lots of buzz about organic cocktails like the Puretini with vodka, mango, and passion-fruit liqueur. ✉ *Contemporary Resort* ☺ *Daily noon–midnight.*

DISNEY SPORTS AND OUTDOOR ACTIVITIES

Tennis, anyone? A round of golf? Or maybe you'd rather surf, parasail, or drive a racecar. You can take part in these activities and many more should you feel the need to stretch your legs and move about beyond the theme parks.

Disney is known for its award-winning golf, but if you'd rather swing a racquet, you'll be happy to know there are several lighted courts—both clay and hard—at five Disney resorts. Disney's Fort Wilderness is the place to saddle up for a ride through the woods, and the Contemporary Resort is number one for water sports, including parasailing.

Got a lead foot? Head over to The Richard Petty Driving Experience, where you can race a NASCAR-style stock car or ride shotgun with a pro. Anglers get hooked on fishing charters; runners and bikers get their adrenaline rush on trails across the property. If you'd rather be a spectator, take yourself out to a ballgame at ESPN Wide World of Sports. Popcorn? Check. Hot dogs? Check. Does it get any better than this? For Disney recreation information, call ☎ 407/939–7529.

TOP EXPERIENCES

Biking. You'll look sweet upon the seat of a bicycle built for two. You can even rent a covered surrey bike for four at the Board-Walk and other resort locations.

Fishing. Depart from the Wilderness Lodge or Contemporary Resort on a Disney fishing charter to tranquil Bay Lake, where odds are good you'll discover a bass bonanza.

Golf. The Tom Fazio–designed Osprey Ridge course keeps competitive players on their toes, and the scenery is lovely. Mini-golf fans can putt-putt their way through the "winter chill" at the whimsical Winter Summerland next to the Blizzard Beach water park.

Parasailing. The sun is bright, and you've got the wind beneath your parasail as you soar hundreds of feet above sparkling Bay Lake.

Surfing. Surf's up in the early hours before Typhoon Lagoon water park officially opens—here's your chance to learn how to hang 10!

EXTREME SPORTS

Auto Racing

The Richard Petty Driving Experience lets you ride in or even drive a NASCAR-style stock car on the real racetrack alongside the road that leads to the Magic Kingdom parking lot. Depending on what you're willing to spend—prices range from $116 to $1,383—you can do everything from riding shotgun for three laps on the 1-mi track to taking driving lessons, culminating in your very own solo behind the wheel. The riding cost for three laps is $116; eight laps, $478; 18 laps, $904; 30 laps, $1,383; the experience, priceless. The Richard Petty organization has a second Central Florida location at the Daytona International Speedway, but prices differ, so check the Web site. ⊠ *Walt Disney World Speedway, 3450 N. World Dr., Lake Buena Vista* ☎ *800/237–3889* ⊕ *www.1800bepetty.com.*

Water Sports

Thanks to **Sammy Duvall's Water Sports Centre** you can get a birds'-eye view of Disney while parasailing on Bay Lake. Flights with 450 feet of line last 8 to 10 minutes ($95); deluxe flights with 600 feet of line last 10 to 12 minutes ($130). You must weigh at least 130 pounds, though lightweights can bulk up with the help of

a lifeguard or family member and a tandem flight (without the tandem charge). But if you want to parasail with a partner from the get-go, tandem flights are $170; deluxe tandem flights are $195.

At the same location, you can try your skills at waterskiing, wakeboarding, and tubing. Up to five people can go on the ski boat that includes equipment and an expert instructor and driver. For a group that large, instructors recommend booking two hours ($165 for the first hour and $125 for each additional hour); couples or smaller groups may want to try one hour, though half-hour rentals ($85) are available. ✉ *Disney's Contemporary Resort* ☎ *407/939–0754.*

SPECTATOR HEAVEN

ESPN Wide World of Sports Complex is proof that Disney doesn't do anything unless it does it in a big way. The 220-acre facility, formerly Disney's Wide World of Sports Complex, is on Osceola Parkway on the route to Animal Kingdom. The huge complex contains a 7,500-seat baseball stadium—housed in a giant stucco structure that, from the outside, looks like a Moroccan palace—a 5,000-seat field house, and a number of fan-oriented commercial ventures such as the Official All-Star Café, ESPN Grill, and shops that sell clothing and other items sanctioned by Major League Baseball, the NBA, and the NFL. During spring training the Atlanta Braves play here.

The complex also hosts more than 170 amateur and professional events each year, including big-ticket tennis tournaments. In all, some 30 spectator sports are represented among the annual events, including Harlem Globetrotters basketball games, baseball fantasy camps held

in conjunction with the Braves at the start of spring training, and track events ranging from the Walt Disney World Marathon to Amateur Athletic Union (AAU) championships. The complex offers bowling, softball, basketball, and other games for group events ranging from family reunions to corporate picnics. ✉ *800 S. Victory Way, Lake Buena Vista* ☎ *407/828–3267 events information* ⊕ *www.disneyworldsports.com.*

TOP SPORTING OPPORTUNITIES

Archery
For 90 minutes you can make like Geronimo at **Fort Wilderness Resort** (☎ *407/939–7529*), where an archery guide oversees novice and expert marksmen (ages 6 and up) who want to get in some target shooting. Non-resort guests are welcome to join campers, and the $25 fee includes use of the compound bow and arrows, plus instruction. You can book up to 180 days in advance.

Biking
Paved trails take you past forests, lakes, wooded campgrounds, and resort villas. If you're 18 or older, you can rent bikes at multiple locations, but you must ride them in the area where you rent them.

Rental locations include Downtown Disney Marketplace (near the Rainforest Café) and nearly every moderate-to-deluxe Disney resort, including the BoardWalk Resort and other Epcot Resort hotels, Coronado Springs Resort near Disney's Hollywood Studios, Old Key West and Saratoga Springs near Downtown Disney, Animal Kingdom Lodge, Grand Floridian Resort, and the Fort Wilderness Bike Barn at Fort Wilderness Resort.

On the Richard Petty Driving Experience, you get to ride in—or even drive—a NASCAR-style stock car.

Most locations have children's bikes with training wheels and bikes with toddler seats. Surrey bikes are also an option. These look like old-fashioned carriages, and are a great way to take your family on a sightseeing tour. The covered tops provide a rare commodity at Disney—shade.

Rates start at $8 to $9 an hour for regular bikes and go up to $20 to $25 per half hour for surrey bikes (depends on whether they have two, four, or six seats). Wear a helmet; it's free with each rental.

Boating

Disney has one of the nation's largest fleets of rental pleasure craft. There are marinas at the Caribbean Beach Resort, Contemporary Resort, Downtown Disney Marketplace, Fort Wilderness Resort, Grand Floridian, Old Key West Resort, Polynesian Resort, Port Orleans Resort, Port Orleans–Riverside Resort, and the Wilderness Lodge.

You can rent 12-foot sailboats, catamarans, motor-powered pontoon boats, pedal boats, kayaks, canoes, and tiny

two-passenger Sea Racers—a hit with children—for use on Bay Lake and the adjoining Seven Seas Lagoon, Crescent Lake at Epcot Resorts, Lake Buena Vista, or Buena Vista Lagoon. You can also sail and water-ski on Bay Lake and the Seven Seas Lagoon; stop at the Fort Wilderness, Contemporary, Polynesian, or Grand Floridian marina to rent sailboats or sign up for waterskiing. Call ☎ 407/939–7529 for more information.

Fishing

You can sign up for two-hour catch-and-release **Disney fishing excursions** (☎ 407/939–2277) on regularly stocked Bay Lake and Seven Seas Lagoon. In fact, Bay Lake is so well stocked that locals joke that you can almost walk across the water on the backs of the bass. Departing from the Fort Wilderness, Wilderness Lodge, Contemporary, Polynesian, Boardwalk, Yacht & Beach Club, Port Orleans Riverside, and Grand Floridian resort marinas, trips include boat, equipment, and a guide for up to five anglers. Similar charters depart at the same times from Cap'n

Jack's Marina at Downtown Disney Marketplace by Lake Buena Vista. Your guide is happy to bait your hook, unhook your catches, and even snap pictures of you with your fish.

Two-hour trips for up to five people depart daily at 7, 10, and 1:30. The cost is $270 (per group) for morning departures and $235 at 1:30. Live bait and fishing equipment are included; a license is not required on Disney property.

At the **Ol' Man Island Fishing Hole** at Port Orleans-Riverside you can enjoy an inexpensive fishing experience from the dock. Cane poles and bait are $4 per half hour or $9 per day. You must rent equipment here to use the dock, and you're required to release any fish that you catch. The Fishing Hole is open daily 11 to 5. Pick up rods and tackle at the **Fort Wilderness Bike Barn** (☎ 407/824–2742), open daily 9–5, for fishing in the canals around Fort Wilderness Resort. Rod and reel with tackle is $6 per hour and $12.50 per day. You must be at least 18 to rent here.

Golf

Where else would you find a sand trap shaped like the head of a well-known mouse? Disney has 72 holes of golf on four championship courses—all on the PGA Tour route—plus a 9-hole walking course. The original Palm and Magnolia 18-hole courses are southwest of the Magic Kingdom near the Grand Floridian and Polynesian resorts, as is the 9-hole Oak Trail walking course. The Lake Buena Vista 18-hole course is northwest of Downtown Disney. The newer 18-hole Osprey Ridge is east of Fort Wilderness Resort.

Tee times are available daily from 6 until 6. You can book them up to 90 days in advance if you're staying at a WDW-owned hotel, 60 days ahead if you're staying elsewhere. One-on-one instruction from PGA-accredited professionals is available at the Palm, Magnolia, and Lake Buena Vista. Prices for private lessons vary: 45 minutes cost $75 for adults and $50 for youngsters 17 and under. For tee times and private lessons, call Walt Disney World Golf & Recreation Reservations at ☎ 407/939–1500. ⇨ *For more information, including individual course reviews, see the Golf section of the Experience Orlando and the Parks chapter at the front of this guide.*

If mini-golf is your game, Disney's Winter Summerland next to Blizzard Beach Water Park has 18 holes on its faux-snow "winter" course and 18 on its tropical "summer" course—sandcastles and all. At the Fantasia Gardens 36-hole mini-golf course adjacent to the Walt Disney World Swan Hotel, dancing hippos and broomsticks remind you of the classic animated film *Fantasia*. There's even a Fantasia Fairways challenge course, with sand traps, water hazards, and par-3 and -4 holes up to 75 feet long for experienced golfers.

Horseback Riding

Fort Wilderness Resort (☎ 407/824–2832) offers tame backwoods trail rides beginning at 8:30 AM and continuing through mid-to-late afternoon. Children must be at least 9 years old and 48 inches tall to ride, and adults must weigh less than 250 pounds. Trail rides are $46 for 45 minutes; hours vary by season. You must check in 30 minutes prior to your ride, and reservations are essential. Both horseback riding and the campground are open to non-resort guests.

Running

The World has several scenic running trails from the Grand Floridian, Polynesian, and Contemporary in the Magic Kingdom area. At the Epcot resorts you can get your heart rate up along the promenade that circles Crescent Lake past the BoardWalk Yacht & Beach resorts. If you're staying at Port Orleans, you can work up a sweat on nearby trails; Coronado Springs guests run along the resort's 1-mi esplanade.

The roads that snake through Downtown Disney resorts are pleasant, and early in the morning traffic isn't too bad. At the **Caribbean Beach Resort** there's a 1½-mi running promenade around Barefoot Bay. **Fort Wilderness Campground** has a woodsy 2-mi course with numerous exercise stations along the way.

Surfing

Surfing? Here, in landlocked central Florida? You bet. Early in the morning, before Typhoon Lagoon opens to water-park visitors, you can hit some man-made waves with 11 other novices and a professional instructor. Run by Craig Carroll's Cocoa Beach Surf School, the 2½-hour session begins with a half-hour beachside lesson on surfing moves and basics. Before you know it, you're in the heated wave pool and headed for your first ride. You must be at least 8 years old, and lessons cost $150 per person. Soft-sided boards are provided. You must have transportation to Typhoon Lagoon; even if you're staying at Disney, buses don't run before the class begins at 6:45 AM. The program is scheduled several days each week for up to 12 participants, but lesson days vary, so call ☎ 407/939–7529.

Tennis

You can play tennis at six Disney hotels: BoardWalk (two hard courts), Fort Wilderness Resort (two hard courts), Old Key West Resort (three hard courts), Disney's Saratoga Springs Resort & Spa (two Hydro-grid clay courts), and Disney's Yacht Club Resort (one hard court). Courts are available without charge on a first-come, first-served basis for resort and non-resort guests. All have lights, and most have lockers and racquets available to rent or borrow. Disney offers lessons at some of its tennis complexes.

The Grand Floridian Tennis Center has two HarTru clay courts and a pro shop that attract a somewhat serious-minded tennis crowd. If you have your own racquet, you can get it restrung or regripped here, and ball machines are available. Court fees are $12.50 per guest, per hour (non-resort guests are welcome, and courts are available on a first come, first served basis—no reservations accepted). You can get an hour-long private lesson for $90 from 8 to 7. Racquets rent for $10; a can of balls goes for $5. ☎ 407/621–1991 ⊙ Mon.–Sat. 9–noon and 4–8, Sun. 9–noon.

The Magic Kingdom

WORD OF MOUTH

"If I had one day only, I would spend it in the Magic Kingdom. Epcot is nice but if you like rides and have never been to Disney, it has to be MK. Nothing beats it."

—Nyetzy

THE MAGIC KINGDOM PLANNER

Park Information

City Hall (☎ *407/824–4521*), to the left in Town Square as you face Main Street, houses Guest Relations (a.k.a. Guest Services), the Magic Kingdom's principal information center. Here you can search for misplaced belongings or companions, ask questions of staffers, and pick up a guide map and a *Times Guide* with schedules of events and character-greeting information.

If you're hoping for a last-minute lunch or dinner reservation, you may be able to book it here, though it's always better to reserve in advance.

At the end of Main Street, on the left as you face Cinderella Castle, just before the Hub, is the **Tip Board,** a large board with constantly updated information about attractions' wait times.

Park Amenities

Baby Care: The quiet Baby Care Center is next to the Crystal Palace between Main Street and Adventureland. Rocking chairs and low lighting make nursing comfortable, though it can get crowded. Toddler-size toilets are a hit with tots. There are also changing tables, formula, baby food, pacifiers, diapers, and children's pain relievers. Most park restrooms also have changing tables.

Cameras: The Camera Center at Town Square Exposition Hall opposite City Hall sells film, batteries, and digital memory cards. If a Disney photographer took your picture in the park, you can purchase the photos here or pick up your PhotoPass to view and order them online. A 5″ × 7″ photo costs $12.95 for the first print and $10 for each copy. An 8″ × 10″ costs $16.95.

First Aid: The First Aid Center, staffed by registered nurses, is beside the Crystal Palace. More than a dozen automated external defibrillators are across the park.

Lockers: Lockers ($5 or $7 plus $5 deposit) are in an arcade under the Main Street Railroad Station. If you're park hopping, use your locker receipt to get a free locker at the next park.

Lost People and Things: Name tags are available at City Hall or the Baby Care Center, which is where children who are lost are taken. Instruct your kids to talk to anyone with a Disney name tag if they lose you. City Hall also has a Lost and Found and a computerized Message Center, where you can leave notes for your companions in the Magic Kingdom and other parks. After a day, found items are taken to the **Ticket and Transportation Center (TTC) Lost and Found** (☎ *407/824–4245*).

Package Pick-Up: Have large purchases sent to Package Pick-Up, next to City Hall, so you won't have to carry them around. Allow three hours for the delivery. You also can have packages delivered to your Disney hotel.

Stroller Rentals: The Stroller Shop is near the entrance on the east side of Main Street. Single strollers are $15 daily, $13 for multiday rental; doubles are $31 daily, $27 for multiday rental.

Guided Tours

Several **Magic Kingdom guided tours** (☏ *407/939–8687*) are available. Ask about discounts when booking, and arrive 15 minutes ahead of time to check in.

Backstage Magic takes you on a tour of the Magic Kingdom, Epcot, Disney's Hollywood Studios, and the resort's behind-the-scenes Central Shop area, where repair work is done. The cost for the seven-hour tour is $219 per person (16 and older only). Tours depart at 9 AM on weekdays. The fee includes lunch but does not include park admission, which isn't required for the tour itself.

The **Family Magic Tour** is a two-hour "surprise" scavenger hunt in which your guide encourages you to find things that have disappeared. Disney officials don't want to reveal the tour's components—after all, it's the Family "Magic" Tour—but they will say that a special character-greeting session awaits you at the end of the adventure. Tours leave City Hall at 10 AM daily ($30 for adults and children 3 and up).

The 4½-hour **Keys to the Kingdom Tour** gives you a feel for the Magic Kingdom's layout and what goes on behind the scenes. The walking tour, which costs $65, includes lunch but not admission to the park itself. No one younger than 16 is allowed. Tours leave from City Hall daily at 8:30, 9, and 9:30 AM. Included are visits to "backstage" zones: the parade staging area, the wardrobe area, and other locations in the web of tunnels beneath the Magic Kingdom.

Magic Behind Our Steam Trains gives you an inside look at the daily operation of the WDW railroad. This tour became so popular that it was lengthened from two to three hours and is offered on six days. Tours begin at the front-entrance turnstile at 7:30 AM Monday through Saturday. Visitors 10 years old and up may participate. The cost is $45 per person, plus park admission.

Mickey's Magical Milestones chronicles the development and influence of the Big Cheese himself, and includes details about how the Disney icon affected pop culture and the Disney theme parks. A VIP meeting with Mickey Mouse and special seating at Mickey's PhilharMagic are included in the two-hour tour, which departs at 9 AM on Monday, Wednesday, and Friday. The cost is $25 per person for guests ages 3 and older, and park admission is required.

If you visit in December, take the 3½-hour daily **Yuletide Fantasy** tour ($79)—an insider's look at how Disney's elves transform its parks and resorts. Reserve a spot several months out. For details, call ☏ *407/939–8687*.

For People with Disabilities

The Magic Kingdom gets decent marks from visitors with disabilities. Level entrances and ramps provide wheelchair access. Frontierland is the only area of the park, aside from Main Street, that has sidewalk curbs; there are ramps by the Mile Long Bar and east of Frontierland Trading Post.

Pick up a *Guide for Guests with Disabilities* at Guest Relations. It gives mobility details and notes where you can use handheld-captioning, assisted-listening, video-captioning, and other devices (free but require a deposit). The guide also indicates which attractions have sign-language interpretation and when, which attractions don't permit service animals, and locations of designated "break" areas for animals.

At the hub by the Tip Board across from Casey's Corner, there's a large Braille map of the park. You can rent wheelchairs only at the park's entrance before passing under the Train Station. for $10 daily, $8 a day for multiday rental. Electronic Convenience Vehicles (ECV) are $45 per day plus a refundable $20 security deposit. ■TIP→ Neither wheelchairs nor ECVs can be booked ahead, so arrive early to rent them—ECV availability is limited.

4

THE MAGIC KINGDOM
ENTER A FAIRYTALE

The Magic Kingdom is the heart and soul of the Walt Disney World empire. It was the first Disney outpost in Florida when it opened in 1971, and it's the park that launched Disney's presence in France, Japan, and Hong Kong.

For a landmark that wields such worldwide influence, the 142-acre Magic Kingdom may seem small—indeed, Epcot is more than double the size of the Magic Kingdom, and Animal Kingdom is almost triple the size when including the park's expansive animal habitats. But looks can be deceiving. Packed into seven different "lands" are nearly 50 major crowd pleasers and that's not counting all the ancillary attractions: shops, eateries, live entertainment, character meet-and-greet spots, fireworks shows, and parades. Many rides are geared to the young, but the Magic Kingdom is anything but a kiddie park. The degree of detail, the greater vision, the surprisingly witty spiel of the guides, and the tongue-in-cheek signs that crop up in the oddest places—"Prince" and "Princess" restrooms in Fantasyland, for instance—all contribute to a delightful sense of discovery.

GETTING ORIENTED

The park is laid out on a north–south axis, with Cinderella Castle at the center and the various lands surrounding it in a broad circle.

As you pass underneath the railroad tracks, symbolically leaving behind the world of reality and entering a world of fantasy, you'll immediately notice the adorable buildings lining Town Square and Main Street, U.S.A., which runs due north and ends at the Hub (also called Central Plaza), in front of Cinderella Castle. If you're lost or have questions, cast members are available at almost every turn to help you.

TOP ATTRACTIONS

FOR AGES 7 AND UP

Big Thunder Mountain Railroad. An Old West–themed, classic coaster that's not too scary; it's just a really good, bumpy, swervy thrill.

Buzz Lightyear's Space Ranger Spin. A shoot-'em-up ride where space ranger wannabes compete for the highest score.

Mickey's PhilharMagic. The only 3-D film experience at Disney that features the main Disney characters and movie theme songs.

Space Mountain. The Magic Kingdom's scariest ride, recently renovated, zips you along the tracks in near-total darkness except for the stars.

Splash Mountain. A long, tame boat ride ends in a 52½-foot flume drop into a very wet briar patch.

Haunted Mansion. With its razzle-dazzle special effects, this classic is always a frightful hoot.

FOR AGES 6 AND UNDER

Goofy's Barnstormer. WDW's starter coaster for kids who may be tall enough to go on Big Thunder Mountain and Space Mountain but who aren't sure they can handle it.

Dumbo the Flying Elephant. The elephant ears get them every time—get in line very early or try later in the day.

The Magic Carpets of Aladdin. On this must-do for preschoolers you can make your carpet go up and down to avoid water spurts as mischievous camels spit at you.

The Many Adventures of Winnie the Pooh. Hang onto your honey pot as you get whisked along on a windy-day adventure with Pooh, Tigger, Eeyore, and friends.

Pirates of the Caribbean. Don't miss this waltz through pirate country, especially if you're a fan of the movies.

VISITING TIPS

■ Try to come toward the end of the week, because most families hit the Magic Kingdom early in a visit.

■ Ride a star attraction during a parade; lines ease considerably. (But be careful not to get stuck on the wrong side of the parade route when it starts, or you may never get across.)

■ At City Hall, near the park's Town Square entrance, pick up a guide map and a *Times Guide*, which lists showtimes, character-greeting times, and hours for attractions and restaurants

■ Book character meals early. Main Street, U.S.A.'s **Crystal Palace Buffet** has breakfast, lunch, and dinner with Winnie the Pooh, Tigger, and friends. All three meals at the **Fairy Tale Dining** experience in Cinderella Castle are extremely popular—so much so that you should reserve your spot six months out. At a **Wonderland Tea Party** weekday afternoons in the Grand Floridian Resort, kids can interact with Alice and help decorate (and eat) cupcakes.

4

By Jennie Hess   Whether you arrive at the Magic Kingdom via monorail, ferry boat, or bus, it's hard to escape that surge of excitement or suppress that smile upon sighting the towers of Cinderella Castle or the spires of Space Mountain. So what if it's a cliché by now? There's magic beyond the turnstiles, and you aren't going to miss one memorable moment.

Most visitors have some idea of what they'd like to see and do during their day in the Magic Kingdom. Popular attractions like Space Mountain and Splash Mountain are on the lists of any thrill seeker. Fantasyland is Destination One for parents of small children. Visitors who steer away from wilder rides are first in line at the Jungle Cruise or Pirates of the Caribbean in Adventureland.

It's great to have a strategy for seeing the park's attractions, grabbing a bite to eat, or scouring the shops for souvenir gold. But don't forget that Disney Imagineers—the creative pros behind every themed land and attraction—are famous for their attention to detail. Your experience will be richer if you take time to notice the extra touches—from the architecture to the music to the costumes. The same genius is even in the landscape, from the tropical setting of Adventureland to the redstone slopes of Frontierland's Big Thunder Mountain Railroad.

Wherever you go, watch for Hidden Mickeys—silhouettes and abstract images of Mickey Mouse—hidden by Imagineers in every corner of the Kingdom. For instance, at the Haunted Mansion, look for him in the place settings in the banquet scene.

Much of the Magic Kingdom's pixie dust is spread by the people who work here, the costumed cast members who do their part to create fond memories for each guest who crosses their path. Maybe the grim ghoul who greets you solemnly at the Haunted Mansion will cause you to break down and giggle. Or the sunny shop assistant will help your daughter find the perfect sparkly shoes to match her princess dress. You get the feeling that everyone's in on the fun; in fact, you wonder if they ever go home!

MAIN STREET, U.S.A.

With its pastel Victorian-style buildings, antique automobiles ahoohga-oohga-ing, sparkling sidewalks, and an atmosphere of what one writer has called "almost hysterical joy," Main Street is more than a mere conduit to the other enchantments of the Magic Kingdom. It's where the spell is first cast.

Like Dorothy waking up in a Technicolor Oz or Mary Poppins jumping through the pavement painting, you emerge from beneath the Walt Disney World Railroad Station into a realization of one of the most tenacious American dreams. The perfect street in the perfect small town in a perfect moment of time is burnished to jewel-like quality, thanks to a four-fifths-scale reduction, nightly cleanings with high-pressure hoses, and constant repainting. And it's a very sunny world thanks to an outpouring of welcoming entertainment: live bands, barbershop quartets, and background music from Disney films and American musicals played over loudspeakers. Horse-drawn trolleys and omnibuses with their horns tooting chug along the street. Vendors in Victorian costumes sell balloons and popcorn. And Cinderella's famous castle floats whimsically in the distance where Main Street disappears.

Although attractions with a capital "A" are minimal on Main Street, there are plenty of inducements—namely, shops—to while away your time and part you from your money. The largest of these, the Emporium, is often the last stop for souvenir hunters at day's end, so avoid the crowds and buy early. You can pick up your purchases later at Package Pick-Up or have them delivered to your Disney hotel or mailed home.

The Harmony Barber Shop is a novel stop if you want to step back in time for a haircut ($14 for children 12 and under, $17 for all others) or a beard and mustache trim ($10). Kids get free Mickey Ears and a certificate if it's their first haircut ever. Tweens like to get colored hair gel applications (only $5 a pop). The Town Square Exposition Hall is actually a shop and exhibit center where you can see cameras of yesteryear and today. Exposition Hall is a good place to stock up on batteries, memory cards, and disposable cameras.

Main Street is also full of Disney insider fun. For instance, check out the proprietors' names above the shops: Roy O. Disney, etched above the Main Street Confectionery, is the name of Walt's brother. Dick Nunis, former chairman of Walt Disney Attractions, has an honored spot above the bakery. At the Hall of Champions, Card Walker—the "Practitioner of Psychiatry and Justice of the Peace"—is the former chairman of the company's executive committee. Longtime CEO Michael Eisner didn't get his own shop. Maybe Disney chief Bob Iger will fare better.

☆☆
Duration
21 mins.
Crowds
Heavy
Audience
All Ages

Walt Disney World Railroad. If you click through the turnstile just before 9 AM with young children in tow, wait at the entrance before crossing beneath the station. In a few moments you'll see the day's first steam-driven train arrive laden with the park's most popular residents: Mickey Mouse, Donald Duck, Goofy, Pluto, and characters from every corner of the World. Once they disembark and you've collected the stars' autographs and photos, step right up to the elevated platform above the Magic Kingdom's entrance for a ride into living history.

Walt Disney was a railroad buff of the highest order—he constructed a one-eighth-scale train in his backyard and named it *Lilly Belle*, after his wife, Lillian. Another *Lilly Belle* rides the rails here, as do *Walter E. Disney, Roy O. Disney*, and *Roger Broggie* (named for a Disney Imagineer and fellow railroad aficionado). All the locomotives date from 1928, the same year Mickey Mouse was created. Disney scouts tracked down these vintage carriers in Mexico (where they transported sugarcane in the Yucatán), brought them back, and overhauled them. They're splendid, with striped awnings, brightly painted benches, authoritative "choo-choo" sounds, and hissing plumes of steam.

Their 1½-mi track runs along the perimeter of the Magic Kingdom, with much of the trip through the woods. Stops are in Frontierland and Mickey's Toontown Fair. The ride is a good introduction to the layout of the park; it's also great as relief for tired feet later in the day. The four trains run at five- to seven-minute intervals. **For people with disabilities:** You must transfer from your wheelchair, which can be folded to ride with you or left at any of the three station stops. Equipped for handheld-captioning. ■ TIP→ If you have your own fold-up stroller, board early for Toontown. (You can't load bulky strollers—like those Disney rents—so if you have one, you must do a round trip). Mid-afternoon when there is no line is a good time to go, too.

ADVENTURELAND

From the scrubbed brick, manicured lawns, and meticulously pruned trees of the Central Plaza, an artfully dilapidated wooden bridge leads to the jungles of Adventureland. The landscape artists went wild here: South African cape honeysuckle droops, Brazilian bougainvillea drapes, Mexican flame vines cling, spider plants clone, and three varieties of palm trees sway, all creating a seemingly spontaneous mess. The bright, all-American sing-along tunes that fill the air along Main Street and Central Plaza are replaced by the recorded repetitions of trumpeting elephants, pounding drums, and squawking parrots. The architecture is a mishmash of the best of Thailand, the Middle East, the Caribbean, Africa, and Polynesia, arranged in an inspired disorder that recalls comic-book fantasies of far-off places.

Pirates are gaining more territory in Adventureland. Once contained within the Pirates of the Caribbean attraction, Captain Jack Sparrow and the crew of the Black Pearl are brazenly recruiting new hardies at The Pirates League, adjacent to the ride entrance. You can get pirate makeovers (for more than a few doubloons) here. Across from the attraction on a stage furnished with pirate booty, the captain instructs scurvy dog recruits on the finer points of brandishing a sword at Captain Jack Sparrow's Pirate Tutorial (several shows each day). Shiver me timbers—it's a pirate's life for ye!

Adventureland Adventure Number 1: Being shipwrecked with the Swiss Family Robinson and exploring their treehouse.

☆

Duration
12 mins.
Crowds
Moderate
Audience
All Ages

Enchanted Tiki Room. Disney's first Audio-Animatronic attraction was originally conceived as the Enchanted Tiki Birds. Its more recent version—"under new management," as the sign out front whimsically notes—includes the avian stars of two popular Disney animated films: Zazu from *The Lion King* and Iago from *Aladdin*. The boys take you on a tour of the original attraction while cracking lots of jokes. A holdover from the original is the ditty "In the Tiki, Tiki, Tiki, Tiki, Tiki Room," which is second only to "It's a Small World" as the Disney song you most love to hate. Speaking of which, many people really do hate this attraction, finding the talking birds obnoxious and the music way too loud and peppy. **For people with disabilities:** Accessible for those in standard wheelchairs; equipped for handheld-captioning and assisted-listening devices. ■ TIP➔ **Go when you need to sit-down with a/c.**

☆☆

Duration
10 mins.
Crowds
Heavy
Audience
All Ages

Jungle Cruise. On this Disney classic you cruise through three continents and along four rivers: the Congo, the Nile, the Mekong, and the Amazon. The canopied launches are loaded, the safari-suited guides make a point of checking their pistols, and the *Irrawady Irma* or *Mongala Millie* is off for another "perilous" journey. The guide's shtick is surprisingly funny in a wry and cornball way. Along the way, you'll encounter Disney's famed Audio-Animatronics creatures of the African veld: bathing elephants, slinky pythons, an irritated rhinoceros, a tribe of hungry headhunters, and a bunch of hyperactive hippos (good thing the guide's got a pop pistol). Then there's Old Smiley, the crocodile, who's always waiting for a handout—or, as the guide quips, "a foot out."

The animals are early-generation and crude by Disney standards—anyone who's seen the real thing at the Animal Kingdom or even a good

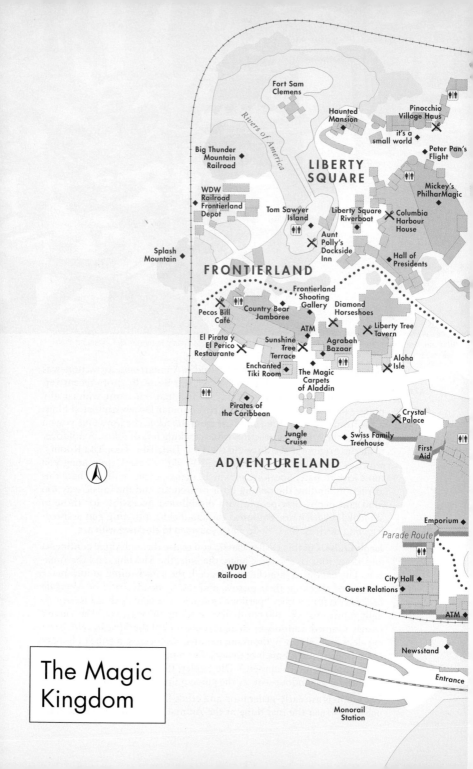

Fort Sam
Clemens

Haunted
Mansion

Pinocchio
Village Haus

it's a
small world

Peter Pan's
Flight

Big Thunder
Mountain
Railroad

**LIBERTY
SQUARE**

Mickey's
PhilharMagic

WDW
Railroad
Frontierland
Depot

Tom Sawyer
Island

Liberty Square
Riverboat

Columbia
Harbour
House

Aunt
Polly's
Dockside
Inn

Hall of
Presidents

Splash
Mountain

FRONTIERLAND

Frontierland
Shooting
Gallery

Pecos Bill
Café

Country Bear
Jamboree

Diamond
Horseshoes

Liberty Tree
Tavern

El Pirata y
El Perico
Restaurante

ATM

Agrabah
Bazaar

Sunshine
Tree
Terrace

Aloha
Isle

Enchanted
Tiki Room

The Magic
Carpets
of Aladdin

Pirates of
the Caribbean

Crystal
Palace

Jungle
Cruise

Swiss Family
Treehouse

First
Aid

ADVENTURELAND

Emporium

Parade Route

WDW
Railroad

City Hall

Guest Relations

ATM

Newsstand

Entrance

Monorail
Station

Rivers of America

The Magic
Kingdom

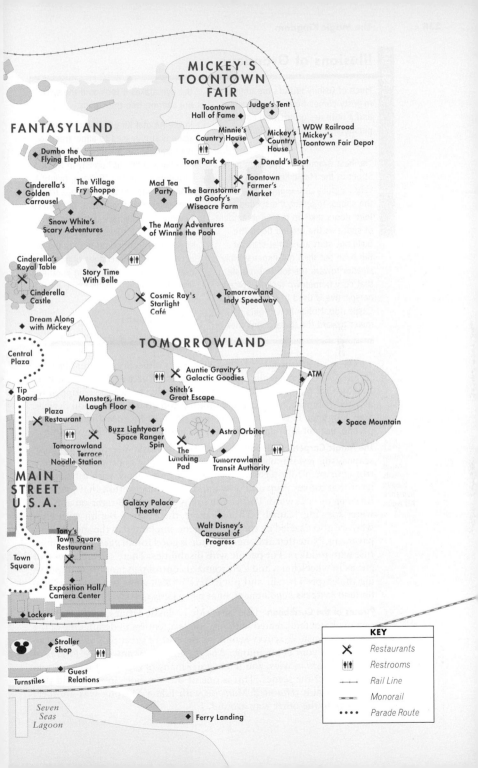

MICKEY'S
TOONTOWN
FAIR

FANTASYLAND

◆ Dumbo the
Flying Elephant

Toontown
Hall of Fame

Judge's Tent

Minnie's
Country House

Mickey's
Country
House

WDW Railroad
Mickey's
Toontown Fair Depot

Toon Park ◆

◆ Donald's Boat

Cinderella's
◆ Golden
Carrousel

The Village
Fry Shoppe

Mad Tea
Party

The Barnstormer
at Goofy's
Wiseacre Farm

✕ Toontown
Farmer's
Market

Snow White's
Scary Adventures

◆ The Many Adventures
of Winnie the Pooh

Cinderella's
Royal Table

Story Time
With Belle

Cinderella
◆ Castle

Cosmic Ray's
Starlight
Café

◆ Tomorrowland
Indy Speedway

Dream Along
◆ with Mickey

Central
Plaza

TOMORROWLAND

◆ Tip
Board

✕ Auntie Gravity's
Galactic Goodies

ATM

Plaza
✕ Restaurant

Monsters, Inc.
Laugh Floor ◆

◆ Stitch's
Great Escape

Space Mountain

Tomorrowland
Terrace
Noodle Station

Buzz Lightyear's
Space Ranger
Spin

◆ Astro Orbiter

The
Lunching
Pad

◆ Tomorrowland
Transit Authority

MAIN
STREET
U.S.A.

Galaxy Palace
Theater

Walt Disney's
◆ Carousel of
Progress

Tony's
Town Square
Restaurant

Town
Square

Exposition Hall/
Camera Center

◆ Lockers

◆ Stroller
Shop

Guest
Relations

Turnstiles

Seven
Seas
Lagoon

◆ Ferry Landing

KEY	
✕	Restaurants
🚻	Restrooms
—•—	Rail Line
━━	Monorail
••••	Parade Route

Illusions of Grandeur

Much of Disney World's breathtaking majesty comes from its architecture and a little design trick called forced perspective, in which buildings appear taller than they actually are.

The best example of this is on Main Street in the Magic Kingdom. Look very carefully at the upper floors of the shops. Together, the second and third floors take up the same amount of space as the ground floor. The buildings start at normal scale at the base but then get imperceptibly smaller toward the top to simulate that cozy hometown feeling. Forced perspective is used in Cinderella Castle, too. Notice how it gets narrower toward the towers. This trick of the eye makes it look as if the spires are soaring into the clouds.

In the Animal Kingdom, architectural scale is suppressed to allow trees to overshadow the buildings. The aim is to relay a sense of humility in the face of nature's wonders. Building height is limited to just 30 feet, whereas trees can tower well above that. But Animal Kingdom's showpiece is the centrally located 145-foot Tree of Life. It's a sculptural masterpiece, too. Its trunk is carved with the images of hundreds of animals, illustrating another important Disney design tenet: every structure must tell a story.

–Ellen Parlapiano

zoo won't be impressed. Unless you're an old-school Disney fan, the Jungle Cruise isn't really worth a Fastpass. **For people with disabilities:** Several boats have lifts that allow wheelchair access; equipped for assisted-listening, handheld-captioning, and audio-description devices. Sign language is provided some days. ■ TIP→ Go during the afternoon parade, but not after dark—you miss too much.

☆☆☆
Duration
3 mins.
Crowds
Heavy
Audience
All Ages

The Magic Carpets of Aladdin. Brightening the lush Adventureland landscape is this jewel-toned ride around a giant genie's bottle. You can control your own four-passenger, state-of-the-art carpet with a front-seat lever that moves it up and down and a rear-seat button that pitches it forward or backward. Part of the fun is dodging the right-on aim of a water-spewing "camel." Though short, the ride is a big hit with kids, who are also dazzled by the colorful gems implanted in the surrounding pavement. Note that although this ride is good for all ages, parents must ride with toddlers. **For people with disabilities:** There's ramp access for guests in wheelchairs and a customized control pendant for manipulating the carpet's height and pitch. ■ TIP→ Visit while waiting for a Frontierland Fastpass appointment; lines move fairly quickly.

☆☆☆
Duration
12 mins.
Crowds
Moderate
Audience
All Ages

Pirates of the Caribbean. This boat ride is classic Disney, with a set and cast of characters created with incredible attention to detail. One of the pirate's "Avast, ye scurvy scum!" is the sort of greeting you'll want to practice on your companions. And if you've seen any of the *Pirates of the Caribbean* movies, you'll recognize many of the colorful characters and some of the scenes. This is one of the few rides in the world that inspired a film (*Haunted Mansion* with Eddie Murphy was another) rather than the other way around.

The gracious arched entrance soon gives way to a dusty dungeon, redolent of dampness and of a spooky, scary past. Lanterns flicker as you board the boats and a ghostly voice intones, "Dead men tell no tales." Next, a deserted beach, strewn with shovels, a skeleton, and a disintegrating map indicating buried treasure prefaces this story of greed, lust, and destruction. Here's where the primary villain from the second *Pirates* film has been added: you'll pass right through a watermist screen featuring the maniacal mug of Davy Jones, complete with squirming tentacle beard and barnacle-encrusted hat. Emerging from a pitch-black tunnel after a mild, tummy-tickling drop, you're caught in the middle of a furious battle. A pirate ship, cannons blazing, attacks a stone fortress. Note the pirate on board: it's gold-hungry Captain Barbossa, evil nemesis of the film's hero, Captain Jack Sparrow. Audio-Animatronics pirates hoist the Jolly Roger while brave soldiers scurry to defend the fort—to no avail.

Politically correct nerves may twinge as the women of the town are rounded up and auctioned, but the wenches rule in another scene, where they chase roguish rapscallions with glee. The wild antics of the pirates—Captain Jack Sparrow pops up in several situations—result in a conflagration; the town goes up in flames, and all go to their just reward amid a catchy chorus of "A Pirate's Life For Me." Don't miss the attraction's revised ending, adjusted in the wake of the first two films— we'll tell no tales at risk of spoiling the fun. **For people with disabilities:** Boarding requires transferring from a standard wheelchair to the ride vehicle; the very small flume drop may make the attraction inappropriate for those with limited upper-body strength or those wearing neck or back braces. Equipped for audio-description and handheld-captioning devices. ■ TIP➡ This is a great destination in the heat of the afternoon, and lines move steadily.

☆☆
Duration
Up to You
Crowds
Moderate
Audience
All Ages

Swiss Family Treehouse. Inspired by the classic novel by Johann Wyss about the adventures of the Robinson family, who were shipwrecked en route to America, the tree house shows what you can do with a big faux tree and a lot of imagination. The rooms are furnished with patchwork quilts and mahogany furniture. Disney detail abounds: the kitchen sink is a giant clamshell; the boys' room, strewn with clothing, has two hammocks instead of beds; and an ingenious system of rain barrels and bamboo pipes provides running water in every room.

As you clamber around the narrow wooden steps and rope bridges that connect the rooms in this split-level dwelling, take a look at the Spanish moss. It's real, but the tree itself—some 90 feet in diameter, with more than 1,000 branches—was constructed by the props department. The 300,000 leaves are vinyl. It all adds up to a species of tree unofficially called *Disneyodendron eximus*, or "out-of-the-ordinary Disney tree." Note that lines, which move slowly here, are artfully camouflaged so you may not see them. Also toddlers unsteady on their feet may have trouble with the stairs. **For people with disabilities:** With its 100 steps and lack of narration, this attraction gets low ratings among those with mobility and visual impairments. ■ TIP➡ If you're with children 4 to 12 who like to explore, visit while waiting for a Jungle Cruise Fastpass appointment.

Adventureland Adventure Number 2: Gliding through the muggy, steamy Caribbean world of pirates. Yo ho ho!

NEED A BREAK?

If you're looking for real refreshment and an energy boost, stop by **Aloha Isle**, where you'll find some of the tastiest and most healthful goodies. Try the fresh pineapple spears, or sip a smoothie or just some fruit juice, while you relax on one of the benches scattered around Adventureland.

FRONTIERLAND

Frontierland evokes the American frontier and is planted with mesquite, twisted Peruvian pepper trees, slash pines, and cacti. The period seems to be the latter half of the 19th century, and the West is being won by Disney cast members dressed in checked shirts, leather vests, cowboy hats, and brightly colored neckerchiefs. Banjo and fiddle music twangs from tree to tree, and snackers walk around munching turkey drumsticks so large that you could best an outlaw single-handedly with one. (Beware of hovering seagulls that migrate to the parks during cooler months—they've been known to snatch snacks.)

The screams that drown out the string music aren't the result of a cowboy surprising an Indian. They come from two of the Magic Kingdom's more thrilling rides: Splash Mountain, an elaborate flume ride; and Big Thunder Mountain Railroad, a roller coaster. The Walt Disney World Railroad tunnels past a colorful scene in Splash Mountain and drops you off between it and Thunder Mountain.

Big Thunder Mountain Railroad. Set in gold-rush days, this thrilling roller coaster simulates a runaway train. It's a bumpy ride with several good drops (pregnant women and guests wearing back, neck, or leg braces should avoid this one). There are also moments when you feel like you're going to fly right off the tracks, but there are no inversions and at least you can see where you're going—unlike in Space Mountain. Overall it's more fun than scary, and you'll see kids as young as 7 lining up to ride. The design is fabulous, too. The train rushes and rattles past 20 Audio-Animatronics figures—including donkeys, chickens, a goat, and a grizzled old miner surprised in his bathtub—as well as $300,000 worth of genuine antique mining equipment, tumbleweeds, a derelict mining town, hot springs, and a flash flood.

The ride was 15 years in the planning and took two years and close to $17 million to build. This 1979 price tag, give or take a few million, equaled the entire cost of erecting California's Disneyland in 1955. The 197-foot mountain landscape is based on the windswept scenery of Arizona's Monument Valley, and thanks to 650 tons of steel, 4,675 tons of concrete, and 16,000 gallons of paint, it replicates the area's gorges, tunnels, caverns, and dry river beds. **For people with disabilities:** You must be able to step into the ride vehicle and walk short distances. Service animals aren't permitted. ■TIP→ Use Fastpass unless the wait is less than 15 minutes. The ride is most exciting at night, when you can't anticipate the curves and the track's rattling really sounds as if something's about to give.

Country Bear Jamboree. Wisecracking, cornpone, lovelorn Audio-Animatronics bears joke, sing, and play country music and 1950s rock-and-roll in this stage show. Even timid youngsters love them. The emcee, the massive but debonair Henry, leads the stellar cast of Grizzly Hall, which includes the robust Trixie, who laments love lost while perching on a swing suspended from the ceiling; Bubbles, Bunny, and Beulah, harmonizing on "All the Guys That Turn Me On Turn Me Down"; and Big Al, the off-key cult figure who has inspired postcards, stuffed animals, and his own shop next door.

Don't miss the bears' seasonal show in late November and December, when they deck the halls for a special concert. **For people with disabilities:** Wheelchair accessible; reflective captioning provided; equipped for assisted-listening devices. If you lip-read, ask to sit up front. ■TIP→ Visit before 11 AM, during the afternoon parade, or late in the day. Stand to the far left in the anteroom, where you wait to end up in the front rows; to the far right if for the last row, so small kids can perch atop the seats to see better.

Splash Mountain. The second-most-popular thrill ride after Space Mountain, Splash Mountain is a log-flume water ride, based on the animated sequences in Disney's 1946 film *Song of the South*. Here the Audio-Animatronics creations of Brer Rabbit, Brer Bear, Brer Fox, and a menagerie of other Brer beasts frolic in bright, cartoonlike settings. When you settle into the eight-person hollowed-out logs, Uncle Remus's voice growls, "Mark mah words, Brer Rabbit gonna put his foot in Brer Fox's mouth one of these days." And this just might be the day.

4

As the boat carries you up the mountain, Brer Rabbit's silhouette hops merrily ahead to the tune of the ride's theme song, "Time to Be Moving Along." Every time some critter makes a grab for the bunny, your log boat drops out of reach. But Brer Fox has been studying his book *How to Catch a Rabbit,* and our lop-eared friend looks as if he's destined for the pot. Things don't look so good for the flumers, either. You get one heart-stopping pause at the top of the mountain—just long enough to grab the safety bar—and then the boat plummets down into a large, wet briar patch. So you know what you're getting into: the drop is 52½ feet—that's about five stories, at a 45-degree angle, enough to reach speeds of 40 mph—and makes you feel weightless. Try to smile through your clenched teeth: as you begin to drop, a flashbulb pops. You can buy a photographic memento of the experience before exiting the ride. Brer Rabbit escapes—and so do you, wet and exhilarated—to the tune of "Zip-a-Dee-Doo-Dah." If you want to get really wet—and you will get splashed from almost every seat—ask the attendant to seat you in the front row.

You may get wet, so plan accordingly. If you need to use Baby Swap you can take the young ones to a play area in a cave under the ride. Note that this ride isn't appropriate if you're pregnant or have heart, back, or neck problems. **For people with disabilities:** You must be able to step into the ride vehicle and walk short distances. Service animals aren't permitted. ■ TIP➔ If you're not in line by 9:45 am, plan to use Fastpass or ride during meal or parade times.

☆☆
Duration
Up to You
Crowds
Light
Audience
Kids and Tweens

Tom Sawyer Island. A creatively ungrammatical sign tells you what to expect: "IF'N YOU LIKE DARK CAVES, MYSTERY MINES, BOTTOMLESS PITS, SHAKY BRIDGES 'N' BIG ROCKS, YOU HAVE CAME TO THE BEST PLACE I KNOW." Aunt Polly would have walloped Tom for his orthography, but she couldn't have argued with the sentiment. Actually two islets connected by a swing bridge, Tom Sawyer Island is a playground of hills, trees, rocks, and shrubs.

Most of the attractions are on the main island, where your raft docks. The Mystery Mine is like a secret passageway to exploration. Children love Injun Joe's Cave, where there are lots of columns and crevices from which to jump out and startle siblings and where the wind wails for a spooky effect. In a clearing atop the hill, there's a rustic playground. As you explore the shoreline on the dirt paths, watch out for the barrel bridge—the whole contraption bounces at every step.

On the other island is Fort Langhorn, a log fortress from which you can fire air guns with great booms and cracks at the passing *Liberty Belle* riverboat. It's guarded by a snoring Audio-Animatronics sentry, working off his last bender. Both islands are sprinkled with lookouts for great views to Thunder Mountain and Frontierland, as well as Liberty Square's Haunted Mansion. **For people with disabilities:** With its stairs, bridges, inclines, and narrow caves, this attraction isn't negotiable by those using a wheelchair. ■ TIP➔ Try it as a refreshing afternoon getaway. Just mind your toddlers, as it's easy to lose track of them here.

Coasting down Splash Mountain in Frontierland will put some zip in your doo dah and some water on your clothes.

LIBERTY SQUARE

The rough-and-tumble Western frontier gently folds into colonial America as Liberty Square picks up where Frontierland leaves off. The weathered siding gives way to solid brick and neat clapboard. The mesquite and cactus are replaced by stately oaks and masses of azaleas. The theme is colonial history, which Northerners will be happy to learn is portrayed here as solid Yankee. The buildings, topped with weather vanes and exuding prosperity, are pure New England.

A replica of the Liberty Bell, crack and all, seems an appropriate prop to separate Liberty Square from Frontierland. There's even a Liberty Tree, a more than 150-year-old live oak found elsewhere on Walt Disney World property and moved to the Magic Kingdom. Just as the Sons of Liberty hung lanterns on trees as a signal of solidarity after the Boston Tea Party, the Liberty Tree's branches are decorated with 13 lanterns representing the 13 original colonies. Around the square are tree-shaded tables for an alfresco lunch and plenty of carts and fast-food eateries to supply the goods.

NEED A BREAK? **Sleepy Hollow** offers quick pick-me-ups in the form of funnel cakes, soft-serve ice cream, espresso drinks, root-beer floats, and caramel corn.

☆☆☆
Duration
25 mins.
Crowds
Mod. to Heavy
Audience
Not Small Kids

Hall of Presidents: A Celebration of Liberty's Leaders. This multimedia tribute to America and its presidents caused quite a sensation when it opened in 1971; it was here that the first refinements of the Audio-Animatronics system of computerized robots could be seen. Today it's still worth a visit, especially after a major rehab of the show and the addition of a latest-generation Audio-Animatronics version of President Barack Obama.

Instead of its previous focus on the U.S. Constitution and civil rights, the show now tells a moving story of the bond between the presidents and "We, the People." Producers re-shot the accompanying film in high-definition video and added more than 130 images culled from the National Archives, Library of Congress, and other collections. A digital soundtrack, LED lighting, and narration by Oscar-winning actor Morgan Freeman further enhance the experience. The film covers 220 years of U.S. history and emphasizes anecdotes about presidents who've reached out to people in times of strife. Both George Washington and Abraham Lincoln get more of the spotlight during the new film, the latter by delivering his famous Gettysburg Address.

For most visitors, the best part of the show is a roll call of all 43 U.S. presidents. (Fun fact: Obama is officially the 44th president because Grover Cleveland is counted twice due to his having served nonconsecutive terms.) Each chief executive responds with a nod, and those who are seated rise (except for wheelchair-bound Franklin Delano Roosevelt, of course). The detail is lifelike, right down to the brace on Roosevelt's leg. The robots can't resist nodding, fidgeting, and even whispering to each other while waiting for their names to come up. The audience might fidget too as they wait for Obama's turn, which includes his presidential Oath of Office (recorded in the White House by Imagineers) and a speech about the American Dream. Anyone interested in presidential artifacts will enjoy the wait in the lobby area, where First Ladies' dresses, presidential portraits, and even George Washington's dental instruments are on display. **For people with disabilities:** Wheelchair accessible; enter through a door marked EXIT either on the right or left. Reflective captioning available; equipped for assisted-listening devices. ■TIP➜ Come in the morning or during the parade.

Fodor'sChoice★
Duration
8 mins.
Crowds
Heavy
Audience
Not Small Kids

Haunted Mansion. The special effects here are a howl crossed with a scream. And Disney Imagineers have kicked the effects up a few notches for some extra thrills and chills. You're greeted at the creaking iron gates of this Hudson River Valley Gothic mansion by a lugubrious attendant, who has one of the few jobs at Disney for which smiling is frowned upon, and ushered into a spooky picture gallery. A disembodied voice echoes from the walls: "Welcome, foolish mortals, to the Haunted Mansion. I am your ghost host." An audio system with 30-plus surround-sound speakers ups the ghost-host fright factor. A scream shivers down, the room begins to "stretch," and you're off into one of Disney's classic attractions. ■TIP➜ Don't rush out of this room when other visitors depart; linger for some ghoulish bonus whispers.

Consisting mainly of a slow-moving ride in a black, cocoonlike "doom buggy," the Haunted Mansion is only really scary for younger children, and that's mostly because of the darkness. Everyone else will just laugh

Liberty Square's Haunted Mansion all lit up—pretty scary or just pretty? You decide.

(or ooh and ah) at the special effects. Watch the suit of armor that comes alive; the shifting walls in the portrait gallery that make you wonder if they're moving up or if you're moving down; the ghostly ballroom dancers; Madame Leota's talking disembodied head in the crystal ball, which floats realistically; and ghostly footprints that move along a staircase. In the "bride in the attic" scene, keep an eye on the portraits. Just when you think the Imagineers have exhausted their bag of ectoplasmic tricks, along comes another one; you suddenly discover that your doom buggy has gained an extra passenger. As you approach the exit, your ghoulish guide intones, "Now I will raise the safety bar, and the ghost will follow you home." Thanks for the souvenir, pal. And speaking of souvenirs, if you can't resist bringing home more than a friendly ghost, you can get Disney's Clue Haunted Mansion board game at the park's Emporium gift shop or at Once Upon a Toy in Downtown Disney. Note that as this is a high-capacity and fast-loading ride, lines usually move along steadily. **For people with disabilities:** Those in wheelchairs must transfer to the "doom buggies" and take one or more steps; however, if you can walk up to 200 feet, you'll enjoy the preshow as well as the ride's sensations and eerie sounds. Equipped for handheld-captioning and audio-description devices. ■ TIP→ Come early or during a parade. Nighttime adds an extra fright factor.

☆
Duration
15 mins.
Crowds
**Light to
Moderate**
Audience
All Ages

Liberty Square Riverboat. An old-fashioned steamboat, the *Liberty Belle* is authentic, from its calliope whistle and the gingerbread trim on its three decks to the boilers that produce the steam that drives the big rear paddle wheel. In fact, the boat misses authenticity on only one count: there's no mustachioed captain to guide it during the ride around the

Rivers of America. That task is performed by an underwater rail. The 1½-mi cruise is slow and not exactly thrilling, except, perhaps, to the kids getting "shot at" by their counterparts at Fort Langhorn on Tom Sawyer Island. But it's a relaxing break for all concerned, and children like exploring the boat. Capacity is high, so lines move quickly. **For people with disabilities:** Wheelchair accessible; enter through exit on right or left. ■ TIP➔ Come when you need a break from the crowds. Check Times Guide—the riverboat is open seasonally.

FANTASYLAND

Walt Disney called this "a timeless land of enchantment." Fantasyland does conjure up pixie dust. Perhaps that's because the fanciful gingerbread houses, gleaming gold turrets, and, of course, rides based on Disney-animated movies are what the Magic Kingdom is all about.

With the exception of the slightly spooky Snow White's Scary Adventures, the attractions here are whimsical rather than heart-stopping. Like the animated classics on which they're based, many of these rides, which could ostensibly be classified as rides for children, are packed with enough delightful detail to engage the adults who accompany them. Unfortunately, Fantasyland is always the most heavily trafficked area in the park, and its rides and shows are almost always crowded.

The good news is that Fantasyland is slated for an expansion—the largest one in the park's history. By sometime in 2013, Ariel of *The Little Mermaid,* will invite you to journey under the sea in her own attraction; Dumbo the Flying Elephant ride will double in size and fly above grounds that include an interactive, three-ring circus tent; and Beast from *Beauty and the Beast* will invite you to "Be Our Guest" for a meal in one of three enchanted dining rooms. You can also join Belle in the library for a story performance. More Disney princess and fairy gatherings are planned.

For now, you can enter Fantasyland on foot from Liberty Square, Tomorrowland, or Mickey's Toontown Fair (until it closes for the Fantasyland expansion), but the classic introduction is through Cinderella Castle. As you exit the castle's archway, look left to discover a charming and often overlooked touch: Cinderella Fountain, a lovely brass casting of the castle's namesake, who's dressed in her peasant togs and surrounded by her beloved mice and bird friends.

From the southern end of Liberty Square, head toward the park hub and stop at the designated Kodak PictureSpot for one of the park's best, unobstructed ground-level views of Cinderella Castle. It's a great spot for that family photo.

Cinderella Castle. Its royal blue turrets, gold spires, and glistening white towers were inspired by the castle built by the mad Bavarian king Ludwig II at Neuschwanstein, as well as by drawings prepared for Disney's animated film of the French fairy tale. Although often confused with Disneyland's Sleeping Beauty Castle, at 180-plus feet this castle is more than 100 feet taller; and with its elongated towers and lacy fretwork, it's immeasurably more graceful. Don't miss the elaborate mosaic murals

DID YOU KNOW?

The quintessential Disney icon, the Cinderella Castle, was inspired by the palace built by the mad Bavarian king Ludwig II at Neuschwanstein. At 180 feet, it's 100 feet taller than Disneyland's Sleeping Beauty Castle.

on the walls of the archway as you rush toward Fantasyland from the Hub. The five panels, measuring some 15 feet high and 10 feet wide, were designed by Disney artist Dorothea Redmond and created from a million bits of multicolor Italian glass, silver, and 14-karat gold by mosaicist Hanns-Joachim Scharff. The mosaics tell the story of the little cinder girl as she goes from pumpkin to prince to happily ever after.

The fantasy castle has feet, if not of clay, then of solid steel beams, fiberglass, and 500 gallons of paint. Instead of dungeons, there are service tunnels for the Magic Kingdom's less-than-magical quotidian operations, such as Makeup and Costuming. These are the same tunnels that honeycomb the ground under much of the park. And upstairs doesn't hold, as rumor has it, a casket containing the cryogenically preserved body of Walt Disney. Instead, there's a suite where some lucky families enjoyed a "dream come true" overnight stay when Disney held its "Year of a Million Dreams" celebration.

Within the castle's archway is the **Bibbidi Bobbidi Boutique,** where the "royal treatment" transforms little girls age 3 and older into princesess or divas. Hair and makeup are by a "Fairy Godmother-in-training." Boys aren't left out of the picture; they can grab a chair for their own "Cool Dude" transformation involving colorful hair gels and other accoutrements. If you're looking for Cinderella's glass slipper, head for **Crystal Arts** on Main Street.

If you have reservations to dine at **Cinderella's Royal Table,** you enter the castle by way of an ascending spiral staircase where costumed waiters attend to your meal. Cinderella, her Fairy Godmother, and other princesses join you at what is one of the most popular character-greeting experiences offered at Walt Disney World. **For people with disabilities:** For those with limited mobility, elevator access to the dining experience is provided. ■TIP→ Call 180 days ahead, or as soon as you can, to reserve the character breakfast, lunch, or dinner known as Fairytale Dining.

☆☆
Duration
2 mins.
Crowds
Mod. to Heavy
Audience
Families

Cinderella's Golden Carrousel. It's the whirling, musical heart of Fantasyland. This ride—which is great for families and for romantics, young and old—encapsulates the Disney experience in 90 prancing horses and then hands it to you on a 60-foot moving platter. Seventy-two of the dashing wooden steeds date from the original carousel built in 1917 by the Philadelphia Toboggan Company; additional mounts were made of fiberglass. All are meticulously painted—it takes about 48 hours per horse—and each one is completely different. One wears a collar of bright yellow roses; another, a quiver of Native American arrows. The horses gallop ceaselessly beneath a wooden canopy, gaily striped on the outside and decorated on the inside with 18 panels depicting scenes from Disney's 1950 film *Cinderella*. As the platter starts to spin, the mirrors sparkle, the fairy lights glitter, and the band organ plays favorite tunes from Disney movies. If you wished upon a star, it couldn't get more magical. **For people with disabilities:** If using a wheelchair, enter through the exit on the right, then transfer to ride vehicles. If you have a service animal, check with a host for boarding information. ■TIP→ Lines move quickly. Come while waiting for your Peter Pan's Flight Fastpass reservation, during the parade, or after dark.

☆☆☆
Duration
2 mins.
Crowds
Mod. to Heavy
Audience
Small Kids

Dumbo the Flying Elephant. Hands down, this is one of Fantasyland's most popular rides. Although the movie has one baby elephant with gigantic ears who accidentally downs a bucket of water spiked with champagne and learns he can fly, the ride has 16 jolly Dumbos flying around a central column, each pachyderm packing a couple of kids and a parent. A joystick controls each of Dumbo's vertical motions, so you can make him ascend or descend at will. Alas, the ears don't flap. Keep an eye out for Timothy Mouse atop the ride's colorful balloon. **For people with disabilities:** If using a wheelchair, enter using the ramp on the right, then transfer to a ride vehicle. ■ TIP→ Lines are perpetual except in very early morning, and there's little shade—in summer, the wait can be brutal.Come as soon as the park opens or head for the similar Magic Carpets of Aladdin instead.

4

☆☆☆
Duration
25 mins.
Crowds
Mod. to Heavy
Audience
Small Kids

Fairytale Garden: Story Time with Belle. Disney's beloved bookworm makes an appearance at the Fairytale Garden several times daily and brings *Beauty and the Beast* to life. If you'd like to be in the show, act enthusiastic—Belle recruits several children and one dad from the audience as cast members. Storytelling was never so much fun. **For people with disabilities:** Wheelchair accessible. Sign language is offered here some days. ■ TIP→ Check your Times Guide for shows. Crowds are heaviest at midday. Arrive at least 15 minutes early for a good seat on a bench.

☆☆
Duration
11 mins.
Crowds
Heavy
Audience
All Ages

it's a small world. Visiting Walt Disney World and not stopping for this tribute to terminal cuteness—why, the idea is practically un-American. The attraction is essentially a boat ride through several candy-color lands, each representing a continent and each crammed with musical moppets, all madly singing. Disney raided the remains of the 1964–65 New York World's Fair for sets, and then appropriated the theme song of international brotherhood and friendship for its own. Some claim that it's the "revenge of the Audio-Animatrons," as 450 simplistic dolls differentiated mostly by their national dress—Dutch babies in clogs, Spanish flamenco dancers, German oompah bands, Russians playing balalaikas, sari-wrapped Indians waving temple bells, Tower of London guards in scarlet beefeater uniforms, Swiss yodelers and goatherds, Japanese kite fliers, Middle East snake charmers, and young French cancan dancers, to name just a few—parade past, smiling away and wagging their heads in time to the song. But somehow, by the time you reach the enchanting snow-white finale populated by dolls from every continent, you're grinning and wagging, too, with the one-verse theme song indelibly impressed in your brain. Now all together: "It's a world of laughter, a world of tears. It's a world of hope and a world of fears." Tots may beg for a repeat ride; it's worth another go-round to see all that you missed on the first trip.

For people with disabilities: You can board without leaving your wheelchair, but only if it's standard size; if you use a scooter or an oversize chair, you must transfer to one of the attraction's standard chairs, available at the ride entrance. Equipped for handheld-captioning and audio-description devices. ■ TIP→ Come back later if there's a long line, since crowds truly do ebb and flow here.

Few can resist being captivated by the 16 chubby, happy, shiny, flying elephants of Fantasyland's Dumbo ride.

☆
Duration
2 mins.
Crowds
Moderate
Audience
Small Kids

Mad Tea Party. This carnival staple is for the vertigo addict looking for a fix. The Disney version is based on its own 1951 film *Alice in Wonderland*, in which the Mad Hatter hosts a tea party for his un-birthday. You hop into oversize, pastel-color teacups and whirl around a giant platter. Add your own spin to the teacup's orbit with the help of the steering wheel in the center. If the centrifugal force hasn't shaken you up too much, check out the soused mouse that pops out of the teapot centerpiece and compare his condition with your own. **For people with disabilities:** If using a wheelchair, enter through the exit on right, then transfer to a ride vehicle. ■TIP→ Lines move slowly; skip this ride if the wait is longer than 30 min and if spinning could ruin your day.

Fodor's Choice★
Duration
3 mins.
Crowds
Heavy
Audience
Small Kids

The Many Adventures of Winnie the Pooh. The famous honey lover and his exploits in the Hundred Acre Wood are the theme for this ride. You can read posted passages from A.A. Milne's stories as you wait in line. Once you board your honey pot, Pooh and his friends wish you a "happy windsday." Pooh flies through the air, held aloft by his balloon, in his perennial search for "hunny," and you bounce along with Tigger, ride with the Heffalumps and Woozles, and experience a cloudburst. When the rain ends at last, everyone gathers again to say "Hurray!" This ride replaced Mr. Toad's Wild Ride; look for the painting of Mr. Toad handing the deed to Owl. **For people with disabilities:** If using a wheelchair, wait in the main queue and then roll onto an individual honey pot to ride along with another member of your party. Equipped for handheld-captioning and audio-description devices. ■TIP→ Use a Fastpass, or if your youngsters need immediate gratification, come early, late in the afternoon, or after dark.

4

Duration
12 mins.
Crowds
Heavy
Audience
Not Small Kids

Mickey's PhilharMagic. Mickey Mouse may be the headliner here, but it's Donald Duck's misadventures—reminiscent of Mickey's as the sorcerer's apprentice in *Fantasia*—that set the comic pace in this gorgeous, 3-D animated film. As you settle into your seat, the on-screen action takes you behind the curtains at a grand concert hall where Donald and Mickey are preparing for a musical performance. But when Donald misuses Mickey's magical sorcerer's hat, he suddenly finds himself on a whirlwind journey that includes a magic carpet ride and an electrifying dip under the sea. And you go along for the ride. On the way you meet Ariel, Simba, Aladdin, and Jasmine, and Peter Pan, Tinker Bell, and others.

The film startles with its special-effects technology—you'll smell a fresh-baked apple pie, feel the rush of air as champagne corks pop, and get lost in the action on one of the larger screens created for a 3-D film: a 150-foot-wide canvas. The film is beautifully scored and marks the first time that classic Disney characters appear in a computer-generated animation attraction. Note that some of the special effects can startle small children, **For people with disabilities:** There's a special viewing area for guests in wheelchairs. Reflective captioning is provided; equipped for assisted-listening and audio-description devices. ■TIP→ **It's a big theater, so you shouldn't have to wait long. Come during the parade for the shortest lines, though.**

☆☆
Duration
2.5 mins.
Crowds
Heavy
Audience
Small Kids

Peter Pan's Flight. This wonderful indoor ride was inspired by Sir James M. Barrie's 1904 novel about the boy who wouldn't grow up, which Disney animated in 1953. Aboard two-person magic sailing ships with brightly striped sails, you soar into the skies above London en route to Neverland. Along the way you can see Wendy, Michael, and John get sprinkled with pixie dust while Nana barks below, wave to Princess Tiger Lily, meet the evil Captain Hook, and cheer for the tick-tocking, clock-swallowing crocodile who breakfasted on Hook's hand and is more than ready for lunch.

Despite the absence of high-tech special effects, children—especially preschoolers—love this ride. Adults enjoy the dreamy views of London by moonlight, a galaxy of twinkling yellow lights punctuated by Big Ben, London Bridge, and the Thames River. The only real downside is the ride's brevity. Avoid the long line or, upon exiting, you may find yourself annoyed at having waited for an hour for a 2½-minute ride. **For people with disabilities:** You must transfer from your wheelchair to the ride vehicles. Service animals aren't permitted. Equipped for handheld-captioning and audio-description devices. ■TIP→ **Use Fastpass here or ride early, late, or during the parade.**

☆
Duration
3 mins.
Crowds
Mod. to Heavy
Audience
Not Small Kids

Snow White's Scary Adventures. What was previously an unremittingly scary indoor spook-house ride where the dwarves might as well have been named Anxious and Fearful is now a kinder, somewhat gentler experience with six-passenger cars and a mini-version of the movie. There's still the evil queen, the wart on her nose, and her cackle, but joining the cast are the Prince and Snow White herself.

The trip is packed with plenty of scary moments for young children. For some, it's too much, but an honest-to-goodness kiss followed by

MAGIC KINGDOM

NAME	Height Req.	Type of Entertainment	Duration	Crowds	Audience	Tips
Adventureland						
Enchanted Tiki Room	n/a	Show	12 mins.	Light	All Ages	Come when you need a refresher in a/c.
Jungle Cruise	n/a	Cruise	10 mins.	Heavy	All Ages	Use Fastpass or come during the parade.
The Magic Carpets of Aladdin	n/a	Thrill Ride for Kids	3 mins.	Heavy	All Ages	Visit while waiting for Frontierland Fastpass appointment.
Pirates of the Caribbean	n/a	Cruise	10 mins.	Moderate	All Ages	A good destination in the heat of the afternoon.
Swiss Family Treehouse	n/a	Walk-through	Up to you	Moderate	All Ages	Visit while waiting for Jungle Cruise Fastpass.
Fantasyland						
Cinderella's Golden Carrousel	n/a	Thrill Ride for Kids	2 mins.	Moderate to Heavy	Families	Come while waiting for Peter Pan's Flight Fastpass, during afternoon parade, or after dark.
Dumbo the Flying Elephant	n/a	Thrill Ride for Kids	2 mins.	Moderate to Heavy	Small Kids	Come at rope drop. No shade in afternoon.
Fairytale Garden	n/a	Show	25 mins.	Moderate to Heavy	All Ages	Check *Times Guide*, and arrive early for a bench.
it's a small world	n/a	Cruise	11 mins.	Moderate	All Ages	Tots may beg for a repeat ride; it's worth it.
Mad Tea Party	n/a	Thrill Ride for Kids	2 mins.	Moderate	Small Kids	Come in the early morning. Skip it if wait is 30 mins.
★ The Many Adventures of Winnie the Pooh	n/a	Thrill Ride for Kids	3½ mins.	Heavy	All Ages	Use Fastpass. Come early, late in the afternoon, or after dark.
★ Mickey's PhilharMagic	n/a	3-D Film	12 mins.	Heavy	All but Small Kids	Use Fastpass or arrive early or during a parade.
Peter Pan's Flight	n/a	Thrill Ride for Kids	2½ mins.	Heavy	All Ages	Try evening or early morning. Use Fastpass first.
Snow White's Scary Adventures	n/a	Thrill Ride for Kids	3 mins.	Moderate to Heavy	All Ages	Come very early, during the afternoon parade, or after dark. May scare toddlers and pre-schoolers.
Frontierland						
★ Big Thunder Mountain Railroad	At least 40"	Thrill Ride	4 mins.	Absolutely!	All but Small Kids	Use Fastpass. Most exciting at night when you can't anticipate the curves.
Country Bear Jamboree	n/a	Show	17 mins.	Heavy	All Ages	Visit before 11 am. Stand to the far left lining up for the front rows.

Name	Height	Type	Duration	Crowds	Audience	Strategy
★ Splash Mountain	At least 40"	Thrill Ride with Water	11 mins.	Yes!	All but Small Kids	Use Fastpass. Get in line by 9:45 am, or ride during meal or parade time. You may get wet.
Tom Sawyer Island	n/a	Playground	Up to you	Light	Kids and Tweens	Afternoon refresher. It's hard to keep track of toddlers here.

Liberty Square

Name	Height	Type	Duration	Crowds	Audience	Strategy
Hall of Presidents	n/a	Show/Film	25 mins.	Moderate	All but Small Kids	Come in the morning or during the parade.
★ Haunted Mansion	n/a	Thrill Ride	8 mins.	Moderate	All Ages	Nighttime adds extra fear factor.
Liberty Square Riverboat	n/a	Cruise	15 mins.	Light to Moderate	All Ages	Good for a break from the crowds.

Main Street U.S.A.

Name	Height	Type	Duration	Crowds	Audience	Strategy
Walt Disney World Railroad	n/a	Railroad	21 mins.	Moderate to Heavy	All Ages	Board with small children for an early start in Toontown or hop on midafternoon.

Mickey's Toontown Fair

Name	Height	Type	Duration	Crowds	Audience	Strategy
The Barnstormer at Goofy's Wiseacre Farm	At least 35"	Thrill Ride for Kids	1 min.	Moderate to Heavy	Small Kids	Come during evening if your child can wait.

Tomorrowland

Name	Height	Type	Duration	Crowds	Audience	Strategy
Astro-Orbiter	n/a	Thrill Ride for Kids	2 mins.	Moderate to Heavy	All Ages	Skip unless there's a short line.
★ Buzz Lightyear's Space Ranger Spin	n/a	Interactive Exp.	5 mins.	Heavy	All Ages	Come in the early morning and use Fastpass. Kids will want more than one ride.
Monster's Inc. Laugh Floor	n/a	Film	15 mins.	Moderate to Heavy	All Ages	Come when you're waiting for your Buzz Lightyear or Space Mountain Fastpass.
★ Space Mountain	At least 44"	Thrill Ride	2½ mins.	You Bet!	All but Small Kids	Use Fastpass, or come at the beginning or the end of day or during a parade.
Stitch's Great Escape	At least 40"	Simulator Exp.	20 mins.	Moderate to Heavy	All but Small Kids	Use Fastpass. Visit early after Space Mountain, Splash Mountain, Big Thunder Mountain, or during a parade.
Tomorrowland Indy Speedway	54" to drive	Thrill Ride for Kids	5 mins.	Moderate	All but Small Kids	Come in the evening or during a parade; skip on a first-time visit; 32" height requirement to ride shotgun.
Tomorrowland Transit Authority	n/a	Railroad	10 mins.	Light	All Ages	Come with young kids if you need a restful ride.
Walt Disney's Carousel of Progress	n/a	Show	20 mins.	Light to Moderate	All Ages	Skip on a first-time visit unless you're heavily into nostalgia.

★ = Fodor's Choice

a happily-ever-after ending might have other wee ones "heigh-ho"-ing on their way out. **For people with disabilities:** Guests using wheelchairs must transfer to ride vehicles. Equipped for handheld-captioning and audio-description devices. ■ TIP➔ Come only if you're a Snow White buff or the line is short.

MICKEY'S TOONTOWN FAIR

This concentrated tribute to the big-eared mighty one was built in 1988 to celebrate the Mouse's Big Six-O, and it became an official Magic Kingdom land soon after. But the times, they are a-changing. As Disney begins to reinvent this area of the park, Toontown Fair is expected to close for good, so if you arrive before it closes, be sure to soak up what's left of the magic here. Once the doors to Mickey's Country House and the Toontown Hall of Fame shut, the site will be a construction zone for the expansion of Fantasyland, with a targeted opening sometime in 2013.

Everything is child size at Toontown Fair; pastel houses are positively Lilliputian, with miniature driveways, toy-size picket fences, and signs scribbled with finger paint. There's some great one-stop shopping (better known as meet-and-greets) for your favorite Disney characters—hug them, get autographs, and take photos. The best way to arrive is on the Walt Disney World Railroad, the old-fashioned choo-choo that also stops at Main Street and Frontierland. Mickey's Toontown Fair is completely accessible.

☆☆☆
Duration
1 min.
Crowds
Mod. to Heavy
Audience
Small Kids

The Barnstormer at Goofy's Wiseacre Farm. Traditional red barns and farm buildings form the backdrop at Goofy's Wiseacre Farm. But the real attraction is the Barnstormer, a roller coaster with ride vehicles that are 1920s crop-dusting biplanes—designed for children but large enough for adults. Hold on to your Mouse ears. This attraction promises tummy-tickling thrills to young first-time coaster riders. If you're uncertain whether your children are up to Big Thunder Mountain Railroad, this is the test to take. Word is that this ride may be reinvented to fit the Fantasyland theme for 2013, but the rumor is unconfirmed. **For people with disabilities:** If using a wheelchair, enter through the exit at left and transfer to a ride vehicle. Service animals aren't permitted. ■ TIP➔ Visit in the evening, when many tykes have gone home.

☆
Duration
Up to You
Crowds
Mod. to Heavy
Audience
Small Kids

Donald's Boat. A cross between a tugboat and a leaky ocean liner, the *Miss Daisy* is actually a water-play area, with lily pads that spray without warning. Although it's intended for kids, grown-ups also take the opportunity to cool off on a humid Central Florida afternoon. ■ TIP➔ Come whenever the kids need some play time.

☆☆☆
Duration
Up to You
Crowds
Moderate
Audience
Small Kids

Judge's Tent. If you want to spend a few moments with the big cheese himself, load your camera, dig out a pen, and get in line here. You can catch Mickey in his personal dressing room for the ideal photo opportunity and autograph session. Shoot fast; your time is limited. **For people with disabilities:** Equipped for video-captioning devices. ■ TIP➔ If you can't get here early, try a lunchtime visit. Plan to wait it out if an audience with Mickey is a priority.

☆☆
Duration
Up to You
Crowds
Moderate
Audience
Small Kids

Mickey's Country House. Begin here to find your way to the mouse. As you walk through this slightly goofy piece of architecture right in the heart of Toontown Fairgrounds, notice the radio in the living room, "tooned" to scores from Mickey's favorite football team, Duckburg University. Down the hall, Mickey's kitchen shows the ill effects of Donald and Goofy's attempt to win the Toontown Home Remodeling Contest—with buckets of paint spilled and stacked in the sink and paint splattered on the floor and walls. The Judge's Tent just behind Mickey's house is where the mouse king holds court as he doles out hugs and autographs and mugs for photos with adoring fans. **For people with disabilities:** Equipped for audio-description devices. ■TIP➔ Come first thing in the morning or during the afternoon parade.

☆☆
Duration
Up to You
Crowds
Moderate
Audience
Small Kids

Minnie's Country House. Unlike Mickey's house, where ropes keep you from going into the rooms, this baby-blue-and-pink house is a please-touch kind of place. In this scenario, Minnie is editor of *Minnie's Cartoon Country Living* magazine, the Martha Stewart of the mouse set. While touring her office, crafts room, and kitchen, you can check the latest messages on her answering machine, bake a "quick-rising" cake at the touch of a button, and, opening the refrigerator door, get a wonderful blast of arctic air while checking out her favorite ice-cream flavor: cheese-chip. **For people with disabilities:** Equipped for audio-description devices. ■TIP➔ Go first thing in the morning or during the afternoon parade.

4

☆☆
Duration
Up to You
Crowds
Light to Moderate
Audience
Small Kids

Toon Park. This spongy green, maize, and autumn-orange play area formerly featured foam farm critters suitable for kiddie climbing. Now the fenced-in area is shaded by an awning and includes a giant tree trunk for scrambling in, around, and under; a tiny yellow-and-blue playhouse; and a gazebo-style structure leading to a tunnel and slide. Festive multi-color lights add a carnival mood by night. ■TIP➔ Come anytime.

☆☆☆
Duration
Up to You
Crowds
Mod. to Heavy
Audience
Small Kids

Toontown Hall of Fame. Stop here to collect an autograph and a hug from Disney princesses like Cinderella and Snow White and the popular fairies from Pixie Hollow. Pluto and Goofy have moved on to other meet-and-greet areas in the park to make room for the popular fairies. Check out the blue ribbon–winning entries from the Toontown Fair. **County Bounty** sells stuffed animals and all kinds of Toontown souvenirs, including autograph books. ■TIP➔ Come first thing in the morning or after the toddlers have gone home.

TOMORROWLAND

The "future that never was" spins boldly into view as you enter Tomorrowland, where Disney Imagineers paint the landscape with whirling spaceships, flashy neon lights, and gleaming robots. This is the future as envisioned by sci-fi writers and moviemakers in the 1920s and '30s, when space flight, laser beams, and home computers were fiction, not fact. Retro Jetsonesque styling lends the area lasting chic.

Gamers who want a break from the crowds can find their favorite video challenges in the arcade attached to Space Mountain. SEGA race car, NASCAR, and Fast and Furious Super Bikes games draw tweens and teens; 'Lil Hoops give young kids a manageable basketball challenge.

Though Tomorrowland Transit Authority isn't a big-ticket ride, it's a great way to check out the landscape from above as it zooms in and out of Space Mountain and curves around the entire land.

☆☆
Duration
2 mins.
Crowds
Mod. to Heavy
Audience
All Ages

Astro Orbiter. This gleaming superstructure of revolving planets has come to symbolize Tomorrowland as much as Dumbo represents Fantasyland. Passenger vehicles, on arms projecting from a central column, sail past whirling planets; you control your car's altitude but not the velocity. The line is directly across from the entrance to the TTA. **For people with disabilities:** You must be able to walk several steps and transfer to the a vehicle. ■TIP➤ The line moves slowly; come while waiting for a Space Mountain Fastpass appointment or if there's a short line. Skip on your first visit if time is limited.

Fodor's Choice★
Duration
5 mins.
Crowds
Heavy
Audience
All Ages—Truly

Buzz Lightyear's Space Ranger Spin. Based on the wildly popular *Toy Story,* this ride gives you a toy's perspective as it pits you and Buzz against the evil Emperor Zurg. You're seated in a fast-moving two-passenger Star Cruiser vehicle with an infrared laser gun in front of each rider and a centrally located lever for spinning your ship to get a good vantage point. You shoot at targets throughout the ride to help Disney's macho space toy, Buzz, defeat the emperor and save the universe—you have to hit the targets marked with a "Z" to score, and the rider with the most points wins. As Buzz likes to say, "To infinity and beyond!" The larger-than-life-size toys in the waiting area are great distractions while you wait. **For people with disabilities:** To board you must transfer to a standard wheelchair. Equipped for audio-description and handheld-captioning devices. ■TIP➤ Come first thing in the morning and get a Fastpass (if available). If you're with kids, time the wait and—if it's only 15 or 20 minutes—ride twice so they can have a practice run.

☆☆
Duration
15 mins.
Crowds
Heavy
Audience
All Ages

Monsters, Inc. Laugh Floor. The joke's on everyone at this interactive attraction starring Mike Wazowski, the one-eyed hero from Disney-Pixar's hit film *Monsters, Inc.* The old Timekeeper theater has been fitted with 400 seats so you can interact with an animated Mike and his sidekicks in the real-time, unscripted way that the character Crush from *Finding Nemo* performs at Epcot in Turtle Talk with Crush at "The Seas with Nemo & Friends." Here the premise is that Mike realizes laughter can be harnessed as a power source, and Mike's new comedy club is expected to generate power for the future. The more the audience yuks it up, jokes, and matches wits with Mike's comedian-wannabes, the greater the power produced. A new technological twist: you can text-message jokes from cell phones to the show's producer; they might even be used in the show. **For people with disabilities:** Wheelchair accessible. Sign language is available some days. Equipped for assisted-listening and video-captioning device. ■TIP➤ Come when you're waiting for your Buzz Lightyear or Space Mountain Fastpass appointment; check Times Guide for hours of operation.

Fodor's Choice★
Duration
2.5 mins.
Crowds
You bet!
Audience
Not Small Kids

Space Mountain. The needlelike spires and gleaming, white, concrete cone of this 180-foot-high attraction are almost as much of a Magic Kingdom landmark as Cinderella Castle. Inside is what is arguably the world's most imaginative roller coaster. Although there are no loop-the-loops, gravitational whizbangs, or high-speed curves, the thrills are amply provided by Disney's masterful brainwashing as you take a trip into the depths of outer space—in the dark.

In Tomorrowland, interplanetary travel is within your reach on the Astro Orbiter.

You can pass the wait time trying to park a spaceship in a station or breaking up meteors with the touch of lighted buttons thanks to big-screen interactive games in the long, dark queue area. As you walk to the loading area, you'll pass whirling planets and hear the screams and shrieks of the riders and the rattling of the cars, pumping you up for your own ride. Once you wedge yourself into the seat and blast off, the ride lasts only two minutes and 38 seconds, with a top speed of 28 MPH, but the devious twists and invisible drops in the dark make it seem twice as long. You can hear the screams from other train cars, but you don't know where they are, adding an additional fright factor. Stow personal belongings securely or have a nonrider hold onto them.

The minimum height is 44 inches, and the ride isn't appropriate for pregnant women or guests wearing back, neck, or leg braces. **For people with disabilities:** You must be able to step into the ride vehicle and walk short distances. Guests in wheelchairs should obtain a Fastpass or enter through the queue on the right. Service animals aren't permitted.
■ TIP→ The wait can be an hour or more. Get a Fastpass ticket, or come early, late, or during a parade.

☆☆
Duration
15 mins.
Crowds
Heavy
Audience
Not Small Kids

Stitch's Great Escape. Once again, Disney seizes upon a hit film to create a crowd-pleasing attraction. This time the film is *Lilo & Stitch,* and the attraction is built around a back-story to the film, about the mischievous alien, Stitch, before he meets Lilo in Hawaii. You're invited, as a new security recruit for the Galactic Federation, to enter the high-security teleportation chamber, where the ill-mannered Stitch is being processed for prison. In the form of a 3½-foot-tall Audio-Animatronics figure, Stitch escapes his captors and wreaks havoc on the room during

MAGIC KINGDOM KIDS TOUR

The Magic Kingdom is alive with thrilling distractions for young children, so let them take the lead now and then. Toddlers may want to jump from their strollers and dance along to the Barbershop Quartet on Main Street. Children who love good stories will be drawn to the Fairy Tale Garden for Story Time with Belle. These may be the most magical moments of your visit.

STOP AND SMELL THE ROSES

Head down Main Street, U.S.A. and, if you're lucky, the park's **Dapper Dans barbershop quartet** will be harmonizing sweet tunes and tossing out one-liners from a small alcove along the street. Small children are jazzed by the music and colorful costumes of these talented singers.

As you continue on toward the park's hub, veer right for the first **Kodak PictureSpot** on the Disney guide map. Take time out to snap one of the prettiest shots in the park: of the kids by the rose garden amid Mickey and Minnie topiaries and with Cinderella Castle in the background. This photo is an ideal family keepsake and perfect for a holiday card.

Fantasyland is dead ahead, and after you've soared on **Dumbo the Flying Elephant** and nabbed a Fastpass for The Many Adventures of Winnie the Pooh, find a bench in the **Fairytale Garden** in the castle's shadow along Tomorrowland's border. Kids love to listen to (some even get to participate in) **Storytime with Belle,** a reenactment of scenes from *Beauty and the Beast.*

PUT THE ZIP IN YOUR DOO-DAH

If your timing is right and Mickey's Toontown Fair hasn't yet closed for the Fantasyland expansion—walk this way. Sure, little ones love the **Barnstormer** kiddie coaster, but they truly can't resist the free-play fun at **Toon Park** and on Donald's (leaky) Boat.

Board the **Walt Disney World Railroad** at Toontown Fair, Main Street, U.S.A., or Frontierland. While in Frontierland, too-short-to-ride kids can burn energy in the cavelike play area beneath **Splash Mountain** while parents take turns riding. And the short raft trip to **Tom Sawyer Island** is worth it for boys and tomboys who like exploring caves and forts. Not far from the Country Bear Jamboree, sure shots can take aim at Western-style targets in the often-missed **Frontierland Shooting Gallery**—at $1 per 35 shots, it's a blast for any aspiring sheriff.

BECOME THE CHARACTER

Girls will get the makeover of a lifetime ($50–$190) at **Bibbidi Bobbidi Boutique** in Cinderella Castle. Hair, nails, makeup—even a sprinkling of pixie dust—it's all here. At **The Pirate's League,** in Adventureland by Pirates of the Caribbean, a scurvy sea-dog makeover ($50–$125 including photos) lets the inner buccaneer emerge.

But the best-buy makeover (and fastest, too) is in Town Square, where the **Harmony Barber Shop** will transform your crowning glory with colored gel at $5 a pop. Of course, neither Mickey nor Goofy cares whether your hair is aglitter or your eye patch is on straight. Be sure not to miss a scheduled Character Meet and Greet (see *Times Guide*) so the little rascals get all the hugs, autographs, photos, and magical memories they deserve.

MAGIC KINGDOM GROWN-UP TOUR

The kids are older, and they're interested in thrills, not magic. Or there aren't any kids in tow, and this is your golden opportunity to enjoy "me" time. Seize the day! The Magic Kingdom is a whole new experience without small children. Maximize the big adventures, take time to dine and shop, and discover your own brand of magic along the way.

CLASSIC THRILLS

As you pass beneath the train station and into Town Square, you're entering the Happiest Place on Earth, and it's time to grab the golden ring. If thrill riding tops your list, work that cardio for a power walk northwest from the park hub through Liberty Square to Frontierland, where you can grab your Fastpass to **Splash Mountain,** then go next door to ride the bumpy, scenic, runaway train at **Big Thunder Mountain Railroad.**

For many, just to see the Johnny Depp–look-alike Audio-Animatronic Captain Jack Sparrow, is reason enough to ride the **Pirates of the Caribbean** in Adventureland, a short stroll from Splash Mountain. Cut back through the park hub and straight to **Space Mountain** in Tomorrowland for your other big-deal Fastpass. While you wait, sip an iced cappuccino or smoothie from **Auntie Gravity's Galactic Goodies** and immerse yourself in the futuristic scene reminiscent of *The Jetsons.*

PLAY, DINE, SHOP

The interactive **Buzz Lightyear's Space Ranger Spin** is addictive for competitive types, who will probably want to ride more than once for a chance to raise their space ranger profile. (This attraction is also one of the best ways to spend time while waiting for your Space Mountain Fastpass to mature—just sayin'.)

Chill out afterward at **Tony's Town Square Restaurant,** a great, full-service, late-lunch spot where you can feast on pasta. Burn the calories shopping on Main Street for a make-your-own Mouse Ears souvenir from **The Chapeau** or a customized watch from **Uptown Jewelers.**

At **Crystal Arts** you could buy a fluted glass bowl then mosey to the rear of the glass shop to see an Arribas Brothers glassblower craft a piece using 2,100°F furnaces, a heated rod, and lots of talent. It takes about 20 minutes for the glassblower to shape a piece of glass and explain each step along the way.

CATCH THE SPIRIT(S)

You can skip the 3 PM parade crowds, and join 999 grim-grinning ghouls at the **Haunted Mansion** in Liberty Square. Afterward, stroll several paces to the Hall of Presidents, featuring President Barack Obama, and catch the patriotic spirit. Just around the corner in Fantasyland, don your goofy 3-D glasses for **Mickey's PhilharMagic,** starring the largest cast of Disney animated stars performing in a single show. Cap the evening with the nighttime **Spectro-Magic** parade—it'll dissolve any cynicism left in your psyche. When the lights go down and the **Wishes** fireworks paint the sky, you'll be glad you stayed for the fairy-tale ending.

4

If Pooh can, you can—enjoy a Main Street parade, that is.

close encounters with the audience in near-darkness. Sensory effects and tactile surprises are part of the package. Beware the chili-dog "belch" odor and a spray that prompts more than a few gasps of surprise (Hint: Stitch is the first Audio-Animatronics figure to spit).

Small children may be frightened by shoulder restraints, periods of darkness, and loud, startling noises. Plus, the minimum height is 40 inches. **For people with disabilities:** Guests in motorized scooters must transfer to an on-site standard wheelchair. Equipped for assisted-listening, handheld-captioning, and video-captioning. Guests with service animals should check with a host before entering. ■ **TIP→ Come during a parade or whenever lines dwindle. Fastpasses are better used on Space Mountain or Buzz Lightyear's Space Ranger Spin (when available).**

☆
Duration
5 mins.
Crowds
Moderate
Audience
**Kids and
Tweens**

Tomorrowland Indy Speedway. This is one of those rides that incite instant addiction in children and immediate hatred in their parents. The reasons for the former are easy to figure out: the brightly colored Mark VII model cars that swerve around the four 2,260-foot tracks with much vroom-vroom-vrooming. Kids will feel like they're Mario Andretti as they "race" around. Like real sports cars, the gasoline-powered vehicles are equipped with rack-and-pinion steering and disc brakes; unlike the real thing, these run on a track. However, the track is so twisty that it's hard to keep the car on a straight course—something the race-car fanatics warming the bleachers love to watch. You may spend a lot of time waiting, first to get your turn on the track, then to return your vehicle after your lap. All this for a ride in which the main thrill is achieving a top speed of 7 mph.

Children riding with an adult must be at least 32 inches tall; those who wish to drive must reach 54 inches. **For people with disabilities:** To drive the cars, you must have adequate vision and be able to steer, press the gas pedal, and transfer into the low car seat. ■TIP→ Skip on a first-time visit, unless you've been through all the major attractions—in which case, come in the evening or during a parade.

☆☆
Duration
10 mins.
Crowds
Light
Audience
All Ages

Tomorrowland Transit Authority. A reincarnation of what Disney old-timers may remember as the WEDway PeopleMover, the TTA takes a nice, leisurely ride around the perimeter of Tomorrowland, circling the Astro-Orbiter and eventually gliding through the middle of Space Mountain. Some fainthearted TTA passengers have no doubt chucked the notion of riding the roller coaster after being exposed firsthand to the screams emanating from within the mountain—although these make the ride sound worse than it really is. Disney's version of future mass transit is smooth and noiseless, thanks to an electromagnetic linear induction motor that has no moving parts, uses little power, and emits no pollutants. **For people with disabilities:** You must be able to walk several steps and step on and off of a moving ramp to transfer to a ride vehicle. Equipped for handheld-captioning and audio-description devices. ■TIP→ Come to view Tomorrowland, to preview Space Mountain, if you have very young children, or if you need a relaxing ride.

☆
Duration
20 mins.
Crowds
Moderate
Audience
All Ages

Walt Disney's Carousel of Progress. Originally seen at New York's 1964–65 World's Fair, this revolving theater traces the impact of technological progress on the daily lives of Americans from the turn of the 20th century into the near future. Representing each decade, an Audio-Animatronics family sings the praises of modern-day gadgets that technology has wrought. Fans of the holiday film *A Christmas Story* will recognize the voice of its narrator, Jean Shepard, who injects his folksy, all-American humor as father figure through the decades. **For people with disabilities:** Wheelchair accessible; equipped for assisted-listening, handheld-captioning, and video-captioning devices. ■TIP→ Skip on a first-time visit unless you're heavily into nostalgia. May close early or entirely in low season.

MAGIC KINGDOM SPECTACLES

☆☆
Duration
25 mins.
Crowds
Heavy
Audience
All Ages

Celebrate A Dream Come True Parade. This 3 PM park mainstay traverses Town Square, Main Street, the castle hub, and Frontierland. Floats feature Mickey, Goofy, and most of the Disney storybook gang. The "Celebrate" theme rings out, though classic Disney tunes are woven into the score to accompany the story told by each float, including "You Can Fly" with Peter Pan and "Chim Chim Cher-ee" with Mary Poppins. Mickey Mouse and main squeeze Minnie lead off on a festive float that spells "party time" with decorations of oversize fireworks and noisemakers. Dozens of performers in bright costumes wave flags and streamers and kick up their heels along the route; the parade stops at three locations for high-energy dance numbers. Six other floats are crowd pleasers, with Disney stars like Pinocchio, Snow White, Cinderella, Belle, Beast, Ariel, Prince Ali, Mary Poppins, Alice (of Wonderland), and others. The villains float scares up laughs with Cruella de Vil,

Maleficent, The Wicked Queen, and Jafar. The warm and fuzzy finale features Pluto, Goofy, and Chip 'n' Dale.

■TIP→ Ask where the parade begins—Frontierland or Town Square—to determine where to camp and how long you'll wait for the parade to arrive. Older kids might want to skip this; rides have shorter lines until the parade ends.

☆☆
Duration
20 mins.
Crowds
Heavy
Audience
All Ages

Dream Along with Mickey. The Cinderella Castle forecourt provides the perfect location for several daily performances of this Disney character spectacle starring Donald Duck, Mickey Mouse, Minnie Mouse, Goofy, and others. As the show begins, Donald is a "dreams-come-true" skeptic, but he has joined his optimistic pals anyway at a party where Disney princes and princesses dance in a romantic, dreamy number. There's adventure, too, when Peter Pan, pirates, and wenches take the stage. When pesky Disney villains crash the party, Donald decides to challenge evil and fight for the dreams of all his character friends and family.

If you want to sit (and don't mind an obstructed view), arrive 30 to 40 minutes before showtime to get a seat on a bench. Pick up a *Times Guide* at City Hall or in most park shops for performance times and a schedule of character meet-and-greets. And, based on Disney's record for creating new live productions, don't be surprised if something has replaced Dream Along with Mickey when you vist. ■TIP→ If you have children, plan to stand or sit on the pavement near the stage for an unobstructed view. Older kids may want to skip this in favor of rides.

Fodor's Choice★
Duration
20 mins.
Crowds
Heavy
Audience
All Ages

SpectroMagic Parade. The magic truly comes out at night when the parade rolls down Main Street, U.S.A., in a splendidly choreographed surge of electro-luminescent, fiber-optic, and prismatic lighting effects that bring to life peacocks, sea horses, fountains, fantasy gardens, and floats full of colorful Disney characters. Plenty of old-fashioned twinkle lights are thrown in for good measure, and familiar tunes are broadcast over 204 speakers with 72,000 watts of power. Mickey, as always, is the star. But Practical Pig, from one of Disney's prewar Silly Symphony cartoons, steals the show. With the flick of a paintbrush, he transforms more than 100 feet of multicolor floats into a gleaming white-light dreamscape. Check *Times Guide* to see if the parade will run; it's presented only on select nights. ■TIP→ Take your place on the curb at least 40 minutes before the parade begins.

☆☆☆
Duration
12 mins.
Crowds
Heavy
Audience
All Ages

Wishes. When the lights dim on Main Street and orchestral music fills the air, you know this fireworks extravaganza is about to begin. In Wishes, Jiminy Cricket's voice comes to life and tries to convince you that your wishes really can come true. He gets plenty of support from the Disney stars of classic films such as *Pinocchio, Fantasia, Cinderella,* and *The Little Mermaid.* Portions of famous film songs play over loudspeakers, and you'll hear the voices of film characters like Peter Pan and Aladdin as more than 680 individual fireworks paint the night sky. Oh, and don't worry that Tinker Bell may have been sealed in her jar for the night—she comes back to fly above the crowd in grand pixie-dust style. Check the *Times Guide* for performance time, which varies seasonally. ■TIP→ Find a place near the front of the park so you can make a quick exit at the end of the show.

Epcot

WORD OF MOUTH

"The food [at Disney] was all good, but one of the highlights was Epcot's Chefs de France. There's a good three-course menu . . . a waiter wheeled a covered tray to our table, and, when the cover was removed, [an Audio-Animatronic] Remy (from *Ratatouille*) stood and started talking. . . . My grandson was speechless."

—jeff49

EPCOT PLANNER

Park Information

Disney's monorail and buses drop you off at the main entrance in front of Future World. But if you're staying at one of the Epcot resorts (the BoardWalk, Yacht Club, Beach Club, Dolphin, or Swan), you can use the International Gateway entrance between World Showcase's France and U.K. pavilions.

Guest Relations (aka Guest Services), to the right of the ticket windows at the park entrance and to the left of Spaceship Earth inside the park, is the place to pick up schedules and maps. You also can get maps at the park's International Gateway entrance and most shops. Guest Relations will also assist with dining reservations, ticket upgrades, and services for guests with disabilities.

Park Amenities

Baby Care: The Baby Care Center at Odyssey Center in Future World has rocking chairs and low lighting. The center sells formula, baby food, pacifiers, and disposable diapers. Changing tables are available here, as well as in all women's and some men's restrooms.

Cameras: Disposable cameras and memory cards are widely available, and you can get your digital memory card downloaded onto a CD for $11.95 plus tax at the Kodak Camera Center in the Entrance Plaza. Other photo services are available at the Imagination! pavilion.

First-Aid: Staffed by registered nurses, First Aid is in the Odyssey Center. More than a dozen Automated External Defibrillators are located across the park.

Lockers: Lockers ($5 and $7, with $5 refundable deposit) are at the International Gateway and to the west of Spaceship Earth. Coin-operated lockers also are at the Bus Information Center by the bus parking lot.

Lost People and Things: Pick up name tags at Guest Relations or the Baby Care Center. Instruct children to speak to someone with a Disney name tag if you become separated. The Baby Care Center has lost-children logbooks; Guest Relations has them, too, as well as a computerized Message Center for contacting companions in any of the parks. **Epcot Lost and Found** (☎ 407/560–7500) is at the Guest Relations lobby east of Spaceship Earth. After one day, all articles are sent to the **Main Lost and Found office** (✉ Magic Kingdom, Ticket and Transportation Center [TTC] ☎ 407/824–4245).

Package Pick-Up: Ask shop clerks to forward large purchases to Package Pick-Up at the Gift Stop in the Main Entrance Plaza and at the World Traveler at International Gateway. Allow three hours for delivery. You also can have packages sent to your Disney hotel.

Stroller Rentals: You can rent strollers on the east side of the Entrance Plaza and at the International Gateway. Singles are $15 daily, $13 for multiday rental; doubles cost $31 daily, $27 for multiple days. Even preschoolers will be glad for a stroller in this large park.

Guided Tours

Reserve with **WDW Tours** (☎ 407/939–8687) up to six weeks in advance for behind-the-scenes tours. In general, participants must be 16 years of age and have an ID. Ever since the Segway Human Transporters were featured at Innoventions, some Disney cast members have used them. You, too, can travel through the World Showcase via Segway on the two-hour guided **Around the World at Epcot Tour.** The price for the daily tour (at 7:45, 8:30, 9, or 9:30 AM) is $95; park admission required.

At 9:45 AM, **Dolphins in Depth** ($175, neither park admission nor diving certification required) guides escort you from the entrance to the Seas with Nemo & Friends pavilion. Tours run weekdays and last about three hours. Participants must be 13 or older; a parent or legal guardian must accompany anyone under 18.

Take the three-hour **Gardens of the World Tour** ($59, plus park admission) to see the World Showcase's realistic replicas of exotic plantings up close. Tours run during the Epcot International Flower & Garden Festival from early to mid-March through late May.

On the three-hour **Epcot Divequest** ($175, park admission not required or included) at the Seas with Nemo & Friends pavilion, you spend 40 minutes in the mammoth aquarium under the supervision of a master diver. The tours take place daily at either 4:30 or 5:30. Guests 10 and up must have open-water adult scuba certification; children under 17 must dive with a parent or legal guardian.

On the **Epcot Seas Aqua Tour** ($140, no park admission required or included) you wear a flotation device and diving gear, but you remain on the water's surface. Anyone age 8 and older can join the tour (those ages 8–11 must be with a parent or legal guardian); tours are limited to 12 guests; meet daily at 12:30; and run about 2½ hours, with 30 minutes in the water.

The UnDISCOVERed Future World ($55, plus park admission) leaves at 9 AM Monday, Wednesday, and Friday from Guest Relations at the main entrance. The four-hour behind-the-scenes walk covers all Future World pavilions and some VIP lounges and backstage areas.

The seasonal 3½-hour **Yuletide Fantasy** visits theme parks and resorts to see how Disney's elves weave holiday traditions. The $69 tour departs daily during December at 9 AM from Epcot and is for guests 16 and older.

For People with Disabilities

Accessibility standards are high. Many attractions and most restaurants and shops are fully wheelchair accessible. There are large Braille park maps at Guest Relations in Future World and International Gateway a well as to the left of the walkway from Future World to the World Showcase Plaza.

At Guest Relations there's a schedule for sign-language presentations at some of the park attractions; you also can pick up special devices for hearing- and sight-impaired visitors.

At World Showcase most people stroll around the promenade, but there are also Friendship boats, which require visitors using oversize wheelchairs or scooters to transfer to Disney chairs.

You can rent wheelchairs at the Gift Stop outside the main entrance, at the Stroller & Wheelchair Rental Shop to the left of Spaceship Earth, or at the International Gateway. A limited number of Electronic Convenience Vehicles (ECV) are available only at the Stroller & Wheelchair Rental.

Wheelchairs are $10 daily, $8 for multiday rental. ECVs are $45 per day plus a refundable $20 security deposit. Arrive early, because neither conveyance can be reserved.

5

EPCOT
TRAVEL THE GLOBE

Nowhere but at Epcot can you explore and experience the native food, entertainment, culture, and arts and crafts of countries in Europe, Asia, North Africa, and the Americas. What's more, employees at the World Showcase pavilions actually hail from the countries the pavilions represent.

Epcot, or "Experimental Prototype Community of Tomorrow," was the original inspiration for Walt Disney World. Walt envisioned a future in which nations coexisted in peace and harmony, reaping the miraculous harvest of technological achievement. The Epcot of today is both more and less than his original dream. Less, because the World Showcase presents views of its countries that are, as an Epcot guide once put it, "as Americans perceive them"—highly idealized. But this is a minor quibble in the face of the major achievement: Epcot is that rare paradox—a successful educational theme park that excels at entertainment, too.

EPCOT BY BOAT

Epcot is a big place at 305 acres; a local joke suggests that the acronym actually stands for "Every Person Comes Out Tired." But still, the most efficient way to get around is to walk.

To vary things, you can cruise across the lagoon in an air-conditioned, 65-foot water taxi; they depart every 12 minutes from two World Showcase Plaza docks at the border of Future World.

The boat closer to Mexico zips to a dock by the Germany pavilion; the one closer to Canada heads to Morocco. You may have to stand in line to board, however.

GETTING ORIENTED

Epcot is composed of two areas: Future World and the World Showcase. The inner core of Future World's pavilions has the Spaceship Earth geosphere and a plaza anchored by the computer-animated Fountain of Nations. Bracketing it are the crescent-shaped Innoventions East and West, with hands-on, high-tech exhibits, and immersion entertainment.

Six pavilions compose Future World's outer ring. Each of the three east pavilions has a ride and the occasional post-ride showcase; a visit rarely takes more than 30 minutes. The blockbuster exhibits on the west side contain rides and interactive displays; each exhibit requires at least 90 minutes.

World Showcase pavilions are on the promenade that circles the World Showcase Lagoon. Each houses shops, restaurants, and friendly foreign staffers; some have films or displays. Mexico and Norway offer tame rides. Entertainment is scheduled at every pavilion except Norway.

TOP ATTRACTIONS

Soarin'. Everyone's hands-down favorite: feel the sweet breeze as you "hang glide" over California landscapes.

The American Adventure. Many adults and older children love this patriotic look at American history; who can resist the Audio-Animatronics hosts, Ben Franklin and Mark Twain?

IllumiNations. This amazing musical laser-fountains-and-fireworks show is Disney nighttime entertainment at its best.

Mission: SPACE. Blast off on a simulated ride to Mars, if you can handle the turbulence.

Test Track. Your car revs up to 60 mph on a hairpin turn in this wild ride on a General Motors proving ground.

MIND GAMES

Although several attractions provide high-octane kicks, Epcot's thrills are mostly for the mind. The park is best for school-age children and adults, but there's interactive entertainment for everyone at Innoventions. And most attractions provide some diversions for preschool children. At the 15 or so **Kidcot Fun Stops**, younger children can try their hands at crafts projects—like designing a mask and adding special touches at each pavilion along the way.

VISITING TIPS

■ Epcot is so vast and varied you really need two days to explore. With just one day, you'll have to be highly selective.

■ Go early in the week, when others are at Magic Kingdom.

■ If you like a good festival, visit during the International Flower & Garden Festival (early to mid-March through May) or the International Food & Wine Festival (late September through mid-November).

5

By Jennie Hess   Wear comfortable shoes—there's *a lot* of territory to cover here. Arrive early, and try to stay all day, squeezing in extras like high-tech games at Innoventions and a relaxing meal. If you enter through International Gateway before 11 AM, cast members will direct you to Future World, which usually opens two hours before World Showcase.

Disney said that Epcot would "take its cue from the new ideas and new technologies that are now emerging from the creative centers of American industry." He wrote that Epcot, never completed, always improving, "will never cease to be a living blueprint of the future, a showcase to the world for the ingenuity of American free enterprise."

But the permanent settlement that Disney envisioned wasn't to be. Epcot opened in 1982—16 years after his death—as a showcase, ostensibly, for the concepts that would be incorporated into the real-life Epcots of the future. (Disney's vision *has* taken an altered shape in the self-contained city of Celebration, an urban planner's dream opened in 1996 on Disney property near Kissimmee.)

Epcot, the theme park, has two key areas: Future World, where most pavilions are collaborations between Walt Disney Imagineering and U.S. corporations and are designed to demonstrate technological advances through innovative shows and attractions; and the World Showcase, where shops, restaurants, attractions, and live entertainment create microcosms of 11 countries from four continents.

For years, Epcot was considered the more staid park, a place geared toward adults. But after its 10th anniversary, Epcot began to evolve into a livelier, more child-friendly park, with interactive fun at Innoventions and such "wow" attractions as Future World's Honey, I Shrunk the Audience, Test Track, and Mission: SPACE

There's something for everyone here. The World Showcase appeals to younger children with the Kidcot Fun Stop craft stations and the Norway pavilion's Princess Storybook Dining. Soarin', in The Land pavilion, is a family favorite. And the Seas with Nemo & Friends—with one of the world's largest saltwater aquariums—is a must-see for all.

FUTURE WORLD

Don't get disoriented as you face the iconic Spaceship Earth and try to figure out which way to go. With Epcot guide map in hand, head straight for one of the two most popular attractions: Soarin' on the west side, or Mission: SPACE on the east. Ride early if you can, or get your Fastpass to return later. Future World's inner core is composed of the Spaceship Earth geosphere and, just beyond it, a plaza anchored by the awe-inspiring computer-animated Fountain of Nations, which shoots water 150 feet skyward. Bracketing it are the crescent-shaped Innoventions East and West.

Six pavilions compose Future World's outer ring. On the east side they are, in order, the Universe of Energy, Mission: SPACE, and Test Track. Each pavilion presents a single, self-contained ride and an occasional post-ride showcase; a visit rarely takes more than 30 minutes, but it depends on how long you spend in the post-ride area. On the west side are the Seas with Nemo & Friends, the Land, and Imagination! These blockbuster exhibits contain both rides and interactive displays; you could spend at least 1½ hours at each of these pavilions, but there aren't enough hours in the day, so prioritize.

■ TIP→ Before you set out, look into the Disney PhotoPass at the Kodak Camera Center in the Entrance Plaza. It tracks photos of your group shot in the parks by Disney photographers so that you can view and purchase them later at the center or online.

☆☆☆
Duration
Up to You
Crowds
Mod. to Heavy
Audience
All Ages

Innoventions. Innoventions is a two-building, 100,000-square-foot, walk-through attraction. Interactive exhibits entertain kids (some are especially designed for preschoolers) and adults as they investigate the innovations now improving the world around us.

Innoventions East is loaded with activities sure to inspire a future engineer. Take Sum of All Thrills by technology company Raytheon, for instance. This is not your typical "design a coaster" ride. Here, you get your own multi-touch-screen table with math- and engineering-based tools (and simple instructions) to design and customize your bobsled, jet, or roller-coaster ride with corkscrews, inversions, and steep hills. Along the way, you'll apply math and engineering principles to measure the energy you need to make it over a hill. Then you and a partner get to climb aboard a robotic simulator for the high-def immersion ride that's as mild or as wild as you design it.

StormStruck, presented by the Federal Alliance for Safe Homes and partners like State Farm, serves up severe weather that'll make you jump and duck in a 3-D theater. You have your own electronic buttons for voting on how you'd protect your property from future storms before the "big reveal" tells you whether you're right or wrong. At the Test the Limits Lab, you can be product testers for Underwriters Laboratories trying to break TV screens, slam doors, crush helmets, and put other home products through their paces. And at Waste Management's Don't Waste It! exhibit, you become an environmental steward working to dispose of a year's worth of trash while creating energy to power a city.

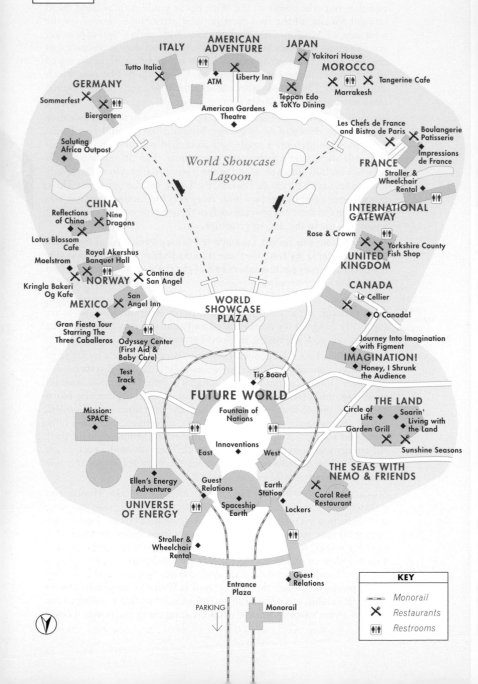

At Innoventions West, you can test drive the Segway Human Transporter at Segway Central. The transporter is so popular that it's used by some Disney personnel to wheel across the park and has been incorporated into guided tours. Liberty Mutual's Where's the Fire? interactive experience is a terrific way to review fire safety and prevention. Your family can enjoy the game house, where you'll team up with other guests to find and extinguish as many fire hazards as possible and learn best ways to stay safe in a fire. The Firefighter Photo station lets you send a photo postcard to family and friends.

> **STARTING EPCOT RIGHT**
>
> Once you go through security and the turnstiles at either the main Future World entrance or the back World Showcase entrance, make a beeline for Mission: SPACE and Test Track (for the fast-paced thrills) or for the Seas with Nemo & Friends and Soarin' (for two terrific family-fun experiences), where the longest lines form first.

At the Velcro Companies' Slap Stick Studios, you can join a very silly, high-energy game show and watch audience members try to solve "sticky" problems using Velcro-branded products. At Smarter Planet, IBM puts you in a game where you can create an avatar of yourself who's able to jump, run, and dance through a video game starring (you guessed it) you! You can even watch your cash reserves grow at the Great Piggy Bank Adventure by T. Rowe Price. Children love the real piggy bank they get to move from one interactive station to another; adults enjoy the fast-paced teamwork involved in choosing a "dream" goal, learning strategies to save, staying ahead of inflation, and diversifying funds.

If you can't resist an interactive escapade with a bit of intrigue tossed in, sign up here for the Kim Possible World Showcase Adventure. You'll receive your own "Kimmunicator"—a handheld wireless controller connecting you with several Kim Possible characters who provide clues to stop comical villains from taking over the world with their mad inventions. At your own pace, you can scour the World Showcase for clues and solve challenges encountered during the experience.

For people with disabilities: This attraction is completely wheelchair accessible—some exhibits inside this always-evolving attraction may require transferring from a wheelchair. Sign-language interpretation is available some days. Guests with service animals should check with an attractions host when entering. ■ TIP→ Come before 11 am or after 2 pm. Sum of All Thrills, StormStruck, and The Great Piggy Bank Adventure have the largest crowds.

NEED A BREAK? With soft drinks going for more than $2 per cup at park concessions, **Club Cool** is the place to visit when you're thirsty and in the mood to be adventurous. Here Coca-Cola's bold red-and-white colors guide you to a room full of soda machines and logo merchandise. You can sample (for free) the cola king's products from around the world, including Vegitabeta from Japan, Smart Watermelon from China, and Kinley Lemon from Israel. It's entertaining to watch kids' faces when their taste buds react to an unfamiliar flavor.

Fodor's Choice ★
Duration
4 mins.
Crowds
You Bet!
Audience
Not Small Kids

Mission: SPACE. It took five years for Disney Imagineers, with the help of 25 experts from NASA, to design Mission: SPACE, the first ride ever to take people "straight up" in a simulated rocket launch. The story transports you and co-riders to the year 2036 and the International Space Training Center, where you are astronauts-in-training about to embark on your first launch. Before you board the four-person rocket capsule, you're assigned to a position: commander, navigator, pilot, or engineer. And at this point you're warned several times about the intensity of the ride and the risks for people with health concerns. (Pregnant women and anyone with heart, back, neck, balance, blood-pressure, or motion-sickness problems shouldn't ride, and the ride-height minimum is 44 inches.)

> **MISSION: SPACE CAUTION**
>
> Parents should exercise caution when deciding whether to let children ride Mission: SPACE. Even if your child meets the height requirement, she may not be old enough to enjoy the ride. In the capsule, you're instructed to keep your head back against the seat and to look straight ahead for the duration of the ride. (Closing your eyes or not looking straight ahead can bring on motion sickness.) Your role as a "crew member" also means you're supposed to hold onto a joystick and push buttons at certain times. All these instructions can confuse younger kids and get in the way of their enjoyment of the ride.

■TIP→ Many people exit this ride feeling nauseated and disoriented from the high-speed spinning, which is what makes you feel as if you're rocketing into space. These effects are often cumulative. You may be OK after your first ride but totally ill after your second or third in a row.

For those who can handle the intense spinning, the sensation of lift-off is truly amazing. You'll feel the capsule tilt skyward and, on a screen that simulates a windshield, you'll see the clouds and even a flock of birds pass over you. Then you launch—a turbulent and heart-pounding experience that flattens you against your seat. Once you break into outer space, you'll even feel weightless. After landing, you exit your capsule into the Advanced Training Lab, where you can rejoin your little ones playing some very entertaining space-related games.

For people with disabilities: This ride requires a transfer from wheelchair to seat. Service animals aren't permitted to board. Video-captioning devices can be used on the ride; assisted-listening devices can be used in the postshow Training Lab. ■TIP→ Arrive before 10 am or use Fastpass during peak season. Don't ride on a full stomach.

☆☆☆
Duration
15 mins.
Crowds
Mod. to Heavy
Audience
All Ages

Spaceship Earth. Balanced like a giant golf ball waiting for some celestial being to tee off, the multifaceted silver geosphere of Spaceship Earth is to Epcot what Cinderella Castle is to the Magic Kingdom. As much a landmark as an icon, it can be seen on a clear day from an airplane flying down either coast of Florida.

Inside the ball, the Spaceship Earth ride transports you past a series of tableaux that explore human progress and the continuing search for better forms of communication. Over the years, both Walter Cronkite and Jeremy Irons have narrated the script by science-fiction writer Ray Bradbury. Today Oscar-winner Dame Judi Dench narrates the journey that begins in the darkest tunnels of time, proceeds through history, and ends poised on the edge of the future. For the first time on a Disney ride, the narration also is offered in French, Japanese, German, Spanish, and Portuguese. Ten-time Emmy winner Bruce Broughton composed the musical score.

RAINY DAYS

Although attractions at Future World are largely indoors, Epcot's expansiveness and the largely outdoor attractions of the World Showcase make the park a poor choice on rainy days. Still, if you can't go another day, bring a poncho and muddle through.

Audio-Animatronics figures present Cro-Magnon man daubing mystic paintings on cave walls, Egyptian scribes scratching hieroglyphics on papyrus, Roman centurions building roads, Islamic scholars mapping the heavens, and 11th- and 12th-century Benedictine monks hand-copying manuscripts. As you move into the Renaissance, Michelangelo paints the Sistine Chapel; Gutenberg invents the printing press; and in rapid succession, the telegraph, radio, television, and computer come into being. A family views the moon landing on TV, and a massive two-story computer room circa 1960s and a '70s garage show where the personal computer was born.

As your ride vehicle swings backward and descends slowly, touch screens ask how you envision your own future, then play back an animated, *Jetsons*-esque scenario based on the answers. Siemans, which presents the higher-tech attraction, created a fun-packed postshow with high-demand interactive games that involve simulated driving, piecing together a digital human body, and managing a growing city's power grid. As you exit the ride and enter the postshow, watch the giant digital map screen to see your photo taken during the ride and posted in your hometown location.

For people with disabilities: You must be able to transfer to a standard wheelchair, then walk four steps to the ride vehicle. Guests with service animals should check with an attraction host for boarding information. The ride is equipped for hand-held captioning or attraction-description devices available at Guest Relations. Although much of the enchantment is in the visual details, the narration is compelling. ■TIP→ Ride while waiting for a Mission: SPACE or Soarin' Fastpass appointment. Lines are longest in the morning and shortest just before closing.

Fodor's Choice★
Duration
5 mins.
Crowds
Heavy
Audience
Not Small Kids

Test Track. This small-scale-with-big-thrills version of a General Motors vehicle proving ground takes you behind the scenes of automobile testing. The line area showcases many of these tests in informative, action-packed exhibits, which make the wait fun, but if you enter with a Fastpass, you'll miss these features.

On the ride, sporty convertible Test Track vehicles take you and five other passengers through seven performance tests. In the Brake Test your ride vehicle makes two passes through a circular setup of traffic cones, and you learn how antilock brakes can make a wildly out-of-control skid manageable. In the Environmental Chamber, vehicles are exposed to extreme heat, bone-chilling cold, and a mist that simulates exposure to corrosive substances. After leaving these test chambers, vehicles accelerate quickly up a switchback "mountain road" in the Ride Handling Test. There's also a too-close-for-comfort view of a Barrier Test.

The best part, the High-Speed Test, is last: your vehicle bursts through an opening in the Test Track building to negotiate a steeply banked loop at a speed of nearly 60 mph. Outside the pavilion, kids can get a soaking in the Cool Wash, an interactive water area that lets them pretend they're in a car wash. Note that the minimum height to ride is 40 inches, but that's OK. The line-area message will be lost on young children anyway, and the speeds and other effects may prove frightening. Also, the ride isn't suitable for pregnant women or guests wearing back, neck, or leg braces.

For people with disabilities: Visitors in wheelchairs are provided a special area in which to practice transferring into the ride vehicle before actually boarding. One TV monitor in the preshow area is closed-captioned, and the ride is equipped for video-captioning and handheld-captioning devices. Service animals aren't permitted on board. ■TIP→ **Go first thing in the morning and get a Fastpass ticket, or you may wait—a long time. Note that the ride can't function on wet tracks, so don't head here after a shower.**

UNIVERSE OF ENERGY

The first of the pavilions on the left, or east, side of Future World, the Universe of Energy occupies a large, lopsided pyramid sheathed in thousands of mirrors—solar collectors that power the attraction inside. Though it's a technologically complex show with a ride, film, and large Audio-Animatronics dinosaurs, the attraction could use some updating. One of the special effects includes enough cold, damp fog to make you think you've been transported to the inside of a defrosting refrigerator. ("We don't want to go through that fog again," one child announced after emerging from the Mesozoic era.)

☆☆
Duration
45 mins.
Crowds
Moderate
Audience
All Ages

Ellen's Energy Adventure. Comedian Ellen DeGeneres portrays a woman who dreams she's a contestant on *Jeopardy!* only to discover that all the categories involve a subject she knows nothing about—energy. Her challengers on the show, hosted by Alex Trebek himself, are Ellen's know-it-all former college roommate (played to the irritating hilt by Jamie Lee Curtis) and Albert Einstein. Enter Bill Nye, the Science Guy, Ellen's nice neighbor and all-around science whiz, who guides Ellen (and you) in a crash Energy 101 course.

First comes the history of the universe—in one minute—on three 70-millimeter screens, 157 feet wide by 32 feet tall. Next the theater separates into six 96-passenger vehicles that lurch into a primeval forest. Huge trees loom out of the mists of time, ominous blue moonbeams waver in the fog, sulfurous lava burbles up, and the air smells of Swamp Thing. Through this landscape, apatosauruses wander trailing mouthfuls of weeds, a tyrannosaurus fights it out with a triceratops,

EPCOT

Future World

NAME	Height Req.	Type of Entertainment	Duration	Crowds	Audience	Tips
The Circle of Life (The Land)	n/a	Film	20 mins.	Moderate to Heavy	All but Small Kids	Come early or for your toddler's afternoon nap.
Ellen's Energy Adventure (Universe of Energy)	n/a	Ride-Through	45 mins.	Moderate	All Ages	Best seats are to the far left and front of the theater.
Honey, I Shrunk the Audience (Imagination!)	n/a	3-D Film	14 mins.	Moderate to Heavy	All Ages	Come in the early morning or just before closing. Take off the 3-D glasses if little kids get scared.
Innoventions	n/a	Walk-Through	Up to you	Moderate to Heavy	All Ages	Come before 11 am or after 2 pm.
Journey into Imagination with Figment (Imagination!)	n/a	Ride-Through	8 mins.	Light	Small Kids	Ride while waiting for Honey, I Shrunk the Audience Fastpass. Warn toddlers about darkness at the end of the ride.
Living with the Land (The Land)	n/a	Cruise	14 mins.	Moderate	All but Small Kids	The line moves quickly, so come anytime.
★ Mission: SPACE	At least 44"	Thrill Ride	4 mins.	You Bet!	All but Small Kids	Come before 10 am or use Fastpass. Don't ride on a full stomach.
The Seas with Nemo & Friends	n/a	Ride- and Walk-Through	Up to you	Moderate to Heavy	Small Kids	Get Nemo fans here early in the morning.

	Height	Type	Duration	Crowds	Audience	Comments
★ Soarin' (The Land)	At least 40"	Simulator Ride	5 mins.	Heavy	All but Small Kids	Use Fastpass, or come early, or just before closing.
Spaceship Earth	n/a	Ride-Through	15 mins.	Moderate to Heavy	All Ages	Ride while waiting for Mission: SPACE Fastpass appointment or just before closing.
★ Test Track	At least 40"	Thrill Ride	5 mins.	Heavy	All but Small Kids	Come in morning with Fastpass. The ride can't function on wet tracks, so don't come after a downpour.

World Showcase

	Height	Type	Duration	Crowds	Audience	Comments
★ The American Adventure Show	n/a	Show/Film	20 mins.	Heavy	All Ages	Arrive 10 mins. before the Voices of Liberty or the Spirit of America Fife & Drum Corps are slated to perform.
America Gardens Theatre	n/a	Live Show	Varies	Varies	Varies	Arrive an hour or so ahead of time for holiday and celebrity performances.
Gran Fiesta Tour Starring the Three Caballeros	n/a	Cruise	9 mins.	Moderate to Heavy	All Ages	Especially good if you have small children.
Impressions de France	n/a	Film	20 mins.	Moderate	All but Small Kids	Come after dinner.
Maelstrom	n/a	Thrill Ride for Kids with Water	10 mins.	Moderate to Heavy	All Ages	Use Fastpass for after lunch or dinner.
O Canada!	n/a	Film	14 mins.	Moderate to Heavy	All Ages	Come when World Showcase opens or in the evening. No strollers permitted.
Reflections of China	n/a	Film	14 mins.	Moderate	All Ages	Come anytime. No strollers permitted.

★ = Fodor'sChoice

EPCOT FAMILY TOUR

A trip to Italy is on hold, but Mom knows she can find a taste of Venice in the World Showcase. Dad, the *Popular Mechanics* devotee, can't wait to check out Test Track and Innoventions. Each can have a great day—in his or her own way.

WE CAN WORK IT OUT

The Beatles had it right, and you can, too, if you just devise a plan before pushing through the Epcot turnstiles. Everyone will want to take off at Soarin' in The Land for the one-ride-fits-all thrill of simulated hang gliding (there are even special safety restraints for little ones). If your kids are too small for the height restrictions at Test Track, let Dad shift into overdrive while the rest of you play Innoventions games like Where's the Fire? Meet up with Dad at the Imagination! pavilion for a wacky visit with Dr. Wayne Szalinski in "Honey, I Shrunk the Audience!" Don't miss an under-the-sea ride at The Seas with Nemo & Friends before meeting the coolest dude of all at Turtle Talk with Crush.

PASSPORTS, PLEASE!

On the way into the World Show-case, let the kids get their own passports, complete with stickers, at any merchandise location. As you visit each country, they can get their passports stamped. But before you cross the Future World border, stop and let young kids play in the danc-ing fountains along the way—it'll be one of their happiest memories. Bring a towel and a change of cloth-ing, and you'll be happy, too.

FOR THE LITTLE ONES (AND MOM)

Younger children can be creative at Kidcot Fun Stops, where a Disney cast member gets them started on a craft activity, such as coloring a Carnivale-style mask on a stick. At each of a dozen or so Fun Stops, the kids can add something to the mask, such as a Viking ship at Norway. Children love Mexico because they can ride the boats at Gran Fiesta Tour Starring the Three Caballe-ros. The Norway ride, Maelstrom, is next door, and offers an adventure involving Viking ships and menacing trolls. Now it's your turn, Mom. Italy is right around the corner, and the kids can watch a juggler or comedy troupe in the courtyard while you participate in a wine-tasting event or go shopping.

THE SHOW GOES ON—AND ON

Back to the Beatles. The Mop Tops themselves (well, almost—some very good impersonators) appear as the British Invasion in the United Kingdom five days each week. Grab a bench and hold hands while nostalgia strikes. Young children are thrilled for the time to explore hedge mazes that surround the gazebo stage.

Live entertainment is one of Epcot's strong suits—best shows for younger kids are the Dragon Legend Acrobats at China, Mariachi Cobre musicians at Mexico, Sergio clown and juggler at Italy, and the JAMMitors Jammin' percussion group at Future World East and West. (Check the daily *Times Guide*).

EPCOT ADULT TOUR

Hang glide over a mountain, blast off into space, then journey to Mexico for a tequila flight and a "moonlit" dinner. Even if the adventures are faux fun, there's so much to soak up here that you'll want to return later to catch up on whatever you missed.

A TICKET TO RIDE

If you're aiming for high adventure, Fastpass is your ticket to Mission:SPACE or Soarin', especially during peak season. With a Fastpass return appointment safely pocketed, you can make tracks for Test Track or head back to Innoventions and design the wildest bobsled, rollercoaster, or jet ride ever—then board a robotic simulator for the total-immersion experience.

Use your Fastpass as soon as you can, then get another while you're in Future World so you don't waste time in a long line. Look for more interactive challenges in the Advanced Training Lab at the end of your Mission:SPACE ride and in the Spaceship Earth postride show by Siemans.

WORLD TRAVEL

You can be in Canada one minute and England the next, once you cross from Future World to the World Showcase. Authentic replicas of famous landmarks like Venice's Piazza San Marco or Norway's 13th-century stave church will grab you. Once inside, you can practice your Italian, French, Spanish—Norwegian, even—with representatives of those countries.

You can also eat your way around the globe from a Biergarten in Germany to a French bistro, and beyond. The Ligurian pasta with pesto and *fagiolini* (green beans) at Tutto Italia delivers the flavor of Italy. Enjoy a glass of Prosecco as you watch passersby in the courtyard, or buy a wine-tasting pass for two tastes at each wineshop in Italy, Germany, and France. You'll find silk (or washable poly) kimonos in Japan's Mitsukoshi store, hefty beer steins at Die Weinachts Ecke in Germany, and belly-dancing garb and finger cymbals at Morocco.

APPLAUSE AND A TOAST

Too many people miss the great, daily live acts around the park, so take time to check your *Times Guide* and choose a performance or two. Top acts include the Voices of Liberty at The American Adventure, Mo'Rockin's brand of Arabic fusion rock at Morocco, the kilt-wearing Off Kilter Canadian-and-Celtic rock band at Canada, and the British Invasion at United Kingdom. The park's comedy troupes are a hoot, and the Matsuriza drummers at Japan are mesmerizing.

Before you venture to the edge of the lagoon for the fireworks-filled closing show, IllumiNations, check out one of Epcot's great watering holes. Cava del Tequila in Mexico serves 90 tequila choices, tequila flights, and specialty margaritas, including unexpected flavors like jalapeño and cucumber. The Rose & Crown pub in the United Kingdom is Epcot's most boisterous spot, where the Hat Lady takes requests for piano numbers—and it's standing-room-only at the bar. Cheers! Salud! Prosit! And take a bus or taxi back to your resort.

5

pterodactyls swoop through the air, and a truly nasty sea snake emerges from the swamp to threaten the left side of the tram. A terrified Ellen is even cornered by a menacing elasmosaurus.

The ride concludes with another film in which Ellen learns about the world's present-day energy needs, resources, and concerns. It's shown on three screens, each 30 feet tall, 74 feet wide, and curved to create a 200-degree range of vision. Does Ellen win in her *Jeopardy!* dream? You'll have to travel back in time for the answer. **For people with disabilities:** This attraction is accessible to guests using standard wheelchairs and those who can transfer to them. Equipped for assisted-listening, handheld-captioning, and attraction-description devices. ■TIP→ To experience the primeval landscape unspoiled by rows of modern heads, sit in the seats to the far left and front of the theater; to get these, position yourself similarly in the preshow area.

THE SEAS WITH NEMO & FRIENDS

This pavilion has always been a draw with its 5.7-million-gallon aquarium filled with 65 species of sea life, including sharks. To capitalize on the popularity of the Disney-Pixar film *Finding Nemo*, Disney Imagineers reworked the attraction using clever technology in a ride that makes it look like Nemo and pals are on an adventure in the aquarium along with the real fish. Don't miss the terrific Turtle Talk with Crush interactive, real-time film attraction.

☆☆☆
Duration
Up to You
Crowds
Mod. to Heavy
Audience
Small Kids

The Seas with Nemo & Friends Experience. Hop into a "clamobile" and take a ride under the sea to look for Nemo, who has wandered off from Mr. Ray's class field trip. This ride adds fresh zip to an aging, but relevant, attraction—an astonishing animation-projection effect makes it appear as if Nemo and his pals are swimming among the marine life of the actual Seas aquarium. As your ride progresses, Dory, Nemo's spacey sidekick, helps Bruce, Squirt, and other pals find him.

After the ride, head for the Sea Base area to line up for Turtle Talk with Crush, starring, of course, Crush, the ancient sea turtle from the *Finding Nemo* film. In this real-time animated show Crush chats and jokes so convincingly with kids in the small theater that young children, eyes wide as sand dollars, have walked up and touched the screen where Crush "swims." There's often a wait for this cartoon chat, but it's a hit with young children, as well as their parents. Walk around the tank at the pavilion's core to Bruce's Shark World for some fun photo ops and shark facts with graphics, plus displays about the endangered Florida manatee and dolphins.

For people with disabilities: Guests in standard wheelchairs can wheel onto an accessible "clamshell" vehicle; those in ECVs must transfer to a standard wheelchair or the ride vehicle; guests using wheelchairs also have access to the aquarium area and Turtle Talk with Crush. Handheld-captioning devices work on the ride; assisted-listening devices can be used in Turtle Talk, where Disney also schedules twice-a-week sign-language presentations. ■TIP→ Come early; the wait for the ride and the interactive Turtle Talk with Crush (20 minutes) will only get longer later on.

THE LAND

Shaped like an intergalactic greenhouse, the enormous, skylighted Land pavilion dedicates 6 acres and a host of attractions to everyone's favorite topic: food. You can easily spend two hours exploring here, more if you take one of the guided greenhouse tours available throughout the day.

NEED A BREAK?

Talk about a self-contained ecosystem: The Land pavilion grows its own produce, including tomatoes and cucumbers, some which show up on the menu at the Sunshine Seasons healthful food court. Much of the fare is cooked on a 48-inch Mongolian grill. The eatery's Asian shop offers chicken noodle bowls and spicy stir-fries. A sandwich shop delivers oak-grilled veggie or ham sandwiches on fresh breads, and a yummy turkey on focaccia with chipotle mayonnaise. The salad shop wows with roasted beets, goat cheese, and seared tuna—among other options—over mixed greens. Wood-fired grills and rotisseries sizzle with chicken, pork, and salmon, and the bakery's pastries are sure bets. To avoid crowds, eat at nonpeak times— after 2 for lunch and before 5 or after 7 for dinner.

5

☆☆
Duration
20 mins.
Crowds
Mod. to Heavy
Audience
Not Small Kids

Circle of Life. Featuring three stars of *The Lion King*—Simba the lion, Timon the meerkat, and Pumbaa the waddling warthog—this film delivers a powerful message about protecting the world's environment for all living things. Part animation, part *National Geographic*–like film using spectacular 70-millimeter live-action footage, Circle of Life tells a fable about a "Hakuna Matata Lakeside Village" that Timon and Pumbaa are developing by clearing the African savanna. Simba cautions about mistreating the land by telling a story of a creature who occasionally forgets that everything is connected in the great Circle of Life. "That creature," he says, "is man." The lilting accompaniment is Tim Rice and Elton John's popular song, and James Earl Jones is the narrator.

For people with disabilities: Wheelchair accessible. Has reflective captioning and is equipped for assisted-listening devices. ■TIP➜ It's enlightening for children and adults; a nap opportunity for toddlers. Squeeze in other attractions and see this before leaving.

☆☆
Duration
14 mins.
Crowds
Moderate
Audience
Not Small Kids

Living with the Land. You climb aboard a canopied boat that cruises, accompanied by recorded narration, through three artificial biomes— rain forest, desert, and prairie ecological communities—and into an experimental live greenhouse that demonstrates how food sources may be grown in the future, not only on the planet but also in outer space. Shrimp, sunshine bass, tilapia, eels, catfish, and alligators are raised in controlled aquacells, and tomatoes, peppers, squash, and other fruits and vegetables thrive in the Desert Farm area via drip irrigation that delivers just the right amount of water and nutrients to their roots. Gardeners are usually interested in the section on integrated pest management, which relies on "good" insects like ladybugs to control more harmful predators.

Everyone enjoys seeing Mickey Mouse–shaped fruits and vegetables (there may be pumpkins, cucumbers, or watermelons) nurtured with the help of molds created by the Land's science team; scientists also have grown a "tomato tree"—the first of its kind in the United States—that yields thousands of tomatoes from a single vine. Many of the growing areas are actual experiments-in-progress, in which Disney and the U.S. Department of Agriculture have joined forces to produce, say, a sweeter pineapple or a faster-growing pepper. The plants (including the tomato tree's golf-ball-size tomatoes) and fish that grow in the greenhouse are regularly harvested for use in the Land's restaurants. **For people with disabilities:** Those using an oversize wheelchair or ECV must transfer to a standard wheelchair. Equipped for handheld-captioning and attraction-description devices. ■TIP→ **The line moves fairly quickly, so come anytime. In case of a crowd, use Fastpass.**

Fodor's Choice★
Duration
5 mins.
Crowds
Heavy
Audience
Not Small Kids

Soarin'. If you've ever wondered what it's like to fly, or at least hang glide, this attraction is your chance to enjoy the sensation without actually taking the plunge. It's based on the popular attraction Soarin' Over California at Disney's California Adventure in Anaheim. It uses motion-based technology to literally lift you in your seat 40 feet into the air within a giant projection-screen dome.

As you soar above the Golden Gate Bridge, Napa Valley, Yosemite, and other California wonders, you feel the wind and smell pine forests and orange blossoms. Navy buffs get a kick out of swooping over a massive aircraft carrier. Duffers can't help but duck when that golf ball heads their way. The accompanying score created by Jerry Goldsmith (*Mulan, Star Trek*) builds on the thrill, and the crispness and definition of the film, projected at twice the rate of a typical motion picture, adds realism.

The only reason this ride isn't suitable for small children is the 40-inch height requirment, The flight is so mild (and the view so thrilling) that even very shy children love it. **For people with disabilities:** Those with mobility impairments must transfer from their wheelchairs to the ride system. Equipped for video-captioning and attraction-description devices. Service animals aren't permitted on the ride. ■TIP→ **Ride early or late or grab a Fastpass.**

IMAGINATION!

The theme here focuses on the fun that can be had when you turn your imagination loose. The fanciful leaping fountains outside the pavilion make the point, as does the big attraction within, the 3-D film *Honey, I Shrunk the Audience.* The Journey into Imagination with Figment ride can be capped by a stroll through Image Works, a sort of interactive fun house devoted to music and art.

☆☆
Duration
14 mins.
Crowds
Mod. to Heavy
Audience
All Ages

Honey, I Shrunk the Audience. This 3-D adventure about the futuristic "shrinking" technologies demonstrated in the films starring comic actor Rick Moranis is one of the older Disney productions, but it has held up well over the years. Moranis reprises his role as Dr. Wayne Szalinski, who's about to receive the Inventor of the Year Award from Dr. Nigel Channing (Eric Idle of Monty Python fame) at the Imagination Institute. While Dr. Szalinski is demonstrating his latest shrinking machine, though, things go terribly wrong. Be prepared for funny and startling moments, courtesy of the special in-theater effects and 3-D

film technology. Try to overlook the women's early-1990s'-style hair and wardrobe. For most, the humor quotient outweighs the few scary moments, but if your small kids frighten easily, you might want to skip this. The large theater capacity generally means a relatively short wait, but the film's popularity can make for big crowds.

> **WATER PLAY**
>
> Preschoolers love to play in the interactive fountains in front of Mission: SPACE and in the walkways between Future World and the World Showcase. Bring swimsuits and a towel!

For people with disabilities: The attraction is wheelchair accessible, although you must transfer to a theater seat to experience some special effects. Equipped with reflective captioning and for assisted-listening, video-captioning, or attraction-description devices. The preshow area has closed-captioned TV monitors for the lovely-but-too-long Kodak commercial and the show intro. Guests with service animals should check with a show host before entering. ■TIP➜ Come early, late, or get a Fastpass.

☆
Duration
8 mins.
Crowds
Light
Audience
Small Kids

Journey into Imagination with Figment. Figment, a fun-loving dragon, is teamed with Dr. Nigel Channing, the presenter of Dr. Szalinski's award in *Honey, I Shrunk the Audience.* The pair takes you on a sensory adventure designed to engage your imagination through sound, illusion, gravity, dimension, and color. After the ride—which could use some imaginative updating—you can check out Image Works, where several interactive displays allow you to further stretch your imagination. Although this ride is geard to smaller kids, be sure to prepare yours for a brief period of darkness.

For people with disabilities: Both ride and postshow hands-on Image Works are wheelchair accessible. Equipped for handheld-captioning and attraction-description devices. ■TIP➜ Ride only to kill time waiting for a Honey, I Shrunk the Audience Fastpass appointment.

WORLD SHOWCASE

Nowhere but at Epcot can you explore a little corner of nearly a dozen countries in one day. As you stroll the 1 mi around the 40-acre World Showcase Lagoon, you circumnavigate the globe-according-to-Disney by experiencing the native food, entertainment, culture, and arts and crafts at pavilions representing countries in Europe, Asia, North Africa, and the Americas. Pavilion employees are from the countries they represent—Disney hires them to live and work for up to a year as part of its international college program.

Instead of rides, you have solid film attractions at the Canada, China, and France pavilions; several art exhibitions; and the chance to try your foreign language skills with the staff. Each pavilion also has a designated Kidcot Fun Stop, open daily from 11 AM or noon until about 8 or 9 PM, where youngsters can try their hand at a cultural crafts project. Live entertainment is an integral part of the pavilions' presentations, and some of your finest moments will be watching incredibly talented

Dragon Legend Chinese Acrobats, singing along with a terrific band of Fab Four impersonators in the U.K. pavilion and the rockin' Off Kilter band in Canada, or laughing along with some improv fun in the Italy courtyard.

Dining is another favorite pastime at Epcot, and the World Showcase offers tempting tastes of the authentic cuisines of the countries that have pavilions. In recent years Disney has worked to increase dining initiatives across its theme-park and resort properties, and Epcot recently debuted several new and enhanced restaurant experiences (*see details in Italy, Japan, China, and Mexico sections*).

FOR PEOPLE WITH DISABILITIES
Attractions at Mexico, American Adventure, France, China, and Canada are all wheelchair accessible, as are the plaza areas where shows are presented. Norway's Maelstrom boat ride requires transferring to the ride vehicle; personal-translator units amplify sound tracks. Most of the live entertainment around the World Showcase feature strong aural as well as visual elements.

EN ROUTE A World Showcase Passport ($9.95) is a wonderful way to keep a kid interested in this more adult area of Epcot. The passports, available at vendor carts, come with stickers and a badge, and children can have them stamped at each pavilion. The World Showcase is also a great place to look for unusual gifts—you might pick up a Oaxacan wood carving in Mexico, a tea seat in China, or a kimonoed doll in Japan.

CANADA

"Oh, it's just our Canadian outdoors," said a typically modest native guide upon being asked about the model for the striking rocky chasm and tumbling waterfall that represent just one of the pavilion's high points. The beautiful formal gardens do have an antecedent: Butchart Gardens, in Victoria, British Columbia. And so does the Hôtel du Canada, a French Gothic mansion with spires, turrets, and a mansard roof; anyone who's ever stayed at Québec's Château Frontenac or Ottawa's Château Laurier will recognize the imposing style favored by architects of Canadian railroad hotels.

Like the size of the Rocky Mountains, the scale of the structures seems immense; unlike the real thing, it's managed with a trick called forced perspective, which exaggerates the smallness of the distant parts to make the entire thing look gigantic. Another bit of design legerdemain: the World Showcase Rockies are made of chicken wire and painted concrete mounted on a movable platform similar to a parade float. Ah, wilderness!

You can browse shops that sell maple syrup; Canadian sports jerseys; and plush huggable bears, beavers, and huskies. Le Cellier Steakhouse is a great place for a relaxing lunch or dinner and may be easier to get into than the higher-demand Chefs de France, Tutto Italia, or Teppan Edo.

☆☆☆
Duration
14 mins.
Crowds
Mod. to Heavy
Audience
All Ages

O Canada! That's just what you'll say after seeing this CircleVision film's stunning opening shot—footage of the Royal Canadian Mounted Police surrounding you as they circle the screen. From there, you whoosh over waterfalls, venture through Montréal and Toronto, sneak up on bears and bison, mush behind a husky-pulled dogsled, and land pluck in the middle of a hockey game. The only downsides: this is a standing-only theater, strollers aren't permitted, and toddlers and small children can't see unless they're held aloft. ■TIP➔ Stop in on your stroll around World Showcase Promenade.

UNITED KINGDOM

Never has it been so easy to cross the English Channel. The United Kingdom rambles between the elegant mansions lining a London square to the bustling, half-timber shops of a village high street to thatched-roof cottages from the countryside. (The thatch is made of plastic broom bristles in deference to local fire regulations.) And of course there's a pair of the familiar red phone booths that were once found all over the United Kingdom.

The pavilion has no single major attraction. Instead, you wander through shops selling tea and tea accessories, Welsh handicrafts, and English lavender fragrance by Taylor of London. There's a Beatles store with T-shirts, CDs, and a Beatles Trivial Pursuit game. Next door is the Historic Research Center, where you can research your family name and purchase printed, hand-painted, or embroidered versions of your family coat of arms.

Outside, the strolling World Showcase Players coax audience members to participate in lowbrow versions of Shakespeare. There's also a lovely garden and park with benches in the back that's easy to miss—relax and kick back to the tunes of the British Invasion, a band known for its on-target Beatles and other Brit-band performances. Kids love to run through the hedge maze as their parents travel back in time to "Yesterday." Check the Times Guide and arrive 30 minutes early for a bench or 15 minutes early for a curb. Restrooms are near the red phone booths.

┌ NEED A
│ BREAK?

Revive yourself with a pint of the best at the **Rose & Crown**, a pub where you'll jostle for space any evening the Hat Lady performs her piano magic. The dining room serves hearty fare for lunch and dinner (reservations often required). The outdoor terrace hosts traditional afternoon tea, and is one of the best spots for watching IllumiNations. Arrive at least an hour or so in advance for a seat. If you're in a hurry, grab fish-and-chips to go from Yorkshire County Fish Shop.

FRANCE

You don't need the scaled-down model of the Eiffel Tower to tell you that you've arrived in France, specifically Paris. There's the poignant accordion music wafting out of concealed speakers, the trim sycamores pruned in the French style to develop signature knots at the end of each branch, and the delicious aromas surrounding the Boulangerie Pâtisserie bakeshop. This is the Paris of dreams, a Paris of the years just before World War I, when solid mansard-roof mansions were crowned with iron filigree, when the least brick was drenched in romanticism.

Here's a replica of the conservatory-like Les Halles—the iron-and-glass barrel-roof market that no longer exists in the City of Light; there's an arching footbridge; and all around, of course, there are shops. You can inspect Parisian impressionist artwork at Galerie des Halles; sample perfume and cosmetics at the Guerlain shop; and acquire a bottle of Bouzy Rouge at Les Vins de France. If you plan to dine at Les Chefs de France, make a reservation for a late lunch or dinner; the second-floor Bistro de Paris (dinner only) is a gourmet treat.

NEED A BREAK? The lines at **Boulangerie Pâtisserie, a small Parisian-style café, are worth the wait.** Have a creamy café au lait and an éclair, napoleon, or another French pastry while enjoying the fountains and floral displays.

☆☆☆
Duration
20 mins.
Crowds
Moderate
Audience
Not Small Kids

Impressions de France. The intimate Palais du Cinema, inspired by the royal theater at Fontainebleau, screens this homage to the glories of the country. Shown on five screens spanning 200 degrees, in an air-conditioned, sit-down theater, the film takes you to vineyards at harvest time, Paris on Bastille Day, the Alps, Versailles, Normandy's Mont-St-Michel, and the stunning châteaux of the Loire Valley. The music sweeps you away with familiar segments from Offenbach, Debussy, and Saint-Saëns, all woven together by longtime Disney musician Buddy Baker.
■ TIP➜ Visit anytime during your stroll around the World Showcase.

MOROCCO

No magic carpet is required to Morocco—just walk through the pointed arches of the Bab Boujouloud gate and you're in the mysterious North African country. The arches are ornamented with wood carvings and encrusted with mosaics made of 9 tons of handmade, hand-cut tiles; 19 native artisans were sent to Epcot to install them and to create the dusty stucco walls that seem to have withstood centuries of sandstorms. Look closely and you'll see that every tile has a small crack or other imperfection, and no tile depicts a living creature—in deference to the Islamic belief that only Allah creates perfection and life.

Koutoubia Minaret, a replica of the prayer tower in Marrakesh, acts as Morocco's landmark. Winding alleyways—each corner bursting with carpets, brasses, leatherwork, and other wares—lead to a tiled fountain and lush gardens. The full-service Restaurant Marrakesh is a highlight if you enjoy eating couscous and roast lamb while distracted by a lithesome belly dancer. One of the hottest fast-food spots in Epcot is Tangierine Café, with tasty Mediterranean specialties like chicken or falafel wraps, lentil and couscous salads, and pita-pocket sliders of lamb, chicken, and falafel. Both eateries are open for lunch and dinner. Restrooms on the France side of the pavilion offer quick access.

5

JAPAN

A brilliant vermilion torii gate, based on Hiroshima Bay's much-photographed Itsukushima Shrine, frames the World Showcase Lagoon and stands as an emblem of Disney's serene version of Japan. During the Epcot International Flower & Garden Festival, the view is more spectacular, as the gate also showcases award-winning bonsai.

PHOTO TIP

You'll get a great shot of Spaceship Earth across the lagoon by framing it in the torii gate.

Disney horticulturists deserve a hand for authenticity: 90% of the plants they used are native to Japan. Rocks, pebbled streams, pools, and pruned trees and shrubs complete the meticulous picture. At sunset, or during a rainy dusk, the twisted branches of the corkscrew willows frame a perfect Japanese view of the five-story winged pagoda that is the heart of the pavilion. Based on the 8th-century Horyuji Temple in Nara, the brilliant blue pagoda has five levels, symbolizing the five elements of Buddhist belief—earth, water, fire, wind, and sky.

The peace is occasionally interrupted by performances on drums and gongs. There are also demonstrations of traditional crafts, such as kite-making or Miyuki, a type of candy art. Mitsukoshi Department Store, an immense three-centuries-old retail firm known as Japan's Sears Roebuck, carries everything from T-shirts to kimonos and row upon row of Japanese dolls. For lunch and dinner, you'll be entertained by the culinary feats of chefs at Teppan Edo (which carries on the chop-toss-applaud antics of the original Teppanyaki Dining Room). Tokyo Dining focuses on presentation of traditional ingredients and cuisine from Japan, including sushi, at slightly lower prices than those at Teppan Edo.

AMERICAN ADVENTURE

In a Disney version of Philadelphia's Liberty Hall, the Imagineers prove that their kind of fantasy can beat reality hands down. The 110,000 bricks, made by hand from soft, pink, Georgia clay, sheathe the familiar structure, which acts as a beacon for those across Epcot's lagoon. The pavilion includes an all-American fast-food restaurant, a shop, lovely rose gardens, and an outdoor theater. Restrooms are tucked away along the far left side of the building.

NEED A BREAK?

What else would you order at the counter-service **Liberty Inn** but burgers, apple pie, and other all-American fare? On a summer evening this is the place to get an ice-cream sundae before IllumiNations starts. On a chilly winter day the hot cocoa is a hit. At the **Fife & Drum** along the promenade you can pair a beer with a turkey leg for a satisfying snack.

Morocco's open-air market is like something out of an Indiana Jones movie. It's a maze of shops selling straw bags, colorful carpets, leather goods, and, of course, ceramics.

Fodor's Choice ★
Duration **20 mins.**
Crowds **Heavy**
Audience **All Ages**

The American Adventure. The pavilion's key attraction is this 100-yard dash through history, and you'll be primed for the lesson after reaching the main entry hall and hearing the stirring a cappella Voices of Liberty. Inside the theater, the main event begins to the accompaniment of "The Golden Dream," performed by the Philadelphia Orchestra. This show combines evocative sets, the world's largest rear-projection screen (72 feet wide), enormous movable stages, and 35 Audio-Animatronics players that are impressive but could use some upgrading (Ben Franklin climbs up stairs, but his movements are more tentative when compared with newer-generation figures).

Beginning with the arrival of the Pilgrims at Plymouth Rock and their grueling first winter, Ben Franklin and a wry, pipe-smoking Mark Twain narrate the episodes, both praiseworthy and shameful, that have shaped the American spirit. Disney detail is so painstaking that you never feel rushed, and, in fact, each speech and scene seems polished like a little jewel. You feel the cold at Valley Forge and the triumph when Charles Lindbergh crosses the Atlantic; you're moved by Nez Percé Chief Joseph's forced abdication of Native American ancestral lands and by women's rights campaigner Susan B. Anthony's speech; you laugh with Will Rogers's aphorisms and learn about the pain of the Great Depression through an affecting radio broadcast by Franklin Delano Roosevelt. ■TIP→ Arrive 10 minutes before the Spirit of America Fife & Drum Corps and Voices of Liberty are slated to perform. See the drum corps outside, then head inside to enjoy the Voices' a cappella tunes.

☆☆
Duration
Varies
Crowds
Vary
Audience
Vary

America Gardens Theatre. On the edge of the lagoon, directly opposite Disney's magnificent bit of colonial fakery, is this open-air, partially tree-shaded venue for concerts and shows. Some are of the "Yankee Doodle Dandy" variety. Others are hot tickets themed to such Epcot events as the Flower Power concerts with '60s pop legends during the March through May Epcot International Flower & Garden Festival and Eat to the Beat! concerts during the late-September through mid-November Epcot International Food & Wine Festival. This is also the setting for the annual yuletide Candlelight Processional—a not-to-be-missed event if you're at WDW during the holidays. The Candlelight Dinner Package (available through Disney's dining reservations hotline) includes dinner in a select World Showcase restaurant and preferred seating for the moving performance. ■TIP➔ Arrive one hour or so ahead of time for holiday and celebrity performances.

ITALY

In WDW's Italy, the star is the architecture: reproductions of Venice's Piazza San Marco and Doge's Palace, accurate right down to the gold leaf on the ringlets of the angel perched 100 feet atop the Campanile; the seawall stained with age, with barbershop-stripe poles to which two gondolas are tethered; and the Romanesque columns, Byzantine mosaics, Gothic arches, and stone walls that have all been carefully antiqued. Mediterranean plants such as grapevines, kumquat, and olive trees add verisimilitude. Shops sell Venetian beads and glasswork, leather purses, perfumes, olive oils, pastas, and Perugina cookies and chocolate kisses.

At Tutto Italia Ristorante, cuisine is from several regions of Italy—Italian wines, handmade mozzarella, and freshly made breads are featured. Limited outdoor dining beneath umbrellas is lovely. At this writing, a 300-seat pizzeria with wood-burning ovens and outdoor dining is expected to open as Italy's second, more casual, eatery.

The World Showcase Players comedy troupe and a clown-juggler bring crowds to the piazza several times each day. This is a great spot for viewing IllumiNations if you're in the vicinity as 9 PM approaches, and there's an outdoor Tutto Italia stand along the promenade where you can cap the evening with an Italian gelato or a refreshing Bellini.

GERMANY

Germany, a make-believe village that distills the best folk architecture from all over that country, is so jovial that you practically expect the Seven Dwarfs to come "heigh-ho"-ing out to meet you. Well, maybe not the Dwarfs, but if you time it right, you will spot Snow White as she poses for photos and signs autographs. The fairy tale continues as a specially designed glockenspiel on the clock tower chimes on the hour. You'll also hear musical toots and tweets from multitudinous cuckoo clocks, folk tunes from the spinning dolls and plush lambs sold at Der Teddybär, and the satisfied grunts of hungry visitors chowing down on hearty German cooking.

The Biergarten's wonderful buffet serves several sausage varieties, as well as sauerkraut, spaetzle, and roasted potatoes, rotisserie chicken, and German breads, all accompanied by yodelers, dancers, and other lederhosen-clad musicians who perform a year-round Oktoberfest show. There are shops aplenty, including Die Weihnachts Ecke (the Christmas Corner), which sells nutcrackers and other Christmas ornaments and Volkskunst, with a folk-crafts collection that includes cuckoo clocks ranging from hummingbird scale to the size of an eagle. It's hard to resist watching the miniature trains that choo choo along a garden track dotted with tiny villages. Restrooms are just steps away.

NEED A BREAK? Bratwurst and cold beer from the **Sommerfest** cart, at the entrance of the Biergarten restaurant, make a perfect quick and hearty lunch, while the soft pretzels and strudel are ever-popular snacks. There's not much seating, so you may have to eat on the run.

The **Saluting Africa–Outpost**, between Germany and China, isn't one of the 11 World Showcase pavilions, but kids love to test their drumming skills on bongos and other drums that invite players to improvise their own African folklore performances. Village Traders sells African handicrafts and—you guessed it—souvenirs relating to *The Lion King*. Buy an ice cream or frozen yogurt at the Refreshment Outpost, and enjoy the break at a table by the lagoon. A cool mist is set up to offer respite on hot days.

CHINA

A shimmering red-and-gold, three-tier replica of Beijing's Temple of Heaven towers over a serene Chinese garden, an art gallery displaying treasures from the People's Republic, a spacious emporium devoted to Chinese goods, and two restaurants. The gardens—planted with a native Chinese tallow tree, water lilies, bamboo, and a 100-year-old weeping mulberry tree—are tranquil.

Piped-in traditional Chinese music flows gently over the peaceful hush of the gardens, which come alive with applause and cheers when the remarkable Dragon Legend Acrobats tumble into a roped-off area for their breathtaking act. At China's popular Nine Dragons Restaurant try the shrimp summer rolls or the salt-and-pepper shrimp with spinach noodles; there are also several chicken and stir-fry favorites.

NEED A BREAK? The open-air **Lotus Blossom Café** offers some authentic Chinese fare: pot stickers, soups, and egg rolls. Entrées include orange chicken with steamed rice, vegetable stir-fry, and a beef noodle soup bowl. The Joy of Tea cart along the promenade serves hot and cold tea, plus trendy green tea frozen drinks and plum wine.

☆☆☆
Duration
14 mins.
Crowds
Moderate
Audience
All Ages

Reflections of China. Think of the Temple of Heaven as an especially fitting theater for a movie in which sensational panoramas of the land and people are dramatically portrayed on a 360-degree CircleVision screen. Highlights include striking footage of Hong Kong, Shanghai, and Macao. This may be the best of the World Showcase films—the

The Temple of Quetzalcoatl (kwet-zel-co-WAH-tal) at Teotihuacán (tay-o-tee-wah-CON), just ouside Mexico City, is the model for the pyramid at the Mexico pavilion.

only drawbacks are that strollers aren't permitted and the theater has no chairs; lean rails are provided. ■TIP→ Come anytime.

NORWAY

Among the rough-hewn timbers and sharply pitched roofs here—softened and brightened by bloom-stuffed window boxes and figured shutters—are lots of smiling young Norwegians, all eager to speak English and show off their country. The pavilion complex contains a 14th-century, fortresslike castle that mimics Oslo's Akershus, cobbled streets, rocky waterfalls, and a stave church modeled after one built in 1250, with wood dragons glaring from the eaves. The church houses an exhibit called "To the Ends of the Earth," which uses vintage artifacts to tell the story of two early-20th-century polar expeditions. It all puts you in the mood for the pavilion's shops, which sell spears, shields, and other Viking necessities.

At the restaurant, Akershus, breakfast is served. Visit the Norwegian *koldtbord* (buffet) for smoked salmon, fruit, and pastries, followed by a family-style hot breakfast of eggs, meats, and other treats served at the table. For lunch and dinner, you'll find cold dishes like chilled shrimp, salads, meats, and cheeses on the traditional *koldtbord*; hot entrées served à la carte may include Norwegian bean stew with venison sausages, mustard-glazed salmon, pan-seared beef tips in brandy-mustard sauce, or the traditional ground beef–and-pork dumpling called *kjottkaker*. Family-style dessert is a treat with warm apple tort, chocolate mousse cake, and rice cream with strawberry sauce.

The restaurant is the only one in the park where you can have breakfast, lunch, or dinner with Disney princesses that may include Aurora, Belle, or Snow White. You can reserve up to 180 days in advance, and we recommend booking as early as possible. However, you can always check at Guest Relations for seats left by cancellations.

NEED A BREAK?

You can order smoked salmon and other open-face sandwiches, pastries, or Norwegian Ringnes beer at **Kringla Bakeri Og Kafe**. Go early or late for speediest service and room to sit in the outdoor seating area.

☆☆
Duration
10 mins.
Crowds
Mod. to Heavy
Audience
All Ages

Maelstrom. In Norway's dandy boat ride you pile into a 16-passenger, dragon-headed longboat for a voyage through time that, despite its scary name and encounters with evil trolls, is actually more interesting than frightful. The journey begins in a 10th-century village, where a boat, much like the ones used by Eric the Red, is being readied for a Viking voyage. You glide steeply up through a mythical forest populated by trolls, who cause the boat to plunge backward down a mild waterfall, then cruise amid the grandeur of the Geiranger Fjord. Then you experience a storm in the North Sea and, as the presence of oil rigs signals the 20th century, end up in a peaceful coastal village. Disembarking, you proceed into a theater for a quick and delightful film about Norway's scenic wonders, culture, and people.

For people with disabilities: You must step down into and up out of a boat to ride. Equipped with reflective captioning and for assisted-listening or handheld-captioning devices. ■TIP→ Grab a Fastpass appointment if the queue is long so you can return after lunch or dinner.

MEXICO

Housed in a spectacular Mayan pyramid surrounded by dense tropical plantings and brilliant blossoms, Mexico welcomes you onto a "moonlit" plaza that contains the Gran Fiesta Tour boat ride; an exhibit of pre-Columbian art; a very popular restaurant; and, of course, shopping kiosks where you can unload many, many pesos.

Modeled on the market in the town of Taxco, Plaza de los Amigos is well named: there are lots of friendly people—the women dressed in ruffled off-the-shoulder peasant blouses and bright skirts, the men in white shirts and dashing sashes—all eager to sell you trinkets from a cluster of canopied carts. The perimeter is rimmed with stores with tile roofs, wrought-iron balconies, and flower-filled window boxes. What to buy? Brightly colored paper blossoms, sombreros, baskets, pottery, jewelry, and maracas.

One of the pavilion's key attractions is the San Angel Inn Restaurante, featuring traditional Mexican cuisine and wine and beer, and overlooking the faux "moonlit" waterway traversed by Gran Fiesta Tour boats. The pavilion's Cava del Tequila bar serves up aged spirits, tapas like blue-crab tostados, and exotic blended margaritas. The more casual, outdoor Cantina de San Angel is being expanded along the World Showcase Lagoon and is slated to have 400 waterside seats for diners eager to sample a new menu of Mexican treats.

☆   **Gran Fiesta Tour Starring the Three Caballeros.** In this attraction—which
Duration   shines with the polish of enhanced facades, sound system, and boat-
9 mins.   ride props—Donald teams with old pals José Carioca (the parrot) and
Crowds   Panchito (the Mexican charro rooster) from the 1944 Disney film *The*
Mod. to Heavy   *Three Caballeros.* The Gran Fiesta Tour film sweeps you along for an
Audience   animated jaunt as the caballeros are reunited for a grand performance
All Ages   in Mexico City. Donald manages to disappear for his own tour of the
country, leaving José and Panchito to search for their missing com-
rade. **For people with disabilities:** The boat is accessible to guests using
wheelchairs, but those using ECVs or oversize chairs must transfer to
a Disney model. Equipped for handheld-captioning devices. ■TIP➔ It's
worth a visit if lines aren't long, especially if you have small children, who
usually enjoy the novelty of a boat ride.

EPCOT SPECTACLE

Fodor's Choice★   **IllumiNations: Reflections of Earth.** This marvelous nighttime spectacular
Duration   takes place over the World Showcase Lagoon every night before clos-
13 mins.   ing. Be sure to stick around for the lasers, lights, flames, fireworks,
Crowds   fountains, and music that fill the air over the water. The show's Earth
Heavy   Globe—a gigantic, spherical, video-display system rotating on a 350-
Audience   ton floating island—is three stories tall with 180,000 light-emitting
All Ages   diodes. It houses six computer processors and 258 strobe lights and
projects images celebrating the diversity and unified spirit of humankind. The globe opens like a lotus flower in the grand finale, revealing
a huge torch that rises 40 feet into the air as additional flames spread
light across the lagoon. Nearly 2,800 fireworks shells paint colorful
displays across the night sky.

Although there's generally good viewing from all around the lagoon,
some of the best spots are in front of the Italy pavilion, on the bridge
between France and the United Kingdom, on the promenade in front of
Canada, at the World Showcase Plaza, and on the bridge between China
and Germany. **For people with disabilities:** During the show, certain
areas along the lagoon's edge at Showcase Plaza, Canada, and Germany
are reserved for guests using wheelchairs. ■TIP➔ For best views (and if
you have young children), find your place 45 minutes in advance.

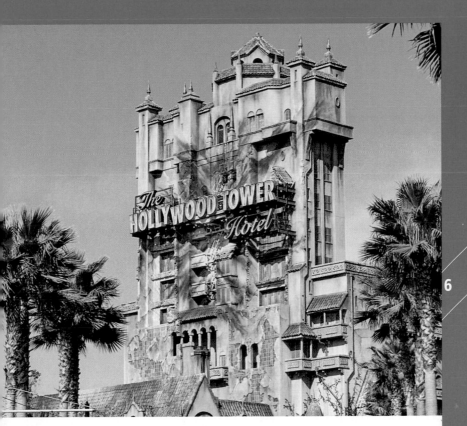

Disney's Hollywood Studios

WORD OF MOUTH

"My 13-year-old daughter *loved* the Aerosmith rollercoaster at Hollywood Studios. Here's a hint: tell the attendant who directs you to the seating that you want to sit in the front row. He or she will direct you to a second line for the front row. You might have to wait a turn or two, but it's worth it."

—chepar

DISNEY'S HOLLYWOOD STUDIOS PLANNER

Park Information

Guest Relations (aka Guest Services) is just inside the turnstiles on the left side of the Entrance Plaza. The Studios Tip Board, with updated information on events and attraction wait times, is at the corner of Hollywood and Sunset boulevards.

Behind the Tip Board is the Hollywood Junction information window, where you can make dining reservations, pick up maps and guides, or get answers to your questions.

If you're staying at one of the Epcot resorts (BoardWalk, Yacht or Beach Club, Swan or Dolphin), getting to the Entrance Plaza on a motor launch is part of the fun. Disney resort buses also drop you at the entrance.

If you're staying off-property and driving, your parking ticket will remain valid for parking at another Disney park later in the day—provided, of course, you have the stamina.

Dinner and a Show

If you're staying through the evening, don't miss the after-dark Fantasmic! show, with its 25 powerful minutes of Disney characters, special effects, fireworks, flames, fountains, and even animation sequences projected onto water screens. If you're not crazy about the idea of arriving at the 6,500-capacity Hollywood Hills Amphitheater 60 minutes ahead of showtime for a good seat, it's worth booking a **Fantasmic! Dinner Package.**

You get a prix-fixe meal at buffet-style Hollywood & Vine or a full table-service dinner at Hollywood Brown Derby or Mama Melrose's, along with a preferred-entry pass to sidestep the main line at the Fantasmic! show. Each dinner includes appetizer, entrée, dessert (the Brown Derby's grapefruit cake is a sweet-tart wonder), and a nonalcoholic beverage.

There's a small catch (well, actually, there are three):

■ You can't book dinner later than 5:30 for the 8:30 show, which means you'll probably have some time to kill before the show. (Disney recommends that you show up at the theater 30 or more minutes ahead of time to choose your seat.)

■ The dinner package is only offered for the 8:30 show on peak nights when Fantasmic! is also performed at 10.

■ If it rains, Fantasmic! might be canceled. You still get dinner, but you lose out on seeing the show and having preferred seating.

It's best to reserve the package a couple of months in advance. You'll have to provide a credit-card number to do so. If you cancel 48 hours or fewer before the show, your card will be charged $10 per person. ⊠ *Disney's Hollywood Studios* ☎ *407/939–3463 reservations* 🎫 *$35–$51 adults, $13–$17 children 3–9 (prices vary by restaurant and exclude tax and gratuity)* ☉ *Fantasmic! usually performed twice weekly during nonpeak seasons; twice nightly during holidays and other peak visiting times.*

Park Amenities

Baby Care: The small Baby Care Center next to Guest Relations has nursing and changing facilities. Formula, baby food, pacifiers, and disposable diapers are for sale next door at Movieland and at Oscar's Super Service. There are also diaper-changing areas in all women's rooms and some men's rooms.

Cameras: At the Darkroom (or next door at Cover Story) on Hollywood Boulevard, you can buy memory cards, film, and disposable cameras. And if a Disney photographer takes your picture in the park, you can pick up a Disney PhotoPass from him or her that lets you see the pictures online. You can also have your memory card downloaded onto a CD for $11.99 plus tax, or you can purchase prints ($16.95 for an 8 inch by 10 inch photo; other sizes available).

First-Aid: The station is in the Entrance Plaza adjoining Guest Relations.

Lockers: You can rent lockers at the Crossroads of the World kiosk in the center of the Entrance Plaza. The cost is $5, with a $5 refundable key deposit. The lockers themselves are located at Oscar's Super Service.

Lost People and Things: Get name tags for your kids at Guest Relations, and instruct them to go to a Disney staffer with a name tag if they can't find you. If you lose them, ask any cast member for assistance; logbooks of lost children's names are kept at Guest Relations, which also has a computerized Message Center, where you can leave notes for companions.

Report lost or found articles at Guest Relations or call **Disney's Hollywood Studios Lost and Found** (☎ *407/560-3720*). Articles lost for more than one day should be sought at the **Main Lost and Found** (✉ *Magic Kingdom, Ticket and Transportation Center [TTC]* ☎ *407/824-4245*).

Package Pick-Up: You can ask shop clerks to forward purchases to your hotel if you're staying on Disney property or to Package Pick-Up next to Oscar's Super Service in the Entrance Plaza, so you won't have to carry them around. Allow three hours for delivery.

Stroller Rentals: Oscar's Super Service rents strollers. Single strollers are $15 daily, $13 for more than one day; doubles are $31 daily, $27 multiday.

For People with Disabilities

Studios restaurants, shops, theaters, and attractions are wheelchair accessible, although there are boarding restrictions on some rides. Parade routes have special sections for guests with disabilities.

Many theater-type attractions, including MuppetVision 3-D, have reflective captioning, and most other attractions are equipped for assisted-listening and video- or handheld-captioning devices. There are large Braille park maps near the Guest Relations lobby and near the Tip Board at Hollywood and Sunset. Note that restaurants don't have Braille menus.

You can pick up Braille Guides ($25 same-day refundable deposit) and assisting devices ($100 deposit) and check on sign-language interpretation schedules at Guest Relations. Although interpreters only appear two days each week, you can request them (at least 14 days in advance) on other days by calling *407/824-4321* or TTY *407/827-5141*.

Oscar's Super Service, to the right in the Entrance Plaza, rents wheelchairs ($10 daily, $8 multiday) and electronic convenience vehicles (ECVs; $45 per day plus a refundable $20 security deposit). Reservations aren't an option, so arrive early, especially to snag an ECV.

6

HOLLYWOOD STUDIOS
MAKE MOVIE MAGIC

Disney's Hollywood Studios were designed to be a trip back to Tinseltown's Golden Age, when Hedda Hopper, not tabloids, spread celebrity gossip and when the girl off the bus from Ohio could be the next Judy Garland.

The result is a theme park that blends movie-production capabilities and high-tech wonders with breathtaking rides and nostalgia. The park's old-time Hollywood ambience begins with a rosy-hued view of the movie-making business presented in a dreamy stage set from the 1930s and '40s, amid sleek Art Moderne buildings in pastel colors, funky diners, kitschy decorations, and sculptured gardens populated by roving actors playing, well, roving actors. There are also casting directors, gossip columnists, and other colorful characters.

Thanks to a rich library of film scores, the park is permeated with music, all familiar, all evoking the magic of the movies, and all constantly streaming from the camouflaged loudspeakers at a volume just right for humming along. The park icon, a 122-foot-high Sorcerer Mickey Hat that serves as a gift shop and Disney pin-trading station, towers over Hollywood Boulevard.

WELCOME TO THE 'HOODS

The park is divided into sightseeing clusters. **Hollywood Boulevard** is the main artery to the heart of the park, and is where you find the glistening replica of Graumann's Chinese Theater.

Encircling it are **Sunset Boulevard**, the **Animation Courtyard, Pixar Place, Commissary Lane, the Streets of America** area, and **Echo Lake**.

The entire park is 135 acres, and has just 20 major attractions (compared with Magic Kingdom's 40-plus). It's small enough to cover in a day and even repeat a favorite ride or two.

TOP ATTRACTIONS

FOR AGES 8 AND UP

Twilight Zone Tower of Terror. The TV classic theming of this free-fall "elevator" screamer is meticulous.

Indiana Jones Epic Stunt Spectacular! The show's Indy double and supporting cast re-enact *Raiders of the Lost Ark* scenes with panache.

Toy Story Midway Mania! 3-D glasses? Check. Spring-action shooter? Check. Ride and shoot your way through with Buzz, Woody, and others.

The Magic of Disney Animation. Take a behind-the-scenes look at the making of Disney films.

Rock 'n' Roller Coaster Starring Aerosmith. Blast off to rockin' tunes on a high-speed, hard-core coaster.

The American Idol Experience. If you don't get chosen to test your pipes, you can vote for your favorite Idol wannabe.

FOR AGES 7 AND UNDER

Block Party Bash. It's a high-energy, interactive parade where you can play along with the toys from *Toy Story* or shout it out with Mike and Sully of *Monsters, Inc.*

Honey I Shrunk the Kids Movie Set Adventure. Youngsters love to romp among the giant blades of grass and bugs at this imaginative playground.

MuppetVision 3-D. Children (and most adults) shriek with laughter during this 3-D movie involving Kermit, Miss Piggy, and other lovable Muppets.

Playhouse Disney—Live on Stage! The preschool crowd can't get enough of the characters here from Disney Channel shows like "Mickey Mouse Clubhouse" and "Little Einsteins."

VISITING TIPS

Visit early in the week, when most people are at Magic Kingdom and Animal Kingdom.

Check the Tip Board periodically for attractions with short wait times to visit between Fastpass appointments.

■ Be at the Fantasmic! amphitheater at least an hour before showtime if you didn't book the dinner package.

■ Need a burst of energy? On-the-run hunger pangs? Grab a slice at Pizza Planet Arcade at **Streets of America**. Alternatively, **Hollywood Scoops Ice Cream** on Sunset is the place to be on a hot day.

■ If you're planning on a fast-food lunch, eat before 11 AM or after 2:30 PM. There are quick-bite spots are all over the park and several stands along Sunset. Get a burger (meat or veggie) or chicken strips at **Rosie's All-American Cafe,** a slice of pizza from **Catalina Eddie's,** or a hunk of smoked bird at **Toluca Legs Turkey Co.**

6

By Jennie Hess The first thing you notice when you pass through the Hollywood Studios turnstiles is the laid-back California attitude. Palm-lined Hollywood Boulevard oozes glamour—but in a casual way that makes you feel as if you belong, even without your Oscar de la Renta outfit and Jimmy Choos.

When the park opened in May 1989 as Disney-MGM Studios, officials welcomed the first guests and VIPs to "the Hollywood that never was and always will be." Attending the lavish, red-carpet affair were Tinseltown icons such as Bette Midler and Warren Beatty. Disney explains the recent name change to Hollywood Studios as a way to "better reflect not only the Golden Age of Tinseltown, but all that today's Hollywood has to offer in movies, music, theater, and television."

Unlike the first movie theme park—Universal Studios in California—Hollywood Studios combined Disney detail with MGM's motion-picture legacy and Walt Disney's own animated classics. Imagineers built the park with real film and television production in mind, and, during its first decade, the Studios welcomed films like *Ernest Saves Christmas* and TV shows like *Wheel of Fortune* to its soundstages.

The Animation Studios, too, were busy. Stories like *Aladdin* and *Lilo & Stitch* came to life on the easels and computers of Disney's Florida animators. Though production has mostly halted at the park, you can enjoy plenty of attractions that showcase how filmmakers practice their craft. Want to see how special effects are created? Visit the Backstage Studio Tour. If you're wowed by action-film stunts, you can learn the tricks of the trade at the Indiana Jones Epic Stunt Spectacular or the Lights, Motors, Action! Extreme Stunt Show. No trip to the Studios would be complete without a tour of The Magic of Disney Animation, where you can sit down and draw a character like Mickey or Donald.

In a savvy effort to grab a big piece of the pop-culture pie, in late 2008 Disney opened its own *American Idol* attraction, where performers earn audience votes to compete in an end-of-day contest for a spot in the TV show's regional audition process. Imagineers continue to "bring it" with big-hit attractions like Toy Story Midway Mania! and new twists on old favorites like the 3-D debut of the Star Tours simulator ride.

HOLLYWOOD BOULEVARD

With its palm trees, pastel buildings, and flashy neon, Hollywood Boulevard paints a rosy picture of 1930s Tinseltown. There's a sense of having walked right onto a movie set of old, with art deco storefronts and roving starlets and nefarious agents—actually costumed actors known as the Citizens of Hollywood. Throughout the park, characters from Disney movies new and old—from *Mickey Mouse* to *Toy Story* friends—pose for photos and sign autographs.

NEED A BREAK?

For a sweet burst of energy, snag a freshly baked chocolate-chip cookie or a pastry and an espresso at Starring Rolls Cafe, at the corner of Hollywood and Sunset near the Brown Derby. Sandwiches are also on the menu here, and outdoor tables offer great people-watching.

☆☆
Duration
22 mins.
Crowds
Moderate
Audience
Not Small Kids

Great Movie Ride. At the end of Hollywood Boulevard, just behind the Sorcerer Mickey Hat, are the fire-engine-red pagodas of a replica of Graumann's Chinese Theater, where you enter this attraction. The line takes you through the lobby past such noteworthy artifacts as Dorothy's ruby slippers from *The Wizard of Oz*, a carousel horse from *Mary Poppins*, and the piano played by Sam in *Casablanca*. You then shuffle into the preshow area, an enormous screening room with continuously running clips from *Mary Poppins, Raiders of the Lost Ark, Singin' in the Rain, Fantasia, Footlight Parade*, and, of course, *Casablanca*. When the great red doors swing open, it's your turn to ride.

Disney cast members dressed as 1920s newsboys usher you onto trams waiting against the backdrop of the Hollywood Hills. Then you're off on a tour of cinematic climaxes—with a little help from Audio-Animatronics, scrim, smoke, and Disney magic. First comes the world of musical entertainment with, among others, Gene Kelly clutching that immortal lamppost as he begins "Singin' in the Rain" and Mary Poppins with her umbrella and her sooty admirers reprising "Chim-Chim-Cher-ee." Soon the lights dim, and your vehicle travels into a gangland shoot-out with James Cagney snarling in *Public Enemy*. Gangsters or Western gunslingers (it depends on which tram you board) hijack your tram and whisk you off to a showdown.

Nothing like a little time warp to bring justice. With pipes streaming fog and alarms whooping, the tram meets some of the slimier characters from *Alien*—look up for truly scary stuff—and then eases into the cobwebby, snake-ridden set of *Indiana Jones and the Temple of Doom*, where your hijacker attempts to steal an idol and gets his or her just desserts.

Each time you think you've witnessed the best scene, the tram moves into another set: Tarzan yodels and swings on a vine overhead; then Bogey bids Bergman goodbye with a "Here's looking at you, kid" in front of the plane to Lisbon. The finale has hundreds of robotic Munchkins cheerily enjoining you to "Follow the Yellow Brick Road," despite the cackling imprecations by the Wicked Witch of the West. Remember to check out Dorothy's tornado-tossed house—you might spot the ruby slippers. The tram follows the Yellow Brick Road, and then there it is:

6

Disney's Hollywood Studios

Catastrophe Canyon

◆ Lights, Motors, Action! Extreme Stunt Show

Mama Melrose's Ristorante Italiano

Toy Story Pizza Planet

Muppet*Vision 3-D

New York Street

Studio Catering Co.

◆ Studio Backlot Tour

Star Tours ◆

Backlot Express

Honey, I Shrunk the Kids Movie Set Adventure

Sci-Fi Dine-In Theater

ABC Commissary

Mickey Avenue

Sounds Dangerous Starring Drew Carey

Indiana Jones Epic Stunt Spectacular!

◆ Toy Story Midway Mania!

Journey into Narnia: Prince Caspian

The American Idol Experience

Great Movie Ride

Echo Lake

Min & Bill's Dockside Diner

Sorceror Mickey's Hat

◆ High School Musical

Walt Disney: One Man's Dream

Earffel Tower

50's Prime Time Café

Tip Board ◆

Brown Derby

Voyage of the Little Mermaid

Hollywood & Vine

Hollywood Boulevard

Hollywood Junction Restaurant Reservations

Animation Courtyard

Guest Relations & Baby Care Center

Entrance Plaza

Playhouse Disney– Live on Stage!

Starring Rolls Cafe

Lockers, strollers

Sunset Boulevard

Toluca Legs Turkey Co.

The Magic of Disney Animation

Rosie's All-American Cafe

Main Entrance

ATM

Catalina Eddie's

Fairfax Fare

Rock 'n' Roller Coaster Starring Aerosmith

Beauty and the Beast– Live on Stage!

Twilight Zone Tower of Terror

◆ Fantasmic!

KEY

✕	Restaurants
🚻	Restrooms
••••	Parade Route

a view of the Emerald City before you're brought back to reality. For people with disabilities: You must transfer to a Disney wheelchair if you use an oversize model or an ECV. The sounds and effects on this ride might scare service animals; check with the host before boarding with yours. ■ TIP→ Come while waiting out a Fastpass appointment for another attraction.

SUNSET BOULEVARD

This avenue honors Hollywood with facades derived from the Cathay Circle, the Beverly Wilshire Theatre, and other City of Angels landmarks. As you turn onto Sunset Boulevard from Hollywood Boulevard, you'll notice the Hollywood Junction information window, where questions are answered and reservations can be made for restaurants throughout the park.

■ NEED A BREAK?

Grab lunch or a quick snack at one of the food stands along Sunset Boulevard. You can get a burger (meat or veggie) or chicken strips at Rosie's All-American Cafe, a slice of pizza from Catalina Eddie's, a fruit salad from the Anaheim Produce Company, or a turkey leg or chili dog at Toluca Legs Turkey Company. Grab a sweet treat at Hollywood Scoops Ice Cream, where you can get two scoops in a cone or cup; the diet conscious can order fat-free, sugar-free vanilla.

☆☆
Duration
30 mins.
Crowds
Mod. to Heavy
Audience
All Ages

Beauty and the Beast—Live on Stage! This wildly popular stage show takes place at the Theater of the Stars, a re-creation of the famed Hollywood Bowl. The long-running production is a lively, colorful, and well-done condensation of the animated film. As you arrive or depart, it's fun to check out handprints and footprints set in concrete of the TV personalities who've visited Disney's Hollywood Studios. For people with dis abilities: Wheelchair accessible. ■ TIP→ Line up at least 30 minutes prior to showtime for good seats. Performance times vary, so check ahead.

Fodor'sChoice★
Duration
1 min., 22 secs.
Crowds
Huge
Audience
Not Small Kids

Rock 'n' Roller Coaster Starring Aerosmith. Although this is an indoor roller coaster like Magic Kingdom's Space Mountain, the similarity ends there. With its high-speed launch (0 to 60 in 2.8 seconds), multiple inversions, and loud rock music, it generates delighted screams from coaster junkies, though it's smooth enough and short enough that even the coaster-phobic have been known to enjoy it. The vehicles look like limos, and the track resembles the neck of an electric guitar that's been twisted. A hard-driving rock sound track by Aerosmith blasts from speakers mounted in each vehicle to accentuate the flips and turns. There's rock-and-roll memorabilia in the line area, and Aerosmith stars in the preshow film.

Pregnant women and guests with heart, back, or neck problems or motion sickness should skip this one, and children under 48 inches tall will have to miss it. For people with disabilities: Guests using wheelchairs must transfer to a ride vehicle. Service animals aren't allowed. ■ TIP→ Ride early, then pick up a Fastpass to go again, especially if visiting with tweens or teens. Another way to avoid a wait—split up and try the Single Rider Queue.

6

Fodor's Choice★
Duration
10 mins.
Crowds
You Bet!
Audience
Not Small Kids

Twilight Zone Tower of Terror. Ominously overlooking Sunset Boulevard is a 13-story structure that was once the Hollywood Tower Hotel, now deserted. You stroll through an overrun, mist-enshrouded garden and then into the dimly lighted lobby. In the dust-covered library, a lightning bolt zaps a TV to life. Rod Serling appears, recounting the story of the hotel's demise and inviting you to enter the Twilight Zone. Then, it's onward to the boiler room, where you climb aboard the hotel's giant elevator ride.

As you head upward past seemingly empty hallways, ghostly former residents appear. The Fifth Dimension awaits, where you travel forward past recognizable scenes from the popular TV series. Faster than you can say "Where's Rod Serling?" the creaking vehicle plunges into a terrifying, 130-foot free-fall and then, before you can catch your breath, shoots quickly up, down, up, and down all over again. No use trying to guess how many stomach-churning ups and downs you'll experience—Disney's ride engineers have programmed random drop variations into the attraction. It's a different thrill every time. After your final plunge, Serling warns, "The next time you check into a deserted hotel on the dark side of Hollywood, make sure you know what vacancy you'll be filling, or you'll be a permanent member of—the Twilight Zone!"

The ride-height minimum is 40 inches. Also, those who are pregnant or have heart, back, or neck problems shouldn't ride. **For people with disabilities:** You must have full upper-body strength and be able to transfer to a ride seat. Unsuitable for service animals. ■ TIP→ Get a Fastpass reserved-time ticket. Otherwise, come early or wait until evening, when crowds thin.

ANIMATION COURTYARD

As you exit Sunset Boulevard, veer right through the high-arched gateway to the Animation Courtyard. Straight ahead are Playhouse Disney—Live on Stage!, the Magic of Disney Animation, and Voyage of the Little Mermaid.

☆
Duration
15 mins.
Crowds
Light
Audience
Not Small Kids

Journey Into Narnia: Prince Caspian. Just after the 2008 motion-picture release of *The Chronicles of Narnia: Prince Caspian,* Disney launched this "behind-the-scenes" tour of props, costumes, concept art, and storyboards similar to an earlier presentation promoting *The Lion, The Witch and The Wardrobe.* As you enter, you step inside a faux-stone-castle interior—standing-room only. Four screens encircling the room play scenes from the film, while a special effect makes it appear that the Ice Witch is emerging from a huge ice block in the "castle" wall. When the video ends, you walk past displays of artifacts and costumes used in the film. If you're not a fan, you may want to skip this one. **For people with disabilities:** Wheelchair accessible and equipped for video-captioning devices. ■ TIP→ Narnia fans can check this out while waiting for a Fastpass appointment elsewhere.

☆☆☆
Duration
15+ mins.
Crowds
Moderate
Audience
All Ages

The Magic of Disney Animation. More than any other backstage peek, this tour truly takes you inside the magic as you follow the many steps of 2-D animation, an art expected to be totally replaced in years to come by computer-generated films such as the Disney/Pixar blockbusters *Toy Story* and *Finding Nemo*. The animation studio was a satellite of Walt Disney's original California studio from 1988 through 2003. It was here that *Brother Bear, Lilo & Stitch*, and *Mulan* were produced, as were several short films and portions of other popular features.

WHO'S THAT GUY?

Keep an eye out for the wacky Citizens of Hollywood characters—detectives, starlets, movie directors, and public works employees—who pop up on Hollywood or Sunset boulevards for impromptu entertainment that usually involves some guest participation. We ran into "movie producer" Alberto Dante of Faux Pas Productions, whose slogan is "If it's a faux pas, I made it!"

You begin in a small theater with a performance of Drawn to Animation, in which an actor plays the role of an animator interacting with Mushu, the wisecracking character from *Mulan*. Mushu prances between two screens above the stage. In their very funny exchange, the two explain how an animated character evolves from original concept. The animators who actually created the spunky dragon appear on screen to help tell the story. Depending on when you visit, new characters from upcoming Disney films may be introduced near the end of this show.

Next, you enter a creative zone where kiosks of computer touch screens invite you to add color to your favorite characters and even find out which one is most like you (answer a brief quiz and you can't help but smile when you find your animated character double). In the Sound Stage area, your interactive computer lets you choose from four film scenes, then cues you to voice the characters—it's a hoot when you play it back! Watch for popular Disney toon stars to appear in this area for autographs and photos.

The final stop is the Animation Academy, a delightful crash course in how to draw an animated character. Children and adults can sit side by side at one of 38 backlighted drafting tables as an artist gives easy-to-follow instructions on drawing a Disney character. Your sketch of Donald Duck (or the character du jour) is your souvenir. As you exit, check out the collection of drawings and cels, the clear celluloid sheets on which the characters were drawn for *Snow White, Fantasia,* and other classics. Here, too, are the actual Academy Awards that Disney has won for its animated films. The whole experience can take 15 to 30 minutes or more if you stop to play at interactive exhibits or take part in the Animation Academy. **For people with disabilities:** Wheelchair accessible, has reflective captioning and closed-captioned TVs (preshow area), and equipped for audio-description devices. ■**TIP→ Come early or late. To test your talents at Animation Academy, get in line for it after the Drawn to Animation show and do interactive stuff later. Toddlers may get bored.**

☆☆☆
Duration
22 mins.
Crowds
Mod. to Heavy
Audience
Small Kids

Playhouse Disney—Live on Stage! This is one of Walt Disney World's best shows for children. A cast of Disney Channel characters joins the show's perky, primary-color-clad host on a larger-than-life storybook stage. Mickey Mouse, Donald Duck, Daisy, and Goofy puppets team up on the Mickey Mouse Clubhouse set to prep for Minnie's surprise birthday bash. As party plans simmer, Handy Manny and his box of tools take the stage for a fix-it project involving a bubble machine—during one viewing, a preschooler tried to storm the stage twice to join Manny and his claw hammer. Next, puppets Leo, Annie, Quincy, and June of the "Little Einsteins" arrive with an animated Rocket and music by Korsakov for a great rocket race with nemesis Big Jet. Finally, Winnie the Pooh and Tigger become supersleuths to rescue Roo's kite trapped high in a tree.

Throughout the 22-minute show, preschoolers and even toddlers sing and dance along as the characters cha-cha-cha their way through lively stories laced with lessons ("when you have a problem, think, think, think!"). Floating bubbles, flying confetti, animated effects, and other treats are icing on Minnie's birthday cake. **For people with disabilities:** Wheelchair accessible, equipped with preshow area TV monitors with closed captioning, and equipped for assisted-listening and video- and handheld-captioning devices. ■TIP➔ Come first thing, when your child is most alert and lines are shorter. Be prepared to sit on the carpet; there aren't any chairs.

6

☆☆
Duration
17 mins.
Crowds
Heavy
Audience
All Ages

Voyage of the Little Mermaid. You join Ariel, Sebastian, and the underwater gang in this stage show, which condenses the movie into a marathon presentation of the greatest hits. In an admirable effort at verisimilitude, a fine mist sprays the stage; if you're sitting in the front rows, expect to get spritzed. Note that although this show is good for all ages, smaller children might be frightened by the dark theater and the evil, larger-than-life Ursula. **For people with disabilities:** Wheelchair accessible, has reflective captioning and preshow-area TVs with closed-captioning, and equipped for assisted-listening devices. ■TIP➔ If you're not riding Rock 'n' Roller Coaster or Tower of Terror, come first thing and put Fastpass (if available) to good use. Or wait until the stroller brigade's exodus after 5.

☆☆
Duration
20+ mins.
Crowds
Light to Moderate
Audience
Not Small Kids

Walt Disney: One Man's Dream. Next door to the Mermaid show, One Man's Dream is a photo, film, and audio tour through Walt's life. You get to peek at his Project X room, where many of his successes were born, and hear him tell much of his own story on tapes never before made public. If you qualify as a baby boomer, it's a real nostalgia trip to see Walt resurrected on film as his Wonderful World of Color intro splashes across the screen. There's also plenty of Walt memorabilia to view as you absorb the history of this entertainment legend. You can spend 20 minutes or longer at this attraction, depending on your interest in artifacts. The film at the end of your self-guided tour is 15 minutes long. **For people with disabilities:** Wheelchair accessible; has reflective captioning; and equipped for assisted-listening, handheld-captioning, and audio-description devices. ■TIP➔ Come while waiting for a Fastpass appointment at a high-demand ride like Rock 'n' Roller Coaster.

PIXAR PLACE

Once known as Mickey Avenue, Pixar Place has a fresh look tied to one of the park's biggest attractions, Toy Story Midway Mania! Where TV- and film-production soundstages once stood, warm brick facades welcome you to the land of Woody and Buzz. Open-air kiosks invite you to browse for themed toys and souvenirs. The brick Camera Department building is the place to mix and mingle with characters from the blockbuster movie *Toy Story*. Check schedules on your *Times Guide*.

Fodor'sChoice★
Duration
7 mins.
Crowds
Heavy
Audience
All Ages

Toy Story Midway Mania! Great toys like Mr. Potato Head, Woody, and Buzz Lightyear from Disney's hit film *Toy Story* never lose their relevance. The action here involves them and takes place inside the toy box of Andy, the boy whose toys come to life when he's gone. The line to enter passes an oversize Audio-Animatronic Mr. Potato Head with a midway-style bark: "It's a ride that's a game! It's a game that's a ride!" Step right up and grab a pair of 3-D glasses before boarding your jazzed-up carnival tram. Soon, you're whirling onto the midway where you can use your car's spring-action shooters to launch darts at balloons, toss rings at aliens, and splatter eggs at barnyard targets.

Just as in the Magic Kingdom's Buzz Lightyear's Space Ranger Spin, you'll rack up points for targets hit and see your tally at ride's end. Frequent riders can hone a rat-a-tat shooting system to increase scores each ride; if you get caught up in intense competition with your riding partner, your shooting arm may ache by the time you've hit your last target. Don't let Rex's fear of failure slow you down—shoot for the stars and you'll deserve a salute from the Green Army Men. **For people with disabilities:** Guests using ECVs must transfer to a standard wheelchair. Equipped for video-captioning devices. Check with a host about boarding with a service animal. ■TIP→ It's so addictive, you might want to come first thing, ride, and get a Fastpass for another go.

STREETS OF AMERICA

It's fun to tour the New York, San Francisco, and Chicago sets here on foot, so that you can check out the windows of shops and apartments, the taxicabs, and other details. If you're lucky (or smart enough to check the *Times Guide* show schedule), you'll join the street party for a performance by Mulch, Sweat & Shears—Live in Concert (aka Los Lawn Boys), as they play a 30-minute set of rock classics.

☆☆☆
Duration
Up to You
Crowds
Moderate
Audience
Small Kids

Honey, I Shrunk the Kids Movie Set Adventure. In this playground based on the movie, youngsters can slide down a gigantic blade of grass, crawl through caves, climb a mushroom mountain, inhale the scent of a humongous plant (which will then spit water back in their faces), and dodge sprinklers set in resilient flooring made of ground-up tires. All the requisite playground equipment is present: net climbs, ball crawls, caves, and slides. Because the area is enclosed, there's often a line to get in—but attraction hosts don't fudge on capacity limits, which maintains a comfort zone for those inside. **For people with disabilities:** Barrier-free, but uneven surfaces make maneuvering a wheelchair difficult.

■TIP→ Come when you've visited several attractions and your kids need to cut loose. Keep a close eye on toddlers—it's easy to lose track of them in the caves and slides.

☆☆
Duration
33 mins.
Crowds
Heavy
Audience
Not Small Kids

Lights, Motors, Action! Extreme Stunt Show. Here Disney designers reveal the secrets behind Hollywood's greatest stunts, including heart-pounding car chases and explosions. The scene is a 177,000-square-foot Mediterranean village movie set inside a 5,000-seat, open-air theater. The premise? Filmmakers are producing a spy thriller, and the director is organizing out-of-sequence stunts. Heroes and villains perform high-speed spinouts, two-wheel driving, jumps, and high falls using various vehicles, including watercraft. In addition to getting to see choreographed stunts live, you learn how filmmakers combine shots of various stunts to create a completed scene.

The theater is large, so you should be able to get in—even on days when there are only two shows or you arrive close to showtime. Note that the show is pretty long, the benches are hard, and babies and some young children become frightened by all the loud noises. Consider sitting toward the back in case you or your kids want to leave early. For people with disabilities: Wheelchair accessible and equipped for assisted-listening devices. ■TIP→ For the best seats, line up for this while others are lining up for the parade.

6

☆☆☆
Duration
25 mins.
Crowds
Mod. to Heavy
Audience
All Ages

Muppet*Vision 3-D. You don't have to be a Miss Piggyphile to get a kick out of this combination 3-D movie and musical revue. All the Muppet characters make appearances, including Miss Piggy in roles that include the Statue of Liberty. In the waiting area, movie posters advertise the world's most glamorous porker in *Star Chores* and *To Have and Have More,* and Kermit the Frog in an Arnold Schwarzenegger parody, *Kermit the Amphibian,* who's "so mean, he's green." Special effects are built into the walls and ceilings of the theater; the 3-D effects are coordinated with other sensory stimulation so you're never sure what's coming off the screen and what's being shot out of vents. For people with disabilities: Wheelchair accessible; has reflective captioning and preshow-area TVs with closed-captioning; and equipped for assisted-listening, video-captioning, and audio-description devices. ■TIP→ Arrive 10 minutes early. And don't worry—there are no bad seats.

☆
Duration
35 mins.
Crowds
Moderate
Audience
Not Small Kids

Studio Backlot Tour. The first stop on this tour, which you enter at the far end of Pixar Place where it meets Streets of America, is an outdoor special-effects water tank, where some of you are recruited for an unforgettable (and very wet) video moment. (In winter, when guests aren't fond of walking through the park with damp clothing, this audience-participation scene is canceled.) The line for the tram ride passes through a huge prop warehouse, which stores everything you could possibly imagine, from chairs to traffic lights to British phone booths.

Board the tram for a tour of different departments—set design, costumes, props, lighting—as well as the movie set for *Catastrophe Canyon.* The tram's announcer swears that shooting for this film is taking a break. But next thing, you experience a simulated earthquake, an oil tanker explodes in a mass of smoke and flame, and a water tower crashes to the ground, touching off a flash flood. As the tram pulls out,

DID YOU KNOW?

Pixar Place's Toy Story Midway Mania! combines the fun of a video game with 3-D technology and interaction with favorite Toy Story characters, like Mr. Potato Head. Man your spring-action shooter and take aim at playful targets along the colorful ride route. Scores are tallied at the end—will yours make you master of the midway?

you see the backstage workings of the catastrophe: the canyon is actually a mammoth steel slide wrapped in copper-color concrete, and the 70,000 gallons of floodwater—enough to fill 10 Olympic-size swimming pools—are recycled 100 times a day, or every 3½ minutes.

You also ride past the Streets of America back lot, where you can glimpse New York Street, with its brownstones, marble, brick, and stained glass that are actually expertly painted fiberglass and Styrofoam facades. Grips can slide the Empire State and Chrysler buildings out of the way anytime. You'll have to walk the Streets set after exiting the tram to see the San Francisco and Chicago side streets. **For people with disabilities:** Wheelchair accessible and equipped for handheld- and video-captioning devices. ■ **TIP→ Come early (it closes at dusk) and remember that people sitting on the left side of the tram get wet.**

ECHO LAKE

In the center of an idealized slice of Southern California is a cool, blue lake—an oasis fringed with trees, benches, and things like pink-and-aqua, chrome-trimmed restaurants with sassy waitresses and black-and-white TVs at the tables; or the shipshape Min and Bill's Dockside Diner; or Gertie, an emotive dinosaur that dispenses ice cream (seasonally); as well as Disney souvenirs and the occasional puff of smoke. (Look for Gertie's giant footprints in the sidewalk.) The hot ticket here is the American Idol Experience, where you can act out your own *American Idol* ambitions. You'll also find two of the park's longest-running attractions, the Indiana Jones Epic Stunt Spectacular! and Star Tours, where a 3-D attraction transformation is slated to take place.

☆☆☆
Duration
25 or 45 mins.
Crowds
Yes!
Audience
Not Small Kids

The American Idol Experience. So you want to be a rock star? How about an American Idol? If you're 14 or older and can sing on key, head to auditions as soon as you enter the park in the morning. You may be chosen by a Disney casting director to belt out a tune during shows at The American Idol Experience stage. At day's end, the top singers are invited back for a grand finale, and the winning performer earns The American Idol Experience "Dream Ticket"—a sort of Fastpass to the front of the line at a future regional audition for the *American Idol* TV show.

Not an *Idol* fan? No problem. This show, performed on a high-tech Hollywood-style stage complete with neon flash and high-energy show hosts, is a blast for all who enjoy live entertainment. Idol wannabes can choose their tunes from many music genres, so performers and songs vary with every show. You might hear the sweet lyrics of "Colors of the Wind" from Disney's *Pocahontas* just before the edgy Aretha Franklin hit "Respect." The best part? You and every other audience member vote for the show's top singer.

A quick-witted warm-up host revs you up while you're waiting in line. He reappears on stage with a fun, fast-paced monologue that explains how to react to singers and judges and how to vote. The show's main host then introduces three judges with show-biz experience who deliver kudos or critiques to each performer. (Don't be afraid to boo one judge

DISNEY'S HOLLYWOOD STUDIOS

NAME	Height Req.	Type of Entertainment	Duration	Crowds	Audience	Tips
Animation Courtyard						
Journey Into Narnia: Prince Caspian	n/a	Walk-Through/ Film	15 mins.	Light	All but Small Kids	Come while waiting for Fastpass appointment.
The Magic of Disney Animation	n/a	Tour	15+ mins.	Moderate	All Ages	Come in the morning or late afternoon. Toddlers may get bored.
Playhouse Disney— Live on Stage!	n/a	Show	22 mins.	Moderate to Heavy	Small Kids	Come first thing in the morning, when your child is most alert and lines are shorter.
Voyage of the Little Mermaid	n/a	Show	17 mins.	Heavy	All Ages	Come first thing in the morning. Otherwise, wait until after 5.
Walt Disney: One Man's Dream	n/a	Walk-Through/ Film	20+ mins.	Light to Moderate	All but Small Kids	See this attraction while waiting for a Fastpass appointment.
Echo Lake						
The American Idol Experience	n/a	Show	25 mins./ 45 mins.	Yes!	All but Small Kids	Check *Times Guide*, for showtimes. Arrive at least 30 minutes early for seats inside the theater.
Indiana Jones Epic Stunt Spectacular!	n/a	Show	30 mins.	Moderate to Heavy	All but Small Kids	Come at night, when the idol's eyes glow. Sit up front to feel the heat of a truck on fire.
Sounds Dangerous Starring Drew Carey	n/a	Show	12 mins.	Moderate	All but Small Kids	Arrive 15 minutes before show. You sit in total darkness.
Star Tours	At least 40"	Simulator Exp.	5 mins.	Moderate to Heavy	All but Small Kids	Come before closing, early morning, or get a Fastpass. Keep to the left in line for the best seats.
Hollywood Boulevard						
Great Movie Ride	n/a	Ride/Tour	22 mins.	Moderate	All but Small Kids	Come while waiting for Fastpass appointment. Lines out the door mean 25-min. wait—or longer.

Pixar Place

Toy Story Midway Mania!	n/a	Interactive Ride	7 mins.	Heavy	All Ages	Come early; use Fastpass.

Streets of America

Honey, I Shrunk the Kids Movie Set Adventure	n/a	Playground	Up to you	Moderate	Small Kids	Come after you've done several shows and your kids need to cut loose. Keep an eye on toddlers who can quickly get lost in the caves and slides.
Lights, Motors, Action! Extreme Stunt Show	n/a	Show	33 mins.	Heavy	All but Small Kids	For the best seats, line up for the show while others are lining up for the parade.
Muppet*Vision 3-D	n/a	3-D Film	25 mins.	Moderate to Heavy	All Ages	Arrive 10 mins. early. And don't worry—there are no bad seats.
Studio Backlot Tour	n/a	Tour	35 mins.	Moderate	All but Small Kids	People sitting on the left can get wet. Come early; it closes at dusk.

Sunset Boulevard

Beauty and the Beast— Live on Stage!	n/a	Show	30 mins.	Moderate to Heavy	All Ages	Come 30 mins. before showtime for good seats. Performance days vary, so check ahead.
★ Rock 'n' Roller Coaster Starring Aerosmith	At least 48"	Thrill Ride	1 min., 22 secs.	Huge	All but Small Kids	Ride early, then use Fastpass for another go later.
★ Twilight Zone Tower of Terror	At least 40"	Thrill Ride	10 mins.	You Bet!	All but Small Kids	Use Fastpass. Come early or late evening.

★ = Fodor's Choice

who enjoys being the caustic critic.) When its time to vote, your armrest keypad lights up for 10 seconds. While votes are tallied, you're treated to a big-screen music video starring 2007 *American Idol* champion Jordin Sparks. Other Idol stars, including host Ryan Seacrest and recent champ David Cook, make video appearances.

Preliminary shows last 25 minutes; finale shows are 45 minutes. Dying to see who wins the Dream Ticket but can't get into the theater for the evening finale? Take heart. A stadium-size LED screen outside the theater offers a live simulcast. To learn about auditions ahead of time, visit ⊕ *www.disneyworld.com/idol.* **For people with disabilities:** Wheelchair accessible. Twice weekly sign-language interpretations. Equipped for assisted-listening and video-captioning devices. ■ TIP➜ **To get a seat inside the theater, arrive at least 30 minutes before showtime.**

☆☆☆
Duration
30 mins.
Crowds
Mod. to Heavy
Audience
Not Small Kids

Indiana Jones Epic Stunt Spectacular! The rousing theme music from the Indiana Jones movies heralds action delivered by veteran stunt coordinator Glenn Randall, whose credits include *Raiders of the Lost Ark, Indiana Jones and the Temple of Doom, E.T.,* and *Jewel of the Nile.* Presented in a 2,200-seat amphitheater, the show starts with a series of near-death encounters in an ancient Mayan temple. Indy slides down a rope from the ceiling, dodges spears that shoot up from the floor, avoids getting chopped by booby-trapped idols, and snags a forbidden gemstone, setting off a gigantic boulder that threatens to render him two-dimensional.

"Okay, I need some rowdy people," the casting director calls. While the lucky few audience members demonstrate their rowdiness, behind them the set crew casually wheels off the temple. Two people roll the boulder like a giant beach ball and replace it with a Cairo street, circa 1940. Then the nasty Ninja-Nazi stuntmen come out, and you start to think that it's probably better to be in the audience.

Eventually Indy comes sauntering down along with his redoubtable girlfriend, Marian Ravenwood, portrayed by a Karen Allen look-alike. She's kidnapped and tossed into a truck while Indy fights his way free with bullwhip and gun, and bad guys tumble from every corner and cornice. Motorcycles buzz around; the street becomes a shambles; and the truck carrying Marian flips and bursts into flame. The final helicopter scene is great fun.

The actors do a commendable job of explaining their stunts. You see how they're set up, watch the stars practice them in slow motion, and learn how cameras are camouflaged behind imitation rocks for trick shots. Only one stunt remains a secret: how do Indy and Marian escape the explosion? That's what keeps 'em coming back. **For people with disabilities:** Wheelchair accessible. Equipped for assisted-listening, audio-description, and handheld-captioning devices. ■ TIP➜ **A high-capacity theater means that all who want to get in usually do; don't waste a Fastpass here. Come at night to see the idols' eyes glow. Sit up front to feel the heat of a truck on fire.**

HOLLYWOOD STUDIOS KIDS TOUR

Although young children prob- ably won't appreciate all the movie nostalgia, they will likely get a kick out of Hollywood Boulevard's wacky street performers, and the park's lively street parades and energetic stage shows.

The minute you enter, head straight to Toy Story Midway Mania! and get in line or grab your Fastpass. This interactive (and high-demand) ride is fun for all, even small children who have to learn how to operate their spring-action shooters to rack up midway points. If you can ride *and* get a Fastpass to come back, you'll be your kids' hero.

Now take a deep breath and lead the little ones to hands-on activities inside The Magic of Disney Anima- tion (where they'll first enjoy a short film) and Honey, I Shrunk the Kids Movie Set Adventure, where they can whoop their way through a larger- than-life playground.

Combine lunch with more play time at the Play 'N Dine at Hollywood & Vine family buffet, where charac- ters from Playhouse Disney mix and mingle with the children. Don't forget your camera and the kids' autograph books!

SEE THE CHARACTERS COME TO LIFE

Shows and attractions based on Dis- ney films and TV series really grab young children. Check schedules in your *Times Guide* for performances of Beauty and the Beast—Live on Stage and Playhouse Disney—Live on Stage! After tots and preschoolers have danced along at the Playhouse show, they can meet the charac- ters in the Animation Courtyard, then catch a Beauty and the Beast

performance or watch Ariel "under the sea" at Voyage of the Little Mermaid.

Check other Character Greeting locations and times—The Green Army Men from *Toy Story* put the kids through their marching paces on Pixar Place, and Mickey Mouse or the Incredibles might turn up at The Magic of Disney Animation. Make time before or after your Honey, I Shrunk the Kids Movie Set Adventure to watch Kermit display his wry wit and Miss Piggy steal the show at MuppetVision 3-D. It's not easy being green. . . .

JOIN THE PARADE

The daily Block Party Bash encour- ages everyone to play in the street. Outgoing children will jump right in to dance along with the perform- ers and characters. If your little one is shy, just pick her up and dance with her! Stilt walkers, acrobats, and dancers in bright costumes paint a Technicolor moving mural that keeps children riveted and bopping along.

If there are *High School Musical* fans in your group, check the park schedule for one of several street performances that also invites kids to kick up their heels and join the party. These may be tweener tunes, but young siblings enjoy Wildcat Fever, too!

6

HOLLYWOOD STUDIOS GROWN-UP TOUR

At the Studios, movie classics like *The Wizard of Oz* and *Casablanca* come to life on The Great Movie Ride, and the best of Disney animation—from *Toy Story* to *Beauty and the Beast*—is reborn as park attractions. The old small-screen favorite *The Twilight Zone* is taken to new heights, and the modern TV phenomenon *American Idol* goes live.

FIND YOUR ADRENALINE RUSH
Two words—"thrills" and "chills"—define the top two attractions for older kids and adults. Head straight to Sunset Boulevard and grab the thrills at Rock 'n' Roller Coaster Starring Aerosmith, where multiple inversions, twists, and turns rock to the tune of "Dude (Looks Like a Lady)." Feel the chills at The Twilight Zone Tower of Terror, when something goes terribly wrong with your elevator car, and it veers off its ghostly course.

A quick walk to Echo Lake lands you in Wookiee territory, where you can climb aboard the Star Tours flight simulator for a wild flight to the Moon of Endor. 3-D upgrades should up the thrill factor.

DISCOVER YOUR TALENT
Are you an actor, an artist, a singer, or a midway-game fanatic? If the Citizens of Hollywood Talent Agent doesn't get your number, you can try out your act at one of several park attractions.

At the Indiana Jones Epic Stunt Spectacular, 10 guests are chosen to perform as show extras. At The American Idol Experience, you can test your pipes in an audition—and maybe even make it onto the show. All those years filling notebooks with doodles might just have been

training for The Magic of Disney Animation experience. At Toy Story Midway Mania! join Woody and Buzz for a manic midway ride past moving targets that test your spring-action-shooter mettle.

LEARN TRICKS OF THE TRADE
Refuel at one of the park's many quick-service stands, let "Mom" serve you meat loaf at the '50s Prime Time Cafe, or boost your image with a plush booth and a Cobb salad at the Hollywood Brown Derby.

Then head for the Studio Backlot Tour and a look at how filmmakers create special effects. Stroll the Streets of America before queuing up for a seat at the Lights, Motors, Action! Extreme Stunt Show! and a peek at how high-speed vehicle action is shot.

Back at Echo Lake, funnyman Drew Carey sheds light in a dark theater on movie sound effects at Sounds Dangerous Starring Drew Carey. The '50s Prime Time Café bar is a great place to grab a mojito or margarita before heading to the night-time extravaganza, Fantasmic! That's a wrap.

☆☆
Duration
12 mins.
Crowds
Moderate
Audience
Not Small Kids

Sounds Dangerous Starring Drew Carey. This show, which runs continuously throughout the day, demonstrates the use of movie sound effects. It employs the techniques of sound master Jimmy MacDonald, who became the voice of Mickey Mouse during the 1940s and invented some 20,000 sound effects during his 45 years at Walt Disney Studios. Most are created using gizmos—a metal sheet that, when rattled, sounds like thunder; a box of sand for footsteps on gravel; and other noises made from nails, straw, mud, leather, and other ordinary components.

The premise is that you will help Drew Carey, who portrays an undercover cop, find out who smuggled the diamonds from the snow globe. To do so, you don headphones to follow Carey's progress and to hear the many sounds that go into a movie or TV show. Carey's bumbling detective provides plenty of laughs for adults and older kids. **For people with disabilities:** Wheelchair accessible. Equipped for assisted-listening and handheld-captioning devices. ■TIP→ Arrive 10–15 minutes before showtime. Most of the show takes place in utter darkness and is *very* loud—some kids may be frightened.

☆☆
Duration
5 mins.
Crowds
Mod. to Heavy
Audience
Not Small Kids

Star Tours. Although the flight-simulator technology used for this ride was long ago surpassed on other thrill rides, this adventure (inspired by the *Star Wars* films) is still a pretty good trip. "May the force be with you," says the attendant on duty, "'cause I won't be!" Piloted by *Star Wars* characters R2D2 and C-3PO, the 40-passenger *StarSpeeder* that you board is supposed to take off on a routine flight to the moon of Endor. But with R2D2 at the helm, things quickly go awry: you shoot into deep space, dodge giant ice crystals and comet debris, innocently bumble into an intergalactic battle, and attempt to avoid laser-blasting fighters as you whiz through the canyons of some planetary city before coming to a heart-pounding halt. We're hoping the anticipated 3-D transformation of this ride adds fresh excitement, fun, and maybe even a higher star rating!

6

Those who are pregnant or have heart, back, neck, or motion sickness issues shouldn't ride. Children less than 40 inches tall can't ride, and those under age 7 must be accompanied by an adult. **For people with disabilities:** Guests using wheelchairs must transfer to a ride seat; those lacking upper-body strength should request an extra shoulder restraint. Equipped for video-captioning devices. Service animals aren't allowed. ■TIP→ Lines swell when the Indiana Jones show lets out. Come early or late or use Fastpass. For the most realistic sensations, keep to the far left in line to snag seats up front, closer to the screen. (In back, the ride is rougher and the sensations less exhilarating).

▌ NEED A
BREAK?

If you have a sweet tooth, save room for some soft-serve Ice Cream of Extinction at **Gertie's** ice-cream bar and snack shop open seasonally inside the big green dinosaur on the shore of Echo Lake. Nearby, **Min & Bill's Dockside Diner** is the spot for a quick sandwich and a shake. You can even buy a beer here. Step right up to the counter.

STUDIOS SPECTACLES

☆☆☆
Duration
25 mins.
Crowds
Heavy
Audience
All Ages

Block Party Bash. Accompanied by pop tunes, the Studios' midday parade wends its up Hollywood Boulevard. The Green Army Men of *Toy Story* lead Disney characters like Woody and Buzz Lightyear from *Toy Story* and Flik and Atta from *A Bug's Life*. Dancers, stilt-walkers, and acrobats draw you into the fun that's enhanced by special effects and floats that double as dance stages and trampoline-style performer launch pads. Watch for a surprise finale with Mr. and Mrs. Incredible. **For people with disabilities:** Disney cast members can direct you to special zones for guests using wheelchairs. ■TIP➔ Stake out your curb spot an hour early and hang on to it. The parade begins at 3.

☆☆☆
Duration
25 mins.
Crowds
Heavy
Audience
Not Small Kids

Fantasmic! The Studios' after-dark show wows huge audiences with its special effects and Disney characters. The omnipresent Mickey, in his Sorcerer's Apprentice costume, plays the embodiment of Good in the struggle against forces of Evil, personified by Disney villains such as Cruella DeVil, Scar, and Maleficent. Animated clips of these famous bad guys (and gals), alternating with clips of Disney nice guys (and dolls), are projected onto screens made of water—high-tech fountains surging high in the air. Disney being Disney, it's Good that emerges triumphant, amid water effects and flames, explosions, and fireworks worthy of a Hollywood shoot-'em-up. All this, plus the villainous action, is why small kids may find this show frightening.

Arrive early at the 6,500-seat Hollywood Hills Amphitheatre opposite the Twilight Zone Tower of Terror. Check ahead for information on show days and times. This show runs twice nightly during peak season; only twice a week in nonpeak periods. **For people with disabilities:** Wheelchair accessible. Equipped with reflective captioning and for assisted-listening devices. ■TIP➔ Arrive at least an hour early and sit toward the rear, near the entrance/exit. Or consider the dinner package, which includes a special block of seating for the show.

☆
Duration
20 mins.
Crowds
Heavy
Audience
All Ages

High School Musical 3: Senior Year. Five or six times each day, pop culture hits Hollywood Boulevard with sing-along, dance-along 'tweener tunes when a lively team of theme-park performers brings Disney Channel's *High School Musical* to the Studios' streets. The live show spreads Wildcat Fever through the crowd, and kids get to sing and dance in the street along with East High performers to the tunes of "A Night to Remember" and "The Boys Are Back." **For people with disabilities:** Disney cast members can direct you to special zones for guests using wheelchairs. ■TIP➔ Stake out a spot near Mickey's Sorcerer's Hat icon 30–45 minutes early; ask Disney cast members for tips on best viewing.

Disney's Animal Kingdom

WORD OF MOUTH

"One of my favorites is Disney's Animal Kingdom. They have a little bit of everything, including character parades (as do other Disney parks). Mt. Everest is the best ride, but the safari is great. . . "

—JillDavis

ANIMAL KINGDOM PLANNER

Park Information

If you're staying on-site, you can take a Disney bus to the Entrance Plaza. If you drive, the $14 parking fee is good at other Disney lots throughout the day.

Although this is technically Disney's largest theme park, most of the land is reserved for the animals. Pedestrian areas are actually quite compact, with relatively narrow passageways. The only way to get around is on foot or in a wheelchair or electronic convenience vehicle (ECV).

Guest Relations (aka Guest Services) will help with tickets at a window to the left just before you pass through the turnstile.

Once you've entered, Guest Relations staffers in the Oasis can provide park maps, schedules, and answers to questions. They can also assist with dining reservations, ticket upgrades, and services for guests with disabilities.

Guided Tours

Reserve with **WDW Tours** (☎ *407/939–8687*) for a behind-the-scenes tour.

Backstage Safari takes an in-depth look at animal conservation every Monday, Wednesday, Thursday, and Friday 8:30–11:30 and 1–4, stopping at the state-of-the-art veterinary hospital, animal nutrition center, and other behind-the-scenes areas. It's a great way to learn about animal behaviors and how handlers manage the diets and health of such a diverse population of critters in captivity.

Don't expect to see many animals on this tour, because most of them will be in the park entertaining guests. There's always the possibility, however, that you'll get a peek at an animal brought in to visit the doc.

Book ahead; you can make reservations up to 180 days in advance. Those in your party must all be at least 16 years old to participate, and the cost is $72 plus park admission.

Wild by Design offers insights into the creation of Animal Kingdom every Monday, Wednesday, Thursday, and Friday from 8:30 to 11:30. The tour touches on the park's art, architecture, history, and landscape, and reveals how stories of exotic lands like Anandapur in Asia and Harambe in Africa are told at the park.

You'll learn about the theming of the park's hub, Discovery Island, where architectural touches include exotic folk art from Bali and where masterful animal carvings grace the iconic Tree of Life. You also get a glimpse of behind-the-scenes buildings where animals receive care. The tour is for ages 14 and older and costs $60; park admission is required as well.

Park Amenities

Baby Care: At Discovery Island you can stop in to nurse babies in the quiet Baby Care Center, which is equipped with rocking chairs and low lighting. There are changing tables, which are also available in restrooms (including some men's restrooms), and you can buy disposable diapers, formula, baby food, and pacifiers.

Cameras: Disposable cameras are widely available, and you can buy film and digital memory cards at several shops throughout the park. If a Disney photographer takes your picture, ask for a Disney PhotoPass—later, you can view and purchase the pictures online or at the park's Photo Center in the Oasis.

First Aid: The First Aid Center, staffed by registered nurses, is in Discovery Island, and at least a dozen automated external defibrillators are in key park areas.

Lockers: Lockers are in Guest Relations in the Oasis. Rental fees are $5 to $7 (depending on size) for a day plus a $5 key deposit.

Lost People and Things: Get name tags for your family at Discovery Island. Instruct your kids to speak to someone with a Disney name tag if you become separated. If you do lose your child, contact any cast member immediately. Lost-children logbooks are at the Baby Care Center in Discovery Island and at the Oasis branch of Guest Relations.

Animal Kingdom Lost and Found (☎ *407/938–2785*) is at Guest Relations. To retrieve lost articles after leaving the park, call Lost and Found on the same day, or call **Main Lost and Found** (✉ *Magic Kingdom Ticket and Transportation Center [TTC]* ☎ *407/824–4245*) if more than a day has passed since you've lost the article.

Package Pick-Up: You can have shop clerks forward purchases to Package Pick-Up near the Main Entrance in the Oasis, so that you won't have to carry them around all day. Allow three hours for the journey. If you're staying at a Disney hotel, you also can have packages delivered there.

Stroller Rentals: Garden Gate Gifts in the Oasis rents strollers. Singles are $15 daily, $13 for more than one day; doubles run $31 daily, $27 for multiday.

For People with Disabilities

Guests using wheelchairs will have ready access to restaurants, shops, and most attractions—including the Festival of the Lion King theater at Camp Minnie-Mickey, Finding Nemo—The Musical theater in DinoLand U.S.A., and the Tree of Life theater showing It's Tough to Be a Bug! (theaters also are accessible to ECVs). Some monitor-equipped attractions (e.g., the Tree of Life) have reflective-captioning boxes.

Scripts and story lines for all attractions are available, and you can book sign-language interpreters with notice of two or more weeks. Large Braille park maps are by Guest Relations and near the Tip Board at the entrance to Discovery Island. Guest Relations is also where you can borrow assisted-listening, handheld-captioning, and video-captioning devices with a refundable deposit. Service animals are allowed in most, but not all, areas of the park.

You can rent wheelchairs ($15 daily, $13 for multiple days) and ECVs ($45 per day plus a refundable $20 security deposit) at Garden Gate Gifts in the Oasis. You can't, however, reserve these items, so arrive early to get one—particularly if you want an ECV.

7

ANIMAL KINGDOM
GO ON SAFARI

Disney's Animal Kingdom explores the stories of all animals—real, imaginary, and extinct. Enter through the Oasis, where you hear exotic background music and find yourself surrounded by gentle waterfalls and gardens alive with exotic birds, reptiles, and mammals.

At 403 acres and several times the size of the Magic Kingdom, Animal Kingdom is the largest in area of all Disney theme parks. Animal habitats take up much of that acreage. Creatures here thrive in careful re-creations of landscapes from Asia and Africa. Throughout the park, you'll also learn about conservation in a low-key way.

Amid all the nature are thrill rides, a 3-D show (housed in the "root system" of the iconic Tree of Life), two first-rate musicals, and character meet and greets. Cast members are as likely to hail from Kenya or South Africa as they are from Kentucky or South Carolina. It's all part of the charm.

GETTING ORIENTED

Animal Kingdom's hub is the Tree of Life, in the middle of Discovery Island. The park's lands, each with a distinct personality, radiate from Discovery Island.

To the southwest is Camp Minnie-Mickey, a character-greeting location and live-show area. North of the hub is Africa, where Kilimanjaro Safaris travel across extensive savanna. In the northeast corner is Rafiki's Planet Watch and conservation activities.

Asia, with thrills like Expedition Everest and Kali River Rapids, is east of the hub, and DinoLand U.S.A. brings T. rex and other prehistoric creatures to life in the park's southeast corner.

TOP ATTRACTIONS

DISCOVERY ISLAND
Tree of Life—It's Tough to Be a Bug! This clever and very funny 3-D movie starring Flik from the Disney film *A Bug's Life* is full of surprises, including "shocking" special effects. Some kids under 7 are scared of the loud noises.

AFRICA
Kilimanjaro Safaris. You're guaranteed to see dozens of wild animals, including giraffes, zebras, hippos, rhinos, and elephants, living in authentic, re-created African habitats. If you're lucky, the lions and cheetahs will be stirring, too.

ASIA
Expedition Everest. The Animal Kingdom's cleverly themed roller coaster is a spine-tingling trip into the snowy Himalayas to find the abominable snowman. It's best reserved for brave riders 7 and up.

CAMP MINNIE-MICKEY
Festival of the Lion King. Singers and dancers dressed in fantastic costumes representing many wild animals perform uplifting dance and acrobatics numbers and interact with children in the audience.

DINOLAND, U.S.A.
DINOSAUR. Extremely lifelike giant dinosaurs jump out as your vehicle swoops and dips. We recommend it for fearless kids 8 and up.

Finding Nemo—The Musical. Don't miss a performance of this outstanding musical starring the most charming, colorful characters ever to swim their way into your heart.

VISITING TIPS

■ Try to visit during the week. Pedestrian areas are compact, and the park can feel uncomfortably packed on weekends.

■ Plan on a full day here. That way, while exploring Africa's Pangani Forest Exploration Trail, say, you can spend 10 minutes (rather than just two) watching vigilant meerkats stand sentry or tracking a mama gorilla as she cares for her infant.

■ Arrive a half hour before the park opens as much to see the wild animals at their friskiest (morning is a good time to do the safari ride) as to get a jump on the crowds.

■ For updates on line lengths, check the Tip Board, just after crossing the bridge into Discovery Island.

■ Good places to rendezvous include the outdoor seating area of Tusker House restaurant in Africa, in front of DinoLand U.S.A.'s Boneyard, and at the entrance to Festival of the Lion King at Camp Minnie-Mickey.

7

By Jennie Hess   If you're thinking, "Oh, it's just another zoo, let's skip it," think again. Walt Disney World's fourth theme park, opened in 1998, takes its inspiration from humankind's enduring love for animals and pulls out all the stops. Your day will be packed with unusual animal encounters, enchanting entertainment, and themed rides that'll leave you breathless.

A large chunk of the park is devoted to animal habitats, especially the forest and savanna of Africa's Kilimanjaro Safaris. Towering acacia trees and tall grasses sweep across the land where zebras, giraffes, and wildebeests roam. A lion kopje, warthog burrows, and elephant watering hole provide ample space for inhabitants.

About 94 acres contain foliage like hibiscus and mulberry, perfect for antelope and many other species. The largest groups of Nile hippos and African elephants in North America live along the winding waterway that leads to the savanna. The generously landscaped Pangani Forest Exploration Trail provides roaming grounds for troops of gorillas and authentic habitats for meerkats, birds, fish, and other creatures.

Beyond the park's Africa territory, similar large spaces are set aside for the homes of Asian animals like tigers and Komodo dragons, as well as for creatures like Galapagos tortoises and a giant anteater.

Disney Imagineers didn't forget to include their trademark thrills, from the Kali River Rapids ride in Asia to the fast-paced DINOSAUR journey in Dinoland U.S.A. Expedition Everest, the park's biggest thrill attraction, is a "runaway" train ride on a faux rugged mountain complete with icy ledges, dark caves, and a yeti legend.

The only downside to the Animal Kingdom layout is that walking paths and spaces can get very crowded and hot in the warmest months. Your best bet is to arrive very early and see the animals first before the heat makes them (and you) woozy.

Just before the park opens, Minnie Mouse, Pluto, and Goofy arrive at the iconic Tree of Life in a safari vehicle to welcome the first guests into the heart of the park. Let the adventure begin!

THE OASIS

This lush entrance garden makes you feel as if you've been plunked down in the middle of a rain forest. Cool mist, the aroma of flowers, and playful animals and colorful birds all enliven a miniature landscape of streams and grottoes, waterfalls, and glades fringed with banana leaves and jacaranda. On the finest Orlando mornings, when the mists shroud the landscape, it's the scene-setter for the rest of your day. It's also where you can take care of essentials before entering the park. Here you'll find guide maps, stroller and wheelchair rentals, Guest Relations, and an ATM.

DISCOVERY ISLAND

The park hub and site of the Tree of Life, this land is encircled by Discovery River, which isn't an actual attraction but makes for attractive views from a bridge in Harambe. The island's whimsical architecture, with wood carvings handmade in Bali, lends charm and a touch of fantasy to this area.

The verdant Discovery Island Trails that lead to the Tree of Life provide habitats for kangaroos, lemurs, Galapagos tortoises, and other creatures you won't want to miss while here. It's hard to tear the kids from the glass panel in a cave-like observation area where you can see river otters frolic underwater and above.

You'll discover some great shops and good counter-service eateries here, and the island is also the site of the daily Mickey's Jammin' Jungle Parade. Visitor services that aren't in the Oasis are here, on the border with Harambe, including the Baby Care Center and the First Aid Center.

Fodor'sChoice★
Duration
20 mins.
Crowds
**Moderate to
Heavy**
Audience
**All but Small
Kids**

Tree of Life—It's Tough to Be a Bug! A monument to all Earth's creatures, the park's centerpiece is an imposing 14 stories high and 50 feet wide at its base. Its 100,000-plus leaves are several shades of green fabric, each carefully placed for a realistic effect. Carved into its thick trunk, gnarled roots, and soaring branches—some of which are supported by joints that allow them to sway in a strong wind—are nearly 350 intricate animal forms that include a baboon, a whale, a horse, the mighty lion, and even an ankylosaurus. Outside, paths tunnel underneath the roots as the fauna-encrusted trunk towers overhead. It's a rich and truly fascinating sight—the more you look, the more you see; perhaps you'll spot ring-tailed lemurs, Galapagos tortoises, and red kangaroos.

The path leads you inside the tree trunk, where you get a bug's-eye view of life. The whimsical 3-D film adventure *It's Tough to Be a Bug!* is modeled vaguely on the animated film *A Bug's Life* from Disney-Pixar. Special film and theater effects spray you with "poison," zap you with a swatter, and even poke you with a stinger. It's all in good fun—and the surprise ending is too playful to give away.

Although the show has something for all ages, it's very loud. Some effects frighten children under 8; there's often at least one screaming toddler during the show. **For people with disabilities:** Wheelchair accessible, but, to fully experience all the special effects, guests using wheelchairs should transfer to a seat. Equipped with reflective captioning and

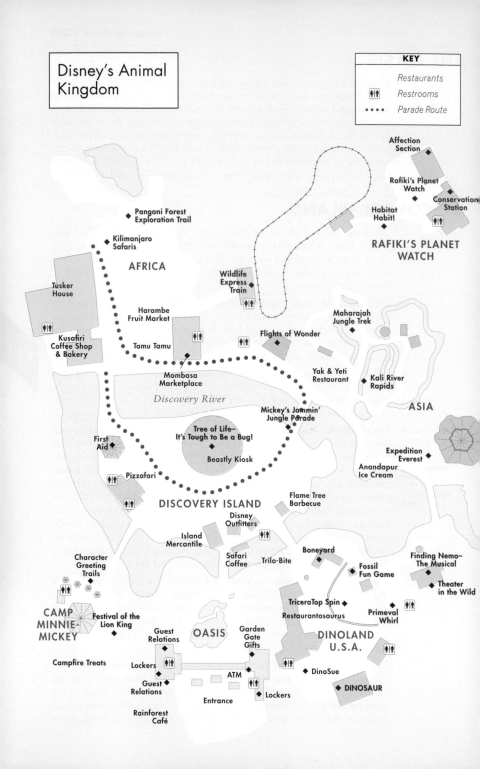

for assisted-listening devices. If you have a service animal, check with a host before entering the theater. ■ TIP→ Get a Fastpass reservation after doing the Kilimanjaro Safari. But if the wait is 40 minutes or less, save your Fastpass for a ride like Expedition Everest, and get into the regular line along the Discovery Island Trails.

DINOLAND U.S.A.

Just as it sounds, this is the place to come in contact with re-created prehistoric creatures, including the fear-inspiring carnotaurus and the gentle iguanodon. The landscaping includes live plants that have evolved over the last 65 million years. In collaboration with Chicago's Field Museum, Disney has added a complete, full-scale skeleton cast of Dino-Sue—also known as "Sue"—the 65-million-year-old Tyrannosaurus rex discovered near the Black Hills of South Dakota.

After admiring "Sue," you can go on the thrilling DINOSAUR ride, play in the Boneyard, or take in the Finding Nemo–The Musical show at the Theater in the Wild. Kids will want to try the TriceraTop Spin and the Primeval Whirl family coaster, which has spinning "time machines." There's no need to dig for souvenirs at Chester and Hester's Dinosaur Treasures gift shop—all you need is your wallet.

NEED A BREAK? Famished, but no time for lunch? Make tracks for **PetriFries** and dig into an order of french fries. Better yet, grab some protein at **Restaurantosaurus** and you'll be ready to take on T. rex.

7

☆☆☆
Duration
Up to You
Crowds
Moderate to Heavy
Audience
Small Kids

Boneyard. Youngsters can slide, dig, bounce, slither, and stomp around this archaeological dig site–cum–playground, the finest play area in any of the four Disney parks. In addition to a huge sand pit where children can dig for mammoth bones, there are twisting short and long slides, climbing nets, caves, and a jeep to climb on. Stomp on the dino footprints to make 'em roar. **For people with disabilities:** This fossil play maze is wheelchair accessible. ■ TIP→ Let the kids burn off energy here while waiting for a DINOSAUR Fastpass appointment. Or head over late in the day when kids need to run free.

☆☆☆
Duration
Under 4 mins.
Crowds
Heavy
Audience
All but Small Kids

DINOSAUR. This wild adventure through time puts you face-to-face with huge dinosaurs that move and breathe with uncanny realism. When a carload of guests rouses a cantankerous carnotaurus from his Cretaceous slumber, it's showtime. You travel back 65 million years on a fast-paced, twisting adventure and try to save the last living iguanodon as a massive asteroid hurtles toward Earth. Exciting Audio-Animatronics and special effects bring to life dinosaurs like the raptor, pterodactyl, styracosaurus, alioramus, and compsognather. Be prepared for a short but steep drop toward the end of the ride.

Guests who are pregnant or have back, neck, or heart problems should avoid this very bumpy ride. The height is minimum 40 inches, which is fine, as all the jostling and realistic carnivores frighten smaller children anyway. **For people with disabilities:** You must transfer from your wheelchair to board this ride. Equipped for video-captioning and assisted-listening devices. No service animals. ■ TIP→ Come first thing in the morning or at the end of the day, or use Fastpass.

Fodor's Choice★
Duration
30 mins.
Crowds
Heavy
Audience
All Ages

Finding Nemo—the Musical. The performance of this fish tale is so creative and fun that many have likened it to a first-rate Broadway show. Indeed, Disney Imagineers collaborated with several Broadway talents to produce it. Original songs by Tony Award–winning *Avenue Q* co-composer-creator Robert Lopez and a-cappella musical *Along the Way* co-creator Kristen Anderson-Lopez add depth and energy. Michael Curry, who co-designed the character puppets of Broadway's *The Lion King,* also created this show's eye-popping puppetry; Peter Brosius, artistic director of the Children's Theatre Company of Minneapolis and winner of a regional theater Tony Award, directed the show.

Multigenerational humor; special effects; and larger-than-life puppets acted by gifted performers, dancers, and acrobats all bring you into Nemo's world. The sweet story remains the same as in the movie— Nemo and his father Marlin go on separate journeys that teach them how to understand each other. Zany Dory, with her memory lapses, Crush the sea turtle dude, tap-dancing sharks, and others give memorable supporting-role turns. **For people with disabilities:** Wheelchair accessible. Equipped with reflective captioning and for assisted-listening devices. ■TIP➜ Arrive 40 minutes before showtime. Bring little kids here while older tweens and teens ride Expedition Everest.

☆
Duration
Up to You
Crowds
Light
Audience
All but Small Kids

Fossil Fun Games. A carnival-style midway in the middle of DinoLand U.S.A., this fun fair draws crowds with games like Whack a Packycephalosaur and the mallet-strength challenge, Dino-Whamma. The prehistoric fun comes at a price, however, and stone currency is not accepted. Prizes are mostly of the plush-character variety—you might win your sweetheart a stuffed Nala. **For people with disabilities:** Wheelchair accessible. ■TIP➜ It costs $2.50 per game on average. Bring a pocketful of change and a stash of ones.

☆☆☆
Duration
2½ mins.
Crowds
Heavy
Audience
All Ages

Primeval Whirl. In a free-spinning, four-passenger vehicle, you head on a brief journey back in time on this outdoor open-air coaster, twisting, turning, and even venturing into the jaws of a dinosaur "skeleton." Crazy cartoon dinosaurs in shades of turquoise, orange, yellow, and purple pop up along the track bearing signs that warn THE END IS NEAR. More signs alert you to incoming METEORS! and suggest that you HEAD FOR THE HILLS!—coaster hills, that is. Halfway through the ride, your car seems to spin out of control and you take the next drop backward. The more weight in the vehicle, the more you spin.

Pregnant women or guests with back, neck, or heart problems should skip this one. The ride-height minimum is 48 inches. **For people with disabilities:** Guests using wheelchairs must transfer to the ride vehicle. No service animals. ■TIP➜ Kids might want to ride twice. Take your first spin early; get a Fastpass to return later if the wait is over 20 minutes.

☆☆
Duration
2 mins.
Crowds
Heavy
Audience
Small Kids

TriceraTop Spin. TriceraTop Spin is designed for playful little dinophiles who ought to get a kick out of whirling around this ride's giant spinning toy top and dodging incoming comets in their dino-mobiles. "Pop!" goes the top and out comes a grinning dinosaur as four passengers in each vehicle fly in a circle and maneuver up and down. **For people with disabilities:** Wheelchair accessible, but guests using ECVs must transfer to standard wheelchairs. ■TIP➜ Ride early or line up while waiting for your Fastpass appointment for DINOSAUR.

On Asia's Expedition Everest, you'll chug, twist, turn, and plunge up, through, and down Mt. Everest on nearly a mile of track. Oh, yeah, and beware of the yeti!

ASIA

Meant to resemble a rural village somewhere in Asia, this land is full of remarkable rain-forest scenery and ruins. Groupings of trees grow from a crumbling tiger shrine, and two massive towers—representing Thailand and Nepal—are the habitat for two families of gibbons, whose hooting fills the air.

Fodor'sChoice★
Duration
2½ mins.
Crowds
Huge
Audience
All but Small Kids

Expedition Everest. At this park's wildest ride the story goes that a fierce yeti guards the route to Mt. Everest. Of course, you're willing to risk running across the big guy in your roller-coaster quest to reach the summit. So, you board an "aging," seemingly innocuous, 34-passenger, steam-engine train into the mountains. You roll past bamboo forests, waterfalls, and glacier fields as you climb higher through snowcapped peaks. Suddenly the train becomes a runaway, barreling forward then backward around icy ledges and through dark snowy caverns.

Nearly a mile of twists and turns cut through the dark mountain, and at one point your train plunges a harrowing 80 feet. Will you find the yeti? Do you even want to? Well, what's a Disney ride without a mammoth, lifelike, Audio-Animatronics monster? (Spoiler alert: this train changes course and drops backward for a short leg, causing some riders temporary discomfort). Buildings in the line look like Himalayan mountain dwellings and teem with things like prayer flags, totems, and other artifacts from Tibet, Nepal, and the entire region.

Since the coaster is supposed to be less intense than, say, Space Mountain, brave children who meet the 44-inch minimum-height requirement can ride. Pregnant women or guests with back, neck, or heart problems

The silverback gorilla is the dominant male and leader of its troop, which is what a group of gorillas is called.

shouldn't ride. **For people with disabilities:** You must transfer from your wheelchair to a ride vehicle. No service animals. ■TIP➜ Unless you prefer to see the animals first, rush here as soon as the park opens and the wait isn't too long. Otherwise, grab a Fastpass.

☆☆
Duration
25 mins.
Crowds
Light
Audience
All Ages

Flights of Wonder. This outdoor show area near the border with Africa has spectacular demonstrations of skill by falcons, hawks, and other rare birds, which swoop down over the audience. Twenty species of birds are part of the show, including the bald eagle. **For people with disabilities:** Wheelchair accessible. Sign-language interpretation sometimes offered. Equipped for assisted-listening devices. ■TIP➜ Arrive 15 minutes before showtime and find a shaded seat beneath one of the awnings—the sun can be brutal in summer.

☆☆
Duration
7 mins.
Crowds
Heavy
Audience
**All but Small
Kids**

Kali River Rapids. Asia's thrilling water adventure ride mixes the fun of a rafting experience with a solemn message to save pristine lands and animal habitats that are threatened by development. Aboard a round raft that seats 12, you run the Chakranadi River. After passing through a huge bamboo tunnel filled with jasmine-scented mist, your raft climbs 40 feet upriver, lurches and spins through sharp twists and turns, and then approaches an immense waterfall, which curtains a giant carved tiger face. Past rain forests and temple ruins, you find yourself face-to-face with the denuded slope of a logged-out woodland burning out of control. There are many more thrills, but why spill the beans?

You will get wet. Actually, there's an 80% chance you will get soaked. Unless you want to wring out your clothing in the nearest restroom afterward (we heard one cast member advise a very wet rider to head to a restroom and dry his wet underwear beneath a hand dryer), bring a poncho. Better yet, bring a change of clothing in a plastic bag. The ride-height minimum is 38 inches. If you are pregnant or have heart, back, neck, or motion-sickness problems, sit this one out. **For people with disabilities:** Guests using wheelchairs must transfer to a ride raft. Equipped for assisted-listening devices. No service animals. ■ TIP➔ Use Fastpass, or come during the parade.

☆☆☆
Duration
Up to You
Crowds
Light
Audience
All Ages

Maharajah Jungle Trek. Get an up-close view of some unusual animals along this trail: a Komodo dragon perched on a rock; Malayan tapirs near a wooden footbridge; giant fruit bats that hang to munch fruit from wires and fly very close to the open and glass-protected viewing areas; and Bengal tigers in front of a maharajah's palace ruins. The tigers have their own view (with no accessibility, of course) of Asian deer and black buck, an antelope species. At the end of the trek, you walk through an aviary with a lotus pool. Disney interpreters, many from Asian countries, are on hand to answer questions. **For people with disabilities:** Wheelchair accessible. Guests with service animals should check with a host before entering the aviary. ■ TIP➔ Come anytime. Crowds stay fairly light, as people are constantly on the move.

AFRICA

This largest of the lands is an area of forests and grasslands, predominantly an enclave for wildlife from the continent. Harambe, on the northern bank of Discovery River, is Africa's starting point. Inspired by several East African coastal villages, this Disney town has so much detail that it's mind-boggling to try to soak it all up. Signs on the apparently peeling stucco walls of the buildings are faded, as if bleached by the sun, and everything has a hot, dusty look.

For souvenirs with both Disney and African themes, browse through the Mombasa Marketplace and Ziwani Traders. Safari apparel, decorative articles for the home, South African wines, and jewelry make souvenir shopping more fun.

■ NEED A
BREAK?

The tantalizing aroma of fresh-baked cinnamon buns leads to the **Kusafiri Coffee Shop & Bakery**, where, after just one look, you may give in to the urge. These buns are worth the banknotes, and they pair well with a cappuccino or espresso. Kids may opt for a giant cookie and milk.

Fodor'sChoice★
Duration
20 mins.
Crowds
Moderate to
Heavy
Audience
All Ages

Kilimanjaro Safaris. A giant Imagineered baobab tree is the starting point for this adventure into the up-country. Although re-creating an African safari in the United States isn't a new idea, this safari goes a step beyond merely allowing you to observe rhinos, hippos, antelope, wildebeests, giraffes, zebras, elephants, lions, and the like. There are illustrated game-spotting guides above the seats in the open-air safari vehicles, and as you lurch and bump over some 100 acres of savanna, forest, rivers, and rocky hills, you'll see most of these animals—sometimes so close you feel like you could reach out and touch them. It's easy to suspend disbelief here because the landscape is so effectively modeled and replenished by Disney horticulturists.

7

This being a theme park, dangers lurk in the form of ivory poachers, and it suddenly becomes your mission to save a group of elephants from would-be poachers. Even without the scripted peril, there's enough elephant excitement on the savanna to impress everyone. In the past several years four baby elephants have been born here. The first, a male calf named Tufani, born May 22, 2003, is the fourth surviving elephant calf in North America resulting from artificial insemination. The second, a female named Kianga, arrived July 6, 2004, as part of the park's breeding program coordinated by the American Zoo and Aquarium Association. On December 19, 2005, the 233-pound female calf Nadirah was born, and a male calf named Tsavo arrived June 28, 2008. Other babies born at the park and thriving in their habitats are a white rhinoceros, a giraffe, and a gorilla.

Parents can hold small tykes and explain the poacher fantasy. The ride is very bumpy and should be avoided by expectant guests or those with heart, back, or neck problems. **For people with disabilities:** Wheelchair accessible, but ECV users must transfer to standard wheelchairs. Equipped for assisted-listening and handheld- or video-captioning devices. Guests with service animals should check with a host for boarding information. ■TIP→ Come first thing in the morning, using Fastpass if necessary. Otherwise come at day's end, when it isn't so hot, and you'll probably see about the same number of animals as in early morning.

☆☆☆
Duration
Up to You
Crowds
Moderate to
Heavy
Audience
All Ages

Pangani Forest Exploration Trail. Calling this a nature walk doesn't really do it justice. A path winds through dense foliage, alongside streams, and past waterfalls. En route there are viewing points where you can watch a beautiful rare okapi (a member of the giraffe family) munching the vegetation, a family and a separate bachelor group of lowland gorillas, hippos (which you usually can see underwater), comical meerkats (a kind of mongoose), graceful gerenuk (an African antelope), exotic birds, an antelope species called the yellow-backed duiker, and a bizarre colony of hairless mole rats. Native African interpreters are at many viewing points to answer questions. **For people with disabilities:** Wheelchair accessible. Guests with service animals should check with a host before entering. ■TIP→ Come while awaiting a safari Fastpass appointment; avoid coming at the hottest time of day, when the gorillas like to nap.

7

RAFIKI'S PLANET WATCH

☆☆☆
Duration
Up to You
Crowds
Moderate
Audience
All Ages

Rafiki's Planet Watch. Take a five-minute *Wildlife Express* steam-train ride to the center of a unique center of eco-awareness named for the wise baboon from *The Lion King*. Rafiki's Planet Watch is divided into three sections. At the Conservation Station you can meet animal experts and gather round for a critter encounter, enjoy interactive exhibits, learn about worldwide efforts to protect endangered species and their habitats, and find out ways to connect with conservation efforts in your own community.

At the Habitat Habit! section, cotton-top tamarins (small white-headed monkeys) play while you learn how to live with all earth's animals. And

ANIMAL KINGDOM

NAME	Height Req.	Type of Entertainment	Duration	Crowds	Audience	Tips
Africa						
★ Kilimanjaro Safaris	n/a	Tour	20 mins.	Moderate to Heavy	All Ages	Do this first thing in the morning. If you arrive at the park late morning, save it for day's end, when it's not so hot.
Pangani Forest Exploration Trail	n/a	Zoo/Aviary	Up to you	Light	All Ages	Come while waiting for your safari Fastpass; try to avoid coming at the hottest time of day, when the gorillas like to nap.
Asia						
★ Expedition Everest	At least 44"	Thrill Ride	2½ mins.	Huge	All but Small Kids	Use Fastpass. This is the park's biggest thrill ride.
Flights of Wonder	n/a	Show	30 mins.	Light	All Ages	Arrive 15 mins. before showtime, and find a shaded seat beneath one of the awnings—the sun can be brutal.
Kali River Rapids	At least 38"	Thrill Ride	7 mins.	Heavy	All but Small Kids	Use your Fastpass or come during the parade. You'll get wet.
Maharajah Jungle Trek	n/a	Zoo/Aviary	Up to you	Light	All Ages	Come anytime.
Camp Minnie-Mickey						
★ Festival of the Lion King	n/a	Show	28 mins.	Light	All Ages	Arrive 40 mins. before showtime. Sit in one of the front rows to increase your kid's chance of being chosen.
DinoLand U.S.A.						
Boneyard	n/a	Playground	Up to you	Moderate to Heavy	Small Kids	Play here while waiting for DINOSAUR Fastpass, or come late in the day.
DINOSAUR	At least 40"	Thrill Ride	4 mins.	Heavy	All but Small Kids	Come first thing in the morning or at the end of the day, or use Fastpass.

★ Finding Nemo–The Musical	n/a	Show	30 mins.	Heavy	All Ages	Arrive 40 mins. before showtime. Take little kids here while big kids wait for Expedition Everest.
Fossil Fun Games	n/a	Arcade/Fair	Up to you	Light	All but Small Kids	Bring a pocketful of change and a stash of ones.
Primeval Whirl	At least 48"	Thrill Ride	2½ mins.	Heavy	All Ages	Kids may want to ride twice. Take your first spin early, then use Fastpass if the wait is more than 20 mins.
TriceraTop Spin	n/a	Thrill Ride for Kids	2 mins.	Heavy	Small Kids	Ride early while everyone else heads for the safari or while waiting for your Fastpass appointment for DINOSAUR.

Discovery Island

★ Tree of Life—It's Tough to Be a Bug!	n/a	3-D Film	20 mins.	Moderate to Heavy	All but Small Kids	Do this after Kilimanjaro Safaris. Fastpass is available. Small children may be frightened.

Rafiki's Planet Watch

Rafiki's Planet Watch	n/a	Walk-Through/Zoo/Aviary	Up to you	Moderate	All Ages	Come in the late afternoon after you've hit all key attractions.
Wildlife Express Train	n/a	Train Ride	5 mins.	Moderate	All Ages	Head straight to Affection Section with little kids to come face-to-face with domesticated critters.

★ = **Fodor's**Choice

ANIMAL KINGDOM KIDS TOUR

Animals fascinate young children, and the more unusual the critters are, the better. From naked mole rats to lowland gorillas, the diverse group at this park gives little ones lots to discover. When their attention wanes, you'll find plenty of kiddie diversions: animated-movie-themed stage shows, fun-filled rides, and one very imaginative playground.

IT'S A CREATURES GREAT AND SMALL WORLD

When you're traveling with young children, there's no better way to kick off a visit to this park than with a ride aboard **Kilimanjaro Safaris.** The animal poaching story that's part of the ride is a teachable moment for schoolchildren. Even if your kids are too young to appreciate the conservation message, they'll enjoy seeing hippos, rhinos, crocodiles, giraffes, zebras, wildebeests, and elephants.

When you disembark, go straight to **Pangani Forest Exploration Trail,** where kids can see the real meerkats behind the animated character Timon from *The Lion King.* Children flock to the glass-walled habitat where tiny naked mole rats scurry through tunnels.

Turn the kids loose on the **Maharajah Jungle Trek** in the park's Asia area to see a Komodo dragon, giant fruit bats, and Bengal tigers. Aviaries on both Pangani and Maharajah walks offer bird-spotting guides so your family can find and compare different species.

RIDE, PLAY, SEE A SHOW, MEET A MOUSE

If the kids meet height requirements (38 inches) and are ready for some adventure, head for **Kali River Rapids**—an exciting family raft ride. Steer smaller children toward **Dino-Land U.S.A.,** where they'll be happy whirling around TriceraTop Spin and exploring The Boneyard play maze with its cool slides and its climbing and sandy fossil-dig areas.

Break for lunch at Restaurantosaurus, and then head around the corner to **Finding Nemo—The Musical,** where kids love the character puppets and lively, Broadway-style music. Toddlers may use this stop to nap in your arms.

Afterward, a visit to **Camp Minnie-Mickey** is a must. You'll meet characters like Mickey or Chip 'n' Dale, and you can take in Festival of the Lion King, where several children get to join "animal" dancers for one show number.

BOARD A TRAIN, SAVE THE PLANET

Try to find time to board the Wildlife Express Train to **Rafiki's Planet Watch,** where the kids can see cotton-top tamarins and learn about taking care of the world's animals. You may be able to take part in a critter encounter with a Disney animal-care specialist at Conservation Station. The Affection Section petting yard is a comfortable place to meet domesticated animals from around the world.

Wrap up your day by celebrating good will toward all creatures in Discovery Island with **Mickey's Jammin' Jungle Parade,** a happy safari led by Disney characters, giant puppets, and lively music.

ANIMAL KINGDOM GROWN-UP TOUR

When the park first opened, Disney went to great marketing lengths to be sure visitors would know that this is "Nahtazu" (as in "not-a-zoo"). Adults and older children, especially, needed assurance that there was plenty to do besides see animals. And there is. Several thrill rides, a hilarious 3-D-and-special-effects-laden film, and two Broadway-style shows with animal and conservation themes can fill a memorable day.

ADVENTURE SEEKERS WANTED

If a trip to the Himalayas is on your wish list but your budget says "dream on," make a beeline for Asia and **Expedition Everest.** Rejoice if there's a wait for the attraction's high-speed train ride, because the queue snakes through authentic rammed-earth and stacked-stone buildings of a Himalayan village, where museum-quality artifacts from Nepal and Tibet are worth browsing. While in Asia, pile into a **Kali River Rapids** raft for a white-water ride on the park's Chakranadi River.

Time travel back to **Dinoland U.S.A.** for a DINOSAUR journey through a primeval forest and white-knuckle encounters with carnivorous creatures like the razor-toothed carnotaurus, a swooping pterodactyl, and other menacing creatures of prehistoric doom.

If it's a cool day, the park's animals should be active, so head to Africa. Your **Kilimanjaro Safaris** open-air journey is a bumpy 20-minute quest for exotic-animal sightings, and you won't be disappointed.

EAT, SHOP, LAUGH

Lunch can be an adventure, too, at **Tusker House Restaurant** in Africa, where a colorful buffet of vegetables and carved meats is enhanced with African-inspired chutneys, hummus, spiced tandoori tofu and couscous salad. You can even choose from a by-the-glass list of South African wines that complement the flavors.

Burn the calories during a shopping excursion to **Mombasa Marketplace,** where you can buy a bottle of that wine you loved or pick up a unique basket crafted with colorful telephone wires by Zulu artisans. Onward to Discovery Island for a stroll along Discovery Island Trails into the Tree of Life show **It's Tough to Be a Bug!** Expect to laugh a lot.

DISCOVER ANIMAL ATTRACTION

Along the **Pangani Forest Exploration Trail,** you can view gorillas through a glassed-in area, but you can also observe them from a bridge as these magnificent primates move among the rocks and lush greenery.

Even though you feel safe from Bengal tigers on the **Maharajah Jungle Trek,** several raised viewing spots offer clear views with no glass or fence to mar your photos. Habitat backdrops like the Maharajah palace ruins create scenic props.

Before your day comes to a close, catch a **Flights of Wonder** performance to see hawks, eagles, and other imposing birds as they exhibit natural behaviors. If you can only squeeze in one live show, choose to take in the beautiful dance moves of "animal" performers at **Festival of the Lion King**.

7

you don't have to be a kid to enjoy the Affection Section, where young children and adults who are giving their inner child free rein get face-to-face with goats and some rare domesticated critters from around the world. **For people with disabilities:** Wheelchair users can board the Wildlife Express train to Rafiki's Planet Watch, but will need their chairs to get from the train stop to the station. Equipped for assisted-listening devices. No service animals in the Affection Section animal petting area. ■ TIP→ Crowds get heavy mid-morning. Go in late afternoon if you've hit all key attractions.

CAMP MINNIE-MICKEY

This Adirondacks-style land is the setting for live performances of the Festival of the Lion King. It's also the place to meet the Disney characters when they gather for autographs and photo ops at four meet-and-greet trails.

Fodor'sChoice★
Duration
28 mins.
Crowds
Light
Audience
All Ages

Festival of the Lion King. If you think you've seen enough *Lion King* to last a lifetime, you're wrong, unless you've seen this show. In the air-conditioned theater-in-the-round, Disney presents a delightful tribal celebration of song, dance, and acrobatics that uses huge moving stages and floats. The show's singers are first-rate; lithe dancers wearing exotic animal-theme costumes portray creatures in the wild. Timon, Pumba, and other Lion King stars have key roles. **For people with disabilities:** The theater is accessible to people in wheelchairs. Sign-language interpretation is sometimes offered. Equipped for assisted-listening and handheld-captioning devices. ■ TIP→ Arrive 40 minutes before showtime. If you have a child who might want to go on stage, sit up front to increase his or her chance of getting chosen.

ANIMAL KINGDOM SPECTACLE

☆☆☆
Duration
12 mins.
Crowds
Heavy
Audience
All Ages

Mickey's Jammin' Jungle Parade. The parade takes off between 4 and 5 PM daily (times may vary, so check *Times Guide*) on a route beginning at the Kilimanjaro Safaris entrance and continuing around Discovery Island with a "characters on safari" theme. Rafiki in his adventure Rover, Goofy in a safari jeep, and Mickey in his Bon Voyage caravan join other popular characters each day for all the fanfare. Adding to the pomp are oversize puppets—snakes, giraffes, frogs, tigers, monkeys, and others—created by famed designer Michael Curry, known for the puppet costumes of Broadway's *The Lion King*. For good measure, Disney throws in some fanciful "party-animal" stilt walkers and animal rickshaws carrying VIPs or lucky park guests. **For people with disabilities:** Guests using wheelchairs should ask a cast member for best viewing location. ■ TIP→ As this is one of Disney's most creative parades, try not to miss it. Choose your spot along the parade route early.

Blizzard Beach and Typhoon Lagoon

WORD OF MOUTH

"Both Typhoon Lagoon or Blizzard Beach have good slides, but Blizzard Beach has the tallest and fastest. . . . Both have nice kiddie sections. If you're really into wave pools and lounging then Typhoon Lagoon is best; its wave pool has a sand beach. . . ."

—spirobulldog

DISNEY WATER PARKS PLANNER

Parks Information	Typhoon Lagoon Amenities

You can either take WDW bus transportation or drive to the water parks. There's no charge to park your car at either. Once inside, your options are to walk, swim, or slide.

During the off-season between October and April, each park closes for several weeks for routine maintenance and refurbishment. Call **WDW Information** (☎ 407/824–4321) or check *disneyworld.com*'s park calendars for days of operation.

The staff at **Typhoon Lagoon's Guest Services** (aka Information) window outside the entrance turnstiles, to your left, can answer many questions; a chalkboard inside gives water temperature and surfing information.

Disney staffers at **Blizzard Beach's Guest Services** window, to the left of the ticket booth as you enter the park, can answer most of your questions.

Dining: Picnicking is permitted, but coolers too large for one person to carry, glass containers, and alcoholic beverages not bought in the park are forbidden. There are tables at Getaway Glen; Typhoon Tilly's, near Shark Reef; and at pavilions across the park. You can always fork out $40 a day for a reserved spot at Getaway Glen. You get chairs an umbrella and small table, and four beach towels. Arrive early, though, and you can stake out a great spot for free.

Park eateries and food stands have salads, burgers, pizza, or other treats. One popular snack is a carton of hot mini-donuts with warm chocolate, vanilla, or strawberry dipping sauce from the Donut Hut.

Dressing Rooms and Lockers: There are thatched-roof dressing rooms and lockers to the right on your way into the park. It costs $8 a day to rent a small locker and $10 for a large one; there's also a $5 deposit. There are restrooms in every nook and cranny. Most have showers and are much less crowded than the dressing rooms. If you forgot your towel, rent ($2) or buy one at Singapore Sal's.

First-Aid: The small First-Aid Stand, run by a registered nurse, is on your left as you enter the park.

Lost People and Things: Ask about your misplaced people and things at the Guest Services window near the entrance turnstiles. Lost children are taken to an area by the Tip Board near the front of the park, where Disney cast members entertain them with games.

Private Patios: The park has seven premium, roped-off Beachcomber Shacks (patios, really) that groups of as many as six can rent. They generally offer both shade and sun as well as plush loungers and other chairs, a table with an umbrella, and an ice chest with two bottles of water per guest (up to six). Each guest also gets two beach towels and a refillable soft-drink mug. The whole group gets a locker to share and an attendant who will take and deliver food orders (cost of meals not included). The patios cost $250 March through October and $150 the rest of the year. Reserve (☎ 407/939–7529) well in advance or arrive very early to book one at High 'N Dry. In summer, any patio that isn't prebooked sells out within a half hour of the park opening.

Blizzard Beach Amenities

Dining: You can't bring oversize coolers, glass containers, or your own alcoholic beverages into the park. Picnicking is welcome, however, and there are several pleasant pavilions and other spots, most notably the terrace outside Lottawatta Lodge. This is also where you can reserve your own picnic spot ($40 for a day), which includes chairs (two of them loungers), an umbrella and small table, and four beach towels. Arrive early enough, and you'll snag a spot for free.

You can get burgers, hot dogs, and salads at Lottawatta Lodge or other eateries and food stands. You could go for the usual snacks—snowballs or ice cream. But a truly sublime nibble is the melt-in-your-mouth mini donut from the Mini Donuts stand across from Lottawatta Lodge.

Dressing Rooms and Lockers: Dressing rooms, showers, and restrooms are in the Village area, just inside the main entrance. There are other restrooms in Lottawatta Lodge, at the Ski Patrol Training Camp, and just past the Melt-Away Bay beach area.

Lockers are near the entrance, next to Snowless Joe's Rentals, and near Tike's Peak (the children's area and the most convenient if you have little swim-skiers in tow). It costs $8 to rent a small locker, $10 for a large one, and there's a $5 deposit. Note that there are only small lockers at Tike's Peak. The towels for rent ($2) at Snowless Joe's are tiny. If you forgot yours, you're better off buying a proper one at the Beach Haus.

First-Aid: The First-Aid Stand, overseen by a registered nurse, is in the Village, between Lottawatta Lodge and the Beach Haus.

Lost People and Things: Instruct youngsters to let a lifeguard know if they get lost. The Lost Children station is beneath a large beach umbrella near the front of the park. And don't worry about the kids—a Disney cast member will keep them busy with activities.

Private Patios: The park has six Polar Patios to rent to groups of as many as six people. For $250 a day in peak season (usually March through Labor Day) and $150 off-peak, you get plush loungers, chairs, a table with umbrella, refillable beverage mugs, an ice chest with two water bottles per person, a group locker, and an attendant who will take your orders for and deliver lunch and snacks (food costs extra). It's best to book a patio ahead of time (☎ *407/939–7529*). If you arrive early enough, there might be an open patio; check at the Shade Shack.

For People with Disabilities

At **Typhoon Lagoon** the paths connecting the different areas are wheelchair accessible, but most of the waterslides are not. There is, however, an elevator that takes you to the loading zone of the Crush 'N' Gusher water coaster. If you transfer from your chair to a raft or inner tube, you can float in Typhoon Lagoon Surf Pool or Castaway Creek.

Wheelchairs—a few built to go into the water—are available at the entrance turnstile area and are free with ID.

Most of **Blizzard Beach**'s paths are flat and level. If you can transfer from your chair a short distance, you can also access all the waterslides except Summit Plummet. Or settle into a large inner tube and float in Cross Country Creek.

A limited number of wheelchairs—some suitable for the water—are available near the park entrance and are free if you leave an ID.

8

DISNEY WATER PARKS
RIDE THE WAVES

There's something about a water park that brings out the kid in us, and there's no denying that these are two of the world's best. What sets them apart? It's the same thing that differentiates all Disney parks—the detailed themes.

Whether you're cast away on a balmy island at Typhoon Lagoon or washed up on a ski resort–turned–seaside playground at Blizzard Beach, the landscaping and clever architecture will add to the fun of flume and raft rides, wave pools, and splash areas. Another plus: the vegetation has matured enough to create shade. The Disney water parks give you that lost-in-paradise feeling on top of all those high-speed wedgie-inducing waterslides. They're so popular that crowds often reach overflow capacity in summer.

Your children may like them so much that they'll clamor to visit more than once. If you're going to Disney for five days or more between April and October, add the Water Park Fun & More option to your Magic Your Way ticket. Of course, check the weather to make sure the temperatures are to your liking for running around in a swimsuit.

SUPPLIES

Typhoon Lagoon: You can get inner tubes at Castaway Creek and inner tubes, rafts, or slide mats at the rides. Borrow snorkel gear at **Shark Reef** (your own isn't allowed) and life vests at **High 'N Dry.** Near the main entrance is **Singapore Sal's,** where you can pick up free life jackets, buy sundries, and rent (or buy) towels and lockers.

Blizzard Beach: Get free life vests or rent towels and lockers at **Snowless Joe's.** Inner tubes, rafts, and slide mats are provided at the rides. Buy beach gear or rent towels or lockers at **Beach Haus. Shade Shack** is the place for a new pair of sunglasses.

WHAT TO EXPECT

Most people agree that kids under 7 and older adults prefer Typhoon Lagoon. Bigger kids and teens like Blizzard Beach better because it has more slides and big-deal rides. Indeed, devoted waterslide enthusiasts generally prefer Blizzard Beach to other water parks.

TYPHOON LAGOON

You can speed down waterslides with names like Crush 'N' Gusher and Humunga Kowabunga or bump through rapids and falls at Mt. Mayday. You can also bob along in 5-foot waves in a surf pool the size of two football fields, or, for a mellow break, float in inner tubes along the 2,100-foot Castaway Creek. Go snorkeling in Shark Reef, rubberneck as fellow human cannonballs are ejected from the Storm Slides, or hunker down in a hammock or lounge chair and read a book. Ketchakiddie Creek for young children replicates adult rides on a smaller scale. It's Disney's version of a day at the beach—complete with friendly Disney lifeguards.

BLIZZARD BEACH

Disney Imagineers have gone all out here to create the paradox of a ski resort in the midst of a tropical lagoon. Lots of verbal puns and sight gags play with the snow-in-Florida motif. The centerpiece is Mt. Gushmore, with its 120-foot-high Summit Plummet. Attractions have names like Teamboat Springs, a white-water raft ride. Themed speed slides include Toboggan Racer, Slush Gusher, and Snow Stormers. Between Mt. Gushmore's base and its summit, swim-skiers can also ride a chairlift converted from ski-resort to beach-resort use—with multihued umbrellas and snow skis on their undersides.

VISITING TIPS

■ In summer, come first thing in the morning (early birds can ride several times before the lines get long), late in the afternoon when park hours run later, or when the weather clears after a thunder-shower (rainstorms drive away crowds). Afternoons are also good in cooler weather, as the water is a bit warmer. To make a whole day of it, avoid weekends, when locals and visitors pack in.

■ Women and girls should wear one-piece swimsuits unless they want to find their tops somewhere around their ears at the bottom of the waterslide.

■ Invest in sunscreen and water shoes. Plan to slather sunscreen on several times throughout the day. An inexpensive pair of water shoes will save tootsies from hot sand and walkways and from grimy restroom floors.

■ Arrive 30 minutes before opening so you can park, buy tickets, rent towels, and snag inner tubes before the crowds descend, and, trust us, it gets very crowded.

By Jennie Hess
Updated by
Nathan Benjamin and Sam Benjamin

The beauty of Disney's water parks is that you can make either experience fit your mood. Like crowds? Head for the lounge chairs along the Wave Pool at Typhoon Lagoon or Melt-Away Bay at Blizzard Beach. Prefer peace? Walk past lush foliage along each park's circular path until you spot a secluded lean-to or tree-shaded patch of sand.

According to Disney legend, Typhoon Lagoon was created when the lush Placid Palms Resort was struck by a cataclysmic storm. It left a different world in its wake: surfboards sundered trees, once-upright palms imitated the Leaning Tower of Pisa, and part of the original lagoon was cut off, trapping thousands of tropical fish—and a few sharks. Nothing, however, topped the fate of *Miss Tilly*, a shrimp boat from "Safen Sound, Florida," which was hurled high in the air and became impaled on Mt. Mayday, a magical volcano that periodically tries to dislodge *Miss Tilly* with huge geysers.

Ordinary folks, the legend continues, would have been crushed by such devastation. But the resourceful residents of Placid Palms were made of hardier stuff—and from the wreckage they created 56-acre Typhoon Lagoon, the self-proclaimed "world's ultimate water park."

With its oxymoronic name, Blizzard Beach promises the seemingly impossible—a seaside playground with an alpine theme. As with its older cousin, Typhoon Lagoon, Disney Imagineers have created a legend to explain the park's origin: after a freak winter storm dropped snow over the western side of Walt Disney World, entrepreneurs created Florida's first downhill ski resort. Sauna-like temperatures soon returned. But as the 66-acre resort's operators were ready to close up shop, they spotted a playful alligator sliding down the 120-foot-tall "liquid ice" slopes. The realization that the melting snow had created the world's tallest, fastest, and most exhilarating water-filled ski and toboggan runs gave birth to the ski resort–water park.

From its imposing ski-jump tower to its 1,200-foot series of rushing waterfalls, Blizzard Beach delivers cool fun even in the hot summertime. Where else can you wear your bikini on the slopes?

TYPHOON LAGOON

The layout is so simple. The wave and swimming lagoon is at the park's center. Note that the waves are born in the Mt. Mayday side and break on the beaches closest to the entrance. Any attraction requiring a gravitational plunge starts around the summit of Mt. Mayday. Shark Reef and Ketchakiddie Creek flank the head of the lagoon, to Mt. Mayday's right and left, respectively, as you enter. The Crush 'N' Gusher water coaster is due right of Singapore Sal's.

☆☆
Duration
Up to You
Crowds
Light to Moderate
Audience
Small Kids

Bay Slides. Kids scramble up several steps tucked between faux-rock formations where a lifeguard sits to supervise their slide into Blustery Bay. The incline is small, but the thrill is great for young kids who whoosh into the bay (sometimes into the arms of waiting parents). These scaled-down versions of the Storm Slides are geared to kids shorter than 60 inches. ■TIP➔ Kids really burn up energy going up the steps and down the slides repeatedly. Parents should be prepared for their wanting to ride over and over and over again. . . .

☆☆☆
Duration
Up to 20 mins.
Crowds
Vary by Season
Audience
All Ages

Castaway Creek. This circular, 15-foot-wide, 3-foot-deep waterway is chill. Snag an inner tube, and float along a creek that winds through the park and around the surf pool and beaches. You pass through a rain forest that showers you with spray, you slide through caves and grottoes, you float by overhanging trees and flowering bushes, and you get dumped on at the Water Works with "broken" pipes. The current flows a gentle 2½ feet per second; it takes about 20 minutes to make a full circuit. Along the way there are landing areas where you can hop in and out. **For people with disabilities:** Guests using wheelchairs must transfer to an inner tube. ■TIP➔ A full circuit takes about 20 minutes, longer if you stop at one of the five lifeguard-manned launches. If you want speed, just swim with the current.

Fodor's Choice★
Duration
1 min.
Crowds
Mod. to Heavy
Audience
Not Small Kids

Crush 'N' Gusher. If flume rides, storm slides, and tube races aren't wild enough for your inner thrill-seeker, get ready to defy gravity on Disney's first water coaster. Designed to propel you uphill and down along a series of flumes, caverns, and spillways, this ride should satisfy the most enthusiastic daredevil. Keeping with park lore, Crush 'N' Gusher flows through what appears to be a rusted-out tropical fruit factory, weaving in and out of the wreckage and debris that once transported fruit through the plant's wash facilities. Three fruit spillways are aptly named Banana Blaster, Coconut Crusher, and Pineapple Plunger. Note that this ride isn't appropriate for guests who are pregnant or who have heart, back, or neck problems. **For people with disabilities:** An elevator takes guests using wheelchairs to the loading area; there's a short distance between this area and the ride. ■TIP➔ Ride first thing in the morning, before lines get too long. And don't forget to say cheese for the cameras!

☆☆
Duration
1 min.
Crowds
Vary by Season
Audience
Not Small Kids

Gangplank Falls. Families who climb up Mt. Mayday for this ride are in for an adventure—in fact, more of an adventure than they might expect. Upon takeoff, a 6½-foot-long inflated raft plunges down the slide with impressive speed. It even gets quite bumpy at times along the 300-foot river. Not too scary for the tykes, and yet not a bore for parents, Gangplank Falls is great family fun! Family members who

8

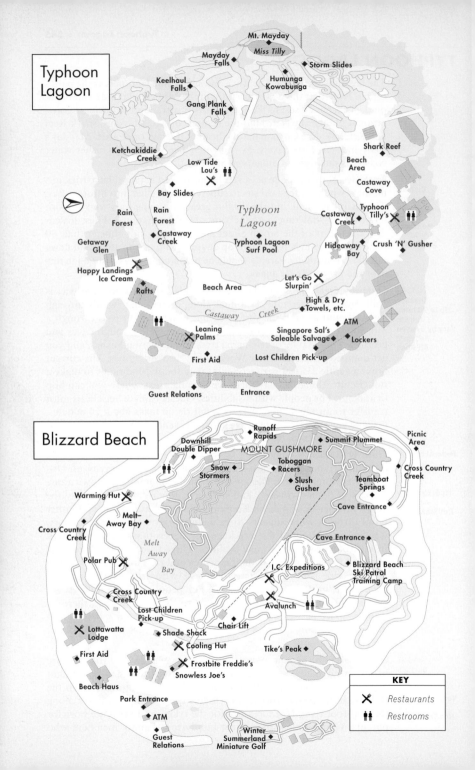

Typhoon Lagoon

Mt. Mayday
Miss Tilly
Mayday Falls
Storm Slides
Keelhaul Falls
Humunga Kowabunga
Gang Plank Falls
Shark Reef
Ketchakiddie Creek
Beach Area
Low Tide Lou's
Castaway Cove
Bay Slides
Typhoon Tilly's
Rain Forest
Rain Forest
Castaway Creek
Typhoon Lagoon
Getaway Glen
Castaway Creek
Typhoon Lagoon Surf Pool
Hideaway Bay
Crush 'N' Gusher
Happy Landings Ice Cream
Rafts
Let's Go Slurpin'
Beach Area
Castaway Creek
High & Dry Towels, etc.
Leaning Palms
ATM
Singapore Sal's Saleable Salvage
Lockers
First Aid
Lost Children Pick-up
Guest Relations
Entrance

Blizzard Beach

Runoff Rapids
Picnic Area
Downhill Double Dipper
Summit Plummet
MOUNT GUSHMORE
Snow Stormers
Toboggan Racers
Cross Country Creek
Warming Hut
Slush Gusher
Teamboat Springs
Cross Country Creek
Melt–Away Bay
Cave Entrance
Melt Away Bay
Cave Entrance
Polar Pub
Blizzard Beach Ski Patrol Training Camp
I.C. Expeditions
Cross Country Creek
Avalunch
Lost Children Pick-up
Chair Lift
Lottawatta Lodge
Shade Shack
Cooling Hut
Tike's Peak
First Aid
Frostbite Freddie's
Snowless Joe's
Beach Haus
Park Entrance
ATM
Winter Summerland Miniature Golf
Guest Relations

KEY	
✗	*Restaurants*
♟	*Restrooms*

are pregnant or have heart, back, or neck problems should sit this one out, though. ■ TIP→ The inner tubes are heavy, so be sure to have at least two willing carriers. Also, be prepared to ride with two to four riders (five if some are kids).

☆☆
Duration
4 secs.
Crowds
Heavy
Audience
Not Small Kids

Humunga Kowabunga. There's little time to scream, but you'll hear just such vociferous reactions as the survivors emerge from the catch pool opposite Shark Reef. The basic questions are: want to get scared out of your wits in four seconds flat—and did you like it enough to go back for more? The three side-by-side Humunga Kowabunga speed slides deserve acclaim among thrill lovers, as they drop more than 50 feet in a distance barely four times that amount. For non-mathematicians, that's very steep. Oh yes, and then you go through a cave. In the dark.

The average speed is 30 mph; however, you can really fly if you lie flat on your back, cross your ankles, wrap your arms around your chest, and arch your back. One caveat: the ride only lasts a few seconds— too short for us—and lines are often too long to re-queue for another plunge. Note that this ride isn't appropriate for guests who are pregnant or who have heart, back, or neck problems. ■ TIP→ Race against your friends or family; there are three slides at the top.

☆
Duration
1 min.
Crowds
Vary by Season
Audience
Not Small Kids

Keelhaul Falls. Do you need to chill out after the Mach 5 speeds of Humunga Cowabunga? Then venture up to Keelhaul Falls, a laid-back trip down the left side of Mt. Mayday. Just kick back and relax as your blue tube cruises down the 400-foot slide and splashes into the pool below. Keelhaul feels a little slow if you ride it right after Mayday Falls, so thrill-seekers may be disappointed. Yet its winding path and scenic descent make for a satisfying ride. Note that this ride isn't appropriate for guests who are pregnant or who have heart, back, or neck problems. ■ TIP→ Ride before or after Mayday Falls.

☆☆☆
Duration
Up to You
Crowds
Light
Audience
Small Kids

Ketchakiddie Creek. Typhoon Lagoon's play area for young children has slides, mini-rapids, faux sand castles, squirting whales and seals, bouncing barrels, waterfalls, sprinklers, and all the other ingredients of a splash fiesta. The bubbling sand ponds, where youngsters can sit in what seems like an enormous whirlpool bath, are special favorites. Little ones also love the tiny-scale tube ride.

Small water canons let kids engage in water-spray wars, and leaky pipes overhead shower kids who duck in and out. Families can camp beneath lots of shady lean-tos when not in the water. Note that on this ride adults must be accompanied by a child or children under 48" and vice versa. **For people with disabilities:** Accessible for people using water-appropriate wheelchairs. ■ TIP→ Parents can take turns watching the kiddies here and riding the thrill slides.

☆☆
Duration
1 min.
Crowds
Vary by Season
Audience
Not Small Kids

Mayday Falls. The 460-foot slide over Mayday Falls in bright yellow inner tubes is the longest and bumpiest of the three falls. It's a long trek up to Mayday falls—even higher than Keelhaul—but the increased speed and longer descent are well worth the climb. It's a relatively straight slide over the falls into a catchment, but it's not as thrilling as the up-and-down water jets on the Crush 'N' Gusher. Note that this ride isn't appropriate for guests who are pregnant or who have heart, back, or neck problems. ■ TIP→ While you're in the neighborhood, ride Keelhaul Falls too.

☆☆
Duration
Up to You
Crowds
Heavy
Audience
Not Small Kids

Shark Reef. If you felt like leaping onto the stage at the Studios' Voyage of the Little Mermaid or jumping into the tank at Epcot's the Seas with Nemo & Friends, make tracks for this 360,000-gallon snorkeling tank. The coral reef is artificial, but the 4,000 tropical fish—including rainbow parrotfish, sting rays, trigger fish, yellowtail damselfish, and amiable leopard and bonnet-head sharks (only 2 to 3 feet long)—are quite real. A sunken ship divides the reef; its portholes give landlubbers access to the underwater scene, though the windows are filmy and viewing is a bit blurry.

During the warmest months (late March through September) adults and children ages 5 and older can rent personal supplied-air snorkeling equipment for $20. If you don't

> ### PARK VIEWS
>
> What goes down can also go up—and up and up. Climbing **Mt. Mayday** "[is] like climbing Mt. Everest," wailed one teenager about a climb that seems a lot steeper than an 85-foot peak should be. However, it's Mt. Everest with hibiscus flowers, a rope bridge, and stepping-stones set in plunging waters. The view encompasses the entire park. Lovers of white-water rafting should head to Mayday Falls, Keelhaul Falls, and Gangplank Falls at Mt. Mayday. These rides in oversize inner tubes plunge down the mountain's left side. They have caves, waterfalls, and intricate rockwork.

like the snorkeling gear, feel free to use goggles. Note that, to prevent algae growth, Shark Reef is kept at a brisk 72°F, which is about 15° cooler than the rest of Typhoon Lagoon. Also, for those who prefer a long, leisurely snorkel, this experience will be a bit too brief. **For people with disabilities:** The sunken-ship viewing area is wheelchair accessible.

■ TIP→ This is a popular attraction, so come early or late in the day. Even in the busy summer months, though, the wait is usually under 20 minutes.

☆☆☆
Duration
15–20 secs.
Crowds
Mod. to Heavy
Audience
Not Small Kids

Storm Slides. Each of these three body slides is about 300 feet long and snakes in and out of rock formations, through caves and tunnels, and under waterfalls, but each has a slightly different view and offers a twist. The one in the middle has the longest tunnel; the others' secrets you'll have to discover for yourself. Maximum speed is about 20 mph, and the trip takes about 30 seconds. Note that this ride isn't appropriate for guests who are pregnant or who have heart, back, or neck problems.

■ TIP→ Try each of the three slides for different twists.

Fodor's Choice★
Duration
Up to You
Crowds
Heavy
Audience
All Ages

Typhoon Lagoon Surf Pool. This is the heart of the park, a swimming area that spreads out over 2½ acres and contains almost 3 million gallons of clear, chlorinated water. It's scalloped by coves, bays, and inlets, all edged with white-sand beaches—spread over a base of white concrete, as bodysurfers soon discover when they try to slide into shore. Ouch! The waves are the draw. Twelve huge water-collection chambers hidden in Mt. Mayday dump their load with a resounding whoosh into trapdoors to create waves large enough for Typhoon Lagoon to host amateur and professional surfing championships.

A piercing double hoot from *Miss Tilly* (the boat that purportedly landed at Mount Gushmore at the park's highest level) signals the start and finish of wave action: every 2 hours, for 1½ hours, 5-foot waves issue

8

From the wreckage—like that shown here—in the wake of a storm, Placid Palms Resort residents created 56-acre Typhoon Lagoon. Or so the story goes....

forth every 90 seconds; the last half hour is devoted to moderate bobbing waves. Even during the big-wave periods, however, the waters in Blustery Bay and Whitecap Cove are protected. Surfers who don't want to risk a fickle ocean can surf here on certain days before the park opens. Instruction and soft-sided surfboard are included in the $150 cost, and the surfing experience (ages 8 and older) lasts for 2½ hours. Reserve your waves by calling ☎ 407/939–7529. **For people with disabilities:** Accessible for people using water-appropriate wheelchairs. ■ **TIP→** Waves come every 90 seconds if you want to time your bodysurfing.

NEED A BREAK? When you need to regain your energy, head to **Leaning Palms**, to your left as you enter the park, for popular beach fare—burgers, pizzas, turkey sandwiches, Asian salads, beer, and, of course, ice cream and frozen yogurt. For adults, **Let's Go Slurpin'** is a beach shack on the edge of Typhoon Lagoon that dispenses frozen margaritas as well as wine and beer. **Typhoon Tilly's,** on the right just south of Shark Reef, serves burgers, dogs, chicken-nugget baskets, pork sandwiches, and salads, and pours mostly sugary, nonalcoholic grog—though you can grab a Davy Jones lager if you must.

BLIZZARD BEACH

The park layout makes it fairly simple to navigate. Once you enter and rent a locker, you'll cross a small bridge over Cross Country Creek before choosing a spot to park your towels and cooler. To the left is the

Melt-Away Bay wave pool. Dead ahead you can see Mt. Gushmore, a chairlift to the top, and the park's many slopes and slides.

If thrills are your game, come early and line up for Summit Plummet, Slush Gusher, and Downhill Double Dipper before wait times go from light to moderate (or heavy). Anytime is a good time for a dip in Melt-Away Bay or a tube trip around Cross Country Creek. Parents with young children should claim their spot early at Tikes Peak to the park's right even before you cross the bridge.

☆
Duration
2 mins.
Crowds
Light to Moderate
Audience
Not Small Kids

Chair Lift. No subtropical skiing paradise would be complete without a chairlift, and this one is an attractive alternative to trekking to the top of Mt. Gushmore over and over again. Instead, sit back and relax as the summit of the mountain approaches. The two-minute ascent also is a great opportunity to scout out other slides, to do some people-watching, and to enjoy the whimsical "ski beach" scenery. Children must be at least 48 inches tall to ride alone or 32 inches tall to ride with an adult. **For people with disabilities:** Guests using wheelchairs can wheel up to the top but then must transfer to the rides. A companion will have to meet you with the wheelchair at the base of Mt. Gushmore. ■TIP→ If you want a shorter wait and don't mind being paired with a stranger, head for the single-riders line. If the wait is too long in either line, why not just hike up?

☆☆☆
Duration
Under 10 secs.
Crowds
Heavy
Audience
Not Small Kids

Downhill Double Dipper. If you're on your way to Snow Stormers or Toboggan Racers on the purple slopes, you may notice a cool-looking slide on the left. This is the Downhill Double Dipper, and it's well worth the stop. The best thing about this slide is that you are timed from blast off to finish line! Competition may get heated as kids vie for the glory of fastest speed slider, but even the least competitive will enjoy tearing down Mt. Gushmore in their racing tubes. Expectant mothers shouldn't ride, nor should guests with heart conditions or neck or back problems. **For people with disabilities:** Guests using wheelchairs must transfer to the tube-launch site. ■TIP→ Ride early; this popular purple-slope attraction gets crowded after lunch. (And, oh, yeah—our fastest time was 5.89 seconds—can you beat that?)

☆☆
Duration
Up to You
Crowds
Vary by Season
Audience
All Ages

Melt-Away Bay. The park's main pool is a 1-acre oasis that's constantly fed by "melting snow" waterfalls. The man-made waves are positively oceanlike. If you're not a strong swimmer, stay away from the far end of the pool, where the waves originate. You can get temporarily stuck in a pocket even if your head is still above water. If you prefer to stay beached, there are plenty of recliner chairs spread out around the bay. This is where moms and dads often relax and watch their kids swim in the lifeguard-protected waters. **For people with disabilities:** Guests using water-appropriate wheelchairs can enjoy shallow waters here. ■TIP→ Get an inner tube if you plan to venture to deeper waters, and arrive early if you want to find a shady spot (there are limited giant umbrellas).

Fodor's Choice★
Duration
15 secs.
Crowds
You Bet!
Audience
Not Small Kids

Slush Gusher. This speed slide, which drops through a snow-banked mountain gully next door to Summit Plummet on the green slopes, isn't quite as intimidating, but it's a real thriller nonetheless. Instead of one scream-inducing steep drop, the Slush Gusher features a fast, hilly descent to the base of Mt. Gushmore. While the Slush Gusher will not disappoint thrill-seekers, it is perfect for those who want some

8

DISNEY'S WATER PARKS

Typhoon Lagoon

Name	Height Req.	Type of Entertainment	Duration	Crowds	Audience	Tips
Bay Slides	Under 60"	Waterslide for Kids	Up to You	Light to Moderate	Small Kids	Parents: be prepared for your kids to ride again and again.
Castaway Creek	n/a	River/Stream Ride	Up to 20 mins.	Vary by Season	All Ages	Spend 20 mins. on a full, leisurely circuit or zoom along with the current.
★ Crush 'N' Gusher	At least 48"	Thrill Ride with Water	1 min.	Mod. to Heavy	Not Small Kids	Ride first thing in the morning to avoid long lines.
Gangplank Falls	n/a	Waterslide	1 min.	Vary by Season	Not Small Kids	It takes two people to carry the heavy inner tubes, and four or five to ride in them.
Humunga Kowabunga	At least 48"	Waterslide	4 secs.	Heavy	Not Small Kids	You can race friends or family as there are three slides here.
Keelhaul Falls	n/a	Waterslide	1 min.	Vary by Season	Not Small Kids	Ride before or after nearby Mayday Falls.
Ketchakiddie Creek	Under 48"	River/Stream Ride	Up to You	Light	Small Kids	Parents can take turns watching kiddies here and riding thrill slides elsewhere.
Mayday Falls	n/a	Waterslide	1 min.	Vary by Season	Not Small Kids	While you're in the neighborhood, ride Keelhaul Falls too.
Shark Reef	n/a	Pool Area; Aquarium	Up to You	Heavy	Not Small Kids	It's popular: come early or late, especially if you want to linger.
Storm Slides	n/a	Waterslide	15–20 secs.	Mod. to Heavy	Not Small Kids	Try each of the three slides for different twists.
★ Typhoon Lagoon Surf Pool	n/a	Wave Pool; Beach Area	Up to You	Heavy	All Ages	Time your bodysurfing to the waves, which come every 90 seconds.

Blizzard Beach

Attraction	Height	Type	Duration	Crowds	Ages	Notes
Chair Lift	At least 48" alone; 32" w/ an adult	Thrill Ride	2 mins.	Light to Moderate	Not Small Kids	Don't want to wait to get up Mt. Gushmore? Head for the single-rider line or just hike up.
Cross Country Creek	n/a	River/Stream Ride	25 mins.	Vary by Season	All Ages	This is the best way to get around the park!
Downhill Double Dipper	At least 48"	Waterslide	Under 10 secs.	Heavy	Not Small Kids	Ride early or face the postlunch crowds.
Melt-Away Bay	n/a	Wave Pool; Beach Area	Up to You	Vary by Season	All Ages	Arrive early to snag an umbrella (for shade) and an inner tube (for deeper waters).
Runoff Rapids	n/a	Waterslide	35 secs.	Light to Moderate	Not Small Kids	Be sure to try both slides.
Ski Patrol Training Camp	n/a	Waterslide; Thrill Ride with Water	Up to You	Light to Moderate	Not Small Kids	Hate lines? Come early or head to the zip-line drop or iceberg obstacle course.
★ Slush Gusher	At least 48"	Waterslide	15 secs.	You Bet!	Not Small Kids	Crowded days see 90-minute waits; come early.
Snow Stormers	n/a	Waterslide	20 secs.	Mod. to Heavy	All Ages	Hold on tight!
★ Summit Plummet	At least 48"	Waterslide	10 crazy secs.	Absolutely	Not Small Kids	Make your first stop! Summer afternoon waits can be two hours.
Teamboat Springs	n/a	River/Stream Ride	1½ mins.	Moderate	Families	There are no age or height requirements, tubes seat groups, and lines move fast.
★ Tike's Peak	48" and under	Pool Area	Up to You	Vary by Season	Small Kids	Adults must be accompanied by children no more than 48' tall!
Toboggan Racers	n/a	Waterslide/Game	10 secs.	Mod. to Heavy	Not Small Kids	It's more fun if you race.

adventure but tremble at the sight of Summit Plummet. For guests who are pregnant or who have heart, back, or neck problems, this ride is less than perfect. **For people with disabilities:** Guests using wheelchairs must transfer to the ride. ■TIP➜ The earlier you ride, the better. On crowded days waits last up to 90 minutes.

☆☆
Duration
20 secs.
Crowds
Mod. to Heavy
Audience
All Ages

Snow Stormers. No water park would be complete without a meandering waterslide, and Blizzard Beach has one. Here three flumes descend from the top of Mt. Gushmore along a switchback course of ski-type slalom gates on the purple slopes. Snow Stormers offers an exciting change of pace from the straight-down slides of the green slopes, and riders are in for a grand total of eight hairpin turns before finally splashing into the pool at the bottom. This ride isn't appropriate for guests who are pregnant or who have heart, neck, or back problems. **For people with disabilities:** Guests using wheelchairs must transfer to slide mat. ■TIP➜ Hold on tight!

Fodor's Choice★
Duration
10 crazy secs.
Crowds
Absolutely
Audience
Not Small Kids

Summit Plummet. This is Mt. Gushmore's big gun, which Disney bills as "the world's tallest, fastest free-fall speed slide." From Summit Plummet's "ski jump" tower at the very top of the green slopes, it's a wild 55-mph plunge straight down to a splash landing at the base of the mountain. It looks almost like a straight vertical drop, and you can't help but feel like a movie stunt double as you take the plunge. If you're watching from the beach below, you can't hear the yells of the participants, but you can bet many of them are screaming their heads off. As you probably guessed, this ride isn't appropriate for guests who are pregnant or who have heart, back, or neck problems. ■TIP➜ Make this one of your first stops. The line will only get longer as the day goes on. (Summer-afternoon waits can be up to two hours.)

☆☆
Duration
1½ mins.
Crowds
Moderate
Audience
Families

Teamboat Springs. Six-passenger rafts zip along green slopes in one of the world's longest family white-water raft rides. Since its original construction, it has doubled its speed of departure onto its twisting, 1,200-foot channel of rushing water, which ends with a refreshing waterfall dousing. This ride is a good place for kids too big for Tike's Peak to test more grown-up waters. Those seeking a speedier descent, however, may want to venture higher up Mt. Gushmore. And those who are pregnant or have heart, neck, or back problems should avoid this one. **For people with disabilities:** Guests using wheelchairs must transfer to the ride. ■TIP➜ This is an excellent ride for the whole family: there are no age or height requirements, tubes seat four to six people, and lines generally move quickly. On busy days, though, waits can be 30 to 45 minutes.

☆☆
Duration
10 secs.
Crowds
Mod. to Heavy
Audience
Not Small Kids

Toboggan Racers. Grab your mat, wait for the signal, and go. You and eight other racers whiz simultaneously down the watery trail on the purple slopes toward the finish line at the base of the mountain. The ride is especially fun if you are racing a group of friends, but it lacks the speed of single-rider green-slope rides like Slush Gusher. For a ride with both speed and friendly competition, check out the Downhill Double Dipper. Expectant mothers shouldn't ride Toboggan Racers, nor should guests with heart, neck, or back problems. **For people with disabilities:** Guests using wheelchairs must transfer to slide mats. ■TIP➜ It's more fun when you race family members or friends—up to eight people can ride at the same time.

NEED A BREAK?

Lottawatta Lodge—a North American ski lodge with a Caribbean accent—is the park's main emporium of fast food. Lines are long at peak feeding times. The **Warming Hut**, which is open seasonally, offers smoked turkey legs, salads, hot dogs, and ice cream. Hot dogs, snow cones, and ice cream are on the menu at **Avalunch**. **Frostbite Freddie's** and **Polar Pub** on the main beach both sell frozen drinks and spirits.

☆☆☆
Duration
Up to You
Crowds
Light to Moderate
Audience
Not Small Kids

Ski Patrol Training Camp. The preteens in your crowd may want to spend most of their time on the T-bar drop, bungee-cord slides, and culvert slides here. In addition, there's a chance to take on Mogul Mania, a wide open area where kids can jump from one slippery mogul to the next. The moguls really look more like baby icebergs bobbing in a swimming pool, and kids don't mind when they miss a berg and plop into the pool. **For people with disabilities:** Guests using water-appropriate wheelchairs can enjoy wading areas here. ■TIP➜ The optimum time to come is early in the day or after a thunderstorm, when crowds thin out. That said, lines are often short at the zip-line drop and the iceberg obstacle course.

☆☆
Duration
35 secs.
Crowds
Light to Moderate
Audience
Not Small Kids

Runoff Rapids. It's easy to overlook this three-track flume ride hidden on the far red slope of Mt. Gushmore. Yet if you have the courage to carry your tube all the way up to the top, you'll eventually come upon three twisting, turning flumes—even one that's in the dark (keep in mind the tunnel slide is single-riders only, while the open slide is for one- or two-passenger tubes). Once you're in, it's way more fun than scary. Still, guests who are pregnant or who have heart, neck, or back problems should skip this one. **For people with disabilities:** Guests using wheelchairs must transfer to inner tubes. ■TIP➜ It's worth riding both the open slide and the tunnel slide, but remember that the tunnel slide is only for single riders.

☆☆☆
Duration
25 mins.
Crowds
Vary by Season
Audience
All Ages

Cross Country Creek. Just grab an inner tube, hop on, and circle the entire park on this creek during a leisurely 25-minute float. Along the way, you'll get doused with frigid water in an ice cave—wonderful on a steamy Florida day. Tubes are provided at seven Creek launch sites, but they're not required. In fact, kids will soon discover that the fastest and most enjoyable way to get around the park is to glide with the current and hop off at whichever exit they wish. **For people with disabilities:** Guests using wheelchairs must transfer to inner tubes. ■TIP➜ There are exits near most thrill rides, and moving through the park this way is oodles more fun than walking.

Fodor's Choice★
Duration
Up to You
Crowds
Vary by Season
Audience
Small Kids

Tike's Peak. Disney never leaves the little ones out of the fun, and this junior-size version of Blizzard Beach, set slightly apart from the rest of the park, has scaled-down elements of Mt. Gushmore, with sand, slides (including one with tubes), faux snow drifts, and igloo-like tunnels. Kids love the whimsical gator fountains and pop jets. Parents can find sun or shade beneath lean-tos while watching over the little ones. Several lifeguards are on hand, but parents should still watch their little ones at all times. Adults must be accompanied by children no more than 48 inches tall. **For people with disabilities:** Guests using water-appropriate wheelchairs can enjoy the wading areas. ■TIP➜ Stake out lounge chairs early, especially for a shady spot. If your tykes don't swim well, get them fitted with a free life vest, and pull your chair up to the water's edge.

8

Part III:
Experience
Universal
Orlando

WELCOME TO UNIVERSAL ORLANDO

TOP REASONS TO GO

★ **More Than You Bargain For:** Universal Orlando is more than just a single Hollywood-themed amusement park; it's also Islands of Adventure theme park, the CityWalk entertainment complex; and the Hard Rock Hotel, Portofino Bay, and Royal Pacific resorts. Wet 'n Wild water park is also affiliated with Universal.

★ **Theme-Park Powerhouse:** Neither SeaWorld nor any of Disney's four theme parks can match the energy at Universal Studios and Islands of Adventure. Wild rides, clever shows, and an edgy attitude all push the envelope here.

★ **A New Experience:** If your Orlando vacations have been based primarily at Disney, Universal will help you expand your range. In time, it may even become your first stop.

★ **Party Central:** Throughout the year, Universal adds special events—Mardi Gras, Halloween Horror Nights, the Rock the Universe Christian-music celebration—to the calendar.

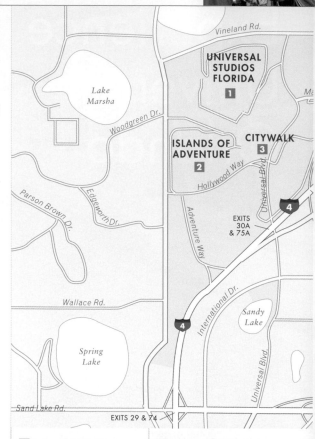

1 Universal Studios. It's a creative and quirky tribute to Hollywood past, present, and future. Overall, the collection of wild rides, quiet retreats, live shows, street characters, and clever movies (both 3-D and 4-D) are as entertaining as the motion pictures they celebrate.

2 Islands of Adventure. IOA has the ability to break new ground—as it did in 2010 with the premiere of an entire land dedicated to Harry Potter. Add a variety of attractions that bring you face-to-face with Spider-Man, the Hulk, velociraptors, and the Cat in the Hat, and there's every reason to head to the islands.

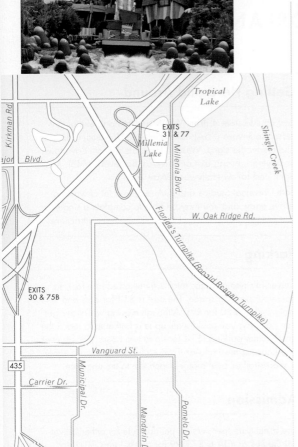

Orlando

CENTRAL FLORIDA

GETTING ORIENTED

Universal Orlando is tucked into a corner created by the intersection of Interstate 4 and Kirkman Road (Highway 435), midway between downtown Orlando and the Walt Disney World Resort. Here you'll be about 15 minutes from each and just 10 minutes from SeaWorld.

3 CityWalk. Locals and visitors come to this sprawling entertainment and retail complex to watch movies; dine at theme restaurants; shop for everything from cigars to surf wear; and stay up late at nightclubs celebrating the French Quarter, Jamaica, and Latin America.

UNIVERSAL ORLANDO PLANNER

Operating Hours

Universal Studios and IOA are open 365 days a year, from 9 AM to 7 PM, with hours as late as 10 PM in summer and at holidays. Wet 'n Wild is also open 365 days a year, weather permitting, but with widely varying hours. Usually it's open from 10 AM to 5 PM, with summer hours from 9:30 AM until 9 PM. Call for exact hours during holiday periods.

Contacts

Universal Dining Reservations: ☎ 407/224-3613 *general,* 407/224-4012 *IOA character meals*

Universal Main Number: ☎ 407/363-8000

Universal Room Reservations: ☎ 888/273-1311

Universal Vacation Packages: ☎ 877/801-9720

Universal Web: ⊕ *www. universalorlando.com*

Wet 'n Wild Main Number: ☎ 407/351-1800 *or* 800/992-9453

Wet 'n Wild Web: ⊕ *www. wetnwild.com*

Getting Here and Around

East on Interstate 4 (from WDW and Tampa), exit at Universal Boulevard (75A); take a left into Universal Orlando, and follow the signs. West on Interstate 4 (from downtown or Daytona, even), exit at Universal Boulevard (74B), turn right, and follow Hollywood Way.

Both Universal Studios and IOA require a lot of walking. Arrive early, and you may be able to complete a single lap that will get you to each of the park's primary attractions.

Parking

Universal's two garages total 3.4 million square feet, so *note your parking space.* The cost is $14 for cars and motorcycles, $20 for RVs. Although moving walkways get you partway, you could walk up to a half mile to reach the gates. Valet parking ($14 for up to two hours $22 for over two hours) is much closer. From Universal hotels, it's either a short stroll or brief motor-launch trip to the entrance.

Admission

The at-the-gate, per-person, per-day rate for either Universal Studios or IOA is $79.99 for adults (ages 10+) and $69.99 for children (ages 3–9). Wet 'n Wild costs $47.95 for ages 10 and up, $41.95 for ages 3 to 9.

Express Passes

At select attractions, watch for **Express Pass** kiosks, where you can get a ticket with a reserved time slot. After procuring one (you can only get one at a time), roam around, return at the appointed hour, and wait in line about 15 minutes—as opposed to as much as an hour. The **Express PLUS Pass** ($26 off-season or $53 in peak season) gets you to the front of each line without an appointment. If crowds are thin and lines are moving fast, skip this pass. Also, if you're a guest at Universal hotel, this perk is free; your room key card serves as the pass.

Universal and Wet 'n Wild Like a Pro

Arrive early—as early at 8 AM if the parks open at 9. Seriously. Better to share Universal or Wet 'n Wild with hundreds of people rather than thousands.

Visit on a weekday. Crowds are lighter, especially fall through spring, when kids are in school.

Don't forget anything in your car. Universal's parking areas are at least a half mile from park entrances and a round-trip will eat up valuable time. At Wet n' Wild parking's closer, but who wants to towel off, get dressed. and walk across the street for a hairbrush?

Consider valet parking. It costs almost twice as much as regular parking, but it puts you much closer to Universal's park entrances and just steps from CityWalk.

Look into the Express PLUS Pass. It really is worth the extra cost to be able to jump to the front of ride lines during peak seasons (summer and holidays).

Ride solo. At Universal some rides have a Single Rider line that moves faster than regular lines.

Take advantage of park concessions. If you're in a hurry to reach the parks and don't feel you can stop for a bite, don't worry—there are plenty of dining options inside. At CityWalk there's a Starbucks, a Cinnabon, and other quick-bite eateries.

Get expert advice. The folks at Guest Services (aka Guest Relations) in both Universal and Wet 'n Wild have great insight. At Universal, reps will create a custom itinerary free of charge.

Check out Child Swap. At certain Universal attractions, one parent can enter the attraction, take a spin, and then return to take care of the baby while the other parent rides without having to wait in line again.

Other Services

All-you-can-eat, daylong **meal deals** are good at three sit-down restaurants in Universal (Mel's Drive-In, Louie's Italian, International Food and Film Festival) and three in IOA (Circus McGurkus Café Stoo-pen-dous, Comic Strip Café, The Burger Digs). The cost is $20 a day for adults, $10 daily for kids; an extra $9 a day buys all-you-can-drink soda.

IOA's **character breakfasts** at Confisco's Grill feature Spider-Man, Scooby-Doo, Woody Woodpecker, Curious George, and Seuss characters. Reservations are a good idea.

For People with Disabilities

The *Studio Guide for Guests with Disabilities* (aka *Rider's Guide*) details special entrances and viewing areas, interpreters, Braille scripts, and assistance devices. In general, if you can transfer from your wheelchair unassisted or with the help of a friend, you can ride many attractions. Some rides have carts that accommodate manual wheelchairs, though not motorized wheelchairs or electric convenience vehicles (ECVs).

Assistive-listening devices are available for shows at Universal (Twister, Men in Black, Terminator, Beetlejuice, Animal Actors, A Day in the Park with Barney) and IOA (Cat in the Hat, Sindbad, Spider-Man).

UNIVERSAL NEWS

For two decades or so Universal and Disney have been going head-to-head. While Disney creates a fantasy world for people—especially young children—who love fairy tales, Universal Orlando is geared to older kids, adults, and anyone who enjoys high-energy thrills and pop culture, and the movies.

Where Disney may roll out a new land or retrofit an old ride once a decade, Universal knows that guests expect something different each time they visit. And the park delivers. In recent years Univeral Studios alone has replaced Alfred Hitchcock with Shrek, Hanna-Barbera with Jimmy Neutron, King Kong with The Mummy, Back to the Future with the virtual-reality Simpsons ride, and Earthquake with Disaster! In 2009 Hollywood Rip Ride Rockit—an interactive roller coaster— was introduced.

Things haven't been static at Islands of Adventure (IOA)—thanks to the opening of the Wizarding World of Harry Potter— or at the CityWalk shopping/nightlife complex. A well-intentionedbut less-than-successful jazz club became a karaoke stage, a Motown restaurant became the Red Coconut Lounge, and a series of stores were switched out to give the complex a new look. In addition, Universal has given the Blue Man Group its very own theater.

A few miles away, on the tourist strip known as International Drive, is Wet 'n Wild—owned by Universal since 1998 and believed to be America's first water park. Wet 'n Wild does with aquatics what Universal does with theatrics: provides over-the-top entertainment, albeit in the form of super waterslides and fantastic plunges. (To wit: Bomb Bay, which drops you 76 nearly-vertical feet down a slide and into the pool. Spooky, splashy fun.)

Despite the adrenaline-charging attractions at Wet n' Wild, it's not hard to chill out lazing about the park's beaches and pools. And, at Universal you can slow down with some leisurely shopping at CityWalk; a concert at Hard Rock Live; and a languorous, elegant dinner at Emeril's.

What's New

The biggest news (for a while it seemed to be the only news) is the 2010 opening of the much-anticipated Wizarding World of Harry Potter. The 35-acre land at IOA includes the Forbidden Forest, Hogsmeade Village, and the iconic Hogwarts castle. If you're a Potter fan, the images you created in your mind (which, incredibly, were captured in the movie series) are largely duplicated here. There's the fantastic Hogwarts Express steam train, and Dervish and Banges shop for wizarding supplies (if you need a wand, though, head to Ollivander's). You can even get a Hogsmeade postmark on postcards and letters mailed from the Owl Post. It's quite a world, this Wizarding World. . . .

But there's more to discover at Universal than just this popular new land. Universal never seems to stop re-inventing and re-formatting shows and attractions. By the time you arrive, it's entirely possible that there will be frsh attractions based on new cartoon characters and revamped stunt shows and spectaculars based on current movie or TV faves. That's the magic of Universal—you never know what they have planned for you next!

UNIVERSAL SHOPPING

Universal makes shopping simple. At the Studios the merchandise is geared toward the attractions themselves; nearly every themed ride channels you from the exit into a gift shop with related merchandise.

At Islands of Adventure the merchandise varies in each section of the park. If you simply must have a Spider-Man T-shirt or Incredible Hulk coffee mug, for example, head to Marvel Superhero Island.

Don't worry if you miss something. You'll find a cross-section of merchandise at the largest stores of both parks: Universal Studios Store at the Studios and the Trading Company at IOA.

TOP AREAS

If you just pass through the parks focused on the main attractions, you may not even notice that you're essentially walking through an outdoor mall. That said, there are a few key shopping areas.

Universal

The largest collection of stores is near the park gates around **Production Central** and **Hollywood.** Here the inventory ranges from silver-screen collectibles to the usual souvenirs and kitsch. The Universal Studios Store offers one-stop shopping.

Islands of Adventure

The largest concentration of stores is near the gates at the **Port of Entry.** And, as at Universal Studios, a central emporium—the Trading Company—carries nearly every coveted collectible from nearly every park shop.

CityWalk

This 30-acre entertainment and retail complex is at the hub of promenades that lead to Universal Studios and Islands of Adventure. Shops here sell fine jewelry, cool beachwear, fashionable clothing, and stylish accessories. Where are the best stores of all? Near the entrance/exit of the complex.

Wet 'n Wild

You may not need a lot when you're hanging out wearing a bathing suit, but even Wet 'n Wild knows that you probably will need (or want) something. One store—the Breakers Beach Shop—carries beachwear, assorted gear, towels, and sundries

TOP SOUVENIRS

Each park has an item or two that tells folks where you've been (and that you're a savvy shopper). Here are a few top picks.

Shop like Homer. At Apu Nahasapeemapetilon's Kwik-E-Mart, near the Simpsons Ride at Universal Studios, Marge wigs and Homer T-shirts or boxer shorts are natural choices.

Shop like an Egyptian. Several stores carry super-hero and film-themed souvenirs—from Spider-Man gear and Incredible Hulk fists to Egyptian hats and clothing from *The Mummy.*

Pair Up. At Seuss Landing in IOA, Thing 1 and Thing 2 T-shirts are always a hit with couples and siblings. Or how about a couple of red-and-white-striped Cat in the Hat mugs?

Make Some Magic. Visit IOA's Wizarding World of Harry Potter and you may find you're one of the first to return home with a Nimbus 2000 broomstick.

Dry Off. Check out Wet n' Wild's beach towels—one of the few souvenirs you may actually use after you go home.

TOP SHOPS

Universal Studios

Brown Derby. Felt fedoras, bush hats that seem straight from wardrobe for *Jurassic Park*, and Cat in the Hat red-and-white stovepipes are among the novelty chapeaus for sale at this Hollywood store.

Kwik-E-Mart. This re-creation of the animated original from the Simpsons is one of the park's most popular stops. Among the finds are Kwik-E-Mart caps and convenience-store smocks, Duff Beer mugs, Lard Lad donuts, Marge-style blue bouffant wigs, and Homer T-shirts packaged in Duff Beer cans.

Nickstuff. An amazingly accurate name for this huge store that sells merchandise dedicated to the many characters of the Nickelodeon network. Check out the do-it-yourself dolls that let you create SpongeBob SquarePants and his undersea friends.

Silver Screen Collectibles. The Queen of Comedy, Lucille Ball, still makes people smile—and makes a wonderful subject for souvenirs that range from cookie jars to aprons. Sepia prints of Richard Gere, Mel Gibson, Marilyn Monroe, and other celebs make great buys. Betty Boop is also featured prominently.

Universal Studios Store. Although impressive in size, this store doesn't have all the merchandise that's sold in individual park gift shops. Only the best-sellers are for sale here—T-shirts, stuffed animals, and limited-edition comic-book artwork, mini movie posters featuring some of Universal's greatest monster movies. It's also one of the few on-site places selling Universal trading pins. Be sure to check the back of the store for clearance racks.

Islands of Adventure

Trading Company. The rambling emporium inside the entrance of IOA is filled with a little something of everything from everywhere. Shrek, SpongeBob, Spider-Man, the Simpsons, and superheroes are plastered on sandals, frames, mugs, cups, caps, and clothing.

Dinostore. Above a juvenile chorus of "I want this!" are adults counseling their kids on what they actually need. It's a monumental task in this large store, which sells dino hats, shorts, necklaces, cards, mugs, squirt guns, figurines, and the clever T-Rex T-shirt emblazoned with the suggestion "Bite Me." There are educational dino toys, too.

Dervish and Banges. Count on cracking open your wallet in the main repository of Potterabilia. There are Hogwarts school uniforms; broomsticks—including top-of-the-line Nimbus 2000 and Firebolt—magical items such as Sneakoscopes, Spectrespecs, Omniculars; and "all your Quidditch needs," including the elusive Golden Snitch.

CityWalk

Cigarz. Still smokin' for a stogie? This is the place to visit for its walk-in humidor, full-length bar, and plenty of tables and ashtrays for enjoying labels like OpusX and Diamond Crown Maximus.

Hart and Huntington Tattoo Company. Universal Studios never wants you to forget that it's edgy and wild, so go ahead, pick out your design and then go home and show off your Orlando ink. It would certainly be one of your most unusual souvenirs.

Quiet Flight. You'll find surf clothes and beachwear here, but no boards. Still, it's a cool, rambling store that opens a little earlier than others at CityWalk, so you can start shopping at 9 AM.

UNIVERSAL

PARTY ON By Gary McKechnie

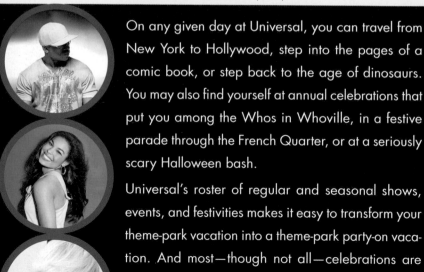

On any given day at Universal, you can travel from New York to Hollywood, step into the pages of a comic book, or step back to the age of dinosaurs. You may also find yourself at annual celebrations that put you among the Whos in Whoville, in a festive parade through the French Quarter, or at a seriously scary Halloween bash.

Universal's roster of regular and seasonal shows, events, and festivities makes it easy to transform your theme-park vacation into a theme-park party-on vacation. And most—though not all—celebrations are included with regular park admission.

(above) Citywalk's Rising Star; (left) summer concert series performers—rapper LL Cool J, R&B artist Jordin Sparks, British pop star Natasha Bedingfield

Mardi Gras, Universal style

YEAR-ROUND ACTIVITIES

HARD ROCK LIVE

Good For: Large groups; couples; singles

When: Almost nightly, usually at 8

Where: CityWalk

Extra Fee: Ticket prices vary

More Info: www.hardrock.com

In a 3,000-seat concert hall adjacent to the world's largest Hard Rock Café, Hard Rock Live gives you the chance to see top-name entertainers. In recent years musical and co-medic talents have included Elvis Costello, Ringo Starr, Snoop Dogg, They Might Be Gi-ants, the Moody Blues, and Craig Ferguson. Although Hard Rock Live shows cost extra, it costs nothing to take in the music-industry memorabilia at the café. Highlights include Buddy Holly's glasses, the doors from the Abbey Road studios, a Beatles poster from their days in Hamburg, and a suit worn by Elvis in *Viva Las Vegas*.

BLUE MAN GROUP

Good For: Families with teens; large groups; couples; singles

When: Nightly (at 6 and 9 if there are two shows; at 7 or 8 if there's one show)

Where: Sharp-Aquos Theatre, CityWalk

Extra Fee: From $25 (children) or $64 (adults)

More Info: www.blueman.com

Every evening, the Blue Man Group pounds out rhythms on PVC pipes, splatters paint on drums, feasts on marshmallows, unrolls a few miles of paper, and engages in something that can only be described as "spin 'n' spit" art.

Audience participation is part of the show. Afterward, you can mingle with the Blue Men in the lobby. It's a great photo op.

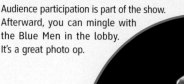

WANTILAN LUAU

Good For: Families; large groups

When: Saturday year-round; also Tuesday in peak season; seating begins at 6

Where: Royal Pacific Resort

Extra Fee: $58 adults, $32 children (including tip)

More Info: www. loewshotels.com

You sit at a table with other guests, taking in the show, and feasting on food from a buffet that includes pit-roasted suckling pig, guava barbecue short ribs, whole-roasted wahoo, tropical fruits, and free beer and wine. Per-formers conduct fire dances and hula navel maneuvers. Luau? No. Lu-wow!

MUSICA DELLA NOTTE

Good For: Large groups; couples

When: Nightly around sunset

Where: Portofino Bay Hotel

Extra Fee: None

More Info: www.loewshotels.com

Each evening, from balconies overlooking the Harbor Piazza, three tenors serenade the audi-ence below with Italian opera classics, Broadway showtunes, and standards made famous by such performers as Andrea Bocelli and Frank Sinatra. If you missed the origi-nal Three Tenors (Plácido Domingo, José Carreras, and Luciano Pavarotti) here's your chance.

VELVET SESSIONS

Good For: Couples; singles

When: Last Thursday of the month, January through October; doors open at 6:30, music begins at 8

Where: Hard Rock Hotel

Extra Fee: None

More Info: www.velvetsessions.com

Most music buffs fantasize about seeing their favorite group perform in a small venue. To help fulfill those fantasies, the Hard Rock Hotel presents Velvet Sessions. They're cleverly billed as a "rock n' roll cocktail party" and are presented in the swanky, sexy Velvet Lounge, just off the hotel's lobby. Die-hard fans have a chance to see groups that could once (and, in some instances, could still) fill large concert halls. Performers have included Orleans, Eddie Money, Joan Jett, the Fixx, ABC, and the Romantics. Some of these acts will take some of you back to your high school days. Rock on!

UNIVERSAL ACCESS

It's not very well promoted, but Universal does offer **backstage tours** (☎ 407/224–4233 ext. 2 for information).

Although they can't begin to compete with the backstage tours of Disney, these may appeal to fans of studio backlots.

Universal also offers five-hour **VIP tours** that usher you around the park (or parks) of your choice and get you front-of-the-line access to major attractions.

A one-day/one park VIP tour costs $120 per person and a one-day/two parks option is $150; this is in addition to park admission.

More exclusive are the one-day/one park tours—including park admission—for groups of up to 12. The price starts at $1,600, with a second park bumping it up to $2,000. Add a second day, and the price hits $3,000.

RISING STAR

Good For: Large groups; couples; singles

When: Nightly; with a live band Tuesday through Saturday. Starts at 8; band plays as late as 2 AM

Where: CityWalk

Extra Fee: $7 cover (singing is free)

More Info: www.citywalk.com

At this 440-seat venue, you can grab a microphone, select a song, and belt it out. But here, instead of having to wail above computerized backing tracks, you get to sing with a live band (and backup singers) whose members seem to know every possible song that every possible guest could ever possibly want to sing. Will it just be a fun evening out, or will it lead to success and a contract? Who knows? Just look what it did for Susan Boyle.

TOTAL NONSTOP ACTION WRESTLING

Good For: Families with teens; singles

When: show nights and times vary

Where: Soundstage 21

Extra Fee: None

More Info: www.tnawrestling.com

Inside Soundstage 21, between CityWalk and Universal Studios, Total Nonstop Action (TNA) Wrestling brings muscle-bound wrestlers to the ring during monthly television tapings—and for theme-park day guests and anyone else who wants to watch, it's a free show (though parking costs). You might see Hulk Hogan, Mick Foley, Kurt Angle, Kevin Nash, or the TNA Knockouts of the woman's wrestling division. The pitch of the die-hard fans becomes fevered as wrestlers leap from the top turnbuckle or rattle the floor while using an opponent as a human jackhammer.

SEASONAL CELEBRATIONS

SUMMER CONCERT SERIES

Universal's free nighttime summer concert series (⊕ www.universalorlando.com) takes place in the open-air Music Plaza during June and July at, more or less, 8. Some of the pop, hip-hop, and R&B performers featured have topped the charts, earned gold and platinum albums, and been nominated for— or won—Grammy awards.

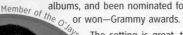
Member of the O'Jays

The setting is great, too. It's patterned after the famed Hollywood Bowl, so as performers take to the 2,400 square foot stage, you relax under the stars on a 15,000-square-foot lawn. It's not a bad way to spend a summer evening.

ROCK THE UNIVERSE

Rock the Universe (⊕ www.rocktheuniverse. com), a two-day, early-September celebration of Christian rock, has a passionate fan base, thanks to performances by some of the biggest names in the industry, including Pillar, Third Day, Casting Crowns, and tobyMac.

The gates open at 4 PM, and music keeps playing till 1 AM. For those who can deal with high decibels and a touch of sleep deprivation, Rock the Universe is truly divine.

Rock the Universe: Group 1 Crew

Entry costs between $50 and $85, depending on the the number of days you attend and whether or not you pay in advance.

MARDI GRAS

When Orlando's other theme parks are ratcheting down after the busy year-end holiday season, Universal Studios looks forward to February and its take on the New Orleans Mardi Gras

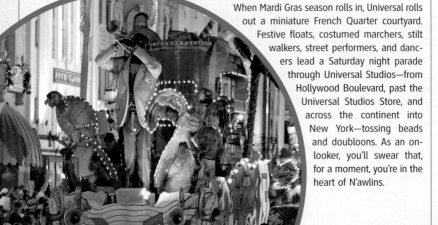

(⊕ www.universalorlando.com). Among the festivities (all of them free) are parades; concerts by headliners in Music Plaza; and performances by popular Louisiana jazz, blues, zydeco, and Cajun bands in the Production Central and Hollywood Boulevard vicinities.

When Mardi Gras season rolls in, Universal rolls out a miniature French Quarter courtyard. Festive floats, costumed marchers, stilt walkers, street performers, and dancers lead a Saturday night parade through Universal Studios—from Hollywood Boulevard, past the Universal Studios Store, and across the continent into New York—tossing beads and doubloons. As an onlooker, you'll swear that, for a moment, you're in the heart of N'awlins.

HALLOWEEN HORROR NIGHTS

Universal Studios pulls out all the stops with Halloween Horror Nights (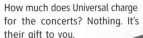 www.halloweenhorrornights.com), which brings the most frightening characters in cinema history to life. Since 1991, Universal has enlisted the talents of maniacal killer clowns, criminally insane morticians, vengeful spinsters, and psychotic psychiatrists (or actors playing them) to scare you silly from late September through Halloween.

Jason is back at Horror Night!

Don't expect a super-sized version of your local Rotary Club's haunted house. The planning for Halloween Horror Nights takes months and utilizes Universal soundstages, movie-ready backlots, skilled makeup artists, existing attractions, eager actors, and horror-flick freaks to create eight haunted houses, six scare zones, and two live shows. It's the most fun you can have with your eyes closed. Prices range between $40 and $60, depending on how close it is to Halloween.

GRINCHMAS

If you owned a theme park that included a place called Seuss Landing, you'd be silly not to stage a holiday celebration starring the legendary Grinch. Each December at Islands of Adventure, Seuss Landing becomes the stage for Grinchmas (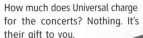 www.universalorlando.com), during which an array of Seussian characters come to life. Actors spend hours in makeup to appear as Whoville's Whos—all adorned in their finest holiday apparel.

There's also a free stage show adapted from the classic *How The Grinch Stole Christmas*. Enjoying the season is simply a cinch... when you spend holidays with a warm-hearted Grinch.

MACY'S HOLIDAY PARADE

If you can't travel to New York on Thanksgiving Day, you can still catch the Macy's parade (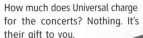 www.universalorlando.com) live. Granted, Universal's version won't be as much of a spectacle as the one in the Big Apple but, then again, New York doesn't have its own Simpsons Ride, either.

Starting in early December, this free nightly holiday event features marching bands, a Christmas tree lighting, and helium-filled balloons paraded through the heart of Universal Studios—down Hollywood Boulevard, through Production Central, and into New York.

In addition, the open-air Music Plaza hosts the Holiday Concert Series, with performers such as Mannheim Steamroller, Chris Isaak, and Natalie Cole.

How much does Universal charge for the concerts? Nothing. It's their gift to you.

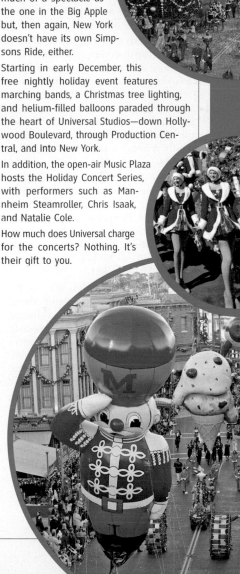

UNIVERSAL NIGHTLIFE

With an attitude that's distinctly non-Disney, Universal has created nightlife for adults who want to party. The epicenter here is **CityWalk**, a 30-acre entertainment and retail complex at the hub of promenades that lead to both Universal parks.

This open and airy gathering place includes an over-the-top discotheque, a theater for the fabulous and extremely popular Blue Man Group, and a huge hall where karaoke's king. There's a New Orleans bar, a Jamaican reggae lounge, and a casual Key West hangout. On weeknights you'll find families and conventioneers; weekends a decidedly younger crowd parties until the wee hours.

Clubs have individual cover charges, but it's far more economical to pay for the whole kit and much of the caboodle. Choose a Party Pass (a one-price-all-clubs admission) for $11.99; a Party Pass-and-a-Movie for $21 (plus tax); a Movie-and-a-Meal for $21.95; or a Party Pass-and-a-Meal for $21.

At AMC Universal Cineplex, with its 20 screens, there's certain to be something you like—including nightly midnight movies. Meals (tax and gratuity included) are served at Jimmy Buffett's Margaritaville, the Hard Rock Cafe, NASCAR Sports Grille, and others. And as if these deals weren't sweet enough, after 6 PM the $14 parking fee drops to $3. However, it's a long haul from the garage to CityWalk—if you prefer, simply call a cab. They run at all hours. ☎ *407/224–2692, 407/363–8000 Universal main line* ⊕ *www.citywalkorlando.com.*

TOP CITYWALK NIGHTSPOTS

With the wide range of nightlife you'll find at Universal, you may get the feeling that you're vacationing in New York, not Orlando. CityWalk's stores open by midmorning, and its restaurants come to life between lunchtime and late afternoon. Eateries that double as nightclubs (e.g., Pat O'Brien's or the Red Coconut Club) start charging a cover before dusk and apply age restrictions (usually 21) at around 9 PM. For details on a particular establishment, check with Guest Services.

Bars and Clubs

Jimmy Buffett's Margaritaville. Buffett tunes fill the air at the restaurant here and at Volcano, Land Shark, and 12 Volt bars. There's a Pan Am Clipper suspended from the ceiling, music videos projected onto sails, limbo and hula-hoop contests, a huge margarita blender that erupts "when the volcano blows," live music nightly—everything that Parrotheads need to roost. Across the promenade, another seaplane is the setting for the Lone Palm Airport, an outdoor bar. ☎ *407/224–2692* ⊕ *www. margaritaville.com* ✉ *$7 after 10 PM* ⊙ *Daily 11:30 AM–2 AM.*

Bob Marley—A Tribute to Freedom. This club, modeled after the so-called King of Reggae's home in Kingston, Jamaica, is like a museum, with more than 100 photographs and paintings showing pivotal moments in Marley's life. Off the cozy bar is a patio where you can be jammin' to a (loud) live band that plays from 8 PM to 1:30 AM nightly. Red Stripe Rastafarian Thursday lasts from 4 PM until closing. ☎ *407/224–2692* ✉ *$7 after 8 PM* ⊙ *Weekdays 4 PM–2 AM, weekends 2 PM–2 AM.*

The Hard Rock Hotel's upscale Velvet Lounge hosts the monthly Velvet Sessions rock-and-roll cocktail party.

the groove. In this cavernous hall images flicker rapidly on several screens and the lights, music, and mayhem appeal to a mostly under-30 crowd. Prepare for lots of fog, swirling lights, and sweaty bodies. The '70s-style Green Room is filled with beanbag chairs and everything you threw out when Duran Duran hit the charts. The Blue Room is sci-fi Jetson-y, and the Red Room is hot and romantic in a bordello sort of way. ☎ 407/224–2692 💷 $7 🕑 Daily 9 PM–2 AM.

Latin Quarter. A tribute to Latin music and dance, this place is spicy hot—salsa hot, even. Although there is a restaurant, most people come for the nightclub—a 21st-century version of Ricky Ricardo's Tropicana, with a design based on Aztec, Incan, and Mayan architecture. There's even an Andes Mountain range, complete with waterfalls, around the dance floor. If you can get your hips working overtime, pick a rumba from 1 to 10 and swivel. Or pick a tango or a merengue or a salsa. ☎ 407/224–2692 💷 $7; price may vary

for certain performances 🕑 Mon.–Thurs. 5 PM–2 AM, Fri. and Sat. noon–2 AM.

Pat O'Brien's. It's an exact reproduction of the legendary New Orleans original, complete with flaming fountain and dueling pianists. The Patio Bar has a wealth of tables and chairs allow you to do nothing but enjoy your potent, rum-based Hurricanes. ☎ 407/224–2692 ⊕ www.patobriens.com 💷 $7 after 9 PM 🕑 Patio Bar daily 4 PM–2 AM; piano bar daily 6 PM–2 AM.

Red Coconut Club. The interior is part Vegas lounge, part Cuban club, and part Polynesian tiki bar—all circa the 1950s. There's a full bar, signature martinis, an extensive wine list, and VIP bottle service. Hang out in the lounge, on the balcony, or at the bar. Have a tight budget? Take advantage of the daily happy hours and gourmet appetizer menu. A DJ or live music pushes the energy with tunes ranging from Sinatra to rock. ☎ 407/224–2692 💷 $7 after 9 PM 🕑 Sun.–Wed. 8 PM–2 AM, Thurs.–Sat. 6 PM–2 AM.

Rising Star. Here you and other hopeful (and hopeless) singers can let loose. Instead of singing to recorded music, you're accompanied by a band complete with backup singers—and all before an audience. Although the band's not here on Sunday and Monday, the backup singers are on hand every night, so you can get yourself one step closer to opening for U2. ☎ *407/224–2692* ☜ *$7* ☽ *Nightly 8* PM–*2* AM, *21 and up; 18 and up on Thurs.*

Shows

Blue Man Group. The Sharp-Aquos Theatre is home to one act and one act only: the Blue Man Group, who give you 90 minutes of surreal and silly routines. How many marshmallows can one Blue Man catch in his mouth? Many. Is it really art when a Blue Man spits paint onto a spinning canvas? Can someone really create music out of a spaghetti twist of PVC tubing? ☎ *407/BLUE–MAN (258–3626)* ☜ *Adults advance purchase from $64, children 9 and under from $25 (add $10 when buying at the box office)* ☽ *Daily showtimes vary, call for schedule.*

Hard Rock Café. The Hard Rock here is the largest on earth. This means more memorabilia than ever, including such Beatles rarities as John Lennon's famous "New York City" T-shirt, Paul's original lyrics for "Let It Be," and the doors from London's Abbey Road studios. The seats are hard, and two-thirds don't face the stage in the Hard Rock Live concert hall, but there's a performance just about every night. Warning: you can't bring large purses or bags inside, and there are no lockers at CityWalk. ☎ *407/224–2692* ⊕ *www. hardrocklive.com* ☜ *Cover prices vary* ☽ *Daily from 11* AM, *with varying closing times, generally around midnight.*

TOP RESORT BARS

After a manic day in the theme parks, or perhaps a brush with hyperactive City-Walk, you may need some quiet. There are several lounges within Universal's resort hotels, each themed and each a sanctuary where you can relax with a soothing libation.

Royal Pacific Resort. Jake's American Bar has a South Pacific look (it's themed as the retreat of an island-hopping airline pilot), English and Asian entrées, cocktails, a full liquor bar, and live background music. The **Orchid Court Lounge and Sushi Bar** is resplendent with orchids, hand-carved Balinese furniture, and South Seas martinis and drinks.

Portofino Bay. At the dockside **Thirsty Fish** bar, sunsets are accompanied by wine and live jazz. **Bar American** specializes in martinis and other cocktails, and grappa.

Hard Rock Hotel. The **Beach Club** is a pool–beach bar and grill where you can sip a tropical drink or cold beer. The evening's certainly more upscale at the **Velvet Lounge**, a hip retreat that's home to the monthly Velvet Sessions rock-and-roll cocktail party.

Universal Studios

WORD OF MOUTH

"You definitely should plan a day each for [Universal Studios and Islands of Adventure]. And it *is* worth it to get the front-of-line privileges . . . but [even with these] you still can spend a day at each park. If you finish one early, check out your hotel pool!"

—FL_Mom

UNIVERSAL STUDIOS PLANNER

Park Information

Entering Universal Studios can be overwhelming, with you and thousands of others flooding through those turnstiles at once. Do yourself a favor: stop and strategize. If you haven't already done so, decide on your must-see attractions.

Pick up a map just past the turnstiles as you enter the park; not only will it help you with the park layout, it also lists show schedules and points out restaurants and any special events. If a host is nearby, ask his or her insider advice on what to see first.

If you're a super-organized type, you can even get strategy advice *before* visiting by calling **Guest Services** at ☎ 407/224–6350.

Park Amenities

Baby Care: There are diaper-changing stations in many of the men's and ladies' restrooms and a nursing station for comfort and privacy at the park's first-aid station near the entrance. Baby supplies (diapers, food, wipes, etc.) are available at larger stores; ask for them at the counter, though, as they're not displayed on shelves.

Cameras: Just inside the main entrance, On Location is a shop with nearly everything you need for a picture-perfect vacation, including disposable cameras and digital memory cards. This is also the pickup location for the souvenir photos taken in the park by Universal's squad of photographers.

First-Aid: There are two first-aid centers: one just inside the turnstiles, to the right near the Studio Audience Center, and the other directly across from the entrance to Beetlejuice's Graveyard Revue.

Lockers: Daily rates for lockers near the park entrance are $8 for a small unit and $10 for a larger one. Some high-speed attractions (e.g., Men In Black and Revenge of the Mummy) have free lockers that you can use for up to 90 minutes. They're usually outside the ride entrance.

Lost People and Things: If you plan to split up, be sure everyone knows where and when to reconnect. Staffers take lost children to Guest Services near the main entrance. This is also where you might find lost personal items.

Stroller Rentals: Just inside the main entrance, there are strollers for $15 (single) and $20 (double) a day.

Wheelchair Rentals: You can rent manual wheelchairs ($12 per day) at the parking garages and inside the main entrance. Because there are limited quantities of ECVs (available in the park for $50), reserve one in advance. A photo ID and a $50 deposit on a credit card are required for wheelchairs.

Guided Tours

Universal has several **VIP Tours** (☎ *407/363–8295*) that are worthwhile if you're in a hurry, if crowds are heavy, if you're with a large group—and if you have the money to burn. The tours include extras like front-of-the-line access (that is, the right to jump the head of the line). You can also arrange for extras like priority restaurant seating, bilingual guides, gift bags, refreshments at check-in, wheelchairs and strollers, and valet parking. Prices cited here do not include sales tax or park admission.

Five-hour nonexclusive (i.e., you'll be touring with other park guests) tours cost $120 per person for one park and $150 for two parks. Each accommodates up to a dozen people.

If you're traveling with a large group (up to 15 people) consider splitting the cost of an exclusive eight-hour tour customized to your interests. The eight-hour one-park price is $1,600; two parks in eight hours will cost you $2,000. What does $3,000 get you? How about a two-day tour of both parks with backstage access and discussions on park history, decorating, and landscaping?

For People with Disabilities

Universal has made it as easy as possible for guests with disabilities to enjoy the park. It starts when you arrive in the parking garage, where you can rent wheelchairs or ECVs before making the long trek to the park entrance (though there's also chair rental at the entrance).

Guest Services (near the entrance just outside and inside the park) is the place to pick assisted-listening and other devices. Other services include special viewing areas for people in wheelchairs, automatic doors, well-equipped restrooms, and walking areas for service animals. Be sure to pick up the *Studio Guide for Guests with Disabilities* (aka Rider's Guide), which is full of details on equipment and other services.

Accessibility information is posted at each attraction. Note that although ride lines can accommodate standard wheelchairs, often you'll be ushered into a waiting area while the rest of your party goes through the line. Many shows have seating to accommodate manual wheelchairs, but, in general, you'll have to transfer from your chair to ride vehicles.

Miscellaneous Tips

■ Although there aren't as many shows taping here as in the past, *Total Non-Stop Action (TNA) Wrestling* often comes for matches featuring stars such as Hulk Hogan, Kevin Nash, and Mick Foley. Tickets are first-come, first-served. Check at the Studio Audience Center.

■ Kids will get drenched at Curious George Goes to Town and Fievel's Playland. Stash a bathing suit or change of clothing in a nearby locker.

■ Want to take a good picture? Universal Studios posts signs that indicate picture spots and show how best to frame your shot.

■ The three Universal Studios restaurants on the Meal Deal plan are Mel's Drive-In, Louie's Italian Restaurant, and the International Food and Film Festival.

■ Don't limit your shopping to the park's stores; kiosks throughout the park are loaded with an assortment of wares.

9

UNIVERSAL STUDIOS
STEP INTO THE MOVIES

Universal Studios appeals primarily to those who like loud, fast, high-energy attractions—generally teens and adults. Covering 444 acres, it's a rambling montage of sets, shops, soundstages housing themed attractions, reproductions of New York and San Francisco, and some genuine moviemaking paraphernalia.

On a map, the park appears neatly divided into six areas positioned around a huge lagoon. There's Production Central, which covers the entire left side of the Plaza of the Stars; New York, with street performances at 70 Delancey; the bicoastal San Francisco/Amity; futuristic World Expo; Woody Woodpecker's KidZone; and Hollywood.

What's tricky is that—since it's designed like a series of movie sets—there's no straightforward way to tackle the park. You'll probably make some detours and do some backtracking. To save time and shoe leather, ask theme-park hosts for itinerary suggestions and time-saving tips.

TOURING TIPS

■ A few things aren't allowed in the park: alcohol and glass containers; hard-sided coolers; soft-sided coolers larger than 8.5 inches wide by 6 inches high by 6 inches deep; coolers, suitcases, and other bags with wheels.

■ Upon entering, avoid the temptation to go left toward the towering soundstages, looping the park clockwise. Head right—bypassing shops, restaurants, and some crowds—to primary attractions like The Simpsons Ride and Men In Black.

■ Good rendezvous points include the Lucy Tribute near the entrance, Mel's Drive-In, and Beetlejuice's Graveyard Revue.

TOP ATTRACTIONS

FOR AGES 7 AND UP
Hollywood Rip Ride Rockit. On this coaster, added in 2009, you select the sound track.

Men In Black: Alien Attack. The "world's first ride-through video game" gives you a chance to plug away at an endless swarm of aliens.

Revenge of the Mummy. It's a jarring, rocketing indoor coaster that takes you past scary mummies and billowing balls of fire (really).

Shrek 4-D. The 3-D film with sensory effects picks up where the original film left off—and adds some creepy extras in the process.

The Simpsons Ride. It puts you in the heart of Springfield on a wild-and-crazy virtual-reality experience.

Terminator 2 3-D. This explosive stage show features robots, 3-D effects, and sensations that all add extra punch to the classic film series.

Twister . . . Ride It Out. OK. It's just a special-effects show—but what special effects! You experience a tornado without having to head to the root cellar.

Universal Horror Make-Up Show. This sometimes gross, often raunchy, but always entertaining demonstration merges the best of stand-up comedy with creepy effects.

FOR AGES 6 AND UNDER
Animal Actors on Location! It's a perfect family show starring a menagerie of animals whose unusually high IQs are surpassed only by their cuteness and cuddle-ability.

A Day in the Park with Barney. Small children love the big purple dinosaur and the chance to sing along.

Curious George Goes to Town. The celebrated simian visits the Man with the Yellow Hat in a small-scale water park.

WHERE TO SNACK

After a morning of rushing around, you can keep up the pace at a fast-food spot. Or slow things down at sit-down restaurant with priority seating, which gives you the first available seat after a reserved time.

■ Full-service restaurants include **Finnegan's Bar and Grille** (Irish pub), and **Lombard's Seafood Grille** (seafood).

■ Among the self-serve restaurants are **Classic Monsters Cafe** (seasonal, with pizzas, pasta, salads, rotisserie chicken); **Richter's Burger Co.** (burgers, salads); the **International Food and Film Bazaar** (pizza, gyros, stir-fried beef, and other multiculti dishes).

■ Other choices include **Mel's Drive-In**, a Happy Days–era soda shop–burger joint; **Beverly Hills Boulangerie** for breakfast croissants and pastries; **Schwab's Pharmacy** for ice cream; **Louie's Italian Restaurant** (pizza, spaghetti, salads); and the **KidZone Pizza Company** for pizza, chicken tenders, and other kid-geared dishes.

9

By Gary
McKechnie

Inspired by the original in California and opened in Orlando in 1990, when the city assumed it would become "Hollywood East," Universal Studios celebrates the movies. The park is a jumble of areas and attractions. But the same is true of backlot sets at a film studio. Suspend any disbelief you might have, and just enjoy the motion-picture magic.

At Production Central large soundstages house attractions based on TV programs and films like Shrek, Jimmy Neutron, and Twister. It's right near the entrance and may be the park's most crowded area, since most visitors are determined to experience every attraction, in order, no matter how long the wait.

Not every film or program based in New York is actually shot in New York. Cleverly constructed sets mean that nearly every studio can own its own Big Apple. Universal is no exception. Here a collection of sparkling public buildings, well-worn neighborhoods, and back alleys are the next best thing to Manhattan itself.

As you enter the area known as San Francisco/Amity, you're roughly one-third of the way through the park. The crowds spread out, and the pace seems to slow. You can stop to see a show starring Beetlejuice, dine on seafood at the waterfront Lombard's Landing, or play midway games in a re-creation of a Cape Cod village.

There's not much shaking between San Francisco/Amity and World Expo and its two large attractions—Men In Black: Alien Attack and The Simpsons Ride. The scarcity of rides here is, however, offset by the abundant attractions at Woody Woodpecker's KidZone. It matches the energy of toddlers and the under-10 crowd with diversions that includes a junior-size roller coaster, a mini water park, and a chance to meet E.T. and Barney the dinosaur. In Hollywood, quiet parks and flashy Rodeo Drive really do make you think you've stepped into vintage Tinseltown.

All in all, Universal Studios fulfills its promise: to put you in the movies.

PRODUCTION CENTRAL

This area has plenty of loud, flashy, rollicking rides that appeal to tweens, teens, and adults. Clear the turnstiles and go straight.

Fodor's Choice★
Duration
2 mins.
Crowds
You Bet!
Audience
Not Small Kids

Hollywood Rip Ride Rockit! Looking like an endless strand of spaghetti, this half-mile-plus coaster loops, twists, dives, and winds above and through Production Central, giving you plenty of time to consider fully whether or not to ride it. Of course, if you're like most people, you will. After what is usually a long wait, you'll select your personal sound track—from heavy-metal, techno, country, rap, and pop—that will accompany the video that's shot as you scream your way along. Next, you'll lower the lap bar on your stadium-seating-style car prior to being hauled up nearly 17 stories. You'll then drop nearly 17 stories before being lifted again into a towering loop and released into what seems like a never-ending series of twists, curves, sideways slings, and snap rolls at speeds up to 65 mph. By the time you return to the station, you may be spent, but you might spend a little more: the video with the sound track you selected is available for purchase. Note that there's a ride-height minimum of 51 inches. **For people with disabilities:** Guests using wheelchairs must transfer to ride vehicles. ■TIP➔ As it's a relatively new attraction, crowds are only natural. Come early or late or use an Express Pass.

☆☆
Duration
8 mins.
Crowds
Mod. to Heavy
Audience
All Ages

Jimmy Neutron's Nicktoon Blast. On this virtual-reality ride, boy genius Jimmy is joined by Nickelodeon characters such as SpongeBob SquarePants and the Rugrats as he demonstrates his latest invention: the powerful Mark IV rocket. Things go awry when evil, egg-shape aliens make off with the rocket and threaten world domination. If your kids are Neutron fans or can sing SpongeBob's theme song, you must do this ride. Be warned: it's geared to those who can handle lots of stimulation and fast-and-furious jostling, bouncing, and shaking. Your rocket car dives, bounces, and skips through Nick-based cartoon settings, where there are lots of computer graphics and high-tech, high-speed gizmos. Like most attractions, this one empties into a gift shop that spotlights Nick merchandise. Kids must be at least 44 inches to ride. **For people with disabilities:** One vehicle has an access door that allows for standard-size wheelchairs, and two vehicles in the back have closed-caption screens. ■TIP➔ If you can talk your kids into waiting, come at day's end (crowds are heavy early in the day because it's near the entrance. Accepts Universal Express Pass.

9

☆☆☆
Duration
12 mins.
Crowds
Heavy
Audience
All Ages

Shrek 4-D. It's been years since *Shrek* hit theaters, but fans still line up at this animated 3-D saga. Mike Myers, Eddie Murphy, Cameron Diaz, and John Lithgow reprise their vocal roles as the swamp-dwelling ogre, Shrek; his faithful chatterbox companion, Donkey; Shrek's bride, Princess Fiona; and the vengeful Lord Farquaad (or rather his ghost). The preshow stars the Gingerbread Man, Magic Mirror, and the Three Little Pigs. It's slightly entertaining, but at nearly 15 minutes long, it lasts longer than the main attraction. Afterward, you're given OgreVision glasses that will enhance your tumultuous ride, during which Shrek tries to rescue Fiona from Lord Farquaad. The adventure includes a battle between fire-breathing dragons and a pretty scary plunge down a 1,000-foot waterfall—all made more intense by special theater seats and surprising sensory effects (mainly blasts of air and sprinkles of

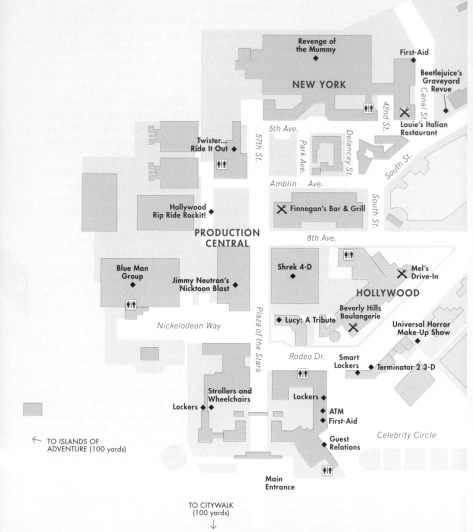

Universal Studios

Revenge of the Mummy

First-Aid

Beetlejuice's Graveyard Revue

NEW YORK

Louie's Italian Restaurant

5th Ave.

42nd St.

Canal St.

Twister...
Ride It Out

57th St.

Park Ave.

Delancey St.

South St.

Amblin Ave.

Hollywood
Rip Ride Rockit!

Finnegan's Bar & Grill

South St.

**PRODUCTION
CENTRAL**

8th Ave.

Blue Man
Group

Shrek 4-D

Mel's
Drive-In

Jimmy Neutron's
Nicktoon Blast

HOLLYWOOD

Beverly Hills
Boulangerie

Plaza of the Stars

Lucy: A Tribute

Universal Horror
Make-Up Show

Nickelodeon Way

Rodeo Dr.

Smart
Lockers

Terminator 2 3-D

Celebrity Circle

Strollers and
Wheelchairs

Lockers

Lockers

ATM

First-Aid

← TO ISLANDS OF
ADVENTURE (100 yards)

Guest
Relations

Main
Entrance

TO CITYWALK
(100 yards)
↓

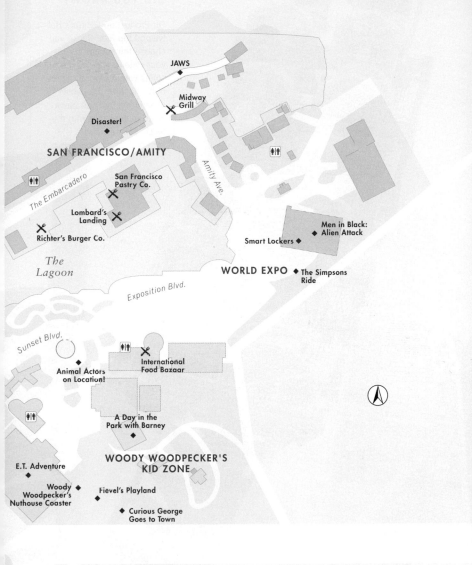

JAWS

Midway
Grill

Disaster!

SAN FRANCISCO/AMITY

Amity Ave.

The Embarcadero

San Francisco
Pastry Co.

Lombard's
Landing

Richter's Burger Co.

Men in Black:
Alien Attack

Smart Lockers

The
Lagoon

WORLD EXPO **The Simpsons**
Ride

Exposition Blvd.

Sunset Blvd.

Animal Actors
on Location!

International
Food Bazaar

A Day in the
Park with Barney

WOODY WOODPECKER'S
KID ZONE

E.T. Adventure

Woody
Woodpecker's
Nuthouse Coaster

Fievel's Playland

Curious George
Goes to Town

TO VINELAND RD. →

KEY	
✗	*Restaurants*
👥	*Restrooms*

water) that create the "4-D" part. **For people with disabilities:** Equipped for assisted-listening devices. Those using wheelchairs don't need to transfer to a ride seat. There are, however, eight seats that allow guests with disabilities to fully experience the sensory effects. ■TIP→ Despite a capacity for 300, you may wait up to an hour to reach the preshow, even with an Express Pass. Come early or late in the day.

NEED A BREAK?

In the heart of Production Central, the self-serve **Classic Monsters Cafe** resembles a mad scientist's lab. When the doors are open (peak season only) it offers wood-fired-oven pizzas, pastas, chef salads, four-cheese ravioli, and rotisserie chicken. Frankenstein's monster and other characters from vintage Universal horror films make the rounds as you eat.

NEW YORK

Universal has gone all out to re-create New York's skyscrapers, commercial districts, ethnic neighborhoods, and back alleys—right down to the cracked concrete. Hidden within these structures are restaurants, arcades, gift shops, and key attractions. And, although they're from Chicago, the Blues Brothers drive from the Second City to New York City in their Bluesmobile for free performances at 70 Delancey.

☆☆☆
Duration
3 mins.
Crowds
Heavy
Audience
Not Small Kids

Revenge of the Mummy. Action, adventure, and horror are in abundance in this $40 million spine-tingling thrill ride that combines roller-coaster technology, pyrotechnics, and some super-scary skeletal warriors. The entrance is set up like the tomb of a pharaoh. You walk by Egyptian artifacts and through winding catacombs before boarding a coaster car and zipping into a haunted labyrinth. Dead ahead, you're given the chance to sell your soul for safety and riches. Regardless of your decision, a mummy sends you hurtling through underground passageways and Egyptian burial chambers. Highlights include running past a phalanx of towering mummy guards, escaping a beetle-infested burial chamber, zipping backwards through fog, and racing full-tilt into the mummified mouth of Imhotep. Take note: you feel the 1.5 g-forces when flying uphill, and much of the ride takes place in the dark. Kids must be at least 48 inches to ride. **For people with disabilities:** Guests using wheelchairs must transfer to a ride vehicle. ■TIP→ Cut down on wait times: head for the single-rider line. Otherwise, use Express Pass or come early or late.

☆☆☆
Duration
3 mins.
Crowds
Heavy
Audience
Not Small Kids

Twister . . . Ride It Out. In just minutes, this attraction accomplishes what it took the movie hours to do: scare the daylights out of you with the experience of being tossed about like a salad. It starts with a slow-moving line and a bland lecture from the movie's stars about the destructive force of tornadoes. You're eventually ushered into a standing-room theater where a make-believe windstorm builds gradually in a country scene. It starts with an ominous five-story-high funnel cloud that weaves in from the background to center stage. Amid the cacophony created by 110 decibels of wind noise, crackling electrical lines, and shattered windows, a truck, signs, car, and a cow earn frequent-flyer points by sailing across the stage. When the roof starts to blow off, your instinct is to head for the root cellar. Don't. Stay to marvel at the work of the

9

special-effects masters who put this together, only to have it torn apart every few minutes. **For people with disabilities:** The theater is wheel-chair accessible. Strong sound effects make it possible for people with vision impairments to enjoy the show. ■TIP→ Use a Universal Express Pass or come first thing in the morning or at closing.

SAN FRANCISCO/AMITY

This area brings the West and East coasts together. One set has the wharves and warehouses of San Francisco's Embarcadero and Fisher-man's Wharf districts. Not far away is the set of a New England fishing village—very much like the town that was terrorized in *Jaws*.

☆☆
Duration
25 mins.
Crowds
**Light to
Moderate**
Audience
Not Small Kids

Beetlejuice's Graveyard Revue. Whew! This is *some* show. In an amphithe-ater, a Transylvanian castle is the backdrop for Beetlejuice, who warms up the audience with his snappy lines, rude remarks, and sarcasm. He then introduces the stars of the show: Frankenstein's monster and his bride, the Wolfman, and Dracula. The monsters doff their traditional garb in favor of glitzy, hip threads to sing hits by such diverse artists as Bruce Springsteen, AC/DC, and Van Halen, albeit with a few changes (e.g., "Jesse's Girl" becomes "Frankie's Girl"). The Ghoul Girl cheer-leaders, Hip and Hop, appear, upping the weirdness factor and adding sex appeal. We are not kidding. This is probably the only place you'll see Frankenstein's monster pretending to play an electric guitar and shout-ing "Are you ready to rock, Orlando?" **For people with disabilities:** The theater is wheelchair accessible and equipped for assisted-listening devices. ■TIP→ You can use Universal Express Pass, but the amphitheater's high capacity means little chance of waiting.

■
NEED A
BREAK?

Richter's Burger Co. (across from Beetlejuice) lets you drop in and create your own burger or grilled-chicken sandwich. It's pretty quick, pretty conve-nient, and there are seats inside and out.

☆☆
Duration
20 mins.
Crowds
Heavy
Audience
Not Small Kids

Disaster! Universal dusted off an attraction based on a forgotten '70s film (*Earthquake*) to create a new one filled with clever comedy and manic energy. Here's how it unfolds: Since all of the movie's stars are in rehab, a harried production assistant must cast park guests for various roles (e.g., a Martha Stewart type without the prison time) in another blockbuster disaster film—*Mutha Earth*. When this guest-star cast is selected, everyone moves to the special-effects set, where disaster-movie producer Frank Kincaid (Christopher Walken) magically appears and interacts with the production assistant. Guest stars are put through some paces before you all board San Francisco–style trams. This is where the attraction really begins. When the trams park at a subway station, a two-minute, 8.3–Richter-scale tremor begins; there are col-lapsing ceilings, blackouts, explosions, fire, and a massive flood that comes at you from every angle. At the end of the experience you get to see the hilarious "finished" film on the tram's monitors: the *Mutha Earth* trailer starring Dwayne "The Rock" Johnson as a heroic park ranger and your fellow guests as his costars.

This ride isn't suitable for pregnant women; guests with heart, back, neck, or motion-sickness problems. Kids must be at least 40 inches tall to ride without an adult. **For people with disabilities:** If you use a standard-size wheelchair or can transfer to a ride vehicle, you can board this attraction. Service animals should not ride. ■ TIP→ Use Universal Express Pass; otherwise, come early or late.

☆☆
Duration
7 mins.
Crowds
Moderate
Audience
Not Small Kids

JAWS. Even though this attraction seems tired (it's based on the 1976 film) it's still popular with park guests who line up for a ride around a 7-acre lagoon aboard what seems like a flimsy pontoon boat. The intent is a pleasure cruise, but things soon go awry when it becomes apparent that a 32-foot killer shark is prowling the waters—and is ready to take a huge bite out of your boat. You'll forget that the film's more than 30 years old when you spy the renegade shark rocketing toward your boat, not once, but in a series of surprise attacks that kick off a series of explosions and teeth-grinding sounds. Don't think you're safe just because you've reached the boathouse. The effects on this ride really shine, especially the heat and fire from electrical explosions that could singe the eyebrows off Andy Rooney.

Pregnant women or guests with heart, back, neck, or motion-sickness problems should skip this one. **For people with disabilities:** If you use a standard-size wheelchair or can transfer to a ride vehicle, you can board this attraction. Service animals shouldn't ride. ■ TIP→ Try it after dark for an extra thrill (you can't see the attack as well but can certainly hear and feel it). And then cancel the next day's trip to the beach.

WORLD EXPO

At the far end of the park is a futuristic set of buildings containing two of Universal Studios' most popular attractions, Men in Black: Alien Attack and The Simpsons Ride. Other than that, there's not much happening in this district.

9

☆☆☆
Duration
4½ mins.
Crowds
Heavy
Audience
Not Small Kids

Men in Black: Alien Attack. This star attraction bills itself as "the world's first ride-through video game." The preshow provides the storyline: To earn membership in MIB you must round up aliens that escaped when their shuttle crashed on Earth. On board your vehicle with a few others, you enter the backstreets of a city where a series of aliens pops out from windows, trash cans, and doorways. Fire at them with that laser gun mounted to your futuristic car. There's no limit to the number of shots you can take, so blast away. Note, though, that the gun's red laser dot is just a pinpoint, so it's hard to see what you've hit. Keep one eye on the aliens and one eye on the onboard scoreboard. Of course, some aliens fire back at you, sending your car spinning out of control. Depending on the collective score, your ride will wrap up with one of 35 endings, ranging from a hero's welcome to a loser's farewell. It's all pretty exciting.

The spinning nature of the cars may cause dizziness, so use caution if you're prone to motion sickness. And don't ride if you have heart, back, or neck problems. Without an adult, kids must be 42 inches tall to ride. **For people with disabilities:** Equipped for assisted-listening devices. Guests using wheelchairs must transfer to the ride vehicle. ■ TIP→ In summer, waits are up to an hour. Come first thing or save time by splitting up and using the shorter singler-riders line.

Fodor's Choice★
Duration
6 mins.
Crowds
Heavy
Audience
Not Small Kids

The Simpsons Ride. As you enter this attraction through Krusty the Clown's gaping mouth, you wonder right away where you'll exit. On video monitors in the carnival-style queue area you'll be greeted by citizens of Springfield, including police chief Clancy Wiggum, who reminds you that if you must get sick, do it in your hat. That sets the tone. Cartoon colors and video clips prepare you for the preshow that explains that the ever-entrepreneurial Krusty has expanded his empire to include a theme park, which his disgruntled former sidekick, Sideshow Bob, plans to sabotage. After a fairly tame start, your coaster is flying all over virtual-reality Springfield, plunging toward the businesses and buildings you know, and narrowly escaping disaster as Sideshow Bob tears up the tracks. You end up safe thanks to the split-second timing of an unexpected hero.

Weigh your love of the Simpsons against the will of your stomach. If you have even a scintilla of motion sickness, this one will throw you for a colorful, cartoonish loop. Guests who are pregnant or who have heart, back, or neck problems shouldn't ride. Kids must be at least 40 inches to ride, and adults must accompany kids between 40 and 48 inches. **For people with disabilities:** Guests in wheelchairs must transfer to the ride vehicle. ■TIP→ Use Universal Express Pass here.

NEED A BREAK?

The International Food and Film Festival, between The Simpsons Ride and Woody Woodpecker's KidZone, is an efficient, multiethnic food court serving Italian (pizza, lasagna), American (fried chicken, meat loaf), Greek (gyros), and Chinese (orange chicken, stir-fried beef) dishes at affordable prices—usually less than $10. This is also one of three places on the Meal Deal (all-you-can-eat) plan.

WOODY WOODPECKER'S KIDZONE

With its colorful compilation of rides, shows, and play areas, this entire section caters to preschoolers. It's a pint-size Promised Land, where kids can try out a roller coaster and get sprayed, splashed, and soaked in a water park area. It's also a great place for parents, since it gives them a needed break after nearly circling the park.

☆☆☆
Duration
20 mins.
Crowds
Mod. to Heavy
Audience
All Ages

Animal Actors on Location! Animal shows are usually fun, and this one is better than most thanks to an arkful of animal stars. The tricks (or *behaviors*) they perform are loosely based on cable-TV shows: *Emergency Vets*, *Planet's Funniest Animals*, and *The Jeff Corwin Experience*. After a raccoon opens the show, Lassie makes a brief appearance and is followed by an audience-participation segment in the clever Dog Decathlon. Next, Gizmo the parrot from *Ace Ventura: Pet Detective* flies in front of a wind machine and blue screen, the televised image showing him soaring across a desert, a forest, and then in outer space. Bailey the orangutan does impressions (how they teach an ape to impersonate Ricky Martin is a mystery), then there's an overpowering ly adorable chimpanzee and, finally, a brief peek at a boa constrictor. Actually,

Save the planet from interstellar invaders in World Expo's interactive Men in Black: Alien Attack. Zap aliens in city streets and compete with other guests to score points.

the storyline is secondary to the fact that you see some of the cutest actors ever to hit the stage. **For people with disabilities: The** theater is equipped for assisted-listening devices and is wheelchair accessible. ■TIP➔ **Come early for a good seat.**

9

☆☆☆
Duration
20 mins.
Crowds
Light
Audience
Small Kids

A Day in the Park with Barney. If your kids can't get enough of the big purple dinosaur, here he is again! A fairly long preshow features a goofy, kid-friendly emcee. Then you and your of preschoolers enter a pleasant theater-in-the-round that's filled with brilliantly colored trees, clouds, and stars. Within minutes, the kids will cheer like baby boomers at a McCartney concert as their beloved TV playmate (and Baby Bop) dance and sing though clap-along, sing-along monster classics including "Mr. Knickerbocker," "If You're Happy and You Know It," and (of course) "I Love You." Following the very pleasing and thoughtful show and a chance to meet Barney up close, you exit to an elaborate play area with hands-on activities—a water harp, wood-pipe xylophone, and musical rocks—that propel the already excited kids to even greater heights. **For people with disabilities: The theater is equipped with assisted-listening devices and is wheelchair accessible.** ■TIP➔ **Arrive 10–15 minutes early for a good seat—up close and in the center.**

☆☆☆
Duration
Up to You
Crowds
Mod. to Heavy
Audience
Small Kids

Curious George Goes to Town. The celebrated simian visits the Man with the Yellow Hat in a no-line, no-waiting, small-scale water park. The main town square has brightly colored building facades, and the plaza is an interactive aqua playground that adults avoid but kids are drawn to like fish to water. Yes, there's water, water everywhere, especially atop the clock tower, which periodically dumps a mighty 500 gallons down a roof and straight onto a screaming herd of preschoolers. Kids

UNIVERSAL STUDIOS GROWN-UP TOUR

A stroll through Universal Studios will make you feel as if you've covered 3,000 mi in just a few hours. California is just a short walk from New York City; San Francisco a stone's throw from Cape Cod. The genius here is in the details, so take your time and notice the second-hand items in the windows of New York shops, for instance, or Amity's nautical touches.

SOUTH SIDE

Upon entering, don't head straight to Production Central; instead, turn right—onto Rodeo Drive. In a few steps you're in the heart of **Holly-wood.** Although you'll probably drop into attractions such as Terminator 2 3-D and the Universal Horror Make-Up Show, you can also have a soda at Schwab's or a hot dog at Mel's. Not even folks in the real Hollywood can do this. Notice the lovely Garden of Allah bungalows that look as if they were actually moved from Tinseltown.

Next stop: Springfield. Although **The Simpsons Ride** is a thrill, so is the amazing pop art that sets the stage for it. The facade is a decorated like a carnival, with games of chance bordering the towering face of Krusty the Clown. Watch for the kiosk that sells Squishees ("America's favorite icy goo").

NORTH SIDE

San Francisco/Amity merges two places into one spot yet keeps them distinct. In Amity, a Cape Cod–style section with weatherworn shingle buildings, midway games, and saltwater taffy booths. There's a welcoming seaside resort feel here—just ignore the 25-foot shark suspended on a hook outside the Jaws ride. San Francisco comes into view with cobblestone streets, redbrick buildings, and a waterfront inspired by Fisherman's Wharf.

New York captures nearly every borough. There are narrow alleys, fire escapes, a Chinese laundry, pawn shops, and secondhand stores. Round a corner and you'll see the Guggenheim Museum, newspaper offices, Italian restaurants, and Irish pubs. It's an amazing assemblage of styles, with clever signage, props, and effects.

Production Central takes you into the world of soundstages, movies, and TV shows. Look for the posters for the movies and albums being released by the stars of Shrek and other witty details.

At Universal Studios, the fun isn't just about the rides.

love the levers, valves, pumps, and hoses that gush at the rate of 200 gallons per minute, letting them get sprayed, spritzed, splashed, and splattered. At the head of the square, footprints lead to a dry play area, with a rope climb and a ball cage where youngsters can frolic among thousands of foam balls. You can get into the act, sit it out on nearby benches, or take a few minutes to buy souvenir towels to dry off your waterlogged kids. **For people with disabilities:** Most of this attraction is barrier-free. ■TIP→ Crowds are heavy in mid-morning: come in late afternoon or early evening.

☆
Duration
5 mins.
Crowds
Mod. to Heavy
Audience
All Ages

E.T. Adventure. This well-meaning ride is looking (and even smelling) a little tired. If it's your first visit, however, you may still get a kick out of the take on Steven Spielberg's *E.T.* Once you've learned that it's your mission to help E.T. return to his planet, you board a bicycle mounted on a movable platform and fly 3 million light years from Earth (in reality just a few hundred feet), past a squadron of policemen and FBI agents to reach E.T.'s home. Here colorful characters climb on vines, play xylophones, and swing on branches in what looks like an alien Burning Man festival. You'll have to listen very, very closely for the payoff: Having given your name to a host at the start of the ride, E.T. is supposed to bid you a personalized good-bye.

This ride isn't suitable for guests with heart, back, neck, or motion-sickness problems. **For people with disabilities:** Guests with mobility issues must be in a standard-size wheelchair or be willing to transfer to the ride vehicle. Service animals aren't permitted. There's some sudden tilting and accelerating, but even those for whom these movements are a concern could ride in E.T.'s orbs (spaceships) instead of the flying bicycles. ■ TIP→ Use Universal Express Pass here; otherwise, come early.

☆☆
Duration
Up to You
Crowds
Light to Moderate
Audience
Small Kids

Fievel's Playland. Based on the Spielberg animated film *An American Tail*, this playground features larger-than-life props and sets designed to make everyone feel mouse-size. An ingenious collection of massive boots, cans, and other ordinary objects disguise tunnel slides, water play areas, ball crawls, and a gigantic net-climb equipped with tubes, ladders, and rope bridges. A harmonica slide plays music when you slide along the openings, and a 200-foot waterslide gives kids (and a parent if so desired) a chance to swoop down in Fievel's signature sardine can. It should keep the kids entertained for hours. The downside? You might have to build one of these for your backyard when you get home. **For people with disabilities:** Unfortunately, this ride isn't fully accessible to people using wheelchairs. ■ TIP→ Crowds generally aren't significant, but waits do develop for the waterslide. On hot days, come after supper.

☆☆
Duration
1½ mins.
Crowds
Mod. to Heavy
Audience
Small Kids

Woody Woodpecker's Nuthouse Coaster. Unlike the maniacal coasters that put you through zero-g rolls and inversions, this is a low-speed, mild-thrill version (top speed 22 MPH) that makes it a safe bet for younger kids (who must be at least 36 inches tall) and action-phobic adults. It races (a relative term) through a structure that looks like a gadget-filled factory; the cars are shipping crates—some labeled "mixed nuts," others "salted nuts," and some tagged "certifiably nuts." Woody's Nuthouse has several ups and downs to reward you for the wait, and children generally love the low-level introduction to thrill rides. **For people with disabilities:** Guests using wheelchairs must transfer to the ride vehicle. ■ TIP→ Use the Universal Express Pass and/or come at park closing, when most little ones have gone home.

9

HOLLYWOOD

The quintessential tribute to the Golden Age of the silver screen, this area to the right of the park entrance celebrates icons like the Brown Derby, Schwab's Pharmacy, and art-deco Hollywood. There are only a few attractions here, but they're all winners.

UNIVERSAL STUDIOS

NAME	Height Req.	Type of Entertainment	Duration	Crowds	Audience	Tips
Hollywood						
Lucy: A Tribute	n/a	Walk-Through	15 mins.	Light	Adults	Save this for a hot afternoon or for on your way out.
Terminator 2 3-D	n/a	3-D Film/ Simulator Exp.	21 mins.	Heavy	All but Small Kids	Come first thing in the morning or use Universal Express Pass.
★ Universal Horror Make-Up Show	n/a	Show	25 mins.	Light	All but Small Kids	Come in the afternoon or evening. Young children may be frightened; older children eat up the blood-and-guts stories.
Production Central						
★ Hollywood Rip Ride Rockit!	At least 51"	Thrill Ride	2 mins.	You Bet!	All but Small Kids	Come early, late, or use a Universal Express Pass. Be patient.
Jimmy Neutron's Nicktoon Blast	At least 40"	Simulator Exp.	8 mins.	Moderate to Heavy	All Ages	Come at the end of the day; use Universal Express or single-rider line.
Revenge of the Mummy	At least 48"	Thrill Ride	3 mins.	Heavy	All but Small Kids	Use Universal Express Pass, or come first thing in the morning.
Shrek 4-D	n/a	3-D Film	12 mins.	Heavy	All Ages	Come early or late, and use Universal Express Pass.
Twister…Ride It Out	n/a	Show/ Simulator Exp.	3 mins.	Heavy	All but Small Kids	Come first thing in morning or at closing. This "ride" involves standing and watching the action unfold.
San Francisco/Amity						
Beetlejuice's Graveyard Revue	n/a	Show	25 mins.	Light to Moderate	All but Small Kids	You can use Universal Express Pass here, but there's really no need as there's little chance of a wait.
Disaster!	At least 40"	Thrill Ride	20 mins.	Heavy	All but Small Kids	Come early, before closing, or use Universal Express Pass. This is loud.
JAWS	n/a	Thrill Ride with Water	7 mins.	Moderate	All but Small Kids	Come after dark for a more terrifying ride.

Woody Woodpecker's KidZone

A Day in the Park with Barney	n/a	Show	20 mins.	Light	Small Kids	Arrive 10–15 mins. early on crowded days for a good seat—up close and in the center.
Animal Actors on Location!	n/a	Show	20 mins.	Moderate to Heavy	All Ages	Stadium seating, but come early for a good seat.
Curious George Goes to Town	n/a	Playground with Water	Up to you	Moderate to Heavy	Small Kids	Come in late afternoon or early evening. Bring a towel.
E.T. Adventure	n/a	Thrill Ride for Kids	5 mins.	Moderate to Heavy	All Ages	Come early morning or use Universal Express Pass.
Fievel's Playland	n/a	Playground with Water	Up to you	Light to Moderate	Small Kids	Generally light crowds, but there are waits for the waterslide. On hot days come late.
Woody Woodpecker's Nuthouse Coaster	At least 36"	Thrill Ride for Kids	1½ mins.	Moderate to Heavy	Small Kids	Come at park closing, when most little ones have gone home.

World Expo

Men in Black: Alien Attack	At least 42"	Thrill Ride	4½ mins.	Heavy	All but Small Kids	Solo riders can take a faster line, so split up. This ride spins.
★ The Simpsons Ride	40"	Thrill Ride/ Simulator Exp.	6 mins.	Heavy	All but Small Kids	Use Universal Express Pass.

★ = **Fodor's**Choice

☆
Duration
15 mins.
Crowds
Light
Audience
Adults

Lucy: A Tribute. If you smile when you recall Lucy stomping grapes, practicing ballet, gobbling chocolates, or wailing when Ricky won't let her be in the show, then a visit to this mini-museum and major gift shop will be a pleasant, nostalgic visit. The low-key attraction pays tribute to Lucille Ball through scripts, props, costumes, awards, and clips from the comedian's estate, and a challenging trivia quiz game on computer monitors has you trying to get Lucy, Ricky, Fred, and Ethel across the country to Hollywood. It's a nice place to take a break and spend time with one of the funniest women of television. **For people with disabilities:** This attraction is wheelchair accessible; the TV-show excerpts shown on overhead screens aren't closed-captioned. ■TIP➔ Save this for your way out or a hot afternoon.

☆☆☆
Duration
21 mins.
Crowds
Heavy
Audience
Not Small Kids

Terminator 2 3-D. The attraction begins with a very entertaining preshow at the headquarters of the futuristic consortium, Cyberdyne, where a "community relations and media control" hostess greets your group and introduces the latest line of law-enforcing robots. Inside, the cyber-patrol goes haywire, which is the reason to introduce a James Cameron–directed 12-minute 3-D movie. With Schwarzenegger, icy fog, live actors, gunfights, and a chilling finale, the pace of the attraction moves at 100 mph (although the 3-D effects seem few and far between). In the end, kids may be scared silly and require some parental counseling. For those who can handle a few surprises, though, this is a must-see attraction. **For people with disabilities:** The theater is wheelchair accessible. ■TIP➔ Use Universal Express Pass, or come first thing in the morning.

■ NEED A
BREAK?

In the heart of Hollywood, **Schwab's Pharmacy** is a re-creation of the legendary drugstore where—studio publicists claim—Lana Turner was discovered. What you'll discover is a quick stop where you can order ice cream as well as hand-carved turkey and ham sandwiches.

Fodor's Choice★
Duration
25 mins.
Crowds
Light
Audience
Not Small Kids

Universal Horror Make-Up Show. This funny, highly entertaining show begins in an intriguing area where masks, props, and rubber skeletons from classic and contemporary horror films make a great backdrop for a family photo. In the theater, your host brings out a special-effects expert, who describes and shares some secrets about what goes into (and oozes out of) creepy movie effects (e.g., corn syrup and food coloring make for a dandy blood substitute).

Despite the potentially frightening topic, most of the audience gets a kick out of the whole show, because the subject is handled with an extraordinary amount of dead-on humor. Older children, in particular, eat up the blood-and-guts stories. One-liners delivered with comedy-club timing, audience participation, knives, guns, loose limbs—all this goes into creating a flat-out great show. **For people with disabilities:** The theater is wheelchair accessible. Good scripts and good shtik mean that those with visual impairments can enjoy the show. ■TIP➔ Use Universal Express Pass or come in the afternoon or evening.

Islands of Adventure

WORD OF MOUTH

"Islands of Adventure is fun and has plenty of good rides (second behind Magic Kingdom)."

—JillDavis

"If your kids like thrill rides, Islands of Adventure will be their dream theme park."

—321go

ISLANDS OF ADVENTURE PLANNER

Park Information	Park Amenities

Park Information

Guest Services (☏ 407/224–6350) is right near the turnstiles, both before and after you enter Islands of Adventure (IOA). Getting your bearings at IOA is far easier than at its sister park, Universal Studios. Grab a brochure from the rack filled with them a few steps beyond the turnstiles. The brochure has a fold-out map that will acquaint you with the park's simple layout (it's a circle).

And, over by the lagoon, boards are posted with up-to-the-minute ride and show information—including the length of lines at the major attractions. From here, you either head left or right, and you're on your way.

Park Amenities

Baby Care: There are diaper-changing stations in many of the men's and ladies' restrooms at IOA, as well as a nursing station for comfort and privacy at the first-aid station near the entrance. Baby supplies (diapers, food, wipes, etc.) are available at larger stores; ask for those items at the counter, though, as they aren't out on the shelves.

Cameras: Just inside the park, on your right after the turnstiles, is DeFotos camera shop. It has nearly everything you need to make your vacation picture-perfect, including disposable cameras and digital memory cards. This is also IOA's pickup location for the souvenir photos taken by the active contingent of park photographers.

First-Aid: There are two health-services/first-aid centers: one at the front entrance inside Guest Services, and another near Sindbad's Village in the Lost Continent. Just look for the red cross symbol on the building across from Oasis Coolers (or ask a park host).

Lockers: There are $8-a-day lockers across from Guest Services at the entrance; for $10 a day you can rent a family-size model. You have unlimited access to both types throughout the day. Scattered strategically throughout the park—notably at the Incredible Hulk Coaster and Jurassic Park River Adventure—are so-called Smart Lockers. These are free for the first 45 to 60 minutes, $2 per hour afterward, and max out at $14 per day. Stash backpacks and cameras here while you're being drenched on a watery ride or going through the spin cycle on a twisty one.

Lost People and Things: If you've misplaced something, head to Guest Services in the Port of Entry. This is also where lost children are taken by park staffers.

Stroller Rentals: You can rent strollers ($15 per day for singles, $20 for doubles) at the Port of Entry to your left after the turnstiles.

Backstage Tour

This is one of the biggest mysteries at Universal. You'll find nothing about it on-line, and perhaps only a brief mention in the guide map. Nevertheless, you can arrange a 2.5-hour guided tour ($50) that takes you to see areas off-limits to other guests (e.g., the maintenance bay area at Spider-Man).

In addition to delivering a lot of technical and production information, this may (or may not) include instant access to one of the attractions. Compared to the VIP tours where you can obtain similar information and far more access to rides (albeit at a greater cost), this one could be a toss-up. You can get information about this little-known tour at Guest Services when you reach the park, or call ahead to the VIP Tours line at 407/363–8295.

For People with Disabilities

Islands of Adventure has made an all-out effort to make the premises accessible for people with disabilities. Most attractions and all restaurants are wheelchair accessible, and all employees attend workshops on how to meet the needs of guests with disabilities. You may occasionally spot staffers using wheelchairs; many employees have had basic sign-language training. There's also a counter in Guest Services where you can pick up assited-listening and other devices

You can rent manual wheelchairs ($12 per day) and electronic convenience vehicles (ECVs; $50 per day) at the Port of Entry to the left after you enter the turnstiles. A photo ID and a $50 deposit on a credit card is required. Since it's a long way between the parking garages and the park entrance, you may want to rent a push wheelchair at the garages and upgrade to an ECV when you reach the park entrance. Quantities of the latter are limited, so reserve in advance.

Even when the crowds are heavy, the park's avenues are wide enough to maneuver a wheelchair. Hosts and hostesss will direct you to a special attraction entrance or a special show seating area. Guide maps indicate with a special icon which o shows include an interpreter.

Miscellaneous Tips

■ Thanks to the roller coasters, architecture, and kid-pleasing ambience of the park, there's a certain level of mania here. There are, however, places where you can relax—by the lagoon, say, or in an upscale restaurant such as Mythos. Take advantage of opportunities to steal some quiet time.

■ Since it's a long haul back to the parking area, don't lug any of these not-allowed items to Islands of Adventure: alcohol, glass containers, picnic lunches, large coolers, or suitcases.

■ Want to take a good picture? Islands of Adventure posts signs that indicate picture spots and show how best to frame your shot.

■ The three Islands of Adventure restaurants on the Meal Deal plan are Circus McGurkus Café Stoo-pendous, Comic Strip Café, and the Burger Digs.

■ Don't limit your shopping to the park's stores; kiosks throughout the park are loaded with an assortment of items.

10

ISLANDS OF ADVENTURE
EXPLORE NEW LANDS

When Islands of Adventure (IOA) opened in 1999 it took attractions to a new level—a practice that continues with The Wizarding World of Harry Potter, opened in 2010. From Marvel Super Hero Island and Toon Lagoon to Seuss Landing and the Lost Continent, most attractions are impressive—some even out-Disney Disney.

You pass through the turnstiles and into the Port of Entry plaza, a bazaar that brings together bits and pieces of architecture, landscaping, music, and wares from many lands—Dutch windmills, Indonesian pedicabs, African masks. Egyptian figurines adorn the massive archway inscribed with the notice THE ADVENTURE BEGINS. From here, themed islands—arranged around a large lagoon— are connected by walkways that make navigation easy.

When you've done the full circuit, you'll recall the fantastic range of sights, sounds, and experiences and realize there can be truth in advertising. This park really *is* an adventure.

TOURING TIPS

■ Invest in a Universal Express Plus Pass for the right to head to the front of the line and see the park without a sense of urgency.

■ Ask hosts about their favorite experiences—and their suggestions for saving time.

■ If the park's open late, split the day in half. See part of it in the morning, head off-site to a restaurant for lunch, then head to your hotel for a swim or a nap (or both). Return in the cooler, less crowded evening.

■ Take time to explore little-used sidewalks and quiet alcoves and other sanctuaries that help counter the manic energy of IOA.

TOP ATTRACTIONS

FOR AGES 7 AND UP

Amazing Adventures of Spider-Man. Get ready to fight bad guys and marvel at the engineering and technological wizardry on this dazzling attraction.

Dudley Do-Right's Ripsaw Falls. Even if its namesake is a mystery to anyone born after the 1960s, everyone loves the super splashdown at the end of this log-flume ride dedicated to the exploits of the animated Canadian Mountie.

Eighth Voyage of Sindbad. Jumping, diving, punching—is it another Tom Cruise action film? No, it's a cool, live stunt show with a love story to boot.

Harry Potter and the Forbidden Journey. This ride truly brings J.K. Rowlings books to life on an adventure through Hogwarts and beyond with Harry, Hermione, and Ron.

Incredible Hulk Coaster. This super-scary coaster blasts you skyward before sending you on no less than seven inversions. It will be hard to walk straight after this one.

FOR AGES 6 AND UNDER

The Cat in the Hat. It's like entering a Dr. Seuss book: all you have to do is sit on a moving couch and see what it's like when the Cat in the Hat drops by to babysit.

Flight of the Hippogriff. Some of the younger Hogswart "students" will enjoy this low-key coaster in Harry Potter's world.

Popeye and Bluto's Bilge-Rat Barges. This tumultuous (but safe) raft ride lets younger kids experience a big-deal ride that's not too scary—just wild and wet.

WHERE TO SNACK

The park's three Meal Deal (all-you-can-eat) options are **Circus McGurkus Café Stoo-pendous** (chicken, pasta, pizza, burgers, salads) in Seuss Landing; **The Burger Digs** (hamburgers, chicken sandwiches, chicken fingers, milk shakes) in Jurassic Park; and the **Comic Strip Café** (Asian, Italian, American, and fish) in Toon Lagoon. Also in Toon Lagoon is **Blondie's Deli** (jumbo sandwiches). **Pizza Predattoria** and the seasonal **Thunder Falls Terrace** (rotisserie chicken and ribs) are in Jurassic Park, and, near the Port of Entry, is **Confisco's Grill,** with its steaks, salads, sandwiches, soups, and pasta. This is also where character breakfasts are held; there's also a neat little pub.

The ultimate dining experience is the Lost Continent's **Mythos Restaurant.** Although its continental dishes change seasonally, the warm, gooey, chocolate-banana cake is a constant.

10

By Gary
McKechnie

More than at just about any other theme park, Islands of Adventure has gone all out to create settings and attractions that transport you from reality into the surreal. What's more, no one island here has much in common with any other, so, in a way, a visit here is almost like a visit to half a dozen different parks.

IOA's unique nature is first revealed when you arrive at the Port of Entry and are greeted by kaleidoscope sights and cacophony of sounds. It's all designed to put you in the frame of mind for adventure.

When you reach the central lagoon, your clockwise journey commences with Marvel Super Hero Island and its tightly packed concentration of roller coasters and thrill rides. Of special note is the amazingly high-tech and dazzling Amazing Adventures of Spider-Man. In just minutes you'll have experienced a day's worth of sensations—and you've only just begun.

Stepping into Toon Lagoon is like stepping into the pages of a comic book, just as entering the upcoming island, Jurassic Park, is like entering a research center where reconstituted dinosaur DNA is being used to create a new breed of brontosaurus.

You move from the world of science into the world of magic when you segue into The Wizarding World of Harry Potter. For the first time anywhere, you—and not just a few fortunate actors—can wander through the magnificently fictional, yet now very realistic, realm of the young wizard and his Hogwarts classmates and tutors.

But that's not the end of it. In the Lost Continent the mood is that of a Renaissance fair, where crafters work inside colorful tents. It's as pronounced an atmosphere as that of the final island, Seuss Landing, which presents the incredible, topsy-turvy world of Dr. Seuss. It's a riot of colors and shapes and fantastic wildlife that pay tribute to the good doctor's vivid imagination.

MARVEL SUPER HERO ISLAND

Head back to the halcyon days of yesteryear, when, perhaps, you could name every Marvel comics hero and villain. The facades along Stanley Boulevard (named for Marvel's famed editor and co-creator Stan Lee) put you smack in the middle of the sometimes pleasant, sometimes apocalyptic comic-book world—complete with cartoony colors and flourishes.

Although the spiky, horrific towers of Doctor Doom's Fearfall and the vivid green of the Hulk's own coaster are focal points, the Amazing Adventures of Spider-Man is the must-see attraction. At various times Doctor Doom, Spider-Man, and the Incredible Hulk are available for photos, and sidewalk artists are on hand to paint your face like your favorite hero (or villain).

Fodor's Choice★
Duration
4½ mins.
Crowds
Absolutely
Audience
All but Small
Kids

Amazing Adventures of Spider-Man. Even if you've never heard of Peter Parker or J. Jonah Jameson, nearly five minutes spent on this ride can make it worth the hour-long wait in a line that moves through the *Daily Bugle* offices. The experience combines moving vehicles, 3-D film, simulator technology, and special effects. You learn that members of the Sinister Syndicate (Doctor Octopus—aka Doc Oc—Electro, Hobgoblin, Hydro Man, and deadly Scream) have used their Doomsday Anti-Gravity Gun to steal the Statue of Liberty. None of this matters, really; once you board your car and don your 3-D glasses, you're swept up into a weird cartoon battle. When Spider-Man lands on your car, you feel the bump; when Electro runs overhead, you hear his footsteps. You feel the sizzle of electricity, the frigid spray of water from Hydro Man, and the heat from a flaming pumpkin tossed by the Hobgoblin. No matter how many times you visit, you cringe when Doc Oc breaks through a brick wall, raises your car to the top of a skyscraper, and then releases it for a 400-foot free fall. The bizarre angles and perspectives are so disorienting, you really do feel as if you're swinging from a web. Do not miss this one.

Youngsters accustomed to action TV shows should be fine, but timid kids won't. The height minimum is 40 inches. Children between this height and 48 inches must be accompanied by an adult—preferably one who isn't a pregnant women and who doesn't have heart, back, or neck problems. **For people with disabilities:** Equipped for assisted-listening devices. Guests using wheelchairs must transfer to a ride vehicle.

■ TIP→ Use Universal Express Pass, or come early in the day or at dusk. If you don't know much about Spider-Man's villains, check out the wanted posters on the walls.

☆
Duration
1 min.
Crowds
Light to
Moderate
Audience
All but Small
Kids

Doctor Doom's Fearfall. Although the 200-foot-tall towers look really, really scary, the ride itself is just kind of scary—but very cool. Four chairs sit side by side, and you and three fellow guests are seated and strapped in out of the sight of other riders. The disembodied voice of Dr. Doom tells you the contraption is designed to extract fear that he can collect and use to rule the world. Without warning, the chairs are quickly snapped skyward to the peak of the tower and then dropped back down before being lifted and lowered again. The ride is so short it

10

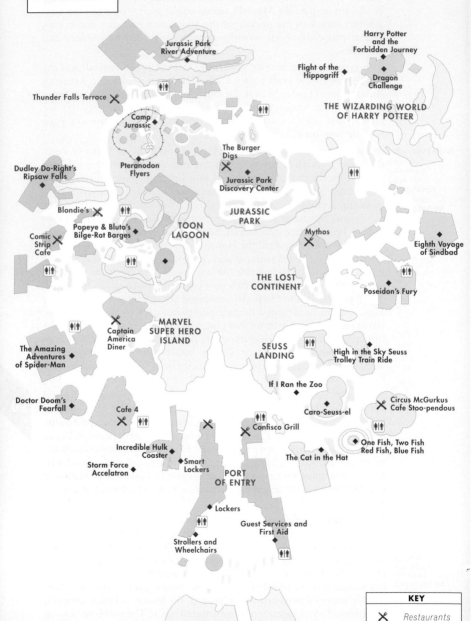

Islands of Adventure

Jurassic Park River Adventure

Harry Potter and the Forbidden Journey

Flight of the Hippogriff

Dragon Challenge

Thunder Falls Terrace

THE WIZARDING WORLD OF HARRY POTTER

Camp Jurassic

The Burger Digs

Dudley Do-Right's Ripsaw Falls

Pteranodon Flyers

Jurassic Park Discovery Center

Blondie's

JURASSIC PARK

Comic Strip Cafe

Popeye & Bluto's Bilge-Rat Barges

TOON LAGOON

Mythos

Eighth Voyage of Sindbad

THE LOST CONTINENT

Poseidon's Fury

Captain America Diner

MARVEL SUPER HERO ISLAND

The Amazing Adventures of Spider-Man

SEUSS LANDING

High in the Sky Seuss Trolley Train Ride

Doctor Doom's Fearfall

If I Ran the Zoo

Circus McGurkus Cafe Stoo-pendous

Cafe 4

Confisco Grill

Caro-Seuss-el

One Fish, Two Fish Red Fish, Blue Fish

Incredible Hulk Coaster

The Cat in the Hat

Storm Force Accelatron

Smart Lockers

PORT OF ENTRY

Lockers

Guest Services and First Aid

Strollers and Wheelchairs

KEY

✕ Restaurants

🚻 Rest rooms

actually feels sort of anticlimactic. It's easy enough to have a second go, as you can actually to step off and get right back into line again.

The minimum ride height is 52 inches, and guests who are pregnant or have heart, back, neck, or motion-sickness problems should sit this one out. **For people with disabilities:** Guests using wheelchairs must transfer to a ride vehicle. ■ TIP➔ Line moves fairly fast, though things can get crowded early in the day; come late or use Universal Express Pass.

☆☆☆
Duration
2¼ mins.
Crowds
Yes!
Audience
All but Small
Kids

Incredible Hulk Coaster. Just seeing this attraction from the sidewalk is a thrill: its cars shoot out from a 150-foot catapult that propels them from 0 to 40 mph in less than two seconds. If this piques your interest, get in line where the walls are illustrated with artwork explaining how the superheroes and villains got their powers. The line for the prized front-row seats is longer than that for other seats. That said, every seat lets you experience flesh-pressing g-forces that match those of an F-16 fighter.

You're whipped into an upside-down, zero-g position more than 10 stories up before being zipped into a dive straight down toward the lagoon at some 60 mph. You then race along the track before spinning through seven rollovers and making a plunge into two deep, foggy subterranean enclosures. Just when you think it's over—it's not. This coaster seems to keeps rolling along well after you've exhausted your supply of screams and shrieks. Powerful.

The minimum height 54 inches, and pregnant women and people with neck, back, or heart problems shouldn't ride. **For people with disabilities:** Guests using wheelchairs must transfer to a ride vehicle. ■ TIP➔ Come here first (effects are best in the morning and in the front row). Use Universal Express Pass.

☆
Duration
2 mins.
Crowds
Light
Audience
All but Small
Kids

Storm Force Accelatron. On this whirling ride X-Men character Storm harnesses the power of weather to battle Magneto by having people like you board Power Orbs. The storyline here is that the containers convert human energy into electrical forces through the power of "cyclospin."

10

Strip away the veneer, however, and what you've got seems like a faster version of Disney World's twirling teacups. Still, it's a high-adrenaline ride that's not for anyone who suffers from motion sickness. It's also not suitable for guests who are pregnant or who have heart, back, or neck problems. **For people with disabilities:** Guests using wheelchairs must transfer to a ride vehicle. ■ TIP➔ Ride whenever—except right after eating.

TOON LAGOON

The main street, Comic Strip Lane, makes use of cartoon characters that are recognizable to anyone—anyone born before 1940, that is. Pert little Betty Boop, gangly Olive Oyl, muscle-bound Popeye, Krazy Kat, Mark Trail, Flash Gordon, Pogo, and Alley Oop are all here, as are the relatively more contemporary Dudley Do-Right, Rocky, Bullwinkle, Beetle Bailey, Cathy, and Hagar the Horrible. With its colorful backdrops, chirpy music, hidden alcoves, squirting fountains, and highly animated scenery, Toon Town is a natural for younger kids.

☆☆☆
Duration
5½ mins.
Crowds
Heavy in Summer
Audience
All but Small Kids

Dudley Do-Right's Ripsaw Falls. In the 1960s, Dudley-Do Right was recognized as the well-intentioned—but considerably dim—Canadian Mountie who somehow managed to always save the damsel and "get his man" (that is, foil the villain). You don't need to be familiar with this character to enjoy the attraction. The twisting, up-and-down flume ride through the Canadian Rockies begins with your mission to help Dudley rescue Nell, his belle, from the evil, conniving Snidely Whiplash. Tucked inside a hollow log, you'll drift gently down the stream until before dropping through the rooftop of a ramshackle dynamite shack. After an explosive dive into a 400,000-gallon lagoon, you're not just damp—you're soaked. If the weather is cold or you absolutely must stay dry, pick up a poncho at Gasoline Alley, opposite the entrance.

The ride isn't suitable for guests who are pregnant or who have heart, back, or neck problems. Kids must be at least 44 inches to ride; those under 48 inches must ride with an adult. **For people with disabilities:** Guests using wheelchairs must transfer to a ride vehicle. ■ TIP→ Use Universal Express Pass, and come in late afternoon, when you're hot as can be, or at day's end, when you're ready to head back to your car. Expect to get wet.

NEED A BREAK?

In Toon Lagoon is Blondie's Deli, home of the Dagwood. The jumbo club sandwich that creates the restaurant's marquee is a hoot, and you can buy the real thing, by the inch, inside. The eatery also sells cookies, hot dogs (Chicago, chili, Reuben, slaw) as well as turkey, roast beef, and tuna sandwiches.

☆☆
Duration
Up to You
Crowds
Heavy
Audience
Small Kids

Me Ship, The Olive. At heart, this is a fantastic playground disguised as a teetering-tottering ship. From bow to stern, there are dozens of participatory activities to keep kids busy as they climb around this jungle-gym that's a boat moored on the edge of Toon Lagoon. Toddlers enjoy crawling in Swee' Pea's Playpen, and older children and their parents can take aim at unsuspecting riders twisting through the rapids over at Popeye and Bluto's Bilge-Rat Barges ride. Primarily, though, this is designed for small kids, with whistles, bells, tunnels, and ladders. Check out the view of the park from the top of the ship. **For people with disabilities:** The playground area is wheelchair accessible. ■ TIP→ Come in the morning or around dinnertime.

☆☆☆
Duration
5 mins.
Crowds
Heavy
Audience
All but Small Kids

Popeye and Bluto's Bilge-Rat Barges. As with every ride at IOA, there's a storyline here, but the real attraction is boarding the wide circular raft with 11 other passengers and then getting soaked, splashed, sprayed, or deluged as it bounces down the twisting stream. The degree of wetness varies, since the direction your raft spins may or may not place you beneath torrents of water flooding from a shoreline water tower or streaming from water guns from an adjacent play area.

Pregnant women and guests with heart, back, neck, or motion-sickness problems should skip this one. The minimum height is 42 inches; children 42 to 48 inches must be accompanied by an adult. **For people with disabilities:** Guests using wheelchairs must transfer to a ride vehicle.

In the Jurassic Park Discovery Center your kids might just learn something about dinosaurs that they didn't already know.

■ TIP→ Come first thing in the morning or an hour before closing. Use Universal Express Pass.

JURASSIC PARK

Just through the towering gates of Jurassic Park, the music is stirring and slightly ominous, the vegetation tropical and junglelike. All of this, plus the high-tension wires and warning signs, does a great job of re-creating the Jurassic Park of Steven Spielberg's blockbuster movie (and its insipid sequels). The half-fun, half-frightening Jurassic Park River Adventure is the island's standout attraction, bringing to life key segments of the movie's climax.

☆
Duration
Up to You
Crowds
Light to Moderate
Audience
All Ages

Camp Jurassic. Remember when you were content with just a swing set and monkey bars? Well, those toys of the past have been replaced by fantastic play areas like this, which are interwoven with the island's theme. Though the camp is primarily for kids, some adults join in, racing along footpaths through the forests, slithering down slides, clambering over swinging bridges and across streams, scrambling up net climbs and rock formations, and exploring mysterious caves full of faux lava. Watch for the dinosaur footprints; when you jump on them, a dinosaur roars somewhere (different footprints are associated with different roars). Also, look out for the watery crossfire nearby—or join in the shooting yourself. **For people with disabilities:** Much of this attraction is wheelchair accessible (its upper levels probably aren't).
■ TIP→ Great anytime.

☆
Duration
Up to You
Crowds
Light
Audience
All but Small Kids

Jurassic Park Discovery Center. If there's a scintilla of information your kids don't know about dinosaurs, they can learn it here. There are demonstration areas where a realistic raptor is being hatched, and where you can see what you'd look like (or sound like) if you were a dino. In the Beasaurus area ("Be-a-Saurus"), you can look at the world from a dinosaur's point of view. There are numerous hands-on exhibits and a quiz game where you can test your knowledge of dinosaur trivia. The casual restaurant upstairs is a nice place to take an air-conditioned break, and tables on the balcony overlook the lagoon. **For people with disabilities:** The attraction is fully wheelchair accessible. ■ TIP➡ Come anytime.

☆☆
Duration
6 mins.
Crowds
Heavy
Audience
All but Small Kids

Jurassic Park River Adventure. It all starts out as a peaceful raft cruise on a mysterious river past friendly, vegetarian dinosaurs. Naturally, something has to go awry. A wrong turn is all that it takes. When you enter one of the research departments, you'll see that it's been overrun by spitting dinosaurs and razor-clawed raptors. This is when things get plenty scary: a towering, roaring T. Rex—with sharp claws and teeth the size of hams—guards the getaway route. Just when you think you're about to become a Cretaceous Era entrée, your raft slips down a tremendously steep 85-foot plunge that will start you screaming. Smile! This is when the souvenir photos are shot. Thanks to high-capacity rafts, the line moves fairly quickly.

The minimum height is 42 inches, and the ride isn't suitable for guests who are pregnant women or who have heart, back, or neck problems. **For people with disabilities:** Guests using wheelchairs must transfer to a ride vehicle. ■ TIP➡ Come early in the morning and/or use Universal Express Pass.

NEED A BREAK?

Thunder Falls Terrace is open for lunch and dinner during peak seasons. One entirely glass side of it is a great place to view the plunge at the Jurassic Park River Adventure. You can also sit outdoors next to the river's thundering waterfall and dine on barbecued ribs, wraps, chicken, turkey legs, soup, and salads. Nearby, Burger Digs and Pizza Predattoria are year-round dining options.

☆
Duration
2 mins.
Crowds
Heavy
Audience
All Ages

Pteranodon Flyers. These prehistoric bird-style gondolas are eye-catching and may tempt you to stand in line for a lift. The problem is that this is a very slow, very low-capacity ride that will eat up a lot of your park time. Do it only if (1) your child asks, (2) you want a prehistoric-bird's-eye view of the Jurassic Park compound, or (3) you've been to the park a dozen times, and this is the last ride to conquer. Children 36 to 56-inches tall must be accompanied by an adult. **For people with disabilities:** Guests using wheelchairs must transfer to a ride vehicle. ■ TIP➡ Crowds are perpetual, since the ride loads slowly, waits can take as much as an hour. Skip this on your first visit.

LOST CONTINENT

Just beyond a wooden bridge, huge mythical birds guard the entrance to a land where trees are hung with weathered metal lanterns, and booming thunder mixes with chimes and vaguely Celtic melodies. Farther along the path, the scene looks similar to a Renaissance Fair as seers and fortune-tellers practice their trade in tents, and, in a huge theater, Sindbad leaps and bounces all over Arabia.

☆☆☆
Duration
25 mins
Crowds
Light
Audience
All but Small Kids

Eighth Voyage of Sindbad. The storyline of this live stunt show is simple: Sindbad and his sidekick Kabob arrive in search of treasure, get distracted by the beautiful Princess Amoura, and are threatened by the evil sorceress Miseria. That's all you really need to know, and it's enough to get the good guy kicking off 25 nonstop minutes of punching, climbing, diving, leaping, and Douglas Fairbanks–ing his way through the performance. Kids are pleased with the action, and women are pleased with Sindbad. The downside is that it's hard to understand the stuntmen who (1) aren't exactly actors and (2) lip-synch to a script that's not as funny as the writer intended. Still, you'll probably be satisfied by the water explosions, flames, and pyrotechnics that end with a daring, flaming high dive. Also, the 1,700-seat theater is a nice place to sit a spell, replenishing your energy. **For people with disabilities:** The theater is equipped for assisted-listening devices and is wheelchair accessible. ■ TIP→ Find seats about 15 minutes before showtime. Don't sit too far up front—the experience is better a few rows back.

☆
Duration
20 mins.
Crowds
Heavy
Audience
All but Small Kids

Poseidon's Fury. After a long walk through cool ruins guarded by the Colossus of Rhodes, a young archaeologist arrives to take you on a trek to find Poseidon's trident. Each chamber you enter looks interesting, but very little happens in most of them. The attraction attempts to bring the entertainment quotient up at the end when, on a 180-degree movie screen, actors playing Poseidon and his archenemy appear. As they shout and point at each other, a memorable fire- and waterworks extravaganza erupts. All around you massive waves crash and scorching fireballs fly. This finale is loud, powerful, and hyperactive. Is it worth the investment of time? That's up to you.

For people with disabilities: The theater is equipped for assisted-listening devices and is wheelchair accessible. ■ TIP→ Stay left against the wall as you enter, and position yourself opposite the central podium In each succeeding section of the presentation, get into the very first row, particularly if you aren't tall.

10

THE WIZARDING WORLD OF HARRY POTTER

In mid 2010, Islands of Adventure fulfilled the fantasy of Harry Potter devotees when it unveiled the biggest theme park addition since the arrival of Disney's Animal Kingdom in 1998. The highly publicized premiere revealed that the land recycles some attractions while seamlessly introducing movie-magic-perfect re-creations of mythical locales such as Hogwarts, Hogsmeade Village, and Diagon Alley. Playing supporting roles are a handful of candy shops, souvenir stores, and restaurants that are each expertly and exquisitely themed to make you believe you've actually boarded the *Hogwarts Express* and arrived in the incredible fantasy world of J.K. Rowling. Expect to be impressed . . . and to wait in line.

CLOSE UP

Hogsmeade Village

In Hogsmeade you'll find the signature restaurant, Three Broomsticks, which serves traditional British fare (as well as an assortment of kids meals), and the Hog's Head Pub, where you can down a pint of Butterbeer or pumpkin juice. The village is also a good place to run errands and pick up sundries. Send a postcard or letter stamped with a novelty (and very real cancellation mark) at Owl Post before selecting (or being selected by) a magic wand at Ollivanders. Pick up some practical jokes (shrunken heads, extendable ears, screaming yo-yos) at Zonko's, and sample strange sweets at HoneyDukes. But the best place to shop for Potterabilia is Dervish and Banges, where there are Hogwarts school uniforms, robes, scarves, T-shirts, and broomsticks—including the legendary Nimbus 2000.

☆☆☆
Duration
3 mins.
Crowds
Heavy
Audience
All but Small Kids

Dragon Challenge. Past guests will recall this as Dueling Dragons, the tandem roller coaster (Fire and Ice) that shot passengers out of the station and into a wild and winding half-mile ride. Now it's the Chinese Fireball and Hungarian Horntail that rocket you in a screaming snap-crackle-pop ride along the rails. In the queue line watch for iconic elements from the Tri-Wizard Tournament; channel those games (or maybe a Quidditch match) when you get hung up in your seat (you're suspended beneath the track) on one of the rides of your life. Making it even more exciting, the coasters are programmed by computer to bring them just feet apart as they blaze through the track at speeds up to 60 miles per hour. There's a 54-inch height requirement. ■TIP➔ Make use of Universal Express Pass. It's perfect for teens and adventurous tweens.

☆☆☆
Duration
1 min.
Crowds
Moderate
Audience
Small Kids

Flight of the Hippogriff. Once known as the Flying Unicorn, this kid-friendly (or at least to kids 36 inches or taller) coaster is a simple way to introduce your children to the pleasures of g-force and vertigo. The queue line takes you past Hagrid's hut and then onboard for a "training flight" above the grounds of Hogwarts Castle. Along the way, there are some nice little twists and dips that'll give them a pint-size dose of adrenaline. An easy alternative to the Dragon Challenge, and one that should please parents and their kids. ■TIP➔ Bring smaller kids here while the older kids ride Dragon Challenge.

Fodor's Choice★
Duration
50–60 mins.
Crowds
Yes!
Audience
All but Small Kids

Harry Potter and the Forbidden Journey. The queue line here is a major part of the attraction. To prepare you for the ride ahead, you'll enter Hogwarts and see the sights you know from the books and films: Headmaster Dumbledore's office, Defence Against the Dark Arts classroom, Gryffindor common room, Room of Requirement, and the greenhouse. You'll also encounter the Sorting Hat, the One-Eyed Witch statue, and several talking portraits. Before reaching the actual ride heroes Harry, Ron, and Hermione appear, and it doesn't take much for them to persuade you to skip a lecture and follow them on a soaring journey. Thanks to a combination of live-action, robotic technology, and innovative filmmaking you come face to face with a flying dragon and the Whomping Willow before being propelled into the heart of a Quidditch

The Cat and his Hat, McGurkus and the Circus, and fish both red and blue are among the attractions geared to the under-7 set at Seuss Landing.

match. You also zip through a dozen scenes and encounter supporting characters Albus Dumbledore, Rubeus Hagrid, Draco Malfoy, and members of the Weasley family. If the visuals aren't enough to fuel this fantasy, a soundtrack from composer John Williams will even the score. To partake of journey, you must be at least 48 inches tall and no more than 6 feet 3 inches tall. You must also weigh under 250 pounds. ■TIP➔ Use your Universal Express Pass and be patient.

SEUSS LANDING

This 10-acre tribute to Dr. Seuss puts you in the midst of his classic children's books. This means spending quality time with the Cat, Things One and Two, Horton, the Lorax, and the Grinch. From topiary sculptures to lurching lampposts to curvy fences to buildings that glow in lavenders, pinks, peaches, and oranges, everything seems surreal. It's a wonderful place to wrap up a day. Even the Cat would approve.

☆☆
Duration
2 mins.
Crowds
Moderate
Audience
All Ages

Caro-Seuss-el. Ordinary horse-centered merry-go-rounds seem passé compared with this menagerie: the cowfish from *McElligot's Pool*, the elephant birds from *Horton Hatches the Egg*, and the Birthday Katroo from *Happy Birthday to You!* It's an entire ark of imaginary and interactive animals: the animals' eyes blink, and their tails wag. It may be a cliché, but there's a good chance you'll feel like a kid again when you hop aboard one of these fantastic creatures. You'll love it. Children under 48 inches must be accompanied by an adult. **For people with disabilities:** Modified mounts let guests using wheelchairs ride without having to transfer to a ride vehicle. ■TIP➔ Use Universal Express Pass,

ISLANDS OF ADVENTURE

NAME	Height Req.	Type of Entertainment	Duration	Crowds	Audience	Tips
Jurassic Park						
Camp Jurassic	n/a	Playground	Up to you	Light to Moderate	All Ages	Come anytime.
Jurassic Park Discovery Center	n/a	Walk-Through	Up to you	Light	All but Small Kids	Come anytime.
Jurassic Park River Adventure	At least 42"	Thrill Ride with Water	6 mins.	Heavy	All but Small Kids	Use Universal Express Pass. Come early or late.
Pteranodon Flyers	At least 36"	Thrill Ride for Kids	2 mins.	Heavy	All Ages	Skip this on your first visit. 36" to 48" can ride but must do so with an adult.
Lost Continent						
Eighth Voyage of Sindbad	n/a	Show	25 mins.	Light	All but Small Kids	Stadium seating, but arrive at least 15 mins. early. Don't sit too far up front.
Poseidon's Fury	n/a	Simulator Exp.	20 mins.	Heavy	All but Small Kids	Come at the end of the day. Stay to the left for best spot. Get in first row each time.
Marvel Super Hero Island						
★ The Amazing Adventures of Spider-Man	At least 40"	Simulator Exp.	4½ mins.	Absolutely	All but Small Kids	Use Universal Express Pass, or come early or late in day. Don't miss the bad guys in the wanted posters.
Doctor Doom's Fearfall	At least 52"	Thrill Ride	1 min.	Light to Moderate	All but Small Kids	Use Universal Express Pass, or come later in the day. Regardless, come with an empty stomach.
Incredible Hulk Coaster	At least 54"	Thrill Ride	2¼ mins.	Yes!	All but Small Kids	Come here first. Effects are best in the morning. The front row is best.
Storm Force Accelatron	n/a	Thrill Ride	2 mins.	Light	All but Small Kids	Come whenever—except right after eating.

Seuss Landing

Caro-Seuss-el	n/a	Thrill Ride for Kids	2 mins.	Moderate	All Ages	Use Universal Express Pass, or end your day here.
The Cat in the Hat	n/a	Thrill Ride for Kids	4½ mins.	Heavy	All Ages	Use Universal Express Pass here, or come early or at the end of the day.
High in the Sky Seuss Trolley Train Tour	At least 34"	Railroad	3 mins.	Heavy	All Ages	Kids love trains, so plan to get in line! 34" to 48" can ride but must do so with an adult.
If I Ran the Zoo	n/a	Playground with Water	Up to you	Heavy	Small Kids	Come toward the end of your visit.
One Fish, Two Fish, Red Fish, Blue Fish	n/a	Thrill Ride for Kids	2+ mins.	Heavy	Small Kids	Use Universal Express Pass, or come early or late in day. Skip it on your first visit.

Toon Lagoon

Dudley Do-Right's Ripsaw Falls	At least 44"	Thrill Ride with Water	5½ mins.	Heavy	All but Small Kids	Ride the flume in late afternoon to cool down, or at day's end. There's ro seat where you can stay dry.
Me Ship, The Olive	n/a	Playground	Up to you	Heavy	Small Kids	Come in the morning or at dinnertime.
Popeye and Buto's Bilge-Rat Barges	At least 42 "	Thrill Ride with Water	5 mins.	Heavy	All but Small Kids	Come early in the morning or before closing. You will get wet.

The Wizarding World of Harry Potter

Dragon Challenge	At least 54"	Thrill Ride	3 mins.	Heavy	All but Small Kids	Use Universal Express Pass.
Flight of the Hippogriff	At least 36"	Thrill Ride for Kids	1 min.	Moderate	Small Kids	Keep an eye on the line, and come when there's an opening.
Harry Potter and the Forbidden Journey	At least 48"	Walk-Through/ Ride-Through/ Thrill Ride	50 mins.	Yes!	All but Small Kids	Come early and use Universal Express Pass.

★ = Fodor'sChoice

DID YOU KNOW?

The Cat in the Hat celebrated its 50th birthday in 2007. The birthday festivities included a nationwide literacy initiative by Random House Children's Books, the publisher of Dr. Seuss's Classic tales.

ISLANDS OF ADVENTURE FAMILY TOUR

As you go through IOA try to see yourself less as a park guest and more as a fledgling explorer and amateur sociologist (sometimes just watching people having fun *is* the fun). Imagine that you're taking in an entirely new world, rather than merely visiting a theme park

In **Marvel Super Hero Island**, most guests race into the Hulk roller coaster and Spider-Man attractions. Instead, spend some time on the bridge or along the waterfront. Watch the frequent launching of the Hulk coaster, and perhaps study the visitors who've gathered for photos and autographs of Marvel superheroes.

In **Jurassic Park**'s Camp Jurassic, a series of paths loop through a prehistoric playground. Why not get lost for awhile? Take time to explore Hogwarts and Diagon Alley over at **The Wizarding World of Harry Potter.** The Lost Continent, with its tents and crafters and colorful bangles, is yet another place to stop and take things in.

Toon Lagoon, the G-rated alternative to Super Hero Island, provides plenty of places to explore, including a marked path that lets you follow the trail of Billy (of Family Circus comic fame), who's wandered off on his own. At **Seuss Landing** find a quiet place to sit and spend some time just watching children (and adults). The closest thing here to a fountain of youth is spinning on a carousel, riding on a Seussian trolley, and meeting the fabled Cat in the Hat.

and/or make this a special end to your day. Lines move pretty well, so don't be intimidated.

☆☆☆
Duration
4½ mins.
Crowds
Heavy
Audience
All Ages

The Cat in the Hat. On this attraction you get to live out the experience of a cat coming to your house to wreak havoc while your mom is out. After boarding a couch that spins, whirls, and rocks through the house, you roll past 18 scenes, 30 characters, and 130 effects that put you in the presence of the mischievous cat. He balances on a ball; hoists china on his umbrella; introduces Thing One and his wild sibling, Thing Two; and flies kites in the house while the voice of reason, the fish in the teapot, sounds the warning about the impending return of the family matriarch. As the tension builds, so does the fun—and kids love pointing out scenes from the book. Children under 48 inches must be accompanied by an adult. **For people with disabilities:** The ride accommodates guests using wheelchairs and is equipped for assisted-listening devices. ■TIP→ Use Universal Express Pass and/or come early or late.

☆☆
Duration
3 mins.
Crowds
Heavy
Audience
Small Kids

The High In The Sky Seuss Trolley Train Ride. Trains on separate tracks embark on a slow and pleasing tour (and aerial view) of the area, with Seuss-like narration along the way. You'll roll right through the Circus McGurkus Café Stoo-pendous and along the shores of the lagoon, where you can see the Sneetches as they enjoy the beaches.

Children 34- to 48-inches tall must be accompanied by an adult. **For people with disabilities:** Guests using wheelchairs must transfer to a ride vehicle. ■TIP→ Kids love trains, so plan to get in line—especially if you have young ones.

10

☆
Duration
Up to You
Crowds
Heavy
Audience
Small Kids

If I Ran the Zoo. In this interactive Seussian maze, kids can ditch the adults and have fun at their level. Here they encounter the trademarked fantasy creatures as they climb, jump, push buttons, and animate strange and wonderful animals. Park designers have learned that kids' basic needs include eating, sleeping, and getting splashed, so they've thoughtfully added interactive fountains. **For people with disabilities:** The area is wheelchair accessible. ■ TIP→ If you can talk your kids into waiting, come at the end of your visit.

■ NEED A
BREAK?

Would you eat ice cream on a boat? Would you drink juice with a goat? Taste vanilla on a cone? Sip some grape juice all alone? Then there are places you must stop. Stop at the **Hop on Pop Ice Cream Shop?** What do you say after Moose Juice Goose Juice? Say, thank you, thank you, Dr. Seuss.

You can also grab a quick bite inside the **Circus McGurkus** fast-food eatery. Check out the walrus balancing on a whisker and the names on the booths: Tum-tummied Swumm, Rolf from the Ocean of Olf, the Remarkable Foon. Occasionally, a circus master–calliope player conducts a sing-along with the diners below. If you prefer dining with large groups of people, keep looking: the cavernous dining room seldom looks even partially full.

☆☆
Duration
2+ mins.
Crowds
Heavy
Audience
Small Kids

One Fish, Two Fish, Red Fish, Blue Fish. Dr. Seuss put elephants in trees and green eggs and ham on trains, so it doesn't seem far-fetched that fish can circle "squirting posts" to a Jamaican beat. After a rather lengthy wait for what seems like a very short experience, you climb into your fish, and, as it spins around a center pole, you (or your child) control its up-and-down motion. The key is to follow the lyrics of the special song—if you go down when the song tells you to go up, you may be drenched courtesy of the aforementioned "squirting post." Mighty silly, mighty fun.

Children under 48 inches must be accompanied by an adult. **For people with disabilities:** Modified mounts let guests using wheelchairs ride without having to transfer to a ride vehicle. ■ TIP→ Use Universal Express Pass and/or come early or late. Consider skipping it on your first visit.

Wet 'n Wild

WORD OF MOUTH

"Wet 'n Wild has great slides but also has a reputation of being [older than the Disney water parks]."

—alpinemccain

WET 'N WILD PLANNER

Park Information

With its array of towers and slides, you can't miss Wet 'n Wild on International Drive. Parking ($10 for cars, vans, and motorcycles and $12 for RVs and cars with trailers) is in a large lot along Universal Boulevard. From here, you'll walk around the corner to the I-Drive entrance. Basic admission for adults (ages 10 and up) is about $48 and $42 for children. Look for coupons in flyers and magazines throughout the I-Drive area. There are other money-saving options, such as the FlexTicket that bundles Wet n' Wild admission with parks and attractions at Universal Orlando, SeaWorld, and Busch Gardens.

Get maps and other information at Guest Services, which is to the left as you enter the park. Initially the park's wide range of attractions, colors, sights, and sounds may overwhelm you. Do yourself a favor: take a few minutes to scan the layout, check your map, and stake out a spot on the beach before heading in.

For general information, call **Wet 'n Wild** (☎ *407/351–3200 recorded information, 407/351–1800 park operations* ⊕ *www.wetnwildorlando.com*) or visit online.

Park Amenities

Baby Care: There's no specific area for baby care at Wet 'n Wild, nor does the park rent strollers. There are changing stations in both men's and women's restrooms.

First-Aid: The First-Aid Stand is between Surf Grill and Pizza & Subs.

Lockers: There are dressing rooms with lockers ($8 plus a $3 deposit) as well as showers and restrooms to the left of the entrance gates. Additional restrooms are near the Bubble Up, the First-Aid Stand, and the Surge.

Lost People and Things: The Lost and Found is at Guest Services, to the left just after you enter the park. This is also where lifeguards and other staffers take lost children.

Picnicking: You're welcome to bring coolers with food into the park, which has many picnic areas—both open and sheltered. Glass containers and alcoholic beverages are not permitted.

Wheelchair Rentals: Near the entrance, you can rent modified wheelchairs (they have large tires that can handle the sand) for $5 per day with a $25 refundable deposit. Note that although many of the paths are flat and accessible, none of the rides accommodates people using wheelchairs.

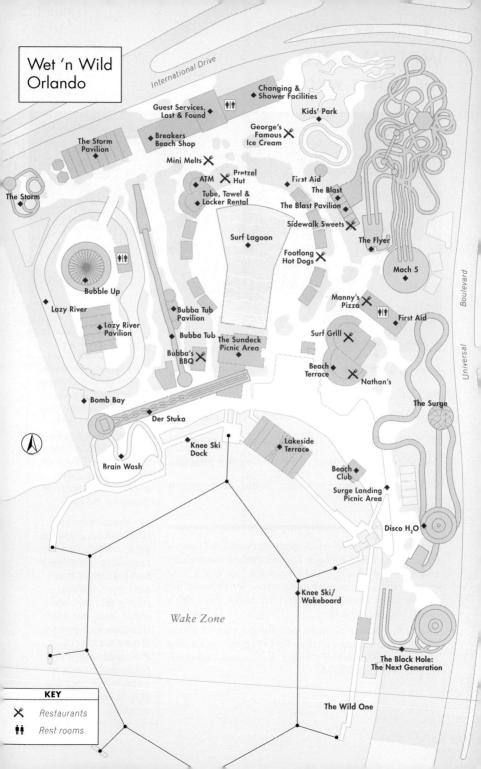

Wet 'n Wild
Orlando

International Drive

The Storm Pavilion

The Storm

Guest Services, Lost & Found

Breakers Beach Shop

Changing & Shower Facilities

Kids' Park

George's Famous Ice Cream

Mini Melts

ATM

Pretzel Hut

Tube, Towel & Locker Rental

First Aid

The Blast

The Blast Pavilion

Sidewalk Sweets

The Flyer

Surf Lagoon

Footlong Hot Dogs

Mach 5

Bubble Up

Lazy River

Lazy River Pavilion

Bubba Tub Pavilion

Bubba Tub

The Sundeck Picnic Area

Bubba's BBQ

Manny's Pizza

First Aid

Surf Grill

Beach Terrace

Nathan's

Bomb Bay

Der Stuka

Knee Ski Dock

Brain Wash

Lakeside Terrace

The Surge

Beach Club

Surge Landing Picnic Area

Disco H$_2$O

Knee Ski/ Wakeboard

Wake Zone

The Black Hole: The Next Generation

The Wild One

Universal Boulevard

WET 'N WILD
THE WATERY WILD SIDE

Since 1977 Wet 'n Wild has been a place to cool off and take a break from the theme parks. Even though the Atlantic Ocean is a mere 50 mi east of Orlando and the Gulf of Mexico is just 90 mi to the west, neither has the massive slides, tube rides, knee-ski lines, and gentle rapids.

Wet 'n Wild has plenty of competition thanks to Disney's Blizzard Beach and Typhoon Lagoon themed water parks and SeaWorld's flashy, splashy Aquatica. But Wet 'n Wild still has the advantage of its location: it's right on the International Drive tourist corridor and a short drive from Universal Orlando.

The park has also earned credit for decades of giving swimmers and aquatic thrill seekers what they're looking for—the most incredible plunges, dives, spins, and swirls they've ever experienced.

WHERE TO EAT

A day here involves nearly nonstop walking, climbing, plunging, and swimming, so eat a high-protein meal and plenty of snacks to keep your energy going. Although there isn't one large restaurant, there are plenty of snack stands and food kiosks scattered throughout the park

Two standouts include **Manny's Pizza** (pizza, spaghetti, and subs) and the main eating establishment, **Surf Grill,** which serves hamburgers, hot dogs, chicken, BBQ beef sandwiches, along with healthier choices such as veggie burgers, baked potatoes, and salads. Smaller kiosks feature cotton candy, ice cream, funnel cakes, and other "carnival-style" selections.

VISITING TIPS

■ Want to save a bundle? Visit after 2 PM, and the admission price drops by half.

■ Note that inner tubes for Surf Lagoon (aka the Wave Pool) are $4 with a $2 deposit. How much are life jackets? Don't be silly—they're free.

■ To claim a prime beach spot, arrive 30 minutes before the park opens, or visit on a cloudy day. If it looks like rain all day, though, head elsewhere.

■ Men should wear a true bathing suit, and women should opt for a one-piece rather than a bikini. Cutoff shorts and garments with rivets, metal buttons, or zippers aren't allowed.

■ Wading slippers are a good idea (put them in a locker or plan to carry them when taking a plunge, though). The rough, hot sidewalks and sandpaper-like pool bottoms can do a number on your feet.

■ Stash money, keys, prescription glasses, and other valuables in a locker.

■ Be patient with the lines here. Just when you think you've arrived, you discover there's another level or two to go.

■ To bypass lines at seven popular rides, get an Express Pass. One-time (i.e., single-use) passes for those rides cost $15. Perpetual passes, which you can use again and again on the popular attractions, cost $25. There are a limited number of passes sold each day; all the more reason to get here early.

■ OK. So you arrived armed with a swimsuit and a towel. But what about sunscreen? You can buy it and other necessities or souvenirs at the Breakers Beach Shop near the park entrance. And if you did forget your towel, renting one here costs $2 with a $2 deposit. Rent a three pack, though, and you'll save $2.

TOP WET 'N WILD ATTRACTIONS

Bomb Bay. You drop through the floor of a cylinder and plummet down a nearly vertical slide—as they say, the first step is a doozie.

Storm. Nestled in an inner tube, you slip into a surreal spin around a massive basin that slowly but surely washes you...down the drain.

Disco H20. Why spin through a watery disco to a 1970s soundtrack? For the aquatic dance-hall sensation that makes this ride so popular.

Brain Wash. Lighting effects and surreal sounds accompany your five-story drop and spin around a 65-foot domed funnel.

Lazy River. This calming stream is a good antidote to all the adrenaline.

Surf Lagoon. If the beach is out of reach, take advantage of the sand and surf here.

Updated
by Gary
McKechnie

When you were a kid, chances are all you needed for unlimited summer fun was a simple inflatable pool and a garden hose or sprinkler. Well, about the same time that you were growing up, so were water parks. They started with a few simple slides, and are now the aquatic equivalents of megamalls.

And it all began with Wet 'n Wild.

As confirmed by *Aquatics International*, Wet 'n Wild, which opened in 1977, was the world's first water park. Although it's now far from alone, it remains extremely popular thanks to its quality; service; and ability to create more heart-stopping waterslides, rides, and tubing adventures than its competitors. There's a complete water playground for kids, numerous high-energy slides for adults, a lazy-river ride, and some quiet sandy beaches on which you can stretch out and get a tan.

Speaking of high energy, this is a park that requires a lot of it. A day here is often a marathon of climbing, sliding, swimming, and splashing. You may not notice just how much your stamina is being drained as you scamper from slide to slide. Plan to take breaks: laze in a beach chair and eat high-protein meals and snacks to maintain your strength. You can bring in a cooler for a picnic or eat at a restaurant in one of several food courts.

If you're not a strong swimmer, don't worry. There are plenty of low-key attractions, and all the ride entrances are marked with warnings to let you know which ones are safe for you. Plus, during peak season, there are as many as 400 lifeguards on duty daily.

Note, too, that the pools here are heated in cooler weather. This, combined with Orlando's temperate climate, means that Wet 'n Wild is one of the few water parks in the country to stay open year-round.

Surf's up!

WET 'N WILD ATTRACTIONS

11

☆☆☆
Duration
1 min.
Crowds
Heavy
Audience
Not Small Kids

Black Hole: The Next Generation. Beneath a massive tower that looks like a UFO, you're hurtled through the cosmos in a two-person "hydra-capsule." All the while there's a dynamic display of lights. Chances are, you'll scream your head off as you zip through space and experience the gravitational effects of Worm Holes and Black Holes before splashdown. The ride-height minimums are 36 inches with an adult, 48 inches without one. ■TIP➔ Try it very early (or late), or invest in an Express Pass.

☆☆
Duration
Under 1 min.
Crowds
Heavy
Audience
Families

The Blast. A pipe has ruptured, and the resulting deluge is enough to create this twisting and turning ride. Aboard a two-passenger inner tube, you and a friend will bump down a series of slides and drops and corners through explosive pipe bursts and drenching waterspouts that lead up to a final waterfall plunge. The ride-height minimums are 36 inches with an adult, 48 inches without one. ■TIP➔ Keep an eye on the line, and hop on as soon as it gets short.

Fodor's Choice★
Duration
Under 1 min.
Crowds
Heavy
Audience
Not Small Kids

Bomb Bay. Lines move quickly here, because a lot of people chicken out once they reach the top. Here's what happens: you step inside a large enclosed cylinder. The attendant looks through the glass door to make sure your arms and legs are crossed (thereby preventing wedgies) and then punches a button to release the trapdoor. Like a bomb dropping out of a plane, you free-fall for 76 feet and then skim down the long, steep slide. The force of the water on your feet, legs, and back rivals the emotional toll it took to take the plunge in the first place. The ride-height minimum is 48 inches. ■TIP➔ The line might look long, but moves quickly. So get on it anytime—if you dare to ride the ride, that is.

Fodor's Choice★
Duration
1 min.
Crowds
Heavy
Audience
Families

Brain Wash. At one of Wet 'n Wild's newest thrill slides, you start by climbing into an inner tube designed for two or four passengers. With lights, video, and surreal sounds washing around you, you and your tube commit to a 53-foot vertical drop—but that's only half of it. Once you've survived the drop, you'll find yourself at the rim of a 65-foot domed funnel and swirl around its massive bowl before finally dropping through into water below. The ride height minimum is 48 inches. ■TIP➔ Try it very early (or very late), or invest in an Express Pass.

☆☆
Duration
Under 1 min.
Crowds
Moderate
Audience
Families

Bubba Tub. Up to four people can ride together. After scaling the platform, your group boards a huge inner tube. It floats over the edge of a six-story slide and into an up-and-down, triple-dip before splashing into the pool. Much of the fun comes from the side-to-side swishing and sloshing of the tube as it travels maniacally down the stream. The ride-height minimums are 36 inches with an adult, 48 inches without one. ■TIP➔ Try it very early (or very late), or invest in an Express Pass.

☆
Duration
Up to You
Crowds
Light
Audience
Small Kids

Bubble Up. Here's a nice twist—an attraction that's off-limits to adults. When kids catch sight of this enormous (about 12 feet tall), wet beach ball, many race right over and try to climb to the top before they're stopped by the laws of gravity and go sliding back down. It's enough to keep them entertained for hours. Surrounding the ball is a wading pool, a respite between attempts to scale the watery mountain. To play you must be between 42 and 64 inches tall. ■ TIP→ When kids spot this, they generally make a beeline for it. Be ready to run with them!

☆☆☆
Duration
1 min.
Crowds
Moderate
Audience
Not Small Kids

Der Stuka. It's a steep slide with thrills similar to those of the adjacent Bomb Bay, but without the trapdoor drop. *Der Stuka* ("Steep Hill" in German) is hard to beat for sheer exhilaration. After climbing the winding six-story platform, you sit down on a horizontal slide, nudge yourself forward a few inches, and then let gravity take over. Before you know it, you're hurtling down a 250-foot-long speed slide that will tax your back and test the security of your bathing suit. This one's a real scream. The ride-height minimum is 48 inches. ■ TIP→ Try it very early (or very late), or invest in an Express Pass.

Fodor's Choice★
Duration
1 min.
Crowds
Heavy
Audience
Families

Disco H20. Here's something even the folks at Studio 54 never dreamed of: a four-person raft that floats into a swirling aquatic nightclub. Once inside the 70-foot-tall building, your raft goes into a spin cycle as disco balls twirl, the lights flash, and the sounds of the '70s greatest hits reverberate. Incredibly, even with the bad music, this is one of the park's most popular attractions. You must be 36 inches (with an adult) or 48 inches in height, or you'll upset the bouncer. ■ TIP→ Try it very early (or very late), or invest in an Express Pass.

☆☆
Duration
1 min.
Crowds
Heavy
Audience
Families

The Flyer. If you've ever visited a ski resort during the summer, you've probably seen a toboggan run that you can take in a retrofitted sled. Well, that's kind of the same principle here, but with one difference: there's water. After getting onto your four-person toboggan, you'll slosh around and race into switchback curves and down suddenly steep drops. The turns are similar to those on a real toboggan run—just much warmer and more refreshing. The ride-height minimums are 36 inches with an adult, 48 inches without one. ■ TIP→ Watch the line, and head over when the timing's right.

☆☆
Duration
Up to You
Crowds
Mod. to Heavy
Audience
Families

Kids' Park. Every few minutes a 5-foot-tall bucket dumps 250 gallons of water onto a seashell-decorated awning, where it splashes off to spray all and sundry. In the center of the attraction is a pool surrounded by miniature versions (designed for children under 48 inches in height) of the more popular grown-up attractions and rides. Children are overjoyed when they see that they can play with a garden hose; they go absolutely nuts when they see that they can slide, splash, squirt, and swim on rides here. There's also a kid-size sand castle to play in. Tables and chairs go fast, with many families settling in for nearly their whole visit. To enjoy the rides, you must be no more than 48 inches tall. ■ TIP→ Come when you need a break but the kids still have energy.

☆
Duration
Over 1 min.
Crowds
Vary by Season
Audience
Tweens & Teens

Knee Ski/Wakeboard. A molasses-slow line marks the entrance to this seasonal attraction, which requires an additional fee: $10 for an all-day pass. A moving cable with ski ropes attached encircles a large lake. After donning protective headgear and a life vest, you kneel on a kneeboard or try to balance yourself on a wakeboard, grab a ski rope, and are given the chance to circumnavigate the lake. The ½-mi ride includes five turns: roughly 75% of the riders wipe out after the first one, and 90% are gone by the second. Only the agile and athletic few make it the distance. Hint: if you wipe out before the first turn, you get to go back and try again. The ride-height minimum is 56 inches. ■ TIP→ An

WET 'N WILD WATER PARKS

Name	Height Req.	Type of Entertainment	Duration	Crowds	Audience	Tips
Black Hole: The Next Generation	36" with an adult, 48" without	Waterslide	1 min.	Heavy	Not Small Kids	Try it very early (or very late) or invest in an Express Pass.
The Blast	36" with an adult, 48" without	Waterslide	Under 1 min.	Heavy	Families	Watch the line.
★ Bomb Bay	At least 48"	Waterslide	Under 1 min.	Heavy	Not Small Kids	Watch the line.
★ Brain Wash	At least 48"	Waterslide	1 min.	Heavy	Families	Try it very early (or very late) or invest in an Express Pass.
Bubba Tub	36" with an adult, 48" without	Waterslide	Under 1 min.	Moderate	Families	Early, late, or EXPRESS Pass.
Bubble Up	42"–64" only	Pool Area	Up to You	Light	Small Kids	Come when your kids are ready.
Der Stuka	At least 48"	Waterslide	1 min.	Moderate	Not Small Kids	Come early, late, or use an Express Pass.
★ Disco H2O	36" with an adult, 48" without	Waterslide	1 min.	Heavy	Families	Come early, late, or use an Express Pass.
The Flyer	36" with an adult, 48" without	Waterslide	1 min.	Heavy	Families	Watch the line.
Kids' Park	Under 48" to ride the rides	Pool Area	Up to You	Mod. to Heavy	Small Kids	Come when you need a break but the kids still have energy.
Knee Ski/ Wakeboard	At least 56"	Thrill Ride with Water	Over 1 min.	Varies by Season	Tweens & Teens	It sosts extra, but the pass is good all day.
Lazy River	n/a	Pool Area	Up to You	Moderate	All Ages	Come whenever you wish
Mach 5	n/a	Waterslide	1 min.	Moderate	Not Small Kids	Come early, late, or when the line looks short.
The Storm	At least 48"	Waterslide	1 min.	Moderate	Not Small Kids	Come early or late.
Surf Lagoon	Under 48" must wear flotation devices	Beach Area	Up to You	Mod. to Heavy	All Ages	Come anytime.
The Surge	36" with an adult, 48" without	Waterslide	Under 1 min.	Moderate	Families	Early, late, or EXPRESS Pass
The Wild One	51"	Thrill ride	Over 1 min.	Varies by Season	Older children and adults	Open seasonally, so early, late, or when the line looks short

extra fee means that the lines may be shorter (but not necessarily faster). The pass is good all day, so return when there's not a wait.

☆☆☆
Duration
Up to You
Crowds
Moderate
Audience
All Ages

Lazy River. Just settle into an inner tube for a peaceful trip down a gently moving stream, guided along by the slow current. As you bask in the sun, you drift past colorful flowers and tropical greenery that grow so incredibly high.

This is a great place to take a break when your body just can't handle any more climbing or free-falling. ■TIP➔ Come and go as you wish!

☆☆
Duration
1 min.
Crowds
Moderate
Audience
Not Small Kids

Mach 5. After grabbing a soft foam board, you scale a few steps and arrive at one of three waterslides. Conventional wisdom says that Lane B is the best, but it's possible all three are the same. Riding on your belly, you zip through some great twists, feel the sensation of hitting the high banks, and then splash down in a flood of water. It's mucho fun. There aren't any height requirements, but you must be able to control the foam board. ■TIP➔ Try it very early (or very late).

☆☆☆
Duration
1 min.
Crowds
Moderate
Audience
Not Small Kids

The Storm. From the top of the tower you'll see that two tubes are flowing with a torrent of water. Climb in a tube, shove off in the midst of a tidal wave, and let the slow, curving arc take you around and around until you reach a 30-foot-diameter bowl. At this point, you spin around again like soap suds whirling around a sink drain. After angular momentum has had its fun, you drop through a hole in the bottom of the bowl and into a small pool. Once you get your bearings, you may be tempted to climb up and do it again. The ride-height minimum is 48 inches. ■TIP➔ Get in line early in the day or later in the evening.

☆☆☆
Duration
Up to You
Crowds
Mod. to Heavy
Audience
All Ages

Surf Lagoon. This 17,000-square-foot lagoon is as close to a beach as you'll get in the park, which explains why it's generally packed. Also known as the Wave Pool, it's just past the turnstiles. Every so often, the lagoon is buffeted by 4-foot-high waves, which elicit screams of delight from kids. Likewise, adults are thrilled to find that the money they spent on the kid's floats, surfboards, and inner tubes was worth it. Children under 48 inches must wear an approved flotation device when swimming in the wave pool. ■TIP➔ Anytime is fine.

☆☆
Duration
Under 1 min.
Crowds
Moderate
Audience
Families

The Surge. The title overstates the thrill of this ride, although it does border on exhilarating. If you or your kids are too nervous for rides like Bomb Bay or the Black Hole, then this may be a good alternative. You and up to three other passengers can fit into its giant rafts. After going over the lip of the first drop, the raft zips down five stories while twisting and turning through a series of steeply banked curves and zooming beneath waterfalls. The ride-height minimums are 36 inches with an adult, 48 inches without one. ■TIP➔ Try it very early (or very late), or invest in an Express Pass.

☆
Duration
Over 1 min.
Crowds
Vary by Season
Audience
Not Small Kids

The Wild One. For this ride, which is open seasonally (usually April through September), you're towed around a lake in a large, two-person inner tube. It's much like being towed behind a water-ski boat, where your ability to stay afloat and atop the tube is challenged by the boat's wake.

Things get bumpy here, too. Like the knee skis, this requires an additional $10 fee for the day. The ride-height minimum is 51 inches. ■TIP➔ Come early or come late.

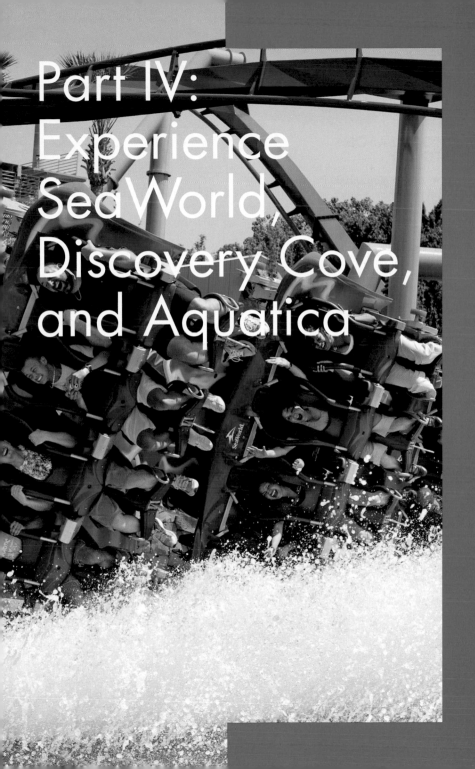

Part IV: Experience SeaWorld, Discovery Cove, and Aquatica

WELCOME TO SEAWORLD, DISCOVERY COVE, AND AQUATICA

TOP REASONS TO GO

★ **Animal Magnetism:** If you love animals—slick, shiny, feathery, or furry—SeaWorld, Discovery Cove, and Aquatica are where you want to be. No robotic wildlife here; just well-cared-for and talented dolphins, whales, seals, otters, penguins, cats, dogs, and an ark-load of other creatures.

★ **A Slower Pace:** The shows and natural settings of SeaWorld and Discovery Cove let you enjoy a theme-park vacation without racing from one attraction to the next. Living in the moment is the lesson here.

★ **Getting Smarter:** No one leaves these parks without learning a little something about nature through shows, back-stage tours, instructional signage, and well-versed educators and naturalists who are always ready to answer questions.

★ **Memories in the Making:** Chances are SeaWorld and Discovery Cove will afford you the chance to pet a penguin, feed a dolphin, or watch a 5-ton whale leap out of the water. You can't forget things like that.

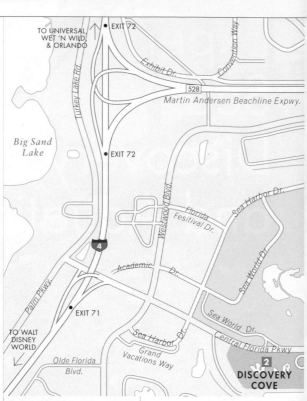

1 SeaWorld. With the exception of a handful of thrill rides, the original park (which opened in 1973 to siphon off visitors heading to the then recently opened Walt Disney World) maintains a slow and easy pace. Here it's all about clever shows, shaded sidewalks, and plenty of opportunities to enjoy the natural grace and intriguing personalities of marine life and other animals.

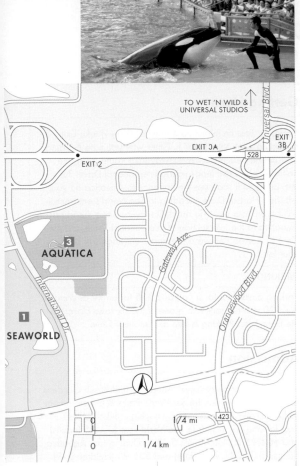

TO WET 'N WILD & UNIVERSAL STUDIOS

EXIT 3A

EXIT 3B

EXIT 2

528

3
AQUATICA

1
SEAWORLD

Universal Blvd.

Gateway Ave.

International Dr.

Orangewood Blvd.

1/4 mi   423

0
0   1/4 km

GETTING ORIENTED

SeaWorld is just off the intersection of Interstate 4 and the Beachline Expressway, equidistant from Universal Orlando and the Walt Disney World Resort, which are about five minutes away. SeaWorld is also a mere 10 minutes from downtown Orlando and 15 minutes from the airport. Discovery Cove is its own oasis across the street from SeaWorld. Aquatica, a little ways down the road from both, is the first of the three that you'll see after exiting the expressway.

2 Discovery Cove. In 2000 SeaWorld spun off this park to give you the chance to enjoy a lot more time (and to spend a little more cash) with the animals. A trip to this park is a daylong, all-inclusive experience that includes breakfast and lunch, drinks, a private beach, snorkeling equipment, and—for an extra $100—the chance to swim with dolphins. Paradise

3 Aquatica. Opened in 2008, SeaWorld's water park offers the chance to slip and slide at adrenaline-rush speeds, relax in the current of two wave pools, laze on a wide beach, and take the wee ones to pint-sized play areas of their very own. All in all, there's something for everyone showcased in a tropical, tiki-themed setting.

Orlando

CENTRAL FLORIDA

SEAWORLD, DISCOVERY COVE, AND AQUATICA PLANNER

Operating Hours

SeaWorld opens daily at 9 AM and closes at 7 PM, with extended hours during the summer and holidays. Hours at Discovery Cove also vary seasonally, although it's generally open daily from 9 to 5:30. Aquatica is open at 9 AM, with closing times varying between 5 and 10 PM depending on the season. Allow a full day to see each attraction.

Contacts

Aquatica: ☎ 888/800–5447 ⊕ www.aquaticabyseaworld. com

Busch Gardens Tampa: ☎ 877/557–7404 ⊕ www. buschgardens.com/bgt

Discovery Cove: ☎ 877/557–7404 ⊕ www.discoverycove. com

SeaWorld: ☎ 888/800–5447 ⊕ www.seaworld.com

Getting Here

Heading west on Interstate 4 (toward Disney) take Exit 72; heaading east, take Exit 71. Either way you'll be heading east on the Beachline Expressway (aka Route 528); the first right-hand exit leads you to International Drive. Turn left, and you'll soon see the entrance to Aquatica on your left. Sea Harbor Drive—leading to SeaWorld's entrance—will be on your right. To reach Discovery Cove, head past Aquatica to the intersection of International Drive and the Central Florida Parkway. The park's entrance will be on your left.

PARKING

Parking costs $12 for a car, and $15 for an RV or camper. For $20 you can pull into a one of the six rows closest to the front gate. Parking is free at Discovery Cove.

Admission

SeaWorld, Discovery Cove, Aquatica, and Busch Gardens Tampa Bay fall under the SeaWorld Parks & Entertainment umbrella, and you can save by buying combo tickets. Regular one-day tickets to **SeaWorld** cost $74.95 (adults) and $64.95 (children ages 3–9), excluding tax. **Aquatica** admission is $41.95 (adults) and $35.95 (children 3–9).

Reserve **Discovery Cove** visits well in advance—attendance is limited to about 1,000 a day. Tickets (with a dolphin swim) start at $199 (off-season) but are generally around $289. Forego the dolphin swim and save $100. Either fee includes access to all beach and snorkeling areas and the free-flight aviary; meals and snacks; use of a mask, snorkel, swim vest, towel, locker, and sunscreen; parking; and a pass for 14 days of unlimited admission to SeaWorld Orlando, Aquatica, or Busch Gardens Tampa.

QUICK QUEUE PASSES

SeaWorld's Quick Queue pass, which costs $14.95–$24.95 per person depending on the season, gets you to the front of the line at major attractions and shows. Neither Discovery Cove nor Aquatica has such a pass.

Smart SeaWorld

Avoid weekend and school-holiday visits. These are the busiest times, so plan around them if you can.

Wear sneakers or water shoes—no heels or slip-on sandals.

Pack dry clothes. You can get wet just by being toward the front at the Shamu show or riding Journey to Atlantis. Alternatively, carry a rain poncho.

Budget for food for the animals. Participating in animal feedings is a major part of the SeaWorld experience. A small carton of fish costs $5.

Pick up a map/show schedule inside the entrance. Spend a few minutes planning so you can casually stroll from show to show and have time for learning, testing out thrill rides, *and* enjoying a leisurely meal.

Be open to learning. SeaWorld's trainers and educators are always at the ready to share information about the park's wildlife.

Discovery Done Right

Make reservations well in advance. Prized June dates, for instance, can sell out in March. If there aren't openings when you call, though, don't despair. Call back often to inquire about cancellations.

Think about your eyewear. Park masks don't accommodate glasses, and there's a limited number of prescription masks (first-come, first-served). Consider wearing contacts as an alternative.

Don't bring your own wet suit or fins. Every guest must wear a Discovery Cove–issued wet suit or vest—not a bad idea, as the water can be cold.

Leave belongings in your locker. The plastic passes you're given are all you need to pick up your meals, soft drinks, and—if you're over 21—alcoholic drinks.

Be flexible when it comes to weather. If weather is really bad (e.g., a daylong thunderstorm) on your reserved day, attempts will be made to reschedule for while you're in town. If that's not possible, you'll have to settle for a refund.

Have a dolphin relay a message. The Special Occasion Package enlists the help of a bottlenose dolphin to deliver love notes, wedding proposals, birthday or anniversary greetings, and the like.

Aquatica Advice

■ **Buy tickets in advance.** Tickets bought ahead of time online or at another park allow early entry to Aquatica, which, in turn, increases your chances of hitting all the big-deal flume and tube rides—possibly more than once.

■ **Be open to animal encounters.** The Commerson's dolphins of Dolphin Plunge have scheduled feeding times, and you can see macaws perched on tree limbs and small mammals on display in Conservation Cabanas—usually attended to by knowledgeable educators.

■ **Pack beach supplies.** You'll save a few bucks by having your own towels, lotion, water shoes, and snacks.

■ **Take care of yourself.** Fight fatigue by eating a good breakfast, drinking plenty of water, and nibbling on high-energy snacks. Avoid sunburn by re-applying sunscreen often—even the waterproof stuff washes off.

■ **Save your soles.** Water shoes protect your feet from hot sand and sidewalks and the rough surfaces in some pools.

DID YOU KNOW?

Commerson's dolphins (*Cephalorhynchus commersonii*) were named after Philibert Commerçon, an 18th-century scientist who saw them swimming in the Strait of Magellan in South America.

SEAWORLD NEWS

SeaWorld and Discovery Cove offer a relatively low-key, ocean-themed experience and are designed for animal lovers and those who prefer the natural to the manmade. Aquatica, on the other hand, suits those who are looking for the action of waterslides, wave lagoons, and beaches.

At SeaWorld you can catch a series of high-energy shows involving dolphins, whales, sea lions, a huge walrus, and even cats and dogs. Plus, you can ride three thrilling coasters: Kraken, considered one of the scariest rides in Florida; Journey to Atlantis, a splashy flume ride; and the park's newest coaster, Manta, which is designed to make you feel like you're sailing along with a giant manta ray.

If you had visited SeaWorld prior to 2010, you might recognize a slight, but important, difference on this trip at shows involving Shamu and his extended family. Trainers are more cautious about their interactions with the killer whales due to the tragic death of one of their colleagues in February 2010.

Discovery Cove is more of a laid-back oasis. In your wet suit or swim vest (provided) you can spend a magical day snorkeling among tropical fish; getting up close to tropical birds in an aviary; relaxing on the beach; and, for a short period and extra charge, interacting with dolphins. You'll pay roughly three times as much as for a ticket to SeaWorld, but your ticket includes 14 days of unlimited access to either SeaWorld or Aquatica or Tampa's Busch Gardens either before or after your visit to Discovery Cove.

There's no denying that SeaWorld's water park, Aquatica, was designed to compete with Disney's Blizzard Beach and Typhoon Lagoon and Universal's Wet 'n Wild. There's also no denying that it does

so—admirably. It's aesthetically pleasing, with tropical, tiki-theme, and eye-popping color schemes. It's also universally appealing, with 36 waterslides of varying thrill levels, six rivers and lagoons, and plenty of calm sandy stretches.

Are you a family with teens looking for adrenaline-rush rides? Do you have toddlers who need pint-size attractions? Are you honeymooners who simply want to sunbathe? All of you can find attractions here, whether lazing on the sands, bobbing in the wave pool, or screaming your heads off in a winding pitch-black tube en route to a super splashdown.

What's New

In 2008 Anheuser-Busch—whose Busch Entertainment Group oversaw SeaWorld and Busch Gardens—was purchased by Belgium's InBev. From the start, onlookers felt that InBev wasn't keen on running theme parks.

Their suspicions were proven correct when, in late 2009, the conglomerate accepted a $2.7 billion offer from the Blackstone Group, a financial services company, for the theme-park branch—that is, three SeaWorld parks (Orlando, San Diego, and San Antonio), Busch Gardens Tampa, and Busch Gardens in Williamsburg, Virginia.

What does it all mean to you? Well, when you visit SeaWorld, you're now visiting the flagship of SeaWorld Parks & Entertainment. And even though you won't receive any free samples of Busch beer or spend time posing for a picture with the iconic Clydesdale horses, don't fret. The real stars of SeaWorld were never draught horses anyway.

SHOPPING SEAWORLD

All three of SeaWorld's parks sell T-shirts, sweatshirts, plush toys, and other park- and marine-themed souvenirs. There are, however, other options—if you know where to look.

SeaWorld

Expect ray-themed merchandise near Manta, dolphin plush toys near the Whale and Dolphin Stadium, polar bear–related items by Wild Arctic, and so on. In an area called the Waterfront, stores carry general SeaWorld merchandise as well as clothing, custom-made dolls, art, and videos.

One standout souvenir is a fresh pearl selected and delivered to you by a diver at the Oyster's Secret. Another is a plush Shamu toy, which you can find at any gift store, including top shop **Shamu's Emporium**. It's just inside the entrance/exit—in case you must pick up yet another plush Shamu toy before leaving.

Discovery Cove

A few shops and kiosks sell sundries and the expected dolphin-themed souvenirs. But at the top shop—the small, cabana-style **Beach Kiosk** between Guest Services and the Laguna Grill—you can also find fine jewelry, marine-themed art, and home-decor items. As the ultimate Discovery Cove thrill is the optional dolphin swim, the ultimate purchase might just be a photo package that includes shots of you splashing in the water with your newfound dolphin pal.

Aquatica

Numerous shops and kiosks sell beach towels, surf wear, and sunglasses—which rank high on the list of top souvenirs— as well as sundries. In addition, be on the lookout for handmade crafts and tropical-themed souvenirs. **Adaptations** gets top-shop points for its beach apparel and surf wear from names like Roxy and Quicksilver.

DINING
SEAWORLD

SeaWorld

participating restaurants—include Voyager's Smokehouse, Spice Mill, Terrace Café, Mango Joe's, Seaport Pizza, and the Seafire Inn—but not at the kiosks. The top dining choice is the classy **Sharks Underwater Grill.** Its broad windows look into a 660,000-gallon aquarium, and its upscale menu has items like filet mignon, New York strip steak, and chicken Portobello. Take time to savor your meal and the surroundings.

The **Makahiki Luau,** held at the Seafire Inn at the Waterfront, begins with a welcome drink and hula lesson before the arrival of the Grand Kahuna. What follows is a family-friendly stage show that includes sing-alongs, a drumming contest, and torch twirling.Reservations are required (call *888/800–5447*) and may be made in advance or on the same day at the information counter near the entrance. The cost is $46 for adults and $29 for children ages 3 to 9, which includes unlimited nonalcoholic drinks and one cocktail for adults. If you have reservations and arrive about an hour before the luau, you can spend a little time inside the park. Alert the parking-lot attendants to your plans, and they'll admit you for free.

Discovery Cove

Discovery Cove's all-inclusive admission means you get to eat and drink as much as you want at snack huts all day. The top dining experience, however, is at the **Laguna Grill.** You'll sit beneath a towering tiki-style ceiling and in open-air dining areas to feast on fresh entrées prepared in the open kitchen.

Aquatica

In addition to many snack spots there's the **Waterstone Grill,** which serves sandwiches, wraps, and kids' meals. If it's peak season, consider the all-you-can-eat **Banana Beach Cookout.** The per-person set prices of $19.99 adults and $11.99 for kids get you burgers, hot dogs, drumsticks, corn on the cob, soft drinks, and salads.

ANIMAL ADVENTURES

SeaWorld has several programs that put you closer to the animals. Basic Spotlight and Behind-the-Scenes tours last 60 to 90 minutes and cost around $30–$50. The seven-hour VIP Tour—which includes instant access to Manta, reserved show seating, the chance to feed the animals, and lunch—is $100.

You can book tours up to three months in advance. For a complete list of them, check the SeaWorld Web site (⊕ *www. seaworld.com*) or give the park a call (☎ *407/351–3600*).

Interactive Programs

For the **Beluga Interaction Program** (from $99) you don a wet suit—which makes it look like you know what you're doing— and assist a trainer in feeding these whales, which average about 15 feet and 2,000 pounds. They're good-natured and well-trained enough to respond to hand signals you learn from the trainer.

The daylong **Marine Mammal Keeper Experience** (from $399) includes lunch, a T-shirt, seven consecutive days of park admission, and, perhaps, a lasting desire to become a SeaWorld trainer. Starting at 6:30 AM, you work side by side with trainers to care for, feed, and train dolphins, manatees, sea lions, and Beluga whales.

The **Shark Deep Dive Program** (from $149) puts you in a steel cage, surrounded by sharks. Wearing a wet suit and a helmet that provides a steady stream of air and a means to communicate, you enter the submerged cage and are towed through the Shark Encounter habitat. Kinda creepy. Kinda cool.

Sleepovers

Sleepovers are arranged primarily for kids, with special programs designed specifically for Boy Scouts, Girl Scouts, and students from grades 2 to 12. Summer sleepovers are geared to families with kids between kindergarten and fifth grade. The sleepovers are held indoors beside a habitat for sharks, manatees, dolphins, Beluga whales, polar bears, penguins, or manta rays. The evening begins at 6 and includes a pizza dinner, a walk around the exhibit with a trainer, and a continental breakfast. Expect to pay $78 for the experience (add $25 for next-day admission to the park).

Trainer For A Day

Discovery Cove's **Trainer For A Day** (from $398) rivals SeaWorld's Marine Mammal Keeper Experience. General Discovery Cove admission includes meals, wet suits, and diving gear; this tour adds a gift bag, waterproof camera, trainer T-shirt, 30-minute dolphin swim, photo session with two dolphins, and an almost exclusive (only eight guests in the entire lagoon) interaction that includes a "double-foot push" (two dolphins propel you across the lagoon by the soles of your feet). Ready for more? Head to the dolphin back area and talk to trainers about how they teach and care for these amazing animals.

VIP Tours

SeaWorld's **VIP Tour** (from $100) provides instant access to Manta and reserved seating at the Believe, Blue Horizons, and Clyde and Seamore shows; a chance to feed sea lions, dolphins, and rays; and a buffet lunch. You'll be traveling with a group of 12. One step up from the VIP Tour is the **Elite VIP Tour** (from $250), which is limited to you and whoever else you'd like—a spouse, some friends. It also adds a penguin encounter and replaces the buffet lunch with a meal at Sharks Underwater Grill.

SEAWORLD SHOWS AND TOURS

	Name	Animal(s)	Duration (approximate)	Cost
	Behind-the-Scenes Tour	Manatees, sea turtles, shark, polar bears, penguins	90 minutes	From $30
★	Believe/Shamu Rocks shows	Killer whales, dolphins	30 minutes	Free
	Beluga Interaction Program	Beluga whales	90 minutes	From $99
	Blue Horizon show	Dolphins, Beluga whales	20 minutes	Free
★	Clyde and Seamore Take Pirate Island show	Sea lions, otters	25 minutes	Free
	Dolphin Spotlight Tour	Dolphins	60 minutes	From $50
	Elite VIP Tour	Penguins, dolphins, sea lions, stingrays, sharks	7 hours	From $250
	Marine Mammal Keeper Experience	Dolphins, Beluga whales, sea lions	Up to 8.5 hours	From $399
	Penguin Spotlight Tour	Penguins, puffins	60 minutes	From $40
	Sharks Deep Dive	Sharks	90 minutes	From $149
	VIP Tour	Killer whales, dolphins, rays, sea lions.	7 hours	From $100

SeaWorld and Discovery Cove

WORD OF MOUTH

"SeaWorld has fewer rides but fewer lines. It also has animal shows . . . the Shamu show is amazing, but Pets Ahoy is terrific."
—321go

"SeaWorld . . . is very manageable on a 100+ heat index day, with all the "splash" potential and air-conditioned areas. . . ."
—rattravelers

SEAWORLD AND DISCOVERY COVE PLANNER

Guest Services

SeaWorld's Main Information Center is near the entrance. Pick up the park map—which also has info on showtimes, services, and amenities—make dinner reservations; and buy tickets for the luau, Discovery Cove, Aquatica, and tours. You can get information at the **Discovery Cove Check-In Lobby** when you arrive, or at **Guest Services** just after you enter.

For People with Disabilities

Get info on services and rent standard wheelchairs ($10 daily) and electric wheelchairs ($45 daily) at SeaWorld's Main Information Center. Discovery Cove has some free wheelchairs equipped with huge balloon-like tires to cross the sand. Reserve one in advance.

At both parks, aquariums, wading areas, theaters, and restaurants are wheelchair accessible. (Note that drinking straws aren't provided, out of concern for the safety of the animals.) Shops are level, but many are so packed with stuff that maneuvering in a wheelchair is a challenge.

Parks Amenities

Baby Care: Diaper-changing tables are in or near most women's restrooms and in the men's restroom at the front entrance. Diaper-vending machines are in all changing areas and at Shamu's Emporium. Areas for nursing are alongside the women's restroom at Friends of the Wild gift shop and beside Shamu's Happy Harbor. Baby food is sold at most restaurants and at the Children's Store. Rent strollers ($14 for a single, $19 for a double per day) at the information center.

First-Aid: SeaWorld first-aid centers, staffed by registered nurses, are behind Stingray Lagoon and near Shamu's Happy Harbor. Discovery Cove's first-aid station is near the Photo Area entrance.

Lockers: One-time-use, coin-op lockers (50¢ to $1.50, depending on size) are near flip-over coasters like Kraken and Manta as well as inside SeaWorld's main entrance. Also near the entrance, next to Shamu's Emporium, are long-term lockers ($7 small, $10 large per day). At Discovery Cove free lockers await you near the cabanas.

Lost and Found: SeaWorld's Main Information Center operates as the park's Lost and Found. Lost children are brought here, and it's the place to report lost children. A parkwide paging system also helps reunite parents with kids. At Discovery Cove lost kids and items eventually find their way to the Check-In Lobby.

Package Pick-Up: If you buy something, you can have it sent to SeaWorld's Package Pick-Up, in Shamu's Emporium, or to the Check-In Lobby at Discovery Cove. Allow two hours for delivery.

Pet Care Center: For $6, SeaWorld's Pet-Care Center, near the main entrance, accommodates dogs, cats, hamsters, and whatever other creatures guests are traveling with. Arrive with a copy of your pet's shot record, updated rabies tag, water bowl, food, and a toy or blanket to remind your pet of home. (Note that dogs must be walked at least once a day.) You can drop off your pet 30 minutes before the park opens and must pick it up 30 minutes before closing.

DID YOU KNOW?

Performers ski atop the backs of two dolphins, divers leap from towers, and an acrobat does an ariel ballet during the Blue Horizons show. It's a show that blends everything SeaWorld does best above and below the water.

SEAWORLD ORLANDO
SWIM WITH THE FISHIES

There's a whole lot more to SeaWorld and Discovery Cove than being splashed by Shamu. You can see manatees face-to-snout, learn to love an eel, swim with dolphins, and be spat at by a walrus. These two parks celebrate all the mammals, birds, fish, and reptiles that live in and near the ocean.

SeaWorld's performance venues, attractions, and activities surround a 17-acre lagoon, and the artful landscaping, curving paths, and concealing greenery sometimes lead to wrong turns. But armed with a map that lists showtimes, it's easy to plan an approach that lets you move fluidly from one show and attraction to the next and still have time for rest stops and meal breaks.

Thanks to Discovery Cove's daily cap on crowds, it may seem as if you have the park to yourself. Navigating the grounds is simple; signs point to swimming areas, cabanas, or the free-flight aviary—aflutter with exotic birds and accessible via a walkway or (even better) by swimming beneath a waterfall.

VISITING TIPS

■ Before investing in front-of-the-line Quick Queue passes, remember that there are only a handful of big-deal rides, and space is seldom a problem at shows.

■ If you bring your own food, remove all straws and lids before you arrive—they can harm fish and birds.

■ Arrive at least 30 minutes early for the Shamu show, which generally fills to capacity. Prepare to get wet in the "splash zone" down front.

■ In Discovery Cove make the aviary one of your first stops, since the 250-plus birds within will be more active in the morning. Check-in starts at 8 AM.

TOP SEAWORLD ATTRACTIONS

Manta. SeaWorld likes to claim that this is two attractions in one: while waiting in line, you walk past 10 supercool aquariums filled with rays and fish. But the big thrill is the amazingly fast coaster at the front of the line.

Kraken. It takes you on a high-speed chase with a dragon. But who's chasing who? Fast and furious.

Pets Ahoy. Anyone who has ever loved a pet, or wanted one, has to see the talented cats, dogs, birds, and pig in this cute and clever show.

Journey to Atlantis. Although it seems a little dated, the Splash Mountain–esque ride still provides thrills—especially on its last, steep, wet drop.

Believe. The park's flagship attraction and mascot are irresistible. In a show four years in the making, you'll see several Shamus performing graceful aquabatics that are guaranteed to thrill.

Clyde and Seamore Take Pirate Island. Head for Sea Lion & Otter Stadium to watch this slapstick comedy routine starring an adorable team of water mammals and their trainers.

TOP DISCOVERY COVE ATTRACTIONS

Snorkeling Pools. The snorkeling pools may well be Discovery Cove's must underhyped attractions. It's a real thrill to float lazily and silently amid tropical fish, to swim beneath a waterfall into an elaborate aviary, and to dive down a few feet to peer at sharks and barracuda through the porthole of a wrecked ship. There's also on-site snorkeling instruction for novices.

Private Cabanas. Granted, admission to Discovery Cove isn't cheap, but if you can pony up a little more (about $175) you'll enjoy complete privacy, personalized service, and a well-stocked mini-refrigerator in these tropical waterfront sanctuaries.

12

HOW IT BEGAN

Hard to believe that four frat brothers intent on creating a restaurant would inadvertently build the foundation for one of the world's most popular theme parks. In the early 1960s UCLA grads Milton Shedd, David DeMott, George Millay, and Ken Norris were ready to parlay their talent and ambition into an underwater restaurant, but as plans changed they ended up building San Diego's SeaWorld, which opened in early 1964.

Within the first year the park welcomed over 400,000 visitors. It took several more years before the second SeaWorld, in Ohio, opened. This was followed in 1973 by Orlando's SeaWorld, and, in 1988—under the then-new ownership of publishing firm Harcourt Brace Jovanovich—a fourth park in San Antonio.

By Gary
McKechnie

Just as you wouldn't expect to arrive at Disney and see nothing but Mickey Mouse, don't expect to arrive at SeaWorld and only see Shamu. There's a lot more going on at this park and its close cousin, Discovery Cove, than you'd expect.

Attractions at both parks are designed not only to showcase the marine world but also to demonstrate ways that humans can protect the earth's waters and wildlife. And because there are more exhibits and shows than rides, you can go at your own pace, without that hurry-up-and-wait feeling.

At SeaWorld, Shamu is, by and very large, the mascot. But you'll also discover a wide range of shows, adventures, attractions, restaurants, and experiences that you likely didn't expect. In addition to entertaining, SeaWorld's goal is also to educate, so you'll see how lumbering manatees live and what they look like up close; watch otters and seals perform slapstick routines in a popular long-running show; learn about the lives of giant tortoises and sea turtles; and be absolutely amazed at the scope of marine life, mammals, and reptiles celebrated throughout the park.

The magnificent menagerie is only part of the appeal. Another pleasing aspect of SeaWorld is that since the shows, attractions, and exhibits are based primarily on nature and animals, the layout is natural as well, so there's never a nagging urge to race through anything. The whole place encourages you to slow down and move at a casual pace.

The pace is even slower at Discovery Cove. Here your mission is to spend an entire day doing nothing but savoring a 32-acre tropical oasis. It's a task made easier by an all-inclusive admission that includes all meals, towels, a wet suit, masks, sunscreen, and the option of springing for the highlight of the day: a unique swimming experience with a bottlenose dolphin.

Even without a dolphin encounter, you can have a great time splashing around coral reefs, swimming into a spacious aviary, floating down a quiet river, or lazing on a sandy beach beneath lovely palms.

Two different parks. Two incredible experiences.

SEAWORLD ATTRACTIONS

☆☆☆
Duration
20 mins.
Crowds
Heavy
Audience
All Ages

12

A'Lure, the Call of the Ocean (Nautilus Theater). SeaWorld never holds back when it comes to stage shows, and its latest presentation, A'Lure is no exception. It's framed by the story of a fisherman who falls overboard and into a new world beneath the waves. The colorful, costumed inhabitants of this underwater kingdom astound the fisherman with their amazing talents on the trampoline, and then rocket themselves through hoops, and leap onto towering poles and stick to them like chameleons. Acrobats march into the audience with festive Chinese dragons, find wonderful new uses for hula hoops, and perform impressive feats with hanging strips of silk. You might want to see this show twice—there's so much taking place you're likely to miss some wonderful moments. ■TIP→ Although the auditorium seats more than 1,000 and you won't feel packed in, arrive at least 15 minutes early for a wider choice of seats.

Fodor's Choice★
Duration
30 mins.
Crowds
Mod. to Heavy
Audience
All Ages

Believe (Shamu Stadium). This is the place. Within this stadium is Shamu, SeaWorld's orca mascot, starring in Believe, which (because we're talking about whales here) took more than four years to perfect. In the show, Shamu performs awe-inspiringly choreographed moves against the backdrop of an elaborate three-story set, and an 80-foot panoramic LED screen within the shape of a tail fluke helps illuminate the action. It's amazing—whales weighing as much as 10,000 pounds perform a ballet to the corresponding beat of an original musical score.

The show is also proof that trainers, who are propelled through the water on the whales' backs or bellies, balance on their noses, and are launched into spectacular high dives, have one of the most exciting—as well as risky—jobs on earth. In peak seasons when the park is open late, the special evening show is the always enjoyable and oddly patriotic Shamu Rocks, which is performed, like all whale shows should be, to the accompaniment of a live guitarist. The anthem-heavy music and visual effects will speak most loudly to you and your teens.

And perhaps you've heard tales of so-called splash zones. They exist. If you sit near the performing pool, when the whales want to soak you all they have to do is wave their massive tail flukes or conduct a well-placed belly flop to throw thousands of gallons of water into the stands. Even in the upper reaches of the splash zones, you'll still get drenched—fun at the time, but less so a few hours later if you didn't bring a change of clothes. ■TIP→ Arrive 30 minutes before early-afternoon shows. Close-up encounters through the Plexiglas walls aren't to be missed, so trot on down.

☆☆☆
Duration
20 mins.
Crowds
Heavy
Audience
All Ages

Blue Horizons. The story of Blue Horizons is a fairy tale of sorts, starting with a young girl's fantasy of life in the sea. It's enough to lead off a high-energy, crowd-pleasing show that features high dives, dolphins, and astounding feats of aquabatics. Dolphins execute perfectly coordinated leaps, arcs, and splashes. Performers ski atop the backs of two dolphins while another performer does an aerial ballet. Divers repeatedly leap from two high towers as two acrobats portraying the story's villains perform impressive and repeated synchronized jumps on bungee cords. It's a show that blends everything SeaWorld does best

SeaWorld Orlando

← TO AQUATICA

TO DISCOVERY COVE →

KEY WEST

- Manatees Rescue
- Dolphin Cove
- Stingray Lagoon
- First Aid
- Captain Pete's Island Eats
- Key West at SeaWorld
- Turtle Point
- Blue Horizons

- Journey to Atlantis
- Kraken
- Penguin Encounter
- Pacific Point Preserve
- Clyde and Seamore Take Pirate Island (Sea Lion & Otter Stadium)
- Antarctic Market
- Voyager's Smokehouse
- Seaport Pizza
- Pets Ahoy (Seaport Theater)
- Manta
- Dolphin Nursery
- Cypress Bakery
- Show Schedules
- Lockers
- Guest Relations, Information
- Main Entrance

- Shark's Underwater Grill
- Shark Encounter
- A' Lure the Call of the Ocean (Nautilus Theater)
- Paddle boats
- Sky Tower
- The Waterfront
- Seafire Inn
- Makahiki Luau

- The Terrace
- Believe (Shamu Stadium)
- Atlantis Bayside Stadium
- Mango Joe's Café
- Coconut Cove Snacks
- Shamu's Happy Harbor
- First Aid
- Wild Arctic

Lagoon

KEY

✕ Restaurants

🚻 Rest rooms

above and below the water. ■TIP→ Arrive 20 minutes before showtime for the best seats.

Fodor's Choice★
Duration
40 mins.
Crowds
Light
Audience
All Ages

Clyde and Seamore Take Pirate Island (Sea Lion & Otter Stadium). Along with presentations starring Shamu and the dolphins, the show here is one of the park's top crowd-pleasers. A multilevel pirate ship forms the set for Clyde and Seamore Take Pirate Island, a drama in which otters, walruses, and California sea lions prevail over piratical treachery. During the performance, these animal thespians prove that they can outperform the human actors in a hilarious swashbuckling adventure that revolves around lost loot, pirate plunder, and misadventure on the high seas.

12

Get ready for plenty of audience interaction, cheap laughs, and good-natured gags designed to please the kids as the animal actors waddle, dive, slide, dance, and scoot through this melodrama. Watching an otter swipe a treasure map, laughing at a seal in a staring contest with a sailor, and enjoying an entire range of silly slapstick is a great way to spend part of your vacation. Be sure to arrive at least 15 minutes early to catch the preshow—the mime is always a crowd favorite. ■TIP→ Sit toward the center for the best view.

☆
Duration
Up to you
Crowds
Light
Audience
All Ages

Dolphin Nursery. Although largely overshadowed by the more magnificent attractions, this large pool has been here since the park opened in 1973, and continues to please guests by allowing them to peer over the side to watch dolphin moms and babies (with birth dates posted on signs) play and leap and splash. You can't get close enough to pet or feed them, so you'll have to be content peering from several feet away and asking the host questions during a regular Q&A session. Here's a popular answer: no, you can't take one home. Hint: if you just *have* to touch a dolphin, head over to Dolphin Cove in the Key West section. ■TIP→ Come during a Shamu show so the kids can be up front.

☆☆☆
Duration
6 mins.
Crowds
Heavy
Audience
Not Small Kids

Journey to Atlantis. SeaWorld's first entry in Florida's escalating coaster wars is a hybrid, combining the elements of a high-speed water ride and a roller coaster with lavish special effects. Like many attractions, it has a story line: the lost continent of Atlantis has risen in the harbor of a quaint Greek fishing village, and you board a rickety Greek fishing boat to explore it. An ominous current tugs at your vessel, and an old fisherman (actually Hermes, the messenger of the gods, in disguise) offers a golden sea horse to protect you from the evil Sirens. The special effects—involving LCD technology, lasers, and holographic illusions—are really cranked up during a watery battle between Hermes and Allura, queen of the Sirens.

Amid this story, you experience frequent twists, turns, and short, shallow dives as well as one hair-raising plunge that sends you nearly 60 feet into the main harbor (plan on getting soaked to the skin). This is followed by a final nosedive into S-shaped, bobsledlike curves. Although the ride is a little dated, it's still not for the faint of heart, for those afraid of the dark, for those who dislike enclosed spaces, or for those under 42 inches tall. **For people with disabilities:** You must transfer from your wheelchair to the ride vehicle. ■TIP→ You could come first thing in the morning or about an hour before closing. But going at night is awesome, and if there's a wait at all, it will be short.

At Believe—the show starring Shamu—it only takes a tail wave or belly flop by one of the performing orcas to send thousands of gallons of water into the stands.

☆
Duration
Up to you
Crowds
Light to Moderate
Audience
All Ages

Key West at SeaWorld. This is simply a laid-back area modeled after Key West, Florida's southernmost outpost, where the sunsets are spectacular, and the mood is festive. There are no distinct "lands" within SeaWorld, but this one comes close, containing individual tropical-style shows and attractions within its loosely defined borders. Along with an obvious Jimmy Buffett–style "island paradise" feel, Dolphin Cove, within the Key West area, is a huge pool where a few-dozen Atlantic bottlenose dolphins skim around and nose up to the edge to be fed fish ($5 a tray) by generous guests. At the far end of the lagoon, a grotto reveals an underwater view of the dolphins that cannot be anything but fascinating and entertaining. ■ TIP→ On your way to or from a show, come see the dolphins. If it's crowded, go shopping until the crowds disperse.

Fodor's Choice ★
Duration
6 mins.
Crowds
Heavy
Audience
Not Small Kids

Kraken. Coaster lovers head straight for Kraken as soon as the park opens, and when you see its loops and dips, you'll know why. Named after an angry monster, this wickedly fast coaster takes you underground three times, lifts you higher (up to 149 feet), drops you longer, and spirals you faster than any other in Florida. Kraken also packs a serious punch thanks to is its floorless seats (your legs dangle loosely), seven inversions, and moments of weightlessness. The line for it moves pretty quickly thanks to a high seating capacity. Note that the ride-height minimum is 54 inches and that bags aren't allowed past the turnstiles. It costs about 50¢ to leave them in a locker, but it's worth the investment. This is one cool coaster. **For people with disabilities:** You must transfer from your wheelchair to the ride vehicle. ■ TIP→ Come as soon as the park opens—especially to snag front-row seats. Otherwise, come at closing or during a Blue Horizons show.

12

☆☆
Duration
Up to you
Crowds
Light to Moderate
Audience
All Ages

Manatees Rescue. If you don't have time to explore Florida's springs in search of manatees in the wild, visit this attraction. The whiskered manatees, which look like a cross between walruses and air bags, were brought here after near-fatal brushes with motorboats and are returned to their homes when they're healthy. Tramping down a clear tunnel beneath the naturalistic, 3½-acre lagoon, you enter Manatee Theater, where a film describes the lives of these gentle giants and the ways in which humans threaten their survival. In Manatee Habitat, a 300,000-gallon tank with a 126-foot seamless acrylic viewing panel, you can look in on the lettuce-chomping mammals as well as such native fish as tarpon, gar, and snook. When you see the mama manatees and their nursing calves, you'll understand why Floridians have been trying to protect them for decades. ■TIP➔ **Come during a Shamu show, when crowds will be light. Avoid it right after a dolphin show, as crowds will be heavy.**

Fodor's Choice★
Duration
6 mins.
Crowds
You Bet!
Audience
Not Small Kids

Manta. While waiting in line for your coaster ride, you'll pass 10 aquariums containing a total of a quarter-million gallons of water and more than 3,000 creatures, including 100 species of fish, graceful rays, and sea dragons and sea horses. This gentle encounter is followed by the sight of row after row of guests being locked down, strapped in, and firmly secured beneath a ray-shaped coaster for . . . what's about to happen. When you board the ride, you're suspended horizontally beneath a 12-foot, ray-shaped, roller-coaster car. You're then whisked off at speeds of up to 56 mph on a ½-mi race of loops and spins around and above the aquarium. At times you'll be so close to the water that the coaster's wings actually skim the surface, though you're not likely to get drenched the way you would on a real water ride. There are also four inversions and a drop of more than 10 stories.

Halfway through, the ride slows down a bit, and you may think it's over—but it's not. When you do finally return to the station, you'll be ready to make your exit—either for some recovery time or for the chance to race back to the entrance and line up again. Kids, who must be at least 54 inches tall to ride, will love the aquarium entrance; daring older children and adults will love the thrill of the ride. **For people with disabilities:** You must transfer to the ride seat, properly use the ride restraint, and be able to grip harness with one hand. ■TIP➔ **Come first thing or late in the day, or use a Quick Queue pass.**

☆☆
Duration
Up to you
Crowds
Light
Audience
All Ages

Pacific Point Preserve. A nonstop chorus of "aarrrps" and "yawps" coming from behind Sea Lion & Otter Stadium will lead you to the 2½-acre home for California sea lions and harbor and fur seals. A naturalistic expanse of beaches, waves, and huge outcroppings of upturned rock designed to duplicate the rocky northern Pacific coast have a calming effect.

The entire area is roughly circular, so as you stroll around the edge of the surf zone you'll see that it's a favorite hangout for fun-loving pinnipeds who are either swimming up close for a share of the smelt you've just bought ($5) or flopped over on their sides and lazing in the Florida sun. On the far side of the complex you can walk down into a grotto where a large Plexiglas wall allows you to peek through and see them darting and diving and playing underwater. ■TIP➔ **Come anytime. It shouldn't be too hard to find a place away from the crowds.**

☆☆
Duration
Up to you
Crowds
Mod. to Heavy
Audience
All Ages

Penguin Encounter. Inside a large white building between the Dolphin and the Sea Lion & Otter stadiums, 17 species of penguin scoot around a refrigerated re-creation of Antarctica. They're as cute as can be, waddling across icy promontories and plopping into frigid waters to display their aquatic skills. A moving walkway rolls you past slowly, so you can watch an average day in their world through the thick see-through walls. You can also step off at one point to stand and marvel at these tuxedo-clad creatures as they dive into 45°F (7°C) water and are showered with three tons of snow a day. Nearby, a similar viewing area for puffins and murres is nearly as entertaining. Afterward, spend a little time in the plaza outside, where there are caricature artists, gift shops, and soothing music. ■TIP➔ Come while the dolphin and sea-lion shows are on and before getting soaked at Journey to Atlantis, or you'll feel the chill.

☆☆☆
Duration
15–20 mins.
Crowds
Mod. to Heavy
Audience
All Ages

Pets Ahoy. About a dozen dogs, a dozen-plus cats, and an assortment of ducks, doves, parrots, and a pig (nearly all rescued from a local animal shelter) are the stars of this lively, hilarious show. The animals perform complex stunts on a stage that looks like a seaside village. From stealing a string of sausages to driving their "girlfriends" on a date, these cute-as-a-button actors perform feats that are each more incredible than the last. Look around and you'll notice that the show is just as appealing to foreign guests; you don't have to speak English to enjoy what is essentially a live version of a silent movie. Stick around and you'll have a chance to shake paws with the stars. ■TIP➔ Gauge the crowds, and arrive early if necessary.

☆☆☆
Duration
Up to you
Crowds
Heavy
Audience
Small Kids

Shamu's Happy Harbor. Sprawling, towering, and incredible, this 3-acre playground has places to crawl, climb, explore, bounce, and get wet. There's even an adjacent arcade with midway games. There are pipes to crawl through, a tent with an air-mattress floor, "ball rooms"—one for toddlers and one for grade-schoolers—with thousands of plastic balls to wade through, big sailing ships to explore, and water to play in and around. **For people with disabilities:** Various areas offer different levels of clearance. Check with attendants about accessibility. ■TIP➔ Don't come first thing, or you'll never drag your child away; that said, it's busy here mid-afternoon or near dusk. Bring a towel to dry them off.

☆☆
Duration
Up to you
Crowds
Light to Moderate
Audience
All Ages

Shark Encounter. Within a large, innocuous, white structure are some thoroughly creepy critters: eels, barracuda, sharks, and poisonous fish. You walk through large transparent corridors as the fish and eels swim all around you. There's a chance you'll spy a few creatures that you've probably never seen (or even imagined) before, like the weedy sea dragon and his cousin, the leafy sea dragon, which look like branches of a tree. But the stars of the show are the sharks, and this attraction doesn't scrimp: a half-dozen species skim silently through the pool around you.

Consider visiting the attraction in conjunction with a meal at the extraordinarily well-designed Sharks Underwater Grill, where you can order fresh fish and Floribbean cuisine while watching your entrées' cousins. ■TIP➔ Spend at least 20 minutes here. Crowds are biggest when the adjacent seal and otter show gets out; time your visit accordingly.

At Discovery Cove's Explorer's Aviary you can attract exotic birds with fruit or feed. You might even get one (or two) to hop onto your shoulder. Get the camera ready.

☆
Duration
6 mins.
Crowds
Light
Audience
All Ages

Sky Tower. The focal point of the park is this 400-foot-tall tower, the main mast for a revolving double-decker platform. During the six-minute rotating round-trip up and down, you'll get the inside scoop on the park's history, its attractions, and surrounding sights. There's a separate $3 admission for this tower ride. Adjacent to it is Pearl Dive, a small area where you can sit and watch pearl divers snag oysters. **For people with disabilities:** The tower can accommodate two wheelchairs per cycle. ■ TIP→ Come whenever there's not a line.

☆
Duration
Up to you
Crowds
Mod. to Heavy
Audience
All Ages

Stingray Lagoon. In this interactive exhibit, dozens of stingrays are close enough to touch, as evidenced by the many outstretched hands surrounding the rim. Buy stingray delicacies (smelts, silversides, shrimp, and squid, available for $5 a tray, two for $9, four for $15) at nearby concessions. When rays flap up for lunch you can stroke their velvety skin. Even though they have stingers they won't hurt you—they just want food. And they're obligingly hungry all day. Check out the nursery pool with its baby rays. ■ TIP→ Walk by if it's crowded, but return before dusk before the smelt concession stand closes.

NEED A BREAK?

Near the Penguin Encounter is the **Antarctic Market,** where you can buy grab-and-go sandwiches, salads, soft-serve ice cream, and frozen drinks.

☆
Duration
Up to you
Crowds
Light
Audience
All Ages

Turtle Point. Just outside the entrance to the heavily themed Manta is its low-key polar opposite. There's nothing flashy or extravagant about this re-creation of a small beach and lagoon, but it's fascinating because you get to watch gigantic sea turtles (loggerheads, green, and hawksbill) basking in the sun or drifting in the water. Many of these lumbering beauties were rescued from predators or fishing nets, and their injuries

SEAWORLD ORLANDO AND DISCOVERY COVE

NAME	Height Req.	Type of Entertainment	Duration	Crowds	Audience	Tips
Sea World						
A'Lure, the Call of the Ocean	n/a	Show	20 mins.	Heavy	All Ages	Plenty of seats, but arrive 15 mins. early for a wide selection.
Blue Horizons	n/a	Show	20 mins.	Heavy	All Ages	Arrive 20 mins. before showtime.
Dolphin Nursery	n/a	Aquarium	Up to you	Light	All Ages	Come during a Shamu show so the kids can be up front.
Journey to Atlantis	At least 42"	Thrill Ride with Water	6 mins.	Heavy	All but Small Kids	You can make a beeline here first thing or come about an hour before closing. But the best time for this is at night.
Key West at SeaWorld	n/a	Walk-Through/ Aquarium	Up to you	Light to Moderate	All Ages	If too crowded, wander until crowds disperse.
★ Kraken	At least 54"	Thrill Ride	6 mins.	Heavy	All but Small Kids	Get to the park when it opens and head straight to Kraken; otherwise, hit it near closing time or during a Blue Horizons show.
Manatees Rescue	n/a	Aquarium	Up to you	Light to Moderate	All Ages	Come during a Shamu show but *not* right after a dolphin show.
★ Manta	At least 54"	Thrill Ride with Water	6 mins.	You Bet!	All but Small Kids	Come first thing or late in the day, or purchase a Quick Queue pass for front-of-ride access.
Pacific Point Preserve	n/a	Aquarium	Up to you	Light	All Ages	Come anytime.
Penguin Encounter	n/a	Aquarium	Up to you	Moderate to Heavy	All Ages	Come during dolphin and sea lion shows, and before you've gotten soaked at Journey to Atlantis, or you'll freeze.
Pets Ahoy	n/a	Show	15–20 mins.	Moderate to Heavy	All Ages	Gauge the crowds, and come here early if necessary.
★ Sea Lion & Otter Stadium	n/a	Show	40 mins.	Light	All Ages	Sit toward the center for the best view, and don't miss the beginning.

				Heavy	Small Kids	
Shamu's Happy Harbor	n/a	Playground with Water	Up to you		All Ages	Don't come first thing in morning, or you'll never drag your child away. Bring a towel to dry them off.
★ Shamu Stadium (Believe)	n/a	Show	30 mins.	Moderate to Heavy	All Ages	Come 30 mins. early for early-afternoon shows. Don't miss close-up encounters.
Shark Encounter	n/a	Aquarium	Up to you	Light to Moderate	All Ages	Come during the sea lion show.
Sky Tower	n/a	Tour/ Thrill Ride	6 mins.	Light	All Ages	Come whenever there's no line. Note the extra $3 charge, though.
Stingray Lagoon	n/a	Aquarium	Up to you	Moderate to Heavy	All Ages	Walk by if it's crowded, but return before dusk.
Turtle Point	n/a	Zoo	Up to you	Light	All Ages	Come anytime.
Wild Arctic	At least 42"	Simulator Exp./ Aquarium	5+ mins.	Moderate to Heavy	All Ages	Come during a Shamu show. You can skip the ride if you just want to see the mammals.
Discovery Cove						
Beaches	n/a	Beach Area	Up to you	Light	All Ages	Arrive early and head to the far side for a private spot.
Coral Reef	n/a	Aquarium/ Pool Area	Up to you	Light to Moderate	All Ages	Monitor crowds and come when they're lightest. Popular with teens.
★ Dolphin Lagoon	n/a	Pool	45–60 mins.	n/a	All but Small Kids	Be mindful of your appointment time.
Explorer's Aviary	n/a	Aviary	Up to you	Light to Moderate	All Ages	Come early, when the birds are most active.
Wind-Away River	n/a	Aquarium	Up to you	Light to Moderate	All Ages	When it gets hot, slip into the water. Popular with teens.

★ = Fodor'sChoice

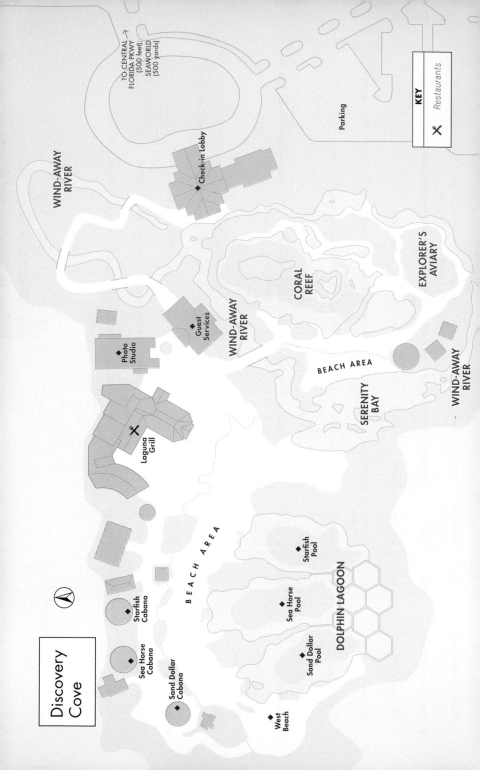

Discovery Cove

WIND-AWAY RIVER

TO CENTRAL FLORIDA PKWY → (500 feet); SEAWORLD (500 yards)

Check-in Lobby

Parking

KEY

✕ *Restaurants*

EXPLORER'S AVIARY

CORAL REEF

WIND-AWAY RIVER

Guest Services

Photo Studio

BEACH AREA

SERENITY BAY

WIND-AWAY RIVER

✕ Laguna Grill

BEACH AREA

Starfish Cabana

Sea Horse Cabana

Sand Dollar Cabana

Starfish Pool

Sea Horse Pool

Sand Dollar Pool

DOLPHIN LAGOON

West Beach

King penguins are one of 17 species in the Penguin Encounter. Here they are comparing notes—perhaps about you. After all, who's really watching who when you're at the zoo?

make it impossible for them to return to the wild. They found a good home here. ■ TIP→ Come anytime. It gets crowded sporadically, but there's generally enough space for all to get a good view.

☆☆
Duration
5+ mins.
Crowds
Mod. to Heavy
Audience
All Ages

Wild Arctic. Inside this pseudo ice station you embark on a simulated helicopter ride that leads to interactive, educational displays. If your stomach can handle the rolls and pitches, it makes for scary but enjoyable fun. Afterward, there are above- and below-water stations where you can watch Beluga whales blow bubble rings, polar bears paddle around with their toys, and groaning walruses hoist themselves onto a thick shelf of ice.

Like the Penguin Encounter, this is a place where you can be entertained doing something as simple as watching wildlife. It's what SeaWorld is all about. The ride-height minimum for the helicopter simulator is 42 inches. **For people with disabilities:** You must transfer from your wheelchair to the ride vehicle. ■ TIP→ Come early, late, or during a Shamu show. You can skip the simulated helicopter ride if you just want to see the mammals.

DISCOVERY COVE ATTRACTIONS

☆☆☆
Duration
Up to you
Crowds
Light
Audience
All Ages

Beaches. Lined with swaying palms, tropical foliage, and quaint thatched huts, and speckled with shady umbrellas, hammocks, lounges, and beach chairs, this is where you claim your own private spot in the sand. Since the park's biggest selling point is its limited guest capacity, the most seductive aspect is lying in the sun and leaving the real world behind. For the most privacy, head to the far west end of Discovery Cove, where the beach chairs will be more plentiful. ■ TIP→ With attendance limited

SEAWORLD GROWN-UP TOURS

Strolling through SeaWorld is comforting. Quiet sidewalks and landscaped lanes abound. Indeed, a number of local senior citizens who were part of mall-walking clubs have learned that an annual pass gives them access to a very pleasant walk in the park—as well as a day filled with wonderful attractions. Follow in their footsteps on a walk of up to a mile, from west to east.

WEST SIDE STORY
The west side has most of the attractions—and the most paths. From the entrance, walk around past the information center and to the left toward **Turtle Point,** where the lazing residents remind you that speed isn't everything.

Turn left into **Key West at Sea-World,** where you can enjoy nature—first by feeding and petting the slippery skates at Stingray Lagoon and then by spending time with the residents of Dolphin Cove. The dolphins are plentiful and always on the go; be sure to head to the far end of the cove and drop down into the grotto, where a wide window reveals their underwater world.

After looping the cove, double back through Key West, passing Turtle Point and walking toward the entrance, before peeling off to your left toward the **Waterfront** area. When you reach the shores of the lagoon, linger by the water for a bit, and then stroll past the **Sky Tower**—unless you'd like a bird's-eye view of the entire park. In that case, head on up and see the sights. You may also want to spend a few minutes watching the action at **Pearl Dive.**

EAST SIDE STORY
Start at the **Seafire Inn,** a great place to grab a bite to eat and cool off in the air-conditioned interior or on the screened patio facing the lagoon. Head to the boardwalk and take it across the lagoon. This pleasing, uncongested walk brings you to the rear of **Shamu Stadium,** and although you can circle it any direction, go right to avoid crowds of kids gathered at Shamu's Happy Harbor.

Walk to **Wild Arctic,** where an observation area affords a glimpse of polar bears and walrus. Spend some time in the frozen North before returning to the sidewalk, which winds its way behind the Atlantis Bayside Stadium and slowly and surely back toward the park entrance, and, all too soon, the real world.

to 1,000 guests, and plenty of sand to share, you should be fine. Just arrive early for the best spot.

☆☆☆
Duration
Up to you
Crowds
Light to Moderate
Audience
All Ages

Coral Reef. You can follow thousands of butterfly fish, angelfish, parrot fish, and a few dozen other species as you snorkel through this authentic-looking coral reef. Stingrays sail slowly and gracefully past, and fish come within touching distance, though when you reach out to them they scatter in nanoseconds. There's even an artificial shipwreck: panels of Plexiglas in its hull reveal a pool filled with barracudas and sharks (thankfully out of reach). Over in the lagoon, dozens of southern and cow-nosed rays skim around the shallows. Don't be afraid to wade in and play—they've had their barbs removed. Often, several rays get together and make loops around the pool, so if you stay in one spot,

To swim with the dolphins, the ultimate Discovery Cove experience, you must book months in advance.

they'll continue to glide past you. And remember: the brighter the day, the more brilliant the underwater colors. ■TIP→ It's easy to monitor crowds; come when they're light. It's suitable for all ages, but teens and adults enjoy it most.

Fodor's Choice ★
Duration
45–60 mins.
Crowds
N/A
Audience
Not Small Kids

Dolphin Lagoon (Dolphin Swim). Before you get too excited about Discovery Cove's top attraction, remember that your "swim" is supervised and restricted to what's safe for both you and the dolphins. The real deal may not line up with your fantasy of frolicking with these playful creatures. Despite the limitations, however, the attraction offers you the truly unique chance to touch, feed, play with, and even kiss a bottlenose dolphin, one of the most social and communicative marine animals.

Before you can get into the lagoon, you have to sit through a somewhat tedious 15-minute orientation, consisting of a film plus a few words from a dolphin trainer. Afterward, you'll proceed to the lagoon where six to eight of you will spend roughly 30 minutes with one of 25 dolphins. Although you'll only be knee-deep in the water most of the time, it's surprisingly chilly, so you'll be grateful for the mandatory, Discovery Cove–provided wet suit.

Trainers teach you about dolphin behavior and reveal the hand signals used to communicate with them. At your command, your dolphin may roll over so you can touch its belly or, at your signal, leap into the air. Near the end of the session you have a chance to swim out to deeper water, catch hold of the dolphin's fin and have it pull you back to shore. You'll even take a moment to pose for a picture with your newfound friend. Be prepared for the photo finish: after you leave the water and return to the orientation cabana the skilled trainers quickly transform into a determined souvenir-photo sales team. **For people with disabilities:** Alert staffers to your hearing, vision, or mobility issues when you're making reservations, and they'll have someone there to offer special assistance—signing or having a modified wheelchair at the ready. Note that the pool here is "zero entry," so there are no steps to contend with. ■ TIP→ Be mindful of the appointment time on your badge. You don't want to miss the experience of a lifetime.

☆☆
Duration
Up to you
Crowds
Light to
Moderate
Audience
All Ages

Explorer's Aviary. The entrance to this 12,000-square-foot birdhouse is a kick. To get here you can walk in from the beach or, better yet, swim into it from beneath a waterfall on the river that snakes through the park. You arrive in a sanctuary populated with more than 250 small exotic birds, including darting hummingbirds, tiny finches, and honeycreepers.

In the large-bird sanctuary, you get up close to perched and wandering toucans, red-legged seriema, and other colorful winged creatures that stand as tall as 4 feet. Look for attendants who have carts filled with complimentary fruit and feed that you can use to attract the birds. It's a beautiful experience—especially when a bird hops onto your shoulder to say hello. Get the camera ready. ■ TIP→ Come early in the morning when the birds are most active.

☆☆
Duration
Up to you
Crowds
Light to
Moderate
Audience
All Ages

Wind-Away River. Wind-Away River meanders through most of Discovery Cove, and, as it flows, river swimmers float lazily through different environments—a sunny beach; a dense, tropical rain forest; an Amazon-like river; a tropical fishing village; an underwater cave; and the aviary. The only drawbacks? The bottom of the river can feel like the bottom of a pool, and the redundant scenery along the way can make it a little tedious. Consider it as a respite from the heat and a unique way to get around the park. ■ TIP→ Slip in when it gets hot. All are welcome, but it appeals most to teens and adults.

Aquatica

WORD OF MOUTH

"[My] advice about going to any water park in Florida: be sure to bring water shoes. The ground is hot, and, even if things are close together, your wait [in line] might have you standing on hot pavement."

—eeyorelvr

AQUATICA PLANNER

Guest Services

Aquatica's Main Information Center is at the park entrance, just past the ticket kiosks. Also at the entrance are an ATM, telephones, and restrooms. This is where you can (and should) pick up a park map (or a couple in case one gets wet), and plan your approach. On the walkways outside the information center and leading into the park, attendants are stationed to help you get your bearings and point out where to find strollers and wheelchairs, help you with lost-and-found inquiries, and describe combination-ticket packages.

Park Amenities

Baby Care: One nursing area is near the center of the park, by the towel- and locker-rental area and the changing rooms; another is at the far north end of the park, near Kata's Kookaburra Cove and Big Surf Shores. The nursing areas and several restrooms—for men and women—have fold-down changing tables. (Keep in mind that children still in diapers must also be wearing waterproof protectors.)

First-Aid: A medical attendant is on duty during regular business hours at the first-aid station at the far end of the park between Kata's Kookaburra Cove and Big Surf Shores.

Lockers: There are three areas with unlimited-access lockers to rent for a day. One is near the splash-down area at Walhalla Wave and HooRoo Run; two others are at the center and far end of the park, where there are also nursing facilities. You pay $5 for a small locker and $10 for a large one; there's also a $5 deposit, which is refunded when you leave. The central locker area also rents towels for $4 ($1 of which is refunded upon return).

Lost and Found: Lost items and people are taken to the main information center near the entrance.

For People with Disabilities

Aquatica was designed to accommodate people with mobility concerns. Paved pathways lead around the entire park; none of the river or family attractions has steps to contend with; and floats, life vests, and inner tubes make it easy for anyone to enjoy the park. This isn't to say there aren't challenges: regular wheelchairs can't handle the sandy beach areas, and several attractions involve climbing to the top of a high tower (although the stairs for each are accessible by ADA guidelines).

There are a limited number of modified wheelchairs—with huge balloon-like tires to handle the sands—available for free near the entrance; as it's first come, first served for these, reserve one online. Basic wheelchairs rent for $10 a day; the motorized numbers cost $40.

DID YOU KNOW?

You can "swim" with the dolphins even if you didn't book a dolphin swim at Discovery Cove. Just take the Dolphin Plunge, a waterslide that jettisons you into a clear tube running through the pool inhabited by Commerson's dolphins.

AQUATICA
SPLASH IN TROPICAL SEAS

Aquatica, which opened in 2008, takes cues from SeaWorld and Discovery Cove in design and mood—marine-life motifs are everywhere. It also gives competitor water parks a run for their money with thrilling slides, broad beaches, calming rivers, and an area for small kids.

The park also takes its cues from the tropics. Right after you clear the parking lot, you'll see a tropical pastiche of buildings. Yup. That's definitely an island vibe you're detecting. Upon entering, you feel as if you've left central Florida for the Caribbean or Polynesia, even.

Go with it. Get into a groove, and relax and enjoy yourself. You might be drawn to the series of super-fast waterslides (some of which conclude by sending you into serene streams). Or you might feel the pull of the white-sand beaches beside the twin wave pools, where you can laze in the sun, venturing out every so often to try a ride or climb into an inner tube and float down a river.

Hey, it's your vacation. You're at Aquatica. Do what you like.

VISITING TIPS

■ **Buy tickets in advance.** Pre-purchased tickets get you early entrance, and this head start will enable you to hit the major flume and tube rides more than once.

■ **Commune with nature.** You can catch Commerson's dolphins at feeding times; spot macaws on tree limbs; or see small mammals in the Conservation Cabanas, where docents answer questions.

■ **Take care of yourself.** Avoid sunburn by reapplying sunscreen often—even waterproof sunblock washes off. Wear sandals or water shoes (or even socks) to protect your feet from hot sand, sidewalks, and rough pool surfaces.

FOOD FOR THOUGHT

Even though the waters are exhilarating, you'll be amazed at how much energy it takes to cover all the rides and attractions at Aquatica. You need to stay hydrated and well-nourished, which can be a costly proposition.

The park allows guests to bring in a small cooler of "serving-size" snacks, bottled water, and baby food in plastic containers. It's not so keen on "family-sized" servings (think sandwiches, pizza, and 2-liter bottles of soft drinks).

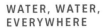

13

TOP AQUATICA ATTRACTIONS

Dolphin Plunge. Aquatica's commercials love to showcase this attraction, where you slip through a winding string of pitch-black tubes and then a stretch of clear tubes through the Commerson's dolphins' habitat.

Wave Pools. The lagoons here aren't too deep and are perfect for cooling off. About every 10 minutes, a series of small waves move across them, enabling you to bob around like a cork.

Tassie's Twisters. After hopping into an inner tube and sloshing at a high speed through an enclosed tube, you're flung into a huge circular basin and spiraled into a drain and down a slide.

Taumata Racer. Eight colorful tubes are lined up and waiting for you. Following a countdown, you launch yourself into your chute, and, following a twisting and turning ride, end up on a long and slippery slide into the splash-down pool.

WATER, WATER, EVERYWHERE

Since the days of the Roman baths, people have been on the lookout for new ways to enjoy water. For Americans, the big breakthrough came after World War II when a growing middle class with a little more money and a well-deserved desire to relax helped inspire the concept of a water park. Early parks included a few standard aquatic thrills: waterslides, tube slides, wave pools, and flowing rivers. Today there are well over 200 water parks in the United States (with Wisconsin claiming about 10% of the total). They range from a simple collection of slides and streams to incredible, over-the-top, exquisitely themed experiences like—Aquatica. For more information on water parks and where they are, check out www.waterparks.com.

By Gary
McKechnie

Just across International Drive from SeaWorld, Aquatica is the 60-acre new kid in town that's angling to lure water-park lovers away from Disney's Typhoon Lagoon and Blizzard Beach and Universal's Wet 'n Wild. And sure, Aquatica has all the slides you'd expect, but it also has plenty of whimsical SeaWorld touches.

Initially, you might find it hard to get your bearings amid the towering slides; Caribbean palms; winding sidewalks; and seemingly random layout of restaurants, rides, slides, and facilities. In reality, the park is easy to navigate. The services (restaurants, changing rooms, shops) form a core around which the attractions are situated. And besides, if you get lost, just ask one of the hundreds of lifeguards or attendants to point you in the right direction.

Hopefully you'll have arrived with some snacks and drinks to combat the fatigue you'll feel after scaling to the tops of all those watery thrill rides. If not, fear not—there are plenty of places to find food and drink.

You should also be toting beach towels, sunscreen, and water shoes. Again, if not, fear not—there are a number of shops and kiosks where you can buy all of this stuff and more.

Many of the rides have height restrictions, so if you're traveling with kids, have their heights checked at the Concierge Cabana, which is to your right as you enter the park. Each child will be issued a colored wristband that alerts attendants to which rides are appropriate for him or her.

After stashing excess supplies in a locker and generally settling in, it's time to explore. Unless it's peak season, several hours should be enough to visit each ride and attraction once or twice. It will also allow for some downtime, lazing on the beach, or enjoying a leisurely meal.

AQUATICA ATTRACTIONS

☆☆
Duration
Up to You
Crowds
Vary by Season
Audience
Tweens and Up

Big Surf Shores and Cutback Cove. Although the names of these side-by-side lagoons (aka wave pools) suggest waves that surfers would fear, the large pool only has modest swells, and the small pool may even be closed if crowds are light. Both edge the park's white-sand beach, and both are pleasant. If you plan on spending a lot of time in the park and need to keep an eye on the kids, the wave pools make great bases of operation. ■TIP➜ If you're establishing base camp here, arrive as early as possible and stake your claim on the beach.

13

Fodor'sChoice★
Duration
1 min.
Crowds
Absolutely
Audience
Tweens and Up

Dolphin Plunge. Thanks to the presence of Commerson's dolphins in the broad bay near the base of this attraction, this has become Aquatica's signature experience. The beginning of the ride is similar to that of other slides within the park. You whiz swiftly through an enclosed tube for about 250 feet. A long stretch immerses you in darkness before the tube turns crystal clear and affords a fleeting glimpse at the water that surrounds you—which happens to be the pool where the dolphins swim. You'll have to look fast to see them, though. A split second later you're making your splash down at the end of the line. The ride-height minimum is 48 inches. ■TIP➜ Keep an eye on the line, and step up when it's light—likely very early or late.

☆☆
Duration
30 secs.
Crowds
Heavy
Audience
Tweens and Up

HooRoo Run/Walhalla Wave. One tower leads to these two attractions, each of which banks on the fact that, after climbing about 10 stories, you'd rather face your fears and slide back down rather than have to climb back down. At the top are a string of yellow rafts that can hold two adults and a child, though some passengers go solo. Walhalla is on your right, HooRoo on your left. After selecting a side, you and your fellow passengers slip into a raft and are pushed into the current by an attendant. Walhalla sends you circling around corners and banking to the edges of tight curves before sliding you into an enclosed tunnel. HooRoo keeps you out in the open, bouncing you down, down, down over a series of slides. Either way you go, you'll want to go again. The ride-height minimum is 42 inches. ■TIP➜ Come early or late—or be patient.

☆☆
Duration
Up to You
Crowds
Mod. to Heavy
Audience
Small Kids

Kata's Kookaburra Cove. If the sight of cool slides and water features finds you wondering who Kata's is meant for, look at the height restrictions and notice that to visit this area, which is in the vicinity of Walkabout Waters, you must be under 4 feet tall (or accompanied by someone who is). The slides and pools and waterspouts are modified for the toddler set, but for them it's a big fun world. ■TIP➜ Adults must be accompanied by a child no more than 48 inches tall.

☆☆
Duration
Up to You
Crowds
Light
Audience
Tweens and Up

Loggerhead Lane. While clinging to a double or single tube, you're taken down and around the bend of a stream by a gentle current. Somewhere along the way, there's a spot where you can exit the river and enter the line for Tassie's Twister. A little farther along, the stream flows to a 10,000-gallon grotto filled with thousands of colorful fish and a view of the Commerson's dolphins. This is indeed a lazy river: there's next to no pull, so you might have to paddle a bit, especially if you choose the turn that leads into the fish grotto. The ride-height minimum is 48

It's easy to make new friends—man or beast—on the sands of Big Surf Shores and Cutback Cove.

inches. ■TIP➔ Although there's plenty of river for everyone, try it when most people are at lunch.

☆☆☆
Duration
Mere Seconds
Crowds
Heavy
Audience
Not Small Kids

Omaka Rocka. New at Aquatica in 2010 is another version of a water flume ride. This one looks like the tentacles on a huge plastic octopus. The multiple series of tunnels provide options for different starting points. Regardless of where you strart, once you slide into the slipstream, you'll be riding through some slick tubes, skim past some half-pipe tunnels, and then slide over some slippery moguls that splash you up on the side during some high-bank turns. You must be at least 48 inches to ride. ■TIP➔ Keep an eye on the line, and hop in when it's short.

☆☆
Duration
Up to You
Crowds
Light
Audience
All Ages

Roa's Rapids. Even though it has "rapids" in its name, this attraction actually has a mild current that winds around numerous curves and "waterfalls" (really just sprays of water from the edge of the channel). There are two entrances (one red, the other blue), where you don a life vest and wade right in. Then, whether you're solo or you're hanging on to the kids, you simply go with the flow. Two advantages: there's no line, so you can always just drop right in, and you can go around and around for as long as you'd like. Guests less than 51 inches tall are required to wear a life vest. ■TIP➔ Like Loggerhead Lane, there's plenty of river for everyone; still, come around lunchtime.

☆☆☆
Duration
1 min.
Crowds
Heavy
Audience
Tweens and Up

Tassie's Twister. This is one of the weirdest attractions at Aquatica. First you settle into an inner tube and launch yourself into the current at the top of the attraction that carries you away at an impressive speed. But that's not the weird part. After that, the enclosed pipe you've been in delivers you to a massive basin where you and your inner tube circle

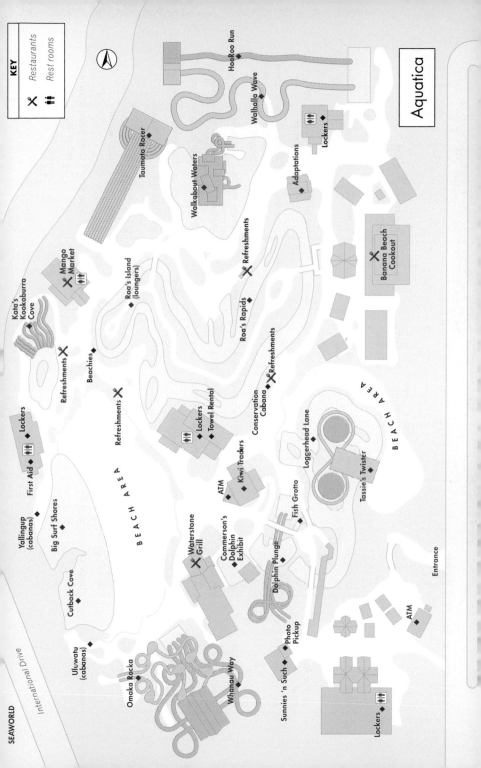

AQUATICA WATER PARK

Name	Height Req.	Type of Entertainment	Duration	Crowds	Audience	Tips
Big Surf Shores and Cutback Cove	n/a	Wave Pool	Up to you	Vary by Season	Tweens and Up	Arrive early to stake your claim on the beach.
★ Dolphin Plunge	At least 48"	Waterslide	1 min.	Absolutely	Tweens and Up	Keep an eye on the line, and step up when it's light.
HooRoo Run/Walhalla Wave	At least 42"	Waterslide	30 secs.	Heavy	Not Small Kids	Arrive early or later—or be patient.
Kata's Kookaburra Cove	Under 48"	Playground with Water	Up to you	Mod. to Heavy	Small Kids	Adults must be accompanied by a child no more than 48 inches tall.
Loggerhead Lane	At least 48"	River/Stream Ride	Up to you	Light	Tweens and Up	Try it during lunchtime.
Omaka Rocka	At least 48"	Waterslide	Mere Seconds	Heavy	Not Small Kids	Keep an eye on the line.
Roa's Rapids	Under 51" must wear life vest	River/Stream Ride	Up to you	Light	All Ages	Visit during lunchtime.
Tassie's Twister	Under 48" must wear life vest	Waterslide	1 min.	Heavy	Tweens and Up	Watch the line.
Taumata Racer	At least 42"	Waterslide	30 secs.	Light to Moderate	Not Small Kids	Watch the line.
Walkabout Waters	36"–42" (main pool); over 42" (large) slides. Under 48" wear life vest on larger slides.	Playground with Water	Up to you	Heavy	Not Small Kids	Save it for when you need a break.
Whanau Way	Under 48" must wear life vest	Waterslide	1 min.	Heavy	Not Small Kids	Come during lunch or end of day.

around and around and around and around like a soap bubble circles a bathtub drain. Eventually gravity takes over, and you slip through an opening in the side of the basin, straight into a short but thrilling slide into the splash-down pool. Yes, weird—but certainly exciting. Guests less than 48 inches tall are required to wear a life vest. ■TIP→ Keep on eye on the line, and head upstairs when it's light.

☆☆☆
Duration
30 secs.
Crowds
**Light to
Moderate**
Audience
Not Small Kids

Taumata Racer. In the aquatic equivalent of a bobsled run, you set yourself up on a blue mat at the opening of a large tube and at the end of a countdown, you and the seven other racers beside you fling yourselves into the chutes. You then slide through 300 feet of enclosed twisting and turning tubes. But that's not all. Things really get going when you enter a stretch that's nearly pitch-black except for a small band of light beside you. After what seems like both an eternity and an instant, you reach the final drop and then slide the last few yards into the splash-down pool. The ride-height minimum is 42 inches. ■TIP→ If you can't see the end of the line, it's probably short—and it's time to head up. Eight lanes keep things moving along.

☆☆
Duration
Up to You
Crowds
Heavy
Audience
Not Small Kids

Walkabout Waters. A colorful 60-foot fortress anchors 15,000 square feet of family slides, pools, water cannons, and two rather large buckets that periodically dump water on frolickers below. This is a well-executed play space; your kids can treat it as a playground and avoid getting too soaked. Plus, the slides attached to the play structure flow slowly enough for beginners (note that kids aren't permitted to ride on grown-ups' laps on this one). An area geared toward young children, Kata's Kookaburra Cove, has more open splashable space as well as fountains and slides. Guests must be from 36 to 42 inches tall for the main pool, and over 42 inches for larger slides. All those under 48 inches must wear a life vest on the larger slides. ■TIP→ Save this area for later, when you're worn out, but the kids want to play.

☆☆
Duration
1 min.
Crowds
Heavy
Audience
Not Small Kids

Whanau Way. Because water-park guests can never get enough slipping and sliding, Aquatica offers this quadruple slide that gives riders an assortment of twists and turns. Depending on which tube you select, you'll enjoy a completely different experience. Like its partner slides, much of the attraction here is sliding straight into a darkened stretch, where you know you're heading somewhere, but you're not exactly sure where. In the end, the answer reveals itself: you're heading down the final stretch on a long slide into the splash-down pool. Rinse and repeat. Guests under 48 inches are required to wear a life vest. ■TIP→ Try it at lunchtime or near day's end.

13

Part V:
Experience
Central Florida

QUINTESSENTIAL CENTRAL FLORIDA

The Sun

Orlando is surrounded by communities that honor Florida's warm, sunny weather. Some were settled by immigrants, others by rich migrants fleeing colder climes.

Peaceful Winter Park, just northeast of Orlando, has brick-paved streets, historic buildings, and a 9-hole public golf course that's listed on the National Register of Historic Places. As its name suggests, town founders used to "winter" here; it also has a lovely park in its center.

Northwest of Orlando, Mount Dora is home to the year-round Renninger's Twin Markets, consisting of a 400-dealer flea market and a 200-dealer antiques and collectibles market.

On the west coast, Ybor City is Tampa's Cuban neighborhood, the town of Dunedin was founded by two Scots, and Tarpon Springs was settled by Greeks who came to dive for sponges.

Nature—Mild and Wild

Florida's climate contributes to some amazing landscapes. It's no wonder that the Spanish explorers called it "la florida" (place of flowers).

In Orlando the 50-acre Harry P. Leu Gardens has one of the east's largest camellia gardens (visit November to March for the best show). Tampa's 100-year-old Sunken Gardens offers cascading waterfalls, koi ponds, a butterfly house, and more than 50,000 tropical plants and flowers.

On the wild side, northwest of Orlando is Wekiwa Springs State Park, whose 6,400 watery acres are filled with otters, alligators, turtles, and other Florida wildlife. On the east coast, Canaveral National Seashore holds 57,000 acres of undeveloped coastline, and the adjacent Merritt Island National Wildlife Refuge protects 500 species of wildlife, 15 of them endangered.

Like the rest of the state, central Florida is synonymous with sunshine, and every year more than 52 million visitors revel in it. The people who live here know that the area's appeal rests on those reliable rays—and so much more.

Fishing

With 1,200 mi of coastline and 11,000 mi of waterways, and more lakes than you can count, Florida is prime fishing territory. Indeed, the fishing in Orlando and Kissimmee is world-renowned.

Top waters include Lake Kissimmee, the Butler and Conway chains of lakes, and Lake Toho. You can lodge in one of the many fish camps and let guides point you to the best spots for bass, perch, and catfish.

Deep-sea aficionados can head east to charter boats in Cocoa Beach or to simply fish off the Cocoa Pier. There are plenty of fishing piers out west as well. Fort De Soto Park in Tampa is a prime spot. South of Tampa, in Bradenton, there's plenty of fresh- and saltwater angling.

Spring Training

Baseball spring training combines professional playing skills with small-town intimacy: it's like Little League played by big boys. Several teams call central Florida home in the spring, including the Atlanta Braves (Disney's ESPN Wide World of Sports), the Houston Astros (Osceola County Stadium in Kissimmee), and the Detroit Tigers (Joker Marchant Stadium in Lakeland, also home to the Class A Minor League Lakeland Flying Tigers).

The Yankees head to Tampa's Steinbrenner Field (naturally) to freshen their tans; the Washington Nationals prefer the Space Coast Stadium. From April through September, Steinbrenner Field belongs to the Tampa Yankees farm team, who play 70 games against the likes of the Daytona Cubs and the Sarasota Red Sox.

IF YOU LIKE

Art

There are a surprising number of world-class art museums in Central Florida—from Orlando and Winter Park to St. Petersburg and Sarasota; from sublime stained glass to surrealist paintings and folk art to circus folk.

Mennello Museum of American Folk Art, Orlando. The Mennello holds the nation's most extensive permanent collection of Earl Cunningham paintings, as well as many other "outsider" artists. Works by Wyeth, Cassatt, Eastman, and others have made their central Florida debuts here.

Charles Hosmer Morse Museum of American Art, Winter Park. Known as the "Tiffany museum," the galleries contain the largest and most comprehensive collection of art by Louis Comfort Tiffany, including stained-glass windows and lamps, blown-glass vases, and gem-studded jewelry.

Salvador Dalí Museum, St. Petersburg. Built upon the collection of an Ohio industrialist, this is the world's most comprehensive gathering of oils, watercolors, drawings, sculptures, photographs, and objets d'art by the Spanish surrealist. At this writing, a new, larger museum is in the work's adjacent to the Mahaffey Theater.

FSU Ringling Center for the Cultural Arts, Sarasota. An artistic compound starring the John and Mable Ringling Museum of Art and the Ringling Circus Museum. Classical masters of art share space with sideshow memorabilia. Don't miss the enchanting scale model of a 1920s Ringling Bros. and Barnum & Bailey Circus.

Culture

A long history, from early Native American occupants, through Spanish, French, and British settlers, has left indelible marks on central Florida. Add to that the influx of wealthy vacationers from the North and hopeful immigrants from Europe, and history comes alive in these repositories of knowledge.

DeSoto National Memorial, Bradenton. Hernando de Soto came ashore with his men and 200 horses near what is now Bradenton in 1539; this federal park commemorates that landing. From mid-December to late April park workers dress in period costumes at Camp Uzita and demonstrate how European explorers lived.

Ybor City, Tampa. One of only four National Historic Landmark districts in Florida, Tampa's rollicking Cuban quarter has antique-brick streets and wrought-iron balconies, hand-rolled cigars, and fresh-roasted coffee. The neighborhood has become one of Tampa's hot spots, as empty cigar factories and social clubs have been transformed into boutiques, art galleries, restaurants, and nightclubs.

Florida Holocaust Museum, St. Petersburg. A permanent History, Heritage, and Hope exhibit; an original boxcar; and an extensive collection of photographs, art, and artifacts give new perspective to one of the largest collections of its kind. Conceived as a learning center for children, many of the exhibits avoid overly graphic content.

Tarpon Springs. Tarpon Springs has been the home of Greek sponge divers for more than 120 years, and the combination of sun, great food, and history can't be beat. Take time to visit St. Nicholas Greek Orthodox Cathedral, a replica of St. Sophia Cathedral in Constantinople.

Critters

There are animals of all stripes outside Disney's Animal Kingdom theme park, some native to Florida, some very exotic indeed, but all a great deal of fun to observe.

Audubon Center for Birds of Prey, Maitland. This is a working conservancy that takes in more than 700 injured wild birds of prey each year. Permanently injured hawks, eagles, owls, falcons, and vultures continue to live at the center. Look for them in the aviaries along the pathways and sitting on outdoor perches.

Gatorland, Kissimmee. Kids get a kick out of this unmanufactured, old-timey Florida experience, complete with Gator Gulley Splash Park, a free train ride through the park, and a Gator Jumparoo Show.

Central Florida Zoo and Botanical Gardens, Sanford. In addition to 400-plus animals, there's a zip-line ride through the treetops; a water playground; a steam-powered 1/5-scale train that puffs around the zoo; and an aquarium with interactive displays, behind-the-scenes tours, and in-water adventures.

Busch Gardens, Tampa. The 335-acre adventure park's habitats offer views of some of the world's most endangered and exotic animals. Other highlights are six fast-paced coasters, a zip-line excursion over the park, and a Sesame Street–themed area for small kids.

Science and Technology

Orlando and environs have a revered reputation for science, from state-of-the-art aircraft to manned space flight. There are many places you can go to augment your scientific knowledge—and have some fun, too.

Orlando Science Center. Kids crazy about science, and adults intrigued by the universe, will love this place. Exhibits about the human body, mechanics, computers, math, nature, and optics feed the inner geek in us all. Check out the Dr. Phillips CineDome with its eight-story screen and the stargazing at the Crosby Observatory.

Valiant Air Command Warbird Museum, Titusville. Aviation buffs will relish memorabilia from World Wars I and II, Korea, and Vietnam, as well as extensive displays of artifacts and vintage warbirds, military flying gear, and uniforms.

Kennedy Space Center. Whether you're a fan of Buzz Aldrin or Buzz Lightyear, this spaceport has the right stuff. See a shuttle launch, admire the rockets, or sign on for the Astronaut Training Experience—a day of training exercises culminating in a simulated mission.

Museum of Science & Industry, Tampa. Florida weather, anatomy, flight, and space are covered here. The Gulf Coast Hurricane Exhibit lets you experience 74-mph winds. The 100-seat Saunders Planetarium has afternoon and evening shows, one of them a trek through the universe. For adventurous spirits, there's a high-wire bicycle ride 30 feet above the floor and a jet-fighter simulator.

GREAT ITINERARIES

If you're like most visitors to Orlando, you've come for a theme park (or two or three). But if you need a break from them, have people in your group who aren't interested in them, or have an extra day or two, know that it's easy to get out and explore Central Florida. A stay in Orlando puts you an hour from the east coast and 90 minutes from the Gulf of Mexico.

■ TIP→ If you're visiting the gulf just for the beaches or fishing, check the state's environmental protection site (www.dep.state.fl.us/deepwaterhorizon) to see how/whether the Deepwater Horizon oil spill has affected the coast.

1 Day: Central Orlando Highlights

Head out midmorning. If it's rainy or hot and humid, visit the Mennello Folk Art Collection, northeast of downtown in Lock Haven Park. If it's a nice day, however, explore the 50-acre Harry P. Leu Gardens, northeast of downtown but not as far as the Mennello. Arrive for one of the day's first guided tours (they start at 10) of the Leu House Museum.

■ TIP→ LYNX Bus 50 runs directly from Disney and I-Drive to downtown Orlando.

Head southwest to downtown's Lake Eola Park. Have a late lunch in the park's Relax Grill or at one of the many eateries nearby—maybe the HUE boutique hotel's contemporary restaurant. Work off some calories in a swan-shape pedal boat. At this point, happy hour and the bars and clubs of Orange Avenue aren't far off. If you feel like dancing later, Firestone Live is a couple of blocks north; Antigua is south and around the corner.

■ TIP→ The Orlando Science Center, in Lock Haven, is a kid-friendly alternative to the museum or gardens, and Johnny's Filling Station (locals love the burgers) or CityFish are good downtown dinner bets.

1 Day: Shopping Highlights

If it's Saturday, head out early so you can start your spree at the Winter Park Farmers Market, where there's free valet parking. There are also stalls that sell locally sourced foods—including breakfast—and crafts. Winter Park is just north of downtown, at Exit 87 off Interstate 4.

■ TIP→ There's no need to rent a car if you're only planning to visit Winter Park; instead hop a LYNX bus from the main Orlando terminal.

Regardless of the day, Winter Park's shopping-and-dining drag, Park Avenue, beckons. Boutiques and galleries—including Jacobsen's, 10,000 Villages, and Timothy's—line the east side, opposite an oak-shaded lawn. An alfresco lunch at a restaurant here will carry you through an afternoon of still more shopping.

Hop on Interstate 4 at the Fairbanks entrance, and head west about 8 mi to Exit 78 (Conroy Road) and the upscale Mall at Millenia. If you'd rather hunt for bargains, take Millenia Boulevard to Oak Ridge Road (at the intersection of International Drive) and its outlet malls—Festival Bay and Prime Outlets International. Farther south, on International Drive at Vineland Avenue, is Orlando Premium Outlets.

■ TIP→ Non-shopping alternatives in Winter Park are the Charles Hosmer Morse Museum of American Art and the town's scenic boat tour. On I-Drive, you'll find Fun Spot, WonderWorks, and Ripley's.

You've spent the day shopping like a local, so you should spend the evening dining like one. Head to Sand Lake Road for a pick of places and cuisines—from Italian and Mediterranean to Thai and Hawaiian-fusion. Splurge on a steak at Morton's of Chicago or go lighter—in terms of both

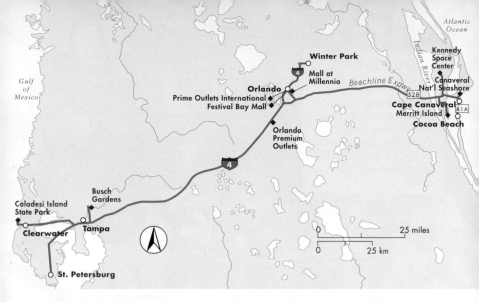

your budget and the food—with seasonal fare at Seasons 52.

1 to 2 Days: The Space Coast

From Orlando, you can be at the Kennedy Space Center in a little over an hour on SR528 (the Beachline Expressway, a toll road), which makes it a good day trip. Also, several Orlando tour companies have trips for about $100 per person. Exhibits on American space travel here have enthralled children of all ages since 1968.

■ TIP→ An overlooked space-center alternative is the Valiant Air Command Warbird Museum. Check out the military-aircraft memorabilia, and then buy a bomber jacket.

With an overnight stay, you can lounge on the blissful beaches of Canaveral National Seashore, catch a wave like surfing legend (and local hero) Kelly Slater, or explore the adjacent 140,000-acre Merritt Island National Wildlife Refuge.

There are also opportunities for horseback riding, hiking, bird-watching, and fishing. Cape Canaveral and Cocoa Beach make great bases thanks to their coastal locations and selection of hotels, restaurants, outfitters, and other amenities.

1 to 3 Days: Tampa and St. Pete

Shamu enthusiasts can include a visit to Busch Gardens Tampa thanks to their SeaWorld Orlando combo ticket (they're owned by the same company). The city is only about 90 minutes southwest on Interstate 4, so you can take in the theme park on a day trip. But many attractions make Tampa, St. Petersburg, and other coastal towns worthy of a car rental, exploration, and an overnight stay.

If you stay, spend an evening in Ybor City, Tampa's Cuban enclave and a nightlife mecca, particularly along Seventh Avenue. In the morning, head to a beach in St. Pete or, maybe, Clearwater. Spend the day sunbathing, or break up the day with an afternoon visit to St. Pete's Salvador Dalí Museum.

■ TIP→ Dalí Museum docents conduct free tours and can explain how works by the Spanish surrealist ended up in Florida.

Alternatively (or in addition), you can hop onto a Segway for a tour of St. Petersburg, catch a spring training or Buccaneers game, bike along Tampa's Bayshore Boulevard Trail or Clearwater's Pinellas Trail, or hunt for shells at Caladesi Island State Park.

Orlando and Environs

WORD OF MOUTH

"Go to Sleuths Mystery Dinner Theatre. The food is average, but the fun is a 10! The actors present a story between courses, and . . . you can question the "suspects" over dessert. Finally, the mystery is solved. There's plenty of comedy built into the show. . . . We always plan at least one night there when we are in Orlando."

—BlueDevlinPA

WELCOME TO ORLANDO AND ENVIRONS

TOP REASONS TO GO

★ **Liberal Arts.** Orlando's theaters host symphony orchestras, Broadway road shows, and local thespians—from the Shakespearean to the progressive. Jazz, blues, world music, and rock are all part of the music scene. Area museums showcase folk art, Tiffany glass, and 19th- and 20th-century American and European painting.

★ **The Sciences.** The Orlando Science Center has exhibits on human biology, technology, nature, and the stars. At WonderWorks, simulators let you survive an earthquake or pilot a jet. The Kennedy Space Center takes you to the final frontier.

★ **Cultivated Spaces.** Gardens devoted to historical blooms, camelias, azaleas, and roses are among the more refined outdoor offerings.

★ **Wild Places.** Go all gator at Gatorland or see rescued winged creatures at the Audubon Center for Birds of Prey. Fish, boat, canoe, or swim in Wekiwa Springs State Park or Ocala National Forest.

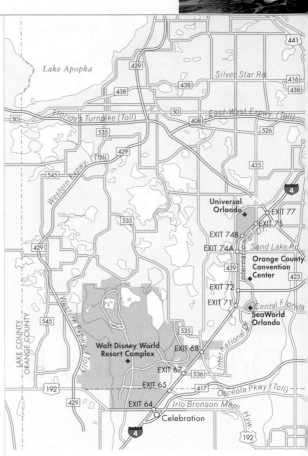

1 Orlando. There's more to Orlando than theme parks: a thriving downtown with ample opportunity to stay, eat, and play. Internationally recognized cultural events, theater, and the evolving music scene makes downtown more than just a stopping point.

2 Orlando Environs. Natural Florida beckons with some of the most unspoiled land and amazing sportfishing in the state. Several towns—Kissimmee, Mount Dora, and Winter Park among them—recall Old Florida *and* have great shopping, world-class museums, or both.

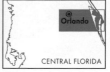

CENTRAL FLORIDA

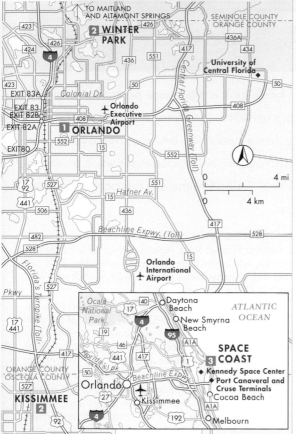

14

GETTING ORIENTED

Central Florida runs from Tampa/St. Petersburg in the west through Orlando and to the Space Coast attractions of Daytona Beach and Cape Canaveral on the east coast. Orlando is more or less equidistant, about 90 minutes by car to the Gulf of Mexico. Walt Disney World is not, contrary to advertising, in Orlando, but lies about 25 mi southwest of the city.

3 Space Coast. More than 70 mi of white-sand beaches (some you can drive on), the magic of the Kennedy Space Center, a dazzling nature preserve, and the down-home charm of small-town Florida. Add in great surfing and fishing and the excitement of Bike Week, and it's hard to imagine staying away.

Revised by
Joseph Reed
Hayes

Most Orlando locals look at the theme parks like an unruly neighbor: it's big and loud, but it keeps a nice lawn. Central Florida's many theme parks can become overpowering for even the most enthusiastic visitor, and that's when an excursion into the "other" Orlando—the one the locals know and love—is in order.

There are so many day trips. If the outdoors is your thing, you can swim or canoe at Wekiwa Springs State Park or one of the area's many other sparkling springs, where the water remains a refreshing 72°F no matter how hot the day. Alternatively, you can hike, horseback ride, canoe, and camp in the Ocala National Forest.

If museums are your thing, charming Winter Park has the Charles Hosmer Morse Museum with its huge collection of Tiffany glass, and the Cornell Fine Arts Museum on the oak-tree-covered Rollins College campus. While in Winter Park, you can indulge in some high-end shopping or dining on Park Avenue or take a leisurely boat tour of the lakefront homes.

Got kids to educate and entertain? Check out WonderWorks or the Orlando Science Center, where you can view live gators and turtles. Even more live gators (some as long as 14 feet) can be viewed or fed (or even eaten) at Gatorland, just south of Orlando. Do the kids prefer rockets and astronauts? Don't miss a day trip to Kennedy Space Center, where you can tour a rocket forest, sit in a space capsule, or climb aboard a shuttle.

Kissimmee is a 19th-century cattle town south of Orlando that proudly hangs on to its roots with a twice-yearly rodeo where real cowboys ride bulls and rope cattle. The town sits on Lake Tohopekaliga, a favorite spot for airboat rides or fishing trips.

ORLANDO

Orlando is a diverse town. The downtown area, though small, is dynamic, thanks to an ever-changing skyline, high-rises, sports venues, museums, restaurants, nightspots, and several annual cultural events—including two film festivals and a world-renowned theater fest. Downtown also has a central green, Lake Eola Park, which offers a respite from otherwise frantic touring.

Neighborhoods such as Thornton Park (great for dining) and College Park (great antiques shopping along Lake Ivanhoe) are fun to wander. Not too far to the north, you can come in contact with natural Florida—its manatees, gators, and crystal-clear waters in spring-fed lakes.

Closer to the theme-park action, International Drive, the hub of resort and conference hotels, offers big restaurants and even bigger outlet-mall bargains. Sand Lake Road, situated between the two, is Orlando's Restaurant Row, with plenty of exciting dining prospects.

GETTING HERE AND AROUND

Orlando is spread out. Most car traffic crawls along the usually crowded Interstate 4, which runs to both coasts. If you're heading east you can also take Route 528 (aka the Beachline), a toll road that heads directly for Cape Canaveral and points along the Space Coast; no such option leads west.

If you avoid rush-hour traffic, traveling to points of interest shouldn't take too much time out of your vacation. Winter Park is no more than 20 minutes from downtown; International Drive and the theme parks are about 30 to 45 minutes away. Orlando International Airport only 9 mi south of downtown, but will take about 30 minutes via a circuitous network of highways (Interstate 4 west to Florida's Turnpike south to Route 528 east).

ESSENTIALS

Hospitals Florida Hospital (⊠ *601 East Rollins Street, Orlando* ☎ *407/303–5600* ⊕ *www.floridahospital.com*). **Orlando Regional Medical Center** (⊠ *1414 Kuhl Ave., Downtown Orlando* ☎ *321/841–5111* ⊕ *www. orlandohealth.com*).

Tourist Information Orlando Travel and Visitors Bureau (☎ *407/363–5872* ⊕ *www.orlandoinfo.com*).

⇨ *For more Essential information, see the Orlando and the Parks Planner in Chapter 1, Planning Your Trip.*

EXPLORING

Numbers in the margin correspond to numbers on the Central Orlando and International Drive maps.

CENTRAL ORLANDO

❸ **Harry P. Leu Gardens.** A few miles outside of downtown—on the former lakefront estate of a citrus entrepreneur—is this 50-acre garden. Among the highlights are a collection of historical blooms (many varieties of which were established before 1900), ancient oaks, a 50-foot floral clock, and one of the largest camellia collections in eastern North

Fodor's Choice
★

The 300-seat Dr. Phillips CineDome, a movie theater with an eight-story screen at the Orlando Science Center, offers large-format IWERKS films.

America (in bloom November–March). Mary Jane's Rose Garden, named after Leu's wife, is filled with more than 1,000 bushes; it's the largest formal rose garden south of Atlanta. The simple 19th-century Leu House Museum, once the Leu family home, preserves the furnishings and appointments of a well-to-do, turn-of-the-20th-century Florida family. ✉ *1920 N. Forest Ave., Lake Ivanhoe* ☎ *407/246–2620* 🌐 *www.leugardens.org* 🎟 *$7; free first Mon. of every month* ⏲ *Garden daily 9–5; guided house tours daily on hr and ½ hr 10–3:30.*

4 **Lake Eola Park.** This beautifully landscaped 42-acre park is the verdant heart of downtown Orlando, its mile-long walking path a gathering place for families, health enthusiasts out for a run, and culture mavens exploring area offerings. The well-lighted playground is alive with children, and ducks, swans, and native Florida birds call the lake home. A farmers' market takes up residence on Sunday afternoon.

The lakeside Walt Disney Amphitheater is a dramatic site for concerts, ethnic festivals, and spectacular Fourth of July fireworks. Don't resist the park's biggest draw: a ride in a swan-shaped pedal boat. Two adults or one adult and two children can fit comfortably into each. (Children under 16 must be accompanied by an adult.)

The Relax Grill, by the swan-boat launch, is a great place for a snack. There are also several good restaurants in the upscale Thornton Park neighborhood along the park's eastern border. The ever-expanding skyline rings the lake with modern high-rises, making the peace of the park even more welcome. At this writing, plans are underway to revamp the landmark fountain, built in 1957 and the victim of a lightning strike in 2009, which temporarily silenced its jetting waters and impressive

Central Orlando

0 1/2 mi

0 1/2 km

light show. ✉ *Robinson St. and Rosalind Ave., Downtown Orlando* ☎ *407/246–2827 park, 407/232–0111 swan boats* 🖃 *Swan boat rental $15 per ½ hr* ☉ *Park daily 6* AM–*midnight; swan boats weekdays noon–dusk, weekends 10–dusk.*

② **Mennello Museum of American Folk Art.** One of the few museums in the United States devoted to folk art has intimate galleries, some with lovely lakefront views. Look for the nation's most extensive permanent collection of Earl Cunningham paintings as well as works by many other self-taught artists. There's a wonderful video about Cunningham and his "curio shop" in St. Augustine. Temporary exhibitions have included the works of Wyeth, Cassatt, Michael Eastman, and others. At the museum shop you can purchase folk-art books, toys, and unusual gifts. ✉ *900 E. Princeton St., Lake Ivanhoe* ☎ *407/246–4278* ⊕ *www.mennellomuseum.com* 🖃 *$4* ☉ *Tues.–Sat. 10:30–4:30, Sun. noon–4:30.*

⑤ **Orange County Regional History Center.** Exhibits here take you on a journey back in time to discover how Florida's Paleo-Indians hunted and fished the land; what the Sunshine State was like when the Spaniards first arrived; and how life in Florida was different when citrus was king. Visit a cabin from the late 1800s, complete with Spanish moss–stuffed mattresses, mosquito netting over the beds, and a room where game was preserved. Seminole Indian displays include interactive screens, and tin-can tourist camps of the early 1900s preview Florida's destiny as a future vacation mecca. ✉ *65 E. Central Blvd., Downtown Orlando* ☎ *407/836–8500 or 800/965–2030* ⊕ *www.thehistorycenter. org* 🖃 *$12; discount coupon available online* ☉ *Mon.–Sat. 10–5, Sun. noon–5.*

① **Orlando Science Center.** With all the high-tech glitz and imagined worlds of the theme parks, is it worth visiting Orlando's reality-based science center? If you're a kid crazy about science, the answer is an overwhelming "yes." With exhibits about the human body, mechanics, computers, math, nature, the solar system, and optics, there's something for every child's inner geek. The four-story internal atrium is home to live gators and turtles and a great spot for simply gazing at what Old Florida once looked like. The 300-seat Dr. Phillips CineDome, a movie theater with a giant eight-story screen, offers large-format IWERKS films and planetarium programs. The Crosby Observatory and Florida's largest publicly accessible refractor telescope are here as are several smaller telescopes; some weekends you can safely view spots and flares on the sun's surface.

Fodor's Choice ★

Adults like the science center, too, thanks to events like Cocktails and Cosmos, quarterly evenings of stargazing in the Crosby Observatory, live music, art, and film (with child care), and Otronicon, a quarterly interactive technology expo. ✉ *777 E. Princeton St., Lake Ivanhoe* ☎ *407/514–2000 or 888/672–4386* ⊕ *www.osc.org* 🖃 *$17; parking $5; tickets include all permanent and special exhibits, films, live science presentations, and planetarium shows* ☉ *Thurs.–Tues. 10–5.*

INTERNATIONAL DRIVE

6 **Fun Spot.** Four go-kart tracks offer a variety of driving experiences for children and adults. Though drivers must be at least 10 years old and meet height requirements, parents can drive smaller children in two-seater cars on several of the tracks, including the Conquest Track. A dozen or so rides range from the dizzying Paratrooper to an old-fashioned Revolver Ferris Wheel to the twirling toddler Teacups. Inside the arcade, traditional Whack a Mole and Spider Stompin' challenges get as much attention as the high-tech video games. From Exit 75A, turn left onto International Drive, then left on Grand National to Del Verde Way. (Older teens looking for "extreme" go-kart and ride thrills may want to take the free shuttle to sister park Fun Spot USA in Kissimmee—check the Web site for details). ⊠ *5551 Del Verde Way, I–4 to Exit 75A, I-Drive area* 🕿 *407/363–3867* ⊕ *www.funspot.tutengraphics.com* 🎫 *$14.95–$34.95 depending on go-kart and ride package (discount coupon online); arcade tokens 25¢ each or $25 for 120* ☉ *Daily 10* AM–*midnight.*

7 **Ripley's Believe It or Not! Odditorium.** A 10-foot-square section of the Berlin Wall. A pain and torture chamber. A Rolls-Royce constructed entirely of matchsticks. A 26-foot-by-20-foot portrait of van Gogh made from 3,000 postcards. These and almost 200 other oddities (shrunken heads included) speak for themselves in this museum-cum-attraction in the heart of tourist territory on International Drive. The building itself is designed to appear as if it's sliding into one of Florida's notorious sinkholes. Give yourself an hour or two to soak up the weirdness, but remember: this is a looking, not touching, experience; it might drive antsy youngsters—and their parents—crazy. ⊠ *8201 International Dr., I-Drive area* 🕿 *407/351–5803 or 800/998–4418 Ext. 3* ⊕ *www.ripleysorlando.com* 🎫 *$18.95; free parking* ☉ *Daily 9:30* AM–*midnight; last admission at 11* PM.

NEED A BREAK?

Café Tu Tu Tango. Here's something unusual: good tapas in a tourist area. With a light, breezy atmosphere (painters work in the Spanish Artist's loft as you eat) and small, shareable dishes, it's a great place for a quick snack while on I-Drive. ⊠ *8625 International Dr., I-Drive area* 🕿 *407/248–2222* ⊕ *www.cafetututango.com* ☉ *Sun.–Thurs. 11:30–11; Fri. and Sat. 11:30* AM–*midnight* 🍴 *AE, D, MC, V.*

8 **WonderWorks.** The building seems to be sinking into the ground. Not only that, but it seems to be sinking into the ground at a precarious angle and upside down. Many people stop to take pictures in front of the topsy-turvy facade, complete with upended palm trees and broken skyward-facing sidewalks. Inside, the upside-down theme continues only as far as the lobby. After that, it's a playground of 100 interactive experiences—some incorporating virtual reality, others educational (similar to those at a science museum), and still others pure entertainment. You can experience an earthquake or a hurricane, pilot a fighter jet or land a space shuttle using simulator controls, make giant bubbles in the Bubble Lab, play laser tag in the largest laser-tag arena and arcade in the world, design and ride your own roller coaster, lie on a bed of real

14

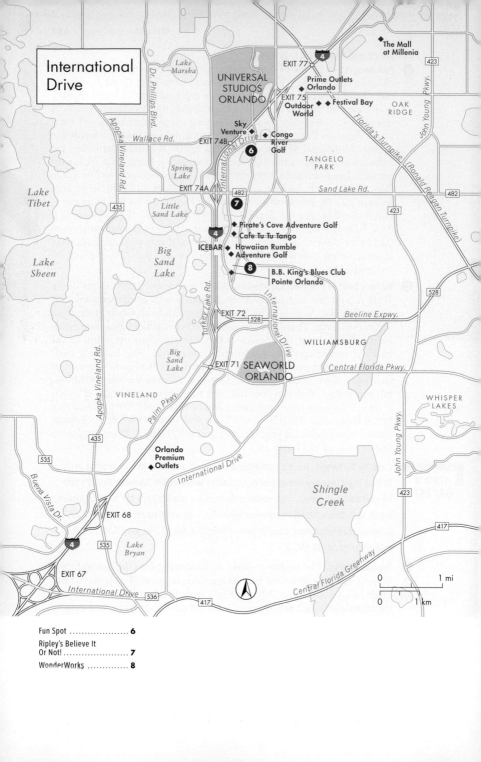

International Drive

- The Mall at Millenia
- EXIT 77
- ④
- 423
- UNIVERSAL STUDIOS ORLANDO
- Prime Outlets Orlando
- EXIT 75
- Outdoor World
- Festival Bay
- OAK RIDGE
- Sky Venture
- EXIT 74B
- ⑥
- Congo River Golf
- TANGELO PARK
- Florida's Turnpike (Ronald Reagan Turnpike)
- John Young Pkwy.
- EXIT 74A
- 482
- ⑦
- Sand Lake Rd.
- 482
- 423
- Pirate's Cove Adventure Golf
- Cafe Tu Tu Tango
- ④
- ICEBAR
- Hawaiian Rumble Adventure Golf
- ⑧
- B.B. King's Blues Club
- Pointe Orlando
- 528
- EXIT 72
- 528
- Beeline Expwy.
- WILLIAMSBURG
- Big Sand Lake
- EXIT 71
- SEAWORLD ORLANDO
- Central Florida Pkwy.
- WHISPER LAKES
- VINELAND
- 435
- Palm Pkwy.
- John Young Pkwy.
- Orlando Premium Outlets
- 535
- International Drive
- Shingle Creek
- 423
- Buena Vista Dr.
- EXIT 68
- 417
- ④
- 535
- Lake Bryan
- EXIT 67
- International Drive
- 536
- 417
- Central Florida Greenway

Dr. Phillips Blvd.
Lake Marsha
Wallace Rd.
Apopka Vineland Rd.
Spring Lake
Lake Tibet
435
Little Sand Lake
Lake Sheen
Big Sand Lake
Turkey Lake Rd.
International Drive

0   1 mi
0   1 km

Kissimmee's Lake Tohopekaliga (affectionately known as Lake Toho) is famous with fishermen the world over. It's also great for wildlife spotting—an especially exhilerating experience when done from an airboat.

nails, and play basketball with a 7-foot opponent. ✉ *9067 International Dr., I-Drive area* ☎ *407/351–8800* ⊕ *www.wonderworksonline.com* ✉ *$19.95; higher-price combo packages include laser tag and Outta Control Magic Comedy Dinner Show; parking $2–$6; look for online coupons* ⊙ *Daily 9 AM–midnight.*

SPORTS AND THE OUTDOORS

There are many ways to enjoy the outdoors here. You can navigate the more than 2,000 lakes and waterways, perhaps on a sportfishing excursion—something to consider in what is one of the bass-fishing capitals of the world. You can also take to the air in a glider or hot-air balloon, or stay firmly planted hiking or biking a trail.

You can tee off at one of the more than six dozen area greens. Indeed, you'll probably be amazed by the country club–like golf courses (and tennis courts) run by the City of Orlando and accessible at bargain prices.

In Orlando a brand-new sports arena and the two pro teams that play in it are bringing in the crowds. Throughout central Florida, professional baseball comes down from the frozen north to warm up during spring training.

BALLOONING

Fodor's Choice ★ **Bob's Balloons.** Bob's offers one-hour rides over protected marshland and will even fly over Disney World if wind and weather conditions are right. You meet in Lake Buena Vista at dawn, where Bob and his assistant take you by van to the launch site. It takes about 15 minutes to get the balloon in the air, and then you're off on an adventure that definitely surpasses Peter Pan's Flight in the Magic Kingdom.

You'll see farm and forest land for miles, along with horses, deer, wild boar, cattle, and birds flying *below* you. Bob may take you as high as 1,000 feet, from which point you'll be able to see Disney's landmarks: the Expedition Everest mountain, the Epcot ball, and more. Several other balloons are likely to go up near you—there's a tight-knit community of ballooners in the Orlando area—so you'll view these colorful sky ornaments from an unparalleled sightline. There are seats in the basket, but you'll probably be too thrilled to sit down. Check the Web site for specials. ☎ 407/466–6380 or 877/824–4606 ⊕ *www.bobsballoons.com* ▧ *$90–$175 per person* ▭ *D, MC, V.*

BASKETBALL

Orlando Magic. The Southeast Division Championship–winning Magic is the only pro sports team in town, and judging by its new, multimillion-dollar, state-of-the art 20,000-seat home at the Amway Center, much beloved by local fans. Many famous names have come out of this team (Shaquille O'Neal, anyone?), and although the team's fortunes have fluctuated, the Magic has consistently been the most successful of the NBA expansion teams. The Magic's season runs from October to June, and tickets for home games, available directly from the Web site, cost as little as $5 (very high promenade seats) and as much as $295 (so-called superstar seating). Parking for home games is an extra $10, $50 in the VIP lot, or park at the Courthouse garage for $7 and take the free city-owned Lymmo bus. ✉ *600 W. Amelia St., Downtown Orlando* ☎ *407/896–2442* ⊕ *www.nba.com/magic.*

BIKING AND RUNNING

Thanks to the Orlando community's commitment to the nationwide Rails to Trails program, the city now has several biking, running, and in-line skating trails—converted from former railroad lines—in both rural and urban surroundings.

Orlando City Transportation Planning Bureau. You can get information about Orlando bike and running trails from this agency. ☎ *407/246–3347* ⊕ *www.cityoforlando.net.*

Cady Way Trail. A favorite of local bikers, joggers, and skaters, the Cady Way connects eastern Orlando with the well-manicured enclave of Winter Park. The pleasant trail is 3½ mi long, with water fountains and shaded seating along the route. **The best access point for the Cady Way Trail is the parking lot on the east side of the Orlando Fashion Square Mall** (✉ *3201 E. Colonial Dr., about 3 mi east of I–4 Exit 83B, Orlando*). **The eastern access to the Cady Way Trail is at Cady Way Park** (✉ *1300 S. Denning Ave., Winter Park*).

Turkey Lake Park. This park, about 4 mi from Disney, has a 3-mi biking trail that's popular with runners, and a lake that attracts the casual fisherman. Several wooded hiking trails also make for a good run. The park closes at 5 PM, and fees are $4 per car. ✉ *3401 S. Hiawassee Rd., West Orlando* ☎ *407/299–5581* ⊕ *www.cityoforlando.net.*

★ **West Orange Trail.** It runs some 20 mi through western Orlando, the neighboring town of Apopka, and the center of the revived suburb of Winter Garden. Highlights are views of Lake Apopka and the xeriscape–butterfly garden a mile east of the Oakland Outpost. **You can access the West Orange Trail at Chapin's Station** (⊠ *501 Crown Point Cross Rd., Winter Garden* ☎ *407/654–1108*). **West Orange Trail Bikes & Blades** (⊠ *17914 State Rd. 438, Winter Garden* ☎ *407/877–0600* ⊕ *www.orlandobikerental.com*) rents bicycles and in-line skates; the cost for either is $6 per hour.

FOOTBALL

Orlando Predators. Professional arena-football team the Predators have been in Orlando since 1991, and have reached the league playoffs for 17 consecutive seasons. The team plays from April to October in the Amway Center. *Parking for home games is an extra $10, $50 in the VIP lot, or park at the Courthouse garage for $7 and take the free city-owned Lymmo bus.* ⊠ *600 W Amelia St., Downtown Orlando* ☎ *407/896–2442* ⊕ *www.orlandopredators.com* 🎟 *$8–$120.*

GOLF

If golf is your passion, you already know that Arnold Palmer, Gary Player, and Tiger Woods—in fact, almost half of the PGA tour—make Orlando their off-road home. It's not by accident that the Golf Channel originates from here. The Bay Hill Invitational, National Golf Team Championship, and several LPGA tourneys (the headquarters is in Daytona) come to Orlando every year. And with more than 80 public and private courses, there's ample opportunity for you to play on worldclass courses such as Grand Cypress or Champions Gate.

⇨ *For details on golfing in Orlando, see Part I: Experience Orlando and the Parks.*

MINIATURE GOLF

☾ **Congo River.** Here mini-putt meets theme park, with multilevel courses wandering amid waterfalls, rocky summits, caves, and rain forests. Kids love the live alligators (not loose on the course), the arcade room, and the treasure hunt. Congo River also has locations on I-Drive near Universal Studios and in East Orlando. ⊠ *6312 International Dr., I-Drive area* ☎ *407/352–0042* ⊕ *www.congoriver.com* 🎟 *$10.95* ☉ *Sun.–Thurs. 10 AM–11 PM, Fri. and Sat. 10 AM–midnight.*

☾ **Hawaiian Rumble Adventure Golf.** Who can resist golfing around an erupting volcano? Hawaiian Rumble combines a tropical setting with waterfalls, tunnels, tiki gods, and flame-belching mountains. There's also a location in the Lake Buena Vista area. ⊠ *8969 International Dr., I-Drive area* ☎ *407/351–7733* ⊕ *www.hawaiianrumbleorlando. com* 🎟 *$9.95–$14.95* ☉ *Sun.–Thurs. 9 AM–11:30 PM, Fri. and Sat. 9 AM–midnight.*

Fodor's Choice
★

☾ **Pirate's Cove Adventure Golf.** Two 18-hole courses wind around artificial mountains, through caves, and into lush foliage. The beginner's course is called Captain Kidd's Adventure; the more advanced course is Blackbeard's Challenge. There's also a branch in the Crossroads of Lake Buena Vista shopping plaza, near Disney. ⊠ *8501 Interna-*

14

tional Dr., I-Drive area ☎ *407/352–7378* ⊕ *www.piratescove.net* ✉ *$10.95–$16.50* ☉ *Daily 9* AM–*11:30* PM.

SKYDIVING

Fodor's Choice **Sky Venture.** OK: you technically aren't skydiving, but you come pretty
★   close in a 12-foot-high, 1,000-horsepower wind tunnel that lets you
experience everything skydivers do, but closer to the ground. The experience starts with instruction, after which you suit up and hit the wind
tunnel, where you soar like a bird under your instructor's watchful
eye. While you're "falling" on the wind stream, you even experience
what divers called ground rush, because you're surrounded by a video
depiction of a dive. It's all so realistic that skydiving clubs come to
hone their skills. You must be less than 250 pounds and at least 4
feet tall to participate. You can purchase a video of your "jump" for
$16. ⊠ *6805 Visitors Circle, I-Drive area* ☎ *407/903–1150* ⊕ *www.
skyventureorlando.com* ✉ *$45 per jump* ☉ *Weekdays 2–midnight,
weekends noon–midnight.*

TENNIS
Tennis awaits on well-tended public tennis courts and on courts in
resort hotels. There are 57 courts run by City Parks & Recreation,
most of which are free.

Fort Gatlin Tennis Complex. Fort Gatlin has the finest city-run courts open
to the public. Ten hard courts equipped for day or night play, a pro
shop that's open daily, and lessons are among this beautiful facility's
offerings. ⊠ *2009 Lake Margaret Dr., Downtown Orlando* ☎ *407/254–
9878* ⊕ *fortgatlintennis.com* ✉ *$3–$5 per court per hour* ☉ *Weekdays,
8* AM–*10* PM, *weekends 8–8.*

Orlando Tennis Centre. Run by the City of Orlando, this fine facility
offers adult tennis clinics (18 and up), private lessons, and youth tennis programs (6 and up). ⊠ *649 W Livingston St., Downtown Orlando*
☎ *407/246–4469* ⊕ *www.ci.orlando.fl.us* ✉ *$5.02 soft court per hour;
$4.02 hard court* ☉ *Weekdays 8* AM–*9:30* PM, *weekends 8–2:30.*

6th Sense Tennis Academy. Based at the Mission Inn Resort, 6th Sense is
run by Olympic gold-medal-winner Justine Henin. It offers one-day,
two-day, and weekly programs for adults ($120–$500) and intensive
children's training ($200–$360) from March through December. The
resort is approximately 40 mi west of Orlando. ⊠ *10400 County Rd.
48, Howie-in-the-Hills* ☎ *352/435–5799* ⊕ *www.6thsenseacademy.com*
☉ *Weekdays 8–8, weekends 8–5.*

SHOPPING

Visitors from as far away as Britain and Brazil have been known to
arrive in Orlando with empty suitcases for their purchases. Although
shopping has all but disappeared from downtown, the metro area is
filled with options. There really is something for everyone—from high-
end fashion to outlet-mall chic, from the world's largest flea market
to a boutique-filled town, from an antique treasure to a hand-hewn
Florida find.

The east end of the Lake Ivanhoe area of College Park is an antiquer's dream, with more than a dozen small shops (including an antiques store–restaurant) running south from Princeton Street along North Orange Avenue.

The simultaneously glitzy and trashy International Drive has almost 500 designer outlet stores and odd, off-brand electronics shops. The factory outlets on the north end of the Drive once consisted of shops with merchandise piled on tables; today the shops here are equal to their higher-priced first-run cousins. The strip also has plenty of restaurants, and, for those in your group who don't feel like shopping, movie theaters.

⇨ *For information on shops at Disney, Universal, and SeaWorld see, respectively, see Part II: Experience Walt Disney World; Part III: Experience Universal Orlando; and Part IV: Experience SeaWorld, Discovery Cove & Aquatica.*

CENTRAL ORLANDO AREA
MALLS
★ **Florida Mall.** With 260-plus stores, 1.9-million square feet of shopping, it's big enough to for you to vacation here—in fact, there's even an attached hotel. Only 7 mi from the airport, the mall attracts crowds of international visitors eager for American bargains. Anchor stores include Sears, JCPenney, Dillard's, Saks Fifth Avenue, Macy's, and Nordstrom. Thirty casual eateries and sit-down restaurants assure that you won't go hungry. Stroller and wheelchair rentals are available; there's even concierge services and a currency exchange. The mall is 4½ mi east of Interstate 4 and International Drive at the corner of Sand Lake Road and South Orange Blossom Trail. ⊠ *8001 S. Orange Blossom Trail, South Orlando* ☎ *407/851–6255* ⊕ *www.simon.com* ⊙ *Mon.– Sat. 10–9, Sun. noon–6.*

Fodor'sChoice **Mall at Millenia.** "Deluxe" is the word for this mall, a high-end col-
★ lection of designer shops, including Gucci, Dior, Burberry, Chanel, Jimmy Choo, Hugo Boss, Cartier, Tiffany, and Ferragamo. You'll also find Neiman Marcus, Bloomingdale's, Bang & Olufsen, and an Apple store. The Mall at Millenia's biggest attraction may be the freestanding IKEA (☎ *407/355–3155* ⊕ *www.ikea.com*) adjacent to Bloomingdale's—it's a great place for lunch or pre-shopping breakfast. The **Millenia Gallery**(☎ *407/226–8701* ⊕ *www.milleniagallery.com*) treats window-shoppers and serious art buyers to paintings by Picasso, pop art by Warhol, and hand-blown glass art by Dale Chihuly. A few minutes northwest of Universal, the mall is easy to reach via Exit 78 off Interstate 4. ⊠ *4200 S. Conroy Rd., South Orlando* ☎ *407/363–3555* ⊕ *www.mallatmillenia.com* ⊙ *Mon.–Sat. 10–9:30, Sun. 11–7.*

SPECIALTY SHOPS
Orlando Harley-Davidson. During Daytona Beach Bike Week in March and Biktober Fest in October, this is Hog Central. Anything Harley is available, from chrome pipes, leather clothing, and cycle GPS units to actual motorcycles to buy or rent—yes, rent. The staff will teach you how to ride or paint flames on the side of your bike, and the calendar includes themed events with free food and live music. There are

Other locations in East Orlando and Kissimmee as well as shops selling gear on International Drive and at the airport. ⊠ *3770 37th St., South Orlando* ☏ *407/423–0346* ⊕ *www.orlandoharley.com* ⊘ *Mon.–Sat. 9–7, Sun. 10–4.*

Rock & Roll Heaven. Apparently, vinyl records are popular again, but according to R&R Heaven, they never left. Thousands upon thousands of LPs, 45s, CDs, and cassettes, in every conceivable (and a few unbelievable) music style can be found here, starting at as little as $1. ⊠ *1814 North Orange Ave., Lake Ivanhoe* ☏ *407/896–1952* ⊕ *www. rock-n-rollheaven.com* ⊘ *Mon.–Sat. 10–7:30, Sun. 11–4.*

Washburn Imports. Here you'll find an eclectic mix of estate-sale antiques, commissioned furniture made in Indonesia and Thailand, and one-of-a-kind home furnishings. ⊠ *1800 N. Orange Ave., Lake Ivanhoe* ☏ *407/228–4403* ⊕ *www.washburnimports.com* ⊘ *Mon.–Sat. 10–6, Sun. 11–4.*

INTERNATIONAL DRIVE AREA
CENTERS AND MALLS

Festival Bay. Taking the "shoppertainment" approach to retailing, Festival Bay, which is opposite the Prime Outlets Mall, has an indoor miniature golf course called Putting Edge, the Money Joe's inflatable play center, and a 55,000-square-foot Vans Skatepark. Shops include the giant Bass Pro Shops Outdoor World and Ron Jon Surf Shop. There's also a 20-screen Cinemark Theater and several restaurants. ⊠ *5250 International Dr., I-Drive area* ☏ *407/351–7718* ⊕ *www.shopfestivalbaymall. com* ⊘ *Mon.–Sat. 10–9, Sun. 11–7.*

Pointe Orlando. What was once an enclosed shopping center is now a dining, shopping, and entertainment hot spot—one that's within walking distance of five top hotels and the Orange County Convention Center. In addition to WonderWorks and the enormous Muvico Pointe 21 IMAX theater, the complex has specialty shops such as Armani Exchange, Tommy Bahama, Chico's, and Victoria's Secret. Restaurants have become a reason to visit, with the very high-end Capital Grille, the Oceanaire Seafood Room, Cuba Libre, and the popular Funky Monkey Wine Company joining B.B. King's Blues Club and Taverna Opa. Parking ($2 for 15 minutes–two hours, $5 daily) can be validated by the movie theater and many of the restaurants. ⊠ *9101 International Dr., I-Drive area* ☏ *407/248–2838* ⊕ *www.pointeorlando.com* ⊘ *Mon.–Sat. noon–10, Sun. noon–8; restaurant hrs vary.*

FACTORY OUTLETS

★ **Prime Outlets Orlando.** This is a "prime" destination for international shoppers who can find shoes, clothing, cosmetics, electronics, and household goods at a fraction of their home-country prices. The massive complex at the north tip of International Drive includes Saks Fifth Avenue OFF 5TH, Neiman Marcus Last Call, Victoria's Secret Outlet, the only outlet store for Baccarat and Lalique crystal, and a Disney outlet. Searching for bargains works up an appetite, and there are plenty of places to eat here, either in the well-lit food court or in one of several sit-down and highly regarded restaurants. Need to relax? Head to the

DID YOU KNOW?

Old Town in Kissimmee—just one of many Orlando area sights outside the theme parks—has 75 shops, 8 restaurants, 18 rides, and 3 or so antique-car shows a week.

day spa. ✉ *5401 W. Oak Ridge Rd., I-Drive area* ☎ *407/352–9600* ⊕ *www.primeoutlets.com* ⊘ *Mon.–Sat. 10* AM*–11* PM*, Sun. 10–9.*

Orlando Premium Outlets. This outlet capitalizes on its proximity to Disney (it's at the confluence of Interstate 4, Route 535, and International Drive). It's easier to see from the highway than to enter, and parking is tedious and scarce, but smart shoppers have lunch on International Drive and take the I-Ride Trolley right to the front entrance (it runs every 15 minutes). The center's design makes this almost an open-air market, so walking can be pleasant on a nice day. You'll find the Kleins (Anne and Calvin), Gap, Nike, Adidas, Timberland, Polo, Giorgio Armani, Burberry, Tommy Hilfiger, Reebok, Mikasa, and about 100 other stores. ✉ *8200 Vineland Rd., I-Drive area* ☎ *407/238–7787* ⊕ *www. premiumoutlets.com/orlando* ⊘ *Mon.–Sat. 10* AM*–11* PM*, Sun. 10–9.*

SPECIALTY STORE

Outdoor World. Inside a 150,000-square-foot Western-style lodge—and with fishing ponds, deer tracks in the concrete, and a massive stone fireplace—the store packs in countless boats, RVs, tents, rifles, deep-sea fishing gear, freshwater fishing tackle, scuba equipment, fly-tying materials (classes are offered, too), a pro shop, outdoor clothing, Uncle Buck's Cabin (a restaurant and snack bar), and a shooting gallery. If you're an outdoors enthusiast, this is a must-visit. ✉ *5156 International Dr., I-Drive area* ☎ *407/563–5200* ⊕ *www.basspro.com* ⊘ *Mon.–Sat. 9* AM*–10* PM*, Sun. 10–8.*

NIGHTLIFE

Outside of Disney's West Side and Universal's CityWalk, the focal point of Orlando nightlife is downtown. If you stand on the corner of Orange Avenue and Church Street long enough, just about every beautiful partier will walk by. The bars and clubs here hop even after the 2 AM last call.

CENTRAL ORLANDO

BARS

Fodor'sChoice ★ **Antigua.** The multi-block-long entertainment complex called Church Street is a restaurant and bar hot spot, with Antigua being a contender for flashiest and hippest of them all. The music in the multilevel, four-bar lounge is loud; the lighting is dramatic; and the waterfall (yes, you read that correctly) cascades 20 feet. No wonder the pretty people pack the place. ✉ *46 West Church St., Downtown Orlando* ☎ *407/649–4270* ⊕ *www.churchstreetbars.com* ⊜ *$5–$10* ⊘ *Wed.–Sat. 10* PM*–2:45* AM*.*

Bull and Bush Pub. One of the most atmospheric places is also one of the few where you can get a hand-drawn pint, play a game of darts, and have a (still) smoky chat. Besides the bar, there are small booths for privacy. The tap lineup covers 11 imported beers and ales. ✉ *2408 E. Robinson St., Downtown Orlando* ☎ *407/896–7546* ⊘ *Mon.–Sat. 4* PM*–2* AM*.*

Monkey Bar. You access this tiny pocket of sophistication amid the frenetic energy of the Wall Street entertainment area by walking through the WaiTiki Retro Tiki Lounge and finding the all-but-hidden elevator at the back. There's a relatively quiet room inside and an almost New

ORLANDO AREA DINNER SHOWS

Dinner shows are an immensely popular form of nighttime entertainment around Orlando, particularly in Kissimmee. What the shows lack in substance and depth they make up for in grandeur and enthusiasm. The result is an evening of light entertainment that youngsters, in particular, enjoy.

For a single price (which seems like an ever-increasing price), you get a theatrical production and a multicourse meal. Performances run the gamut from jousting matches to jamborees, and meals tend to be better than average. Unlimited beer, wine, and soda are usually included, but mixed drinks (and often *any* drinks before dinner) cost extra.

Seatings are usually between 7 and 9:30, and there are usually one or two performances a night, with an extra show during peak periods. You might sit with strangers at tables for 10 or more, but that's part of the fun. Always reserve in advance, especially for weekend shows, and always ask about discounts, although you can often find online coupons (sometimes for half off) that you can print out yourself. Since performance schedules can vary by season, it's always smart to call in advance to verify showtimes. When buying tickets, ask if the cost includes a gratuity.

Orleans–style balcony. The martinis are half price during happy hour (and you will be happy, as they are huge) from 5 to 7 Tuesday to Friday. ⊠ *26 Wall St., Downtown Orlando* ☎ *407/481–1199* ⊘ *Tues.–Fri. 5* PM*–2* AM*, Sat. 9* PM*–2* AM*.*

Wally's. One of Orlando's oldest bars (circa 1953), this longtime local favorite is a hangout for a cross section of cultures and ages. Some would say it's a dive, but that doesn't matter to the students, bikers, lawyers, and barflies who land here to drink surrounded by the go-go-dancer wallpaper and '60s-era interior. Just grab a stool at the bar to take in the scene and down a cold one. ⊠ *1001 N. Mills Ave., Downtown Orlando* ☎ *407/896–6975* ⊘ *Mon.–Sat. 7:30* AM*–1* AM*, Sun. noon–10.*

MUSIC CLUBS

Bösendorfer Lounge. One of only two Imperial Grand Bösendorfer pianos takes center stage at this, perhaps the classiest gathering spot in Orlando. The highly civilized (but not stuffy) lounge attracts a cross section of trendy Orlandoans, especially the after-work crowd, among whom the conversation and camaraderie flow as smoothly as the champagne, beer, wine, and cocktails. Art on the walls, comfortable couches, rich fabrics, sleek black marble, and seductive lighting invite you to stay awhile. If music is what attracts you, call in advance for the schedule of jazz combos and solo pianists who perform in the lounge. Many are among the area's finest and most talented musicians. ⊠ *Westin Grand Bohemian Hotel, 325 S. Orange Ave., Downtown Orlando* ☎ *407/313–9000* ⊕ *www.grandbohemianhotel.com* ⊘ *Thurs.–Sat. 11* AM*–2* AM*, Sun.–Wed. 11* AM*–midnight.*

Firestone Live. Based in an old automotive repair shop, this multilevel, high-energy club draws international music acts. Something's always going on to make the crowd hop: DJ mixes, big band, jazz, hip-hop, rock. Often the dance floor is more like semicontrolled chaos than a place to just listen, so be prepared. Hours and prices vary by event; check the Web site. ⊠ *578 N. Orange Ave., Downtown Orlando* ☎ *407/872–0066* ⊕ *www.firestonelive.net.*

Fodor's Choice ★ **Social.** Beloved by locals, Social is a great place to see touring and area musicians. It serves full dinners Wednesday through Saturday and offers up live music seven nights a week. You can sip trademark martinis while listening to anything from alternative rock to rockabilly to undiluted jazz. Several now-national acts got their start here, including Matchbox Twenty, Seven Mary Three, and other groups that don't have numbers in their names. Hours vary. ⊠ *54 N. Orange Ave., Downtown Orlando* ☎ *407/246–1419* ⊕ *www.thesocial.org* ⊠ *$7–$30, depending on entertainment.*

Tanqueray's. Of all the entertainment possibilities in Downtown Orlando, the most interesting one may be the hardest to find. Housed in a former bank vault, Tanqueray's is a belowground hideaway featuring live music and a small but interesting menu. Mondays are for reggae, weekends are the time for jazz and Orlando's own brand of folk, rock, and electro dance music. The multiroom setup is linked by giant monitors, so the stage can be seen from everywhere. ⊠ *100 S Orange Ave., Downtown Orlando* ☎ *407/649–8540* ⊕ *www.myspace.com/tanqueraysbar* ⊙ *Daily 5 PM –2 AM.*

NIGHTCLUB

Parliament House Resort. For those enamored of gay, lesbian, and high-camp entertainment, Parliament House is legendary and welcoming to every kind of audience. The 250-seat art-deco performance space, which has been open since 1975, hosts live theater, musical acts, karaoke, cabaret, dance, and bawdy and hilarious drag shows. Le Club disco and dance bar, along with four other bars, draw thousands of partiers weekly. Unfortunately Orange Blossom Trail remains a sketchy area, so wandering around the neighborhood isn't advised. ⊠ *410 N. Orange Blossom Trail, Downtown Orlando* ☎ *407/425–7571* ⊕ *www. parliamenthouse.com* ⊙ *Mon.–Sat. 9 PM–2 AM, Sun. 3 PM–when they decide to close.*

THEATER

Bob Carr Performing Arts Centre. Want to see the latest Broadway touring company strut its stuff? This is the place. It's also where the Orlando Philharmonic Orchestra, Florida Symphony Youth Orchestra, and the Broadway Across America series entertain 2,500 fans at each performance. (Note that the long-rumored, multimillion-dollar Dr. Phillips Center may replace the Bob Carr in two or three years). Parking is $8 before 5 PM, $10 after. ⊠ *401 W. Livingston St., Downtown Orlando* ☎ *407/849–2577* ⊕ *www.orlandovenues.net.*

Mad Cow Theatre. Orlando's longest-standing professional theater company is where risks are taken. Regional premieres, new works, and thoughtful interpretations of seldom-seen classics make this a stage

14

The beloved music club, Social, is the heart of downtown Orlando's nightlife scene—appropriate given its location on Orange Avenue, the main nightlife artery.

worth seeking out, and local actors eager to show their talents line up to work here. ⊠ *105 S Magnolia Ave., Downtown Orlando* ☎ *407/297–8788* ⊕ *www.madcowtheatre.org.*

Orlando Shakespeare Theater. "Orlando Shakes" has four stages, where a typical season includes six classics (Shakespeare and more), plays for young audiences, and the very popular Orlando International Fringe Festival, the oldest in America. The season runs September through April, with the Fringe Festival in May. The Harriett Lake Festival of New Plays in April ("Playfest") offers staged and reading opportunities for new playwrights. The theater is in Loch Haven Cultural Park, just a few minutes north of downtown, where the science center and the museum of art also stand. ⊠ *812 E. Rollins St.,Lake Ivanhoe* ☎ *407/447–1700* ⊕ *www.orlandoshakes.org.*

INTERNATIONAL DRIVE AREA
DINNER SHOW

Fodor's Choice
★

Sleuths Mystery Dinner Show. If Sherlock Holmes has always intrigued you, head on over for a four-course meal served up with a healthy dose of conspiracy. Sleuths is a hotbed of local acting talent, with 14 rotating whodunnit performances staged throughout the year in three different theaters. The show begins during your appetizer, and murder is the case by the time they clear your plates for this course. You'll get to discuss clues and question still-living characters over dinner and solve the crime during dessert. ⊠ *8267 International Dr.* ☎ *407/363–1985 or 800/393–1985* ⊕ *www.sleuths.com* ☎ *$52.95–$55.95* ☉ *Performances usually daily at 7:30 but call ahead* ▤ *AE, D, MC, V.*

MUSIC CLUB

★ **B.B. King's Blues Club.** The blues great was doing quite well as a musician before becoming a successful entrepreneur, with blues clubs in Memphis, Nashville, Las Vegas, and West Palm Beach as well as Orlando. Like the others, the root of the club is music. There's a dance floors and two stages for live performances by the B.B. King All-Star Band or visiting musicians. You can't really experience Delta blues without Delta dining, so the club doubles as a restaurant with fried dill pickles, catfish bites, po' boys, ribs, and other comfort foods. Oh, yeah, and there's a full bar. ✉ *Pointe Orlando, 9101 International Dr., I-Drive area* ☏ *407/370–4550* ⊕ *www.bbkingclubs.com* ☺ *Daily 11* AM–2 AM.

NIGHTCLUB

ICEBAR. Thanks to the miracle of refrigeration, this is Orlando's coolest bar—literally and figuratively. Fifty tons of pure ice is kept at a constant 27°F and has been cut and sculpted by world-class carvers into a cozy (or as cozy as ice can be) sanctuary of tables, sofas, chairs, and a bar. The staff loans you a thermal cape and gloves, and when you enter the frozen hall you receive a complimentary drink served in a glass made of crystal-clear ice. There's no cover charge if you just want to hang out in the Chill Lounge or outdoor Polar Patio, but you will pay $30 to spend 45 minutes in the subfreezing ICEBAR. There's no beer or wine inside; it's simply too cold. ✉ *Pointe Orlando, 8967 International Dr., I-Drive area* ☏ *407/426–7555* ⊕ *www.icebarorlando.com* ☺ *Daily 11* AM–2 AM.

14

ORLANDO ENVIRONS

Although the small towns around Orlando aren't historic in a European sense, they reflect the early settlers' desire to capitalize on the subtropical climate—much as you and other visitors do today.

To the south lies Kissimmee, a former cattle town on Lake Tohopekaliga, one of Florida's largest. Locals call it Lake Toho, and it's a good place to go fishing or take an airboat ride. Kissimmee retains its ranching roots, with a twice-annual rodeo that's worth a visit.

Winter Park, to the northeast, offers a more intellectual look at Florida's past. The town exudes charm, with brick streets lined with Spanish moss–draped oaks. Park Avenue, the main drag, is lined with unique shops edged by a landscaped park. You can take a leisurely boat tour on waterways that snake through town or visit the large collection of Tiffany glass in the Morse Museum of American Art.

To the northwest of Orlando is Mount Dora, built with citrus money in the 19th century. It's on Lake Dora, and the shops and restaurants lining its charming streets often have a water view.

KISSIMMEE

18 mi south of Orlando, 10 mi southeast of Walt Disney World (WDW).

Although Kissimmee is primarily known as the gateway to Disney (technically, the park is in both Osceola and Orange counties), its non-WDW attractions just might tickle your fancy. They range from throwbacks to old-time Florida or to dinner shows for you and 2,000 of your closest. Orlando used to be prime cattle country, and the best sampling of what life was like is here during the Silver Springs Rodeo in February and October.

With at least 100,000 acres of freshwater lakes, the Kissimmee area brings anglers and boaters to national fishing tournaments and speedboat races. A 50-mi-long series of lakes, the Kissimmee Waterway, connects Lake Tohopekaliga—a Native American name that means "Sleeping Tiger"; locals call it Lake Toho—with huge Lake Ocheechobee in south Florida, and, from there, to both the Atlantic Ocean and the Gulf of Mexico.

GETTING HERE AND AROUND

From Downtown Orlando it's easy to reach Kissimmee's main road, U.S. Highway 192, from Interstate 4, Exit 64, just past the last Disney exit. Osceola Parkway (Toll Road 522) heads directly from Disney property, and Florida's Turnpike runs north–south through Kissimmee.

ESSENTIALS

Visitor Info Florida Fish And Wildlife. To be able to catch those big Lake Toho bass, you need a license. (☎ *850/488–4676* ⊕ *www.myfwc.com/recreation* ✉ *Nonresident licenses: $17 for three consecutive days, $30 for seven consecutive days, $47 for one year*).

Kissimmee Convention and Visitors Bureau. Get a travel guide and discount coupons in person or online. (✉ *1925 E. Irlo Bronson Memorial Hwy., Kissimmee* ☎ *407/742–8200* ⊕ *www.visitkissimmee.com*).

⇨ *For information on Kissimmee hotels and restaurants, see Chapter 2, Where to Stay and Chapter 3, Where to Eat.*

EXPLORING

Numbers in the margin correspond to numbers on the Kissimmee map

❶ **Gatorland.** This campy attraction near the Orlando–Kissimmee border
☞ on U.S. 441 has endured since 1949 without much change, despite competition from the major parks. Over the years, the theme park and registered conservancy has gone through some changes while retaining its gator rasslin' spirit. Kids get a kick out of this unmanufactured, old-timey thrill ride. The Gator Gulley Splash Park is complete with giant "egrets" spilling water from their beaks, dueling water guns mounted atop giant gators, and other water-park splash areas. There's also a small petting zoo and an aviary. A free train ride is a high point, taking you through an alligator breeding marsh and a natural swamp setting where you can spot gators, birds, and turtles. A three-story observation tower overlooks the breeding marsh, swamped with gator grunts, especially come sundown during mating season.

For a glimpse of 37 giant rare and deadly crocodiles, check out the Jungle Crocs of the World exhibit. To see eager gators leaping out of the water to catch their food, come on cool days for the Gator Jumparoo Show (summer heat just puts them to sleep). The most thrilling is the first one in the morning, when the gators are hungriest. There's also a Gator Wrestlin' Show, and although there's no doubt who's going to win the match, it's still fun to see the handlers take on those tough guys with the beady eyes. In the educational Up Close Animal Encounters Show, 30 to 40 rattlesnakes fill a pit around the show's host. This is a real Florida experience, and you leave knowing the difference between a gator and a croc. ☒ *14501 S. Orange Blossom Trail, between Orlando and Kissimmee* ☎ *407/855–5496 or 800/393–5297* ⊕ *www.gatorland. com* ☒ *$22.99; discount coupons online* ☉ *Daily 9–6.*

14

❷ **Old Town.** A collection of shops, restaurants, and giant amusement-park rides, Old Town was literally the heart of tourist Kissimmee before Disney moved in. It's made a good go at keeping families coming by maintaining a Ferris wheel; the 150-foot-tall Super Shot free-fall ride; the *Windstorm* steel roller coaster; go-karts; and classic car shows on Wednesday, Thursday, and Saturday. ☒ *5770 W. Irlo Bronson Memorial Hwy., Kissimmee* ☎ *407/396–4888* ⊕ *www.old-town.com* ☒ *Free (admission and parking)* ☉ *Daily 10* AM*–11* PM *(bars open until 2* AM*).*

SPORTS AND THE OUTDOORS
ICE SKATING
The Ice Factory. Ice-skating in Florida? Yup! This Olympic-class facility has two rinks that are open daily. Friday is Teen Night, and there are family-night rates on Saturday. ☒ *2221 Partin Settlement Rd., Kissimmee* ☎ *407/933–4259* ⊕ *www.icefactory.com* ☒ *$6–$7; $3 skate rental* ☉ *Hours vary by rink and day; check Web site.*

FISHING
Fishermen the world over congregate in central Florida to catch bass, speckled perch, bream, stripers, and catfish. Top fishing waters include Lake Kissimmee, the Butler and Conway chains of lakes, and Lake Toho. Your best chance for trophy fish is between November and April on Toho or Kissimmee. For good creels, the best is usually the Butler area, which has the additional advantage of its scenery—lots of live oaks and cypresses, plus the occasional osprey or bald eagle.

Toho and Kissimmee are also good for record-setting largemouth bass. The Butler chain yields largemouth, some pickerel, and the occasional huge catfish. Services range from equipment and boat rental to full-day trips with guides and guarantees. Like virtually all lakes in Florida, these are teeming with alligators, which pose little threat unless you engage in the unwise practice of swimming at night.

To fish in Florida waters (though not those at Disney) anglers over 16 need a fishing license, available at bait-and-tackle shops, fishing camps, most sporting-goods stores, and Wal-Marts and Kmarts. Some locations may not sell saltwater licenses, so call ahead if this matters. For nonresidents of Florida, freshwater or saltwater licenses cost $17 for three consecutive days, $30 for seven consecutive days, and $47 for one

Go gator! After a visit to authentic, rustic Kissimmee's Gatorland, you'll truly know the difference between a gator and a croc.

year. ■TIP→ Fishing on a private lake with the owner's permission—which is what anglers do at Disney—doesn't require a state fishing license.

Guides fish out of the area's fishing camps, and you can usually make arrangements to hire them through the camp office. Rates vary, but for two people a good price is $250 for a half day and $350 for a full one. Many area guides are part-timers who fish on weekends or take a day off from their full-time job.

Bass Challenger Guide. BCG takes you out onto the St. Johns River—Florida's longest and one of the few that runs north—which is a prime bass site. Indeed, bass is the only quarry. Half-day trips for one or two people begin at $250; six-hour trips are $300; full-day trips begin at $350. Each additional person pays $75 more. BCG also sells licenses and bait, arranges for transportation to and from your hotel, organizes multiday trips, and books area accommodations ($59 a night). ✉ *195 Heather Lane Dr., Deltona* ☎ *407/273–8045 or 800/241–5314* ⊕ *www.basschallenger.com.*

East Lake Fish Camp. Eastern Lake Toho's camp has a restaurant and country store, sells live bait and propane, and rents boats. You can also take a ride on an airboat from here. The camp has 286 RV sites ($40–$45 per night, $168 a week, or $425 per month) and simple, rustic cabins ($65 per night for two people and $5 per night for each additional person with a limit of five per cabin). Try to reserve the 24 cabins at least two weeks in advance in winter and spring. ✉ *3705 Big Bass Rd., Kissimmee 34744* ☎ *407/348–2040* ⊕ *www.eastlakefishcamp.com.*

Lake Charters. This outfitter conducts trips from November to May on Lake Toho (January through April is high season, so reserve accordingly), and has done so for more than 20 years. It's possible to catch a 14-pound bass here. Rods and reels are included in the costs, and transportation is available. Half-day freshwater trips are $250, six-hour trips are $300, and full-day trips are $350. Prices are for one to two people. A third participant costs $50 more. You can also buy your licenses here. ⊠ *1650 Justin Matthew Way, St. Cloud* ☎ *407/891–2275 or 877/326–3575* ⊕ *www.lakecharter.com.*

Lake Toho Resort. Although most of the full hookups at the 200 RV sites here are booked year round, electrical and water hookups are usually available, as are live bait, food, and drinks. Sites are $28 per night or $350 per month, plus electricity and an initial $100 refundable deposit. Boat slips start at $45 a month, depending on the length of your boat. ⊠ *4715 Kissimmee Park Rd., St. Cloud* ☎ *407/892–8795* ⊕ *www.laketohoresort.com.*

Richardson's Fish Camp. This camp on western Lake Toho has seven cabins with kitchenettes, 16 RV sites, and six tent sites as well as boat slips and a bait shop. The RV sites are $30 per night, tent sites are $24.50; cabins run $44 for one bedroom, $68 for two bedrooms, and $79 for three bedrooms. ⊠ *1550 Scotty's Rd., Kissimmee* ☎ *407/846–6540.*

HORSEBACK RIDING

Horse World Riding Stables. Here's a way to get a taste of the days when the Orlando area had more horse and cattle farms than Texas. Horse World offers lessons and rides for groups or individuals on three unspoiled Florida woods trails. Trail rides take about an hour, and cost $43.95–$74.95 per person (weeklong ride passes cost $99–$149). Call at least a week ahead for reservations in winter and spring. ⊠ *3705 Poinciana Blvd., Kissimmee* ☎ *407/847–4343* ⊕ *www.horseworldstables.com.*

Silver Spurs Rodeo. Every February and October since the 1920s, bull riders and cowboys have been competing in the Silver Spurs Rodeo, the largest east of the Mississippi. The event at Osceola Heritage Park features competition in bull- and bronc-riding, steer-wrestling, and barrel racing. Take Interstate 4 west to Exit 77 and Florida's Turnpike South, then take Exit 244 (Kissimmee–St. Cloud). ⊠ *1875 Silver Spur Ln., Kissimmee* ☎ *407/677–6336* ⊕ *www.silverspursrodeo.com* ⊠ *$15* ☾ *Sat. 6:30* PM, *Sun. 1* PM.

SHOPPING

Lake Buena Vista Factory Stores. Although it has scant curb appeal, it does have a good collection of standard outlet stores for Aeropostale, Bass, Eddie Bauer, Fossil, Gap, Izod, Liz Claiborne, Nike, Tommy Hilfiger, and Old Navy. Check out the coupons on the Web site, too. Take Exit 68 off Interstate 4, then go 2 mi south on *Route 535.* ⊠ *15657 S. Apopka Vineland Rd., Lake Buena Vista* ☎ *407/238–9301* ⊕ *www.lbvfs. com* ☾ *Mon.–Sat. 10–9, Sun. 10–6.*

192 Flea Market Outlet. With 400 booths, this market is about a fourth the size of Flea World in Sanford, but it's much more convenient and is open daily. The all-new merchandise includes tons of items: toys, luggage, sunglasses, jewelry, clothes, beach towels, sneakers, electronics,

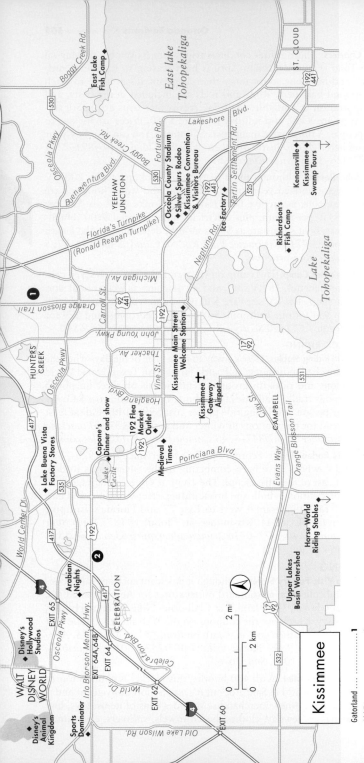

Kissimmee

KISSIMMEE TOURS

Historic Downtown Kissimmee. Founded 128 years ago, Kissimmee has a story rooted in the founding of the state. It was an important air base during World War II, and it was vital in the development of the Orlando cattle and orange industries. You can learn more on this self-guided audio tour available at the Main Street Welcome Station. ☒ 421 Broadway, Kissimmee ☎ 407/846–4643 ⊕ www.kissimmeemainstreet.com ⊙ Weekdays 9–5, Sat. 10–2.

Haunted Kissimmee. This 90-minute tour takes you through the shadowy streets and alleys of historic downtown. The community has amassed a huge store of paranormal activity over the years, and the docents who lead these outings know where the bodies are buried. ☒ 421 Broadway, Kissimmee ☎ 321/251–5204 ⊕ www.hauntedkissimmee.com ☒ $19 ⊙ Daily at 8:30 PM.

Kissimmee Swamp Tours. The 60- or 90-minute cruises in high-powered airboats take you through the marshes and swamps of Lake Kissimmee—home to hundreds of species of birds and other critters. There are also twilight tours. ☒ 4500 Joe Overstreet Rd., Lake Kissimmee, Kenansville ☎ 407/436–1059 ⊕ www.kissimmeeswamptours.com ☒ $47–$59.

14

and the obligatory T-shirts. ☒ 4301 W. Vine St., Hwy. 192, Kissimmee ☎ 407/396–4555 ⊕ www.192fleamarketprices.com ⊙ Daily 9–6.

Sports Dominator. The huge, multilevel Sports Dominator could probably equip all the players of Major League Baseball and the NFL, NBA, and NHL combined. Each sport receives its own section, crowding the floor with soccer balls, golf clubs, catcher's mitts, jerseys, and a few thousand more pieces of sports gear. The prices may not be lower than anywhere else, but the selection makes it a winner. Its location between Disney and Universal Studios isn't bad either. ☒ 7550 W. Irlo Bronson Hwy., Kissimmee ☎ 407/397–4700 ⊕ www.sportsdominator.com ⊙ Daily 9 AM–10 PM.

NIGHTLIFE

Fodor's Choice
★
Arabian Nights. An elaborate palace on the outside, this arena has seating for more than 1,200 on the inside. Its 25-act dinner show, complete with about 60 horses, centers around the quest of an Arabian princess to find her true love, and includes a buffoonish genie who may or may not be amusing, a chariot race, and an intricate dance on horseback. Dinner is served during the show, so you might end up not paying much attention to the food, which is a shame; the kitchen has serves such things as USDA Choice and certified Black Angus sirloin. Extra shows are added in summer. Make reservations and ask about discounts, which are also available when booking online. ☒ 3081 Arabian Nights Blvd., Kissimmee ☎ 407/239–9223, 800/553–6116, 800/533–3615 in Canada ⊕ www.arabian-nights.com ☒ $63.99, including tax ⊙ Shows nightly, times vary ⊟ AE, D, MC, V.

Capone's Dinner and Show. This show brings you back to gangland Chicago of the 1930s, when mobsters and their molls were the height of underworld society. The evening begins in an old-fashioned ice-cream parlor, but say the secret password, and you're ushered inside Al Capone's private Underworld Cabaret and Speakeasy. Capone's is different from the other themed dinner shows in the area, hiring talented local actors to perform, often improvisationally. Dinner is an all-you-can-eat American and Italian buffet that includes beer, alcoholic mixed drinks, and cocktails for kids. Check the Web site for a 50%-off coupon. ⊠ *4740 W. Irlo Bronson Memorial Hwy., Kissimmee* ☎ *407/397–2378* ⊕ *www.alcapones.com* ⊠ *$49.99* ⊘ *Daily 7:30* ⊟ *AE, D, MC, V.*

Medieval Times. In a huge, ersatz-medieval manor you'll see a tournament of sword fights, jousting matches, and other games on a good-versus-evil theme. No fewer than 30 charging horses and a cast of 75 knights, nobles, wizards, and maidens participate. Sound silly? It is. But it's also a true extravaganza. That the show takes precedence over the meat-and-potatoes fare is obvious: everyone sits facing forward at long, narrow banquet tables stepped auditorium-style above the tournament area. Kids love eating without forks; adults are swept away by the tremendous horse-riding artistry. Check the Web site for discount specials. ⊠ *4510 W. Irlo Bronson Memorial Hwy., Kissimmee* ☎ *407/396–1518 or 800/229–8300* ⊕ *www.medievaltimes.com* ⊠ *$59.95; $20 per person "royalty" upgrade includes first-row seating* ⊘ *Castle daily 9–4, village daily 4:30–8, performances usually daily at 8 but call ahead* ⊟ *AE, D, MC, V.*

BOK TOWER GARDENS

57 mi southwest of Orlando; 42 mi southwest of WDW.

Fodor's Choice
★
You'll see citrus groves as you ride south along U.S. 27 to the small town of Lake Wales and the **Bok Tower Gardens.** This appealing sanctuary of plants, flowers, trees, and wildlife has been something of a local secret for years. Shady paths meander through pine forests with silvery moats, mockingbirds and swans, blooming thickets, and hidden sundials. The majestic, 200-foot Bok Tower is constructed of coquina—from seashells—and pink, white, and gray marble. The tower houses a carillon with 57 bronze bells that ring out each day at 1 and 3 PM during 30-minute live recitals that might include early American folk songs, Appalachian tunes, Irish ballads, or Latin hymns. The bells are also featured in recordings every half hour after 10 AM, and sometimes even moonlight recitals.

The landscape was designed in 1928 by Frederick Law Olmsted, Jr., son of the planner of New York's Central Park. The grounds include the 20-room, Mediterranean-style Pinewood Estate, built in 1930 and open for self-guided touring. Guides will lead you on a 60 minute tour of the gardens (included in the admission price); tours of the inside of the tower are a benefit of membership ($85 and up).

Take Interstate 4 to Exit 55, and head south on U.S. 27 for about 23 mi. Proceed past Eagle Ridge Mall, then turn left after two traffic lights onto Mountain Lake Cut Off Road and follow the signs. ⊠ *1151 Tower Blvd., Lake Wales* ☎ *863/676–1408* ⊕ *www.boktower.*

org ✉ *$10 adults, Pinewood Estate general tour $6. 50% off admission Sat. 8–9 AM; holiday tour prices higher* ⊙ *Daily 8–6.*

NEED A BREAK?

Chalet Suzanne Country Inn. While at Bok Gardens, it's worth stopping at time-worn but charming Chalet Suzanne for the kitsch factor and the restaurant's renowned soups, which are served at every meal (take a can home). ✉ *3800 Chalet Suzanne Dr., Lake Wales* ☎ *800/433–6011* ⊕ *www. chaletsuzanne.com* ⊟ AE, D, MC, V

WEKIWA SPRINGS STATE PARK

13 mi northwest of Orlando, 28 mi north of WDW.

☾

Fodor'sChoice

★

"Wekiva" is a Creek Indian word meaning "flowing water"; "wekiwa" means "spring of water." The river, springs, and surrounding 6,400-acre **Wekiwa Springs State Park** are well suited to camping, hiking, picnicking, swimming, canoeing, and fishing. The area is also full of Florida wildlife: otters, raccoons, alligators, bobcats, deer, turtles, and birds.

Canoe trips can range from a simple hour-long paddle around the lagoon to observe a colony of water turtles to a full-day excursion through the less congested parts of the river that haven't changed much since the area was inhabited by the Timacuan Indians. You can rent canoes ($16 for two hours and $3.20 per hour after that) in the town of Apopka, near the park's southern entrance.

The park has 60 campsites: some are "canoe sites" that you can only reach via the river, and others are "trail sites," meaning you must hike a good bit of the park's 13.5-mi trail to reach them. Most, however, are for the less hardy—you can drive right up to them. Sites go for $24 a night with electric hookups. Tents are available for $4 per night, and it costs $6 per vehicle to enter the park.

To get here, take Interstate 4 Exit 94 (Longwood) and turn left on Route 434. Go 1¼ mi to Wekiwa Springs Road; turn right and go 4½ mi to the entrance, on the right. ✉ *1800 Wekiva Circle, Apopka* ☎ *407/884–2008, 800/326–3521 for campsite bookings* ⊕ *www.floridastateparks. org* ✉ *$2 per pedestrian or bicycle; $6 per vehicle* ⊙ *Daily 8–dusk.*

MOUNT DORA

35 mi northwest of Orlando; 50 mi north of WDW.

The unspoiled Lake Harris chain surrounds remote Mount Dora, an artsy valley community with a slow and easy pace, a rich history, New England–style charm, and excellent antiquing. Although the town's population is only about 10,000, there's plenty of excitement here, especially in fall and winter. The first weekend in February is the annual Mount Dora Art Festival, which opens central Florida's spring art-fair season. Attracting more than 250,000 people over a three-day period, it's one of the region's major outdoor events.

During the year there's also the annual Taste of Mount Dora event (April), a sailing regatta (April), a bicycle festival (October), a crafts fair (October), and many other happenings. Mount Dora draws large

14

Wildlife rich Wekiwa Springs State Park is a great place to camp, hike, picnic, canoe, fish, swim, or snorkel.

crowds during monthly (third weekend, except December) antiques fairs and thrice-yearly antiques "extravaganzas" (third weekends of January, February, and November) at popular Renninger's Twin Markets, an antiques center plus farmers' and flea markets.

GETTING HERE AND AROUND

Take U.S. 441 (Orange Blossom Trail in Orlando) north or take Interstate 4 to Exit 92, then Route 436 west to U.S. 441, and follow the signs. A historic train depot serves as the offices of the Mount Dora Chamber of Commerce. Stop in and pick up a self-guided tour map. Don't forget to ask about the trolley tour, during which a guide gives you the skinny on local historical spots and throws in a ghost story.

ESSENTIALS

Tourist Info Mount Dora Chamber of Commerce. (⊠ *341 Alexander St., at 3rd Ave., Mount Dora* ☎ *352/383–2165* ⊕ *www.mountdora.com* ⊙ *Weekdays 9–5, Sat. 10–4, Sun. 10–2; after hrs, maps on display at kiosk.*)

EXPLORING

Lakeside Inn. A stroll around the lakefront grounds here, a country inn built in 1883, makes you feel as if you've stepped out of the pages of *The Great Gatsby*; there's even a croquet court. ⊠ *100 N. Alexander St., Mount Dora* ☎ *352/383–4104*

Mount Dora Center for the Arts. Local and national artists are highlighted in this compact center that grew out of the annual arts festival. The center is a focal point for the community, serving as headquarters of the arts festival and a place to take art lessons. ⊠ *138 E. 5th Ave., Mount Dora* ⊙ *Daily sunrise–sunset.*

SHOPPING

The Renaissance. Built in the 1920s, what was once known as the Dora Hotel is now The Renaissance, a shopping arcade with restaurants and an Icelandic pub. The Eustis Arts League calls this center home, creating jewelry and ceramics for sale. ⊠ *413 Donnelly St. Mount Dora* ☎ *352/735–2608.*

★ **Renninger's Twin Markets.** Renninger's may be Florida's largest gathering of antiques and collectibles dealers. Atop the hill, 400 flea-market dealers sell household goods, garage-sale surplus, produce, baked goods, pets, and anything else you can think of. Below, 200 antiques dealers purvey ephemera, old phonographs, deco fixtures, antique furniture, and other stuff Granny had in her attic. If you have the time, hit the flea market first, since that's where antiques dealers find many of their treasures. Both markets are open every weekend, but on the third weekend of the month the antiques market has a fair attracting about 500 dealers. The really big shows, however, are the three-day extravaganzas held on the third weekends of November, January, and February—these draw approximately 1,500 dealers. Summers are very slow, the pace picks up from October through May. These events can be all-day affairs; otherwise, spend the morning at Renninger's and then move on to downtown Mount Dora in time for lunch. From Interstate 4, take the Florida Turnpike north to Exit 267A to reach Highway 429 east and, 8 mi later, Highway 441 north to Mount Dora. ⊠ *U.S. 441, Mount Dora* ☎ *352/383–8393* ⊕ *www.renningers.com* ⊠ *Markets and Antiques Fairs free; Extravaganzas $10 Fri., $6 Sat., $4 Sun.* ☉ *Markets, weekends 9–5; Antiques Fairs, Mar.–Oct., 3rd weekend of month, 9–5; Extravaganzas Nov., Jan., and Feb., 3rd weekend of month, Fri. 10–5, weekends 9–5.*

Uncle Al's Time Capsule. This is a great place to sift through some terrific Hollywood memorabilia and collectibles. ⊠ *140 E. 4th Ave., Mount Dora* ☎ *352/383–1958.*

| NEED A BREAK? |

Pisces Rising. This upscale, New Orleans–themed seafood and steak house with a deck overlooks Lake Dora. It's open every day except Christmas for lunch and dinner. ⊠ 239 W. 4th Ave., Mount Dora ☎ 352/385-2669 ⊕ www.piscesrisingdining.com ▭ AE, D, MC, V.

WINTER PARK

6 mi northeast of Orlando; 20 mi northeast of WDW.

This peaceful, upscale community may be just outside the hustle and bustle of Orlando, but it feels like a different country. The town's name reflects its early role as a warm-weather haven for those escaping the frigid blasts of Northeast winters. From the late 1880s until the early 1930s, wealthy industrialists and their families would travel to Florida by rail on vacation, and many stayed, establishing grand homes and cultural institutions. The lovely, 8-square-mi village retains its charm with brick-paved streets, historic buildings, and well-maintained lakes and parkland. Even the town's bucolic nine-hole golf course is on the National Register of Historic Places.

14

On Park Avenue you can spend a few hours sightseeing, shopping, or both. The street is lined with small boutiques and fine restaurants and bookended by world-class museums: the Charles Hosmer Morse Museum of American Art, with the world's largest collection of artwork by Louis Comfort Tiffany, and the Cornell Fine Arts Museum, on the campus of Rollins College (the oldest college in Florida).

GETTING HERE AND AROUND

From downtown Orlando, take Interstate 4 4 mi to Exit 87, and head east on Fairbanks Avenue for 3 mi to Park Avenue. LYNX Buses 1, 9, and 23 run from the main depot to Winter Park.

ESSENTIALS

Bus Info LYNX Bus (✉ *455 N. Garland Ave., Downtown Orlando* ☎ *407/841–2279* ⊕ *www.golynx.com).*

Hospital Winter Park Hospital (✉ *200 N. Lakemont Ave., Winter Park* ☎ *407/646–7000* ⊕ *www.winterparkhospital.com).*

Tour Scenic Boat Tour. Head north from Park Avenue, and at the end of Morse Avenue you'll find the launching point for this tour, a Winter Park tradition since 1938. The one-hour cruise takes in 12 mi of waterways, including three lakes and oak- and cypress-shaded canals built in the 1800s as a transportation system for the logging industry. A well-schooled skipper shares stories about the moguls who built their mansions along the shore and points out wildlife and remnants of natural Florida still hidden amid the expensive houses. ✉ *312 E. Morse Blvd., Winter Park* ☎ *407/644–4056* ⊕ *www.scenicboattours. com* ✍ *$10* ☉ *Daily 10–4.*

Visitor Info City of Winter Park (✉ *401 Park Ave. S, Winter Park* ☎ *407/599–3399* ⊕ *www.cityofwinterpark.org).*

⇨ *For information on Winter Park hotels and restaurants, see Chapter 2, Where to Stay and Chapter 3, Where to Eat.*

EXPLORING

Numbers in the margin correspond to numbers on the Winter Park map.

❹ Albin Polasek Museum and Sculpture Gardens. Stroll along on a guided tour through gardens showcasing the graceful sculptures created by internationally known sculptor Albin Polasek (1879–1965). The late artist's home, studio, galleries, and private chapel are centered on 3 acres of exquisitely tended lawns, colorful flower beds, and tropical foliage. Paths and walkways lead past classical life-size, figurative sculptures and whimsical mythological pieces. Inside the museum are works by Hawthorne, Chase, Mucha, and Saint-Gaudens. ✉ *633 Osceola Ave., Winter Park* ☎ *407/647–6294* ⊕ *www.polasek.org* ✍ *Gardens free; house tour $5* ☉ *Sept.–June, Tues.–Sat. 10–4, Sun. 1–4; July and Aug., only gardens open weekdays 10–4.*

❷ Central Park. Given to the City of Winter Park by the Genius family (benefactors of the Morse Museum), this 11 acre green spot has manicured lawns, specimen plantings, a rose garden, a fountain, and a gazebo. If you take a seat and listen as the Amtrak passenger train rolls

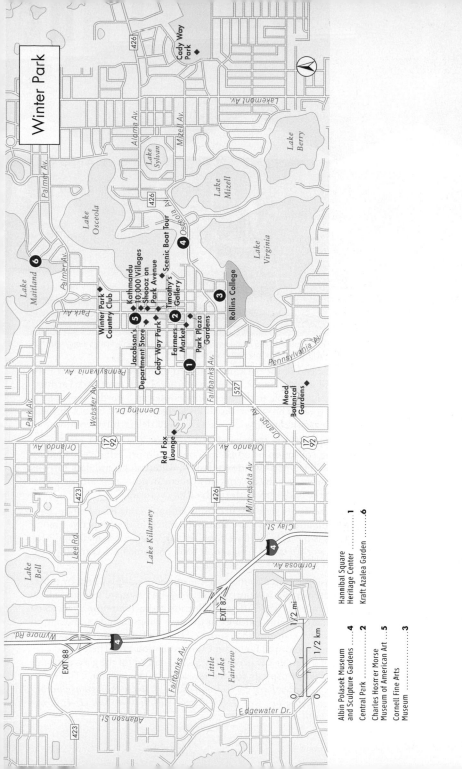

Winter Park

426
Cady Way Park

Palmer Av.

Aloma Av.

Mizell Av.

Lakemont Av.

Lake Berry

Lake Sylvan

Lake Mizell

426

Lake Osceola

Scenic Boat Tour

Osceola

Lake Virginia

Palmer Av.

Lake Maitland

Park Av.

Kathmandu
10,000 Villages
Shoooz on
Park Avenue
Timothy's
Gallery

Winter Park
Country Club

Jacobson's
Department Store
Cady Way Park
Farmers
Market

Park Plaza
Gardens

Rollins College

Fairbanks Av.

Pennsylvania Av.

Park Av.

Pennsylvania Av.

Webster Av.

Denning Dr.

527

Mead
Botanical
Gardens

Orlando Av.

17
92

Red Fox
Lounge

17
92

Orlando Av.

423

Lee Rd.

Lake Bell

Lake Killarney

426

Minnesota Av.

Clay St.

Formosa Av.

EXIT 88

Wymore Rd.

EXIT 87

Fairbanks Av.

Adanson St.

Little
Lake
Fairview

Lake Bell

423

Edgewater Dr.

0   1/2 mi

0   1/2 km

A café culture: in ritzy Winter Park, restaurants and boutiques are tucked into historic buildings along brick-paved streets. Here, even the 9-hole golf course is a national landmark.

by the west end of the park, it's not hard to imagine how Winter Park looked and sounded in the late 19th century. The Winter Park Farmers' Market draws people to the southwest corner on Saturday morning. If you don't want to browse in the shops across the street, a walk through the park beneath the moss-covered trees is a delightful alternative.

⑤ **Charles Hosmer Morse Museum of American Art.** The world's most com-
Fodor's Choice prehensive collection of work by Louis Comfort Tiffany—including
★ immense stained-glass windows, lamps, watercolors, and desk sets—is in this museum, which also contains American decorative art and paintings from the mid-19th to the early-20th centuries.

Many of the works were rescued from Tiffany's Long Island estate, Laurelton Hall, after a 1957 fire destroyed much of the property. Among the draws is the 1,082-square-foot Tiffany Chapel, originally built for the 1893 world's fair in Chicago. It took craftsmen 2½ years to painstakingly reassemble the chapel here.

An expansion is slated to increase the museum's display area by 6,000 square feet, increase its courtyard area by 4,450 square feet, and allow for much more of the Tiffany collection from Laurelton Hall to be displayed at one time. Exhibits in the new wings include architectural and decorative elements that survived the fire from Laurelton's dining room, living room, and Fountain Court reception hall. There's also a re-creation of the estate's Daffodil Terrace, so named for the glass daffodils that serve as the capitals for the terrace's marble columns. ⊠ 445 N. Park Ave. , Winter Park ☎ 407/645–5311 ⊕ www.morsemuseum.org ⊠ $3; Nov.–Apr., Fri. free 4–8 ☉ Tues.–Sat. 9:30–4, Sun. 1–4; Nov.–Apr., Fri. until 8.

③ Cornell Fine Arts Museum. On the Rollins College campus, this museum houses Florida's oldest art collection (its first paintings acquired in 1896)—one with more than 6,000 works, from Italian Renaissance to 19th- and 20th-century American and European paintings. Special exhibitions feature everything from Native American artifacts to Soviet propaganda posters. Outside the museum, a small but charming garden overlooks Lake Virginia. ⊠ *Rollins College, 1000 Holt Ave., Winter Park* ☎ *407/646–2526* ⊕ *www.rollins.edu/cfam* ⊠ *$5* ☉ *Tues.–Fri. 10–4, weekends noon–5.*

④ Hannibal Square Heritage Center. Almost crowded out by glitz of new shops, restaurants, and art galleries is the original, once-thriving town of Hannibal Square, one of the oldest African-American communities in the country and home to Pullman porter families to this day. The Heritage Center hosts a permanent photographs and oral-history collection of the significant West Winter Park area. It's a touching and important memorial to a neighborhood that influenced American history. ⊠ *642 West New England Ave., Winter Park* ☎ *407/539–2680* ⊕ *www.hannibalsquareheritagecenter.org* ⊠ *$5* ☉ *Tues.–Fri. noon–4, Sat. 10–2.*

⑥ Kraft Azalea Garden. A 5-acre public park on the shores of Lake Maitland is alive with heady color from January through March. The thousands of blooming azaleas (hence the name) make a perfect backdrop for romantic strolls or the regularly scheduled wedding parties. ⊠ *1365 Alabama Dr., Winter Park* ☎ *407/599–3334* ⊕ *www.cityofwinterpark.org.*

NEED A BREAK?

Park Plaza Gardens. The bistro with sidewalk tables at the Park Plaza Hotel serves great sandwiches, and has beer on tap, an extensive selection of wines, and great people-watching. If the weather is bad, you can always head inside to the grand atrium. ⊠ *319 Park Ave. S, Winter Park* ☎ *407/645–2475* ⊕ *www.parkplazagardens.com* ⊟ *AE, D, MC, V.*

SPORTS AND THE OUTDOORS

Winter Park Country Club. At the north end of Park Avenue the historic Country Club offers nonresidents access to its immaculate golf course. Opened in 1914, the nine-hole course was modeled after authentic Scottish links. Play between November and April costs $15; it's $14 from May to October. ⊠ *761 Old England Ave., Winter Park* ☎ *407/599–3339* ⊕ *www.winterparkcountryclub.com.*

SHOPPING

Park Avenue in downtown Winter Park is definitely a shopper's heaven. This inviting brick street has chic boutiques, sidewalk cafés, and hidden alleyways that lead to peaceful nooks and crannies with even more restaurants and shops. The last couple of years have seen a mass exodus of the chain stores that came to dominate shopping on Park Avenue, leaving the street open to the return of boutiques. Most of these stores are privately owned and offer merchandise that cannot be easily found elsewhere.

A stroll across the railroad tracks that run through Winter Park brings you to the recently gentrified Hannibal Square. Centered on the

14

These lamps are just some of the stained-glass works at Winter Park's Charles Hosmer Morse museum, home to the world's largest collection of pieces by Louis Comfort Tiffany.

intersection of New England and Pennsylvania avenues, the upscale dining and shopping found here has revitalized the area.

Farmers' Market. Try to schedule your visit to Winter Park for a Saturday morning, so you can begin your day at the weekly Winter Park Farmers' Market, which takes place from 7 AM to 1 PM at the city's old train depot, two blocks west of Park Avenue. It's a bustling, vibrant market with vendors selling farm-fresh produce, dazzling flowers, and prepared foods. On any given morning you may find a chef stirring a steaming pot of Irish oatmeal or a woman selling made-to-order crepes. Pick up locally harvested honey, locally made cheese, and freshly baked croissants. ⊠ *200 West New England Ave., Winter Park* ☎ *407/599–3397* ⊕ *www.cityofwinterpark.org.*

SPECIALTY SHOPS

Charles Hosmer Morse Museum Gift Shop. The obvious reasons to shop here are for the representations of Tiffany glass, silk scarves with stained-glass motifs, and fine-art glass that Louis Comfort himself would have treasured. There are also many objects from world museum gift collections and a wide assortment of books about the Arts and Crafts movement. ⊠ *445 N. Park Ave., Winter Park* ☎ *407/645–5316* ⊕ *www. morsemuseum.org.*

Fodor's Choice ★ **Jacobson's Department Store.** That rarest of things—a local, independent department store—is also a Winter Park legend. Open since 1945, the original chain folded in 2002, but two neighborhood entrepreneurs reopened this single store two years later. High-end, stylish, and pricy women's fashions and boutique men's accessories are the norm. ⊠ *216 N. Park Ave., Winter Park* ☎ *407/539–2528* ⊕ *www.jacobsons.com.*

Kathmandu. The unique items here comes from exotic locales like India, Indonesia, Nepal, and Turkey. Hats, turquoise and crystal jewelry, and brass figures of Indian gods are among the merchandise. ⊠ *352 N. Park Ave., Winter Park* ☏ *407/644–8464* ⊕ *www.tribalasia.com/artstore/.*

Shoooz on Park Avenue. Mephisto, Nota Bene, and Betsey Johnson just begin the list of designers in this cozy, shoe-only shop. ⊠ *303 N. Park Ave., Winter Park* ☏ *407/644–0110.*

Ten Thousand Villages. This fascinating little store sells fair-trade, artisan-crafted home decor and gifts from the smaller corners of the world. ⊠ *346 N. Park Ave., Winter Park* ☏ *407/644–8464* ⊕ *winterpark. tenthousandvillages.com.*

Timothy's Gallery. It's not a museum gallery, rather Timothy's sells wearable, sittable, usable art. Hand-carved exotic woods crafted by local artists become jewelry; blown, fused, and shaped glass turns into showcase vases and bowls; and carved furniture can turn a room into a masterpiece. ⊠ *236 N. Park Ave., Winter Park* ☏ *407/629–0707* ⊕ *www. timothysgallery.com/.*

14

NIGHTLIFE

Rollins College. The gorgeous Mediterranean-revival campus is home to two prominent cultural venues and one renowned festival. The Annie Russell Theatre produces student-acted classic and modern plays and dance programs in its beautiful (and, some say, haunted) building. The music department hosts local and international classical, jazz, and world-music artists in a multimillion-dollar performance hall. The annual Bach Festival in late February and early March honors all things classical and is held in the historic Knowles Memorial Chapel in the center of the campus. ⊠ *1000 Holt Ave., Winter Park* ☏ *407/646–2501* ⊕ *www.rollins.edu.*

Red Fox Lounge. Fans of camp, connoisseurs of the bygone lounge era, and those who just want a beer in a 1960s setting come to the Red Fox at the Best Western Mount Vernon Hotel. It's the home of Mark and Lorna, two cabaret singers who have performed here for 20 years. Songs are from the 1940s through the 1970s. ⊠ *110 S. Orlando Ave., Winter Park* ☏ *407/647–1166.*

MAITLAND

10 mi northeast of Orlando; 25 mi northeast of WDW.

An Orlando suburb with an interesting mix, Maitland is home to both the Florida Save the Manatee Society and one of Central Florida's larger office parks. A number of spectacular homes grace the shores of this town's various lakes, and there's a bird sanctuary and an art center as well.

GETTING HERE AND AROUND

Take Interstate 4 Exit 90A, then Maitland Boulevard east, and turn right (south) on Maitland Avenue.

EXPLORING

Audubon Center for Birds of Prey. More than 20 bird species, including hawks, eagles, owls, falcons, and vultures, make their home at this wildlife rehabilitation center on Lake Sybelia. You can take a self-guided conservation tour with interactive exhibits and walkways through the wetlands, or you can call ahead for a free private tour. There's an earnestness to this working facility, which takes in more than 700 injured wild birds each year. Fewer than half the birds can return to the wild; permanently injured birds continue to live at the center and can be seen in the aviaries along the pathways and sitting on outdoor perches. The center also tracks eagles and occasionally sets up a closed-circuit monitor to observe a nest, so you can watch a genuine nature show. From Maitland Avenue, turn right onto U.S. 17–92, right onto Kennedy Boulevard, and then right again onto Audubon Way. ⊠ *1101 Audubon Way, Maitland* ☎ *407/644–0190* ⊕ *fl.audubon.org* ☜ *$5* ⊙ *Tues.–Sun. 10–4.*

Maitland Arts Center. Hidden down a tree-lined side street is this collection of 23 buildings in the Mayan Revival style—with Mesoamerican motifs—that contains an art gallery and artists studios. Recognized by Florida as a historic site and on the National Register of Historic Places, the center was founded as an art colony in 1937 by American artist and architect André Smith (1880-1959). It continues his tradition of art instruction and contains a major collection of his works. ⊠ *231 W. Packwood Ave., Maitland* ☎ *407/539–2181* ⊕ *www.maitlandartcenter. org* ☜ *$3* ⊙ *Wed.–Sat. 9–5:30, Sun. noon–5:30.*

Zora Neale Hurston National Museum of Fine Arts. This museum is in Eatonville, just a few minutes west of Maitland, the first African-American town to be incorporated after the Civil War. It showcases works by artists of African descent during five six-week-long exhibits each year, with one reserved for up-and-comers. The museum is named after former resident Zora Neale Hurston (1891–1960), a writer, folklorist, and anthropologist best known for her novel *Their Eyes Were Watching God.* This is the home of Zora Fest, a street festival and cultural arts and music event celebrating Hurston's life, which is held every January. ⊠ *227 E. Kennedy Blvd., Eatonville* ☎ *407/647–3307* ⊕ *www.zoranealehurstonmuseum. com* ☜ *Donations accepted* ⊙ *Weekdays 9–4.*

NEED A BREAK?	**Jeremiah's Italian Ice.** There's always a long line in front of this little corner shop thanks to the fresh fruit ices and dozens of gelato flavors. It's also thanks to the pleasant staff, who give "pup cups" to well-behaved dogs. Bring your sweet tooth. ⊠ *111 S. Orlando Ave., Maitland* ☎ *407/599-9991* ⊕ www.jeremiahsice.com ⊟ AE, MC, V.

SANFORD

30 mi northeast of Orlando; 45 mi northeast of WDW.

At one time Sanford was the heart of Central Florida—a vital vacation spot and transportation hub on the St. John's River. But that was before vacationers focused on Orlando. In an attempt to turn things around, Sanford has been slowly rebuilding its picturesque downtown overlooking Lake Monroe and steadily increasing the size of its airport (Orlando–Sanford International), which is favored by flights from the United Kingdom. But the main reason most folks make the 30-mile, traffic-choked haul northeast of downtown Orlando (about 45 minutes), is Flea World, which claims to be America's largest flea market under one roof. The town also has the Orlando area's only zoo.

EXPLORING

★ **Central Florida Zoo and Botanical Gardens.** Sanford has had a zoo since 1923, and while there's nothing here to rival San Diego or New York, there's a certain charm about the place. In addition to 400-plus animals (say hi to Maude, the very friendly Asian elephant), there's the ZOOm Air Adventure Park; a zip-line ride through the treetops; and the Wharton-Smith Tropical Splash Ground, a mini water playground. And frankly, the steam-powered 1/5-scale train that puffs around the zoo is as fun for adults as it is for kids. Take U.S. 192 for 3 mi east of Interstate 4 to South Poinciana Boulevard; turn right and drive 5 mi. ⊠ *3755 N.W. Hwy. 17–92,Sanford* ☎ *407/323–4450* ⊕ *www.centralfloridazoo. org* ⊠ *$11.95; parking free* ⊘ *Daily 9–5.*

SHOPPING

Flea World. Merchants at more than 1,700 booths sell predominately new merchandise—car tires, Ginsu knives, pet tarantulas, gourmet coffee, biker clothes, darts, NASCAR souvenirs, rugs, books, incense, leather lingerie, and beaded evening gowns. It's also a great place to buy cheap Florida and Mickey Mouse T-shirts. In one building 50 antiques and collectibles dealers cater to people who can pass up the combination digital ruler and egg timer for some good old junk and authentic collectibles. A free newspaper, distributed at the parking-lot entrance, provides a map and directory. Children are entertained at Fun World next door. It has two unusual miniature golf courses, arcade games, go-karts, bumper cars, bumper boats, children's rides, and batting cages. Flea World is 3 mi east of Interstate 4. Take Exit 98 to Lake Mary Boulevard, then go 1 mi south on U.S. 17–92. ⊠ *U.S. 17–92, Sanford* ☎ *407/321–1792* ⊕ *www.fleaworld.com* ⊠ *Free* ⊘ *Fri.–Sun. 9–6.*

OCALA NATIONAL FOREST

65 mi north of Orlando; 90 mi north of WDW

This breathtaking 383,000-acre wilderness with lakes, springs, rivers, hiking trails, campgrounds, and historic sites has three major recreational areas (listed here from east to west): **Alexander Springs** (⊠ *Off Rte. 40 via Rte. 445 S*) has a swimming lake and a campground; **Salt Springs** (*visitor center,* ⊠ *14100 State Rd. 19*) has a natural saltwater spring where Atlantic blue crabs come to spawn each summer (and appreciate the sidewalk and landscaping update the area received in the latter half of 2009); and **Juniper Springs** (⊠ *14100 Rte. 40 N*), which includes a stone waterwheel house, a campground, a natural-spring swimming pool, and hiking and canoe trails. About 30 campsites are sprinkled throughout the park and range from bare sites to sites with electric hookups, showers, and bathrooms. Credit cards are not accepted. To get here, take Interstate 4 east to Exit 92, and head west on Route 436 to U.S. 441, which you take north to Route 19 north. ⊠ *Visitor center, 17147 Rte. 40 E, Salt Springs* ☎ *352/625–2520* ⊕ *www.fs.fed.us/r8/florida* ☜ *Alexander Springs, Salt Springs, Juniper Springs: $4.*

SPORTS AND THE OUTDOORS

CANOEING

The 7-mi **Juniper Springs run** is a narrow, twisting, and winding canoe ride, which, although exhilarating, is not for the novice. Canoe rentals and guided tours are available through **Juniper Springs Canoe Rentals** (☎ *352/625–2808*) inside the park.

FISHING

Captain Tom's Custom Charters (☎ *352/236–0872*) allows you to charter fishing trips ranging from three hours to a full day, and offers sightseeing cruises as well. Trips are by reservation only.

HORSEBACK RIDING

JNB Horse Haven Farm (⊠ *Rte. 42 between Weirsdale and Altoona, Lady Lake* ☎ *352/821–4756 or 800/731–4756* ⊕ *www.jnbhorsehavenfarm. com*), located within the Ocala National Forest, offers nature trail rides for beginner, intermediate, and advanced riders, as well as group and private lessons.

▌ NEED A BREAK? **Terry's Place.** If your trip through the national forest left you with an appetite, consider a stop here. It's more of a sports bar than a restaurant, but the kitchen still manages to crank out huge sandwiches and giant (and delicious) burgers. ⊠ *4121 N.E. 36th Ave., Ocala* ☎ *352/732–3820* ☐ *AE, MC, V.*

THE SPACE COAST

The Space Coast offers the closest beaches to Orlando, unspoiled nature, and outer-space thrills. Along the Atlantic Ocean, south of Daytona Beach, are the Canaveral National Seashore, Merritt Island National Wildlife Refuge, and the John F. Kennedy Space Center. This region, just 50 miles east of Orlando, is home to the laid-back town of Cocoa Beach (famous from I Dream of Jeannie), which attracts visitors on weekends year-round.

ESSENTIALS

Visitor Information Space Coast Office of Tourism (⊠ *430 Brevard Ave., Suite 150, Cocoa Village* ☎ *321/433–4470* ⊕ *www.space-coast.com).*

CANAVERAL NATIONAL SEASHORE

★ Miles of grassy, windswept dunes and a virtually empty beach await you at this remarkable 57,000-acre park on a barrier island with 24 mi of undeveloped coastline spanning from New Smyrna to Titusville. The unspoiled area of hilly sand dunes, grassy marshes, and seashell-sprinkled beaches is a large part of NASA's buffer zone, and is home to more than 1,000 species of plants and 300 species of birds and other animals. Surf and lagoon fishing are available, and a hiking trail leads to the top of an American Indian shell midden at Turtle Mound. For an additional charge visitors can take a pontoon-boat tour ($20) or participate in the turtle-watch interpretive program ($14). Reservations required. A visitor center is on Route A1A at Apollo Beach. Weekends are busy, and parts of the park are closed before, during, and after launches, so call ahead. ⊠ *Visitor Information: 7611 S. Atlantic Ave., Titusville* ☎ *386/428–3384* ⊕ *www.nps.gov/cana* ⊠ *$3 per person* ☉ *Nov.–Mar., daily 6–6; Apr.–Oct., daily 6* AM–8 PM.

SPORTS AND THE OUTDOORS
BEACHES

Apollo Beach. In addition to typical beach activities (lifeguards are on duty May 30 to September 1), visitors to this beach on the northern end of Canaveral National Seashore can also ride horses here (with a permit), hike self-guided trails, and tour the historic Eldora Statehouse (currently closed for renovations). ⊠ *Rte. A1A to the southern end of New Smyrna Beach* ☎ *386/428–3384* ⊠ *$3 per person (admission to the National Seashore)* ☉ *Nov.–Mar., daily 6–6; Apr.–Oct., daily 6* AM–8 PM.

Playalinda Beach. The southern access for the Canaveral National Seashore, remote Playalinda Beach has pristine sands and is the longest stretch of undeveloped coast on Florida's Atlantic seaboard. Its isolation explains why there are limited services (no phones, food service, drinking water, or lifeguards from May 30 to September 1) and why a remote strand of the beach is popular with nude sunbathers. Aside from them, hundreds of giant sea turtles come ashore here from May through August to lay their eggs. Eight parking lots anchor the beach at 1-mi intervals. To get here, take Interstate 95 Exit 220 east and follow the signs. Take bug repellent in case of horseflies. ⊠ *Rte. 402/Beach Rd.* ☎ *321/867–4077* ⊕ *www.nps.gov/cana* ⊠ *$3 per person (admission to the National Seashore)* ☉ *Nov.–Mar., daily 6–6; Apr.–Oct., daily 6–8.*

TITUSVILLE

67 mi east of Orlando, off I–95.

It's unusual that such a small, easily overlooked community as Titusville could accommodate what it does, namely the magnificent Merritt Island National Wildlife Refuge and the entrance to the Kennedy Space Center, the nerve center of the U.S. space program *(⇨ See In-Focus feature, "Soaring High at Kennedy Space Center").*

American Police Hall of Fame & Museum. You know police officers deserve your respect, and you'll be reminded why at this intriguing attraction. In addition to memorabilia like the Robocop costume and Blade Runner car from the films, informative displays offer insight into the dangers officers face every day: drugs, homicides, and criminals who can create knives from dental putty and guns from a bicycle spoke (really). Other historical exhibits include invitations to hangings, police patches, how you collect evidence at a crime scene, and a rotunda where more than 7,000 names are etched in marble to honor police officers who have died in the line of duty. The 24-lane shooting range provides rental guns

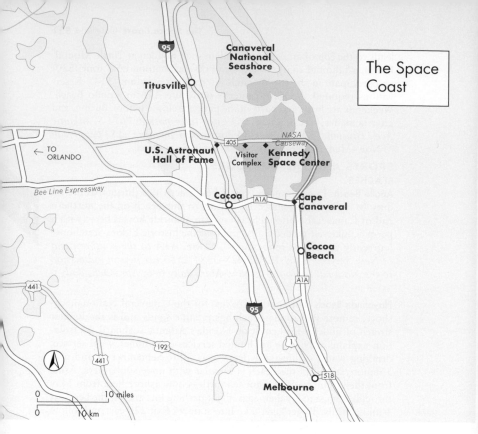

The Space Coast

(Tuesday to Friday noon–8, weekends noon–6). ✉ *6350 Horizon Dr.* ☎ *321/264–0911* ⊕ *www.aphf.org* ✉ *$12* ⊙ *Daily 10–6.*

Valiant Air Command Warbird Museum & Tico Airshow. Although its exterior looks sort of squirrelly, what's inside here is certainly impressive. Aviation buffs won't want to miss memorabilia from World Wars I and II, Korea, and Vietnam, as well as extensive displays of vintage military flying gear and uniforms. There are posters that were used to identify Japanese planes, plus a Huey helicopter and the cockpit of an F-106 that you can sit in. In the north hangar it looks like activity day at the senior center as a volunteer team of retirees busily restores old planes. It's an inspiring sight, and a good place to hear some war stories. The lobby gift shop sells real flight suits, old flight magazines, bomber jackets, books, and T-shirts. ✉ *6600 Tico Rd.* ☎ *321/268–1941* ⊕ *www. vacwarbirds.org* ✉ *$18* ⊙ *Daily 9–5.*

SPORTS AND THE OUTDOORS

Fodor'sChoice
★ **Merritt Island National Wildlife Refuge.** Owned by the Florida Fish and Wildlife Service as well as National Aeronautics and Space Administration (NASA), this 140,000-acre refuge, which adjoins the Canaveral National Seashore, acts as a buffer around Kennedy Space Center while protecting 1,000 species of plants and 500 species of wildlife, including 15 considered federally threatened or endangered. It's an immense

area dotted by brackish estuaries and marshes and patches of land consisting of coastal dunes, scrub oaks, pine forests and flatwoods, and palm and oak hammocks. You can borrow field guides and binoculars at the visitor center (4 mi east of Titusville) to track down falcons, ospreys, eagles, turkeys, doves, cuckoos, owls, and woodpeckers, as well as loggerhead turtles, alligators, and otters. A 20-minute video about refuge wildlife and accessibility—only 10,000 acres are developed—can help orient you. You might take a self-guided tour along the 7-mi **Black Point Wildlife Drive.** The dirt road takes you back in time, where there are no traces of encroaching malls or mankind and it's easy to visualize the tribes who made this their home 7,000 years ago. On the **Oak Hammock Foot Trail** you can see wintering migratory waterfowl and learn about the plants of a hammock community. If you exit the north end of the refuge, look for the **Manatee Observation Area** just north of the Haulover Canal (maps are at the visitor center). They usually show up in spring and fall. There are also fishing camps scattered throughout the area. Most of the refuge is closed 24 hours prior to a shuttle launch. ⊠ *Rte. 402, across Titusville Causeway* ☎ *321/861–0667, 321/861–0668 visitor center* ⊕ *www.fws.gov/merrittisland* ⊠ *Free* ☉ *Daily sunrise–sundown; visitor center weekdays 8–4:30, weekends 9–5 (Nov.–Mar.).*

> ## WORD OF MOUTH
>
> "We have been to KSC several times. Keep to the basic tour. The Astronaut Hall of Fame is also nice. My children's only complaint was that they showed pretty much the same film at each stop. I would recommend staying at the Hilton on Cocoa Beach; it is in a quieter area with a nice beach. There are lots of good restaurants in the area." —cbr

14

WHERE TO EAT AND STAY

$

SEAFOOD

★

✕ **Dixie Crossroads.** This sprawling restaurant is always crowded and festive, but it's not just the rustic setting that draws the throngs—it's the seafood. The specialty is the difficult-to-cook rock shrimp, which are served fried, broiled, or steamed. Diners with a hearty appetite can opt for the all-you-can-eat rock shrimp, small shrimp, tilapia, or catfish. You might have to wait (up to 90 minutes) for a table, but if you don't have time to wait, you can order takeout or eat in the bar area. And a word to the wise: as tempting as those corn fritters dusted with powdered sugar are, don't fill up on them. ⊠ *1475 Garden St., 2 mi east of I–95 Exit 220* ☎ *321/268–5000* ⊕ *www.dixiecrossroads.com* ⌂ *Reservations not accepted* ▭ *AE, D, DC, MC, V.*

$$

🏨 **Hampton Inn Titusville.** Proximity to the Kennedy Space Center and reasonable rates make this four-story hotel a top pick for visitors wanting to see a launch in person (though rates do generally go up just before launches). Guests deem the rooms clean, comfortable, and quiet (when the sky isn't reverberating with the sound of rocket thrusters, that is) and larger than those in comparable hotels. The property also scores points for conveniences like 24/7 coffee and tea service in the lobby, complimentary hot breakfast, and microwaves and refrigerators in every room. **Pros:** free Internet; extra-comfy beds; convenient to Interstate 95. **Cons:** thin walls; no restaurant on-site; no room service. ⊠ *4760 Helen*

Continued on page 534

The astronauts prepare for the launch
of Endeavour STS-118 on Pad 39-A.

SOARING HIGH

by John Blodgett

AT THE KENNEDY SPACE CENTER

Ever since the National Aeronautics and Space Administration (NASA) was founded, in 1958, the United States has been working on missions that launch us heavenward. When these dreams are about to become reality, and it's time for blastoff, Kennedy Space Center in Cape Canaveral, Florida, is where the action is.

NASA FROM COAST TO COAST

The Vehicle Assembly Building houses the space shuttle before a launch.

You've heard the words: "Houston, the *Eagle* has landed." And *Apollo 13*'s "Houston, we have a problem." But have you wondered, "Why are they talking to Houston if they left from Florida?"

NASA actually has operations at centers scattered across the United States. Its major centers are in Florida, Texas, and California. NASA's Launch Operations Center, known as the Kennedy Space Center, in Cape Canaveral, Florida, is where the famous countdowns are heard as a mission prepares for launch. You could say this is like NASA's big airport for outbound flights.

Once a mission (with a crew inside) is airborne, Houston takes over. In addition to operating all manned space flights, the Lyndon B. Johnson Space Center in Houston, Texas, is home base for American astronauts. They train here in laboratories that simulate weightlessness and other space-related concepts.

Not to be left out, the West Coast also gets a piece of the space-action pie. At Moffet Field, in California's Silicon Valley, the Ames Research Center is research and development central for NASA technology. If a mission can't happen because the technology isn't there yet, it's the job of the Ames Research Center to figure it out. Also in California is the Dryden Flight Research Center, at Edwards Air Force Base in Southern California. The center is where a lot of smart people who know a lot of about aerodynamics get to test out their ideas; it's also where space shuttle orbiters land.

So, in a nutshell, you could say California is the brains of NASA's operations, Texas is its heart, and Florida is its wings.

NASA TIMELINE

OCT. 1958: NASA begins operating with 8,000 employees and $100 million. Ten days later, *Pioneer* I takes off.

MAY 1961: Alan B. Shepard, Jr., becomes the first person in space.

FEB. 1962: John Glenn is the first American to orbit the Earth.

JUNE 1965: Edward H. White II is the first American to walk in space.

DEC. 1968: Three astronauts orbit the moon aboard *Apollo 8*.

JULY 1969: *Apollo 11* brings man to the moon.

JULY 1976: *Viking 1* lands on Mars.

APRIL 1981: First space shuttle orbiter launches two astronauts into space.

JAN. 1986: Space shuttle *Challenger* explodes 73 seconds after launch; seven onboard astronauts die.

APRIL 1990: Hubble telescope launches.

JULY 1997: Mars Pathfinder lands on the red planet.

JULY 1999: Eileen Collins is the first woman to command a space shuttle mission.

FEB. 2002: Mars Odyssey begins mapping the red planet.

FEB. 1, 2003: Space shuttle *Columbia* explodes over Texas 15 minutes before scheduled landing; seven astronauts on board die.

JULY 2004: Cassini–Huygens spacecraft begins orbiting Saturn.

MARCH 2009: Shuttle *Discovery* launches for a two-week mission to the International Space Station.

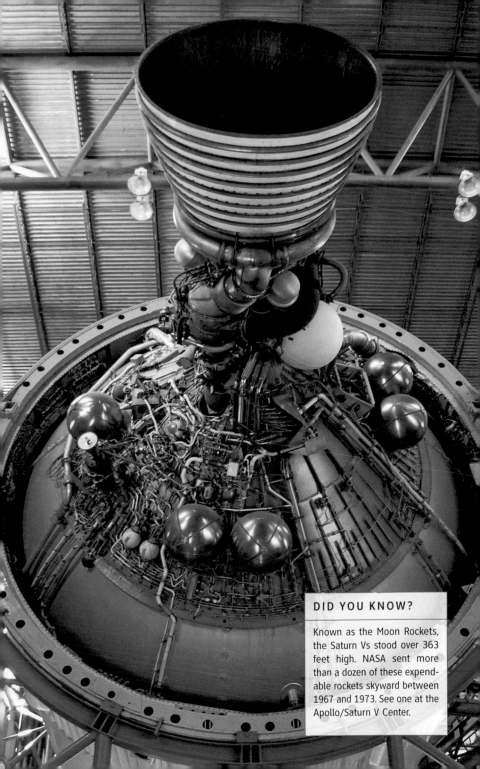

DID YOU KNOW?

Known as the Moon Rockets, the Saturn Vs stood over 363 feet high. NASA sent more than a dozen of these expendable rockets skyward between 1967 and 1973. See one at the Apollo/Saturn V Center.

THE KENNEDY SPACE CENTER

The 140,000-acre Kennedy Space Center is one of central Florida's most popular sights. The must-see attraction gives you a hands-on opportunity to learn about the past, present, and future of America's space program. View old rockets and other artifacts from space flight operations, talk with astronauts during Q&As, experience a simulated launch, and become part of the awed crowd on launch days as you watch the blastoff from a viewing site on the grounds or nearby.

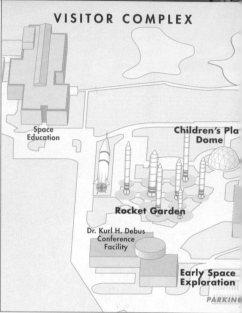

VISITOR COMPLEX

Space Education

Children's Pla Dome

Rocket Garden

Dr. Kurl H. Debus Conference Facility

Early Space Exploration

PARKING

VISITOR COMPLEX

The Kennedy Space Center Visitor Complex is the starting place for your visit. It's home to several attractions and is also where you can board the bus for tours of the center beyond the visitor complex.

EXHIBITS

The **Early Space Exploration** display highlights the rudimentary yet influential Mercury and Gemini space programs; **Robot Scouts** is a walk-through exhibit of unmanned planetary probes; and the **Exploration Space: Explorers Wanted** exhibit immerses visitors in exploration beyond Earth. Don't miss the outdoor **Rocket Garden,** with walkways winding beside rockets, from early Atlas spacecraft to a Saturn IB. The most moving exhibit is the **Astronaut Memorial.** The 70,400-pound black-granite tribute to astronauts who lost their lives in the name of space exploration stands 42½ feet high by 50 feet wide.

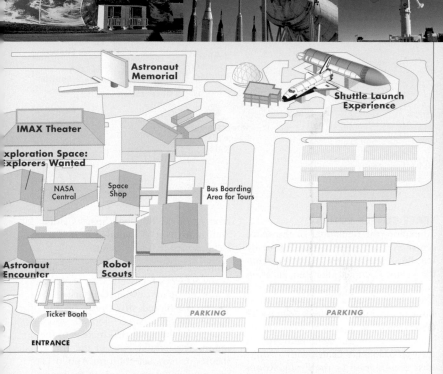

Map labels: Astronaut Memorial · Shuttle Launch Experience · IMAX Theater · Exploration Space: Explorers Wanted · NASA Central · Space Shop · Bus Boarding Area for Tours · Astronaut Encounter · Robot Scouts · Ticket Booth · PARKING · PARKING · ENTRANCE

INTERACTIVE SHOWS AND RIDES

Astronaut Encounter Theater has two daily programs where NASA astronauts share their adventures in space travel and show a short film. More befitting Walt Disney World or Universal Studios (complete with the health warnings), the **Shuttle Launch Experience** is the center's newest and most spectacular attraction. Designed by a team of astronauts, NASA experts, and renowned attraction engineers, the 44,000-square-foot structure uses a sophisticated motion-based platform, special-effects seats, and high-fidelity visual and audio components to simulate the sensations experienced in an actual space-shuttle launch, including MaxQ, Solid Rocket Booster separation, main engine cutoff, and External Tank separation. The journey culminates with a breathtaking view of Earth from space. For those under 48 inches, the redeveloped **Children's Play Dome** enables kids to play among the next generation of spacecraft, climb a moon-rock wall, and crawl through rocket tunnels.

MOVIES

At the world's only back-to-back twin **IMAX Theater** the dream of space flight comes to life on a movie screen five stories tall with dramatic footage shot by NASA astronauts during missions. Realistic 3-D special effects will make you feel like you're in space with them. Films alternate throughout the year.

BEYOND THE VISITOR COMPLEX

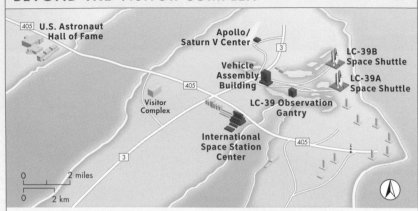

405 U.S. Astronaut
Hall of Fame

Apollo/
Saturn V Center

LC-39B
Space Shuttle

Vehicle
Assembly
Building

LC-39A
Space Shuttle

Visitor
Complex

LC-39 Observation
Gantry

International
Space Station
Center

405

0   2 miles

0   2 km

SPACE CENTER TOURS

To explore the remainder of the space center, you will need to take a tour by bus. Buses depart every 15 minutes from the Visitor Complex; the tour duration is two hours, but you can get off and back on again at will at various sites. Bus stops include the **Launch Complex 39 Observation Gantry,** which has an unparalleled view of the twin launchpads; the **Apollo/Saturn V Center,** with a don't-miss presentation at the Firing Room Theatre, where the launch of America's first lunar mission, 1968's *Apollo VIII,* is re-created with a ground-shaking, window-rattling liftoff; and the **International Space Station Center,** where NASA is building pieces of the space station. This bus tour is included with admission; two others are available for additional fees (*see Add-Ons*).

U.S. ASTRONAUT HALL OF FAME

The original Mercury 7 team and the later Gemini, Apollo, Skylab, and shuttle astronauts contributed to make the United States Astronaut Hall of Fame the world's premium archive of astronauts' personal stories. Authentic memorabilia and equipment from their collections tell the story of human space exploration. This stand-alone attraction is across the

river from the Kennedy Space Center; admission to it is included with your Kennedy Space Center ticket.

You can see one-of-a-kind items like Wally Schirra's relatively archaic Sigma 7 Mercury space capsule, Gus Grissom's spacesuit (colored silver only because NASA thought silver looked more "spacey"), and a flag that made it to the moon. The exhibit First of the Moon focuses on crew selection for Apollo 11 and the Soviet Union's role in the space race. One of the more challenging activities at the hall of fame is a space-shuttle simulator that lets you try your hand at landing the craft—and afterward replays a side view of your rolling and pitching descent. Don't miss Astronaut Adventure, an area with interactive exhibits about space travel. There are also videos of historic moments.

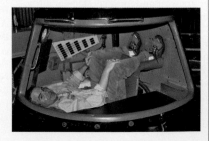

The life of an astronaut can mean a tight squeeze! See for yourself at the U.S. Astronaut Hall of Fame.

ADD-ONS

The following tours and programs are available for extra cost beyond admission and should be reserved in advance.

■ **Discover KSC: Today and Tomorrow** ($21) brings visitors to sites seldom accessible to the public, such as the Vehicle Assembly Building, the shuttle landing strip, and the 6-million-pound crawler that transports the shuttle to its launch pad.

■ See how far the space program has come on the **Cape Canaveral: Then and Now Tour** ($21). It puts you up close to the original launch pads, brings you to the Air Force Space and Missile Museum, and lets you watch the active unmanned rocket program.

■ During **Lunch with an Astronaut** ($23), astronauts talk about their experiences and engage in Q&A (kids often ask "How do you eat/sleep/relieve yourself in space?").

■ If you or one of your little ones wants to live the life of an astronaut, you can enroll in **Astronaut Training Experience** (ATX). The $145 cost includes astronaut gear, lunch, a VIP tour of the Kennedy Space Center, and a half day of hands-on learning. Held at the United States Astronaut Hall of Fame, this is an intense half-day experience where you can dangle from a springy harness for a simulated moonwalk, spin in ways you never thought possible in a multi-axis trainer, and either work Mission Control or helm a space shuttle (in a full-scale mock-up) during a simulated landing. Reserve your spot well in advance.

Cape Canaveral Then and Now Tour.

PLANNING YOUR TRIP

GETTING HERE

The Kennedy Space Center and the U.S. Astronaut Hall of Fame are near Titusville on Cape Canaveral, about a 45- to 60-minute drive from Orlando. From Orlando International Airport, take the north exit to 528 East (the Beeline Expressway) and drive east to the exit marked "407, Titusville, Kennedy Space Center." Take 407 until you reach Rte. 405 (Columbia Boulevard/NASA Parkway) and then turn right. After approximately 1 mi you will see the U.S. Astronaut Hall of Fame on your right. Continue another 5 mi until you reach the visitor complex, your starting point for all tours.

BUDGETING YOUR TIME

Plan to spend a full day at the center and hall of fame, or at the very least, several hours.

ADMISSION

Your $38 admission ticket grants you access for two days (within the span of one week) to Kennedy Space Center Visitor Complex and related tours as well as the U.S. Astronaut Hall of Fame, which is just across the causeway.

CONTACT INFORMATION

✉ Off Rte. 405

☎ 321/449–4444

🌐 www.kennedyspacecenter.com

🎫 $38

🕐 Daily 9 AM to 5:30 PM. (Call ahead for restrictions if you're visiting on a launch day.)

SHUTTLE COMPONENTS

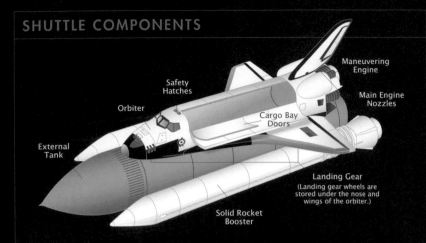

Maneuvering Engine

Safety Hatches

Main Engine Nozzles

Orbiter

Cargo Bay Doors

External Tank

Landing Gear
(Landing gear wheels are stored under the nose and wings of the orbiter.)

Solid Rocket Booster

ROCKET VS. SHUTTLE

When the space shuttle orbiter *Columbia* blasted off on April 12, 1981, NASA launched its Space Transportation System—a planned fleet of manned, reusable spacecraft that can transport crew, cargo, and experiments into space and return to Earth to land like an aircraft. The system is a radical departure from the days when manned lunar modules were thrust into space at the tip of a disposable rocket, to return to the planet by parachute and then be plucked from the ocean. (Shuttles are launched piggyback on a huge, single-use fuel tank; its two solid rocket boosters return via parachute.) Modern traditional rockets are used only to deploy instruments like unmanned probes into space.

EXTERNAL TANK—provides a platform for the shuttle and fuel for the two booster rockets that transport the shuttle into space. It separates from the shuttle within the first 10 minutes of the flight and falls into the ocean.

SOLID ROCKET BOOSTER—one of two rockets used to launch the shuttle into space. Each returns to Earth via parachute to be restored for use on a future mission.

ORBITER—another name for the space shuttle, which rides piggyback on the fuel tank until it can launch into space under its own rocket power. The crew is inside.

CARGO BAY DOORS—the two long doors on the back of the orbiter that open to allow payload to be deployed into space by means of a manipulating arm.

LANDING GEAR—the retractable wheels under the nose and wings of the orbiter, which allow it to land like a typical aircraft.

ENTRY HATCH—this door allows astronauts to enter the shuttle, and doubles as an escape hatch.

MANEUVERING ENGINES—a number of smaller orbiter engines, on the nose and in the tail section, which allow the craft to make fine positioning adjustments while in space.

MAIN ENGINE NOZZLES—the three engines at the rear of the orbiter that propel the craft to space.

BLASTOFF!

From Kennedy Space Center's numerous launch pads the majority of unmanned space flights and all manned space missions have found their origin, with many of them being momentous events—the first satellite launched into space, the first man in space, that giant leap onto the moon's surface. Over the years many flights have become rather routine in a sense, happening with a fair amount of frequency, but hundreds of spectators still line the cape's nearby roads to watch the countdown, the great explosions of rocket power, and the always exciting liftoff—proving that what is routine at NASA is never boring.

When visiting the area, you can become part of the awed crowd on launch days watching the blastoff or liftoff (rocket blast, shuttles lift).

WATCHING A LAUNCH

A limited number of tickets are available for viewing a launch from within the Kennedy Space Center at the Visitor Complex ($28–$38); prices include admission to the center. Popular off-site vantage points:

■ Along the Indian River on Hwy. 1, especially in Titusville

■ Beach Line Expressway (Rte. 528), especially where it crosses over the Indian or Banana Rivers

■ Rte. A1A in Cocoa Beach

■ Jetty Park at Port Canaveral, just south of the Cape Canaveral Air Force Station border (park admission is $5)

Hauser Blvd. ☎ *321/383–9191* ⊕ *www.hamptoninn.com* ↪ *86 rooms, 4 suites* ⚴ *In-room: refrigerator, Internet. In-hotel: pool, gym, laundry facilities, laundry service, parking (free), Wi-Fi hotspot* ⑩ *CP.*

COCOA

17 mi south of Titusville, on U.S. 1.

Not to be confused with the seaside community of Cocoa Beach, the small town of Cocoa sits smack-dab on mainland Florida and faces the Intracoastal Waterway, known locally as the Indian River. There's a planetarium and a museum, as well as a rustic fish camp along the St. Johns River, a few miles inland.

Folks in a rush to get to the beach tend to overlook Cocoa's Victorian-style village, but it's worth a stop, and is perhaps Cocoa's most interesting feature. Within the cluster of restored turn-of-the-20th-century buildings and cobblestone walkways you can enjoy several restaurants, indoor and outdoor cafés, snack and ice-cream shops, and more than 50 specialty shops and art galleries. The area hosts music performances in the gazebo, arts-and-crafts shows, and other family-friendly events throughout the year. To get to Cocoa Village, head east on Route 520—named King Street in Cocoa—and when the streets get narrow and the road curves, make a right onto Brevard Avenue; follow the signs for the free municipal parking lot.

EXPLORING

⟳ **BCC Planetarium & Observatory.** Based at Brevard Community College, this planetarium and observatory has one of Florida's largest public-access telescopes. The 24-inch telescope allows visitors to view objects in the solar system and deep space. The on-campus planetarium has two theaters, one showing a changing roster of nature documentaries, the other hosting laser-light shows as well as changing planetarium shows. Science Quest Exhibit Hall has hands-on exhibits, including scales calibrated to other planets (Vegas-era Elvis would have weighed just 62 pounds on the moon). The International Hall of Space Explorers displays exhibits on space travel. Show schedules and opening hours may vary, so it's best to call ahead. ⊠ *1519 Clearlake Rd., Bldg. 19* ☎ *321/433–7373* ⊕ *www.brevardcc.edu/planet* ⊡ *Observatory and exhibits free; film or planetarium show $7; both shows $11; laser show $7, triple combination $16* ⊗ *Call for schedule.*

SPORTS AND THE OUTDOORS

AIRBOAT RIDES

Twister Airboat Rides. If you haven't seen the swampy, alligator-ridden waters of Florida, then you haven't really seen Florida. Guests on these rides go on a unique and thrilling wildlife tour, where eagles and wading birds coexist with water moccasins and gators. The Coast Guard–certified deluxe airboats hit speeds of up to 45 mph and offer unparalleled opportunities to photograph native species. The basic tour lasts 30 minutes, but 60- and 90-minute ecotours are also available at an additional cost. Twister Airboat Rides is inside the Lone Cabbage Fish Camp, about 9 mi west of Cocoa's city limits, 4 mi west of Interstate

95. ⊠ *8199 Rte. 520 at St. Johns River* ☎ *321/632–4199* ⊕ *www. twisterairboatrides.com* 🖼 *$22* ☉ *Daily 10–5:30.*

SHOPPING

You could spend hours browsing in the more than 50 boutiques and shops of **Cocoa Village** (⊠ *Rte. 520 and Brevard Ave.* ☎ *321/631–9075*) along Brevard Avenue and Harrison Street, which has the densest concentration of shops. Although most are of the gift and clothing variety, the village is also home to several antiques shops, art galleries, florists, bookstores, and even a tattoo parlor and a spa.

NIGHTLIFE AND THE ARTS

In 1918 the building that now holds the **Cocoa Village Playhouse** (⊠ *300 Brevard Ave.* ☎ *321/636–5050*) was a Ford dealership that sold Model Ts. After that, it evolved into the Aladdin Theater, a vaudeville house, and then did a turn as a movie theater before being purchased by Brevard Community College. The September-through-June performance schedule has musicals starring local talent. The rest of the year the stage hosts touring professional productions, concerts, and, in summer, shows geared to children on vacation.

WHERE TO EAT

$$$
CAFÉ
Fodor's Choice
★

✕ **Café Margaux.** Eclectic, creative, and international is the perfect way to describe the cuisine and the decor at this charming Cocoa Village spot. The menu blends French, Italian, and Asian influences with dishes like tenderloin of beef brochette, sesame-seared ahi with green-tea and bamboo risotto, and braised veal scaloppine, and also features more exotic fare such as duck and ostrich. The themed dining rooms are elaborately decorated with dramatic but not necessarily coordinating window treatments, wallpaper, and artwork. ⊠ *220 Brevard Ave.* ☎ *321/639–8343* ⊕ *www.margaux.com* ⊟ *AE, D, MC, V* ☉ *Closed Sun.*

$
ECLECTIC

✕ **Lone Cabbage Fish Camp.** The word "rustic" doesn't even begin to describe this down-home, no-nonsense restaurant (translation: you eat off paper plates with plastic forks) housed in a weathered, old, clapboard shack along with a bait shop and airboat-tour company. Set your calorie counter for plates of catfish, frogs' legs, turtle, and alligator (as well as burgers and hot dogs). Dine inside or on the outdoor deck overlooking the St. Johns River with live music every Sunday. Who knows, you might even see your dinner swimming by. ⊠ *8199 Rte. 520 at St. Johns River* ☎ *321/632–4199* 🚣 *Reservations not accepted* ⊟ *AE, MC, V.*

CAPE CANAVERAL

5 mi east of Cocoa via Rte. A1A.

The once-bustling commercial fishing area of Cape Canaveral is still home to a small shrimping fleet, charter boats, and party fishing boats, but its main business these days is as a cruise-ship port. Cocoa Beach itself isn't the spiffiest place around, but what is becoming quite clean and neat is the north end of the port, where the Carnival, Disney, and Royal Caribbean cruise lines set sail, as well as Sun Cruz and Las Vegas Casino Lines. Port Canaveral is now Florida's second-busiest cruise port for multiday cruises, which makes this a great place to catch a glimpse of these giant ships even if you're not headed out to sea.

EXPLORING

The Cove at Port Canaveral. Whether you're at Port Canaveral for a cruise or are just passing through, this retail marketplace on the south side of the harbor has enough restaurants, entertainment venues, and shops to keep you occupied. Since most of the bars and eateries are located on the public waterfront area, you'll have a unique view of the cruise ships—and their colorful passengers. ⊠ *Glen Cheek Dr. and Scallop Dr., Port Canaveral* ⊠ *Free* ⊙ *Hours vary by business.*

SPORTS AND THE OUTDOORS

Jetty Park. Come here for a wonderful taste of the real Florida. The 4½-acre beach and oceanfront campground has more than 150 camp-sites for tents and RVs, picnic pavilions, bike paths, and a 1,200-foot-long fishing pier that doubles as a perfect vantage point from which to watch a liftoff of the space shuttle. Lifeguards are on duty all year, and beach wheelchairs are available for rent. A jetty constructed of giant boulders adds to the landscape, and a walkway that crosses it provides access to a less populated stretch of beach. Real and rustic, this is Florida without the theme-park varnish. ⊠ *400 E. Jetty Rd., Port Canaveral* ☎ *321/783–7111* ⊕ *www.jettypark.org* ⊠ *$5 per car, $7 for RVs for fishing or beach; camping $18–$29 for basic, $22–$32 with water and electric, $25–$34 full hookup* ⊙ *Daily 7 AM–9 PM.*

WHERE TO STAY

$$$ ⊡ **Radisson Resort at the Port.** For cruise-ship passengers who can't wait to get under way, this splashy resort, done up in pink and turquoise, already feels like the Caribbean. Guest rooms have wicker furniture, hand-painted wallpaper, tropical-theme decor, and ceiling fans. The pool is lushly landscaped and features a cascading 95-foot mountain waterfall, tiki bar, and occasional appearances by the "Radisson par-rots," about a dozen renegade birds who call the resort home (can you blame them?). This resort, directly across the bay from Port Canaveral, is not on the ocean, but it does provide complimentary transportation to the beach, Ron Jon Surf Shop, and the cruise-ship terminals at Port Canaveral. **Pros:** cruise-ship convenience; pool area; free shuttle. **Cons:** three-day cancellation policy; rooms around the pool can be noisy; loud air-conditioning in some rooms; no breakfast. ⊠ *8701 Astronaut Blvd.* ☎ *321/784–0000 or 888/201–1718* ⊕ *www.radisson.com/ capecanaveralfl* ⤵ *284 rooms, 72 suites* ⚬ *In-room: kitchen (some), refrigerator (some), Internet, Wi-Fi. In-hotel: restaurant, bar, tennis court, pool, gym, laundry facilities, laundry service, Wi-Fi hotspot* ⊟ *AE, D, MC, V.321/784–0000*

$$$ ⊡ **Residence Inn Cape Canaveral/Cocoa Beach.** Billing itself as the closest all-suites hotel to the Kennedy Space Center, this four-story Residence Inn, painted cheery yellow, is also convenient to other area attractions such as the Cocoa Beach Pier, the Brevard Zoo, and Cocoa Village, and is only an hour from the Magic Kingdom. Considerably larger than traditional hotel rooms, the one- and two-bedroom suites include a full kitchen—dishwasher and all—and separate living and sleeping areas.

The morning buffet and nightly manager's reception are popular with guests who aren't hoping to remain incognito. **Pros:** helpful staff; free breakfast buffet; pet friendly. **Cons:** less than picturesque views; street noise in some rooms. ✉ *8959 Astronaut Blvd.* ☎ *321/323–1100 or 800/331–3131* ⊕ *www.marriott.com* ➔ *150 suites* ♿ *In-room: kitchen, Internet, Wi-Fi. In-hotel: pool, gym, laundry facilities, laundry service, parking (free), some pets allowed, Wi-Fi hotspot* ═ *AE, D, MC, V* ❍ *BP.321/323–1100*

COCOA BEACH

5 mi south of Cape Canaveral.

After crossing a long and high bridge just east of Cocoa Village, you'll drop down upon a barrier island. A few miles farther and you'll reach the Atlantic Ocean and picture-perfect **Cocoa Beach** at Route A1A. This is one of the Space Coast's nicest beaches, with many wide stretches that are excellent for biking, jogging, power walking, or strolling. In some places there are dressing rooms, showers, playgrounds, picnic areas with grills, snack shops, and surf-side parking lots. Beach vendors offer necessities, and guards are on duty in summer. As the closest beach to Orlando, Cocoa Beach is popular with Central Floridians looking for a quick getaway or vacationers looking to extend their stay. The city is also considered the capital of Florida's surfing community.

ESSENTIALS

Visitor Information Cocoa Beach Convention and Visitors Bureau (✉ *8501 Astronaut Blvd., Suite 4, Cape Canaveral* ☎ *321/454–2022 or 877/321–8474* ⊕ *www.visitcocoabeach.com*).

SPORTS AND THE OUTDOORS

BEACHES

Alan Shepard Park. Named for the former astronaut, this 5-acre ocean-front park, aptly enough, provides excellent views of shuttle launches. Facilities include 10 picnic pavilions, shower and restroom facilities, and more than 300 parking spaces. Those spaces are in high demand on launch days, but the park's a nice break any other day, too. Parking is $7 per day, $10 per day on weekends and holidays from early March through Labor Day. Shops and restaurants are within walking distance. ✉ *East end of Rte. 250* ☎ *321/868–3274.*

Sidney Fischer Park. The 10-acre oceanfront has showers, playgrounds, changing areas, picnic areas with grills, snack shops, and plenty of well-maintained, inexpensive surf-side parking lots. Beach vendors carry necessities for sunning and swimming. The parking fee is $5 for cars and RVs. ✉ *2100 block of Rte. A1A* ☎ *321/868–3252.*

FISHING

The **Cocoa Beach Pier** (✉ *401 Meade Ave.* ⊕ *www.cocoabeachpier. com* ☎ *321/783–7549*) has a bait-and-tackle shop and a fishing area. Although most of the pier is free to walk on, there's a $1 charge to enter the fishing area at the end of the 800-foot-long boardwalk, and a $3.50 fishing fee. You can rent rods and reels here. ■**TIP**➔ **The pier is a great place to watch space-shuttle launches.**

14

A stand of palms, beautiful blue water, and Kennedy Space Center—the reasons why this region is called the Space Coast.

KAYAKING

Specializing in manatee encounters, **Adventure Kayak of Cocoa Beach** (✆ 321/480–8632 ⊕ *www.kayakcocoabeach.com*) takes guests on one- and two-person kayak tours of mangroves, channels, and islands.

SURFING

If you can't tell a tri-skeg stick from a hodaddy shredding the lip on a gnarly tube, then you may want to avail yourself of the **Ron Jon Surf School** (✉ *150 E. Columbia La.* ✆ *321/868–1980*) or the **Cocoa Beach Surf Company** (✉ *4001 N. Atlantic Ave.* ✆ *321/799–9930*). They teach grommets (dudes) and gidgets (chicks) from kids to seniors in groups and one-on-one. **Ron Jon Watersports** (✉ *4275 N. Atlantic Ave.* ✆ *321/799–8888*) and the **Cocoa Beach Surf Company** (✉ *4001 N. Atlantic Ave.* ✆ *321/799–9930*) rent surfboards, body boards, and wet suits, as well as umbrellas, chairs, and bikes.

SHOPPING

Cocoa Beach Surf Company (✉ *4001 N. Atlantic Ave.* ✆ *321/799–9930*) is the world's largest surf complex, with three floors of boards, apparel, sunglasses, and anything else a surfer, wannabe-surfer, or souvenir-seeker could need. Also on-site are a 5,600-gallon fish and shark tank, the Shark Pit Bar & Grill, and the **East Coast Surfing Hall of Fame and Museum.**

Fodor's Choice
★ It's impossible to miss the **Ron Jon Surf Shop** (✉ *4151 N. Atlantic Ave., Rte. A1A* ✆ *321/799–8888* ⊕ *www.ronjonsurfshop.com*). With a giant surfboard and an aqua, teal, and pink art-deco facade, Ron Jon takes up nearly two blocks along Route A1A. What started in 1963 as a small T-shirt and bathing-suit shop has evolved into a 52,000-square-

foot superstore that's open every day 'round the clock. The shop has water-sports gear as well as chairs and umbrellas for rent, and sells every kind of beachwear, surf wax, plus the requisite T-shirts and flip-flops. ■TIP➜ For up-to-the-minute surfing conditions, call the store and press 3 and then 7 for the Ron Jon Surf and Weather Report.

NIGHTLIFE

The **Cocoa Beach Pier** (✉ *401 Meade Ave.* ☎ *321/783–7549*) is for locals, beach bums, surfers, and people who don't mind the weather-worn wood and sandy, watery paths. The Mai Tiki Bar claims that "No Bar Goes This Far," which is true, considering it's at the end of the 800-foot pier. Come to The Boardwalk Friday night for the Boardwalk Bash, with live acoustic and rock-and-roll music, drop in Saturday for more live music, and come back Wednesday evening to catch the reggae band. For great live jazz, head to **Heidi's Jazz Club** (✉ *7 Orlando Ave. N* ☎ *321/783–4559*). Local and nationally known musicians (Boots Randolph and Mose Allison have taken the stage) play Tuesday through Sunday, with showcase acts appearing on weekends.

> ## LIFE IMITATES ART
>
> In the early 1960s Cocoa Beach was a sleepy, little-known town. But in 1965 the sitcom *I Dream of Jeannie* premiered. The endearing show centered around an astronaut, played by Larry Hagman, and his "Jeannie" in a bottle, Barbara Eden, and was set in Cocoa Beach. Though the series was never shot in Florida, creator Sidney Sheldon paid homage to the town with local references to Cape Kennedy (now known as the Kennedy Space Center) and Bernard's Surf.

WHERE TO EAT

$$$

GERMAN

✕**Heidelberg.** As the name suggests, the cuisine here is definitely German, from the sauerbraten served with potato dumplings and red cabbage to the beef Stroganoff and spaetzle to the classically prepared Wiener schnitzel. All the soups and desserts are homemade; try the Viennese-style apple strudel and the rum-zapped almond-cream tortes. Elegant interior touches include crisp linens and fresh flowers. There's live music Friday and Saturday evenings. You can also dine inside the jazz club, Heidi's, next door. ✉ *7 N. Orlando Ave., opposite City Hall* ☎ *321/783–6806* ⊕ *www.heidisjazzclub.com* ▭ *AE, MC, V* ⊗ *Closed Mon. Closed Tues. in summer. No lunch Sun.*

$

SEAFOOD

✕**Oh Shucks Seafood Bar.** At the only open-air seafood bar on the beach, at the entrance of the Cocoa Beach Pier, the main item is oysters, served on the half shell. You can also grab a burger here, crab legs by the pound, or Oh Shucks' most popular item, coconut beer shrimp. Some diners complain that the prices don't jibe with the ultracasual atmosphere (e.g., plastic chairs), but they're also paying for the "ex-Pier-ience." There's live entertainment on Friday and Saturday. ✉ *401 Meade Ave., Cocoa Beach Pier* ☎ *321/783–7549* ▭ *AE, D, MC, V.*

WHERE TO STAY

$$

⊡ **Best Western Ocean Beach Hotel & Suites.** Folks who loved Cocoa Beach's Ocean Suite Hotel will love this Best Western property since it now encompasses the five-story, all-suites building that's particularly

14

Popular with families, Cocoa Beach is an easy day trip for Orlando or Kennedy Space Center visitors.

popular with families. Just a half block from the Cocoa Beach Pier, the former Ocean Suite Hotel is in a great location, especially for shuttle launches. The newly renovated suites are still modest, but feature two TVs, a separate living room, wet-bar area with sink, refrigerator, microwave, sofa bed, and a private balcony. ■ TIP→ **Skip the standard motel rooms and stick with the suites in the "Tower." Pros:** free Internet; complimentary breakfast. **Cons:** not all rooms have an ocean view; small bathrooms; noise from the pier. ⊠ *5600 N. Ocean Beach Blvd.* ☎ *321/784–4343 or 800/367–1223* ⊕ *www.bestwesterncocoabeach. com* ⌁ *50 suites ⚑ In-room: refrigerator, Internet. In-hotel: 2 restaurants, pools, laundry facilities* ⊟ *AE, D, MC, V* ⦿ *CP.*

$$ ⛱ **Doubletree Hotel Cocoa Beach Oceanfront.** Proximity to the beach and comforts like microwaves and refrigerators—and Doubletree's famous chocolate-chip cookies—make this five-story hotel a favorite of vacationing families as well as Orlandoans on weekend getaways. Guest rooms are West Indies–inspired, with dark oak furniture, colorful tropical prints, and sunny yellow walls. Most rooms are oceanfront with private balconies, though all offer ocean views. **Pros:** private beach; refrigerator and microwave in every room; comfy beds. **Cons:** extra charge for beach-chair rental; loud air-conditioning in some rooms; slow elevators; no breakfast with standard room. ⊠ *2080 N. Atlantic Ave.* ☎ *321/783–9222* ⊕ *www.cocoabeachdoubletree.com* ⌁ *148 rooms, 12 suites ⚑ In-room: refrigerator, Wi-Fi. In-hotel: restaurant, room service, bar, pool, gym, beachfront, laundry facilities, laundry service, parking (free)* ⊟ *AE, D, DC, MC, V.*

$$$ ⛱ **Hilton Cocoa Beach Oceanfront.** You can't get any closer to the beach
★ than this seven-story oceanfront hotel. Most rooms have ocean views,

but for true drama get a room on the east end, facing the water. If sand isn't your thing, enjoy the ocean breeze and live music on the 10,000-square-foot deck surrounding "the largest pool on the Space Coast." The property also offers a variety of water-sport rentals and surf lessons. With purple, gold, and green soft goods, room decor is more Mardi Gras than beach resort, and yet rooms also feature Hilton Serenity Beds. **Pros:** beachfront; friendly staff; clean. **Cons:** small bathrooms; no balconies; room windows don't open; breakfast not included with standard rate. ⊠ *1550 N. Atlantic Ave.* ☎ *321/799–0003* ⊕ *www. hiltoncocoabeach.com* ⇨ *285 rooms, 11 suites* ♿ *In-room: refrigerator, Wi-Fi. In-hotel: 3 restaurants, room service, bar, pools, gym, beachfront, laundry facilities, laundry service, parking (free)* ⊟ *AE, D, DC, MC, V.*

14

$$$ 🏨 **Inn at Cocoa Beach.** One of the area's best, this charming oceanfront
★ inn has spacious, individually decorated rooms with four-poster beds, upholstered chairs, and balconies or patios; most have ocean views. Deluxe rooms are much larger, with a king-size bed, sofa, and sitting area; most also have a dining table. Jacuzzi rooms are different sizes. Included in the rate are afternoon socials in the breezeway, evening wine and cheese, and a continental breakfast. **Pros:** quiet; romantic; honor bar. **Cons:** no on-site restaurant; "forced" socializing. ⊠ *4300 Ocean Beach Blvd.* ☎ *321/799–3460, 800/343–5307 outside Florida* ⊕ *www.theinnatcocoabeach.com* ⇨ *50 rooms* ♿ *In-room: safe, DVD (some). In-hotel: pool, beachfront, parking (free), Wi-Fi hotspot* ⊟ *AE, D, MC, V* ❏ *CP.*

$$$$ 🏨 **The Resort on Cocoa Beach.** Even if the beach weren't in its back-
♻ yard, this family-friendly, oceanfront property offers enough activities
Fodor's Choice and amenities—from tennis and basketball courts to a game room and
★ 50-seat movie theater—to keep everyone entertained. Organized activities begin at 9 and run through 2:30, with offerings including arts-and-crafts projects and scavenger hunts for kids and pool volleyball and bingo for adults. The two-bedroom, two-bathroom suites won't win any interior design awards, but they offer all of the comforts of home with a separate living room, dining area, and fully equipped kitchen. 42-inch plasma TV with DVD player, whirlpool tub, and washer and dryer. **Pros:** full kitchens; in-room washers and dryers; large balconies. **Cons:** check-in not until 4 and check out at 10; not all rooms are oceanfront; slow elevators. ⊠ *1600 N. Atlantic Ave.* ☎ *321/783–4000* ⊕ *www.theresortoncocoabeach.com* ⇨ *124 suites* ♿ *In-room: kitchen, DVD, Internet. In-hotel: restaurant, bars, tennis court, pools, gym, Wi-Fi hotspot, children's programs (ages 4–12), laundry facilities, parking (free)* ⊟ *AE, D, MC, V.*

$–$$ 🏨 **Wakulla Suites Resort.** This kitschy two-story motel in a converted 1970s apartment building is clean and comfortable, surrounded by tropical gardens, and just off the beach. Some rooms are a block away from the water, and a few are just a walk down the boardwalk. The bright rooms are fairly ordinary, decorated in tropical prints. Completely furnished suites, designed to sleep six, are great for families; each includes two bedrooms and a living room, dining area, and fully equipped kitchen. The throw-back property isn't for everyone, but those who dig it return year after year. **Pros:** kitchen; barbecue grills. **Cons:** lots of kid noise; a hike to the beach; seven-day cancellation policy. ✉ *3550 N. Atlantic Ave.* ☎ *321/783–2230 or 800/992–5852* ⊕ *www. wakullasuites.com* ⮌ *117 suites* ⚖ *In-room: kitchen, Internet, Wi-Fi. In-hotel: pool, laundry facilities, parking (free), Wi-Fi hotspot* ═ *AE, D, MC, V.*

MELBOURNE

20 mi south of Cocoa, on U.S. 95.

Despite its dependence on the high-tech space industry, this town is decidedly laid-back. The majority of the city is on the mainland, but a small portion trickles onto a barrier island, separated by the Indian River Lagoon and accessible by several inlets, including the Sebastian Inlet.

EXPLORING

ⓒ **Brevard Zoo.** At the only American Zoo and Aquarium Association–
Fodor's Choice accredited zoo built by a community, stroll along the shaded board-
★ walks and get a close-up look at alligators, crocodiles, giant anteaters, marmosets, jaguars, eagles, river otters, kangaroos, exotic birds, and kookaburras. Alligator, crocodile, and river-otter feedings are held on alternate afternoons—although the alligators do not dine on the otters. Stop by Paws-On, an interactive learning playground where kids and adults can crawl into human-size gopher burrows, beehives, and spider webs; get cozy with several domestic animals in Animal Encounters; hand-feed a giraffe in Expedition Africa or a lorikeet in the Austra-lian Free Flight Aviary; and step up to the Wetlands Outpost, an ele-vated pavilion that's a gateway to 22 acres of wetlands through which you can paddle kayaks and keep an eye open for the 4,000 species of wildlife that live in these waters and woods. ✉ *8225 N. Wickham Rd.* ☎ *321/254–9453* ⊕ *www.brevardzoo.org* ▨ *$12.50 for general admis-sion; $17 for admission, a train ride, and food for the lorikeets* ⊙ *Daily 9:30–5, last admission at 4:15.*

SPORTS AND THE OUTDOORS

BASEBALL

Even though they play in our nation's capital during the regular season, the **Washington Nationals** (✉ *5800 Stadium Pkwy., Viera* ☎ *321/633–4487* ⊕ *www.nationals.com*), formerly the Montréal Expos, use Melbourne's Space Coast Stadium for their spring-training site. For the rest of the sea-son, the facility is home to the **Brevard County Manatees** (☎ *321/633–9200*), one of the Milwaukee Brewers' minor-league teams.

NIGHTLIFE AND THE ARTS

The **Maxwell C. King Center for the Performing Arts** (✉ *3865 N. Wickham Rd.* ☎ *321–242–2219 box office* ⊕ *www.kingcenter.com*) is one of the premier performance centers in Central Florida. Oddly enough, top-name performers often bypass Orlando to appear in this comfortable 2,000-seat hall. Call for a performance schedule.

The Tampa Bay Area

WORD OF MOUTH

"The north beach (at Fort DeSoto park) is huge. You can escape the crowds if you want—head to an area where there is nothing but beach, water, and scrubby trees."

—Malesherbes

WELCOME TO THE TAMPA BAY AREA

Ybor City.

TOP REASONS TO GO

★ **Art Gone Wild:** Whether you take the guided tour or chart your own course, experience the one-of-a-kind collection at the Salvador Dalí Museum in St. Petersburg.

★ **Cuban Roots:** You'll find great food and engaging shops in historic Ybor City, which is just east of downtown Tampa.

★ **Beachcomer Bonanza:** Caladesi Island State Park has some of the best shelling on the Gulf Coast, and its five-star sunsets are a great way to end the day.

★ **Culture Fix:** If you love the arts, there's no finer offering in the Bay Area than at the Florida State University Ringling Center for the Cultural Arts in Sarasota.

1 **Tampa/St. Petersburg Area.** State-of-the-art zoos and museums in the communities north and west of Tampa Bay promise to broaden your imagination, and some of Florida's best beaches tempt you with sparkling waters. The area includes Clearwater, Dunedin, and Tarpon Springs.

2 **South of Tampa Bay: Sarasota County.** Barrier islands lure travelers to another battery of white-sand beaches, but Sarasota's cultural treasures are the true draw for many of its visitors.

Ringling Museum of Art.

Orlando

CENTRAL FLORIDA

Home of John Ringling,
Sarasota.

Cosme
598
Gunn Hwy.
Fletcher Ave.
597
Fowler Ave.
586
Carrollwood
Waters
41
Temple
Terrace
Busch Blvd.
Oldsmar
580
Sheldon Rd.
583
Hillsborough
Tampa
International
Airport
92 Ave.
574
Ybor City
Courtney Campbell Causeway
Rocky
Point
60
Adamo St.
Old Tampa
Bay
Kennedy Blvd.
St Petersburg-
Clearwater
International
Airport
Howard Frankland Bridge
92
BUS
41
BIG ISLAND
Gandy Bridge
TAMPA
1
Hillsborough
Bay
41
92
East Tampa
WEEDON I.
MacDill
Air Force
Base
Gibsonton
62nd Ave. N
ROSS I.
Gadsden Point
Adamsville
ST.
PETERSBURG
Tampa Bay
Apollo Beach
Ave. S
Boyd Hill
Nature Park
Mangrove Point
54th
Ave. S
COQUINA KEY
Pinellas Point
Gulf City
Ruskin
Sun City
Valroy
41
Piney Point
301
2
TO
SARASOTA
Gillette
275
Parrish
19
75

GETTING
ORIENTED

On the east side of the
bay, industry- and business-
oriented Tampa also offers
attractions such as Busch
Gardens. To the west, St.
Petersburg and Clearwater
use beaches and barrier
islands as calling cards.
Moving to the south,
Sarasota's arts scene is
among the finest in Florida.

15

Busch Gardens.

TAMPA BAY AREA PLANNER

When to Go

Winter and spring are high season, and the level of activity is double what it is in the off-season. In summer there are huge afternoon thunderstorms, and temperatures hover around or above 90°F during the day. Luckily the mercury drops to the mid-70s at night, and beach towns have a consistent onshore breeze that starts just before sundown, which enabled civilization to survive here before air-conditioning arrived.

Visitor Information

Greater Tampa Chamber of Commerce (⊠ 615 Channelside Dr., Box 420, Tampa ☎ 813/228-7777 or 800/298-2672 ⊕ www. tampachamber.com).

Getting Here

Tampa International Airport (☎ 813/870-8700 ⊕ www. tampaairport.com), the area's largest and busiest with 19 million passengers a year, is served by most major carriers and offers ground transportation to surrounding cities. Many of the large U.S. carriers also fly into and out of Sarasota–Bradenton International Airport (☎ 941/359-2777 ⊕ www.srq-airport.com). Meanwhile, St. Petersburg–Clearwater International Airport (☎ 727/453-7800 ⊕ www.fly2pie.com), 9 mi west of downtown St. Petersburg, is much smaller and has limited service. SuperShuttle (☎ 727/572-1111 or 800/282-6817 ⊕ www.supershuttle.com) and Blue One Transportation (☎ 813/282-7351 ⊕ www.blueonetransportation.com) provide Tampa International Airport service to and from Hillsborough (Tampa, Plant City), Pinellas (St. Petersburg, St. Pete Beach, Clearwater), and Polk (Lakeland) counties. Taxi fare from the airport within 10 mi (including downtown Tampa) is $15–$30. Amtrak (☎ 800/872-7245 ⊕ www.amtrak.com) trains run from the Northeast, the Midwest, and much of the South into Tampa; the station is at 601 N. Nebraska Avenue.

Getting Around

Interstates 75 and 275 span the Bay Area from north to south. Coming from Orlando, you're likely to drive west into Tampa on Interstate 4. Along with Interstate 75, U.S. 41 (the Tamiami Trail) stretches the length of the region and links the business districts of many communities; it's best to avoid it and all bridges during rush hours (7–9 AM and 4–6 PM). Hillsborough Area Regional Transit (☎ 813/254-4278 ⊕ www.hartline.org) serves the county, and TECO Line Street Cars (☎ 813/254-4278 ⊕ www. tecolinestreetcar.org) replicate the city's first electric streetcars, transporting cruise-ship passengers to Ybor City.

About the Restaurants

Fresh gulf seafood is plentiful—raw bars serving oysters, clams, and mussels are everywhere. Tampa's many Cuban and Spanish restaurants serve spicy paella with seafood and chicken, *boliche criollo* (sausage-stuffed eye-round roast) with black beans and rice, *ropa vieja* (shredded flank steak in tomato sauce), and other treats. Tarpon Springs adds classic Greek specialties. In Sarasota the emphasis is on ritzier dining, but many restaurants offer extra-cheap early-bird menus for those dining before 6 PM.

About the Hotels

Many convention hotels in the Tampa Bay Area double as family-friendly resorts—taking advantage of nearby beaches, marinas, spas, tennis courts, and golf links. However, unlike Orlando and some other parts of Florida, the area has been bustling for more than a century, and its accommodations often reflect a sense of its history. You'll find a turn-of-the-20th-century beachfront resort where Zelda and F. Scott Fitzgerald stayed, a massive all-wood building from the 1920s, plenty of art deco, and throwbacks to the Spanish-style villas of yore. But one thing they all have in common is a certain Gulf Coast charm.

Assume that hotels operate on the European Plan (EP, no meals), unless we specify that they use the Breakfast Plan (BP, with full breakfast), Continental Plan (CP, continental breakfast), Full American Plan (FAP, all meals), or Modified American Plan (MAP, breakfast and dinner), or are all-inclusive (AI, all meals and most activities).

WHAT IT COSTS

	¢	$	$$	$$$	$$$$
Restaurants	under $10	$10–$15	$15–$20	$20–$30	over $30
Hotels	under $80	$80–$100	$100–$140	$140–$220	over $220

Restaurant prices are per person for a main course at dinner. Hotel prices are for a standard double room, excluding 6% sales tax (more in some counties) and 1%–4% tourist tax.

Boat Tours

Dolphin Landings Charter Boat Center (✉ *4737 Gulf Blvd., St. Pete Beach* ☎ *727/360-7411* ⊕ *www.dolphinlandings. com*) has daily four-hour cruises to unspoiled Egmont Key at the mouth of Tampa Bay. Aboard the glass-bottom boats of **St. Nicholas Boat Line** (✉ *693 Dodecanese Blvd., Tarpon Springs* ☎ *727/942-6425*) you take a sightseeing cruise of Tarpon Springs' historic sponge docks and see a diver at work. The *Starlite Princess* (✉ *Clearwater Beach Marina, at the end of Rte. 60, Clearwater Beach* ⊕ *www. starlitecruises.com*), an old-fashioned paddle wheeler, and *Starlite Majesty*, a sleek yacht-style vessel, make sightseeing and dinner cruises.

Oil Spill

After an April 20, 2010 explosion, the Deepwater Horizon oil rig leaked huge quantities of oil into the Gulf of Mexico near Louisiana, initally affecting over 50 mi of Louisiana shoreline before spreading to other coastal areas. For updates on the impact on Florida's coast, see Florida's Department of Environmental Protection Web site: ⊕ *www.dep.state.fl.us/ deepwaterhorizon*.

Florida's state tourism board also posts updates and links to local communities at ⊕ *www.visitflorida.com/ florida_travel_advisory*.

15

TAMPA BAY BEACHES

Tampa Bay gets rave reviews for having some of the state's best beaches. The allure includes warm water from spring through fall, gentle waves (when there are any at all), good shelling, and usually smaller crowds than ocean-front beaches. These are great places to go for romantic walks, or enjoy spectacular sunsets.

Tampa Bay–area beaches include Madeira Beach (called Mad Beach by locals), where you can see dolphins at play, and North Redington Beach, once a vacation spot for Marilyn Monroe and Joe DiMaggio. In Sarasota County, beaches range from artsy Siesta Key to the mansion-fronted Casey Key. Farther south, Venice beaches are good for shelling, but they're most known for their wealth of sharks' teeth and fossils, washed up from the ancient shark burial grounds just offshore. To learn more, contact **Tampa Bay Beaches Chamber of Commerce** (⊠ *6990 Gulf Blvd., St. Pete Beach* ☎ *800/944–1847* ⊕ *www.tampabaybeaches.com*) or **Sarasota Convention & Visitors Bureau** (⊠ *701 N. Tamiami Trail (U.S. 41), Sarasota* ☎ *800/800–3906* ⊕ *www.sarasotafl.org*).

WHEN TO GO

Tampa Bay area beaches are very popular but also very crowded in the summer, when families flock here, as well as in the winter, when snowbirds land to escape the cold in their home states. Arguably, the best times to visit are early fall and late spring, when there are fewer people and milder temperatures. But do check on red tide, an occasionally appearing algae that can cause breathing difficulty and itchy eyes; it is most common September to November, but it can happen at any time of year (⊕ *research.myfwc.com*).

TAMPA BAY'S BEST BEACHES

BEACH AT SOUTH LIDO PARK

At the southern tip of Sarasota's island, at 2201 Ben Franklin Drive in Lido Key, South Lido Park has one of the best beaches in the region, but note that there are no lifeguards. The sugar-sand beach offers little for shell collectors, but try your luck at fishing, take a dip in the gulf, or picnic as the sun sets through the Australian pines into the water. Facilities include nature trails, canoe and kayak trails, restrooms, and picnic grounds.

CALADESI ISLAND STATE PARK

The beach at Caladesi, accessible by ferry from Honeymoon Island State Recreation Area, offers three reasons to visit: pure white beaches, beautiful sunsets and, by Florida standards, relative seclusion. Oh, we left out the fact that this is an excellent spot for bird-watching.

CLEARWATER BEACH

You will find crowds on weekends and during spring break, which are a turn-off for some, but this sun-worshippers' shrine off State Road 60 is the west coast's best muscle beach. Expect to see tanned bods draped with minimal bikinis and Speedos, plenty of hot cars, and sunsets nearly as grand as at Caladesi.

PASS-A-GRILLE BEACH

Located where Tampa Bay meets the Gulf of Mexico in southern Pinellas County, this long-popular beach is wide and still dotted with small dunes and sea oats, two throwbacks that are rapidly vanishing in Florida. Pass-a-Grille (also called St. Pete Beach) tends to be crowded on weekends and during summer and spring break.

SIESTA BEACH

This 40-acre park at 948 Beach Road in Siesta Key, Sarasota, has nature trails, a concession stand, fields for soccer and softball, picnic facilities, a playground, restrooms, a fitness trail, and tennis and volleyball courts. This beach has fine, powdery, quartz sand that squeaks under your feet, very much like the sand along the state's northwestern coast. It has been ranked as one of the country's top beaches.

TURTLE BEACH

Only 14 acres, this beach park at 8918 Midnight Pass Road in Siesta Key, Sarasota, is popular with families, and is more secluded than most gulf beaches. It doesn't have the soft sand of Siesta Beach, but it does have boat ramps, a canoe and kayak launch, bay and gulf fishing, picnic facilities, restrooms, and a volleyball court.

15

Updated
by Christina
Tourigny

Planning and preserves have partially shielded pockets of the Tampa Bay Area from the overdevelopment that saturates much of the Atlantic coast. Tampa has Florida's third-busiest airport and a vibrant business community, and is one of the state's largest metro areas. Even so, it is less fast-lane than Miami.

Whether you feel like long walks on white-sand beaches, testing your nerve on thrill rides, or wandering through upscale shopping districts, there's something to your liking in the diverse Bay Area. Bright, modern Tampa is the area's commercial center. It's a full-fledged city, with a modest high-rise skyline and highways jammed with traffic. Across the bay, St. Petersburg's compact downtown has interesting restaurants, shops, and museums on the southeast side of the Pinellas County peninsula. The county's western periphery is rimmed by barrier islands with beaches, quiet parks, and little, laid-back beach towns. To the north, communities such as Tarpon Springs, settled by Greek sponge divers, celebrate their ethnic heritage. To the south lie resort towns, including sophisticated Sarasota, which, like the Pinellas County beaches, fill up in winter with snowbirds escaping the cold.

TAMPA/ST. PETERSBURG AREA

The core of the northern bay comprises the cities of Tampa, St. Petersburg, and Clearwater. A semitropical climate and access to the gulf make Tampa an ideal port for the cruise and freight industries. The waters around Clearwater and St. Petersburg are often filled with pleasure and commercial craft, including boats with day and night trips featuring gambling in international waters.

It's fitting that an area with a thriving international port should also be populated by a wealth of nationalities. The center of the Cuban community is the east Tampa enclave of Ybor City, whereas north of Clearwater, in Dunedin, the heritage is Scottish. North of Dunedin, Tarpon Springs has supported a large Greek population for decades, and is the largest producer of natural sponges in the world. Inland, to the east and north of Tampa, it's all suburban sprawl, freeways, shopping malls, and—the main draw—Busch Gardens.

TAMPA

84 mi southwest of Orlando via I–4.

Tampa, the west coast's business and commercial hub, has a sprinkling of high-rises and heavy traffic. A concentration of restaurants, nightlife, stores, and cultural events is amid the bustle.

GETTING HERE AND AROUND

Downtown Tampa's **Riverwalk**, on Ashley Drive at the Hillsborough River, connects waterside entities such as the Florida Aquarium, the Channelside shopping and entertainment complex, and Marriott Waterside. The landscaped park is 6 acres and extends along the Garrison cruise-ship channel and along the Hillsborough River downtown. The walkway is being expanded as waterside development continues.

ESSENTIALS

Visitor Information Tampa Bay & Company (⌂ *401 E. Jackson St., Suite 2100, Tampa* ☎ *800/368–2672 or 813/223–1111* ⊕ *www.visittampabay.com*). **Ybor City Chamber Visitor Bureau** (⌂ *1600 E. 8th Ave., Suite B104, Tampa* ☎ *813/241–8838* ⊕ *www.ybor.org*).

EXPLORING

TOP ATTRACTIONS

Numbers in the margin correspond to the Downtown Tampa map.

❶ **Florida Aquarium.** Although eels, sharks, and stingrays are the headliners, the Florida Aquarium is much more than a giant fishbowl. This architectural landmark features an 83-foot-high, multitier, glass dome, 250,000 square feet of air-conditioned exhibit space, and more than 20,000 aquatic plants and animals representing species native to Florida and the rest of the world. Floor-to-ceiling interactive displays, behind-the-scenes tours, and in-water adventures allow kids to really get hands-on—and even get their feet wet. Adventurous types (certified divers age 15 and up) can dive with mild-mannered sharks and sea turtles, participate in shark-feeding programs (age 12 and up), or shallow-water swim with reef fish such as eels and grouper (age six and up). However, you don't have to get wet to have an interactive experience: boasting the most high-tech aquarium gallery in the country, the Ocean Commotion exhibit offers virtual dolphins and whales, multimedia displays and presentations, and even allows kids to upload video to become a part of the exhibit. The Coral Reef Gallery is a 500,000-gallon tank with viewing windows, an awesome 43-foot-wide panoramic opening, and a walk-through tunnel that gives the illusion of venturing into underwater depths. There you see a thicket of elkhorn coral teeming with tropical fish and a dark cave reveals sea life you would normally see only on night dives. If you have two hours, try *Bay Spirit*'s Wild Dolphin Ecotour, which takes up to 130 passengers onto Tampa's bay in a 72-foot catamaran for an up-close look at bottlenose dolphins and other wildlife. The outdoor Explore a Shore exhibit, which gives

15

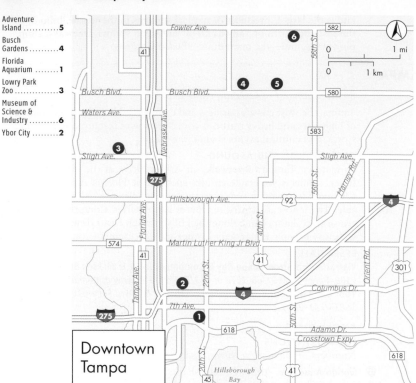

Downtown
Tampa

younger kids a chance to release some energy, is an aquatic playground
with a waterslide, water-jet sprays, and a climbable replica pirate ship.
Last but not least, two black-footed African penguins make twice daily
appearances in the aquarium lobby. ⊠ *701 Channelside Dr., Downtown, Tampa* ☎ *813/273–4000* ⊕ *www.flaquarium.org* ⊠ *Aquarium
$19.95, Ecotour $21.95; Aquarium/Ecotour combo $35.95; parking
$6* ☉ *Daily 9:30–5.*

❷ **Ybor City.** Tampa's lively Latin quarter is one of only four National
Fodor'sChoice Historic Landmark districts in Florida. It has antique-brick streets and
★ wrought-iron balconies. Cubans brought their cigar-making industry to
Ybor (pronounced *ee*-bore) City in 1886, and the smell of cigars—hand-
rolled by Cuban immigrants—still wafts through the heart of this east
Tampa area, along with the strong aroma of roasting coffee. These days
the neighborhood is one of Tampa's hot spots, if at times a rowdy one,
as empty cigar factories and historic social clubs have been transformed
into trendy boutiques, art galleries, restaurants, and nightclubs.

Step back into the past at **Centennial Park** (⊠ *8th Ave. and 18th St.*),
which re-creates a period streetscape and hosts the Fresh Market every
Saturday. The **Ybor City Museum State Park** provides a look at the history of the cigar industry. Admission includes a tour of La Casita, one of
the shotgun houses occupied by cigar workers and their families in the

late 1890s. ✉ *1818 E. 9th Ave., between Nuccio Pkwy. and 22nd St., from 7th to 9th Ave., Tampa* ☎ *813/247-6323* ⊕ *www.ybormuseum. org* ⌨ *$4, walking tours $6* ⊙ *Daily 9–5; walking tours Sat. 10:30.*

3 **Lowry Park Zoo.** Natural-habitat exhibits such as the white tiger cubs and clouded leopards in Asia Gardens make the 56-acre Lowry Park Zoo one of the best small-scale animal parks in the country. Safari Africa is the home of Tamani, an elephant born in 2005, and residents of the nearby Ituri Forest include cheetahs and lovably plump pygmy hippos. The stars at Primate World range from cat-size red-ruffed lemurs to a colony of heavyweight Bornean orangutans that love to ham for the camera. For hands-on experiences, Lowry has more options than most large parks, including chances to ride a camel, feed a giraffe, or serve as a perch for energetic lorikeets. Majestic red-tailed hawks and other raptors are displayed in the Birds of Prey Center, and you can come face-to-face with American alligators, Florida panthers, black bears, and red wolves at the Florida Wildlife Center. Kookaburras and kangaroos populate the Wallaroo Station children's zoo, and gentle creatures of another kind star at the Manatee Aquatic Center. Speaking of manatees, they are among the occasional sights on the hour-long Hillsborough River Odyssey Ecotour, where you also may spot wild hawks and herons. There are also water-play areas, rides, shows, and restaurants. ✉ *1101 W. Sligh Ave., Central Tampa* ☎ *813/935–8552* ⊕ *www.lowryparkzoo.com* ⌨ *$20.95* ⊙ *Daily 9:30–5.*

4 **Busch Gardens.** *See the highlighted listing in this chapter.*

Fodor's Choice

WORTH NOTING

5 From spring until fall, rides named Tampa Typhoon, Gulf Scream, and Key West Rapids promise heat relief at **Adventure Island**, a corporate cousin and neighbor of Busch Gardens. Tampa's most popular "wet" park features waterslides and artificial wave pools in a 30-acre package. One of the attraction's headliners, Riptide, challenges you to race three other riders on a sliding mat through twisting tubes and hairpin turns. Planners of this park also took the younger kids into account, with offerings such as Fabian's Funport, which has a scaled-down wave pool and interactive water gym. Along with a volleyball complex and a surf pool, there are cafés, snack bars, picnic and sunbathing areas, changing rooms, and, the newest addition, private cabanas. ✉ *1001 Malcolm McKinley Dr., less than 1 mi north of Busch Gardens, Central Tampa* ☎ *813/987- 5660 or 888/800–5447* ⊕ *www.adventureisland. com* ⌨ *$44.95; parking $10* ⊙ *Mid-Mar.–late Oct., daily 10–5.*

6 The **Museum of Science & Industry** is a fun and stimulating scientific playground, though at times some exhibits aren't working properly. When it's hitting on all cylinders, you learn about Florida weather, anatomy, flight, and space by seeing *and* by doing. At the Gulf Coast Hurricane Exhibit you can experience what a hurricane and its 74-mph winds feel like, though crowds sometimes mean a long wait. The BioWorks Butterfly Garden is a 6,400-square-foot engineered ecosystem project that demonstrates how wetlands can clean water plus serve as a home for butterflies. The 100-seat Saunders Planetarium—Tampa's

15

BUSCH GARDENS
ENTER AFRICA

Busch Gardens was opened in Tampa on March 31, 1959, by the Anheuser-Busch company. It was originally designed as an admission-free animal attraction to accompany the plant, but it eventually was turned into a theme park, adding more exotic animals, tropical landscaping, and rides to entertain its guests.

Today the 335-acre park has nine distinct territories packed with roller coasters, rides, eateries, shops, and live entertainment. The park is best known for its incredible roller coasters and water rides, which draw thrill-seekers from around the globe. These rides tend to cater to guests over the age of 10. With this in mind, Busch Gardens created the **Sesame Street Safari of Fun,** which is designed solely with children under 5 in mind. There's a lot packed into this area: junior thrill rides, play areas (some with water), and shows—all of which make it exciting for the kids.

GETTING ORIENTED

The park is set up on a north–south axis with Nairobi being the center of the surrounding areas.

Your first encounter at the park is the Moroccan market (grab a map here). There are several small eateries and souvenir shops in this area. If you head west from Morocco you'll get to the Bird Gardens, Sesame Street Safari of Fun, Stanleyville, and Jungala. Heading north you'll find Nairobi, Timbuktu, and the Congo. Heading east takes you to Egypt and the Serengeti Plain. If you get lost, there are team members available almost everywhere to help you.

TOP ATTRACTIONS

FOR AGES 7 AND UP

SheiKra. The newest roller coaster is 200 feet tall and has a 200-foot vertical descent, and isn't for the faint of heart.

Montu. This 150-foot tall inverted coaster reaches speeds of 60 mph, and has a zero-G roll and seven inversions.

Gwazi. The largest, fastest wooden dueling roller coaster in the world, boasting crossing speeds of 100 mph.

Kumba. Riders on this coaster experience weightlessness, cobra rolls, corkscrews, and inverted rolls.

Wild Surge. You're shot out of a mountain crater up a 40-foot structure and then bounced up and down, creating a freefall experience.

Rhino Rally. A Land Rover takes passengers on an off-road safari with up-close animal encounters and a raging river adventure. Sometimes the river adventure isn't working.

Cheetah Chase. It's a pint-size roller coaster with twists and turns throughout.

FOR AGES 6 AND UNDER

Air Grover. Take a ride on Grover's plane and soar through the Sahara on this junior coaster.

Rosita's Djembe Fly-Away. Rosita takes you on a swing ride that sends you above the African canopy.

Oscar's Swamp Stomp. Get wet stomping and splashing your way through this cool water area.

Bert and Ernie's Watering Hole. It's a water adventure filled with bubblers, geysers, jets, dumping buckets, and more.

Zoe-Petra & the Hippos of the Nile. A kid-size flume ride with Zoe's hippo friends that gives children a river glimpse of Africa.

VISITING TIPS

■ The park is least crowded during the week, with weekends bringing in a lot of locals. Summer and the holidays also are crowded.

■ Ride the thrill rides as early as possible. Think about purchasing a Quick Queue pass for $14.95, which grants you no-wait access. It's only good once per ride, but insures you will hit all the big rides quickly.

■ Bring extra quarters for all the locker rentals at each of the coasters.

■ You can pick up a map at the entrance, which lists show times, meet-the-keeper times, and special hours for attractions and restaurants.

■ Vegetarians will enjoy **Zagora Café** veggie burgers or **The Colony House's** delicious vegetable platter. Your best food bet's the All Day Dining Deal, $29.95 per adult and $13.95 per child. It's accepted at most dining venues. If eating at the Colony House, you'll want to make your reservations immediately upon entering the park.

15

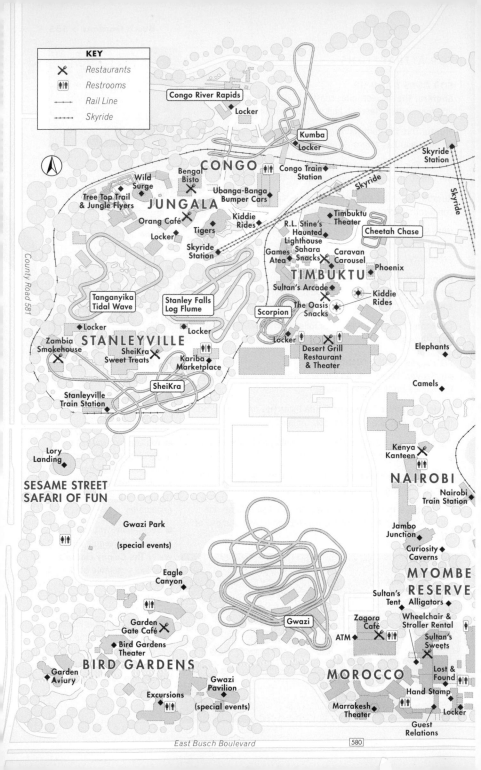

KEY

✕ Restaurants
🚹🚺 Restrooms
�┼┼ Rail Line
•••• Skyride

Congo River Rapids
Locker

Kumba
Locker

CONGO

Congo Train Station

Skyride

Skyride Station

Skyride

Wild Surge

Bengal Bisto

Ubanga-Banga Bumper Cars

Tree Top Trail & Jungle Flyers

JUNGALA

Orang Café

Kiddie Rides

Timbuktu Theater

R.L. Stine's Haunted Lighthouse

Cheetah Chase

Tigers

Locker

Skyride Station

Games Atea

Sahara Snacks

Caravan Carousel

Phoenix

TIMBUKTU

Sultan's Arcade

Kiddie Rides

Tanganyika Tidal Wave

Stanley Falls Log Flume

Scorpion

The Oasis Snacks

Elephants

Locker

Locker

Locker

Desert Grill Restaurant & Theater

Zambia Smokehouse

STANLEYVILLE

SheiKra Sweet Treats

Kariba Marketplace

Camels

SheiKra

Stanleyville Train Station

Kenya Kanteen

NAIROBI

Lory Landing

Nairobi Train Station

SESAME STREET SAFARI OF FUN

Gwazi Park

(special events)

Jambo Junction

Curiosity Caverns

MYOMBE RESERVE

Eagle Canyon

Garden Gate Café

Bird Gardens Theater

Gwazi

Sultan's Tent

Alligators

Zagora Café

Wheelchair & Stroller Rental

ATM

Sultan's Sweets

Garden Aviary

BIRD GARDENS

Excursions

Gwazi Pavilion

(special events)

MOROCCO

Lost & Found

Hand Stamp

Marrakesh Theater

Guest Relations

Locker

County Road 581

East Busch Boulevard

580

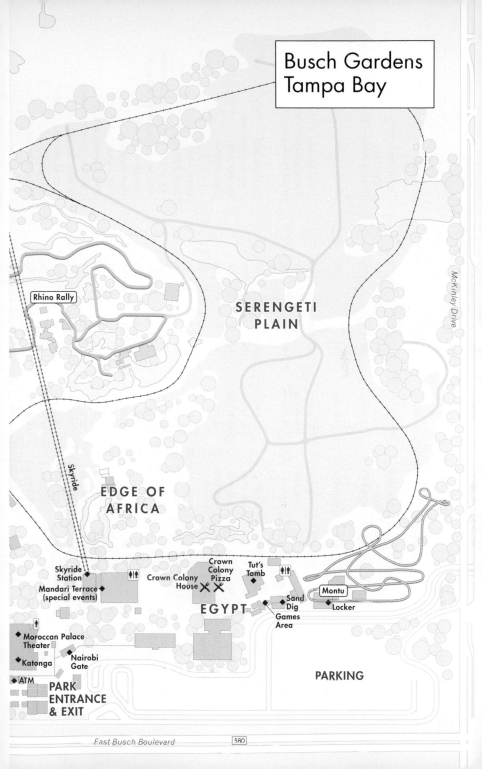

BUSCH GARDENS

Name	Min. Height	Type of Entertainment	Duration	Suits	Crowds	Strategy
Egypt						
Montu	54"	thrill ride	3 min.	14 & up	Yes!	Go here first
Skyride	n/a	ride	5 min.	All	Yes	Can get busy
Tut's Tomb	n/a	walk thru	10 min.	All	OK	Go after Montu
Morocco						
Edge of Africa	n/a	walk thru	up to you	All	OK	Go after lunch
GWAZI	48"	thrill ride	2.5 min.	10 & up	Yes!	Expect to wait
Myombe Reserve	n/a	walk thru	up to you	All	OK	Before noon photo op
Rock-A-Doo-Wop	n/a	show	20 min.	All	Yes	Arrive 15 min early
Bird Gardens						
Critter Castaway	n/a	show	25 min.	All	Yes	Do after Gwazi
Lory Landing	n/a	walk thru	up to you	All	OK	Bring money to feed
Garden Aviary	n/a	walk thru	up to you	All	OK	Go after lunch
Backyard Wildlife Habitat	n/a	walk thru	up to you	All	Yes	Good anytime
Sesame Street Safari of Fun						
Air Grover	n/a	junior thrill ride	2 min.	Under 6	Yes!	Expect a wait
Zoe-Petra & the Hippos of the Nile	n/a	junior thrill ride	3 min.	Under 6	Yes	Good cool off spot
Elmo's Treehouse Trek	n/a	play area	up to you	Under 6	OK	May be hard to keep track of toddlers.
Rosita's Djembe Fly-Away	n/a	junior thrill ride	2 min.	Under 6	Yes	Older toddlers may enjoy this more.
The Count's Zambezi Rally	n/a	Ride	up to you	Under 6	Yes	Go early in the day.
Elmo's Safari Go-Round	n/a	Ride	3 min.	Under 6	Yes	Good anytime
Oscar's Swamp Stomp	n/a	play area	up to you	All	OK	Bring a towel
Bert and Ernie's Watering Hole	n/a	play area	up to you	All	OK	Bring a bathing suit
Slimey's Sawara Sand	n/a	play area	up to you	All	OK	Chance for parents to relax
Big Bird's Whirly Birdy	n/a	ride	3 min.	Under 6	OK	Excellent for toddlers
Cookie Morster's Canopy Crawl	n/a	play area	up to you	Under 6	OK	Good for energetic children
Telly's Jungle Jam	n/a	play area	up to you	All	OK	Slow paced area
Big Bird's 123-Smile With Me	n/a	walk thru	up to you	All	Yes	Photo/autograph op

Stanlyeville

Ride	Height	Type	Duration	Age	Priority	Notes
SheiKra	54"	thrill ride	2.5 min.	14 & up	Yes!	Use the lockers
Stanley Falls Flume	46"	thrill ride	3 min.	10 & up	Yes	Lengthy lines
Tanganyika Tidal Wave	48"	thrill ride	2 min.	10 & up	Yes	Bring a change of clothes or poncho

Jungala

Ride	Height	Type	Duration	Age	Priority	Notes
Jungle Flyers	48"	junior thrill ride	3 min.	6 to 13	Yes	Skip for other rides
Wild Surge	38"	thrill ride	2 min.	5 & up	Yes!	
Tree Top Trails	n/a	walk thru	up to you	All	Yes	Gets crowded
Tiger Lodge	n/a	walk thru	up to you	All	Yes	Close-up views
Orangutan Overlook	n/a	walk thru	up to you	All	Yes	Morning photo op
Jungala Stiltwalkers	n/a	show	15 min.	All	ok	Very entertaining

Congo

Ride	Height	Type	Duration	Age	Priority	Notes
Congo River Rapids	42"	thrill ride	6 min.	10 & up	Yes!	Bring extra clothes or poncho
Kumba	54"	thrill ride	3 min.	14 & up	Yes!	Go early or before closing
Ubanga-Banga Bumper Cars	42"	ride	2 min.	8 & up	yes	Long wait times

Timbuktu

Ride	Height	Type	Duration	Age	Priority	Notes
Carousel Caravan	n/a	ride	3 min.	All	ok	Slow paced ride
Cheetah Chase	46"	junior thrill ride	2 min.	All	yes	Very popular
Pirate 4-D Movie	n/a	show	15 min.	All	ok	Arrive 15 min early
Phoenix	48"	thrill ride	2 min.	12 & up	yes	Go after Scorpion
Scorpion	42"	thrill ride	2 min.	14 & up	yes	Go during Dance to the Music show
Dance to the Music	n/a	Seasonal show	20 min.	All	yes	Arrive 15 min. before show
Lights, Camera, Action!	n/a	show		All	yes	Good break from the sun

Nairobi

Ride	Height	Type	Duration	Age	Priority	Notes
Rhino Rally	39"	vehicle ride	10 min.	10 & up	yes	This ride is rough and can get wet and often breaks down.
Serengeti Express	n/a	vehicle ride	12-35 min.	All	no	Great way to relax and see the park
Curiosity Caverns	n/a	walk thru	up to you	All	no	Good to get out of the sun.
Elephant Habitat	n/a	walk thru	up to you	All	ok	Go during Meet the Keeper
Rhino Habitat	n/a	walk thru	up to you	All	yes	Earlier the better
Edge of Africa	n/a	walk thru	up to you	All	ok	Great break from the crowds

DID YOU KNOW?

One of six roller coasters at Busch Gardens, the steel, 60-foot-tall Scorpion twists and turns at speeds near 50 mph and then throws you into a 360-degree vertical loop. During the 1½-minute ride you'll experience a 3.5 G-force.

only planetarium—has afternoon and evening shows, one of them a trek through the universe. For adventurous spirits, there's a high-wire bicycle ride 30 feet above the floor. There's also an impressive IMAX theater, where films are projected on a hemispherical 82-foot dome. ✉ *4801 E. Fowler Ave., 1 mi north of Busch Gardens, Northeast Tampa* ☎ *813/987–6100 or 800/995–6674* ⊕ *www.mosi.org* ✉ *$23.95* ⊙ *Weekdays 9–5, weekends 9–6.*

SPORTS AND THE OUTDOORS

BASEBALL

Locals and tourists flock each March to see the **New York Yankees** (✉ *George M. Steinbrenner Field, 1 Steinbrenner Dr., near corner of Dale Mabry Hwy. and Martin Luther King Jr. Blvd., off I–275 Exit 41B, Central Tampa* ☎ *813/879–2244 or 813/875–7753*) play about 17 spring-training games at 11,000-seat Steinbrenner Field. Call for tickets. From April through September, the stadium belongs to a Yankee farm team, the **Tampa Yankees,** who play 70 games against the likes of the Daytona Cubs and the Sarasota Red Sox.

FOOTBALL

Seeing the National Football League's **Tampa Bay Buccaneers** (✉ *Raymond James Stadium, 4201 N. Dale Mabry Hwy., Central Tampa* ☎ *813/879–2827* ⊕ *www.buccaneers.com*) play isn't easy without connections, since the entire stadium is booked by season-ticket holders years in advance. But tickets can be found in the classifieds of newspapers such as the *Tampa Tribune* and *St. Petersburg Times.* The Arena Football League **Tampa Bay Storm** (✉ *St. Pete Times Forum, 401 Channelside Dr., Downtown* ☎ *813/301–6900* ⊕ *www.tampabaystorm.com*) plays about 16 games in its March–June season. The Storm has a hot rivalry with the Orlando Predators.

GOLF

Babe Zaharias Golf Course (✉ *11412 Forest Hills Dr., Northeast Tampa* ☎ *813/631–4374*) is a challenging par-70, 18-hole public course with water hazards on eight holes; greens fees $26/$48. A pro is on hand to give lessons. **Bloomingdale Golfers Club** (✉ *4113 Great Golfers Pl., Southeast Tampa* ☎ *813/685–4105*) is an 18-hole, par-72 course with a two-tiered driving range, a 1-acre putting green, and a restaurant; greens fees $30/$80. **The Claw at USF** (✉ *13801 N. 46th St., North Tampa* ☎ *813/632–6893*) is named for its many dog-legged fairways. The 18-hole, par-71 course is on a preserve with moss-draped oaks and towering pines; greens fees $20/$45. **The Club at Eaglebrooke** (✉ *1300 Eaglebrooke Blvd., Lakeland* ☎ *863/701–0101*) is a par-72, 18-hole course about 30 mi east of Tampa; greens fees $55/$65. The public 18-hole 71-par course at **Tournament Players Club of Tampa Bay** (✉ *5300 W. Lutz Lake Fern Rd., Lutz* ☎ *813/949–0090*), 15 mi north of Tampa, was designed by Bobby Weed and Chi Chi Rodriguez; greens fees $99/$109. About 10 mi north of Tampa International Airport, **Westchase Golf Club** (✉ *11602 Westchase Golf Dr., Tampa* ☎ *813/854–2331*) has a wooded 72-par, 18-hole course with bridges and bulkheads; greens fees $49/$59. Golfers rotate from the back nine holes to the front nine.

15

SHOPPING
MALLS
Ybor City's destination within a destination is the dining and entertainment palace **Centro Ybor** (⌧ *1600 E. 8th Ave., Ybor City*). It has shops, trendy bars and restaurants, a 20-screen movie theater, and GameWorks, an interactive playground developed by Steven Spielberg. **Channelside** (⌧ *615 Channelside Dr., Downtown*) offers movie theaters, shops, restaurants, and clubs. The official Tampa Bay visitor center is also here. If you want to grab something at Neiman Marcus or Nordstrom on your way to the airport, the upscale **International Plaza** (⌧ *2223 N. West Shore Blvd., Airport Area*) has Betsey Johnson, J.Crew, L'Occitane, Louis Vuitton, Tiffany & Co., and many other shops. **Old Hyde Park Village** (⌧ *Swan Ave. near Bayshore Blvd., Hyde Park*) is a typical shopping district, just like the ones you find in every major American city. Williams-Sonoma and Brooks Brothers are mixed in with bistros and sidewalk cafés.

SPECIALTY SHOPS
For the mildly unusual to the downright bizarre, stop at **Squaresville** (⌧ *508 S. Howard Ave., near Downtown* ☎ *813/259–9944*), which stocks everything from Cuban clothing to Elvis posters to Bettie Page clocks. If you are shopping for hand-rolled cigars, head to Ybor City, where a few hand-rollers practice their craft in small shops. One of the more popular stops is the **King Corona Cigar Factory** (⌧ *1523 E. 7th Ave., Ybor City* ☎ *888/248–3812*).

NIGHTLIFE AND THE ARTS
NIGHTLIFE
Although there are more boarded storefronts than in the past, the biggest concentration of nightclubs, as well as the widest variety, is found along 7th Avenue in Ybor City. It becomes a little like Bourbon Street in New Orleans on weekend evenings. **Centro Cantina** (⌧ *1600 E. 8th Ave., Ybor City* ☎ *813/241–8588*) has a balcony overlooking the crowds on 7th Avenue. There's live music Thursday through Sunday nights, a large selection of margaritas, and more than 30 brands of tequila. Food is served until 2 AM.

At International Plaza, **Blue Martini Lounge** (⌧ *2323 N. West Shore Blvd., West Tampa* ☎ *813/873–2583*) has live entertainment nightly, except Monday, and a menu of killer martinis. International Plaza's **Bay Street** (⌧ *2223 N. West Shore Blvd., Airport Area*) has become one of Tampa's dining and imbibing hot spots. Considered something of a dive—but a lovable one—by a loyal and young local following that ranges from esteemed jurists to nose-ring-wearing night owls, the **Hub** (⌧ *719 N. Franklin St., Downtown* ☎ *813/229–1553*) is known for having one of Tampa's best martinis and one of its most eclectic jukeboxes.

Skippers Smokehouse (⌧ *910 Skipper Rd., Northeast Tampa* ☎ *813/971–0666* ⊕ *www.skipperssmokehouse.com*), a junkyard-style restaurant and oyster bar, has live reggae on Wednesday, rock on Thursday, and great smoked fish every night.

THE ARTS

On the Hillsborough River, the 345,000-square-foot **Tampa Bay Performing Arts Center** (⊠ *1010 W. C. MacInnes Pl., Downtown* ☎ *813/229–7827* ⊕ *www.tbpac.org*) is the largest such complex south of the Kennedy Center in Washington, D.C. Among the facilities are the 2,500-seat Carol Morsani Hall, a 1,047-seat playhouse, the 200-seat Teco Theater, a 300-seat cabaret theater, and a 120-seat black-box theater. Opera, concerts, drama, and ballet performances are presented here. In a restored 1926 movie palace, the **Tampa Theatre** (⊠ *711 N. Franklin St., Downtown* ☎ *813/274–8982* ⊕ *www.tampatheatre.org*) hosts films, concerts, and special events.

WHERE TO EAT

$$$$
STEAK
Fodor'sChoice
★

✕ **Bern's Steak House.** With the air of an exclusive club, this is one of Florida's finest steak houses. Rich mahogany paneling and ornate chandeliers define the legendary Bern's, where the chef ages his own beef, grows his own organic vegetables, roasts his own coffee, and maintains his own saltwater fish tanks. There's also a Cave Du Fromage, housing a selection of artisanal cheeses from around the world. Cuts of topmost beef are sold by weight and thickness. There's a 60-ounce strip steak that's big enough to feed your pride (of lions), but for most appetites the veal loin chop or 8-ounce chateaubriand is more than enough. The wine list includes approximately 7,000 selections (with 1,000 dessert wines). After dinner, tour the kitchen and wine cellar before having dessert upstairs in a cozy booth. The dessert room is a hit. For a real jolt, try the Turkish coffee with an order of Mississippi mud pie. Casual business attire is recommended. ⊠ *1208 S. Howard Ave., Hyde Park* ☎ *813/251–2421* ⊕ *www.bernssteakhouse.com* ⚶ *Reservations essential* ▤ *AE, D, MC, V.*

$$
ECLECTIC

✕ **Café Dufrain.** Dogs can tag along if you dine on the patio at pet-friendly Café Dufrain, a riverside eatery popular with an upscale crowd. Fido gets a little treat from the staff, while diners get a treat from the chef with the pan-seared sea bass served with polenta and wilted arugula or Dufrain's cioppino—a delightful dish with sea bass, lobster, shrimp, and spicy sausage. Seal the deal with the mango cheesecake. In mild weather, opt for the waterfront view of downtown Tampa. ⊠ *707 Harbour Post Dr., Downtown* ☎ *813/275–9701* ⊕ *www.cafedufrain. com* ▤ *AE, D, MC, V.*

$$
SPANISH
Fodor'sChoice
★

✕ **Columbia.** Make a date for some of the best Latin cuisine in Tampa. A fixture since 1905, this magnificent structure with an Old World air, spacious dining rooms, and a sunny courtyard takes up an entire city block, and seems to feed the entire city—locals as well as travelers—throughout the week, but especially on weekends. The paella, bursting with seafood, chicken, and pork, is arguably the best in Florida, and the 1905 salad—with ham, olives, cheese, and garlic—is legendary. The menu has Cuban classics such as *boliche criollo* (tender eye of round stuffed with chorizo sausage), *ropa vieja* (shredded beef with onions, peppers, and tomatoes), and *arroz con pollo* (chicken with yellow rice). Don't miss the flamenco dancing show every night but Sunday. ⊠ *2117 E. 7th Ave., Ybor City* ☎ *813/248–4961* ⊕ *www.columbiarestaurant. com* ▤ *AE, D, DC, MC, V.*

15

$ ✕ **Estela's.** Despite its nondescript storefront, Estela's is a favorite among
MEXICAN those who enjoy authentic Central American cuisine and Mexico's best
★ beers. Expect the usual entrées (enchiladas, fajitas, and chiles rellenos)
mixed with delightful starters (chicken soup with avocado slices) and a
palate-pleasing rib-eye steak with rice, beans, and guacamole. Warning:
the place gets very crowded for weekday lunches. ⊠ *209 E. Davis Blvd.,
Downtown* ☎ *813/251–0558* ⊕ *www.estelas.com* ▭ *MC, V.*

$ ✕ **Kojak's House of Ribs.** Few barbecue joints can boast the staying power
SOUTHERN of this family-owned and -operated pit stop, which had its debut in
1978. In the last three decades it has earned a following of sticky-
fingered regulars who have turned it into one of the most popular barbecue stops in Central Florida. It could pass for a century-old Cracker
house complete with veranda, pillars supporting the overhanging roof,
and brick steps. Day and night, three indoor dining rooms and an outdoor dining porch have a steady stream of hungry patrons digging into
tender pork spareribs that are dry-rubbed and tanned overnight before
visiting the smoker for a couple of hours. Then they're bathed in the
sauce of your choice. Kojak's also has a nice selection of sandwiches,
including sloppy chicken and country-style sausage. ⊠ *2808 Gandy
Blvd., South Tampa* ☎ *813/837–3774* ⊕ *www.kojaksbbq.com* ▭ *AE,
D, MC, V* ☾ *Closed Mon.*

¢ ✕ **Mel's Hot Dogs.** Talk about a tubular experience. Visitors as well as
AMERICAN passersby usually are greeted by a red wiener-mobile (you have to see
it to believe it), parked on the north side of the highway near Busch
Gardens. Those lucky enough to venture inside find walls dotted with
photos from fans and a hot-diggity menu that's heaven for tube-steak
fans. You can order a traditional dog, but try something with a little
more pizzazz, such as a bacon-cheddar Reuben-style bow-wow on a
poppy-seed bun, or the Mighty Mel, a quarter-pounder decked out with
relish, mustard, and pickles. To avoid lunch crowds, arrive before 11:30
or after 1:30. ⊠ *4136 E. Busch Blvd., Central Tampa* ☎ *813/985–8000*
⊕ *www.melshotdogs.com* ▭ *No credit cards* ☾ *Closed Sun.*

¢ ✕ **Papito's Cuban Café & Bar.** It's one of the best budget eateries in Tampa,
CUBAN and while the cafeteria-style line can be a bit slow, the tasty home
★ cooking—roast pork, chicken and yellow rice, and more—is worth
waiting for. If you prefer something a little more casual, just inside the
front door you can order a pressed Cuban sandwich. Dine in with the
locals or take out. ⊠ *5305 Ehrlich Rd., North Tampa* ☎ *813/849–7675*
▭ *MC, V.*

$$$ ✕ **Roy's.** Chef Roy Yamaguchi's Pan-Asian restaurant has fresh ingre-
ASIAN dients flown in every day from around the Pacific. Some menu choices
change daily, so call ahead if you don't want to be surprised. Regular
dishes include roasted macadamia-nut-crusted mahimahi with lobster
sauce and blackened ahi tuna with spicy soy-mustard sauce. Can't
decide? Try the prix-fixe menu, usually around $35 for three courses.
For dessert, choices include chocolate soufflé and fruit cobbler. ⊠ *4342
Boy Scout Blvd., Airport Area* ☎ *813/873–7697* ⊕ *www.roysrestaurant.
com* ▭ *AE, D, DC, MC, V.*

$$ ✕ **Stumps Supper Club.** The menu is as lively as the entertainment at one
SOUTHERN of Tampa's more popular restaurant-nightclub combos. Southern vittles

are the house specialty—they're reminiscent of Sunday dinner at one of our aunts' houses. The Brunswick stew (chicken mingling with butter beans and veggies in tomato broth) is close to perfection. The meat loaf comes under creamy ham gravy, and the obligatory country-fried steak does not disappoint. Sides include corn bread, cheese grits, black-eyed peas, and collard greens. Decorated in flea-market chic, Stumps takes food quite seriously. Friday and Saturday nights after 9 you'll bump into Jimmy James & the Velvet Explosion, a six-piece band that relives Elvis, ABBA, Motown, and KC & the Sunshine Band. ⊠ *615 Channelside Dr., Downtown* ☎ *813/226–2261* ⊕ *www.stumpssupperclub.com* ▭ *AE, D, DC, MC, V* ☺ *No lunch weekdays.*

WHERE TO STAY

$$$
★
☷ **Don Vicente de Ybor Historic Inn.** Built as a home in 1895 by town founder Don Vicente de Ybor, this inn shows that the working-class cigar city had an elegant side, too. From the beige-stucco exterior to the white-marble staircase in the main lobby, this boutique hotel is an architectural tour de force. Rooms have parquet floors, canopy beds, and private baths; most have wrought-iron balconies. Common areas have crystal chandeliers, Tiffany lamps, and Persian carpets. **Pros:** elegant rooms; rich in history; walking distance to nightlife. **Cons:** rowdy neighborhood on weekend nights. ⊠ *1915 Republica de Cuba, Ybor City* ☎ *813/241–4545 or 866/206–4545* ⊕ *donvicenteinn.com* ↩ *13 rooms, 3 suites* ♿ *In-room: Internet, Wi-Fi. In-hotel: restaurant, bar, laundry service, Wi-Fi hotspot* ▭ *AE, D, DC, MC, V* ˢ⧄ *BP.*

$$–$$$
★
☷ **Hilton Garden Inn Tampa Ybor Historic District.** Although its modern architecture makes it seem out of place in this historic district, this chain hotel's location across from Centro Ybor is a plus. There is an on-site restaurant that serves breakfast, but be sure to take at least one day off to visit one of the nearby eateries for a traditional breakfast of *café cubano* or *café con leche* with a wedge of Cuban bread slathered with butter. **Pros:** good location for business travelers; reasonable rates. **Cons:** chain-hotel feel; far from downtown. ⊠ *1700 E. 9th Ave., Ybor City* ☎ *813/769–9267* ⊕ *www.hiltongardeninn.com* ↩ *93 rooms, 2 suites* ♿ *In-room: refrigerator, Internet, Wi-Fi. In-hotel: restaurant, pool, laundry facilities, laundry service, Wi-Fi hotspot* ▭ *AE, D, DC, MC, V.*

$$$–$$$$
★
☷ **Saddlebrook Resort Tampa.** If you can't get enough golf and tennis, here's your fix. Saddlebrook is one of west Florida's top resorts, largely because it has so many things in one spot—36 holes of championship golf; the Arnold Palmer Golf Academy; 45 clay, grass, and artificial-surface tennis courts; a Harry Hopman tennis program; a full-service spa; a fitness center; and a kids' club. Varied accommodations include one- and two-bedroom suites, making it a good choice for families. **Pros:** away from urban sprawl; great choice for the fitness minded. **Cons:** a bit isolated. ⊠ *5700 Saddlebrook Way, Wesley Chapel* ☎ *813/973–1111 or 800/729–8383* ⊕ *www.saddlebrookresort.com* ↩ *540 rooms, 407 suites* ♿ *In-room: safe, kitchen (some), Internet, Wi-Fi. In-hotel: 4 restaurants, room service, bars, golf courses, tennis courts, pools, gym, spa, bicycles, children's programs (ages 4–12), laundry service, Wi-Fi hotspot* ▭ *AE, D, DC, MC, V* ˢ⧄ *MAP.*

15

$$$–$$$$ 📺 **Tampa Marriott Waterside Hotel & Marina.** Across from the Tampa Convention Center, this downtown hotel was built for conventioneers but is also convenient to tourist spots such as the Florida Aquarium and the Channelside and Hyde Park shopping districts. At least half the rooms and most of the suites overlook the concrete-walled channel to Tampa Bay, which has sparse boat traffic except on weekends; the bay itself is visible from the higher floors of the 27-story tower. The pillared lobby has real palm trees growing out of the gleaming tile floors, and the coffee bar overlooks the water. Il Terrazzo is the hotel's formal dining room. **Pros:** great downtown location; near shopping. **Cons:** gridlock during rush hour; area sketchy after dark; chain-hotel feel. ✉ *700 S. Florida Ave., Downtown* 📞 *888/268–1616* ⊕ *www.marriott. com* ☛ *681 rooms, 36 suites* ♿ *In-room: safe, kitchen (some), Internet, Wi-Fi. In-hotel: 3 restaurants, room service, bars, pool, gym, spa, laundry facilities, laundry service, Wi-Fi hotspot, parking (paid)* ⊟ *AE, D, DC, MC, V.*

$$$–$$$$ 📺 **Westin Tampa Harbour Island.** Few folks think of the islands when visiting Tampa, but this 12-story hotel on a 177-acre man-made islet is a short drive from downtown Tampa. The rooms are decorated in whites and bright colors, and many have terrific views of the water or the downtown skyline. Service is attentive. There's a marina and a new fitness center with free weights and the latest exercise equipment. **Pros:** close to downtown; nice views; on the TECO streetcar line. **Cons:** a bit far from the action; chain-hotel feel. ✉ *725 S. Harbour Island Blvd., Harbour Island* 📞 *813/229–5000* ⊕ *www.starwoodhotels.com/westin* ☛ *299 rooms, 19 suites* ♿ *In-room: safe, refrigerator (some), Internet, Wi-Fi. In-hotel: restaurant, room service, bar, pool, laundry service, Wi-Fi hotspot, parking (paid), some pets allowed* ⊟ *AE, DC, MC, V.*

ST. PETERSBURG

21 mi west of Tampa.

St. Petersburg and the Pinellas coast form the thumb of the hand that juts out of Florida's west coast and grasps Tampa Bay. There are two distinct parts of St. Petersburg: the at-times-snobbish downtown and cultural area, centered on the bay; and the more laid-back but pricey beach area, a string of barrier islands that faces the gulf and includes St. Pete Beach, Treasure Island, and Madeira Beach. Causeways link beach communities to the mainland peninsula.

GETTING HERE AND AROUND

U.S. 19 is St. Petersburg's major north–south artery; traffic can be heavy, and there are many lights, so use a different route when possible. One viable option is the Veterans Expressway/Suncoast Parkway, a toll road that runs from west Tampa to northern Hernando County. Interstate 275 heads west from Tampa across Tampa Bay to St. Petersburg, swings south, and crosses the bay again on its way to Terra Ceia, near Bradenton. Along this last leg—the Sunshine Skyway and its stunning suspension bridge—you'll get a bird's-eye view of bustling Tampa Bay. U.S. 92 yields a spectacular view of Tampa Bay, and Route 679 takes you along two of St. Petersburg's most pristine islands, Cabbage and

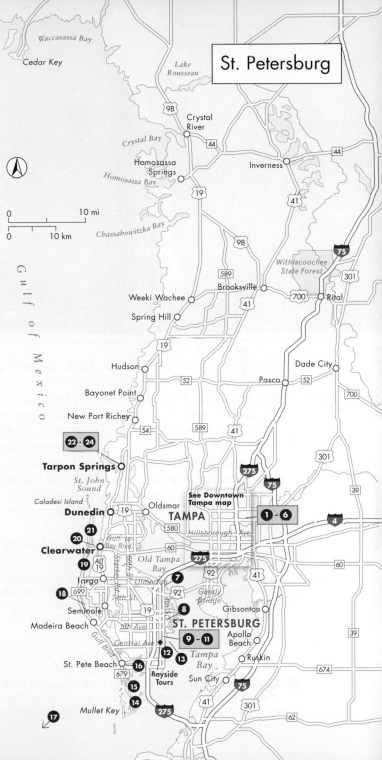

A St. Petersburg pelican stares down passersby on the wharf; photo by Seymour Levy, Fodors.com member

Mullet keys. Around St. Petersburg, **Pinellas Suncoast Transit Authority** (☎ 727/540–1900 ⊕ *www.psta.net*) serves Pinellas County.

TAKE A TOUR

All About Fun Tours (✉ *335 NE 2nd Ave.* ☎ *727/896-3640* ⊕ *www. gyroglides.com* 🖃 *Tours $35–$50* ⊙ *Tues.–Sat. 10:30 and 2, Sun. 12:30 and 2:30, Mon. call for availability*) is a carefree way to see downtown St. Petersburg, the park system, and the waterfront while learning about local history. What sets this tour apart from others is that you are not going by bus or boat—your self-guided chariot is a motorized Segway. Each tour starts with an easy 15- to 20-minute training session. Tours are 60 or 90 minutes and are offered up to three times daily. Reservations are required.

ESSENTIALS

Transportation Contacts Pinellas Suncoast Transit Authority (☎ 727/540–1900 ⊕ www.psta.net).

Visitor Information St. Petersburg Area Chamber of Commerce (✉ 100 2nd Ave. N, St. Petersburg ☎ 727/821-4069 ⊕ www.stpete.com). **St. Petersburg/Clearwater Area Convention and Visitors Bureau** (✉ 13850 58th St. N, Suite 2200, St. Petersburg ☎ 727/464-7200 or 877/352-3224 ⊕ www.floridasbeach.com).

EXPLORING

Numbers in the margin correspond to the St. Petersburg map.

TOP ATTRACTIONS

17 **Egmont Key.** In the middle of the mouth of Tampa Bay lies the small (350 acres), largely unspoiled but critically eroding island Egmont Key, now a state park, national wildlife refuge, national historic site, and bird sanctuary. On the island are the ruins of Fort De Soto's sister fortification, Fort Dade, built during the Spanish-American War to protect Tampa Bay. The primary inhabitants of the less-than-2-mi-long island are the threatened gopher tortoise and box turtles. Shelling and nature-viewing are rewarding. The only way to get here is by boat. **Dolphin Landings Tours** (☎ *727/367–4488* 🌐 *www.dolphinlandings.com*) runs a four-hour shelling trip, a two-hour dolphin-sighting excursion, back-bay or party-boat fishing, and other outings.

⓬ Fodor's Choice ★ **Salvador Dalí Museum.** The Spanish surrealist certainly had a different way of viewing our world, as evidenced by exhibits at this museum, which holds the world's most comprehensive collection of his work. The mind-expanding paintings in this downtown headliner include *Eggs on a Plate Without a Plate*, *The Hallucinogenic Toreador,* and more than 90 other oils. You'll also discover more than 2,000 additional works including watercolors, drawings, sculptures, photographs, and objets d'art. Free hour-long tours are led by well-informed docents. How did the collection end up here? A rich industrialist and friend of Dalí's, Ohio magnate A. Reynolds Morse, was looking for a museum site after his huge collection began to overflow his mansion. The people of St. Petersburg vied admirably for the collection, and the museum was established here as a result. At press time, a new museum—twice the size of this facility—was scheduled to open just south of the Mahaffey Theater and Baker in January 2011. ✉ *1000 3rd St. S* ☎ *727/823–3767 or 800/442–3254* 🌐 *www.salvadordalimuseum.org* 🎟 *$15* ⏲ *Mon.–Wed. and Sat. 9:30–5:30, Thurs. 9:30–8, Fri. 9:30–6:30, Sun. noon–5:30.*

15

❽ **Sunken Gardens.** This is a 100-year-old botanical paradise. Check out photos of its colorful past in the gift shop. Explore the cascading waterfalls and koi ponds, and walk through the butterfly house and exotic gardens where more than 50,000 tropical plants and flowers thrive amid groves of some of the area's most spectacular palm trees. The on-site restaurant and hands-on kids' museum make this place a family favorite. ✉ *1825 4th St. N* ☎ *727/551–3102* 🌐 *www.sunkengardens.org* 🎟 *$8* ⏲ *Mon.–Sat. 10–4:30, Sun. noon–4:30.*

WORTH NOTING

❼ **Bayshore Boulevard Trail.** If you like to get out and walk, talk, jog, bike, and inline skate with locals, you might want to take to this 8.6-mi trail in the downtown area and convenient to anywhere in the south Tampa area. It's a good spot for just standing still and taking it all in, too, with its spectacular views of downtown Tampa and the Hillsborough Bay area. Locals gather here when there's a launch at Cape Canaveral—views are superb. The trail is open from dawn to dusk daily. ✉ *Bayshore Blvd.* ☎ *727/549–6099.*

⓫ **BayWalk.** Downtown St. Petersburg gets an infusion of vibrancy from BayWalk, a shopping, dining, and entertainment mall in a square-block complex incorporating California Mission–style design and courtyard areas lined with trendy eateries, bars, shops, and a 20-screen movie theater. It's best for adults to stroll the plaza and restaurants in the afternoon and early evening, since teenagers overtake BayWalk at night. ✉ *Bordered by 2nd St. N, 2nd Ave. N, 1st St. N, and 3rd Ave. N* ☎ *727/895–9277.*

⑨ **Florida Holocaust Museum.** The downtown Florida Holocaust Museum is one of the largest of its kind in the United States. It has the permanent History, Heritage, and Hope exhibit, an original boxcar, and an extensive collection of photographs, art, and artifacts. One compelling display includes portraits and biographies of Holocaust survivors. The museum, which also has a series of rotating exhibits, was conceived as a learning center for children, so many of the exhibits avoid overly graphic content; signs are posted outside galleries if the subject matter might be too intense for kids. ⊠ *55 5th St. S* ☎ *727/820–0100* ⊕ *www. flholocaustmuseum.org* ⊠ *$12* ⊙ *Daily 10–5.*

WORD OF MOUTH

"My favorite beach is Ft. De Soto. it's just outside St. Pete Beach, but it's a county park and you can't stay there—which is part of its beauty. Aside from the old fort, there are no structures there, just dunes, sea oats, and beach (great shelling too)." —OO

⑭ **Fort De Soto Park.** Spread over five small islands, 1,136-acre Fort De Soto Park lies at the mouth of Tampa Bay. It has 7 mi of beaches, two fishing piers, a 4-mi hiking-skating trail, picnic and camping grounds, and a historic fort that kids of any age can explore. The fort for which it's named was built on the southern end of Mullet Key to protect sea lanes in the gulf during the Spanish-American War. Roam the fort or wander the beaches of any of the islands within the park. ⊠ *3500 Pinellas Bayway S, Tierra Verde* ☎ *727/582–2267* ⊠ *Free* ⊙ *Beaches, daily sunrise–sunset; fishing and boat ramp, 24 hrs.*

⑬ **Great Explorations.** "Don't touch" are words never spoken here. The museum is hands-on through and through, with a Robot Lab, Climb Wall, Lie Detector, Fire House, Vet's Office, and other interactive play areas, including the new Tree House. Smart exhibits like the Tennis Ball Launcher, which uses compressed air to propel a ball through a series of tubes, and Sound Waves, where Styrofoam pellets in a clear tube show differences in sound frequencies, employ low-tech to teach kids (and parents) high-tech principles. ⊠ *1925 4th St. N* ☎ *727/821– 8992* ⊕ *www.greatexplorations.org* ⊠ *$9* ⊙ *Mon.–Sat. 10–4:30, Sun. noon–4:30.*

⑩ **Museum of Fine Arts.** One of the city's cornerstones, this museum is a gorgeous MediterraneanRevival structure that houses outstanding collections of European, American, pre-Columbian, and Asian art. Major works here by American artists range from Whistler to O'Keeffe to Rauschenberg and Lichtenstein, but the museum is known for its collection of French artists, including Fragonard, Cézanne, Monet, Rodin, Gauguin, and Renoir. There are also photography exhibits that draw from a permanent collection of more than 1,200 works. In 2008 the Hazel Hough Wing opened, more than doubling the museum's exhibit space. A new café offers visitors a lunch respite and a beautiful view of the bay. Docents give narrated gallery tours. ⊠ *255 Beach Dr. NE* ☎ *727/896–2667* ⊕ *www.fine-arts.org* ⊠ *$14* ⊙ *Tues.–Sat. 10–5, Sun. 1–5.*

SPORTS AND THE OUTDOORS

BEACHES

⑮ **Pass-A-Grille Beach,** at the southern end of St. Pete Beach, has parking meters, a snack bar, restrooms, and showers. It and Clearwater Beach are two of the area's most popular saltwater swimming holes. ⊠ *Off Gulf Blvd. (Rte. 699), St. Pete Beach.*

⑯ **Treasure Island** (⊠ *11260 Gulf Blvd.*) is a free beach north of Pass-A-Grille with dressing rooms, metered parking, and a snack bar.

BASEBALL

Major League Baseball's **Tampa Bay Rays** (⊠ *Tropicana Field, 1 Tropicana Dr., off I–175* ☎ *727/825–3137* ⊕ *tampabay.rays.mlb.com*) completed an improbable worst-to-first turnaround when they topped the American League Eastern Division in 2008. Tickets are available at the box office for most games, but you may have to rely on the classifieds sections of the *Tampa Tribune* and *St. Petersburg Times* for popular games.

SHOPPING

Designer boutiques, movie theaters, and trendy restaurants can be found at the downtown shopping plaza **Florida Craftsmen Galleries** (⊠ *501 Central Ave.* ☎ *727/821–7391* ⊕ *www.floridacraftsmen.net*), which gives 125 local craftsmen a chance to exhibit glassware, jewelry, furniture, and more. **John's Pass Village and Boardwalk** (⊠ *12901 Gulf Blvd., Madeira Beach* ⊕ *www.johnspass.com*) is a collection of shops and restaurants in an old-style fishing village, where you can pass the time watching pelicans cavorting and dive-bombing for food. A five-story structure on the bay front, the **Pier** (⊠ *800 2nd Ave. NE* ⊕ *www. stpete-pier.com*), near the Museum of Fine Arts, looks like an inverted pyramid. Inside are numerous shops and eating spots.

More than 150 art dealers sell their wares at **Art & Antiques** (⊠ *Beach St. between 1st and 2nd Aves.*). One of the state's more notable bookstores is **Haslam's** (⊠ *2025 Central Ave.* ☎ *727/822–8616* ⊕ *www.haslams. com*), a family-owned emporium that's been doing business just west of downtown St. Petersburg for more than 70 years. The store carries some 300,000 volumes, from cutting-edge best sellers to ancient tomes. If you value a good book or simply like to browse, you could easily spend an afternoon here.

NIGHTLIFE

Joyland Country Music Nightclub (⊠ *5520 14th St.* ☎ *941/756–6060* ⊕ *www.joylandcountry.com*) is the local hot spot Wednesday to Saturday for live country music and dancing. At **Cha Cha Coconuts** (⊠ *The Pier* ☎ *727/822–6655* ⊕ *www.chacha-coconuts.com*) crowds catch live contemporary music Friday through Sunday year-round. **Coliseum Ballroom** (⊠ *535 4th Ave. N* ☎ *727/892–5202*) has ballroom dancing and group lessons on most Wednesday afternoons and Saturday nights.

At **Marchand's** (⊠ *Vinoy Hotel, 501 5th Ave. NE* ☎ *727/894–1000* ⊕ *www.marchandsbarandgrill.com*) sophisticated locals and well-informed out-of-towners gather at the bar for after-dinner cocktails and dancing to top-notch jazz bands Friday and Saturday. It's the most genteel place in town for a nightcap. The **Rare Olive** (⊠ *300 Central Ave.,*

15

corner of 3rd St. ☎ *727/822–7273* ⊕ *www.rareolive.com*) adds a touch of class to an otherwise jeans-and-T-shirt nightlife scene.

WHERE TO EAT

$ ✕ **Crabby Bill's.** Nothing fancy about the crab-man's place—just some of
SEAFOOD the area's tastiest seafood served family-style (picture long picnic-style tables) in a friendly atmosphere. The fried-grouper sandwich is tasty, but you can also order it grilled, broiled, or blackened. Crustaceans are the house specialty, meaning your choice of blue, soft-shell, king, and, from October to May, delicious though costly stone crabs, among others. There's also a good selection of other treats, including flounder, bay scallops, and farm-raised oysters. Diners usually dress in the official uniform of Florida beaches: shorts, T-shirts, and flip-flops. ⊠ *5100 Gulf Blvd.* ☎ *727/360–8858* ⊕ *www.crabbybills.com* ⊟ *D, MC, V.*

$ ✕ **Hurricane Seafood Restaurant.** Sunsets and gulf views are the bait that
SEAFOOD hooks regulars as well as travelers who find their way to this somewhat hidden St. Pete Beach pit stop. Dating to 1977, it's mainly heralded as a watering hole where you can hoist a cold one while munching on one of the area's better grouper sandwiches. (Speaking of this sweet white fish, it's the real deal here, which—be warned—isn't always a guarantee in some restaurants.) There's also a range of seafood and steak entrées. The aforementioned sunsets are best seen from the rooftop sundeck. ⊠ *807 Gulf Way, St. Pete Beach* ☎ *727/360–9558* ⊕ *www.thehurricane. com* ⊟ *AE, D, MC, V.*

$$$$ ✕ **Marchand's Bar & Grill.** Opened in 1925, this wonderful eatery in the
ECLECTIC posh Renaissance Vinoy Resort has frescoed ceilings and a spectacular
★ view of Tampa Bay. Upscale and special-occasion diners are drawn to Marchand's by an imaginative and ever-changing menu. A visit might offer a deliciously rare lamb duo (T-bone and double chop) with cheese and pesto-smashed spuds, halibut poached in vanilla-bean olive oil, or lump-crab-and-cheese ravioli with crunchy duck cracklings. The wine list is extensive, including a number of by-the-glass selections. There's live jazz Friday and Saturday nights. ⊠ *Renaissance Vinoy Resort, 501 5th Ave. NE* ☎ *727/824–8072* ⊕ *www.marchandsbarandgrill.com* ⊟ *AE, D, DC, MC, V.*

$$ ✕ **PJ's Oyster Bar & Seafood Restaurant.** Follow the crowds to this back-
SEAFOOD alley eatery where 60 varieties of beer flow as freely as the rolls of paper towels mounted on wire hangers overhead. Seafood selections range from fried catfish and grouper to more elegant options such as blackened yellowfin tuna. The all-day menu includes sandwiches and pasta. Come after work weekdays or on weekends if you enjoy making new friends. ⊠ *7500 Gulf Blvd.* ☎ *727/367–3309* ⊕ *www.pjsoysterbar. com* ⊟ *AE, MC, V* ☉ *No lunch.*

$$$ ✕ **Salt Rock Grill.** This hot spot is where tourists and locals converge to
SEAFOOD enjoy a fun and lively beachside atmosphere. A band plays Saturday and Sunday nights during summer, and couples get close on the patio bar and beach. But the rock-solid (if slightly less than imaginative) menu is the best reason to come. Don't believe the Caribbean lobster is a "monster"—at 1¼ pounds it's on the small side, but it's twice cooked including a finish on the grill and quite tasty. The showstopper is the cioppino (shrimp, king crab, lobster, mussels, fish, and clams with a

Continued on page 578

SPRING TRAINING, FLORIDA-STYLE

by Jim Tunstall

Sunshine, railroads, and land bargains were Florida's first tourist magnets, but baseball had a hand in things, too. The Chicago Cubs led the charge when they opened spring training in Tampa in 1913— the same year the Cleveland Indians set up camp in Pensacola.

Over the next couple of decades, World War I and the Great Depression interrupted normal lives, but the Sunshine State became a great fit for the national pastime. Soon, big-league teams were flocking south to work off the winter rust.

At one point, the Florida "Grapefruit League" held a monopoly on spring training, but in 1947 Arizona's "Cactus League" started cutting into the action.

Today, roughly half of Major League Baseball's 30 teams arrive in Florida in February for six weeks of calisthenics, tryouts, and practice games. The clubs range from the Detroit Tigers, who have been in the same city (Lakeland) longer than any other team (since 1934), to the Tampa Bay Rays, who moved to a new spring home (Port Charlotte) in 2009.

The Los Angeles Dodgers play the Washington Nationals in Viera during a spring training game.

HERE COME THE FANS

Cardinals fans take advantage of spring training's easier access to players.

Florida's spring training teams play 25 or 30 home and away games, to the delight of 1.68 million annual ticker buyers. Die-hards land as soon as the first troops—pitchers and catchers—come to practice around the third week of February. Inter-squad games start in the fourth week, while the real training schedule begins by the end of February or first of March and lasts until the end of the month or early April. These games don't count in the regular season, but they give managers and fans a good idea of which players will be on the opening-day rosters, and who will be traded, sent to the teams' minor leagues, or told it's time to find a regular day job.

Spring training games provide a great excuse for local base-ball fans to cut out of work early, while visitors from the North can leave ice, snow, and sleet behind. And who doesn't want a few chili dogs, brats, burg-ers, and brews on a March day?

Spring training's draw is more than just a change of venue with an early sample of concession-stand staples. There is also the ample choice of game sites. Teams are scattered around most of the major tour-ist areas of central and southern Florida, so those coming to watch the games can try a different destination each spring—or even make a road trip to several. Baseball fans also like that it's a melting pot—teams from more than a dozen cit-ies are represented here.

Finally, you can't beat the price—tick-ets are usually cheaper than during the regular season—nor the access you have to baseball celebrities. In fact, the relaxed atmosphere of spring training makes most play-ers more willing to sign your ball, glove, or whatever. You can get autographs during pregame work-outs (practice sessions), which are free, as well as after the game.

World champion Jimmy Rollins.

3 TIPS

■ **Have a game plan.** Don't just show up. Most teams only have about 15 home games, and those involving the Yankees, Red Sox, and other popular clubs often are sold out weeks in advance. Consider buying tickets ahead of time, and if needed, make hotel room reservations at the same time.

■ **Beat the crowds.** The best chance to do this is to go to a weekday game. You'll still encounter lots of fans, but weekday games generally aren't as stuffed as weekenders. Also, every team only has a few night games; if you want to attend one, book it by Christmas.

■ **Pack a picnic.** Some stadiums let you bring coolers through the turnstiles. Many game attendees also gather for a tailgate party, grilling burgers and sipping a lemonade or beer while jawing with fellow fans (have a chair in tow).

(above) Hammond Stadium in Ft. Myers is where the Minnesota Twins practice.
(right) St. Louis Cardinals Chris Duncan is tagged out at Tradition Field in Port St. Lucie.

Atlanta Braves	2	New York Yankees	4
Baltimore Orioles	7	Philadelphia Phillies	1
Boston Red Sox	14	Pittsburgh Pirates	10
Detroit Tigers	9	St. Louis Cardinals/	
Houston Astros	11	Florida Marlins	12
Minnesota Twins	8	Tampa Bay Rays	3
New York Mets	6	Toronto Blue Jays	5
		Washington Nationals	13

15

IN FOCUS SPRING TRAINING, FLORIDA-STYLE

PLAY BALL!

Spring training schedules are determined around Thanksgiving. Ticket prices change each year; 2009 prices are shown here. For all of these teams, you also can order spring training tickets through Ticketmaster (☎ 866/448–7849 ⊕ www.ticketmaster.com) or through the respective team's box office or team Web site. For more information about any of the teams, visit ⊕ www.floridagrapefruitleague.com.

SPRING TRAINING GUIDE
Order a free Guide to *Florida Spring Training* from the **Florida Sports Foundation** (✉ 2930 Kerry Forest Parkway, Tallahassee, FL ☎ 850/488–8347). Published in February each year, it's packed with information about teams, sites, tickets, and more.

New York Mets catcher Ramon Castro.

ATLANTA BRAVES
Home Field: Champion Stadium, Walt Disney World Wide World of Sports, 700 S. Victory Way, Kissimmee. **Tickets:** $15–$32
☎ 407/939–4263 ⊕ www.braves.mlb.com

BALTIMORE ORIOLES
Home Field: Ed Smith Stadium, 1090 N. Euclid Ave., Sarasota. **Tickets:** $10–$22
☎ 954/776–1921 ⊕ www.orioles.mlb.com

BOSTON RED SOX
Home Field: City of Palms Park, 2201 Edison Ave., Fort Myers. **Tickets:** $10–$26
☎ 239/334–4700, 877/733–7699 ⊕ www.redsox.mlb.com

DETROIT TIGERS
Home Field: Joker Marchant Stadium, 2301 Lakeland Hills Blvd., Lakeland. **Tickets:** $12–$22
☎ 863/686–8075 ⊕ www.tigers.mlb.com

FLORIDA MARLINS
Home Field: Roger Dean Stadium (shared with St. Louis Cardinals), 4751 Main St., Jupiter. **Tickets:** $14–$31
☎ 561/775–1818 ⊕ www.marlins.mlb.com

HOUSTON ASTROS
Home Field: Osceola County Stadium, 631 Heritage Parkway, Kissimmee. **Tickets:** $10–$22
☎ 321/697–3200 ⊕ www.astros.mlb.com

MINNESOTA TWINS
Home Field: Hammond Stadium, 14100 Six Mile Cypress Parkway, Fort Myers. **Tickets:** $12–$23
☎ 239/768–4270 ⊕ www.twins.mlb.com

NEW YORK METS
Home Field: Tradition Field, 525 NW Peacock Blvd., Port St. Lucie. **Tickets:** $7–$22
☎ 772/871–2115 ⊕ www.mets.mlb.com

NEW YORK YANKEES
Home Field: Steinbrenner Field, 1 Steinbrenner Dr., Tampa **Tickets:** $18–$33
☎ 813/879–2244 ⊕ www.yankees.mlb.com

PHILADELPHIA PHILLIES
Home Field: Bright House Networks Field, 601 N. Old Coachman Rd., Clearwater. **Tickets:** $11–$30
☎ 727/467–4457 ⊕ www.phillies.mlb.com

PITTSBURGH PIRATES
Home Field: McKechnie Field, 17th Avenue W. & 9th St., Bradenton. **Tickets:** $10–$18
☎ 941/748–4610 ⊕ www.pirates.mlb.com

ST. LOUIS CARDINALS
Home Field: Roger Dean Stadium (shared with Florida Marlins), 4751 Main St., Jupiter. **Tickets:** $14–$27
☎ 561/775–1818 ⊕ www.cardinals.mlb.com

TAMPA BAY RAYS
Home Field: Charlotte County Sports Park, 2300 El Jobean Rd., Port Charlotte. **Tickets:** $9–$23
☎ 727/825–3250 ⊕ www.rays.mlb.com

TORONTO BLUE JAYS
Home Field: Dunedin Stadium, 373 Douglas Ave., Dunedin **Tickets:** $15–$22
☎ 727/733–0429 ⊕ www.bluejays.mlb.com

WASHINGTON NATIONALS
Home Field: Space Coast Stadium, 5800 Stadium Parkway, Viera. **Tickets:** $9–$26
☎ 321/633–4487 ⊕ www.nationals.mlb.com

15

IN FOCUS SPRING TRAINING, FLORIDA-STYLE

sourdough crust). In fair weather, dine on the dock; otherwise ask for a table with a view of the water. ⊠ *19325 Gulf Blvd.* ☎ *727/593–7625* ⊕ *www.saltrockgrill.com* ▤ *AE, MC, V.*

$
SEAFOOD
Fodor's Choice
★

✕**Ted Peters Famous Smoked Fish.** Picture this: flip-flop-wearing anglers and beach-towel-clad bathers lolling on picnic benches, soaking up a beer, and devouring oak-smoked salmon, mullet, and mackerel. Everything comes to the table with heaped helpings of potato salad or coleslaw. If you're industrious enough to have hooked your own fish, the crew will smoke it for about $1.50 per pound. If not, there's always what many consider to be the best burger in the region. The popular smoked-fish spread is available to go. There's also indoor seating at Ted's, which has been a south-side fixture for more than six decades. Closing time is 7:30 PM. ⊠ *1350 Pasadena Ave. S, South Pasadena* ☎ *727/381–7931* ⚑ *Reservations not accepted* ▤ *No credit cards* ☯ *Closed Tues.*

$
AMERICAN

✕**TooJay's.** Kippered salmon and roast brisket with potato pancakes are the mainstays at this kosher-style deli that's busy at breakfast, lunch, and dinner. Other selections include salmon cakes, shepherd's pie, and shrimp salad. Don't miss the éclair, a house specialty. The restaurant is nothing fancy, but it's bright and friendly, and management ensures you're waited on promptly. Everything on the menu is available for takeout. ⊠ *141 2nd Ave. N, BayWalk* ☎ *727/823–3354* ⊕ *www.toojays. com* ⚑ *Reservations not accepted* ▤ *AE, D, DC, MC, V.*

WHERE TO STAY

$$$–$$$$
Fodor's Choice
★

▣ **Don CeSar Beach Resort.** You have to love the story—real or imagined—about Thomas Rowe's ghost. As legend has it, the man who built this Roaring Twenties–era hotel came back after death to meet his beloved. Some guests and staff swear they see the couple occasionally having a rendezvous in the garden (more romantic than spooky); others say Rowe appears in corridors and rooms. On a more documented level, the Don once was a favorite of F. Scott and Zelda Fitzgerald, Babe Ruth, and Clarence Darrow. Today the "Pink Palace," as it's called thanks to its paint job, is a gulf-coast landmark with remarkable architecture. Its exterior and public areas have turn-of-the-last-century elegance. Ditto for the rooms, and the staff is known for friendly Old World service. The hotel's fitness center and spa have recently undergone extensive renovations. The restaurant, Maritana Grille, specializes in Florida seafood and is lined with huge fish tanks. **Pros:** romantic destination; great beach; tasty dining options. **Cons:** quite pricey. ⊠ *3400 Gulf Blvd., St. Pete Beach* ☎ *727/367–6952 or 800/282–1116* ⊕ *www.doncesar.com* ⭧*277 rooms, 40 suites, 70 condos* ⚘ *In-room: safe (some), Internet, Wi-Fi. In-hotel: 3 restaurants, room service, bars, pools, gym, spa, beachfront, children's programs (ages 4–12), laundry service, Wi-Fi hotspot, parking (paid), some pets allowed* ▤ *AE, D, DC, MC, V.*

$$$–$$$$
Fodor's Choice
★

▣ **Renaissance Vinoy Resort & Golf Club.** Built in 1925, making it the same vintage as the Don CeSar, the Vinoy is a luxury resort in a quiet, quaint neighborhood. Thoughtful renovations keep its yesteryear glamour and place on the National Register of Historic Places. Some of the units are cramped by today's standards, so ask for one of the spacious rooms for more comfort. Those on the bay side have better views of Tampa Bay.

A tiny bay-side beach several blocks away is good for strolling (but not swimming). Transportation is provided to better beaches 30 minutes away. Other offerings include access to a Ron Garl–designed golf course with a stunning clubhouse, an expansive marina, and pool attendants who deliver drinks. **Pros:** charming property; friendly service; close to downtown museums. **Cons:** pricey; not on the beach. ⊠ *501 5th Ave. NE* ☎ *727/894–1000* ⊕ *www.vinoyrenaissanceresort.com* ↘ *345 rooms, 15 suites* ⚿ *In-room: Internet. In-hotel: 5 restaurants, room service, bars, golf course, tennis courts, pools, gym, spa, laundry facilities, laundry service, Wi-Fi hotspot* ⊟ *AE, D, DC, MC, V.*

$$$–$$$$ 🖵 **TradeWinds Islands Resort.** The TradeWinds is very popular with foreign travelers who enjoy the indoor waterways complete with paddleboats. It's also one of the few pet-friendly resorts in the area, boasting a play area and a room-service menu for dogs and cats. Most rooms have a view of the beach, though you may have to crane your neck in some. The best views are from gulf-front suites with balconies or those overlooking the Intracoastal Waterway. All rooms are currently receiving furniture, lighting, and linen upgrades. There are on-site swimming lessons for children and adults. **Pros:** great beachfront location; close to restaurants. **Cons:** lots of conventions. ⊠ *5500 Gulf Blvd., St. Pete Beach* ☎ *727/363–2212* ⊕ *www.justletgo.com* ↘ *584 rooms, 103 suites* ⚿ *In-room: safe, kitchen, refrigerator, Internet, Wi-Fi. In-hotel: 11 restaurants, bars, tennis courts, pools, gym, spa, beachfront, children's programs (ages 4–15), laundry facilities, laundry service, Wi-Fi hotspot, parking (paid)* ⊟ *AE, D, DC, MC, V.*

CLEARWATER

12 mi north of St. Petersburg via U.S. 19.

Residential areas are a buffer between the commercial areas that center on U.S. 19 and the beach, which is moderately quiet during winter but buzzing with life during spring break and summer. There's a quaint downtown area on the mainland, just east of the beach.

ESSENTIALS

Visitor Information Clearwater Regional Chamber of Commerce (⊠ *1130 Cleveland St., Clearwater* ☎ *727/461–0011* ⊕ *www.clearwaterflorida.org*).

EXPLORING

Numbers in the margin correspond to the St. Petersburg map.

18 When pelicans and other birds become entangled in fishing lines, locals sometimes carry them to the nonprofit **Suncoast Seabird Sanctuary,** founded by Ralph Heath and dedicated to the rescue, repair, recuperation, and release of sick and injured birds. At times there are hundreds of land and sea birds in residence, including egrets, herons, gulls, terns, sandhill cranes, hawks, owls, and cormorants. ⊠ *18328 Gulf Blvd., Indian Shores* ☎ *727/391–6211* ⊕ *www.seabirdsanctuary.com* ✆ *Donations* ☺ *Tours Wed. and Sun. at 2.*

19 South of Clearwater Beach, on Sand Key at Clearwater Pass, **Sand Key Park** has a lovely beach, plenty of green space, a playground,

Clearwater's Bait House lures in those heading to the pier to fish; photo by watland, Fodors.com member.

and a picnic area in an otherwise congested area. ⊠ *1060 Gulf Blvd.* ☎ *727/588–4852.*

❷⓿ The **Clearwater Marine Aquarium** is a laid-back attraction offering an opportunity to participate in the work of saving and caring for endangered marine species. Many of the sea turtles, dolphins, and other animals living at the aquarium were brought here to be rehabilitated from an injury or saved from danger. The dolphin exhibit has an open-air arena giving the dolphins plenty of room to jump during their shows. The aquarium conducts tours of the bays and islands around Clearwater, including a daily cruise on a pontoon boat (you might just see a wild dolphin or two), and kayak tours of Clearwater Harbor and St. Joseph Sound. ⊠ *249 Windward Passage* ☎ *727/441–1790* ⊕ *www. cmaquarium.org* ➲ *$13* ⊙ *Mon.–Thurs. 9–5, Fri. and Sat. 9–7, Sun. 10–5.*

SPORTS AND THE OUTDOORS
BEACHES

❷❶ Connected to downtown Clearwater by Memorial Causeway, **Clearwater**
Fodor'sChoice **Beach** (⊠ *Western end of Rte. 60, 2 mi west of downtown Clearwater*)
★ is on a narrow island between Clearwater Harbor and the gulf. It has a widespread reputation for beach volleyball. There are lifeguards here as well as a marina, concessions, showers, and restrooms. Around Pier 60 there's a big, modern playground. This is the site of a nightly sunset celebration complete with musicians and artisans. It's one of the area's nicest and busiest beaches, especially on weekends and during spring break, but it's also one of the costliest in terms of parking fees, which can reach $2 per hour.

BASEBALL

The **Philadelphia Phillies** (⊠ *Bright House Networks Field, 601 N. Old Coachman Rd.* ☎ *727/441–8638*) get ready for the season with spring training here (late February to early April). The stadium also hosts the Phillies' farm team.

BIKING

The **Pinellas Trail** is a 35-mi paved route that spans Pinellas County. Once a railway, the trail runs adjacent to major thoroughfares, no more than 10 feet from the roadway, so you can access it from almost any point. The trail, also popular with in-line skaters, has spawned trailside businesses such as repair shops and health-food cafés. There are also many lovely rural areas to bike through and plenty of places to rent bikes. Be wary of traffic in downtown Clearwater and on the congested areas of the Pinellas Trail, which still needs more bridges for crossing over busy streets. To start riding from the route's south end, park at Trailhead Park (37th Street South at 8th Avenue South) in St. Petersburg. To ride south from the north end, park your car in downtown Tarpon Springs (East Tarpon Avenue at North Stafford Avenue). ☎ *727/464–8201.*

MINIATURE GOLF

The live alligators advertised on the roadside sign for **Congo River Golf** (⊠ *20060 U.S. 19 N* ☎ *727/797–4222*) are not in the water traps but in a fenced-off lagoon. The reptiles do, however, add a Florida touch to this highly landscaped course tucked into a small parcel of land adjacent to Clearwater's busiest north–south thoroughfare. Admission is $9.50–$10.50. Closed mid-October through April, weekends only April, May, October.

WHERE TO EAT

$$$
AMERICAN
✕ **Bob Heilman's Beachcomber.** The Heilman family has fed hungry diners since 1920. Although it's very popular with tourists, you'll also rub shoulders with devoted locals. Despite the frequent crowds, the service is fast and friendly. The sautéed chicken is an American classic—arriving with mashed spuds, gravy, veggie du jour, and fresh-baked bread. Or try the New Bedford sea scallops, broiled with lemon and capers, or pan-seared with roasted peppers. ⊠ *447 Mandalay Ave., Clearwater Beach* ☎ *727/442–4144* ⊕ *www.heilmansbeachcomber.com* ▭ *AE, D, DC, MC, V.*

$
SEAFOOD
✕ **Frenchy's Rockaway Grill.** Quebec native Mike "Frenchy" Preston runs four eateries in the area, including the fabulous Rockaway Grill. Visitors and locals alike keep coming back for the grouper sandwiches that are moist and not battered into submission. (It's also real grouper, something that's not a given these days.) Frenchy also gets a big thumbs-up for his she-crab soup, and, on the march-to-a-different-drummer front, the cheddar-stuffed shrimp. In mild weather, eat on the deck, though the screaming yellow-and-turquoise paint job can be nearly as blinding as the sun. ⊠ *7 Rockaway St.* ☎ *727/446–4844* ⊕ *www.frenchysonline. com* ▭ *AE, MC, V.*

15

WHERE TO STAY

$$$-$$$$ ⊞ **Safety Harbor Resort & Spa.** Although it's not for everyone, those who enjoy old-school pampering love this hotel's 50,000-square-foot spa, which has the latest in therapies and treatments. Request a treatment room overlooking Tampa Bay—the sunsets can be gorgeous—and plan to spend a little downtime in the tranquillity garden. Accommodations are continuously being upgraded, so expect to find high-end mattresses and luxurious linens. The pleasant hamlet of Safety Harbor is also a point of interest, with charming shops along the nearby main street. The resort was built over hot springs on Tampa Bay in 1926, but little of the original architecture remains. The springs still function, however, feeding into pools, the spa, and water coolers. **Pros:** charm to spare; good choice for pampering. **Cons:** far from attractions; staff can be chilly. ⊠ *105 N. Bayshore Dr., Safety Harbor* ☎ *727/726–1161 or 888/237–8772* ⊕ *www.safetyharborspa.com* ⤳ *175 rooms, 16 suites* ⚓ *In-room: a/c, Internet, Wi-Fi. In-hotel: restaurant, tennis courts, pools, gym, spa, laundry facilities, laundry service, Wi-Fi hotspot* ⊟ *AE, D, DC, MC, V.*

$$$-$$$$ ⊞ **Sheraton Sand Key Resort.** Expect something special—a modern prop-
★   erty and one of the few uncluttered beaches in the area. The nine-story resort is set on 10 well-manicured acres, and many rooms have excellent gulf views; others keep an eye over an adjacent park. All rooms have balconies or patios, those on higher floors have beautiful views of the water. Considered one of the top convention hotels in the area, the resort has amenities—such as a beautiful private beach—that make it ideal for leisure travelers, too. **Pros:** private beach; great views; flat-screen TVs and Nintendo Wii in room. **Cons:** near crowded Clearwater Beach; views come with a high price tag. ⊠ *1160 Gulf Blvd., Clearwater Beach* ☎ *727/595–1611* ⊕ *www.sheratonsandkey.com* ⤳ *375 rooms, 15 suites* ⚓ *In-room: Wi-Fi. In-hotel: 4 restaurants, room service, bars, tennis courts, pool, gym, beachfront, water sports, children's programs (ages 3–15), Wi-Fi hotspot* ⊟ *AE, D, DC, MC, V.*

$$-$$$ ⊞ **Wingate Inn—Clearwater/St. Pete.** The Wingate is a pleasant motel close to the attractions of northern Pinellas County. Rooms are clean, modern, and not cramped, but this is a chain. **Pros:** friendly staff; waffle station at breakfast. **Cons:** a bit far from the sights. ⊠ *5000 Lake Blvd., Clearwater* ☎ *727/299–9800* ⊕ *www.wingateinnclearwater.com* ⤳ *84 rooms* ⚓ *In-room: refrigerator, Internet, Wi-Fi. In-hotel: pool, gym, laundry facilities, Wi-Fi hotspot* ⊟ *AE, D, DC, MC, V.*

DUNEDIN

3 mi north of Clearwater.

If the sound of bagpipes and the sight of men in kilts appeals to you, you might catch an earful or a glimpse if your timing is right. Founded and named by two Scots in the 1880s, this town hosts the Highland Games in March and the Celtic Festival in November, both of which pay tribute to the town's heritage. Dunedin also has a nicely restored historic downtown—only about five blocks long—that has become a one-stop shopping area for antiques hunters and is also lined with gift shops and good nonchain eateries.

GETTING HERE AND AROUND

From Clearwater, take U.S. 19 to Route 580, then go west about 8 to 10 mi.

ESSENTIALS

Visitor Information Greater Dunedin Chamber of Commerce (⊠ *301 Main St., Dunedin* ☎ *727/733-3197* ⊕ *www.dunedin-fl.com*).

SPORTS AND THE OUTDOORS

BEACHES

Caladesi Island State Park. Quiet, secluded, and still wild, this 3½-mi-long barrier island is one of the best shelling beaches on the Gulf Coast, second only to Sanibel. The park also has plenty of sights for birders—from common sandpipers to majestic blue herons to rare black skimmers—and miles of trails through scrub oaks, saw palmettos, and cacti (with tenants such as armadillos, rabbits, and raccoons). The landscape also features mangroves and dunes, and the gradual slope of the sea bottom makes this a good spot for novice swimmers and kids. You have to get to Caladesi Island by private boat (there's a 108-slip marina) or through its sister park, Honeymoon Island State Recreation Area, where you take the hourly ferry ride across to Caladesi. Ferry rides cost $9 per person. ⊠ *Dunedin Causeway* ☎ *727/469-5942* ⊘ *$5 per car* ☉ *Daily 8–sunset.*

BASEBALL

The **Toronto Blue Jays** (⊠ *Knology Park, 373 Douglas Ave., north of Hwy. 580* ☎ *727/733-9302*) play about 18 spring-training games here in March.

WHERE TO EAT

$$$
CONTINENTAL
✕ **Bon Appétit.** Known for its creative fare, this waterfront restaurant has a menu that changes frequently, offering such entrées as broiled rack of lamb in herbed walnut crust and sautéed veal sweetbreads with mushrooms in brown butter. The roasted grouper in garlic and lemon butter gets well-deserved plaudits from many patrons. Bon Appétit has staying power, serving at the same location for more than three decades. It's a great place to catch a sunset over the Gulf of Mexico. There's a pianist Wednesday through Sunday evenings and a Sunday brunch. ⊠ *148 Marina Plaza* ☎ *727/733-2151* ⊕ *www.bonappetitrestaurant. com* ⊟ *AE, D, DC, MC, V.*

$$
MEXICAN
★
✕ **Casa Tina.** Vegetarians can veg out here on roasted chiles rellenos (cheese-stuffed peppers), enchiladas with vegetables, and a cactus salad that won't prick your tongue but will tickle your taste buds with the tantalizing flavors of tender pieces of cactus, cilantro, tomatoes, onions, lime, and *queso fresco* (a mild white cheese). There also are tamales, tacos, and tortillas prepared dozens of ways. The place is often crowded, and service can be slow as a result, but there's a reason why everyone's eating here. ⊠ *369 Main St.* ☎ *727/734-9226* ⊟ *AE, D, MC, V* ☉ *Closed Mon.*

$$$
STEAK
✕ **Spoto's Italian Grille.** It's a simple formula: aged Angus beef expertly prepared and pasta cooked to perfection. This restaurant serves about

every cut of beef you can imagine, from a huge porterhouse to a petit fillet to succulent prime rib. If red meat isn't what you're looking for, there's also a variety of fresh fish entrées. ✉ *1280 Main St.* ☎ *727/734–0008* ⊕ *www.spotossteakjoint2.com* ▭ *AE, D, MC, V* ⊙ *No lunch.*

TARPON SPRINGS

10 mi north of Dunedin on Alternate U.S. 19.

Tucked into a little harbor at the mouth of the Anclote River, this slowly growing town was settled by Greek immigrants at the end of the 19th century. They came to practice their generations-old craft of sponge diving. Although bacterial and market forces seriously hurt the industry in the 1940s, sponging has had a modest return, mostly as a focal point for tourism. The docks along Dodecanese Boulevard, the main waterfront street, are filled with sweet old buildings with shops and eateries. Tarpon Springs' other key street is Tarpon Avenue, about a mile south of Dodecanese. This old central business district has become a hub for antiques hunters. The influence of Greek culture is omnipresent; the community's biggest celebration is the annual Greek Orthodox Epiphany celebration in January, in which teenage boys dive for a golden cross in Spring Bayou, a few blocks from Tarpon Avenue, during a ceremony followed by a street festival in the town's central business district.

ESSENTIALS

Visitor Information Tarpon Springs Chamber of Commerce (✉ *11 E. Orange St.* ☎ *727/937–6109* ⊕ *www.tarponsprings.org*).

EXPLORING

Numbers in the margin correspond to the St. Petersburg map.

㉒ **St. Nicholas Greek Orthodox Cathedral** is a replica of Hagia Sophia in Istanbul and an excellent example of New Byzantine architecture. It's the home of a weeping icon that received national and international headlines in the 1970s. ✉ *36 N. Pinellas Ave.* ☎ *727/937–3540* ▭ *Donation suggested* ⊙ *Daily 9–4.*

㉓ **The Sponge Factory** is a shop, museum, and cultural center that reveals more than you ever imagined about how a lowly sea creature created the industry that built this village. See a film about these much-sought-after creatures from the phylum *porifera* and how they helped the town prosper in the early 1900s. You'll come away converted to (and loaded up with) natural sponges. ✉ *510 Dodecanese Blvd., off U.S. 19* ☎ *727/938–5366* ⊕ *www.spongedocks.net* ▭ *Free* ⊙ *Daily 10–6.*

㉔ Although it's not on par with larger tanks in Tampa and Clearwater, the **Konger Tarpon Springs Aquarium** is an entertaining destination. There are some good exhibits, including a 120,000-gallon shark tank complete with a coral reef. (Divers feed the sharks several times daily.) Also look for tropical fish exhibits and a tank where you can touch baby sharks and stingrays. ✉ *850 Dodecanese Blvd., off U.S. 19* ☎ *727/938–5378* ⊕ *www.tarponspringsaquarium.com* ▭ *$6.75* ⊙ *Mon.–Sat. 10–5, Sun. noon–5.*

WHERE TO STAY

$$$-$$$$ ⚇ **Innisbrook Resort & Golf Club.** A massive pool complex with a 15-foot
★ waterslide and a sandy beach are part of the allure of this sprawl-
ing resort. But 72 holes of golf, including the challenging Copperhead
course, are the real magnets. Bald eagles and herons are sometimes
seen on the grounds, which are beautifully maintained. Guest suites
are in 24 two- and three-story lodges tucked among the trees between
golf courses. Some of the roomy suites have balconies or patios. Inn-
isbrook has enough restaurants and lounges to make it self-contained,
though there are other dining options in the area. **Pros:** great for seri-
ous golfers; varied dining options. **Cons:** far from attractions. ⊠ *36750
U.S. 19 N, Palm Harbor* ☎ *727/942–2000 or 800/456–2000* ⊕ *www.
innisbrookgolfresort.com* ⇅ *620 suites* ⚇ *In-room: a/c, kitchen (some),
Internet, Wi-Fi. In-hotel: 4 restaurants, bars, golf courses, tennis courts,
pools, gym, spa, bicycles, laundry facilities, laundry service, Wi-Fi
hotspot* ▭ *AE, D, MC, V.*

SOUTH OF TAMPA BAY: SARASOTA COUNTY

Sarasota County anchors the southern end of Tampa Bay. A string of
barrier islands borders it with 35 mi of gulf beaches, as well as two state
parks, 22 municipal parks, and more than 30 golf courses, many open
to the public. The city of Sarasota has a thriving cultural scene dating
to circus magnate John Ringling, who chose this area for the winter
home of his circus and his family.

BRADENTON

49 mi south of Tampa.

Named for early physician Joseph Braden, this Manatee River city has
some 20 mi of beaches and is well situated for access to fishing, both
fresh- and saltwater. It also has its share of golf courses and historic
sites dating to the mid-1800s.

EXPLORING

Numbers in the margin correspond to the Sarasota County map.

❶ **South Florida Museum & Parker Manatee Aquarium.** Snooty, the oldest man-
ⓒ atee in captivity, is the headliner here. Programs about the endangered
marine mammals run four times daily. View changing exhibits such as
digital images of water and other natural resources in the East Gallery;
glass cases and roll-out drawers on the 2nd floor allow you to look at
exhibits normally out of public view. At the Bishop Planetarium (with
a domed theater screen), programs presented range from black holes
to Jimi Hendrix, Pink Floyd, and other rockers. ⊠ *201 10th St. W*
☎ *941/746–4131* ⊕ *www.southfloridamuseum.org* ⚑ *$15.95* ☉ *Jan.–
Apr. and July, Mon.–Sat. 10–5, Sun. noon–5; May, June, and Aug.–Dec.,
Tues.–Sat. 10–5, Sun. noon–5.*

❷ **De Soto National Memorial.** One of the first Spanish explorers to land in
Fodor's Choice North America, Hernando de Soto, came ashore with his men and 200
★ horses near what is now Bradenton in 1539; this federal park heralds
that landing. During the height of tourist season, mid-December to

late April, park workers dress in period costumes at Camp Uzita, demonstrate the use of 16th-century weapons, and show how European explorers prepared and preserved food for their overland journeys. The season ends with a reenactment of the explorer's landing. The site also offers a film and short nature trail through the mangroves. ⊠ *75th St. NW, Bradenton* ☎ *941/792-0458* ⊕ *www.nps.gov/deso* ⊠ *Free* ⊗ *Visitor center daily 9–5, grounds daily dawn–dusk.*

SARASOTA

30 mi south of Tampa and St. Petersburg.

Sarasota is a winter destination and in some cases permanent home to some of Florida's most affluent residents. Circus magnate John Ringling and his wife, Mable, started the city on the road to becoming one of the state's hotbeds for the arts. Today cultural events are scheduled year-round, and there is a higher concentration of upscale shops, restaurants, and hotels than in much of the Tampa Bay area. Across the water from Sarasota lie the barrier islands of **Siesta Key, Longboat Key,** and **Lido Key,** with myriad beaches, shops, hotels, condominiums, and houses.

15

GETTING HERE AND AROUND

Sarasota is accessible from Interstate 75 and Interstate 275, and U.S. 41. The town's public transit company is **Sarasota County Area Transit (SCAT)** (☎ *941/316–1234*). Fares for local bus service range from 75¢ to $3 (for an all-day pass); exact change is required.

ESSENTIALS

Transportation Contact Sarasota County Area Transit (SCAT) (☎ *941/316–1234*).

Visitor Information Sarasota Convention and Visitors Bureau (⊠ *701 N. Tamiami Trail, Sarasota* ☎ *941/957–1877 or 800/522–9799* ⊕ *www.sarasotafl.org*).

EXPLORING

Numbers in the margin correspond to the Sarasota County map.

TOP ATTRACTIONS

❸ **Florida State University Ringling Center for the Cultural Arts.** Along Sarasota Bay, Ringling built a grand home that was patterned after the Palace of the Doges in Venice. This exquisite mansion of 32 rooms, 15 bathrooms, and a 61-foot Belvedere Tower was completed in 1925, and is a must-visit today. Its 8,000-square-foot terrace overlooks the dock where Ringling's wife, Mable, moored her gondola. The **John and Mable Ringling Museum of Art** is the state art museum of Florida and houses 500 years of art, including a world-renowned collection of Rubens paintings and tapestries. The **Ringling Circus Museum** displays circus memorabilia from its ancient roots to modern day. The Tibbals Learning Center, which opened in early 2006, focuses on the American circus and the collection of Howard Tibbals, master model builder, who spent 40 years building the world's largest miniature circus. This impressive to-scale replica of the circa 1920s and '30s Ringling Bros. and Barnum & Bailey Circus is authentic from the number of pancakes the circus cooks are flipping, to the exact likenesses and costumes of the performers (painstakingly recreated from photography and written accounts), to the correct names

Fodor's Choice
★

DID YOU KNOW?

Sometimes called "sea cows," manatees are aquatic relatives of elephants. They can weigh more than 1,500 pounds and live 50-plus years. There are more than 3,000 in Florida's coastal waters.

of the animals marked on the miniature mess buckets. Tibbals's passion to re-create every exact detail continues in his on-site workshop, where kids can ask him questions and watch him carving animals and intricate wagons. ✉ *U.S. 41, ½ mi west of Sarasota-Bradenton Airport* ☎ *941/359–5700* ⊕ *www.ringling.org* 🖙 *$25* ⊙ *Daily 10–5.*

❺ Marie Selby Botanical Gardens. A don't-miss attraction for plant and flower lovers—especially those attracted to orchids, which make up nearly a third of the 20,000 species here. You can stroll through the Tropical Display House, home of orchids and colorful bromeliads gathered from rain forests, and wander the garden pathway past plantings of bamboo, ancient banyans, and mangrove forests along Little Sarasota Bay. Although spring sees the best blooms, the greenhouses make this an attraction for all seasons. The added bonus is a spectacular view of downtown. There are rotating exhibits of botanical art and photography in a 1924 restored mansion. Enjoy lunch at the Selby Café. ✉ *811 S. Palm Ave.* ☎ *941/366–5731* ⊕ *www.selby.org* 🖙 *$17* ⊙ *Daily 10–5.*

WORTH NOTING

❻ Mote Marine Aquarium. The 135,000-gallon shark tank here lets you view bull, sandbar, and other sharks from above and below the surface. Other tanks show off eels, rays, and other marine creatures native to the area. There's also a touch tank where you can get friendly with horseshoe crabs, conchs, and other creatures. Hugh and Buffett are the resident manatees and, though not as venerable as Snooty at the Parker Manatee Aquarium, they have lived here since 1996 as part of a research program. There's also a permanent sea-turtle exhibit. Many visitors take the 105-minute boat trip onto Sarasota Bay, conducted by **Sarasota Bay Explorers** (☎ *941/388–4200* ⊕ *www.sarasotabayexplorers.com*). The crew brings marine life on board, explains what it is, and throws it back to swim away. You are almost guaranteed to see bottlenose dolphins. Reservations are required. ✉ *1600 Ken Thompson Pkwy., City Island, Sarasota* ☎ *941/388–4441* ⊕ *www.mote.org* 🖙 *Aquarium $17, boat excursion $26, combined ticket $36* ⊙ *Aquarium daily 10–5; boat tours daily 11, 1:30, and 4.*

❹ Sarasota Jungle Gardens. One of Florida's better throwback attractions, Sarasota Jungle Gardens fills 10 acres with native and exotic animals as well as tropical plants. The lush gardens date to 1936, and still have the small-world feel of yesterday's Florida. You'll find red-tailed hawks and great horned owls in the birds of prey show, American alligators and a variety of snakes in the reptile encounter, and bugs of many varieties in a show called Critters and Things. You can talk to trainers and get to know such plants as the rare Australian nut tree and the Peruvian apple cactus in the gardens. Also on-site are flocks of flamingos, reptiles, and a butterfly garden. ✉ *3701 Bay Shore Rd.* ☎ *941/355–1112* ⊕ *www. sarasotajunglegardens.com* 🖙 *$15* ⊙ *Daily 10–5.*

OFF THE BEATEN PATH

Solomon's Castle shows off Florida's wackier side. Namesake Howard Solomon got an itch in 1972 to build a castle. The 12,000-square-foot work in progress is constructed of thousands of offset aluminum printing plates. Inside, you'll find tons of odd sculptures, including a knight assembled from Volkswagen parts and an elephant made of oil drums.

15

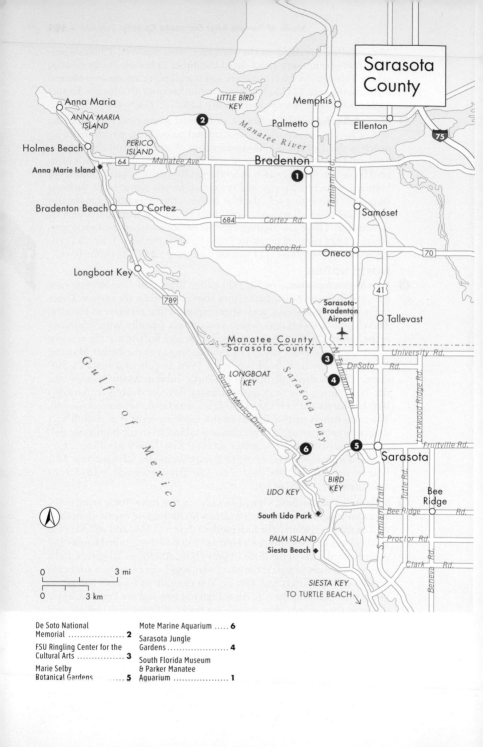

There's also a restaurant (open Friday and Saturday nights in season) that's a full-scale model of a Spanish galleon. The castle is 40 minutes east of Sarasota. ⊠ *4533 Solomon Rd., Ona* ☎ *863/494–6077* ⊕ *www. solomonscastle.com* ➩ *$10* ⊙ *Oct.–June, Tues.–Sun. 11–4.*

SPORTS AND THE OUTDOORS

BASEBALL

The Baltimore Orioles (⊠ *Ed Smith Stadium, 1090 N. Euclid Ave.* ☎ *954/776–1921*) have spring training here in March.

GOLF

Bobby Jones Golf Course (⊠ *1000 Circus Blvd.* ☎ *941/955–8097*) has 45 holes and a driving range; greens fees $36/$27. **Bobcat Trail Golf Club** (⊠ *1350 Bobcat Trail, North Port* ☎ *941/429–0500*) is a semiprivate 18-hole course 35 mi from Sarasota; greens fees $49/$27. Semiprivate **Forest Lakes Golf Club** (⊠ *2401 Beneva Rd.* ☎ *407/654–4653*) has a practice range and 18 holes; greens fees $45/$32. **Heron Creek Golf & Country Club** (⊠ *5303 Heron Creek Blvd., North Port* ☎ *941/423–6955 or 800/877–1433*) has a semiprivate 27-hole course; greens fees $52/$37. There are 27 holes at the Ron Garl–designed **University Park Country Club** (⊠ *7671 Park Blvd., University Park* ☎ *941/359–9999*). This club is private but does allow nonmembers limited play after 11 AM; greens fees $70/$50.

SHOPPING

The **Ringling Art Museum Store** (⊠ *5401 Bay Shore Rd.* ☎ *941/359 5700* ⊕ *www.ringling.org*) is a fun place to pick up clown noses, ringmaster hats, and circus-themed T-shirts. **L. Boutique** (⊠ *610 S. Pineapple Ave., Downtown* ☎ *941/906–1350* ⊕ *www.lboutiques.com*) features the trendiest fashions and most stylish handbags from top designers. **St. Armands Circle** (⊠ *John Ringling Blvd. at Ave. of the Presidents*) is a cluster of oh-so-exclusive shops just east of Lido Beach.

THE ARTS

One of the best theaters in Sarasota, the $5 million **Asolo Repertory Theatre** (⊠ *5555 N. Tamiami Trail* ☎ *941/351–8000* ⊕ *www.asolo. org*) stages productions November to June. The **Sarasota Opera** (⊠ *The Edwards Theater, 61 N. Pineapple Ave.* ☎ *941/366–8450*) performs from February through March in a historic 1,033-seat downtown theater. Internationally known artists sing the principal roles, supported by a professional chorus of young apprentices. Performers at the **Sarasota Orchestra** (⊠ *709 N. Tamiami Trail* ☎ *941/953–4252* ⊕ *www.fwcs.org*) include members of the Florida West Coast Symphony, Florida String Quartet, Florida Brass Quintet, Florida Wind Quintet, and New Artists Piano Quartet.

WHERE TO EAT

$$

ITALIAN

✕ **Café Baci.** A longtime favorite for its northern Italian cuisine, Café Baci attracts loyal locals as well as savvy travelers. Menu highlights include veal simmered with white wine, lemon, and capers; red snapper with tomatoes, black olives, rosemary, and white wine; and sautéed shrimp, scallops, fish, mussels, and clams bathed in a broth and served over risotto. The interior is not as enticing as the entrées, but resembles an English garden, with splashes of green and white and slightly outdated floral accents. ⊠ *4001 S. Tamiami Trail* ☎ *941/921–4848* ⊕ *www.cafebaci.net* ▭ *AE, D, DC, MC, V.*

$$$$
STEAK/SEAFOOD
Fodor's Choice
★

✕ **Euphemia Haye.** Named for its original owner, this place has good food, a friendly staff, and intimate lighting, though the prices can cause credit cards of the unsuspecting to light up. Treats include lamb shank braised in a red-wine garlic sauce, crispy barbecued duckling in a sweet and spicy sauce, and a very tasty pistachio-crusted red snapper. The upstairs Haye Loft, once the home of the original owner's grandson, has been converted into a lounge and dessert room. ⊠ *5540 Gulf of Mexico Dr., Longboat Key* ☎ *941/383–3633* ⊕ *www.euphemiahaye. com* ▭ *AE, D, MC, V.*

$
AMERICAN

✕ **The Old Salty Dog.** A view of New Pass between Longboat and Lido keys and affordable eats make this a popular stop, especially for visitors to Mote Marine Aquarium. Its open-air dining area is comfortable even in summer, thanks to a pleasant breeze. Quarter-pound hot dogs, fish-and-chips, wings, and burgers set the menu's tone. Locals hang out at the bar, shaped from the hull of an old boat. ⊠ *1601 Ken Thompson Pkwy., City Island* ☎ *941/388–4311* ⊠ *5023 Ocean Blvd., Sarasota* ☎ *941/349–0158* ⊕ *www.theoldsaltydog.com* ⌖ *Reservations not accepted* ▭ *MC, V.*

$$$$
AMERICAN

✕ **Ophelia's on the Bay.** The view is the first thing to lure you to this intimate waterfront spot. During the day you'll get glimpses of Little Sarasota Bay, its mangrove trees, and wildlife like ospreys and dolphins; at night, plan to sit outside (except in the buggier months of July and August) for a delightful view. The menu changes nightly, but entrées might include braised lamb osso buco with button mushrooms, plum tomatoes, and spuds; plump sea scallops (expect at least a half pound) accompanied by polenta and maple-glazed pancetta; and tuna (big-eye, yellowfin, and more), which owner Jane Ferro, who is also the grandniece of the restaurant's namesake, has flown in from Hawaii. ⊠ *9105 Midnight Pass Rd., Siesta Key* ☎ *941/349–2212* ⊕ *www. opheliasonthebay.net* ▭ *AE, D, DC, MC, V* ⊗ *No lunch.*

$
AMERICAN

✕ **Yoder's.** Pies—key lime, egg custard, strawberry rhubarb, and others—are the main event at this family restaurant in the heart of Sarasota's Amish community, but don't miss enjoying at least one meal here. Entrées are served family style—feeding two to three people—and typically include meat loaf, liver and onions, turkey and dressing, and a wonderful goulash. Breakfasts include big stacks of pancakes. If you're in the mood for a sandwich, there are plenty to choose from, including belly-filling Manhattans (roast beef, turkey, or meatloaf on homemade bread and joined with mashed potatoes and gravy). The place gets crowded around noon and early evening. ⊠ *3434 Bahia Vista* ☎ *941/955–7771* ⊕ *www.yodersrestaurant.com* ⌖ *Reservations not accepted* ▭ *MC, V* ⊗ *Closed Sun.*

WHERE TO STAY

$$–$$$

▦ **Best Western Midtown.** Here's a three-story motel that's comfortable and very affordable, especially from mid-April through early February. Set back from U.S. 41 and somewhat removed from traffic noise, it's within walking distance of a shopping center and several restaurants—including the popular Michael's on East—and is central to area

"When my granddaughter saw the beach for the first time at Longboat Key the sand was so white that she thought it was snow and wanted to make angels."—photo by Elizabeth Shevloff, Fodors.com member.

attractions and downtown. Rooms have sitting areas. **Pros:** central location; good rates. **Cons:** chain-hotel feel; bland furnishings. ⊠ 1425 S. Tamiami Trail ☎ 941/955–9841 or 800/937–8376 ⊕ www.bwmidtown. com ⤶ 100 rooms ♻ In-room: a/c, refrigerator (some), Internet. In-hotel: pool, laundry facilities ⊟ AE, D, DC, MC, V ⦿ CP.

$$$–$$$$ ★ 🖭 **Colony Beach & Tennis Resort.** If tennis is your game, this is *the* place to stay—it's one of Florida's best racquet clubs, and tennis greats such as Björn Borg have made it their home court. Ten of its courts are clay hydrosurfaced (the other 11 are hard), and the pros are all USPTA–certified. It runs clinics and camps at all levels, and with the guaranteed match-making program, you can play with a pro when no one else is available. There are even rackets and lessons for children, plus excellent free kids' programs. The Colony dining room has a reputation for good food and wine. Suites sleep up to eight. Among the suites are a two-story penthouse and three private beach houses that open onto sand and sea. The exterior and interior of the lodging buildings are truly outdated; the bed linens could have come from Motel 6. **Pros:** a must for tennis fans; not far from trendy St. Armands shopping. **Cons:** pricey; not for those who don't love tennis; rooms lack polish of pricey resorts. ⊠ 1620 Gulf of Mexico Dr., Longboat Key ☎ 941/383–6464 or 800/426–5669 ⊕ www.colonybeachresort.com ⤶ 235 suites ♻ In-room: safe, kitchen, Internet, Wi-Fi. In-hotel: 2 restaurants, bars, tennis courts, pool, gym, spa, beachfront, water sports, bicycles, children's programs (ages 3–17), laundry facilities, laundry service, Wi-Fi hotspot ⊟ AE, D, DC, MC, V.

$$$$ 🖭 **Longboat Key Club & Resort.** This beautifully landscaped property is one of the best places to play golf in the state, and among the top

tennis resorts in the country. Water is the test on both golf courses, which have excellent pro shops. Hobie Cats, kayaks, and deep-sea charters are available. If you just want to chill, check out the hammocks between buildings 1 and 2. All rooms have balconies overlooking the golf course, beach, or private lagoon where manatees and dolphins are occasionally spotted. Golf and dining facilities are for guests only. **Pros:** upscale vibe; lovely grounds. **Cons:** service can

feel snooty. ⊠ *301 Gulf of Mexico Dr., Longboat Key* ☎ *941/383–8821, 800/237–8821, or 888/237–5545* ⊕ *www.longboatkeyclub.com* ⇆ *23 rooms, 95 suites* ♿ *In-room: a/c, kitchen (some), refrigerator, Internet, Wi-Fi. In-hotel: 5 restaurants, room service, bars, golf course, tennis courts, pool, gym, spa, beachfront, water sports, bicycles, children's programs (ages 5–12), laundry facilities, Internet terminal, Wi-Fi hotspot* ▭ *AE, DC, MC, V.*

$$$$ ⊡ **Ritz-Carlton, Sarasota.** Developers like to say that this hotel is circus
★   magnate John Ringling's realized dream, and it certainly has a style the impresario would have coveted. Fine artwork and fresh-cut flowers decorate marble-floored hallways. Rooms have marble bathrooms, and private balconies with views of the bay, the marina, or the downtown skyline. A private 18-hole Tom Fazio–designed golf course is 12 mi northeast of the property on the Braden River. A European-style spa and guest-and-members-only beach facility on Lido Key, about 4 mi away, make this city resort full-service. Vernona restaurant serves regional organic cuisine and overlooks yachts in the marina. **Pros:** Ritz-style glitz; lots of amenities. **Cons:** long distance to golf course; not on the beach. ⊠ *1111 Ritz-Carlton Dr.* ☎ *941/309–2000 or 800/241–3333* ⊕ *www. ritzcarlton.com/resorts/Sarasota* ⇆ *266 rooms, 30 suites* ♿ *In-room: safe, Wi-Fi. In-hotel: 2 restaurants, room service, bars, golf course, tennis courts, pool, gym, spa, children's programs (ages 5–12), laundry service, Wi-Fi hotspot, some pets allowed* ▭ *AE, D, DC, MC, V.*

INDEX

PHOTO CREDITS

1, © Disney. 2, I'll Never Grow Up/Flickr. 5, SeaWorld Parks & Entertainment. **Part I: Experience Orlando:** 8-9 and 11, Universal Orlando Resort. 12, Busch Entertainment Corporation. 13 (left), Universal Orlando Resort. 13 (right), PrincessAshley/Flickr. 14 (left), versageek/Flickr. 14 (top center), tom.arthur/Flickr. 14 (top right and bottom right), Thomas_Jung/Flickr. 15 (top left), Troy House. 15 (bottom left and top center), Universal Orlando Resort. 15 (right), Busch Entertainment Corporation. 16, SeaWorld Parks & Entertainment. 17 (left), Stig Nygaard/Flickr. 17 (right), liangjinjian/Flickr. 18 (left), lrargerich/Flickr. 18 (right), Sky Hotels & Resort. 19 (left), The School House/Flickr. 19 (right), sanctumsolitude/Flickr. 20, PrincessAshley/Flickr. 21 (left), Universal Orlando Resort. 21 (right), PrincessAshley/Flickr. 23 and 24 (all), © Disney. 25, Rennett Stowe/Flickr. 26 (left), Cruise News Weekly/Flickr. 26 (right), sanctumsolitude/Flickr. 27, Richard Cummins / age fotostock. 28 (left and right), flickrized/Flickr. 29 (left), Cruise News Weekly/Flickr. 29 (right), sanctumsolitude/Flickr. 30, © Disney. 31, Visit Florida. 34 (left), © Disney. 34 (right), 35 (both), and 36 (left), Orlando CVB. 36 (right), © Disney. 37 and 38 (left), SeaWorld Parks & Entertainment. 38 (right), liangjinjian/Flickr. 39 (left), Universal Orlando Resort. 39 (right), Sleuths Mystery Dinner Shows. 40 (left), Orlando CVB. 40 (right), Joe Shlabotnik/Flickr. **Chapter 1: Planning an Orlando Vacation:** 41, LimeBye/Flickr. 44, Universal Orlando. 46, ©Disney. 47, @ LaRsNoW @/Flickr. 48, Orlando CVB. 51, whiteafrican/Flickr. 55, Caza_No_7/Flickr. 60, © Disney. 66, Orlando CVB. 79, © Disney. **Chapter 2: Where to Stay:** 85, Daniels & Roberts INC/The Waldorf Astoria Orlando. 86, Greencolander/Flickr. 87 and 89, coconut wireless/Flickr. 104, © Disney. 108, Buena Vista Palace Hotel & Spa. 114, Universal Orlando Resort. 120, Dan Forer. 125, Rosen Shingle Creek. 126 (top), The Waldorf Astoria Orlando. 126 (bottom), Yanik Chauvin/Shutterstock. 127 (top), Troy House. 127 (bottom), doga yusuf dokdok/iStockphoto. 128, © Disney. 129 (left), Rosen Shingle Creek. 129 (right), Buena Vista Palace Hotel and Spa. 130, Troy House. 131 (left), Marianne Campolongo/Shutterstock. 131 (center and right), Poznyakov/Shutterstock. **Chapter 3: Where to Eat:** 139, Emeril's. 140, Orlando CVB. 143-45, Seasons 52. 150, © Disney. 151 (top), meshmar2/Flickr. 151 (bottom), ckramer/Flickr. 155, Orlando CVB. 159-60, © Disney. 161 (left), ffg/Flickr. 161 (right), Thomas_Jung/Flickr. 162 (top), JeffChristiansen/Flickr. 162 (bottom), Loren Javier/Flickr. 163 (left and top right), PrincessAshley/Flickr. 163 (bottom right), marada/Flickr. 164 (top), Thomas_Jung/Flickr. 164 (bottom), PrincessAshley/Flickr. 165 (left), jason tinder/Flickr. 165 (right), JeffChristiansen/Flickr. 166, Thomas_Jung/Flickr. 174 and 175 (top), Emeril's. 175 (bottom), Robert Quailer. 185, Seasons 52. 193, Douglas Nesbitt. **Part II: Experience Disney World:** 194-95, © Disney. 196, d4rr3ll/Flickr. 197, vanguardist/Flickr. 198, © Disney. 200, Joe Shlabotnik/Flickr. 201, Orlando CVB. 203, dpape/Flickr. 204, Photos 12 / Alamy. 205 and 206 (left and top right), Everett Collection. 206 (bottom right), WALT DISNEY PICTURES / Ronald Grant Archive / Mary Evans/Everett Collection. 206 (bottom), Dashu Pagla/Flickr. 207 (top left), ©Walt Disney Co./ Everett Collection. 207 (bottom left and right), Everett Collection. 207 (bottom), daryl_mitchell/Flickr. 208 (top left), Flickr. 208 (bottom left), Bob B. Brown/Flickr. 208 (right), seanosh/Flickr. 208 (bottom), ©Buena Vista Pictures/Courtesy Everett Collection. 209 (top left), ©Walt Disney Co./Courtesy Everett Collection. 209 (top right), Prosthetic Lips/Flickr. 209 (bottom), ©Walt Disney Co./Courtesy Everett Collection. 210, ckramer/Flickr. 211 (left), J&E's photos/Flickr. 211 (right), Sam Howzit/Flickr. 212, Allie_Caulfield/Flickr. 213 (left), yeowatzup/Flickr. 213 (right), Allie_Caulfield/Flickr. 214, Stéfan/Flickr. 215, © Disney. 216 and 217 (left), J&E's photos/Flickr. 217 (right), Loren Javier/Flickr. 218, eschipul/Flickr. 219 (left), d4rr3ll/Flickr. 219 (right), Don Sullivan. 220, breezy421/Flickr. 221, Orlando CVB. 223 (left), PrincessAshley/Flickr. 223 (right), Torres, Leoraúl from Orlando, FL, USA/Wikimedia Commons. 224, Nick Traveller/Flickr. 225 (left), Jeff Kern/Flickr. 225 (right), 2Eklectik/Flickr. 226, coconut wireless/Flickr. **Chapter 4: The Magic Kingdom:** 227, hyku/Flickr. 228, Loren Javier/Flickr. 230, Paul Beattie/Flickr. 231 (top), PrincessAshley/Flickr. 231 (bottom), Loren Javier/Flickr. 232, The School House/Flickr. 235, ckramer/Flickr. 240, Bob B. Brown/Flickr. 243, JoshMcConnell/Flickr. 245, Loren Javier/Flickr. 247, Orlando CVB. 250, Thomas_Jung/Flickr. 257, ckramer/Flickr. 260, Growl Roar/Flickr. **Chapter 5: Epcot:** 263, yeowatzup/Flickr. 264, yeowatzup/Flickr. 266, Orlando CVB. 267 (top), Joe Shlabotnik/Flickr. 267 (bottom), Orlando CVB. 268, ckramer/Flickr. 275, © Disney. 283, yeowatzup/Flickr. 289, ckramer/Flickr. 292, yeowatzup/Flickr. **Chapter 6: Hollywood Studios:** 295, © Disney. 296, travislopes/Flickr. 298, edanley/Flickr. 299 (top and bottom), © Disney. 300, CCRcreations/Flickr. 305, tom.arthur/Flickr. 310, daryl_mitchell/Flickr. **Chapter 7: Animal Kingdom:** 319, Jason Pratt/Flickr. 320 (top), mrkathika/Flickr. 320 (bottom), coconut wireless/Flickr. 322, Joe Shlabotnik/Flickr. 323 (top), Thomas_Jung/Flickr. 323 (bottom), Allie_Caulfield/Flickr. 324, Paul Beattie/Flickr. 329, tom.arthur/Flickr. 330, marada/Flickr. 332, dawnzy58/Flickr. **Chapter 8: Blizzard Beach and Typhoon Lagoon:** 339, © Disney. 340, Alex1961/Flickr. 341-42, © Disney. 343 (top), PrincessAshley/Flickr. 343 (bottom), © Disney. 344, PrincessAshley/Flickr. 347, © Disney. 350, PrincessAshley/Flickr. **Part III: Experience Universal:** 356-58,

Universal Orlando Resort. 359 (top), bea&txm/Flickr. 359 (bottom), Universal Orlando Resort. 361, Wet 'n Wild. 363-64, Universal Orlando Resort. 365 (left), Copyright Donabel and Ewen Roberts. 365 (right) and 366-71, Universal Orlando Resort. 373, Orlando CVB. **Chapter 9: Universal Studios:** 375-89, Universal Orlando Resort. **Chapter 10: Islands of Adventure:** 395, Universal Orlando Resort. 396-97, Jessica Walsh. 398, Universal Orlando Resort. 399 (top), Jessica Walsh. 399 (bottom), Universal Orlando Resort. 400, divemasterking2000/Flickr. 405, Jessica Walsh. 409, PCL / Alamy. 412, Universal Orlando. **Chapter 11: Wet 'n Wild:** 415-23, Wet 'n Wild. **Part IV: Experience SeaWorld, Discovery Cove, and Aquatica:** 426-27, Jason Collier/SeaWorld Parks & Entertainment. 428, Cybjorg/Wikimedia Commons. 429 (top), Fantaz/Flickr. 429 (bottom), Wendy Piersall (@eMom)/Flickr. 430-31, SeaWorld Parks & Entertainment. 432, Orlando CVB. 433, Stig Nygaard/Flickr. 434, psyberartist/Flickr. 435, SeaWorld Parks & Entertainment. 437, Peter Titmuss / Alamy. **Chapter 12: SeaWorld and Discovery Cove:** 439-42 and 443(top), SeaWorld Parks & Entertainment. 443 (bottom), Visit Florida. 444-51, SeaWorld Parks & Entertainment. 455, Richard Lindie/iStockphoto. 457, SeaWorld Parks & Entertainment. **Chapter 13: Aquatica:** 459, Jason Collier/SeaWorld Parks & Entertainment. 460, Fantaz/Flickr. 461-62 and 463 (top), Jason Collier/SeaWorld Parks & Entertainment. 463 (bottom), Fantaz/Flickr. 464-66, SeaWorld Parks & Entertainment. **Part V: Experience Central Florida:** 470-71, Mike Sharp. 472-73, Orlando CVB. 474, Busch Entertainment Corporation. 475 (left), jking89/Flickr. 475 (right), Stig Nygaard/Flickr. 476, Visit Florida. 478, Paddy Eckersley / age fotostock. **Chapter 14: Orlando and Environs:** 479-80, Visit Florida. 481 (both), Orlando CVB. 482, Kissimmee - The Heart of Florida/ Flickr. 484, Orlando CVB. 489, Kissimmee - The Heart of Florida/Flickr. 493-96, Orlando CVB. 500, Kevin N. Murphy/Flickr. 504, Orlando CVB. 510, spakattacks/Flickr. 514, Joe in DC/Flickr. 516, Orlando CVB. 524-25, jurvetson/Flickr. 526, thelastminute/Flickr. 527, yeowatzup/Flickr. 528 (top left), hyku/Flickr. 528 (top right and bottom) and 529 (left), thelastminute/Flickr. 529 (center), yeowatzup/ Flickr. 529 (right), divemasterking2000/Flickr. 530, by jonworth/Flickr. 531, bnhsu/Flickr. 532-33, jurvetson/Flickr. 538, bastix.net/Flickr. 540, breezy421/flickr. **Chapter 15: The Tampa Bay Area:** 543, Joe Stone/Shutterstock. 544 (top), gppilot, Fodors.com member. 544 (bottom), Visit Florida. 545 (top), Marje Cannon/iStockphoto. 545 (bottom), William Hamilton / SuperStock. 546, iStockphoto. 548, St. Petersburg/Clearwater Area CVB. 549 (top), Visit Florida. 549 (bottom), Graca Victoria/Shutterstock. 550, iStockphoto. 554-55, Busch Entertainment Corporation. 560, Martin Bennett / Alamy. 568, jaxlor, Fodors.com member. 573, Ed Wolfstein/Icon SMI. 574 (top), Palm Beach Post/ZUMA Press/Icon SMI. 574 (bottom), Cliff Welch/Icon SMI. 575 (top), Evan Meyer/Shutterstock. 575 (bottom) and 576 (top), GARY I ROTHSTEIN/Icon SMI. 576 (bottom background photo), Ed Wolfstein/Icon SMI. 577 (background photo), Ed Wolfstein Photo/Icon SMI. 576-77 (logos), wikipedia.org. 580, watland, Fodors. com member. 585, Richard T. Nowitz / age fotostock. 588, TIPTON DONALD / age fotostock. 593, Elizabeth Shevloff, Fodors.com member.

NOTES

ABOUT OUR WRITERS

Los Angeles—based freelancer **Elise Allen** (www.eliseallen.com), who wrote the Planning Your Trip chapter, visits Disneyland in Anaheim, California, all the time and Disney World in Orlando at least once a year with her extended family for Marathon Weekend. (She has four Mickey marathon medals, three half-marathon Donalds, and three Goofys—for running the half *and* full marathons during the one weekend). In addition to writing for Fodor's, Elise has also worked on episodes of PBS's *Sid the Science Kid* and *Dinosaur Train* and has written a young-adult novel, *Populazzi*.

Brothers **Nathan** and **Sam Benjamin**, who've lived in Orlando since birth, slid their way through Blizzard Beach and Typhoon Lagoon to revise the Water Parks chapter. Nathan, a senior at Cypress Creek High School, plays piano and is on the tennis team. Sam, a junior at William R. Boone High School, is a percussionist and is in the marching band. Both enjoy writing, and although they're fans of all central Florida's theme-park thrills, speeding down slides and catching some rays at the water parks are favorite diversions.

Rona Gindin, who worked on the Where to Eat chapter, is a freelance writer, editor, and TV personality specializing in restaurants and travel. She's the host of *On Dining*, a TV show that celebrates central Florida restaurants; is the dining editor of *Winter Park Magazine;* is the author of *The Little Black Book of Walt Disney World* and *WHERE—Eat! Orlando: Great Meals Wherever You Are*; and contributes to Zagat, *Go, American Way,* and other publications.

Where to Stay chapter writer, **Jennifer Greenhill-Taylor,** has been a journalist for more than two decades—working as a travel editor, theater and film critic, wire editor, and freelance writer/editor. She was born in Edinburgh, Scotland, has lived in four countries and a dozen states, and travels widely for pleasure and profit. She lives in Orlando with her partner, playwright and freelance writer Joseph Reed Hayes, with whom she runs two web-sites for writer: Inked-In (http://inkedin.ning.com) and The Burry Man Writers Center (www.burryman.com).

Orlando-based travel and feature writer (and former Disney publicist) **Jennie Hess** covered just about all of the World for this edition, and what she didn't cover (the water parks) her teenage sons, Nathan and Sam Benjamin, did. When she's not trekking through theme parks, she's enjoying Orlando's many treasures, from local spas and restaurants to museums and historic sites. Jennie gives the inside scoop on the city's growth and the evolving Disney kingdom, with added perspective gleaned from her husband, Walter, and her sons.

Gary McKechnie, who covered all of Universal and SeaWorld, knows a lot about Florida—his native state—and its many attractions. During his student days, he worked as a Walt Disney World ferryboat pilot, Jungle Cruise skipper, steam-train conductor, double-decker bus driver, and was also an improv comedian at Epcot. His award-winning book *Great American Motorcycle Tours* is the nation's best-selling motorcycle guidebook and, following years of travel and research, in May 2009 released *National Geographic's USA 101*, a book that highlights 101 American icons, events, and festivals. He's also a lecturer on the Cunard Line ship *Queen Mary 2*.

Orlando and Environs section writer **Joseph Reed Hayes** (www.jrhayes.net) has written about travel, food, and the arts for print and online publications for more than 15 years. He's also a playwright, whose work has been produced in New York, California, Florida, and the United Kingdom; a jazz entrepreneur; and a performance artist. Born in Manhattan, Hayes worked in publishing in New York before moving to central Florida to take up writing as a full-time career.